Evolutionary Psychology
THE SCIENCE OF HUMAN BEHAVIOR AND EVOLUTION

Evolutionary Psychology

THE SCIENCE OF HUMAN BEHAVIOR AND EVOLUTION

Matthew J. Rossano

Southeastern Louisiana University

JOHN WILEY & SONS, INC.

SENIOR EDITORS   Patrick Fitzgerald/Tim Vertovec
MARKETING MANAGER   Kevin Malloy
ASSOCIATE PRODUCTION MANAGER   Kelly Tavares
COVER AND TEXT DESIGNER   Susan Brown Schmidler
PRODUCTION MANAGEMENT SERVICES   Chestnut Hill Enterprises, Inc.

This book was set in Minion by The Format Group, LLC and printed and bound by Malloy Lithographers. The cover was printed by Phoenix Color. The cover photos are by Michael Nichols/NGS (left) and Reza/Webistan (right).

Between the time Website information is gathered and published, some sites may have closed or changed. Also, the transcription of URLs may result in typographical errors. John Wiley & Sons would appreciate notification where these occur so that they may be corrected in subsequent editions.

Library of Congress Cataloging in Publication Data:
Rossano, Matthew J.
  Evolutionary psychology : the science of human behavior and evolution / Matthew J. Rossano.
      p. cm.
  Includes bibliographical references and index.
  ISBN 1-891786-12-1 (alk. paper)
   1. Genetic psychology. 2. Human evolution. I. Title

BF701′.R74′2002
155.7--dc21

                                                                                    2002027121

Printed in the United States of America

10 9 8 7 6 5 4 3 2 1

To my kin, both ancestral and descendent.
To my wife Rhonda, whose love and support make endeavors such as this possible.
To the girls, Dani, Talia, Alicia, and Julia, someday you'll have to read this.
And to my parents, Joe and Judy Rossano, who had to tolerate an awful lot before being able to say "my son, the author."

Contents

SECTION III
COOPERATION   189

Preface

Evolutionary Psychology: The Science of Human Behavior and Evolution is intended to serve as a text for college and university courses that focus on the central role of evolution in the shaping of human behavior. For the most part, such courses are usually found in departments of psychology, anthropology, or biology and are offered to advanced undergraduates and graduate students. However, the broad range of topics included here touch on the subject matter of many other courses across the social and behavioral sciences. My hope is that instructors and students coming to evolutionary psychology from different disciplines will find the text to be useful and enjoyable reading. The only prerequisite for students is a course in general psychology. I have provided a review of human evolution and evolutionary biology topics in the early chapters; in my experience, many psychology students benefit from this coverage and find the topics fascinating.

Inspiration

The ultimate inspiration for this book can be traced back, I think, to a rather off-hand comment a colleague made to me several years ago. As we discussed what (if any) attributes of the human intellect could be considered "unique," he casually remarked that it was really only language that separated humans from other animals, and all of our cherished intellectual accomplishments (science, culture, art, etc.) could be traced back to this one faculty. Take away language, and humans become nothing more than naked, rather incompetent, apes. A sobering thought and maybe even a correct one, but one that just seemed a bit overly simplistic to me. Computers programmed with rational and algorithmic powers far exceeding that of humans still struggle with elementary language comprehension. It seemed to me that language was more a manifestation of human intellectual uniqueness than the cause of it. So, if there are distinctly human mental attributes, one must dig deeper to find their origins.

Over the next decade, I began teaching a series of graduate and undergraduate seminars exploring the nature of human thinking. Because my training was in cognitive psychology, I began with comparisons of human thought and machine (artificial intelligence) thinking. Here an inevitable and profound difference quickly emerges: unlike the machine "mind," the human mind is the product of a long, slow process of biological evolution. As an evolutionary product, the human mind (it seems) has been endowed with attributes that make language learning a nearly effortless affair for us, whereas for machines it has proved a formidable challenge. But what are our very special attributes? The mind of every other creature on earth is the product of that very same process—why is language absent in them?

Over the next few years, my seminars moved away from human–machine comparisons and concentrated on interspecies comparisons, with special emphasis on our primate relatives. Eventually we broadened out to include extinct species, spending one semester comparing humans with Neanderthals. Why were we still here, and why did they become extinct? Were the differences intellectual, possibly? With every class I taught and book I read, the same unmistakable message emerged: *If we are to truly understand the human mind, we must understand human evolutionary history.* There is simply no escaping this fundamental fact. My biologist friends had been telling me this for years, and now I completely and wholeheartedly agree. Psychologists, psychology students, and, indeed, anyone who wishes to understand humans and human nature must be competent Darwinists, capable of interacting and exchanging ideas with evolutionists in a variety disciplines. Ergo this book!

The Promise of Evolutionary Psychology

What makes evolutionary psychology so exciting for me is that it provides the vehicle whereby psychology is brought into meaningful conversation with all of the varied disciplines that explore evolution, especially primate and human evolution. My goal was to create a book that would further this interdisciplinary interaction. I envision evolutionary psychology with the broadest possible scope of inquiry. If the psychologists' mission is to understand human nature, then evolutionary biologists, primatologists, anthropologists, zoologists, and archeologists have much to tell us, and we must be capable of listening. The next generation of psychologists must be prepared to constructively engage with evolutionary theory and with those whose disciplines directly apply an evolutionary framework. The next great advances in the behavioral sciences, I believe, will come from those with broad and deep intellects, whose competencies span across the traditional disciplines and unite them in creative ways. Humans are complex. It will take incisive, sophisticated thinkers working from an array of perspectives to unravel the mysteries of being human. So be it. We have been deluded to think narrowness could possibly explain the goings-on among the trillion interconnections of the human brain.

This book, then, seeks to place evolutionary psychology within the broad sweep of our primate heritage and the full scope of our evolutionary story. As with any book that crosses disciplinary boundaries, it will, I am sure, prove inadequate on many counts. Despite the best of efforts, anytime a nonspecialist attempts to communicate with students about topics outside his or her field of formal training, oversimplifications and misinterpretations are inevitable. Moreover, I do not pretend that a single book (any single book) can accurately convey the breadth of knowledge necessary to make the reader the competent Darwinist that I think future psychologists must be. My only ambition is that this book will serve as a respectable step in the right direction.

Plan of the Book

I have tried to lay out the subject matter in an orderly, logical fashion. The first three chapters define and provide background on evolutionary psychology itself. Here, I hope to convey the historical antecedents of this new approach and provide a reasonably thorough and balanced assessment of its methods, potential, and the criticisms leveled against it. The next two chapters cover the basics of evolution and unpack the far-ranging saga of human evolution. This is presented in as much of a narrative form as possible to capture all of the intrigue and fascinating detail that make up the human epic. The next section (chapters 6–8) covers motor behavior and emotions. My desire here is to elevate the status of these often neglected topics. I take a firmly antidualistic stance here: We must not divorce the evolution of the mind from the evolution of the body. Human intelligence is embodied intelligence, and although I'm not sure that we yet appreciate all that that entails, I am sure that future psychologists will have to consider carefully how the mind's representations and operations are constrained by and act in service to the body's design. Likewise, our appreciation of how emotions interact and affect our thought processes is expanding tremendously. As I emphasize in the text, the legacy of our evolutionary heritage is found most directly in our emotional lives. The attractions and repulsions that served our ancestors' fitness needs continue to be with us today.

Section three (chapters 9–12) on cooperation makes up what many consider to be the core of evolutionary psychology—sexual behavior and mate selection. I try to embed this topic within the larger issue of cooperative behavior, with male–female relations being a specific instance of the evolution of human cooperativeness. This is not to deny that there are competitive aspects to these relationships. Certainly there are, and these are discussed. But, at bottom, if natural selection had not honed cooperative skills in our hominin ancestors, we would not be here.

The next section (chapters 13—14) deals with developmental and familial issues. This is another area in which the cooperative/competitive dynamic intertwines in fascinating and often complicated ways. This section should provide insights into the way family relations can become the focus of so many intense emotions, both positive and negative.

The final section (chapters 15—18) on higher cognition is, admittedly, the most scientifically underdeveloped and speculative. Despite its relatively immaturity, however, a number of promising and intriguing lines of research have been initiated addressing the evolution of thought, rationality, language, and morality. It seemed to me that students should at least be aware of how scientists are attempting to address these issues. It may inspire a few of them to get involved.

Supplementary Material

The following supplementary materials are available to instructors online at www.wiley.com/college/rossano:
- Instructor's Manual, containing learning objectives and lecture outlines for each chapter.
- Test Bank, containing approximately 60–100 multiple choice test questions for each chapter.

Acknowledgments

An author sits in an interesting position. He or she is simply at the forefront of what is really a collaborative effort. The comments, suggestions, and criticism of a number of dedicated reviewers helped me immeasurably. Of course, any shortcomings in the book are the responsibility of the author.

I wish to express my appreciation to the reviewers who have patiently read through all or significant parts of the manuscript, generously sharing their expertise:

Jeff Baker, Southeastern Louisiana University
Colin Beer, Rutgers University, Newark
Thomas Bouchard, University of Minnesota
Kelley Brennan, State University of New York at Brockport
Al Burstein, Southeastern Louisiana University
Charles Crawford, Simon Fraser University
Brian Crother, Southeastern Louisiana University
Judith Horowitz, Medaille College
Elizabeth Ince, Richard Stockton College of New Jersey
Lee Kirkpatrick, College of William & Mary
Margery Lucas, Wellesley College
Kevin MacDonald, California State University Long Beach
Linda Mealey, College of Saint Benedict
Jack Pasternak, University of Waterloo
Brian Richmond, University of Illinois at Urbana–Champaign
Nicholas Thompson, Clarke University.

Daniel Povinelli of the University of Louisiana–Lafayette and Robert Foley of Cambridge University (UK) were also kind enough to read over sections and offer helpful comments and encouragement.

A special thanks is owed to those reviewers from disciplines outside my own. They cheerfully suffered my naivete, listened to my questions, and did their level best to bring me up to speed and keep me on track. One of the great privileges of working in academia is the collegiality and professionalism of those with whom one is allowed to rub shoulders. I can only hope that when called upon, I can show the same degree of respect and cordiality to others that my reviewers have shown to me, and I am embarrassed for the times I know I did not. In this regard, I reserve a special thanks to Brian Richmond of the University of Illinois and Brian Crother of Southeastern Louisiana University, both of whom went "above and beyond" the call to aid me in this project. Thanks are also due to my tireless and dedicated graduate assistant, Samata Elmore Amedee. She never failed when I said "find this." It's no exaggeration to say that without her help this book simply could not have happened. Thanks, Sam!

Finally, I must say that it has been pleasure to work with Patrick Fitzgerald and everyone associated with John Wiley & Sons. Patrick had unflagging faith in this idea from the start and was nonstop with encouragement ("This is going to be a great book!"). Nancy Knight was a superb editor and real treat to work with (I'm sure she would flag the preposition at the end of that sentence!). Her clarity of thought and expression have contributed significantly to the quality of the final product.

My name may be on the front cover, but the hard work was shared by many. Thanks to you all!

Matt Rossano
mrossano@selu.edu

BACKGROUND: HISTORY AND EVOLUTION

Explaining Human Nature

What Is to Be Explained?

WHAT SHOULD A USEFUL THEORY of human nature explain? Most people would say that such a theory ought to explain why people are the way they are. The extraordinary number of features shared in common by humans around the globe would seem to make constructing such a theory a straightforward task. We all communicate with language. We all like to eat sweets. We are all comfortable with the air temperature around 75°F. We all prefer to marry someone who is beautiful rather than someone who is ugly. We find koalas endearing. Excrement repulses us. By explaining the origins of these and other common traits, we would be well on our way to a useful theory of human nature.

But what about extreme examples of human behavior that fall outside the bounds of these shared common traits? Two individuals drawn from recent news accounts serve as examples.

> On a late spring evening in 1997, a New Jersey teenager, like so many of her peers, was attending her high school prom at the Garden Manor banquet hall. Shortly after she arrived, she excused herself, went to the restroom, gave birth to a healthy 6.6-lb baby boy and left him in a trash receptacle to die. After freshening up, she returned to the dance floor. A little more than a year later, she tearfully pleaded guilty to aggravated manslaughter and was sentenced to 15 years in prison.

> A young publications mogul has amassed a personal fortune of more than $325 million by turning his personal interests in sex, music, and politics into edgy magazines. He owns five homes and, although he does not drive, has five Rolls-Royces to go with them. Over the years, he has managed to trim down his list of girlfriends from 14 to just 1, although he admits to lapses of fidelity and continues to vehemently oppose monogamy. When he strays, his current companion consoles herself by purchasing a "whopping big watch."

Most of us are not like either of these individuals. Perhaps we should simply consider them "exceptional" and therefore beyond the bounds of any general theory of human nature. But consider the large numbers of other people who might be considered exceptional. Were the 900 people who engaged in mass suicide as part of Jim Jones's cult in Guyana exceptional? And what of the thousands who participated, to one degree or another, in the Holocaust? Or, on the positive side, what about the thousands, including Albert Schweitzer and Mother Theresa, who have

3

devoted their lives to the poor? Should all these individuals fall outside the scope of our theory of human nature? In fact, although most of us are neither Nazi sympathizers nor Nobel Peace Prize winners, we do regard ourselves as unique in some way. Perhaps because of our unique individuality we, too, are outside the bounds of any general theory of human nature.

To be useful, any such theory must be able to explain both why people share many traits in common and why glaring exceptions to the norm are also present. An insightful understanding of why humans are the way we are cannot be content with tackling just the mundane—why we get up every morning, go to work, eat supper, go to bed, and then do it all again the next day. It also must explain why, in each of us, there exists the potential to be exceptional: both exceptionally virtuous and exceptionally evil.

In centuries past, philosophers explained human nature by proposing the existence of a **rational soul**. This attribute was often thought of as simply a gift from God (or the gods) that gave humans the capacity for logical thought and reasoning. Although our culture owes much to the wisdom of the ancient Greek and Medieval philosophers, the idea of a rational soul is scientifically problematic. Because one cannot test for a divine gift, any effort to analyze the origins and properties of human nature would be thwarted before it began.

Another theory that seeks to explain the basis of human nature is **cultural determinism**, which credits the culture in which we are raised with shaping everything about the way we are. This notion sees humans as virtual blank slates to be written upon and molded by the cultural environment. Culture plays an undeniably important role in influencing the ways people think and behave, but it fails to provide a complete explanation for a number of issues fundamental to human nature. One might wonder, for example, from where cultural norms themselves arise. Or, why do certain universal human behavior traits exist despite very different cultural environments?

Almost any approach to explaining human nature faces serious obstacles. The theory must address the wide diversity of human behavior and at the same time allow for the emergence of certain universal traits. It must be testable, so that it can be verified or refuted, and must take into account the vast potential for learning and adaptive change possible in individuals. A tall order for any theory!

The Evolutionary Approach

Evolutionary psychology is an emerging approach to understanding human nature, based on Darwinian principles. This approach has shown great promise and has been adopted by increasing numbers of researchers. It begins with a simple principle: the traits we observe in an organism, such as brown eyes or an excitable personality, are related to the genes that organism inherited from its parents. Extending from this principle is the more central claim that many of the traits humans possess today are present because they held survival and reproduction advantages for individuals over the course of our evolution. Put another way, in the past, our ancestors with advantageous traits reproduced more, thus spreading the genes associated with those traits. Humans today are the ultimate products of this process.

This is a powerful and not entirely uncontroversial claim. Part of its power and appeal lies in the fact that, unlike claims of a rational soul, it lends itself to empirical testing, and, unlike cultural determinism, it has the potential for providing a complete and comprehensive understanding of human nature.

An example from another species may help us understand this approach. If one were trying to understand "gorilla nature," then one might identify a specific gorilla behavior and propose a theoretical explanation for it. One frequent male gorilla behavior is water splashing. Male gorillas love to make grand displays by leaping into pools of water or by creating massive plumes of spray with their powerful hands. Why? One could argue that gorillas simply have been given a divine gift of a playful soul (rather than a rational soul) and that water play is one expression of it. But how could the existence of a playful soul be tested? Conversely, one could argue that gorillas simply learn splashing as part of their upbringing in gorilla culture. But why, then, do only male gorillas splash and only at certain times? An evolutionary approach would argue that splashing offered some survival or reproductive advantage to male gorillas over the course of their evolution, and, therefore, the genes associated with splashing behavior spread in the gorilla population.

Recently, two researchers tested just this idea. Parnell and Buchanan-Smith (2001) proposed that male gorillas engage in spectacular water-splashing displays to intimidate other males and keep them away from the local females. If this were so, then we would expect to find gorillas splashing in social settings in which such behavior is clearly observable by other males. Over a 3-year period, the researchers catalogued the splashing activities of lowland gorillas in the Nouabale-Ndoki National Park in the Democratic Republic of the Congo. They found that the displays often occurred in swampy forest clearings, called *bais*, where different gorilla groups congregated for feeding. More than 70% of the displays were by dominant males and could be seen by other males from distances up to 20 m. More than half of the displays occurred when no females were present. Thus, the displays gave every indication of being directed at strange males who might pose a threat to the dominant male's control of his group. Over the course of gorilla evolution, males who failed to prevent other males from stealing females from their groups left fewer offspring than those who didn't fail. Thus the tendency to splash and look tough when strange males are around persists in the male gorilla population today because the genes associated with those behaviors provided a reproductive advantage in the past.

Psychologists and other researchers who adopt the evolutionary approach apply a similar type of logic to understanding humans. Like splashing gorillas, we exhibit a number of traits that are present today because they proved valuable for survival and reproduction over the course of human evolution. Like Parnell and Buchanan-Smith (2001), evolutionary psychologists look for ways to test these ideas to gather supportive evidence.

Evolution and Human Nature

We began by noting that any theory of human nature must explain not only the many routine commonalities present among humans but also the exceptional traits and behaviors, including those of individuals such as the New Jersey teen and the hedonistic magazine entrepreneur. Can an evolutionary approach meet this challenge? Take some of the everyday commonalities we mentioned earlier. How would an evolutionary approach address such things as: (1) eating sweets, (2) finding koalas "cute" and excrement "disgusting," and (3) preferring to marry someone who is beautiful rather than ugly? A moment's reflection offers a number of ideas about the ways in which these traits might have offered survival and reproductive advantages to our ancestors. (1) Sweets provided energy, a valuable commodity when food was scarce and life difficult. (2) Round-headed, toddler-sized koalas remind us of our own infants. The emotional bond between our ancestors and their infants helped ensure the survival of offspring. Excrement was (and is) rife with potentially deadly bacteria. Our ancestors who avoided it enjoyed a survival advantage over those who found it appealing. (3) In our past, "beautiful" people were probably also healthy people and therefore more likely to produce healthy offspring. Given that these traits all provided some survival or reproductive advantage in our past, it is not surprising to find them widespread in humans today.

But how would an evolutionary approach address those exceptional examples mentioned at the beginning of the chapter? It seems almost absurd to suggest that infanticidal tendencies could have been advantageous during the course of our evolution. Wouldn't destroying one's own offspring be disadvantageous? Not necessarily. With humans, a reproductive advantage would not necessarily have gone to those who *produced* many babies but to those who managed to *raise* more of them to reproductive maturity. Distinct signs may have indicated to our ancestors circumstances (lack of resources, poor health, no social support) in which the chances of successfully raising a newborn to maturity were quite low. New mothers who were sensitive to these foreboding signs and willing to act on them by engaging in infanticide preserved their energy for future reproduction. In doing so, they reaped an advantage over those who expended energy and resources in vain. This seems callous and immoral when judged by modern standards. However, the past history of our species was not entirely pretty. For better or worse, we carry the imprint of that past with us today.

As for the extravagance and consumption displayed by our magazine entrepreneur, evolutionary psychologists would contend that these serve as indicators of status and resources. Given the vast resources required to successfully raise a child, a smart female in our evolutionary past would have done well to choose a mate with plenty to offer—and the more he had to offer, the more females he was likely to attract. Males have evolved with a tendency to seek wealth and status, because, in the past, these things could be "cashed in" reproductively. The fact that our entrepreneur boasts of 14 girlfriends suggests that this dynamic still exists today.

Evolutionary psychology does not claim to have an explanation for every quirk and eccentricity known to man and woman. Moreover, many other explanations, outside of those provided by evolutionary psychology, are possible and plausible for these traits and behaviors. But the evolutionary approach has great potential for generating testable hypotheses concerning why people are the way they are. Through those tests, the explanatory power of the approach can be realized or its limitations exposed. For the many tests conducted thus far, the results are impressive.

Historical Background of Evolutionary Theory

Before the 19th century, most philosophers and scientists agreed that the various animal species populating the earth were each separately and specially created, an idea that can be traced all the way back to the Greek philosopher Aristotle (384–322 BCE) Medieval Christian philosophers continued in the Aristotelian tradition, attributing creative activity to God. However, beginning in the 18th and early 19th centuries, scholars began to question the notion of a separate, special creation for each species and, instead, posited the idea of a slow, gradual evolutionary process whereby a new species might emerge from a pre-existing one. What led them to this idea?

An important shift occurred in the first half of the 19th century when the geological notion of **catastrophism**, championed by Georges Cuvier, was replaced by the **uniformitarianism** of James Hutton and Charles Lyell. Catastrophism was the idea that the earth had been the subject of intermittent cataclysmic events, such as the Biblical great flood, that accounted for its various geological features. Uniformitarianism, by contrast, argued that the forces affecting the earth's geology today were a reasonable approximation of the forces that had always been present, with no global catastrophes affecting its development. The critical implication of uniformitarianism was that the earth had to be incredibly old for certain geological features to have emerged. For example, Lyell noted that the slopes of Mount Etna had been built up over the years as a result of lava flows. By studying the frequency of the flows and the amount that each would deposit, he determined that there were not enough eruptions in all of recorded history to account for the size of the mountain's slope (Brooke, 1991, pp. 249–250). If the earth was very old, then the time necessary to allow for species to gradually emerge one from another was available. Furthermore, deep within these very old layers of rock, scientists had catalogued numerous fossils, indicating that life on earth also had a long history.

Around this same time, other scientists were grappling with the physical and anatomical similarities that existed across different species. For example, a century before Darwin's *Origin of Species*, the French naturalist Georges de Buffon published his 44-volume epic *Histoire Naturelle*. In it, he observed physical similarities between humans and apes and speculated about a possible common ancestry. Even today, the anatomical similarities among different species (including humans) provide compelling evidence for a common heritage (Fig. 1.1). Scientists had noted not only physical similarities between humans and other animals but behavioral ones as well. Darwin himself made an extensive case for similar behavioral tendencies in humans and other animals, implying that the emotions and thoughts behind those behaviors might also be similar.

Darwin and Wallace

It was against this background that the work of two important scientists, Charles Darwin and Alfred Russel Wallace (Fig. 1.2), elevated the idea of evolution to full scientific credibility. The events that led to the emergence of evolution as an accepted scientific theory began in the spring of 1858, when Darwin received an unexpected letter that abruptly ended his quiet methodical work on an idea that he called "descent with modification." The letter, with attached manuscript, was from

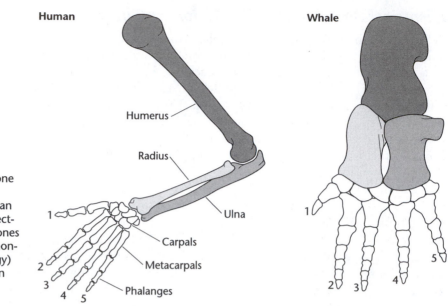

Figure 1.1 The common bone structure of different species' forelimbs. Note that all have an upper (humerus) bone connected to a paired set of lower bones (radius and ulna). This commonality of structure (or homology) argues strongly for a common ancestry. (Adapted from Cambridge Press.)

Figure 1.2 The minds behind natural selection. Working independently, both Charles Darwin and Alfred Russel Wallace formulated the notion of natural selection as the primary mechanism producing evolutionary change. Though generally collegial colleagues, Darwin and Wallace were two men from different backgrounds with sharply contrasting world views: Darwin was thorough-going materialist, Wallace a spiritualist. As will be explored in the text, this difference in backgrounds and world views contributed to their opposing views on the relevance of evolution to human nature. (From Wisdom and internet)

fellow naturalist Wallace. Independently, Wallace had arrived at a theoretical viewpoint concerning the history of life similar to that of Darwin. In the summer of that year, Joseph Hooker presented papers by both Darwin and Wallace to the Linnean Society, outlining their ideas and providing the first official public airing of the theory of evolution by natural selection. In the decades to follow, it was to become one of the most scientifically important and socially controversial theories in history. The theory fundamentally changed the generally accepted view of humanity and human nature. Scientists, philosophers, theologians, and Darwin and Wallace themselves, clashed over its interpretation and implications.

Darwin Versus Wallace: Is Evolution Relevant to Humans?

How relevant is evolution when it comes to understanding humans and human nature? Almost as soon as evolution emerged as a respected scientific theory, this question became the subject of a pointed debate that continues to some extent even today. The initial debate involved Darwin and Wallace. Darwin saw unbroken continuity between the thought and behavior of humans and other species. Wallace saw a qualitative leap between humans and other animals, one that could be bridged only by divine intervention. Evolution, it seemed, only rekindled the smoldering notion of the rational soul.

Darwin: Continuity

A keystone of Darwin's theory was the idea that an organism's physical and behavioral traits are the products of a slow adaptive process. The human animal, in all its physical and intellectual glory, is the product of the same long, incremental process of adaptation that molded all animals. Humans did not arrive fully formed from clay onto this earth; instead they emerged gradually from other species, specifically from the primate line (which includes the orangutans, gorillas, and chimpanzees). Human nature has a deep history, and, if we look carefully, we can find something of ourselves in other creatures. Humans represent nothing dramatically new, just peculiar augmentations of the already present. This was certainly the attitude that Darwin adopted.

In *Origin of Species* (1859), Darwin rigorously laid out the evidence for evolution by natural selection and established it as a credible scientific theory. Recognizing the inherent controversy that it would engender, he specifically avoided any direct discussion of human evolution in that important work. It was not until more than a decade later, with the publication of *The Descent of Man* (1871) and *The Expression of Emotions in Man and Animals* (1872), that Darwin tackled the issue. He was convinced that the evolutionary process moved by gradual increments over long spans of time and saw no need to abandon this principle when it came to understanding human mental traits. In his view, the ample evidence of intelligent behavior in nonhuman animals confirmed the notion that human mental capacities were evolutionarily linked to those of other species.

To make his case, Darwin provided numerous examples of the intellectual capacity of animals. For example, he noted how many species had well-developed powers of imitation. Birds could mimic the sounds of their local environments. A dog raised with cats would lick its paws and face in a fashion similar to its feline compatriots. Apes (but not other animals) were capable of imitating many human actions. Animals, he noted, could also deliberately focus attention, citing as an example a cat that lies in wait, staring at a mouse hole. Many animals showed evidence of highly developed memory abilities and some appeared to recognize another animal or human after years of separation. Darwin noted that monkeys were especially gifted intellectually. He recounted an incident in which a baboon poured water into a dirt hole to create mud, which he then poured on a military officer passing by in a parade. Not only did this baboon show evidence of deliberation and planning, but for weeks afterward the animal seemed mockingly joyful each time he encountered the officer, as if recalling with pleasure his earlier triumph. Monkeys also showed exceptional curiosity, poking and exploring at new objects, even when those objects could be potentially dangerous (such as a stuffed snake). Darwin also described incidents of learning and reasoning. Apes and monkeys presented with boiled eggs initially smashed them. Later, they learned to carefully peel and pick off the shells to retrieve the contents.

Darwin also observed that animals were exquisitely emotional. It seemed difficult to deny the presence of affective quality when a dog licked and caressed an injured or dying master. Emotional response in humans, he believed, was an extension of the practical facial and bodily expressions of animals. For example, a dog bares its teeth to eat and bite. This practical response could easily become linked to other physiological responses associated with aggression to produce an emotion of anger. It is not difficult to see how these responses could evolve into human emotional expressions, such as clenching teeth and fists when angry. Anger and aggression, however, are not the only emotions with animal precedents. Darwin noted that many group-living species, such as wolves, elephants, and apes, appear to develop strong affiliative bonds. He observed that these animals often cooperated, shared food, and defended each other. In one incident, Darwin described how a large male baboon placed himself at risk to save a young member of the group from a pack of wild dogs. It was in these social animals that Darwin found the roots of human emotional, relational, and even moral aptitudes. For Darwin then, human reasoning, memory, emotion, and even morality were not qualitatively different from those of other species, only extensions and elaborations of what was already present in nature.

Wallace: Discontinuity

Although Darwin is a well-known figure, Alfred Wallace has remained more obscure. He was born in 1823 in the village of Usk of Monmouthshire in Wales. After the early death of his father, young Alfred took up surveying with his brother William. He learned the importance of careful observation and accurate measurement. His skills helped him secure a position on the faculty of the Collegiate College in Leicester, where he befriended botanist Henry Walter Bates. The two sailed to South America on a scientific expedition. In 1852, after 4 years exploring the Amazon River and Brazilian jungles, Wallace secured passage back to England. His ship caught fire and sank at sea. Wallace was rescued but lost his specimens and notes. In 1854, he set sail again, this time for Singapore. There, he embarked on an 8-year expedition to study the plant and animal life of southeast Asia. There, too, he identified the famous "Wallace line," a zoological dividing line separating the plants and animals of Malaysia from those of Australia.

It was also in southeast Asia that Wallace formulated a theory of evolution following the same explanatory principles as those of Charles Darwin. But for Wallace, something about humans did not seem to fit with the theory. Humans appeared to possess an intelligence that far exceeded their survival needs, suggesting that something more than just natural selection must have been at work on them. Humans had what Wallace referred to as an "extraordinary latent intellectual capacity." Given the right schooling, a primitive tribesman could master calculus as well as a cultured English gentleman, indicating that a vast reservoir of potential intellect (mathematical and otherwise) resided in the tribesman's mind. This latent knowledge was obviously not essential to the tribesman's survival and reproduction. How, then, could natural selection account for its evolution?

Humans appeared to possess an embarrassing wealth of these latent intellectual capacities that seemed to offer no survival or reproductive advantages. Examples included musical and artistic abilities, humor, speech, reasoning, and geometric and spatial understanding. The fact that nascent forms of these abilities were largely lacking in other species compounded the paradox of how they could have evolved naturally. Apes may be able to distinguish four bananas from two and, when offered a choice, may take the larger quantity. But how was this in any way a precursor to the sophisticated mathematics of human beings? Why was there no evidence of simple musical forms, art, or primitive religious systems in the animal world? What could natural selection have operated on in order to hone these abilities in humans? These were traits that seem to have appeared nearly full blown in the human animal and with little direct survival advantage. For Wallace, those mental attributes that seemed most uniquely human were also those with origins and purposes most deeply shrouded in mystery—a mystery that seemed beyond the explanatory power of natural selection.

Was Wallace Right?

It was because he saw the evolutionary process as inadequate to explain the totality of the human intellect that Wallace resorted to supernatural and mystical explanations for human uniqueness. If Wallace was correct, then the implications for evolutionary psychology are devastating. If humans have somehow "escaped" the processes that shape evolution, then those processes can hardly be used as means of understanding why humans are as we are. Most scientists, however, would object to Wallace's analysis and his invocation of the divine. Why?

First, science has a track record of filling in explanatory gaps and lifting veils of mystery. For example, as we will see later, studies have demonstrated that such faculties as mathematical thinking and linguistic abilities are present in other species and may very well provide the bases for those traits in humans. Second, evolutionary biologists are quick to point out that no adaptive trait can be assumed to have a direct linear history. For example, the bones of our middle ear, which are now used to help conduct sound vibrations, did not evolve from the "simpler" auditory bones of other animals. Instead, these bones were part of the jawbones of reptiles, which require a flexibly hinged chewing system. These intricate jawbone hinges were later co-opted (or "exapted," as biologist say) for use in auditory processing. Because similar convoluted histories may be behind a number of human traits, including intellectual ones, we might not expect to be able to identify simplified versions of human traits in other species.

Moreover, given the contortions of evolution, it becomes difficult to sort out the "selected for" traits from their accidental side effects. For example, the ability to operate effectively in a social context is directly tied to one's survival and ability to reproduce. An enlarged brain may have an advantage, because it can support more sophisticated communication and relational skills. But other brain-based abilities with no adaptive significance would also benefit from the expanding brain. So, as the brain grows, reasoning power, musical ability, and other mental traits improve, even though it is really socializing ability that accounts for the survival and reproductive advantage. Other abilities, in essence, come along for the ride.

Wallace may have been correct in pointing out the immense gap that appears to exist when comparing human intellect with that of other species. He may have been too quick, however, to conclude that that gap could not be understood scientifically and from an evolutionary perspective.

At the same time that evolutionary theory was making great strides at the hands of Darwin and Wallace, another approach to understanding human nature was also emerging: psychology. Although they coincided in both time and place, evolution and psychology would remain all but strangers to each other for many decades.

The Historical Background of Evolutionary Psychology

Evolution's Influence on Psychology

It is somewhat ironic that both Darwinian evolution and experimental psychology emerged in the latter half of the 19th century in the milieu of British and European academia but were almost entirely unrelated. The founders of evolutionary theory, such as Darwin, Wallace, Haeckel, and Huxley, were naturalists and biologists. The founders of experimental psychology, such as Wundt, Weber, and Fechner, were physiologists trained in a strongly reductionist tradition. Wundt, who established the first laboratory in experimental psychology, in Leipzig in 1879, was interested in the fundamental structure of conscious experience, not the adaptive history of that experience. American psychology emerged at the turn of the 20th century and largely inherited the European indifference to evolutionary ideas. The one notable exception was William James, who wholeheartedly embraced evolutionary thinking in his functional approach to psychology. However, James's influence was quickly eclipsed by behaviorism.

The behaviorist movement, ushered in by John Watson's seminal article in *Psychological Review* in 1913, defined scientific psychology as the study of observable causes and measurable behaviors. Most behaviorists saw little need to distinguish between the behaviors of various nonhuman animal species or between those of humans and animals. The same explanatory principles of stimulus and response were believed adequate for understanding the nature of all creatures. For example, behaviorists argued that learning exhibited **equipotentiality**. This meant that the same mechanisms of learning applied, regardless of the specific stimuli or responses involved. Thus, the evolutionary history of an organism was largely irrelevant when it came to how and what it learned from its environment.

Interest in evolutionary notions was not rekindled until the late 1950s and early 1960s, when behaviorism began to tire and ethology and cognitive science began to build steam. A number of factors contributed to this transition. First, some findings in behaviorist psychology itself called into question the concept of equipotentiality and implicated evolutionary factors in animal learning. A rat exposed to nausea-inducing radiation hours after eating a particular food had no problem associating the nausea with the food. However, associating the nausea with a buzzer or a flash of light was nearly impossible (Garcia, Ervin, & Koelling, 1966). It seemed rats were naturally "prepared" to learn certain associations but not others, and these learning biases were not random. Associating nausea with food has great adaptive value; associating nausea with lights has very little. How might such a bias arise? The presence of **prepared learning** in animals pointed many scientists, even behaviorists, in the direction of an organism's evolutionary history.

Second, the limitations of a strict behaviorist approach were becoming increasingly apparent in both animal and human research. For example, B.F. Skinner's (1957) attempt to explain human language based on the principles of operant conditioning was subjected to a devastating critique from Noam Chomsky (1959), who vividly illustrated just how much of language was left unexplained when viewed from the behaviorist's prism.

Third, in Europe, where behaviorism was never as dominant, **ethology** was flourishing in the expert hands of Konrad Lorenz and Niklaus Tinbergen. Ethologists took an evolutionary approach to understanding animal behavior and saw behavior as having adaptive value. For example, Tinbergen and Kuenen (1939) found that baby blackbirds would gape (present wide-open mouths) to a very specific visual stimulus. If two adjacent disks were placed before the nestling, with one disk about one third the diameter of the other, the nestling would gape (Fig. 1.3). If the relative sizes of the two disks deviated too much from this ratio, the nestling would not gape. It appeared that baby blackbirds were born with a visual template of "mom," and, when a stimulus matched that template, they would gape for food. The adaptive value of this behavior lies in the fact that if mom is present the only way to get fed is to gape. If mom is not present, then it is better to conserve energy. Although this behavior may make the unsuspecting nestlings subject to the tricks of devious ethologists, in the natural world the behavior works pretty well to get the nestling fed.

Studies like the blackbird experiment led to the development of the concept of a **fixed action pattern**; that is, a behavior that is triggered by an external event

"Mom"   Not "Mom"   Not "Mom"

Figure 1.3 Examples of stimuli used to elicit gaping response from nestling blackbirds. (Adapted from Hoffman, 1998.)

and that, once triggered, will be executed to its completion. For ethologists, fixed action patterns represented behaviors honed by natural selection for their adaptive value. In 1973, Lorenz, Tinbergen, and fellow ethologist Karl von Frisch were awarded the Nobel Prize for their contributions to the understanding of behavior and its causes. It did not go unnoticed that it was ethologists and not psychologists who were honored with science's most prestigious award for research on behavior (Plotkin, 1994). To add insult to injury, not only was the stodgy world of academia rewarding nonpsychologists for behaviorally oriented work, but the unwashed masses had joined in as well. In 1967, zoologist Desmond Morris published *The Naked Ape*, a best-selling book that used a comparative/evolutionary approach to address the question: what kind of animal is the human? Collectively, the growing shortcomings of behaviorism and the successes of alternative (including evolutionary) approaches eroded behaviorism's hegemony over psychology and energized a new generation of researchers to try out new paradigms.

One of the new paradigms that emerged at this time was the cognitive approach to psychology, which sought to directly address issues of mental processes. The cognitive revolution did not immediately embrace evolutionary thinking as part of its agenda. But the influence was important, because it legitimized "unobservables" as causal theoretical structures. Although no one had directly seen a short-term memory store or schema, these concepts were admitted as necessary and valid structures for understanding the working of the human mind. In addition, as the study of cognition moved steadily toward neuroscience, the evolutionary history of the brain became increasingly germane. By the 1970s, psychology's door was opening wider to evolution's influence.

Darwinian Motivations in Animal Behavior

Although psychologists historically were coy or even cold to evolution's overtures, evolutionists seem to have always evinced an interest in psychology, at least when it came to understanding the motivation behind certain animal behaviors. This is not to say that evolutionists think that explaining animal motivations requires "high-level" cognitive theorizing; quite the contrary. Evolutionists have made great strides fitting animal motivations into a satisfying Darwinian framework.

To illustrate what all this means, think of a familiar scene from a Nature or National Geographic television episode. Down on haunches, slinking low in the grass, the lioness moves ever closer to the antelope herd. Suddenly she springs, quickly identifies the slower moving youngster or the limping elderly animal, and, as the other antelope run past, pulls down her prey. Others in the pride soon join in, and the grizzly feast has begun. "Nature red in tooth and claw," "survival of the fittest": these are the common platitudes of Darwinism. Although possibly overstatements, they are not devoid of truth. Predators ensure that the slower and weaker of their prey are less likely to reproduce. Natural selection is not a compassionate or pretty process; it can be brutal. Each creature seems to be solely out for itself, preying on others while avoiding becoming another's prey, living just long enough to reproduce and then exit (often not so gracefully) from the scene.

Yet something has always seemed a bit wrong with this picture. It bothered Darwin from the very start. He took as the starting point for his dilemma the presence of sterile castes in many insects. If every creature was simply out to survive and reproduce, then what were these nonreproducing insects doing on the scene? Their sole purpose seemed to be the care and maintenance of their breeding counterparts, but such generosity seemed wholly inconsistent with the dog-eat-dog world of evolution. For those who came after Darwin, the dilemma only deepened. Look, for instance, at the behavior of some birds and wild dogs. Among Florida scrub jays, "helpers" in the nest are a common phenomenon. Some male birds will assist in the care and protection of another pair's nestlings (Woolfenden & Fitzpatrick, 1984). African wild dogs, jackals, and hyenas show a similar behavior pattern, with "helpers" caring for and feeding another's offspring (Bueler, 1973; Malcolm & Marten, 1982; Moehlman, 1979; Owens & Owens, 1984). Even the lions, at close inspection, are not nearly as self-absorbed as one might assume. Lionesses are not exclusive in their suckling of young in the pride. A female can and sometimes does nurse another's cubs (Packer et al., 1988; Packer, Lewis, & Pusey, 1992). This is remarkable when one considers the fact that lionesses have few concerns about predation, so the likelihood of a lion cub losing its mother is very small. Why would evolution bother making sure that other females would nurse an orphaned cub, when there are so few orphans around?

The problem with these seemingly altruistic behaviors is that they appear to put the altruist at a reproductive disadvantage compared with those who are not so inclined. Ponder for a moment what would happen if you put an altruistic lioness in a typical pride. Motivated as she is by her generous genes, our self-sacrificing lioness goes about nursing and caring for other lioness's cubs. The other lionesses are all too happy to receive her aid, because she is helping to ensure the survival of their offspring. However, because our altruist is expending her energy on other's cubs, she has less energy to bear and rear her own. Thus, the likelihood of her altruistic genes being propagated into the next generation is relatively small. It would seem that altruistic traits would be selected against, because they hold no advantage for the individual in reproduction.

So what's going on here? In 1964, graduate student William Hamilton (Box 1.1) argued that the key to understanding the seemingly altruistic behaviors of animals was **kinship**. What he meant by this was that when animals engage in helping behaviors, they most often are helping other animals who are related to them. The closer the relationship, the more likely an animal is to help. If the ultimate goal of each organism is the propagation of its own genetic material, then helping to ensure the survival of a brother or sister can be just as effective a strategy as producing an offspring, because half of one's genetic makeup is shared with direct offspring and with full siblings. Hamilton formalized this notion with the concept of **inclusive fitness**. Inclusive fitness refers to the success one has in spreading his or her genes into the next generation, not just through direct offspring but also through the descendants of kin (nieces, nephews, etc.). Thus, by helping relatives, one is (at least in a genetic sense) helping oneself.

Confirmation of Hamilton's ideas came when researchers began to study the genetic relatedness of animals engaging in altruistic acts. The "helper" scrub jays and African dogs, it turns out, are older siblings who have "hung around" to help raise their younger brothers and sisters (Bueler, 1973; Woolfenden & Fitzpatrick, 1984). Females in the lion pride are also genetically related, so again the help is

WILLIAM HAMILTON
Inclusive Fitness

PROFILE *William Hamilton was born in 1936 and was a graduate student at University College, London, in 1963 when he began working on the idea of inclusive fitness. The idea's originality, coupled with its highly mathematical presentation, aroused suspicion among Hamilton's supervisors, who initially rejected his dissertation work. Despite this early setback, he went on to hold positions at the Imperial College, London, the University of Michigan, and Oxford. He died in March 2000 after contracting malaria on an expedition to the Congo. Robert Trivers called Hamilton "one of the greatest evolutionary theorists since Darwin."*

BOX 1.1

Before Hamilton, the measure of an organism's fitness was defined narrowly as its relative reproductive success, or, how many surviving direct offspring it had compared with others. If, for example, I have four surviving offspring and you have only three, I have been more reproductively successful than you. Hamilton, however, realized that from a gene-centered point of view, this definition was too simplistic. Copies of an organism's genes are not only found in its direct offspring but also in its relatives and their offspring. My children share half of their genes with me but so do my sisters and brothers, and their children share a quarter of their genes with me. As far as my genes are concerned, a cadre of nieces and nephews can be just as "reproductively successful" as a few children. This was what Hamilton meant by inclusive fitness, the idea that reproductive success included direct offspring plus the offspring of relatives appropriately weighted by their degree of relatedness (i.e., a niece counts more than a cousin).

This idea had actually been discussed before Hamilton by both R.A. Fisher and J.B.S. Haldane. Nearly a decade before Hamilton's landmark 1964 article, Haldane noted that a gene for altruism might have a chance of spreading in a small population provided that the altruistic acts (jumping into a river to save a drowning child, for example) were directed at close relatives (Haldane, 1955). Strangely, however, neither Haldane nor Fisher, who proposed much the same idea, seemed impressed enough with the theory to devote much time to it. Hamilton's success forever changed our view of evolution. Gone was the idea of evolution as an unremitting contest among purely self-interested parties. Inclusive fitness meant that an organism's self-interest could lie in helping others, albeit a restricted set of others. Hamilton went on to make important contributions in other areas, such as reciprocal altruism and the role of parasites in sexual reproduction. He was working on the origins of the AIDS virus when he died.

"The last time I saw Bill," wrote Robert Trivers, "[was] at Oxford in December 1998. He pointed with pride to the two, possibly three, species of moss growing on his Volvo...and told me that this was a clear advantage of Oxford over Cambridge, the latter climate being too dry."

Source: Quotes taken from Robert Trivers's obituary of William Hamilton, (2000) *Nature, 404,* 828.

extended to a relative or a relative's offspring. Although genetics in beehives and ant colonies can be complex, inclusive fitness is found to be in effect there, too. The sterile workers are helping themselves by helping relatives who reproduce (Oldroyd, Smolenski, Cornuet, & Corzier, 1994; Ratnieks, 1988).

A second major development occurred in understanding the social behavior of animals in the early 1970s, when Robert Trivers (1971, 1972, 1974) formulated the notions of **reciprocal altruism** and **parental investment**. Reciprocal altruism refers to the fact that, in some animals such as chimpanzees, non-kin will form cooperative relationships based on a "tit-for-tat" arrangement. For example, chimp A grooms chimp B, and, later, chimp B returns the favor by sharing food with chimp A. (Technically this is referred to as interchange rather than reciprocity. However, evidence for both has been found in chimps; de Waal, 1989; de Waal & Luttrell, 1988.) Through their cooperation, both A and B stand better chances of moving themselves to more dominant positions in the chimpanzee social hierarchy, thus increasing their access to females and their reproductive potential.

Although reciprocal altruism seems to imply the building up of "credits" and the paying of "debts" as the basis for non-kin cooperative relationships, parental investment highlights the way in which even the most direct familial relationships also can be subject to a cost/benefit type of analysis. It seems obvious that parents would expend considerable time, energy, and resources taking care of their young, because their offspring are their direct genetic contribution to the next generation. What is less obvious is that a parent's investment in current offspring comes at a cost to future offspring. If the goal is to maximize the propagation of one's genes, then there may come a point at which investment in current offspring must end, so that time, energy, and resources can be directed toward another offspring. This concept explains both why a parent would defend its offspring against a predator and why it might give up that defense, saving itself and leaving the youngster to its fate. Formally stated, parental investment refers to parental energy expended on one offspring at the cost of investing in another. Related and of special importance to most mammalian species (such as humans) is the fact that greater parental investment is required of females than of males, because of the the extended period of internal gestation and postnatal suckling. This fact becomes central to understanding some observed sex differences.

The Grand Synthesis

The critical contribution of Hamilton and Trivers was that they gave the complex, social behaviors (including altruistic behaviors) of intelligent mammals a Darwinian explanation. Lions, dogs, and antelope do what they do for the same fundamental reason that frogs, fish, and fireflies do what they do: they all just want to maximize the propagation of their genes. As Oxford biologist Richard Dawkins likes to say, genes are "selfish." They "care" only about spreading and replicating themselves, and it matters little whether cockroaches, camels, or kittens are the vehicles for that transmission. The stage had been set for a grand synthesis, whereby a single theoretical viewpoint, that of the selfish gene, would serve as the explanatory principle for the behavior of all organisms great and small, microscopic to gigantic, bacterium to blue whale.

That task was left to Harvard biologist Edward O. Wilson (Box 1.2), who in 1975 published *Sociobiology: The New Synthesis*. A specialist in ants, Wilson methodically worked his way from insects to mammals, demonstrating the explanatory breadth and power of Darwinism as complemented by Hamilton and Trivers (and others). In his final chapter, Wilson did the unspeakable: he claimed that the same explanatory principles also held for humans. Although at the time he had little supportive data, Wilson confidently proclaimed that a complete understanding of human nature, extending even to such honored attainments as culture, art, religion, and ethics, would necessarily have to include the principle of "selfish genes."

Needless to say, all hell broke loose. For a time, Wilson's mere presence at a conference or meeting would bring protests and howls of disapproval. Certainly, critics argued, the same primitive motivation behind a frog's croak could not

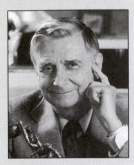

EDWARD O. WILSON
Sociobiology

PROFILE *Paradise Beach in Florida is special place for E.O. Wilson. As a boy, he was sent there to avoid the unpleasantness of his parent's divorce. Its fish, birds, and abundant beauty provided an escape from a rather rocky home life and instilled in him a lifelong passion for the natural world. Later, it was there that a fishing accident caused him to lose the sight in one eye, which, coupled with his already poor hearing seemed to eliminate any thoughts of being a field biologist—unless, of course, he wanted to study the minute, silent world of ants. Although a world-renowned entomologist, Wilson is best known as the champion of sociobiology, the idea that much of animal (including human) social behavior can be understood from an evolutionary perspective.*

BOX 1.2

Sociobiology and Its Critics

At first blush, ants may seem to be a strange starting point for developing a comprehensive theory of animal social behavior. However, ants are highly social creatures, and the ant colony is nothing less than a well-ordered, sophisticated society. As a practicing entomologist at Harvard, Wilson teamed up with Stuart Altmann, a specialist in the social behavior of rhesus monkeys. Together, they began to uncover common themes in social behavior that seemed to generalize across species. Wilson also underwent a self-described personal "paradigm" shift in 1965 while reading Hamilton's paper on inclusive fitness. On a long, slow train ride from Harvard to Florida, he plowed through Hamilton's dense prose. North of New Haven, he began reading the paper, greeting it skeptically. By the New Jersey marshes, he was dissecting it line by line, searching for the fatal flaw. Rolling across Virginia, he was frustrated and angered by the meticulous correctness of Hamilton's logic. As the train screeched into Miami, Wilson had given up. "I was a convert, and put myself in Hamilton's hands," he later said in his autobiography (Wilson, 1994, p. 320).

But it was a fruitful conversion. Hamilton's logic was crucial to Wilson's synthesis. Inclusive fitness provided a means of understanding the diverse social behavior of a wide range of animals, thus putting scientific force behind Wilson's sociobiological view. In 1975, Wilson published *Sociobiology: The New Synthesis*, a more-than-600-page volume, with a final chapter on humans that numbered less than 30 pages. It was this slim ending chapter that provoked a firestorm of controversy. By arguing that the fundamental origins of human behavior lie in genetics and evolution, Wilson was going against the political and social tide of the 1970s. He was accused of being a right-wing extremist bent on providing scientific cover for racism and discrimination. The tumult reached its zenith at the 1978 meeting of the American Association for the Advancement of Science, where Wilson had a jug of ice water dumped on his head while protesters chanted "racist Wilson you can't hide. We charge you with genocide!"

For Wilson, the public anger was regrettable but not entirely unexpected. Nonscientists often misinterpret scientific ideas. What he did not anticipate and found truly hurtful was animosity from his own Harvard colleagues. Among Wilson's most severe critics were Stephen Jay Gould and Richard Lewontin, fellow Harvard faculty members. In his autobiography, Wilson laments the fact that they never approached him personally or privately to discuss their concerns but, instead, savaged him publicly and without warning. Although the "evolution wars" were trying, Wilson has remained a congenial, southern-bred gentleman and an unrepentant believer in the power of biology. Over the years, he has continued to contribute books dealing with the evolutionary origins of human nature, culture, religion, and the arts. He latest book, *Consilience: The Unity of Knowledge* (1998), continues in this vein, arguing that a biological perspective will eventually pervade the humanities and social sciences.

Sources: Those interested in his role in the sociobiology controversy are encouraged to read Wilson's autobiography, *Naturalist* (1994), and *Defenders of truth: The sociobiology debate* (2000), by Ullica Segerstrale.
Photo: Courtesy of Edward O. Wilson. Photo by Jon Chase, Harvard News Office.

explain Shakespeare's sonnets! The human sense of beauty, concern for justice and truth, human love and spirituality—these characteristics were self-evidently and qualitatively different from anything evolution had managed to squeeze out of the earth's more "primitive" inhabitants. For a while at least, these arguments tended to hold sway among most social scientists. Although they were aware of the rumblings in evolutionary biology, most psychologists, sociologists, and other practitioners of human studies remained smugly confident that Wilson's Godzilla would not threaten their academic terrain.

Their security, however, was an illusion. Certain trends in psychology had already pried open its gates to evolution's influence. One of the first indications that the evolutionary approach was seeping its way into psychology came from a series of provocative studies in the early and mid 1980s dealing with family violence. Martin Daly and Margo Wilson of McMaster University in Canada examined homicide data from Detroit police records of 1972. They were motivated by what seemed to be an evolutionary conundrum. Why would most homicides occur between family members when, according to evolutionary theory, our selfish genes should motivate us to help, not harm, our kin? The answer they uncovered was that most family homicides were not, genetically speaking, between family members at all but were spousal homicides (Daly & Wilson, 1982). Moreover, they found that homicide rates for children, parents, and other genetic relatives were actually lower than those for nonrelatives. Within a household, nonrelatives (such as roommates or boarders) were 11 times more likely to be homicide victims than were blood kin. According to Daly and Wilson, there was no conundrum when it came to understanding lethal behavior among humans. Hamilton's principles still applied, just as they did with every other animal.

In 1989, psychologist Leda Cosmides and her husband, anthropologist John Tooby, produced evidence that human reasoning ability was tailored specifically for solving problems of social exchange, just as evolutionary theory would predict (given our heritage as a group-living species). In 1992, Cosmides, Tooby, and Jerome Barkow edited *The Adapted Mind*, a collection of writings that was instrumental in helping to define the emerging field of evolutionary psychology. Finally, in the early and mid 1990s, University of Texas (Austin) psychologist David Buss undertook an ambitious cross-cultural research project assessing human mate preferences. The findings, consistent with evolutionary expectations, showed that regardless of differences in culture, religion, race, etc., women tend to prefer older men with status and resources, whereas men tend to prefer younger, attractive, healthy-looking women (Buss & Schmitt, 1993). What these pioneers in the evolutionary psychology movement had demonstrated was that in our habits of love, sex, thought, and murder, humans show just as much evidence of operating by evolutionary principles as any other animal. Wilson may have been overly exuberant about the potential of sociobiology two decades ago. However, as the 20th century drew to a close, more and more social scientists were recognizing that being overly exuberant was not the same as being wrong! The evolutionary approach to understanding human nature had matured into a credible enterprise.

Humanity: A Soul from Dirt

For more than 2,000 years, humanity has sought to understand itself. For as long as we can remember we have yearned to know what it is that makes us human. The evolutionary perspective and the tools of modern science are only the latest vehicles for continuing this ancient and noble quest. The philosophers of old have told us that we possess a rational soul. It was our soul that accounted for our intellect, reasoning power, self-control, and even immortality. Lacking the rational soul, animals were governed by desire or they were lifeless automata. But how did this magnificent soul arise? Plato and the Christian thinkers who followed him believed it to be simply a gift from God. The soul was heavenly, not earthly. It was, in Plato's view, made of stardust and to the stars it would return when freed by death from its imprisonment within the body—a lofty and romantic notion that crashed and burned in the shadow of Darwinism. Our souls, however one wishes to define the term, were not bestowed from the heavens but instead arose from the dirt at our feet. Through a long, arduous, and meandering evolutionary process, humans emerged from the countless forms and families that came before. The uniqueness of human nature did not fall as dust from the wings of passing angels but bore up battle-hardened and bloodied from the clay below. A steep price was paid for what we have, and recognizing this fact may shake us into a deeper appreciation of what it means to be human. In this volume we will take a detailed look at the process that forged our distinctly human nature, with a keen eye toward identifying the unique attributes of our species.

SUMMARY

Throughout history, humans have been keenly interested in what made us different from other animals. Ancient philosophers ascribed this difference to our rational souls. With the emergence of Darwinism in the 19th century, we became aware of the extent of our interconnections with the natural world, and arguments for our continuity (as well as potential discontinuity) with other species followed. Psychology remained largely separate from developments in evolutionary biology until the 1950s and 1960s. Important theoretical concepts, such as inclusive fitness and parental investment, helped to explain animal social behaviors and seemed to have implications for human behavior as well. By the 1980s and 1990s, increasing numbers of psychologists were borrowing concepts from evolution and using them as bases for investigating human behavior. Their success spawned a new approach called evolutionary psychology.

KEY TERMS

catastrophism	inclusive fitness	reciprocal altruism
cultural determinism	kinship	sociobiology
ethology	parental investment	uniformitarianism
evolutionary psychology	prepared learning	
fixed action patterns	rational soul	

REVIEW QUESTIONS

1. What problems are associated with postulating a rational soul as an explanation for human nature?

2. What are the basic principles espoused by evolutionary psychology concerning human nature and the origins of many human traits?

3. Describe some of the factors that led 18th- and 19th-century scholars to adopt a more evolutionary perspective on the emergence of different species.

4. What arguments were used by Darwin to support the notion of evolutionary continuity between humans and other animals and by Wallace to support discontinuity?

5. How did Hamilton's notion of inclusive fitness change the current view of evolution?

6. Describe how "prepared learning" and the work of European ethologists served to bring psychology into closer contact with evolution.

SUGGESTED READINGS

Eisley, L. (1958). *Darwin's century.* New York: Doubleday.

Kemp, S. (1990). *Medieval psychology.* Westport, CT: Greenwood Press.

Raby, P. (2000). *Alfred Russel Wallace.* London: Chatto & Windus.

Segerstrale, U. (2000). *Defenders of truth.* Oxford, UK: Oxford University Press.

Wilson, E.O. (1994). *Naturalist.* Washington, D.C.: Island Press.

WEB SITES

http://psychclassics.yorku.ca/ classic readings in the history of psychology.

www.philosophypages.com/hy/ readings in the history of philosophy.

http://www.ucmp.berkeley.edu/history/evolution.html readings in the history of evolution from Aristotle to the Modern Synthesis.

Evolutionary Psychology: Basic Concepts

History Matters

ANCIENT GREECE IS OFTEN CITED as the birthplace of democratic ideals. Yet Plato (428–347 BCE), one of ancient Greece's most famous philosophers, argued in his *Republic* that the ideal society would be ruled by a king surrounded by a small clique of elites. Plato's utopia hardly fits our concept of a democracy. However, his disenchantment with democracy is easier to understand if one is aware that, as a young man, Plato watched Athenian democracy descend into mindless excess, a path that would lead ultimately to the condemnation and death of his mentor, Socrates. In that historical context, Plato's *Republic* and its antidemocratic overtones make more sense.

Plato's story is a reminder of an important lesson: history matters. To have a complete understanding of an individual, it is necessary to know something of the history of that individual. The same is true for a species. We cannot fully appreciate why a species is the way it is unless we understand something about its evolutionary history. The history of the person or species leaves its mark on the present state—that is precisely the lesson that Darwinian evolution teaches (Gould, 1986). Evolutionary psychology seeks to understand humanity and human nature in light of its evolutionary history. For centuries, philosophers have ruminated over what it is that lies at the heart of human nature. Before Darwin and Wallace, those ruminations remained only speculative, with little or no evidence or empirical testing. Evolutionary theory, however, has provided a new tool for addressing this question. By understanding how our evolutionary past has molded our modern psyches, evolutionary psychology has the potential to extend our age-old philosophical quest to understand ourselves in unprecedented and highly productive ways. The ancient Greeks would be envious!

Evolutionary Psychology

Simply put, evolutionary psychology is the study of the imprint left upon us by our species' evolutionary journey. More formally, evolutionary psychology is the application of Darwinian principles to the understanding of human nature. At the heart of the evolutionary approach is the idea that the human mind is an evolved, adapted organ. As such, it does not confront the world as a tabula rasa (blank slate) but with evolutionarily designed predispositions, such as a propensity toward learning language, recognizing faces, an attraction to sweet-tasting foods, and a revulsion to feces. These predispositions owe their existence to our species' evolutionary history.

About 5 million years ago, two evolutionary branches diverged. One eventually produced humans, and the other evolved into the chimpanzees, our closest primate relatives (Sarich & Wilson, 1967; Sibley & Alquist, 1987). That 5-million-year stretch of time has been marked by dramatic climate change, long periods of stasis, and the emergence and extinction of numerous species before the existence of our own species, *Homo sapiens*. When *H. sapiens* arrived, however, we were not cut from whole cloth (so to speak) but instead were mended and patched from what had gone before. The physical and behavioral structures of our ancestors provided the foundation upon which the human species emerged. The echoes of our journey can be found deep within our particular and peculiar human nature.

The Environment of Evolutionary Adaptedness

A central concept in evolutionary psychology is the **environment of evolutionary adaptedness** or the **EEA**. This is the environmental context in which most of the mental and behavioral traits we think of as specifically human evolved. There are really two notions of the EEA used by evolutionary psychologists. The first is a more generalized or species-level EEA. Bowlby (1969), for example, defined the EEA for *H. sapiens* as the Pleistocene hunter–gatherer stage of history. By this he was referring to two things: (1) the Pleistocene epic, which is a term used to describe a block of time on the geologic time scale beginning about 2 million years ago and ending about 10,000 years ago; and (2) the lifestyle in which our ancestors engaged, involving survival in mobile, tribal units in which game hunting and local foraging were the primary means of obtaining food. Thus, for almost 2 million years our ancestors were confronted with repeated problems of how to survive, reproduce, and live more or less peaceably in relatively small, mobile, kin-based groups that had to hunt and search for edibles in their environments.

Thinking of the EEA as a certain period in history when our ancestors were engaged in a consistent lifestyle may be a valuable heuristic. It can be criticized, however, for being far too general. A second and more frequent interpretation of the EEA is that it represents the sum total of the selection pressures confronted by ancestral humans relative to a specific trait in their more recent evolutionary history (say in the last 200,000 rather than 2 million years). Put another way, one should think of the EEA as the particular aspects of the recent Pleistocene environment that were critical in the evolution of a certain trait. We should think in terms not of a single EEA but of many EEAs, different ones or different combinations for each trait that might be studied (Crawford, 1998). For example, many evolutionary psychologists would contend that female nurturance is an evolved adaptive trait. However, this trait probably had little to do with the need for foraging Pleistocene females to discriminate ripe from rotten fruits. It probably had more to do with the fact that the Pleistocene environment was rife with predators, environmental hazards, and other hominins who presented a constant mortal threat to an unattended infant or child. It was most likely these specific elements of the ancestral environment that were relevant in shaping our mothers with a heightened sensitivity and concern about the well-being of their children and a tendency to keep those children in close proximity. Mothers who lacked these traits were less likely to successfully pass on their genetic material.

Furthermore, over the course of tens of thousands of years, the interaction of a species and its environment may change significantly. The same adaptation may be subject to different environmental conditions (or selection pressures) at different times. Consider this possible scenario for the evolution of human communication. Early in our evolution, the males who could make the deepest, loudest, most threatening sounds were at an advantage when it came to reproduction. They could scare away other males and thereby gain access to more females. Later, however, as hominin groups grew larger and the need to cooperate with other group members became more critical, the environment favored those males who could speak fluently and articulate precisely, rather than the large, loud "boomers." The EEA for male speech patterns then cannot be defined as any one specific moment in time but must be considered an aggregation of separate circumstances occurring at different times. This is why the EEA is often thought of in statistical terms as a "multivariate and dynamic niche space that mathematically describes selection pressures on evolving humans" (Mealey, as quoted in Crawford, 1998, p. 281).

Assumptions of Evolutionary Psychology

By taking an evolutionary approach to understanding human nature, evolutionary psychology makes certain assumptions or adopts certain premises about human thought and behavior.

Proximate and Ultimate Explanations

The first assumption is that human behavior can be explained at both a **proximate** and an **ultimate** level of analysis. Evolutionary explanations are ultimate in nature rather than proximate. An example will clarify this distinction. Why is it that people, especially adolescents, are so concerned about keeping up with popular trends in looks, fashion, music, and talk? A proximate explanation might be that people want to "fit in." They want to belong to the right crowd and have the right friends. But one can push the question further. Why do people want to fit in? Why are they concerned (sometimes to a pathological extent) about being "in" with the "right" crowd?

An ultimate explanation, which incorporates an evolutionary perspective, would be that people are actually concerned about their reproductive success. In our evolutionary past, being part of the group was not an option but a necessity. One simply could not survive alone. To be banished from the group and, therefore, separated from the group's protection and resources was a death sentence. Moreover, establishing status and respect within the group could produce rewards in increased resources and greater access to mates, thus increasing possible offspring. The motivation to be a respected member of a premier group is a deeply ingrained and evolved psychological attribute. One would expect the drive toward establishing strong group ties to be especially keen in adolescence, when reproductive potential is just emerging and adult patterns are being established. The fact that people sometimes work so hard to be good group members that they actual-

Figure 2.1 Specialized structure for solving an adaptive problem. Note the exceptionally long claws and extended bony middle "finger" on this aye-aye (a small prosimian that lives in the forests of Madagascar). Aye-ayes feed on insect larvae that live below the surface bark of trees. The aye-aye's protruding claw is a specialized tool for probing deep within a tree's cracks and fissures to extract the larvae. (Courtesy of the Duke Primate Center. Photo by David Haring)

ly risk their health and future well-being suggests that this adaptation, once so useful in our evolutionary history, is now often problematic.

Evolutionary psychologists would not argue that people are consciously aware of their ultimate concern in this matter. Conscious awareness of ultimate motivations is not necessary as long as the proximate mechanisms are sufficient to achieve the desired end. However, it is the ultimate explanation that the evolutionary psychologist wants to understand and test empirically.

Domain Specificity

A second important assumption is that of **domain specificity**. This refers to the idea that the human mind has evolved to solve specific adaptive problems. Domain specificity is a key concept in evolutionary psychology's understanding of the mind, so we will consider this assumption carefully. First, we need to understand what is meant by an **adaptive problem**. An adaptive problem has two characteristics: (1) it was recurrently present in the EEA, and (2) it affected the individual's success in reproduction. The most obvious example of an adaptive problem would be finding a mate. Generation after generation, consistently over the hundreds of thousands of years of human evolution, our ancestors had to find mates in order to produce offspring. Thus, the "mate finding" challenge easily qualifies as a recurrent problem. Even more obvious is the fact that if one failed to find a mate, success at reproduction would be seriously affected. Our ancestors were those who were the most successful at solving this particular adaptive problem. Examples of other adaptive problems might include: distinguishing kin from non-kin, identifying life-threatening circumstances, avoiding pathogens, discriminating ripe from rotten edibles, communicating with others, and identifying safe and productive habitats.

Next, we need to understand that evolution solves adaptive problems through specific, narrowly tailored physical and behavioral structures. Again, some simple examples will help. How could one solve the adaptive problem of distinguishing between ripe and rotten edibles? Organs capable of processing light energy and providing information about the color, size, and shape of objects would certainly fill the bill. Eyes allow an organism to process light information, thus providing the capacity to visually distinguish ripe from rotten fruit. Another example is the immune system, which protects an organism from pathogens, thus providing it with a defense against potentially fatal infections. Lungs oxygenate blood, livers detoxify blood, and hearts circulate blood, all providing metabolic energy for the organism. Each of these structures is highly effective at its specific objective but woefully ineffective at tasks for which it was not designed. Immune systems, for instance, are all but useless when it comes to processing light energy, and eyes make extraordinarily incompetent blood pumps. The lesson here is clear: to solve adaptive problems, evolutionary processes create domain-specific (rather than generalized) problem-solving structures.

For evolutionary psychologists, the brain (whose functioning gives rise to the mind) simply represents another evolved physical structure designed to solve adaptive problems, similar to other organs of the human body, such as the lungs or stomach. As such, it is specialized for performing certain functions critical to the survival and reproductive success of the organism. The important implication is that the mind is not a general learning device (as some cognitive scientists have claimed) but, instead, is a collection of narrowly focused problem-solving specialists. A recent review by Gallistel (2000) has offered broad support for the notion of functionally specialized learning programs in various species. Gallistel analyzed a broad range of learning problems faced by different animals, such as desert ants, pigeons, bees, and others, and concluded that only task-specific learning mechanisms attuned to the organism's environmental niche could account effectively for how these animals learned what they did. Evolutionary psychologists simply contend that what is true of other species extends to humans as well.

Evolutionary psychologist Leda Cosmides likens the mind to a Swiss army knife: not a single, all-purpose cutting instrument but a varied collection of separate tools, each designed for effectively performing a specific task (Cosmides, 1994). For example, it has been shown that normally difficult reasoning tasks are relatively simple for people to solve when recast as problems that require the detection of cheaters (for example, determining whether someone did or did not carry through on a promise). The reason for this, it is claimed, is that we evolved as a group-living species and it was important for tribe members to be proficient at determining which other members were trustworthy and which were not (Cosmides, 1989; Cosmides & Tooby, 1989). Thus, rather than evolving a generalized abstract reasoning system, our minds evolved a specialized reasoning subsystem for making judgments about social justice (a cheat-detecting program).

These different specially programmed subsystems are often referred to as **mental modules**. A module can be thought of as a relatively self-contained mental system with its own acquisition, retention, and retrieval processes and its own rules of operation (Fodor, 1983; Sherry & Shacter, 1987). These properties mean that a module is informationally encapsulated or functionally independent of other mental functions. A good illusionist takes great advantage of this property when he or she appears to saw off limbs or pull rabbits out of a hat. Although rational thought tells you that these events are impossible, this does little to dispel the illusion. The rules by which the visual system determines cause and effect are encapsulated from or functionally independent of higher level logic. The functioning of a module represents an evolved solution to a recurrent problem posed by the EEA. Examples of modules might be: human face recognition ability, language acquisition and use, cheat detection mechanisms, interpreting physical causality, and ascribing mental states to others (see Duchaine, Cosmides, & Tooby, 2001, for a review of the various modules of the brain).

Interactionist Approach

A third assumption is that human nature must be explained using an **interactionist** approach to the ongoing nature/nurture controversy. Nature/nurture refers to whether the human mind is best understood as a product of one's genetic endowment (nature) or if it is best understood as a product of the environment (nurture). For centuries, debates have raged over whether humans are the products of the genes they inherit or the learning they acquire. Evolutionary psychologists firmly reject both genetic determinism and environmental determinism and, instead, contend that both genes and environment must be considered in understanding the human mind. Thus, neither nature nor nurture alone can adequately explain why humans are they way they are. Our genes are programmed to respond differently to varying environmental circumstances. It is within this gene–environment interaction that an understanding of both human diversity and universality can be found.

Consider, for example, human mating strategies. Undoubtedly, a genetic factor is important in the mating strategies that we employ. However, our genes may be designed so that we are highly sensitive to environmental feedback indicating our own mate value (e.g., are we beautiful or ugly?), and that input triggers a tendency toward a certain mating strategy (Landolt, Lalumiere, & Quinsey, 1995). A male swooned over by throngs of females is more likely to adopt a strategy of many short-term matings to maximize his genetic contribution to the next generation, whereas a more homely male may opt for loyalty to a single mate. Both strategies could have genetic roots; only their manifestations are influenced by the environment.

As an example of universality, consider incest taboos. Prohibitions against sexual relations with close kin have been present in nearly all human societies. A genetic component seems likely, given that inbreeding has deleterious effects on an organism's fitness, often producing malformed and/or sterile offspring. Moreover, the presence in nonhuman animals of mechanisms to avoid sex with close relatives, such as the dispersal of adolescents from their natal groups in apes and monkeys, further supports the involvement of genetics in the avoidance of inbreeding. However, this cannot be the entire story in understanding human incest taboos.

Wolf (1995) has convincingly demonstrated that another key element of incest avoidance involves consistent, close interaction between individuals before 30 months of age. When nonrelated children are raised together in close quarters as brother and sister, as often occurs, for example, on an Israeli kibbutz, they tend to have little if any sexual interest in one another. It is as if the genes are programmed to turn sexual interest "off" toward anyone who was consistently present in the early years of life. Notice that this is both a fairly effective means of avoiding incest and a mechanism that depends on environmental input for its functioning.

It is also important to note how, in both of these examples, the genetic contribution was not something that appeared "at birth." Often, claiming that there is a genetic factor to a trait is misinterpreted as meaning that the trait was present at birth. Certainly the genes were present at birth, but notice how the unfolding of environmental events over time affected the ultimate expression of the genetic tendency. An evolutionary approach sees humans as endowed with various genetic propensities that come to fruition (or fail to) over an individual's lifetime, based on feedback from the environment. Neither mapping an infant's genome nor thoroughly dissecting his or her social environment can adequately provide the full picture of personality or potential.

The Primacy of Emotions and the Unconscious Mind

Science can sometimes make strange bedfellows! In a rather ironic twist, the evolutionary approach emerging at the dawn of the 21st century finds itself dusting off an old Freudian idea popular at the dawn of the 20th century: the **unconscious mind**. For evolutionary psychologists, the vast majority of what drives our thinking and behaviors occurs below our level of conscious awareness. Freud was deeply right about the pervasive influence of the unconscious on our waking lives. He was deeply wrong, however, about the nature of the unconscious (see Box 2.1 for a discussion of the connection between Freud and Darwin).

A fourth important assumption of evolutionary psychology is that most of our evolved mental endowment resides unconsciously and manifests itself emotionally. Why is this so? First, regardless of whether one takes an evolutionary approach or not, modern science reveals that most of our mental processing occurs below our level of awareness. We know, for example, that the visual system processes incoming light energy using separate channels for color, motion, edges, and contrasts. But none of this decomposition process is part of visual awareness. Instead, we can immediately and effortlessly perceive a specific visual scene, such as grandma's face or a bucolic landscape. Similar things can be said for auditory processing, the understanding and production of language, and execution of motor behaviors. A great deal of our mental lives is simply not available to consciousness. Given this fact, it would be rather surprising if our evolved mental solutions to adaptive problems faced in the EEA were conscious. After all, millions of species were solving adaptive problems long before anything resembling conscious deliberation appeared on the scene. Our ancestors just inherited that machinery and put it to use in their specific context.

But if our evolved mental solutions to adaptive problems are largely unavailable to conscious inspection, why would they manifest themselves in our emotions? The answer is that "feeling" is one of evolution's oldest mechanisms for attracting

Freud, Darwin, and Unconscious Motivations

BOX 2.1 Sigmund Freud maintained that children went through a series of psychosexual stages of development, which included the oral, anal, phallic, and genital stages. Today, most developmentalists see little scientific value in Freud's original proposal. Some researchers, however, are breathing new Darwinian life into old Freudian ideas. At first blush, the notion of uniting Freud with Darwin seems almost laughable. To many, Freud represents psychology's flawed, unscientific past, whereas Darwin offers a brighter, more rigorous future. Although many important differences separate the Freudian and Darwinian approaches, they share a central theme: the importance of the unconscious mind. Freud saw a child's progression through the different psychosexual developmental stages as driven by the largely unconscious interplay of id, ego, and superego. Evolutionary psychologists see many of our behaviors and emotional responses as driven by largely unconscious strategies for maximizing fitness. Perhaps Freud and Darwin are more akin than one might suspect.

As Freud originally envisioned it, the oral stage was one in which the infant gained libidinal gratification from getting objects into the mouth. Darwinian-minded Freudians now suggest that the oral stage may have more to do with the infant's fitness rather than sexual interests. Breastfeeding has a contraceptive effect, and hunter–gatherer women are known to breastfeed an infant for up to 3 years to space out the timing of pregnancies. A 3- or 4-year birth interval is not just good for women, it also helps to ensure an infant's survival. The arrival of a newborn sibling often leads to early weaning of an older child, a situation so dangerous for the older child's nutritional welfare that in West Africa it is

actually described as a disease: the disease of the displaced one. An infant's exaggerated oral behaviors, especially those directed at mother's nipples, may hold fitness advantages, not only in helping to supply the infant with nutrition but also in forestalling the birth of a younger sibling who might threaten its very survival.

Freud's most (in)famous concept was that of Oedipal conflict. During the phallic stage, Freud argued, a young boy would be sexually attracted to his mother and view his father as a rival for her affection. From a perspective of parental investment, the Oedipal conflict really is not so crazy. Mother is normally the far more heavily investing parental figure, and a child's affectionate displays directed at mother are likely to promote increases in investing behaviors, all of which is in the fitness interests of the child. As the child gets older, however, father's fitness interests shift from facilitating mother's continued investment in the current child to impregnating her to produce more offspring. It seems reasonable that at some point the conflicting interests of father and child over how mother invests her energies will come to a peak, with the child displaying ever-increasing affectionate behaviors and father becoming increasingly resentful of mother/child closeness. One problem with this, of course, is that it should apply equally to both young boys and girls, contrary to the male emphasis put forth by Freud.

It remains to be seen whether Freud and Darwin prove to be a comfortable fit, and if Freud enjoys a resurgence in a Darwinian guise. The tentative steps being taken to find common ground between these two influential thinkers certainly merit attention and no doubt will continue to arouse interest and controversy.

Source: **Badcock, C.R. (1998).** PsychoDarwinism: The new synthesis of Darwin and Freud. In C. Crawford & D.L. Krebs (Eds.), *The handbook of evolutionary psychology* (pp. 457–483). Mahwah, NJ: Erlbaum.

an organism toward beneficial stimuli and repulsing it from harmful ones. The capacity to discriminate between beneficial and harmful stimuli was present in the earliest mobile single-celled life forms more than 3 billion years ago. These cells used **chemotaxis** or the ability to sense chemicals in the environment and move either toward or away from them. Few would argue that these cells had any subjective "feeling" associated with their attraction toward or repulsion away from the chemicals they encountered. As nervous systems became more complex, however, internal attractive and repellant states (primitive pleasures and pains) evolved to pull organisms toward life-enhancing stimuli and push them away from life-threatening ones. Organisms with relatively large brains experience these attractive and repulsive states as "emotions," which continue to serve the same adaptive function.

Over the course of human evolution, emotions represented an efficient means of compelling us to engage in behaviors beneficial to our survival and reproduction while causing us to avoid those that were detrimental. Efficient is the key term here. Consider the fate of two long-ago humans confronted by a snake. One used conscious deliberation to decide whether the snake really was dangerous, pondered the various exit routes for escape, considered the cost/benefits of trying to kill the snake for food, and weighed the ethical arguments for and against the killing of other living organisms for survival. The other just ran off, screaming. By the time our first human had decided on a course of action, he or she may already have been nursing a potentially fatal snake bite. By merely following emotions, the second human enhanced the probability of passing on his or her genes. In our evolutionary past, quick reactions could have been the difference between reproductive success or failure. Emotion provided a fast, efficient way of sizing up dangers and opportunities in the environment.

A skeptic might respond, "That all may be well and good, but if natural selection designed my emotions to attract me to things beneficial to survival and reproduction and repel me from things harmful to survival and reproduction then why am I so attracted to chocolate? It's bad for my health, ruinous to my physique, and makes me break out. How is any of that good for my survival and reproduction?" This type of question raises a very important point about the evolutionary process: it does not have the power to ensure that creatures produce numerous offspring. Instead, *all natural selection can do is design creatures with physical structures and behavioral tendencies that in the past history of the species have been associated with higher rates of reproduction.* Emotions are the vehicles by which natural selection compels us to engage in those behaviors that were associated in the past with relatively higher rates of reproduction.

Let's look carefully at what this means. It would do no good for a creature to be born with the single echoing thought in its head, "Go reproduce! Go reproduce!" Such a creature would forget to eat, would walk unknowingly into the clutches of predators, and would waste time trying to mate with anything and everything that passed by. Reproduction is a complicated business with a whole host of related activities as prerequisites. One has to survive to sexual maturity, be able to identify receptive mates, secure food, avoid becoming food, fend off competitors, build a nest, and engage in a number of other activities. Going back to our earlier example, running away from snakes in no way assures one of having lots of offspring. In our evolutionary past, however, it did make it more likely that one would survive long enough to have the opportunity to reproduce (as compared with those who were not afraid). In addition, craving energy-rich foods would also have made it more likely in the past that one might survive long enough to have reproductive opportunities. Thus, the attraction to sugars would have been advantageous, especially in an environment in which resources were scarce. Although our environment has changed significantly from that of our ancestors, our emotions have not. They still push and pull us to act in ways that made our long-ago ancestors more likely to survive and reproduce.

This can be summed up with the following statements: (1) natural selection has filled our minds with specific solutions to adaptive problems faced in our ancestral past, and (2) this mental inheritance is largely unconscious but (3) will manifest itself in emotions designed to get us to engage in certain behaviors that were associated in the past with high rates of reproduction.

Contrast Between Current and Ancestral Environments

A fifth important assumption of evolutionary psychology is the notion that there is a significant contrast between the current and the ancestral environments. In other words, our modern environment differs in important ways from the environment in which the human species evolved. For almost 2 million years, hominins lived in small hunter–gatherer groups. Today, most of us live in densely populated urban centers, surrounded by unrelated co-workers and strangers and challenged by technological devices and symbolically represented information utterly foreign to our evolutionary heritage. We are strangers in a strange land—of our own making! Many of our adaptations may be out of step with our current context. As alluded to previously, our craving for sweet-tasting morsels may have been quite functional in a setting in which sugar was a highly valued and rare energy source. Being attracted to sweet-tasting fruits helped keep our bodies energized in an environment in which rigorous work and constant movement were the norm. The "sweet tooth," however, is disadvantageous given the sedentary lives that most of us now lead. The result in terms of health and dental problems has been devastating for many.

Two signs often point to a significant difference in the ancestral and current environments. The first is evidence of widespread physical or psychological malfunction or maladjustment. For example, the presence of numerous stress-related diseases and infections has led some to conclude that the current environment activates the human stress response in an "unnatural" way (Neese & Williams, 1994; Sapolsky, 1994). We can imagine hunters during the Pleistocene spending long hours patiently stalking prey. In a few frenzied moments of high energy, the mortal chase commenced. In this scenario, the rush of adrenaline, the rapid increase in heart rate and respiration, and other aspects of sympathetic nervous system activity would explode into action only rarely and briefly in the course of a typical day. Our modern world, however, may cause many of us to remain at a level of high tension for most of the working day. Because our stress response did not evolve to deal with an environment that calls for its constant use, the result may be stress-related illness, brought on by environmental conditions significantly varied from those of our evolutionary history.

A second important sign of environmental difference is the rarity of some behavior patterns in the ethnographic record. If researchers study 100 different cultures around the world and find only 1 or 2 that practice a certain behavior pattern, we might conclude that the peculiar behavior pattern has been brought on by the unique conditions of that culture, conditions that are very likely different from the ancestral conditions of our evolution. An example of this might be the rarity of polyandry in human societies. Polyandry refers to a single wife sharing many husbands. Although monogamy (one husband, one wife) and polygyny (one husband, many wives) are fairly common across human cultures, polyandry has been found in only 4 of 849 cultures studied (Daly & Wilson, 1983). These cultures usually are found in extremely harsh environmental conditions in which the resources of many men are required to support a single family.

It should be pointed out, however, that not all researchers are in agreement about the meaning of the differences between current and ancestral environments. One could argue that when it comes to the basic functions of human existence, our environments are pretty much the same as they were 1 million years ago and that whatever differences are present are trivial. Crawford (1998), for example, points out that, just as in the Pleistocene, we humans continue to successfully mate, raise children, form communities and coalitions, settle disputes, detect cheaters, and cheat occasionally ourselves when we can get away with it. Dunbar (1996) estimates that the average person, whether he or she lives in a small town or large city, has around 150 friends and social acquaintances—a number that, given the average size of hunter–gatherer tribes, has probably remained fairly constant since Pleistocene times. It may be an oversimplification to say that the current environment is the same as or different from the ancestral one. Instead, we must look at more specific aspects of each and evaluate them individually.

Evolutionary Psychology and Psychology

Psychology defines itself broadly as the study of behavior and mental processes. Given the generality of this endeavor, it is hardly surprising that over the past century "psychology" has splintered into a diverse collection of subdisciplines, each jealously guarding its defined slice of the psychological pie. A sampling of these subdisciplines includes:

Cognitive: focuses on mental processes, such as memory, language, and problem solving;

Physiological: focuses on the anatomy and physiology of the brain and nervous system;

Developmental: focuses on the physical, intellectual, and emotional changes that occur over the lifespan of individuals;

Social: focuses on how group dynamics affect individual thought and behavior;

Sensation and perception: focuses on how sense information is processed and interpreted; and

Clinical: focuses on pathologies of thought, behavior, and affect.

Given the defined focus of each subdiscipline, certain questions naturally emerge as better suited to be targets of research. For example, asking whether episodic and semantic memory constitute independent systems or simply different aspects of the same system makes far more sense within a cognitive framework than, say, a social one. Likewise, asking how the capacity to empathize changes over the childhood years is an appropriate developmental pursuit but not a well-formulated question for a physiologist. The important point here is that each subdiscipline addresses issues in a manner fitting to its domain. The issues may overlap. For example, a physiologist may address the issue of empathy, but the questions asked about empathy will not be the same as those posed by a developmentalist (e.g., what neurotransmitters are released during an empathic response?).

How does evolutionary psychology fit within this framework? One of the most important points about evolutionary psychology is that it is *not* aimed at creating just another of the already too numerous psychological subdisciplines!

If, 20 years hence, introductory textbooks simply include an evolutionary chapter along with the biological, social, and developmental ones, then evolutionary psychology will have been a monumental failure as a scientific movement. Instead, evolutionary psychology attempts to define new issues and formulate new questions that cut across the various subdisciplines of psychology. For example, if evolutionists are right and the mind is composed of a collection of evolved problem-solving modules, then this will necessarily have implications for all other areas of psychology. Cognitive psychologists will want to define the information-processing characteristics of each module in terms of capacity, speed of processing, and representation. Physiologists will want to explore the biological foundation of these modules and the ways in which they compare with those of other animals. Developmentalists will want to chart the course of a module's emergence and functioning over a lifespan. Clinicians will want to know how the functioning or malfunctioning of a module can produce pathologies or problems of adjustment.

Let's take a specific example from the clinical literature. Certain psychopathologies are known to differ dramatically based on sex. Males, far more than females, exhibit criminal aggressive tendencies, sociopathological behaviors, and antisocial personalities. Females, on the other hand, are far more likely than males to suffer from depression and pathologies associated with the need for social and personal acceptance and approval (e.g., histrionic and dependent personality disorders). For decades, each area of psychology has addressed this issue from its own perspective. Freudians conjectured about the unconscious minds of males and females. Developmentalists pointed to differences in upbringing between boys and girls. Social psychologists fretted over the cultural and social roles of males and females. Physiologists tested for chemical differences between male and female brains, and cognitivists studied individual and gender-based differences in information-processing styles. Each group asked its own proximate questions and derived their own answers about why the phenomenon exists.

Evolutionists seek to reformulate this issue by posing a more fundamental question about this sex difference. Evolutionists would ask: What was the evolutionary significance of these emotions and behaviors? What adaptive problem was solved by male aggressiveness and female empathy and emotional sensitivity? Let's suppose that we are able to gather evidence supporting the notion that male aggression and female empathy are, in fact, evolved adaptations. In our ancestral past, males had to compete for mates, with more aggressive males being more likely than more conciliatory males to secure and hold mates. Females of the past, however, faced a different challenge. They needed to cultivate a supportive community around them to help in the care and maintenance of their offspring. Females who possessed greater empathy and emotional sensitivity may well have accomplished this feat more successfully, thus producing more viable offspring than their more stoic counterparts.

Assume for a moment that the evolutionary perspective just outlined is more or less correct. How does this ultimate, evolutionary understanding affect the various subdisciplines actively looking at the question of why males engage in more aggressive criminal acts and females suffer with more depression? The evolutionary explanation serves as a foundation from which more proximate subdiscipline-specific questions can be formulated. For example, developmentalists could address the question of when male aggression is most problematic and whether this corresponds to the ages in our ancestral past when mate competition would have been most intense (adolescence and young adulthood). Physiologists could look at the chemical and hormonal bases for aggression and depression and compare these findings across species to look for evolutionary trends. Clinicians could assess how long-standing male and female adaptations could produce pathologies in a modern world that is so starkly different from that of our ancestral past. Cognitivists could look to see how males and females differ in their interpretation of information and if, in fact, similar circumstances are processed in more "competitive" terms by males and more "relational" terms by females. The point is that the various subdisciplines of psychology will continue to address issues and construct questions appropriate to their domains. These pursuits only change in that they are informed and united by a common evolutionary framework.

Only time will tell if the evolutionary approach fulfills the lofty ambitions set for it by its faithful enthusiasts. The track record of Darwinism, however, is a strong one. From its unquestioned success in biology, the evolutionary framework has been successfully extended into other widely divergent areas, such as cosmology, anthropology, and economics. At this point, it does not seem unreasonable that it could find a highly productive home in psychology as well.

SUMMARY

Evolutionary psychology refers to the application of Darwinian principles in understanding human nature. A key concept in evolutionary psychology is the environment of evolutionary adaptedness, which refers to the selection pressures that have formed the suite of our mental and behavior adaptations. Evolutionary psychology operates on a number of basic premises or assumptions, including the search for ultimate explanations, domain specificity, the primacy of the unconscious and the emotions, the importance of gene–environment interaction, and the contrast between ancestral and current environments. Finally, evolutionary psychology sees itself not as another subdiscipline of psychology but as a new perspective with relevance to all of psychology's various subdisciplines.

KEY TERMS

domain specificity

environment of evolution-
ary adaptedness (EEA)

interactionist approach

ultimate and proximate
explanations

unconscious mind

REVIEW QUESTIONS

1. What is the EEA? Why is it important in understanding the evolution of human nature?

2. Define domain specificity, and describe what is meant by an adaptive problem.

3. Give some examples of ways in which our current environment differs from the ancestral environment of human evolution. What effect(s) do these differences have on us?

4. How does the unconscious mind as envisioned by evolutionary psychologists differ from that described by Sigmund Freud?

5. Why will evolutionary psychology be considered a failure if it becomes recognized as another subdiscipline within psychology?

SUGGESTED READINGS

Barkow, J., Cosmides, L., & Tooby, J. (1992). *The adapted mind: Evolutionary psychology and the generation of culture.* New York: Oxford University Press.

Baron-Cohen, S. (1997). *The maladapted mind: Classic readings in evolutionary psychopathology.* East Sussex, UK: Psychology Press.

Crawford, C. (1998). Environments and adaptations: Then and now. In C. Crawford & D.L. Krebs (Eds.), *The handbook of evolutionary psychology* (pp. 275–302). Mahwah, NJ: L. Erlbaum.

Crawford, C. (1998). The theory of evolution in the study of human behavior: An introduction and overview. In C. Crawford & D.L. Krebs (Eds.), *The handbook of evolutionary psychology* (pp. 3–41). Mahwah, NJ: L. Erlbaum.

WEB SITES

www.psych.ucsb.edu/research/cep/primer.html a basic introduction to evolutionary psychology provided by the Center for Evolutionary Psychology at the University of California, Santa Barbara.

www.anth.ucsb.edu/projects/human/evpsychfaq.html answers to frequently asked questions about evolutionary psychology.

www.hbes.com/ homepage of the Human Behavior and Evolution Society, provides access to a wide range of good information and research in evolutionary psychology.

www.evoyage.com/ general information about evolutionary psychology plus some discussion of evolution/creationist issues.

3

Evolutionary Psychology: Methods and Criticism

Testing the Idea

SUPPOSE YOU TURN ON YOUR LAMP one evening and it doesn't work. You think the bulb is okay but have a hunch that something is wrong with the lamp itself. Testing this hunch seems straightforward enough: try another light bulb, or take the bulb out of this lamp and try it in another. If we dissect this simple process, we find that you did two things: (1) assumed the lamp was broken and (2) tested a consequence of that assumption. Notice that you did not directly test whether the lamp was broken. You did not, for example, go into its internal wiring and see if something was awry. Instead, you tested a logical consequence based on the assumption that the lamp was broken: if it is broken, then other bulbs would not work in it. The scientific process of evaluating theories operates in a similar fashion. Your idea that the lamp was broken is a **core theory**, and the logical consequence of this theory (the fact that other bulbs will not work) is a **hypothesis**. It is the hypothesis that is put to the direct test.

Let's look at a more scientifically minded example. In the 17th century, Italian astronomer/mathematician Galileo Galilei became convinced that the Copernican or sun-centered view of the universe was correct, as opposed to the more widely accepted Ptolemaic or Earth-centered view. The Copernican view thus constituted the core theory that Galileo assumed was true. To test the core theory, Galileo identified a specific hypothesis, dealing with the phases of the planet Venus, that flowed logically from the core theory. If Venus and Earth were rotating around the sun, then Venus should show a certain sequence of phases, similar to those of the moon as it rotates around Earth. Galileo then set about testing this hypothesis by regularly observing Venus in the night sky to see if it did, in fact, show the predicted sequence of phases. (It did, of course!) In this example, it is important to recognize that Galileo was not directly testing his core heliocentric theory. Instead, he simply assumed heliocentrism to be true and set about testing a predicted consequence of that idea.

Formulating Hypotheses in Evolutionary Psychology

How does evolutionary psychology go about testing its ideas? Like any other theoretical approach to understanding the natural world, evolutionary psychology

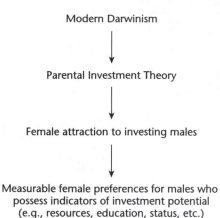

Figure 3.1 Theoretical hierarchy depicting core theory at the top, with more specialized theories below, along with specific predictions derived from those theories. Specific hypotheses subject to testing are found at the lowest levels.

Modern Darwinism

Parental Investment Theory

Female attraction to investing males

Measurable female preferences for males who possess indicators of investment potential (e.g., resources, education, status, etc.)

begins with a core theoretical idea (or set of ideas) that is assumed to be true. From that core, more concrete, specific hypotheses are identified and put to empirical tests. In evolutionary psychology, the process is best envisioned in terms of a theoretical hierarchy, with the core theory being placed at the top. Figure 3.1 provides a graphic depiction. The top two levels describe the theoretical foundations of the evolutionary approach. At the highest level is the core theory of all evolutionary psychology, modern Darwinism (evolution by natural selection). At the second level are somewhat more refined theories that extend from that core theory. Because evolution by natural selection is quite broad in scope, a series of more narrowly tailored midlevel theories, such as Hamilton's concept of kin selection and Trivers's ideas about parental investment and reciprocal altruism, have emerged from it. Evolutionary psychology does not claim to provide any direct tests of the theories of Darwin, Hamilton, or Trivers. Instead, it assumes these theories to be correct and tests the different ways in which they can be applied to understand human nature. In terms of our hierarchy, the real testing and validating go on between the bottom two levels, where specific hypotheses are constructed, and not in the top two levels, where the theories reside.

A specific example will help illustrates the process of constructing a testable hypothesis. In many different cultures, female mate preferences show remarkable consistency. Females tend to prefer men who are older and have greater resources or status as long-term mates. Using the graph, we can understand how this finding relates to the different levels involved in testing evolutionary hypotheses.

1. At the highest level, we see that all organisms have been naturally selected for their ability to survive and reproduce in the environment. Human females, as naturally selected organisms, ought to have biological and behavioral tendencies that permit them to maximize their reproductive success.
2. At the middle level, we encounter Trivers's notion of parental investment, a refinement of the more general evolutionary theory, which states that parental investment in one offspring will necessarily reduce investment in others. Thus, we would expect that nature has selected females so that they

will possess strategies for optimizing the amount of investment needed to produce the maximum number of viable offspring.

3. At the third level of the hierarchy, we apply the middle level theory directly to our understanding of human nature to form a general evolutionary hypothesis. In this example, the hypothesis takes the following form: Because humans are one species in which males can and often do contribute to the raising of offspring, one naturally selected strategy that females might possess would be a tendency to mate only with males who are willing and able to share some of the investment burden. This makes sense if you think about the fact that a female who has a partner sharing the load of raising offspring has more energy and resources available to allow for more total offspring. Over long spans of time, females who were attracted to high-quality partners should out-reproduce those who either "went it alone" or who settled for poor-quality partners, until eventually the female population became dominated by those who possess this trait (natural selection at work).

4. At the lowest level, we must take our evolutionary hypothesis and form it into a specific prediction that can be tested empirically. For example, we might predict that women will show a preference for men who possess indicators of investment potential and resources. Thus, a man who has land, money, a college degree, and a good reputation in the community will be preferred over one who has fewer or none of these same assets.

Testing Hypotheses

What distinguishes the evolutionary approach is not the use of any specific methodology but the nature of the hypotheses being tested. Unlike other psychologists, evolutionary psychologists derive their hypotheses from within a Darwinian framework. However, once a hypothesis is formulated, the full spectrum of scientific methods is available for testing.

Experimental Tests

Experimental tests have the advantage of strict controls and direct manipulation of variables, allowing for credible cause-and-effect inferences. But how can an evolutionary hypothesis, formulated on the basis of what presumably happened hundreds of thousands of years ago, be put to a rigorous test? One such example is provided by McBurney, Gaulin, Devineni, and Adams (1997) in testing what has been called the "gathering hypothesis." To derive this hypothesis, McBurney and his colleagues began with the core theory of parental investment. Because males and females invest differently in offspring, they would be subject to different selection pressures over evolutionary time. One of those selection pressures would be related to the securing of food resources for themselves and their children.

It is widely believed that in our evolutionary history males tended to roam broadly about while hunting, whereas females tended to gather food closer to home (McBurney et al., 1997; Silverman & Eals, 1992). Thus, for 100,000 years or more, men faced a recurring problem of how to navigate across long distances to find game. Those who were most skilled at maintaining their orientation in space and adjusting their cognitive maps as they moved were more likely to successfully capture prey and provide for themselves and their families. Females, on the other hand, faced a recurring problem of how to find and identify locally occurring edibles. Those with good landmark identification skills and locational memories were more likely to successfully find food for themselves and their offspring. Based on this evolutionary history, McBurney and colleagues hypothesized that men today should excel at tasks of mental rotation and spatial orientation, whereas women should be proficient at tasks involving local landmark location.

The researchers put these spatial sex differences to an experimental test by giving both males and females tests of mental rotation and local object location. The mental rotation test was presented as a test of "object relations" that required the subject to determine whether members of pairs of three-dimensional figures were identical. The object location test involved randomly placing 33 pairs of cards face down on a table and asking subjects to turn as few of them over as possible to identify locations of the pairs (like playing the Milton Bradley board game "Memory"). As predicted, men outperformed women on the mental rotation test, whereas women outperformed men on the landmark location test, thus offering support for the idea of differently evolved spatial competencies in men and women.

The Survey/Questionnaire Approach

Evolutionary psychologists also frequently have used **survey and questionnaire** data as means of testing their hypotheses. Probably the most well-known example of this approach was the massive cross-culture work on mate preferences completed by David Buss (1989). Buss was interested in looking for "universals" in human mate preferences that cut across cultural boundaries. In doing so, he and his collaborators questioned more than 10,000 people across 37 different cultures. The questions he posed were designed to test whether long-term mate preferences would conform to evolutionary-based predictions that transcended specific cultural circumstances. For example, on a scale of 0–3, with 0 = irrelevant or unimportant and 3 = indispensable, he had people rate the importance of a long-term mate's financial prospects and physical attractiveness. He reasoned that if evolutionary theory was correct, then females should be far more concerned with a mate's financial prospects, whereas males should be more concerned with physical attractiveness. Again, we can understand these hypotheses as extending from the core theory of parental investment. As the sex that invests more in offspring, women presumably have evolved to select men based on their ability to provide resources for those offspring. As the sex that invests relatively less in offspring, men have evolved to select women based on indicators of fertility. Across all 37 cultures studied, Buss found that women rated the importance of a mate's financial prospects higher than did men, whereas men rated physical attractiveness higher than did women.

The fact that these preferences are present despite vast cultural differences among the groups sampled makes a strong argument for an evolutionary factor at work. However, Buss's critics have contended that culture could still explain these preferences, because all the cultures in the study were to one degree or another patriarchal in nature and may have conditioned men and women to assume certain roles in close relationships (with males being more dominant). In response,

Buss did additional work in which women who already had adequate resources for raising offspring were questioned about the preferred amount of resources they desired for a mate. These women showed a preference for a man with even greater resources. Although this still did not satisfy some critics, it does show how evolutionary hypotheses can be posed, tested, refined, and retested using survey and questionnaire data.

Archival Data

Evolutionary hypotheses also can be addressed using **archival data** to see whether historical trends and patterns follow evolutionary predictions. Economist Anne Case, for example, has done extensive analyses of the ways in which resources are allocated in biological and nonbiological (step-, foster-, adoptive-) families. She has used the University of Michigan's Panel Study of Income Dynamics, which contains information on resource allocations in thousands of households from 1968 to 1985. In addition, Case and her colleagues have analyzed the ways in which health care services and resources are allocated within families, using the 1988 National Health Interview Survey, an annual health survey administered to more than 50,000 households. Based on evolutionary theory, she predicted that, within households, biological offspring would receive preferential allocation of resources compared with nonbiological offspring. This hypothesis extends logically from the core theory of inclusive fitness, which contends that humans, like other animals, seek to maximize their genetic contribution to the next generation through direct offspring as well as the offspring of genetic relatives. Her findings confirmed that food, health care services, and educational resources were preferentially bestowed upon biological offspring compared with nonbiological offspring, especially stepchildren (Case, Lin, & McLanahan, 1999; Case, Lin, & McLanahan, 2000a; Case, Lin, & McLanahan, 2000b; Case & Paxon, 2001).

The work of Daly and Wilson (1988b) provides another example of the use of archival data for evaluating evolutionary hypotheses. They examined official Detroit police records for homicides in 1972 to determine whether homicide rates varied based on kinship. The results were startling. Homicides within households rarely involved genetic relatives and, instead, were far more frequent between (genetically) unrelated spouses. These examples show that evolutionary thinking can generate a broad range of questions which, in turn, can be tested using existing data bases.

Comparing Across Species

Evolution highlights the interconnectedness of humans with other species. Specifically, as primates, humans are closely related to the other great ape species: chimpanzees, orangutans, and gorillas. Given these close relationships, evolutionary hypotheses often can be tested by comparing across different species. For example, suppose we were interested in the origins of marriage in our evolutionary history. Were our evolutionary ancestors romantic, faithful monogamists or philandering, self-indulgent sexual opportunists? One way of addressing this question would be to look at the sexual lifestyles of different species and the ways in which this behavior affects their physical makeup. An important relationship exists between **sexual dimorphism** in body size and the degree of male-on-male competition over access to females in a given species. Sexual dimorphism in body size refers to the fact that (usually) males are physically larger than females, a result of the fact that males compete with each other to mate with females (Reynolds & Harvey, 1994). When males compete, the bigger ones usually win. Over long spans of time and many generations, the size of males tends to increase. Two of our primate relatives, the gibbon and gorilla, are especially valuable as examples. Gibbons are relatively small, arboreal apes who live largely monogamous lives. Males and females live in pair bonds, sharing fairly equally in the care and maintenance of their young. As committed monogamists, gibbons participate in relatively little male-on-male competition for females, and, as expected, very little size difference separates male and females. Gorillas, on the other hand, live in harems in which a single male controls a group of females and their offspring. Gaining and keeping control of a harem requires serious effort on the part of the male, who must constantly be on guard against other males who threaten his supremacy. Because male gorillas compete for the females, it is unsurprising to find a high degree of sexual dimorphism in size, with males being about twice as large (in weight) as females. What is learned when we extend this comparison to humans?

Humans are sexually dimorphic in size, with the average female only about 84% the size of the average male. Human size dimorphism has led many researchers to argue that monogamy was not the predominant practice among our evolutionary ancestors (Miller, 1998). However, the degree of dimorphism does not approach the extremes seen in the gorilla. Instead, human size dimorphism is similar to that of the chimpanzee, our closest primate relative. This has led some to speculate that our ancestral social/sexual structure was similar to that of chimpanzees, in which coalitions of males work together to control reproductive access to females. Although this conclusion is not without controversy, the point is to see how comparisons across species can begin to provide us with information about human nature and allow for tests of different hypotheses.

Comparing Across Cultures

Another approach often used by evolutionary psychologists involves looking for "universals" in human behavior that seem to transcend different environments and cultures. Because all humans share a common evolutionary history, an evolutionist would expect to find certain commonalities in human nature (**universals**) despite considerable variations in culture. The work of Buss (1989) on mate preferences falls into this category. However, one of the first studies of this type was performed by Ekman (1973), who investigated the understanding and expression of emotions in humans. He found that across widely different cultures (from America, Sweden, Japan, Kenya, and New Guinea) the understanding and expression of emotion were largely consistent and based on species-typical facial configurations and body states. This is precisely what an evolutionary psychologist would predict, given our common ancestry as a group-living primate for whom communicating with and "reading" the intentions of others was a necessary life skill.

Evolutionary cross-cultural studies need not be aimed exclusively at uncovering "universals." The evolutionary approach also provides a means of interpreting cultural variability. For example, from an evolutionary perspective, human judgments of beauty are understood as evolved strategies for choosing healthy, fertile mates (i.e., beauty is seen as an indicator of health and fertility). Gangestad and Buss (1993) reasoned that the degree to which people would use physical attractiveness as a high priority in choosing a mate would vary, depending upon the prevalence of harmful parasites in the local environment. They compared the relative value placed on physical attractiveness with the danger posed by parasitic infection in 29 countries. The results revealed a highly significant correlation: the higher the danger of parasitic infection, the greater the value placed on physical attractiveness in a mate. In this example, the cross-cultural comparison was not used to find a commonality but to test for an evolution-based variation in cultures.

Testing for Sex Differences

An important element of our evolutionary past was the fact that men and women played different social roles. These varying roles have left their imprint on male and female bodies and psyches, thus allowing evolutionists another avenue for hypothesis testing: identifying evolution-derived sex differences. The study by McBurney et al. (1997) on spatial cognition is one example. Another can be found in the now classic experiment conducted by Goodenough and Brian (1929) on sex differences in throwing ability. Over the course of 50 days, they tested preschool children on throwing accuracy. Throughout the testing, boys maintained a significant advantage in throwing accuracy over girls. Given the young age of the subjects, many researchers argued that it is unlikely that this was the result of differences in socialization. Instead, it reflects physical differences in male and female bodies resulting from variant selection pressures over evolutionary time (Geary, 1998; Watson, 2001). Males, more than females, would have been under selection pressure for accurate throwing for hunting and intrasexual competition for mates and territory.

Sex difference research always evokes a justifiable degree of skepticism, because it is very difficult to tease apart the extent to which male/female differences are attributable to social or biological factors. Furthermore, social and biological factors often interact and reinforce one another in ways that make it almost impossible for researchers to disentangle them. Are little boys more rambunctious because parents play more roughly with them (a social influence)? Do parents play more roughly with them because boys are naturally more active (a biological predisposition)? Or are both true and therefore mutually reinforcing? These questions are always legitimate and often laden with emotional, social, and political implications. Moreover, a sex difference must always be assessed in light of the degree of commonality that exists between the sexes. Sometimes the difference is the exception and commonality is the rule. Thus, a single study demonstrating a sex difference rarely constitutes powerful evidence in favor of some evolutionary hypothesis. Instead, a body of work, replicating a specific type of difference under a variety of circumstances, is necessary to make a convincing argument. The differences in throwing ability between boys and girls, for example, has been replicated many times, with large skill differences observed, and has been related to physical differences in arm structure, some of which can be observed in utero, and to throwing differences in other primate species (French & Thomas, 1985; Jardine & Martin, 1983; Watson, 2001; Geary, 1998 for review). The accumulated evidence suggests a "real" difference that may well be linked to our evolutionary past.

Evolutionary Hypotheses Versus Hypotheses from Other Models

It is important to contrast hypotheses drawn explicitly from evolutionary considerations with those from other theoretical viewpoints to see which best explain the data. An example is the Daly and Wilson (1982) study of domestic violence. An evolutionary hypothesis would contend that homicide rates can be correlated inversely with genetic relatedness. Because of kin selection, one would be more likely to murder nonrelatives than relatives. Another hypothesis, however, is that homicide is also a function of victim access or availability. Persons to whom the culprit has the easiest access are most likely to be victimized. Thus, it is not surprising that many murders occur within households, because other household members are easily accessible to the perpetrator. To compare these hypotheses in a direct test, Daly and Wilson examined police records for homicide rates involving spouses and offspring within households. Because both a spouse and children are equally accessible within a household, the accessibility hypothesis predicts that rate of homicides should be roughly equal between them. The kin selection hypothesis, however, predicts that rates of homicide will be much higher for spouses because they are not genetic kin. The results were strongly supportive of the kin selection hypothesis, not the accessibility hypothesis.

Directly comparing evolutionary predictions with those of other theories will be increasingly important in future research. One current weakness of the evolutionary approach is that it does not always lead to predictions that are distinct from those of other approaches. For example, in a re-analysis of Buss's work on mating preferences, Eagly and Wood (1999) found that many of the results were also consistent with predictions based on an alternative "social roles" hypothesis. In addition, the notion of a cheater-detection module (see chapter 2) has drawn criticism because its predictions often overlap with those of other theories (Fodor, 2000; Riesberg, 2001, pp. 420–426). Evolutionary theories need to generate not only testable but also unique hypotheses that distinguish it from competing views.

Criticisms of Evolutionary Psychology

Evolutionary psychology is not without its critics, and often they raise credible and important issues that should be addressed seriously and thoughtfully. The issues presented here should not be considered an exhaustive list of the criticisms leveled against evolutionary psychology but merely some of the more prominent and most often cited. Interested readers can examine *Alas, Poor Darwin*, edited by Hilary and Steven Rose (2000), for an extensive polemic against evolutionary psychology and sociobiology. (For more, see Web sites on p. 51.)

"Just So" Stories

A **"just so" story** refers to an untested (and perhaps untestable) account about the way in which a particular trait came into existence. It is quite tempting to observe a current behavior and construct an evolutionary story about how that behavior evolved for some adaptive purpose. However, because evolutionary explanations are historical in nature, it is often difficult to test and verify the story's credibility. One of the best examples of this comes from the neuroscientist V. S. Ramachandran, who became so frustrated with what he considered to be the excess of unsubstantiated "just so" stories in evolutionary psychology that he made one up himself and called it "Why do gentlemen prefer blondes?" He proceeded to weave an imaginative tale about how, in our evolutionary history, fair-skinned females would have been preferable as mates because indicators of health, fertility, and sexual fidelity would have been more clearly visible than on their darker complexioned counterparts. He had no evidence, of course—just a plausible story. Much to his amazement, the article was accepted for publication! (Details of this can be found in Ramachandran & Blakeslee, 1998, p. 202. In fairness, it should be mentioned that the article was not accepted in a journal specializing in evolutionary psychology). Ramachandran's experience highlights the problem: a creative mind can make up a believable adaptive history for just about any currently observed behavior or trait. Critics of evolutionary psychology contend such stories have proliferated in the field, straining the credibility of the discipline.

Dealing with the "just so" criticism is tricky. On the one hand, the criticism has some validity. Scientific hypotheses often begin with imaginative ideas, and a profusion of imaginative ideas is a hallmark of an emerging field. Given that the evolutionary approach to psychology is currently in its formative stage, an abundance of adaptionist stories is to be expected (it may even be a sign of healthy vigor). It is certainly fair to point out that many of these stories still must generate testable hypotheses and accrue solid evidence before they are taken seriously. In this sense, the "just so" criticism cautions evolutionary psychologists not to elevate creativity above verification or equate plausibility with evidence.

On the other hand, this criticism is often used unfairly to smear the entire field of evolutionary psychology as nothing but "just so" stories. Many "stories" have progressed through the hypothesis generating stage, accumulated quite a bit of solid evidence, and deserve reputable places at the scientific table. For example, the notion that there is an evolved tendency to be biased toward genetic kin has generated a number of testable (and tested) hypotheses in both humans and animals. Cross-species studies, anthropological studies, and sociological and economic data all converge in finding that biological offspring enjoy considerable advantages over stepchildren in a family setting. As evolutionary psychology matures, more and more "just so" stories will work their way through the rigors of proper scientific evaluation. Some will flourish, and others will wither as the data dictate.

Can We Truly Know the EEA?

Another often-leveled criticism of evolutionary psychology is its use of the concept of the environment of evolutionary adaptedness (EEA). Human nature is supposedly the result of our adaptation to the hunter–gatherer environment of a half a million (or so) years ago. But how much confidence can we have in our understanding of that environment? If the EEA is little more than a murky haze of our primordial past, then do we have any basis for saying that the way we think and behave today reflects adaptations to it? Furthermore, as Tattersall (1998) has pointed out, it was not so much our ability to adapt to a specific environment that made humans successful but that we could roam far beyond that environment and survive in a wide range of varied habitats.

This criticism has two parts. One deals with the EEA and the other with supposed adaptations to it. Let's begin with the EEA. Evolutionary psychologists would acknowledge that some aspects of the EEA will forever be mysterious. However, despite the fact that evolutionary psychology deals with prehistory, we can be fairly confident about a number of aspects of humanity's evolutionary past and the prevailing selection pressures. For example, our EEA was one in which pregnancy was risky; infant mortality rates were high; diseases, parasites, and other mortal dangers were prevalent; hunting and foraging for sustenance were common; tribal groups were kin based; and other humans were both cooperators and competitors. It must be remembered that the EEA does not necessarily refer to a specific time or place. These characteristics would apply to a wide variety of specific geographic environments and would require adaptations that were generalized to a range of places and times.

Second, evolutionary psychologists readily admit that not all human mental and behavioral traits are adaptations. The process of evolution produces not only adaptations but other observable products in an organism. For example, the protruding of the human nose helps prevent a sunburned chin and provide a secure base upon which to place spectacles. However, the shape and size of the nose did not evolve to serve either of these functions. Technically speaking, these are **evolutionary byproducts**, not directly adaptive in and of themselves but related to other naturally selected adaptive traits.

Evolutionary psychologists recognize that some aspects of human nature may not reflect adaptations to the EEA but may be byproducts. For example, the research of Daly and Wilson (1988a) on domestic violence has never attempted to portray spousal homicide as an adapted trait. Instead, it is regarded as a byproduct of other adaptations, such as male sexual jealousy. Distinguishing adaptations from byproducts or other random effects can be challenging. Currently, a debate rages over whether language is best understood as an adaptation or a mere byproduct (Gould, 1991; Pinker, 1994). However, evolutionary psychologists have specific guidelines for identifying adaptations. For example, the complexity of a trait, how well the trait fits within its environmental niche, and whether a trait was subject to intense selection pressures can serve as indicators of an adaptation as opposed to a byproduct or random effect (Plotkin, 1997; Williams, 1966).

What About Culture?

One of the most passionate criticisms of evolutionary psychology is that it ignores a potent factor affecting human behavior: culture. This criticism becomes further enflamed by the misperception that evolutionary psychology is tantamount to **genetic determinism**, the notion that genes determine our behaviors and personalities. Many worry that genetic determinism can be used as a scientific justification for such ills as social inequality and gender discrimination. Because these are delicate issues that often arouse strong emotions, one must tread slowly and cautiously through this territory.

First, evolutionary psychologists would contend that they do not ignore culture. Instead, they see it as the "...mental, behavioral, or material commonalities shared across individuals..." (Tooby & Cosmides, 1992, p. 117). They would expect different cultures to exhibit both deep commonalities (as a result of our common

Figure 3.2 Lions kill a zebra: natural does not mean moral. (© Stephen Krasemann/ PhotoResearchers.)

evolutionary history) and more conspicuous variability (resulting from local circumstances) (Fig. 3.2). A simple example of this would be the fact that, as social creatures, we have a universal need to communicate with spoken language. Although all cultures will have language, the specific form of language will vary. Moreover, as social creatures, humans also must organize social relationships in some fashion. However, the specific conventions used for that organization will vary from culture to culture. In France, for example, people greet one another with a kiss on each cheek; in America, they shake hands; and, in Japan, they bow. The point is that culture emerges in various ways but always under the constraining hand (or leash, as sociobiologists like to say) of our biological human natures.

But how strong is that constraining hand? The real meat of this criticism is that the extreme cultural variability exhibited by humans renders useless any notion of underlying evolution-based commonalities. Many philosophers and scientists would contend that human nature is so varied and culturally malleable that we have, in effect, "broken free" of any meaningful evolutionary constraints. Voice was given to this view recently by philosopher John Troyer, who expressed skepticism about the idea that evolutionary history offers much assistance in understanding human nature.

> I am doubtful that either knowledge of our evolutionary history or the study of other species can add much to what we learn about human nature from more direct investigation.... What this direct investigation shows is that human nature is compatible with a very wide range of behaviour; people can live together as peacefully and cooperatively as the Old Order Amish, but they can also engage in internecine wars, torture innocent children, and practice "ethnic cleansing."
>
> (TROYER, 2000, P. 63)

For Troyer and others, human variability defies evolutionary explanations. Evolutionary psychologists, of course, beg to differ. They would point out that the very examples Troyer uses to bolster his case may, in fact, reflect the deep commonalities rooted in our evolutionary past. Humans evolved as a tribal species in which in-group and out-group distinctions were fundamental to survival. This tribalism may provide the foundation upon which all of Troyer's examples are set. The Old Order Amish are highly cooperative *with one another* but reject the wider world. Ethnic cleansing occurs across, not within, tribal boundaries. Humans do torture innocent children but are much more likely to do so when those children have no genetic, racial, or cultural connection to their torturers. Finally, warfare almost necessarily requires the exacerbation of group distinctions. Even within a nation or group, some tribal "split" almost always precedes hostilities and serves to ignite violent passions and define friend and foe. Americans only fought Americans when we could first redefine ourselves as North and South, Yank and Reb. Pointing out the potential underlying commonality present in Troyer's argument does not mean that evolutionists are right and Troyer is wrong. Instead, it simply means that before dismissing the evolutionary approach out-of-hand because of what seems to be wide variability in human nature, one needs to explore (and test) the notion that outward differences mask more subtle universals.

This introduces the second, even more contentious issue. If there is a universal human nature with an evolutionary (and therefore genetic) foundation, then is evolutionary psychology providing scientific endorsement to social inequity? For example, suppose we find evidence that men and women have different evolved tendencies, with men being more aggressive and competitive and women more nurturant and verbal. Does this mean that we are providing scientific evidence that men should be soldiers and CEOs and that women should be nurses and teachers (or stay-at-home moms)? Evolutionary psychologists would respond with an emphatic "no," for two reasons. One is the *naturalistic fallacy*. No rational justification supports the transition from naturalistic statements ("women tend to be more nurturant and verbal") to moral ones ("women should be or ought to be teachers," which, of course, is not the same as merely observing that more teachers are women or that more women express a desire to be teachers).

Another reason evolutionary psychologists would reject this is because it is suggestive of **genetic determinism** or the idea that genes determine what a person is and therefore what kind of profession he or she ought to pursue. Evolutionary psychology is committed to gene–environment interaction, not genetic determinism. Having male genes does not automatically make one aggressive and therefore a good soldier. It simply means that *on average* a male is relatively more likely to have aggressive tendencies than a female, and those tendencies can be damped or exaggerated by the environment. In addition, *genetic variability* is an essential element of the evolutionary process. We would also expect that *by nature* men will vary in their genetic predisposition toward aggressiveness, with some actually being less aggressive than some females. It is therefore inappropriate to view evolutionary psychology as a grand scheme to return us all to medieval feudalism. It is a scientific pursuit with the goal of understanding human nature. There are evolved human tendencies, and some of them vary based on sex. However, the decision is ours as to how this information will be used in living our lives and building good societies.

Evolution and Morality: The Naturalistic Fallacy

The **naturalistic fallacy** is a straightforward concept: one cannot logically deduce moral tenets from the *natural* state of the world. In other words, recognizing that something is natural does not necessarily imply that it is *good* or *moral*. It is often said that the *is* of nature should not be confused with the *ought* of morality. Most evolutionary biologists are quite clear on this issue. For example, population geneticist Francisco Ayala has commented: "Biology is insufficient for determining which moral codes are, or should be, accepted" (Ayala, 1995, p. 134). Renowned evolutionist John Maynard Smith is even more emphatic: "A scientific theory—Darwinism or any other—has nothing to say about the value of being human....Scientific theories say nothing about what is right but only about what is possible...we need some other source of values" (Maynard Smith, 1984, pp. 11, 24).

The problem is that although the naturalistic fallacy is well known and understood in scientific circles, it is often lost when scientists communicate their ideas and theories to the general public. Critics of evolutionary psychology sometimes claim that by describing certain human tendencies as products of evolution, these traits are somehow being justified or excused. What is found to be "natural" for humans is often misread as meaning what is right or acceptable. For example, consider an article in *The New York Times Magazine* by evolutionary psychologist Steven Pinker on the issue of mothers killing their newborns (neonaticide). The title of the article included the line: "Neonaticide may be a product of maternal wiring." In the body of the article Pinker stated: "...a capacity for neonaticide is built into the biological design of our parental emotions....Parental investment is a limited resource, and mammalian mothers must 'decide' whether to allot it to their newborn or their current and future offspring. If a newborn is sickly, or if its survival is not promising, they may cut their losses and favor the healthiest in the litter or try again later on" (Pinker, 1997, p. 52).

Although Pinker's point was not unreasonable from a scientific standpoint and he took pains in the article to make it clear he was not condoning the act, the article inevitably caused public controversy. It would be easy for some readers to shrug their shoulders and say, "Well, if scientists say it is natural then it must be OK." What the general public (and students) often fail to recognize is that even when scientists study and describe humans as *animals*, few, if any, would argue that we should use the same judgmental criteria on humans that we do for animals. By this I mean that when we observe a lion killing an antelope, we do not hold the lion morally responsible for the act or say that he or she is evil. After all, the lion is just doing what is natural. That's fine for lions, because lions have no *moral systems* for guiding their actions. Lions have no *moral oughts*, so we can not expect them to abide by them. But the same is not true for humans. One of the qualities that makes humans unique is that we do have moral systems, and those systems should influence human behaviors just as our natural tendencies do. Thus, the criteria we use to judge humans cannot and should not be based solely on nature. One important challenge for evolutionary psychologists will be to communicate this message clearly to students and the public. Evolutionary psychology promises to uncover quite a bit about human nature, some of which may not be pleasant. Those unpleasant tendencies are not excused just because they may be natural.

The Promise of Evolutionary Psychology

One of the reasons that psychologists and other researchers have become excited about the emergence of evolutionary psychology is because of its integrative potential. Within the field of psychology, evolutionary principles have the potential for providing a theoretical framework for organizing and interconnecting the often disparate areas of psychology. Currently, few avenues of substantive interaction connect such areas as developmental, cognitive, personality, clinical, and social psychology. Each has its own professional societies, journals, theories, and, of course, class offering(s) in the typical psychology curriculum. The common human nature espoused by evolutionary psychologists should manifest itself in some fashion across these different approaches to the mind, and this commonality can provide a basis for interactions among the subdisciplines. For example, developmentalists have long wondered how it is that children can so effortlessly acquire the complexities of language but at the same time demonstrate such glaring deficits in logical reasoning (the failure to conserve, for example). Similarly, cognitivists have grappled with the fact that adults can easily solve reasoning problems when they are posed in practical social terms but fail those same problems when posed more abstractly. The evolutionary approach offers an answer to both in that humans have evolved biases in learning and reasoning.

Our evolved tendencies extend beyond just learning and reasoning to encompass our emotional and social lives. Numerous theories have been proposed in social psychology to explain the tremendous importance and power of social groups in molding individual behavior. Baumeister and Leary (1995) applied evolutionary thinking to the understanding of this issue in their "need to belong" theory. The fact that when the need to belong goes unsatisfied one can suffer mental and emotional stress shows the way in which this approach interconnects quite seamlessly with issues in clinical and abnormal psychology. Increasing numbers of researchers are finding great utility and success in addressing mental illness from a Darwinian perspective (Baron-Cohen, 1997; Neese & Williams, 1994). Many areas of psychology are recognizing the value of incorporating the evolved human nature into theorizing in their field. This common Darwinian framework will aid in communication and integration across subfields in psychology.

As the evolutionary approach fosters connections within psychology, it also promises integration with other sciences. Understanding the evolved human nature will naturally require that psychologists gain a greater understanding of evolution, evolutionary biology, and human evolution. Such areas as comparative psychology or ethology, which have recently diminished in prominence in psychology curriculums, may be reinvigorated with new relationships forged with primatologists and ecologists. Finally, anthropologists, prehistorians, and even paleontologists may find new common interests with psychologists as all explore important issues in human evolution and ancestral human conditions.

Scientist Theodosius Dobzhansky once titled an article "Nothing in biology makes sense except in the light of evolution" (Dobzhansky, 1973). Physicists and cosmologists have also recognized that the universe itself has been subject to evolutionary forces. The evolution of life, especially human life, may yet provide the attractive force that spans psychology's internal rifts and affixes bridges to other sciences.

SUMMARY

Evolutionary psychologists test their hypotheses using all the standard methodologies available in the social and behavioral sciences, including experiments, surveys and questionnaires, archival records, and comparisons across species and cultures. Evolutionary psychologists do not directly test Darwinian evolution but instead test predictions based on evolutionary theory to see how well these predictions explain human behavior. The evolutionary approach has stirred criticisms, including concerns about the naturalistic fallacy, the failure to appreciate culture, vagueness concerning the EEA, and a proliferation of "just so" adaptionist stories.

KEY TERMS

archival data

core theory

cross-cultural comparisons

cross-species comparisons

evolutionary byproduct

experimental test

genetic determinism

hypothesis

just so stories

naturalistic fallacy

survey/questionnaire approach

universals

REVIEW QUESTIONS

1. What is meant by cultural universals, and how do evolutionary psychologists often interpret these?

2. What is the logic behind using a cross-species comparison in testing an evolutionary hypothesis?

3. What is the naturalistic fallacy? Why is it important when dealing with evolutionary findings?

4. Can we truly know the EEA? What impact does this have on interpreting evolutionary findings?

5. What is a "just so" story? In what ways is the criticism valid and in what ways is it not?

SUGGESTED READINGS

Buss, D. (1999). Evolutionary psychology: A new paradigm for psychological science. In Rosen, D.H., & Luebbert, M.C. (Eds.), *The evolution of the psyche.* Westport, CT: Praeger Publishing.

Holcomb, H.R. III. (1998). Testing evolutionary hypotheses. In C. Crawford & D.L. Krebs (Eds.), *The handbook of evolutionary psychology* (pp. 303–334). Mahwah, NJ: L. Erlbaum.

Rose, H., & Rose, S. (2000). *Alas, poor Darwin: Arguments against evolutionary psychology.* London: Crown Publishing

WEB SITES

http://www.human-brain.org/evolpsy2.html Web site critical of the concept of "innateness" in evolutionary psychology.

http://human-nature.com/nibbs/02/apd.html gives Ian Pitchford's critique of the book *Alas Poor Darwin.*

http://www.psych.ucsb.edu/research/cep/ramachandran.html discusses the "just so" story.

http://www.socsci.kun.nl/psy/cultuur/voestermans_baerveldt.html deals with evolutionary psychology and culture.

Sites listed in chapter 2 are relevant here as well.

4

Human Evolution I: Foundations

The Paradox of Evolution

WE HAVE DEFINED EVOLUTIONARY PSYCHOLOGY as the application of Darwinian principles to the understanding of human nature. We must take a closer look at those Darwinian principles and the central role they play in illuminating the history of life and of our own species. **Evolution** simply refers to "descent with modification." Over time, the traits that species exhibit change, sometimes even to a point where new species emerge. **Natural selection** is the major mechanism by which that change occurs. It was really natural selection and not evolution that was Darwin's great contribution to science. Evolution by natural selection is paradoxical. It is at once both very simple and exceedingly complex. Its basic principles are so straightforward that when Darwin first articulated them, his colleague T.H. Huxley is reported to have wondered out loud how he could have been so foolish not to think of them first. However, as simple as they may be, once these principles are implemented in a natural system, they give rise to a process of almost unimaginable complexity. We'll address the simple part first.

Evolution by natural selection can be summarized in four basic principles (for simplicity's sake, these are assumed to relate to sexually reproducing species):

1. All species are capable of producing more offspring then there are resources to support those offspring;
2. Offspring will vary in the physical and behavioral traits that they possess, and those physical and behavioral traits are associated with the genes they inherit from their parents;
3. An offspring with a trait that allows it to more effectively exploit the limited resources of the environment will be more likely to survive and reproduce than another that lacks that trait; and
4. The gene or genes associated with that advantageous trait are therefore more likely to propagate and spread in that species.

Let's use an example and apply each of these principles. Suppose you have a litter of rabbits born in the cold north country of the Yukon. There are many rabbits and very little vegetation (principle 1). Some of the rabbits are gray, and some are white (principle 2). Given the scarcity of grass and other edibles, the rabbits must scavenge widely to find enough to eat. This puts them at risk of being preyed upon by hungry wolves. However, given the nature of the environment, the white rabbits are more difficult to detect in winter. They can forage in areas where the gray rabbits would be at greater risk. In other words, they have a trait that gives them an advantage in exploiting the limited resources in their environment (principle 3). The white rabbits are more likely to survive and reproduce, thus passing on their genetic predisposition toward white fur to the next generation (principle 4). Over many generations, then, we would expect the population of rabbits to be dominated by "white coat" genes and not "gray coat" genes. Another way to put this is to say that white coats were *naturally selected* from the many variations of coat color as the best adapted for that environment.

Probably the most famous example of the evolutionary process at work comes from Darwin himself. In 1832, the HMS *Beagle*, with Darwin on board, landed on the remote Galapagos Islands, a few hundred miles off the coast of Ecuador. Darwin traveled from island to island, closely observing the natural diversity of life and collecting specimens for later study. One immensely curious item was the fact that each island seemed to have its own type of finch, each with unique characteristics. Darwin surmised that the different finches were descendants of an original population that migrated long ago from the mainland. The original population was a land-dwelling, seed-eating finch that sported a relatively large, strong bill. As the birds migrated from one island to another, however, they encountered varying conditions, both from island to island and from the mainland. On many islands, the large, seed-crushing bill was no longer an advantage. On one island, Darwin found warbler finches with slender, pointed bills for extracting insects. On another, he found the vegetarian tree finch, with a short, broad bill for tearing at buds and leaves. On yet another, he found the tool-using finch, which held cactus spines in its long straight bill and fished out insects from the bark of trees. Over generations, each population of finch had adapted to the specific environmental conditions of each island. The birds that possessed the traits (in this case bill shapes) that were most functional for exploiting the resources of each island survived and passed on their traits to their descendants, until each island had its own particular bird. Natural selection was at work sifting through the variants of beak shape to find the ones most fit for the conditions of each island.

Important Terms and Concepts

To understand the evolutionary process, one must be acquainted with a number of important terms and concepts:

Mutation. A mutation refers to a mistake or copying error in the replication of deoxyribonucleic acid (DNA). This mistake is then transmitted from parent to offspring and may manifest itself in the physical makeup of the offspring (its phenotype). Most mutations are either detrimental or neutral in terms of affecting the organism's functioning in the environment. Occasionally, however, a mutation may be beneficial, thus conferring a selective advantage on an organism. It is possible that the first white-coated rabbit in the Yukon resulted from a genetic mutation. Mutations are important because they provide one source of variability (along with sexual recombination) on which natural selection can operate in sifting and sorting for more fit phenotypes.

Competition. Because species can produce more offspring than the available resources will support, organisms (both within and across species) will be in competition with each other for those scarce resources. Resources include not just food but any and all aspects of the environment necessary for the survival and reproduction of the organism, including adequate habitat range, nesting materials, access to mates, and many others. Any genetic mutation that confers a competitive advantage on a particular organism is likely to enhance that organism's chances of survival and reproduction, thus making it more likely that its genetic information (genotype), mutations included, will be passed on to future generations.

Reproductive success or fitness. Reproductive success or fitness refers to the extent to which certain genes have been propagated relative to other genes in the population. If organism A has 2 viable offspring, and organism B has 10, B has had more reproductive success (or enhanced fitness), in the sense that B's genes are more prevalent in the subsequent generation than A's (assuming kin descendancy is equal or nonexistent). The fact that the reproductive success of different organisms within a population will vary is often captured in the term *differential reproductive success*. The differential reproductive success of organisms within a population is the very essence of natural selection and is what drives evolutionary change over time.

Chance and law. The evolutionary process is often thought of as one characterized by a combination of chance and law. The chance part comes from the fact that the mutations, which are an integral part of the evolutionary process, occur (for the most part) randomly. Thus, that first white-coated rabbit in the Yukon was just plain lucky. However, whether a mutation survives and spreads in a population is not just a matter of chance or luck (here is where the law part comes in). Generally speaking, a mutation must confer some fitness advantage on the organism if that mutation is to successfully propagate into subsequent generations. Natural selection is lawful and deterministic. Regardless of the time, place, or organism, it unfailingly favors those traits that make one organism more adaptive than another. Despite this, one must not think of natural selection as necessarily "rewarding" "better" organisms with greater reproductive success. Environments often change in unpredictable ways, making what would have been a disadvantageous trait only a few generations ago into an advantageous one and vice versa. So even though evolution is lawful, it is not necessarily predictable, nor is it necessarily "improving" or "perfecting" species. It is only making them more adapted. What makes a creature more fit is often simply a serendipitous combination of genes and circumstances.

Preadaptation. Preadaptation refers to the fact that natural selection does not "design" adaptations from scratch. Instead, it works with what is already structurally present in the organism. Sometimes, a structure that evolved for one purpose can serve a second function. Such was the case with the reptilian jawbone hinges that later converted to middle ear bones (discussed in chapter 1). Another classic example involves certain fish with fins that could be used to move about on lake bottoms and muddy shorelines as well as to swim in the open water. This alternate use provided the basis from which terrestrial locomotion could evolve. It is often said that natural selection is not a designer but a tinkerer (Jacob, 1982). It adjusts, tweaks, and tinkers with what is already there to construct an adaptation that works "well enough" for a given purpose. Because adaptations are not designed from scratch but built ad hoc onto what is already present, adaptations are not necessarily perfect for their functions. We humans are all too aware of the

Evolution typically moves at a glacial pace. However, the evolution of scientific terms to describe the process seems to change at light speed. Until very recently, the species that emerged along the evolutionary branch that eventually produced us (*Homo sapiens*) were referred to as **hominids**, indicating that they were classified under the family Hominidae. The Hominidae family was separate from another family, the Pongidae, whose members include the great apes, chimpanzees, gorillas, and orangutans. However, this classification system has been called into question, because it fails to reflect genetic evidence that indicates that humans are more closely related to chimpanzees than are chimpanzees to gorillas or orangutans. An alternative system places both humans and chimpanzees under the family Hominidae, with humans under the tribe Hominini and chimpanzees under the tribe Panini (Wood & Richmond, 2000). This means that all the species emerging along the human evolutionary branch are labeled **hominins** instead of hominids. Furthermore, under this system the term Australopithecines has been replaced by the Australopiths as the general label for the pre-*Homo* genus that emerged on this branch. Although hominid and Australopithecine are still commonly used in the scientific and popular literature, we will adopt the newer system in this text.

The term *Homo sapiens* also needs some clarification. *Homo sapiens* (or *H. sapiens*) generally refers to modern humans (us), and the term will be used in that manner in this book. However, another general species designation, **archaic *Homo sapiens***, is also commonly used to refer to the relatively large-brained hominins that emerged immediately before *H. sapiens*. Although archaic *H. sapiens* shared many more characteristics in common with modern humans than did earlier hominin species (such as *Homo erectus* or *Homo ergaster*), they were still dissimilar enough from *H. sapiens* be considered a separate species. Thus, to clearly distinguish modern humans from archaic *H. sapiens*, the term **Homo sapiens sapiens** is sometimes used as the designation for modern humans. In this book, *H. sapiens* and *H. sapiens sapiens* will always refer to the same species: modern humans. The term archaic *H. sapiens* will refer exclusively to that species the immediately preceded modern humans.

flawed character of evolutionary adaptations. Our bodies are adapted for bipedal locomotion, but the prevalence of lower back problems in the population testifies to the fact that this adaptation was not "perfectly designed." It was, instead, modified piecemeal from the quadrupedal and tree-climbing adaptations present in our primate ancestors.

Blindness. The processes that drive evolution are blind to the future. This reflects the fact that genes can only code for what was adaptive in the past and cannot predict what is to come. The genetic information inherited by an offspring represents the sum total of the information that allowed its ancestors to be reproductively successful. Whether that information will be as productive for the offspring is a good bet but not a certainty. If a violent volcanic eruption should drastically reorder the ecology of one of the Galapagos Islands, the next generation of finches might be out of luck.

Thus, evolutionary process might be summarized in a sentence: Given that variation based on genetic inheritance exists within a population and that the environmental resources to support the population are limited, those variants with advantageous traits are more likely to propagate their genetic material to the next generation (differential reproductive success), thereby driving adaptive change in the population over time.

The Complicated Part: The Ever-Branching Tree

If we take the basic premises of evolution and put them into practice, an explosion of creativity ensues. To gain an appreciation of the immensity of this creativity we will concentrate on that very tiny twig of the evolutionary tree that gave rise to humanity. Once we see how quickly this minuscule portion of the evolutionary

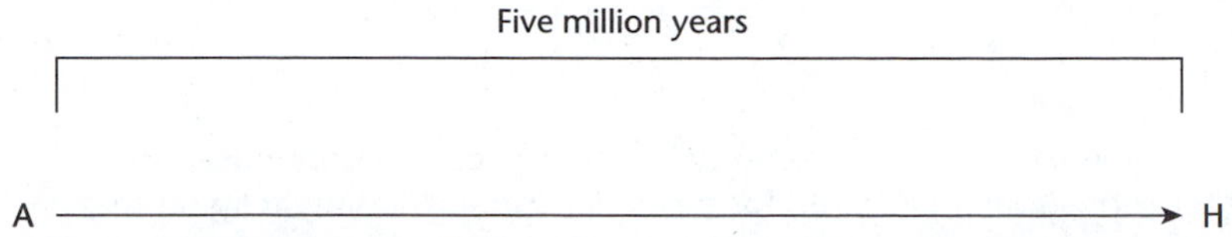

Five million years

A ——————————————————————→ H

Figure 4.1 An oversimplified depiction of the evolutionary emergence of humans (H) from the common ancestor (A) of humans and chimpanzees that existed some 5 million years ago.

tree overflows with life forms, we should more clearly recognize how enormously complex the patterns of evolution can become. We start with a simple line graph showing A leading to H (Fig. 4.1).

In the late 19th century, after the introduction of Darwinian evolutionary theory, one of Darwin's most stalwart supporters, T.H. Huxley, engaged in a celebrated debate with Samuel Wilberforce, the Bishop of Oxford. Wilberforce is reported to have sardonically asked if the apes in Huxley's family line came from his grandfather's or grandmother's side (see Box 4.1). The bishop's question betrays a misunderstanding of human origins that is still quite common today. Humans did not evolve from what we commonly think of as "apes." It is inaccurate from an evolutionary standpoint to gaze upon a chimpanzee or gorilla and wonder whether that is what we used to be like. This leads to an important point about the notation in the first figure. It is easy to interpret this figure as showing apes at one end (A), with a 5-million year period of time leading ultimately to the emergence of humans (H) at the other end. The A does not stand for apes but for the **common ancestor** of humans and chimpanzees. Both humans and chimpanzees evolved from a primate that lived roughly 5–6 million years ago. To look at a chimpanzee today and believe that humans were once similar assumes that chimpanzees have not changed at all from that common ancestor—an assumption that is unlikely if not absurd. Chimpanzees have evolved just as humans have.

If the evolutionary process were simple, then Figure 4.1 would capture the essence of what led to the emergence of humans. One species, an ancestral primate, simply changed into a second one, modern humans. Over the course of 5 million years, the common ancestor steadily lost its hair, enlarged its brain, and straightened its back until, on some fateful day, it emerged fully human. Let's look carefully at this oversimplified depiction until it becomes a closer approximation of reality. Figure 4.2 shows a slightly more complex process leading to the emergence of humans. A evolved into a second species, A′, which had characteristics somewhat different from A but was still markedly distinct from anything that would be

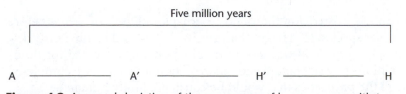

Five million years

A ———————— A′ ———————— H′ ———————— H

Figure 4.2 A second depiction of the emergence of humans, now with two intervening species between the common ancestor (A) and humans (H). This is still too simplistic to capture what happened in the 5 million years between the common ancestor and humans.

Evolution and Religion

BOX 4.1

Evolution has been one of the most important theories in science. Yet it remains socially controversial, as it was when first proposed by Darwin. One of the major reasons for this controversy is that Darwinism challenges some traditional religious views on the origin of humanity and the nature of God and the universe. In recent years, especially in the United States, some groups have reacted to this challenge by exerting political pressure on educators to remove evolution from the science curriculum. This is nothing short of tragic, given that humanity is poised on the brink of unprecedented challenges in such areas as genetics, medicine, environmental conservation, and technological advancement. These challenges can only be adequately met with a more—not less—scientifically sophisticated public. The stakes involved in this volatile mix of science, religion, and politics are high, and it is important for students to be well informed on issues surrounding the apparent conflict between Darwinism and deity.

To some, any conflict between the world of science and that of the sacred is mere illusion. Science, they contend, deals with *how* the universe operates, whereas religion deals with *why* the universe exists at all. Thus, these two modes of inquiry, science and religion, inhabit utterly distinct realms and ask entirely different questions about the natural world and humanity's place within it. In this view, the two modes of inquiry cannot conflict because they do not overlap. This point of view has most recently been argued by Harvard paleontologist Steven Jay Gould (1998) in his NOMA principle, or the notion that science and religion have **nonoverlapping magisteria**. A magisterium simply refers to one's domain of authority. In this case, science has authority over natural laws, whereas religion deals with issues of morals and meaning.

Although many find Gould's approach appealing, for others it merely represents an unwillingness to confront tough issues. Theologian John Haught (2000), for example, argues that any religion that envisions purpose or meaning in the universe must come to grips with the implications of Darwinism. Evolution necessarily entails a universe ruled by the blind forces of natural selection and random chance, fraught with gratuitous suffering and cruelty, and leading only to inevitable extinction for everyone involved. For many, this seems to leave little room for the benevolent Creator of Judaism and Christianity, the merciful Allah of Islam, or even the transcendent wisdom of Buddhism. It was on this very point that Darwin himself was led to doubt, if not entirely reject, religious belief. In a letter to his friend, American botanist Asa Gray, Darwin confided:

> There seems to me too much misery in the world. I cannot persuade myself that a beneficent and omnipotent God would have designedly created the Ichneumonidae [a type of wasp] with the expressed intention of their feeding on the living bodies of caterpillars, or that cats should play with mice. (Darwin, 1860/1898, p. 105)

For Darwin it was the inherent misery of the evolutionary process that seemed incompatible with his understanding of God. Others have pointed to the contingent nature of the evolutionary process as a refutation of the idea of a "divine design" to the universe. **Contingency** refers to simple dumb luck, or, put more formally, the confluence of circumstances that directs evolution down a specific pathway out of a potential multitude of possible options. Probably the most dramatic example of contingency at work was the meteorite that struck the earth 65 million years ago and put an end to the dinosaurs. For more than 100 million years, the dinosaurs had managed to survive and adapt to a vast array of different environmental conditions and circumstances. What more could evolution ask of them? Yet, through no fault or weakness of their own, they unceremoniously disap-

considered human. A′ existed for thousands, perhaps millions of years, before evolving into another species, H′. H′ had characteristics that made it obviously distinct from the A species but still was not quite fully human. H′ existed for thousands, perhaps millions of years before enough evolutionary changes accumulated for it to possess all the properties that would be considered fully human.

Figure 4.2 is still vastly too simple to be realistic. Its two most significant flaws are that it underestimates the number of species that emerged during the 5-million-year period depicted, and it gives the impression of a steady, progressive march

peared from the face of the earth, victims of a giant rock from the sky. What more stunning evidence of the universe's capricious and indifferent character could one want?

The idea that evolution implies an impersonal, meaningless universe has spawned two diametrically opposed reactions. One camp sees this as a devastating blow to religion and adopts a strictly materialistic and atheistic view of the universe. Biologist Richard Dawkins, for example, sees evolution as the decisive argument for atheism. "Darwin made it possible to be an intellectually fulfilled atheist," he claimed in his book *The Blind Watchmaker* (1986; p. 6). Dawkins was even more blunt in his later book *River out of Eden:* "The universe we observe has precisely the properties we should expect if there is, at bottom, no design, no purpose, no evil, no good, nothing but blind, pitiless indifference" (1995, p. 133).

Dawkins's understanding of evolution led him to reject religion. Ironically, another camp agrees with Dawkins on evolution's message about our universe but instead chooses to reject evolution and the science upon which it is based. In the Christian West, this view is generally referred to as **creationism**, a perspective that adopts a literalist interpretation of scripture to retain some semblance of meaning in the universe. Its adherents have been the most vocal advocates against the teaching of evolution in public schools. Although creationists are a minority among religious believers, their movement has gained considerable political force in the United States and recently has begun to spread to other countries, including Turkey, Australia, and some parts of Europe (Koenig, 2001; Numbers, 1998).

Although confrontations between strident atheists and ardent creationists often attract the glare of media attention, it is important to recognize that most religious people and religious denominations accept evolution. For example, in an essay recently published in none other than the *Quarterly Review of Biology*, Pope John Paul II made the following statement:

The theory of evolution is more than a hypothesis. It is indeed remarkable that this theory has been progressively accepted by researchers, following a series of discoveries in various fields of knowledge. This convergence, neither sought nor fabricated,…is itself a significant argument in favour of the theory." (John Paul II, 1997, p. 382)

This statement reflects the fact that many religious people (including some scientists) desire a form of engagement between science and religion that avoids the extremes represented by Dawkins or the creationists. In this vein, some theologians have argued that evolution reinforces important and long-standing religious themes. One of these is the idea of kenosis, which refers to self-denial or self-renunciation (Murphy & Ellis, 1996). For these theologians, evolution presents us with a picture of a God who willingly denies him- or herself the power to control the universe, so that it will have the freedom to be a fully formed "other" rather than merely a divinely dictated subordinate. The kenotic God desires not to coerce the universe toward goodness and perfection but to gently persuade it, never determining the universe's course but encouraging some directions over others. For many religious people, this image of God is in perfect harmony with the humility and self-sacrificial ethic embodied in the life of Jesus, the teachings of Buddha, the passive power of the Tao, and Isaiah's discourse on the suffering servant. A universe given maximal freedom, of course, may take paths of corruption, destruction, and evil; such is the cost of freedom. However, it also will explore endless variety, diversity, and novelty (Haught, 2000). "When we look at the glory of stars and galaxies in the sky and the glory of forests and flowers in the living world around us, it is evident that God loves diversity," said physicist Freeman Dyson. "Perhaps the universe is constructed according to a principle of maximum diversity" (Dyson, 2000, p. 3).

Ideas such as these offer the hope that in the future religious people will not find it necessary to invoke creationism when trying to reconcile faith with science.

toward humanity. This erroneously implies that species A′ and H′ were not really fully formed species each in its own right but were transitional, intermediate steps on the way to some predetermined destination. Let's try to remedy these flaws. Figure 4.3 shows a more complex process with a number of A′ and H′ species emerging.

Starting at the left of Figure 4.3, we once again have the common ancestor of humans and chimpanzees. That common ancestor gave rise to four different A′ species, called A1′, A2′, A3′, and A4′. A moment's reflection will verify that this is a

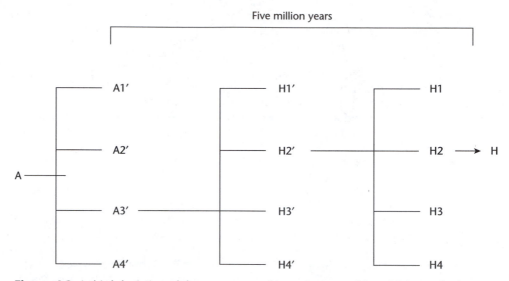

Figure 4.3 A third depiction of the emergence of humans, now with multiple species intervening between the common ancestor and humans. This is getting closer to reality, except that it gives the impression that the various A and H species never overlapped in existence.

much more realistic state of affairs. Think about how many different species of monkeys (capuchin, macaque, colobus, baboon, etc.) or bears (grizzly, polar, brown, panda, etc.) exist today. To assume that only four different species might have emerged from the common ancestral primate is still rather conservative. Note that only one, A3′, evolved into the early H species (H3′), whereas the other A's went extinct. As with the A's, a multitude of H′ species emerged. Only one eventually gave rise to a later series of Hs, whereas other H's eventually went extinct. Finally, one of the later H species, H2, gave rise to the human species as we know it today. This figure is getting closer to reality, but even it is misleading, because it gives the impression that all the A's emerged at roughly the same time and all went extinct before the H's emerged. Similarly, it suggests that all the early H's emerged at roughly the same time and went extinct before the later Hs arrived on the scene.

Figure 4.4 attempts to deal with this problem and shows the common ancestor with a number of A variants emerging. A dotted line shows the presumed connection between A2 and an early H species (H2′). The connection is assumed, because there may have been other A or H variants that came between A2 and H2′. Note that a number of As are shown overlapping with the emergence of the early H's. One of the emergent H's (H3′) is shown with a presumed connection to a later H species (H3). At this later stage, a number of H species emerged. Notice, however, that many of the early versions of H′ were still present. Finally, one of the later Hs (H1) is shown with a presumed connection to modern humans. Even this illustration is oversimplified, because the number of A and H species shown is too small and the connections among them too straight and simple.

The important point is this: the emergence of humans was marked by a proliferation of hominin species living contemporaneously. Each had its own set of characteristics and adaptations and successfully existed for hundreds of thousands

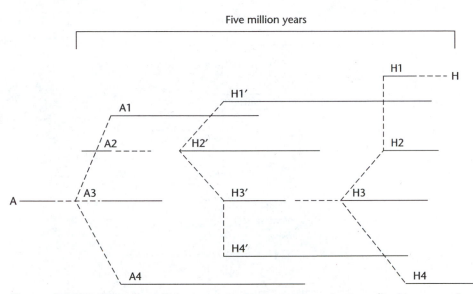

Figure 4.4 This illustration of human origins begins to approximate reality. Numerous A and H species emerged in the 5-million-year interval separating the common ancestor from humans. These species overlapped in both time and space, and the evolutionary connections among them may have been indirect.

of years or more. None should be considered a "transitional" or "temporary" form on the way to creating a modern human. The choice of using As and Hs to distinguish the different species was not arbitrary. Figure 4.5 is a graph or phylogeny depicting the evolutionary relationships among hominin species from a book on human origins (Foley, 1995). On the graph, human ancestors are lumped into two general A and H categories. The As stand for ***Australopithecus,*** and the Hs stand for the genus ***Homo.***

Recognizing the complexity of just one tiny part of the evolutionary tree illustrates how prolific the evolutionary process is and how deeply varied are its products. Our infinitesimal twig depicts the evolution of just the hominins over the last few million years. It has been estimated that among the Australopiths alone, 12–14 different species probably existed (Foley, 1991). It is further estimated that at least 6,000 different primates have existed since their emergence about 50 million years ago (Martin, 1990). Primates represent just one of the more than 25 different orders of mammals, not to mention the reptiles, amphibians, birds, insects, flowers, trees, and other life forms. The diversity of life on earth currently includes tens of millions (maybe up to a billion) different species. However, evolution is not simply an ever-branching tree of increasing numbers of species. At least five major extinction phases have occurred in the past 500 million years and have periodically decimated the number of species. Those that exist today constitute only about 1% of all the species that have ever existed (Foley, 1995; Wilson, 1992). Imagine for a moment the vastness of life that has shared our fortuitously wet and warm little orb since multicellular organisms first emerged more than 700 million years ago! Evolution is paradoxical—simple, yet simply overwhelming in its productivity.

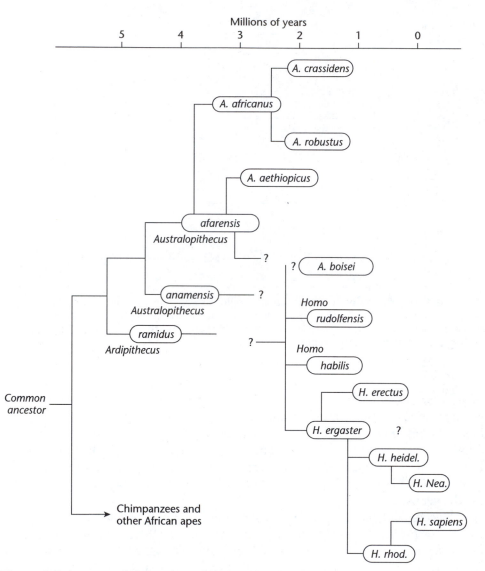

Figure 4.5 A more realistic graph or phylogeny showing the various Australopith and *Homo* species that preceded the emergence of *Homo sapiens* (modern humans). (Adapted from Foley, 1995, p.99.)

The Background of Human Evolution

Evolutionary psychology looks to humanity's evolutionary past as a basis for understanding our current nature. Human evolution, however, cannot be understood as a unique, isolated process. We are but one species among the countless species that have emerged over time. Thus, to fully understand our past, we must first understand some basic concepts about how new species emerge and explore the specific context relevant to the emergence of our species. The saga of human evolution is truly an epic worthy of Hollywood's golden age. However, before it became our story—the human story—it was the primate story. Before that, it was just another story about the arrival of one of the innumerable species occupying the earth.

The Origin of New Species

Humans, as new species, emerged over millions of years from a common ancestor that we shared with other apes. Two basic patterns are associated with the emergence of new species. The first is known as **anagenesis**. Anagenesis describes the process that occurs when one species evolves slowly into another over an extended period of time. This can occur when a species is subject to various selection pressures and changing environmental conditions over the course of time, so that an accumulation of adaptive changes causes it to transform into something new. Figure 4.1 might be viewed as a very simplified version of anagenesis.

A second pattern is referred to as **cladogenesis**, which describes the process that occurs when a subgroup of a population splits from the main group and begins to follow its own evolutionary course. This is often the result of a peripheral or marginalized group becoming isolated from the larger group and therefore encountering a unique set of selection pressures and environmental conditions (a process referred to as **allopatric speciation**). Darwin's finches, which developed into different species on different islands in the Galapagos, are classic examples of cladogenesis. As the birds migrated, groups became isolated from one another and each began to follow its own evolutionary path. This helps to explain why so many different species can emerge in relatively short periods of time (evolutionarily speaking) and why it is believed that many different species of Australopiths and *Homo* emerged over the course of human evolution. A vigorous debate is currently underway in the anthropological community over whether the evolution of *Homo sapiens* is best described in an anagenic or cladogenic pattern.

Primates and Primate Adaptations

Whether by cladogenesis or anagenesis, the human species is unquestionably part of the primate order. Our primate heritage is reflected in many aspects of our physical and behavioral characteristics. However, defining exactly what is meant by primate has proven difficult for many researchers. Anthropologist Alison Jolly summarized the essence of being primate as simply the "progressive evolution of intelligence as a way of life" (quoted in Lewin, 1998, p. 125). Jolly's comment reflects our intuitive inclination to think of monkeys and apes as smarter than most other animals. Our intuition is not entirely baseless. Primates do tend to have brains that are larger relative to body size than do other mammals, and among primates, apes have relatively larger brains than monkeys. (Martin, 1990; Jerison, 1973). Perhaps even more compelling than primate intellect is primate sociability. Where other mammals are distinctive for their physical characteristics such as antlers, long necks, or retractable claws, primates are extraordinarily gregarious (Jolly, 1972). Of the nearly 150 species of monkeys and apes, only 1 (orangutans) does not live in some sort of social group setting (Dunbar, 1988; Smuts, Cheney, Seyfarth, Wrangham, & Struhsaker, 1985). In a survey of 167 different primates, Lee (1994) found that 83% were social rather than solitary, with the vast majority of the nonsocial primates being prosimians (non-monkeys and non-apes). Furthermore, among the social primates, female kin-based groupings and monogamous groupings formed the core of the most social systems.

Martin (1990) focused his definition of primates around the universal or near universal anatomical and behavioral attributes of primates. For example, primates are generally arboreal (tree dwelling) and live in tropical or subtropical forests.

Furthermore, primate hands and feet are adapted for grasping with opposable thumbs and great toes. Primate locomotion is variable, consisting of brachiation, tree climbing, clinging, leaping, and quadrupedal walking. It is, however, generally dominated by the hindlimbs, and the body is often held vertically, thus making a shift to bipedalism less radical for primates than for other mammals. Unlike other mammals, primate sensory systems are visually rather than olfactorily dominated, with the eyes set close together at the front of the head, providing for well-developed stereoscopic vision. In primates, then, one can already see the foundations in place for many human characteristics, such as the enlarged brain, bipedalism, grasping hands, well-developed visual capacities, and a strong social inclination.

The Primate Branch and the Ape/Human Common Ancestor

Figure 4.6 depicts the evolutionary relationships among some of the higher primates and the approximate times when different species branched off from one another. Humans are part of the primate branch of the evolutionary tree, but we are not equally related to all the different primate species. By comparing the genomes of different species, estimates of relatedness can be made. (Genetic comparisons are not the only way to estimate relatedness, and different procedures can produce somewhat different estimates. For simplicity, we will stay with this approach.)

The foundations of the human epic were laid more than 50 million years ago, after the dinosaurs had been banished from the scene and mammals had begun to expand into the territory once occupied by the giant reptiles. By this time, early primates had already emerged. Figure 4.6 shows that an important divergence among the primates occurred about 25 million years ago when the branch that ultimately gave rise to the Old World monkeys (colobus, macaque, etc.) separated from the one that gave rise to the apes. Estimates for this split vary, ranging from 34 to 21 million years ago (see Klein, 1999, pp. 88–90, for discussion). It is important to understand what this split means. Roughly 25 million years ago, there were no monkeys, chimps, or gorillas. Instead, there was a population of small primates. A subgroup of that population most likely became isolated from the main group, and each set out on its own evolutionary course. If we track the evolution of those two groups, we find that eventually one provided the basis for the apes we know today (chimps, gorillas, us, etc.) and the other for the Old World monkeys. The original population that existed 25 million years ago (or so) constitutes the common ancestor of the apes and Old World monkeys.

Although the split between the monkeys and apes took place more than 25 million years ago, its ramifications are critical for understanding some uniquely human qualities. Sociability is a distinctive feature of primates, but monkeys and apes are not social in the same way. Among Old World monkeys, the primary social grouping is among related females, who remain in their natal groups, whereas males disperse to other groups as they approach maturity. In apes, female kin groups are rare if not absent, and the social structure varies from species to species with, for example, most gorillas having a harem-based system, chimpanzees having multimale/multifemale groups, and gibbons having monogamous pairs (Foley, 1989; Foley & Lee, 1995; Giglieri, 1987; Wrangham, 1987). About 10 million years ago, the ancestors of today's monkeys and apes were faced with an ecological transformation that challenged their adaptability. Natural selection adapted monkeys in a variety of physical and behavioral ways; however, they retained their basic social

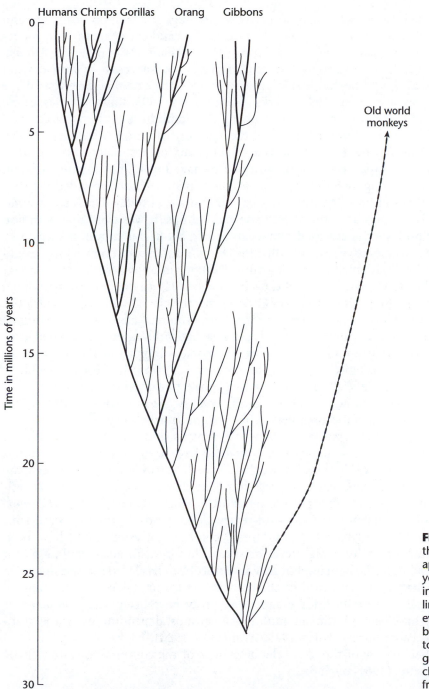

Humans Chimps Gorillas   Orang   Gibbons

Old world
monkeys

Figure 4.6 A graph depicting
the evolution of monkeys and
apes over the past 30 million
years. The thick lines indicate living species, whereas the thinner
lines show ones that emerged but
eventually went extinct. Major
branchings can be seen that lead
to the Old World monkeys,
gibbons, orangutans, gorillas,
chimps, and humans. (Adapted
from Foley, 1995, p. 69.)

structure. Such was not the case with apes. As selection operated on them, they
began to explore a wide range of varied social structures. Humans, of course,
emerged from the socially "avant-garde" apes, not the more conservative monkeys.

By following the ape branch in Figure 4.6, we can see that the next divergence
occurred about 17 million years ago, when the gibbon branch was established.
About 5 million years after that (about 12 million years ago), the orangutans

emerged. The last two branchings occurred at roughly 8 million years ago and between 5 and 6 million years ago, when the gorillas and chimpanzees, respectively, diverged (Hasegawa, Kishino, & Yano, 1989; Pilbeam, 1986; Sibley & Alquist, 1987). Researchers disagree over whether the common ancestor of humans and chimpanzees should be considered separately from the one that gave rise to the gorillas (Goodman et al., 1994; Marks, 1994; Rogers, 1993; Ruvolo, 1994). Some have argued that a three-way split involving the hominin line, chimpanzees, and gorillas is the simplest interpretation of the data (Corruccini, 1992; Rogers, 1993). Although this may be true, for the sake of simplicity the last divergence, between humans and chimpanzees, will be assumed to have involved a unique common ancestor. Thus, roughly 5 million years ago, a primate creature provided the evolutionary basis for both the chimpanzees and humans of today. That creature was the shared common ancestor of humans and chimps. It was from that common stock that both species emerged. What can be said about this common ancestor?

Some analyses have suggested that the chimp/human common ancestor would have been relatively small in size. Martin (1990), for example, estimated its size at about 19 kg (42 lb), with a cranial capacity at about 210 cc or about on par with a small baboon. Noble and Davidson (1996) generally agreed with such figures but cautioned that these are likely overestimates. Furthermore, it has often been assumed that the common ancestor was primarily arboreal but with some ground-based locomotion as well. Its locomotion would have been some combination of branch swinging with occasional bipedal walking, both in trees and on the ground (Noble & Davidson, 1996). While all four limbs were probably involved in its locomotion, it probably was not a knuckle walker (Lewin, 1998; Noble & Davidson, 1996). This view of the common ancestor, however, has not gone unchallenged.

Given the close association between humans and chimpanzees, Pilbeam (1996) argued that the common ancestor would have been chimplike. His claim is bolstered by fossil evidence indicating that the earliest species to emerge along the human evolutionary branch had some chimplike characteristics. A recent analysis by Richmond, Begun, and Strait (2001) added further support to Pilbeam's conclusion. After an extensive anatomical review, Richmond, Begun and Strait concluded that the most recent chimp/human common ancestor would have been about chimp-size, with a high level of sexual dimorphism and adaptations for knuckle walking. The high level of sexual dimorphism has led some researchers to conclude that the social world of the common ancestor was one with extensive male-on-male competition for mates. Males may have been harem holders, or there may have been multimale, multifemale groups, depending upon the availability of local resources (Foley, 1995; Wrangham, 1980).

In their review of the likely characteristics of the common ancestor, Noble and Davidson (1996) concluded:

> The common ancestor more than 5 million years ago lived and nested in trees on the edge of the tropical forests of Africa, was rarely bipedal, and had a small brain but, for its small body size, one similar in size to chimpanzees. [Its] diet...was fruit and leaves with some invertebrates but little meat. Communication was primarily nonvocal, this and limited vocal utterances being honed through observational learning and conditioning. Symbols were not part of either form of communication. Females associated with each other but did not form alliances, and males were sometimes solitary, and little involved in rearing offspring. (p. 142)

By understanding the basic primate and (potential) common ancestor traits, we can get a handle on the "starting point" of human evolution. This much seems sure: humans evolved from a moderate-size, partly arboreal primate with good vision, grasping hands, limited bipedal locomotion, some degree of sociality, and a diet consisting largely of fruits, leaves, and bugs.

The Context of Human Evolution

Here's a fanciful experiment that, if successfully completed, would ensure the author of winning a Nobel Prize. Locate an animal with all the presumed traits of the common ancestor and allow it 5 million years to evolve; check then to see if it has become human. Of course, this would not work—but why not? True, the right animal subject no longer exists, and no one could live long enough to inspect the results. But even setting those practicalities aside, there is a more fundamental reason why the experiment would fail. The mortal flaw is that the experiment assumes that the environmental context of the ancestral animal could be reproduced. Without the environment imposing the demands that it did over the 5-million-year period of human evolution, the ancestral animal would never have accumulated the suite of adaptations that constitute the unique signature of humanity. What, then, was the context of human evolution?

We should not be too surprised that humans evolved where they did. The tropics are currently and always have been the region of greatest species diversity. For example, only 20 species of land mammals live at 66° latitude near the Arctic and Antarctic circles, whereas 160 species live at 8° latitude near the equator (Myers & Giller, 1988). One of the main reasons for this is simple energy: more radiant energy is present nearer the equator and provides greater opportunities for life forms to flourish. Thus, the deck is stacked in favor of the tropics as the region most likely to produce a wide range of life forms, including primates and, eventually, humans. Beyond this, however, is the fact that, about 10 million years ago, African primates were being exposed to climatic changes that affected their food resources. Eastern Africa, especially, was experiencing a cooling and drying phase, which slowly transformed its once unbroken tropical forests into a region of patchy forests surrounded by open grasslands. This changing and fragmenting habitat stressed and isolated the indigenous primate populations, forcing them to adapt and bringing about speciation (the creation of new species). One group of primates adapted by becoming increasingly more bipedal, possibly because this proved to be a more energy-efficient way of getting from one "patch" of resources to another (Rodman & McHenry, 1980; Isbell & Young, 1996). The ecological changes, however, had more than just physical effects on these primates. As resources became more widely dispersed, a harem-like social structure would have been more difficult to maintain. Females would be forced to forage for food separately and over longer distances. The most likely male response would be to try to form kin-based alliances to defend wide territories within which the females were present (Foley & Lee, 1995). Thus, one theory regarding the social system of early hominins was that it looked somewhat chimpanzee-like, with groups of territorial males controlling groups of females. The degree of sexual dimorphism in early hominins suggests that if this type of system was in fact in place, it involved as much competition among males as it did cooperation.

Foley (1995) attempted to describe the general course of human evolution in terms of alternate strategies adopted in response to the demands of changing environments. In response to the breaking up of the African forests, one group of primates (from which humans evolved) was selected for bidpedalism, so that they could more efficiently get from one resource patch to another. The other (which gave rise to the other African apes) clung to the remaining forests, expertly combining knuckle walking and tree climbing to survive. It was a fateful divergence of strategies: the bipedal apes ultimately expanded to cover the globe, while the forest apes dwindled. As additional environmental stresses occurred affecting the bipedal apes, one group was adapted by the enlargement of the brain and another by changes to the jaw and dental structure that allowed the eating of coarse vegetable material. Finally, as additional environmental stresses occurred affecting the large-brained, bipedal apes, one group evolved a sophisticated culture, including symbols and language, and another relied on brawn and strength. The important lesson is that the environmental context places demands on the organism to adapt in certain ways or face extinction. Certain traits, then, including many of those that we think of as being uniquely human, owe their character and quality to the stresses and strains of the context of the past (for more on Robert Foley's ecological approach to human evolution, see Box 4.2).

Perhaps we could revisit our hypothetical experiment and modify it slightly to salvage that coveted Scandinavian trophy. Let's assume that we could reconstruct the cooling and drying forests of East Africa along with the other environmental changes that occurred over the 5 million years of human evolution. Let's further assume that we could place a primate population within that context and wait the obligatory amount of evolutionary time. Could we get our human then? No. In fact, nature has already tried something similar. Consider the baboon. Baboons evolved under similar circumstances as those that faced early hominins, but they were derived from different stock. Their primate ancestor was a monkey, not an ape, and, as such, was a committed quadruped. As the ancestral baboons' habitat dried, cooled, and became patchy, they transferred their quadrupedal ways onto terra firma and set off down an entirely different evolutionary path. The essential lesson of this second, failed variant of our original (doomed) experiment is the following: uniquely human characteristics resulted from an evolutionarily unique combination of circumstances—a merging of currents never to be repeated. That is, these characteristics evolved from a certain ancestral organism with bipedal potential (our common ancestor) that encountered a specific array of environmental conditions (Foley, 1995).

Natural selection can only shape a future with the materials provided by the past. When the African forests started changing, the past histories of all the creatures facing that calamity imposed constraints on and opened possibilities for their evolutionary futures. Natural selection is a conservative, incremental tinkerer with current designs. Our ancestors could hardly be expected to fly or grow scales or anything of that sort in response to their circumstances. But they could get upright and grow bigger brains. That's what they did, and that's why we are here. It was by virtue of our primate heritage that our ancestors possessed the potential for what later evolved into the distinctive markings of humanity: big brains, rationality, sociality, language, and morality. We are what we are because of the peculiarities of the stock from which we were drawn and the selection pressures we endured.

ROBERT FOLEY
Questions and Answers on Human Evolution

PROFILE: *Robert Foley is the director of the Leverhulme Center for Human Evolutionary Studies and a Fellow and Director of Studies at King's College of Cambridge University. He has done important and pioneering work in understanding how environmental and ecological factors have affected the course of human evolution.*

BOX 4.2

Human Evolution's Critical Questions: What are human beings?

On one level this question is simple: human beings are a species of hominin of the genus *Homo*, specifically *Homo sapiens sapiens*. If, however, we ask what are the defining characteristics of this particular species, the question becomes more complicated. Humans seem to posses some unique physical and behavioral attributes, such as bipedalism, language, tool use, and big brains. However, on close inspection we can see that none of these features is entirely unique to our species. Kangaroos are (and some dinosaurs probably were) bipedal. With proper training, apes can demonstrate a limited use of language, and wild chimpanzees fashion and use tools. Whales have bigger brains. It may be that humans are the only species to possess this entire suite of characteristics and to have developed them to such a degree. For any single characteristic, the difference between humans and other animals is a matter of degree. However, the cumulative effect of these differences may indeed be qualitative.

When did we become human?

The various characteristics we associate with humans emerged at different times over the course of our evolution. Because of bipedalism, our ancestors were quite distinct from apes by at least 4 million years ago. However, it was only in the last 2 million years that the brain began to enlarge significantly to near modern size. If we went back in time about a million years and located our upright, large-brained ancestor would he (she) have appeared "human" to us? Certainly not. The physical form of humans today was not in place until about 150,000 years ago, and human-like behavior (including art, complex tools, large social groups, and probably language as we know it) was not present until about 100,000–50,000 years ago. Becoming human was a long, mosaic process, not a sudden cataclysmic event.

Why are humans so rare in evolution?

As humans, we generally have a high opinion of ourselves. What other creature wouldn't want to have the collection of traits we possess? Given how successfully we have populated the planet and modified our environments for our own sake, surely our evolved characteristics must be highly adaptive and advantageous. And certainly they are to some extent, but human-like characteristics also have costs. A large brain can make you intelligent (an advantage), but it also imposes a heavy burden: our brain is only 3% of our total body weight, but it consumes 20% of all our metabolic resources and greatly increases mortality during childbirth. For most other animals, it is far more adaptive to devote that energy to more muscle, hair, or bone. A big brain means other organs must reduce their size and energy requirements. The human digestive tract is relatively small and, unlike that of gorillas or cows, cannot deal with highly abundant but low-quality foods, such as grasses or leaves. Thus, humans must expend energy hunting and scavenging for meat and fruits and other high-protein, easily digestible foods. Other costs also are associated with bipedalism (lack of speed), naked skin (lack of protection), and upright posture (bad for climbing trees). Only under very rare conditions indeed did the particulars of humanity prove to be advantageous, thus leading to our rarity.

Does human evolution matter?

It unquestionably matters to us: it's better to be around than not. But the consequences of human evolution go far beyond just the fact that we are here. In the last few thousand years, humans have affected the planet in unprecedented ways. Vast ecosystems have been rearranged as a result of human activities. Deserts have expanded, forests reduced, and mounting evidence suggests that human agriculture and industry are affecting our climate. Humans also have affected the very course of evolution itself. Centuries of selective breeding have produced animal and plant populations adapted to our needs and desires, rather than adapted for their own reproductive success. This effect will only accelerate given the emergence of powerful new genetic engineering technologies. There is nothing modest about Project Humanity, and we cannot fully anticipate how our influence will ultimately affect the planet and ourselves.

Source: **Foley, R. (1995).** *Humans before humanity.* Oxford, UK: Blackwell.

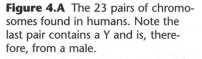
NOTE: *Genetics is complicated, and any attempt to provide a concise explanation of terms and concepts will inevitably suffer from oversimplification. The following should help to clarify some important genetic concepts and dispel some inaccurate myths but is not intended as a thorough exploration of each issue raised.*

What is a gene?

A gene is a unit of heredity. That unit is typically (although not exclusively) located on a segment of chromosome, and it serves the function of coding for a protein. Bodies, including human bodies, are made of many different kinds of cells, such as nerve cells, muscle cells, skin cells, etc. Inside each cell are chromosomes that carry information about the cell's functioning and design. Humans have 46 chromosomes in each cell, or 23 pairs, half inherited from each parent (Fig. 4.A). Each chromosome

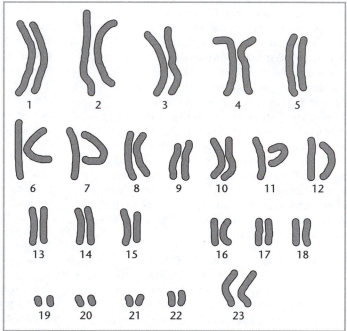

Figure 4.A The 23 pairs of chromosomes found in humans. Note the last pair contains a Y and is, therefore, from a male.

is made up of thousands of genes. It is the gene that carries the information that ultimately determines whether the cell is part of the nervous system, digestive system, or another part of the body. The genes do this by supplying a code for constructing various proteins, which are then assembled into cells of different types. At its very simplest, then, a gene is merely a bit of information on how to construct a protein inside a cell. The effects of genes, however, are enormous. They constitute the recipe for creating a body (a phenotype), and it is that body's success in survival and reproduction that will determine whether the genes multiply and spread in a population or diminish to oblivion.

What is an allele?

An allele is also a gene, but the term refers specifically to a form or variant of a gene that may produce a different effect on the body (phenotypic effect) compared with another allele. A good example would be the different alleles that determine whether one's ear lobe is free-swinging or attached. These genes occupy a specific location within the genome and vary slightly from each other (via the proteins they produce), so that those who inherit one allele end up with attached lobes and those who inherit the other allele of this same gene have free-swinging lobes. Suppose that, for some strange reason, those with free-swinging lobes have an advantage in survival and reproduction (perhaps some predator has emerged that prefers to eat "attached lobers"). Those organisms with the "free-swinging" gene variant at that location will tend to survive longer and reproduce more than those with the "attached-lobe" variant at that location. Thus, the "free-swinger" allele will spread in the population. This example makes it clear that it is really the phenotypic effects produced by some alleles that are under the pressure of natural selection. Certain alleles end up producing phenotypic effects in bodies that give those bodies advantages over others.

What is a mutation?

A mutation is a mistake or copying error in the replication of DNA. Genes are made of DNA sequences. Sometimes, when these sequences are replicated, a mistake is made and the gene is altered slightly. (Mutations may also occur as a result of environmental factors, such as the ingestion of certain chemicals or exposure to X rays.) If this slightly altered form of the gene contributes to some phenotypic effect that gives an organism an advantage in survival and reproduction, then the mutation will likely spread in the population. Most mutations are either neutral or disadvantageous to their organism, but, very rarely, a mutant confers an advantage and, in doing so, helps to drive the evolutionary process. Mutations provide the genetic variability that is the basis for natural selection.

What is genetic determinism?

Genetic determinism is the idea that genes *determine* a person's physical and psychological make-up. In other words, genes are *it*! If you were lucky enough to get good ones, good for you. If not, then too bad. From this perspective, everything about an individual is determined at conception. Whether one is weak or strong, a success or failure, happy or depressed, beautiful or ugly—all are decided by which genes a person inherited from his or her parents. This is one of the key misunderstandings about genetics that needs to cleared up.

Let's go back to basics. Genes code for proteins that do the work of assembling a certain cell structure. Bodies are composed of various cells. Bodies are not built in a day. They take time. Thus, genetic effects are long, drawn-out affairs. Because the effects of genes are spread out over months and years, they are open to environmental influences. Suppose that when you were conceived you inherited genes that, generally speaking, will affect your body so that at maturity you will be tall (you have "tall" genes). Does that mean that 18 years after conception you will, in fact, be tall? What if you are badly malnourished during childhood? What if you contract some terrible growth-stunting disease? What if your mother ingests some toxic chemical while you are in utero? A whole host of environmental factors could affect whether or not the tall trait encoded in the genes actually comes to fruition.

Take another example. We know that genetic factors are involved in addictions. Suppose someone is born with a genetic predisposition to alcohol addiction. Will that person be an alcoholic? Almost certainly not if he or she is born in Saudi Arabia, a strict Muslim country where alcohol is nowhere to be found. But if he or she is born in Russia, where vodka flows freely, the situation could be very different. The effects of the environment and other external factors usually are even more pronounced when dealing with psychological factors than with physical ones. Genes are players in the system that ultimately produces humans, not dictators.

Aren't there genes for certain things, like a gene for homosexuality or a gene for intelligence?

In a word, no! Genes provide information for creating proteins, not for intelligence or homosexuality. These proteins then interact with other proteins coded by other genes and the environment to produce traits in bodies. Genes are players, so, yes, there are genetic effects in sexuality, intelligence, temperament, and just about any other trait (physical or psychological), but tracing a trait back to a single gene is overly simplistic.

Continued

It is unfortunate that much of the publicity surrounding the Human Genome Project has latched onto the term "blueprint" as a way of describing genes. Genes are not blueprints for building human beings or any other organism. A blueprint conjures up images of a finished building (the body) with a primal sketch (genes) behind it. You can point to some aspect of the building (an electrical outlet in a room, for example) and go back to the blueprint and see its representation there. This gives one the idea that there is a one-to-one match between the finished product and the primal sketch that preceded it. The blueprint analogy tends to reinforce the "gene for" something idea. A much better analogy (from Richard Dawkins) is the idea of a recipe. The instructions you see for making a cake look very different from the finished product. Furthermore, it makes no sense whatsoever to point to a particular crumb of the cake and claim that a certain ingredient in the recipe was responsible for it. The point-to-point reductionism just doesn't work here. All the ingredients *and* the way in which they were combined and how they were cooked are jointly responsible for the finished cake in its totality. It is the same with genes. It is their joint effort, combined with the environment, that produces the body in total.

The recipe analogy works in many other ways as well. How does changing one ingredient affect the finished cake? It depends, of course, on the specific ingredient, but usually the effects will be subtle and perhaps even undetectable. A little less salt and no one will be the wiser. So it is with genes: a change in one will usually have only subtle effects. Of course, there can be exceptions. You can't replace the eggs with ground beef and still expect to have a cake. Furthermore, the oven contributes to the finished product, just as the environment contributes significantly to the finished body. Again, genes must be thought of as part of the system responsible for producing the human finished product, and their influence within that system waxes and wanes depending upon the specific trait.

Why do some genetic disorders produce debilitation and death? Shouldn't natural selection have removed them?

Seemingly destructive genes remain in a population for a number of reasons, only a few of which will be addressed here. First, remember that genes can be dominant or recessive. Unlike a dominant gene, a recessive one can be present in the genome but remain unexpressed in the body. Someone can carry a gene for a certain trait and pass that trait (or disorder) along without having the trait themselves. In this way, the gene is actually somewhat "invisible" to selection. It's there, and it gets passed along, but its expression pops up so rarely that selection really cannot operate on it in any effective way.

Second, remember that selection is primarily "concerned" with reproduction, not necessarily survival. A gene may contribute to a trait that is advantageous for reproduction but disadvantageous to survival. Suppose there is a gene that diverts a large proportion of a male's metabolic energy at sexual maturity from immune system function to the creation of colors highly attractive to the opposite sex. When the gene kicks in, our male is inundated with females ready to copulate. Within a short period of time, however, his depleted immune system will no longer be able to fend off pathogens and he will die. If he has managed to spread his genes in larger proportion than competitors without his genetic "disorder," then that "disorder" will actually spread in the population. It improves fitness even though it ends life earlier.

Finally, the detrimental effects of some genes may be outweighed by their benefits in certain environments. The most well-known example is the allele that produces sickle-cell anemia, a fatal disease found almost exclusively in populations of African descent. The allele that produces the disease actually serves a protective function for those living in environments where malaria is rampant. Malarial environments, then, favor a selection pressure that maintains a certain prevalence of the sickle-cell gene because of its protective effects. However, when Africans move (or are moved) to environments in which malaria is not a threat, the benefits of the gene are gone and only its devastation remains.

What is genetic drift?

Genetic drift refers to random changes in allele frequency from one generation to the next. The effects of drift are typically confined to small breeding populations. The result can be that certain alleles may be relatively common in small populations but have much lower frequencies in a larger group. As an example, take a large population in which nearly everyone has straight hair. Over time, a small subgroup becomes isolated from the main group and begins to follow its own evolutionary path. Simply as a function of sampling error, a relatively high number of that smaller group has curly hair. The genes associated with curly hair now have an opportunity to become established and spread within this smaller population, thus making the descendants genetically (and phenotypically) dissimilar from the parent population. Notice that this change was not necessarily for adaptive reasons (curly hair was not selected because of a fitness advantage) but resulted simply from the increased curly allele frequency in the originally isolated group. This is often referred to as the **founder effect**.

Why are genes important in evolution?

Natural selection operates on phenotypes (bodies). Genes are the recipe for building phenotypes, and therefore, it is this recipe that either is passed along or fails to get passed along to subsequent generations. Thus, as selection operates on phenotypes it indirectly sifts and sorts through genes as well.

What is the difference between evolution and natural selection?

One of the best ways to differentiate these concepts is to keep in mind that evolution is the *effect*, whereas natural selection is the cause. Natural selection produces evolution. Thus, evolution refers to descent with modification, that is, organisms changing with passing generations. Natural selection is the major mechanism by which that change occurs, this mechanism being that, by virtue of their inherited traits, some organisms have advantages in survival and reproduction over others and are therefore more likely to pass those traits along to offspring. Natural selection is not the only mechanism that can bring about evolution, but it is generally accepted to be the most important.

Is evolution progressive?

Entire books have been written arguing for and against the notion of progress in evolution. A critical problem in trying to assess whether evolution is progressive or not is in defining what is meant by "progress." Progress is often defined in terms of increasing complexity, such as increasingly complex nervous systems (bigger, more sophisticated brains, for example). With this definition, one can go back and observe a general trend over time toward more complex nervous systems with more neocortex and claim that, indeed, there has been progress in evolution. But this strategy is problematic. First, the definition of progress is somewhat arbitrary. Why is complexity necessarily progressive? Second, even if one accepts that complexity equals progress, observing that complexity has increased does not necessarily mean that evolution is inherently designed to produce greater levels of complexity. Greater levels of complexity may be simply an incidental byproduct of selection, not a necessary or "intended" consequence. All we can say for sure is that the process of evolution is designed to produce adaptation. Going beyond that takes us out of the realm of science and into metaphysical speculation, something most scientists try to avoid.

What is an "arms race" in evolution?

The best way to tackle this is to give an example. Foxes eat rabbits. Thus, those rabbits that inherit traits that make them better able to avoid foxes (for example, better ears with which to detect the approaching fox) will have a selective advantage. In time, rabbits with sensitive ears will come to dominate the population. Keen-eared rabbits put pressure on foxes, so that only those foxes with traits that make them stealthier hunters manage to capture the rabbits they need to survive and reproduce. Thus, foxes that have inherited such traits as sharp eyes, quiet approach, and fast acceleration will have a distinct advantage in a world full of good-eared rabbits. Stealthier foxes put pressure on rabbits, so that rabbits with even better ears (and possibly other traits associated with predator detection and avoidance) have an advantage, and so on. The idea is that when organisms are in a competitive relationship with one another, they will exert reciprocal selection pressures on each other for the increasing "improvement" of traits necessary for engaging in the competition. This is the idea of an arms race.

Although he was generally an antiprogressive, Darwin toyed with the idea that there might be "progress" in evolution in situations such as this. One of the important implications of evolutionary arms races is that they can exert a distinct, **directional pressure** on the evolution of certain traits. This is one reason why some researchers have looked to the arms race notion as a means of explaining the trend toward the increasing size of the hominin brain.

If competition is such an important factor in evolution does that mean that evolution is always directional in nature?

No. Competition is a critical factor in evolution, but as we will see in upcoming chapters, an organism's survival and reproductive success often depends on its ability to fit in and work with others. This often produces what are called **stabilizing selection** pressures rather than directional ones.

Stabilizing selection pressure refers to the fact that sometimes extreme values of a trait are disadvantageous and selection acts to find some moderate value that optimizes the competing interests of different organisms. A good example is the human infant's birth weight. From the infant's perspective, heavier birth weight would be advantageous for its survival, but increasing birth weight can be disadvantageous for the mother, causing complications in pregnancy and childbirth. A smaller baby makes things easier on the mother but places the baby at greater risk. Thus, over time there has been selection pressure against extremes in birth weight, with the most advantageous weight being one somewhere in the middle. In cases in which there are competing interests rather than directional selection, stabilizing selection sometimes can operate to find a mutually adaptive "compromise."

What are evolutionary homologies and analogies?

Homologies and analogies refer to traits shared across different organisms. The difference between the two is whether or not the shared trait is the result of inheritance from a common ancestor. Homologous traits trace back to a common ancestor, and analogous traits do not. For example, both chimpanzees and humans have frontally placed eyes with good stereoscopic vision. This trait was probably one that we share because of our common primate ancestry and would be a homologous trait. But common traits need not be the result of common ancestry. Two distinct and independently evolved versions of saber-toothed big cats once prowled the earth. The saber-toothed tigers of the Northern Hemisphere were mammals and relatives of today's tigers and panthers. The saber-toothed cats of the Southern Hemisphere were marsupials, most closely related to today's opossums and kangaroos (Fig. 4.B). Despite their widely varying ancestry, these two animals evolved nearly identical exaggerated canines that were used for similar purposes. Analogous traits such as these provide examples of what is called **convergent** evolution, that is, parallels in evolution with independently origins. Convergent evolution suggests that constraints on the evolutionary process result in a finite number of ways to solve the adaptive problems posed by the earth's environments.

Figure 4.B Example of convergent evolution. Left: Southern Hemisphere saber-toothed marsupial cat. Right: better-known Northern Hemisphere saber-toothed tiger. The canines evolved independently but serve a similar function in each animal. (Adapted from Marshall, 1981 and Conway Morris, 1998.)

How does evolution unfold?

Two points of view currently address the question of how the evolutionary process tends to unfold over time. Darwin proposed originally that evolution was a slow, gradual process with incremental genetic and phenotypic changes (microevolution) accumulating over time to produce more major

Continued

ones (macroevolution). Many evolutionists continue to defend this type of process. However, it has been proposed that evolution may unfold in a more uneven manner, with long periods of evolutionary stasis punctuated by shorter bursts of evolutionary change (called **punctuated equilibrium**). The origins of this debate stem from the fossil record itself. The traditional argument has been that the lack of "transitional" species in the fossil record results from the incompleteness of that record (very, very few living organisms ever become fossils). Others have argued that the incompleteness of the fossil record reflects the actual tempo of evolutionary change. Species may go long periods with little if any evolutionary change (stasis) and then rather rapidly (by geological time scales) undergo significant evolutionary change. Because of the speed of these changes, one would not expect to find much record. The debates between these camps have occasionally become quite bitter and bombastic. Two of the most prominent and media-savvy evolutionists, Richard Dawkins and Stephen Jay Gould, are standard bearers for the different positions.

Is evolution predictable?

Generally speaking, no. However, some evolutionists (most notably Stephen Jay Gould) have taken this to an extreme and argued that the forces of chance and contingency reduce evolution to something bordering on a cosmic crapshoot, with extinction and survival separated by only a roll of the dice. Rewind and rerun the evolutionary tape and wildly different scenarios might easily emerge. Although this viewpoint has some truth, others (e.g., Stuart Kauffman and Simon Conway Morris) argue that it fails to acknowledge the constraints that exist in the evolutionary process. Evolution tends to be a very conservative process with an underlying lawfulness. The presence of convergence in evolution, they contend, epitomizes the constraints under which evolution operates. Certainly, no evidence of predestination in evolution exists, and we will probably never be able to predict the specific branches of the evolutionary tree. However, we may be able to discern some general patterns. As with the issue of progress, discussions on the predictability of evolution often exceed what can be tested scientifically and enter the realm of metaphysics.

SUMMARY

Evolution refers to descent with modification. The major mechanism driving evolutionary change is natural selection, a process whereby adaptive traits are preserved in a species. Because organisms must compete for scarce resources, those with traits offering an advantage in competition are likely to leave more offspring or, put another way, possess greater reproductive success or fitness. Evolutionary change over generations can lead to the emergence of new species. This emergence generally follows either an anagenetic or cladogenetic pattern. The foundations of human evolution were laid more than 5 million years ago along the primate line. The human/chimpanzee common ancestor was probably a small, arboreal primate that subsisted on fruits, leaves, and bugs. Around 10 million years ago, the East African forests began a slow drying phase that broke up their contiguous nature and created a more scattered wooded environment. Selection pressures arising from this change affected all creatures in this environment, including our common ancestor, who presumably came down from the trees and began spending more time on the ground searching for food.

KEY TERMS

allopatric speciation	common ancestor	mutation
anagenesis	competition	natural selection
Australopithecus	contingency	preadaptation
blindness	evolution	reproductive success
chance and law	fitness	
cladogenesis	*Homo*	

REVIEW QUESTIONS

1. What is the difference between evolution and natural selection? What is the relationship between the two concepts?

2. Discuss how chance and law, preadaptation, mutation, and competition play roles in the evolutionary process.

3. Describe what is meant by the concept of a human/chimpanzee common ancestor. How is this different from the idea of humans "evolving from apes"?

4. Describe some important primate characteristics that may have provided the foundation for many distinctively human characteristics.

5. Describe how a combination of selection pressures and common ancestor characteristics played an important role in our evolution.

SUGGESTED READINGS

Foley, R.A. (1995). *Humans before humanity*. Oxford, UK: Blackwell Publishers.

Jolly, A. (1972). *The evolution of primate social behavior*. London: McMillan.

Martin, R.D. (1990). *Primate origins and evolution: A phylogenetic reconstruction*. Princeton, NJ: Princeton University Press.

Noble, W., & Davidson, I. (1996). *Human evolution, language and mind*. Cambridge, UK: Cambridge University Press.

WEB SITES

www.emory.edu/LIVING_LINKS/ Emory University Center for the study of primate and human evolution.

www.primate.wisc.edu/pin/evolution.html primate/human evolution page of the University of Wisconsin. Provides links to numerous resources on both human and non-human primate evolution.

www.escalix.com/freepage/galago/links.html#top page providing numerous links dealing with both primate and human evolution.

5

Human Evolution II: From Hominin to Human

The Importance of Human Evolution

WE ARE NOW READY TO TRACE out the course of evolution from the chimp/human common ancestor to modern humans. Before proceeding, however, one might ask what possible relevance events beginning over 5 million years ago could have on the psychological make-up of present-day men and women. The answer is found in the human body itself. Philosophers, cognitive scientists, and psychologists recognize increasingly that critical aspects of our psychology are intimately related to our embodiment (Clark, 1997, 2001; Dennett, 1996; Thelen & Smith, 1994). One of the reasons we think the way we do is because of the ways in which our bodies actively engage the environment around us. The biomechanical nature of our bodies necessarily means that we act upon and think about our environments in ways unique to our species.

For many years, anthropologists debated which came first: human brains or human bodies. The answer is now clear: bodies first, brains later. As far back as we can trace the fossil record, our ancestors walked upright with free, grasping hands operating under visual guidance. More than 4 million years ago, our ancestors were striding about on two legs. By 2.5 million years ago, we were scavenging about and making stone tools, and, by a million years ago, we were hunting and gathering. Our brains, however, did not reach their current size until about 200,000 years ago. This means that our minds (which arise from brain activity) evolved in service to bodies that had related to our environment in a species-specific way for millions of years.

The evolutionary interaction of body on brain and vice versa contributed to the evolution of human rationality, cooperative behavior, language, motor learning and development, and even our sense of self. For example, human language very well may have been built upon the unprecedented levels of motor control made possible, in part, by bipedalism and the resulting visual guidance of the hands. Moreover, hands adapted for grasping can fashion artifacts, such as tools, that both reflect and enlarge thought processes. Body designs (including our own) also impose adaptive constraints on learning and development (see chapter 14). Our very sense of self may have emerged by virtue of the way human bodies engage and explore the objects around us. Human intelligence is embodied intelligence, and our bodies came early in the evolutionary story.

The Hominin Branch

We will concentrate here on the evolutionary branch that extends from the chimp/human common ancestor and leads ultimately to the emergence of humans, beginning with a note on terminology. The species that emerged along this line usually have been referred to as the **hominids**, indicating that they were classified under the family Hominidae. The Hominidae family was separate from another family, the Pongidae, with members including the great apes, chimpanzees, gorillas, and orangutans. Recently, however, this classification system has been called into question because it fails to reflect genetic evidence that indicates that humans are more closely related to chimpanzees than are chimpanzees to gorillas or orangutans. An alternative system places both humans and chimpanzees under the family Hominidae, with humans under the tribe Hominini and chimpanzees under the tribe Panini (Wood & Richmond, 2000). This means that all the species emerging along the human evolutionary branch are labeled **hominins** rather than hominids. Although this new system has not yet been universally adopted, we will use it here (Corballis, 1999).

The Australopiths

In 1922, Raymond Dart became professor of anatomy at the University of Witwatersrand in Johannesburg, South Africa. To help develop a collection for a planned museum, Dart asked his students to collect fossils on their vacations. Two years later, one of Dart's ambitious students brought him a baboon skull recovered from the Buxton lime quarry about 320 km (200 miles) southwest of Johannesburg. Dart contacted the quarry manager and convinced him to send two crates of material from a cave recently uncovered at the quarry. In November of that year, after sifting through countless specimens of useless rock, Dart discovered what appeared to be a small, ape-like skull. He quickly realized, however, that this was no ordinary ape head. In a paper published in the journal *Nature* in February 1925, he announced the discovery as an early form of human and called it *Australopithecus africanus*, southern ape from Africa. The scientific community, however, largely dismissed Dart's discovery. It did not fit with the prevailing view of human origins, which held that the brain evolved and enlarged before other physical characteristics distinctive to humans. Dart's *A. africanus* showed just the opposite constellation of features: a small, ape-like brain but with more human-like teeth, and a spinal/cranial connection characteristic of a biped. Furthermore, most scientists were of the view that Asia and not Africa was the likely spawning ground of humanity (Lewin, 1987). Dart, they believed, had, in a fit of unprofessional excitement wholly unbecoming of a British-trained anatomist, simply misinterpreted what was obviously nothing more than an ape fossil.

In the late 1930s, however, paleontologist Robert Broom made a series of finds in other sites near Johannesburg. Broom's discoveries both reinforced Dart's original *A. africanus* species and introduced a second species called *Australopithecus robustus*. As the name implies, the *A. robustus* was a more powerfully built species, especially in the dental and chewing mechanics. Although different dating techniques have not always yielded consistent estimates for the age of these fossils, it does appear that the more gracile form (*africanus*) is older, in the range of

3.5–2.5 million years ago, and the robust species is somewhat more recent, in the range of 2–1.5 million years ago.

In the 1970s, a dramatic find in the Hadar region of Ethiopia was made by a team led by Donald Johanson. Many specimens were uncovered, but a nearly 40% reconstruction of a single skeleton, dubbed **Lucy**, was the most spectacular. Johanson and his co-workers concluded that they had discovered another, more primitive *Australopithecus* species and named it *Australopithecus afarensis*. *A. afarensis* was characterized by a very ape-like head set on a body with ape- and human-like characteristics. The species also showed extreme sexual dimorphism, with females being only about two thirds (67%) the size of males. By comparison, human females are about 84% the size of males, and female gorillas are about 50% the size of males (McHenry, 1991). As Johanson suspected, dating revealed the finds to be older than other *Australopithecus* species, with ages ranging from 3.9–2.9 million years ago. Because so much of Lucy was preserved, a wealth of knowledge about the physical structure and, to some extent, the behavior of *A. afarensis* has been revealed (see chapter 6).

Since Johanson's discoveries, even older specimens have been found. *Ardipithecus ramidus* currently holds the distinction as the earliest hominin. Fossil remains of this species were found in Ethiopia in the early 1990s, dating from 5–4.4 million years ago. *Australopithecus anamensis* was discovered in 1995 in northern Kenya. It appears to be somewhere between 4.2 and 3.9 million years old. Other species of Australopiths also have been identified. Currently, depending on how different specimens are classified, seven or eight species are recognized (Klein, 1999).

No scheme has been agreed upon entirely for ordering the ancestor/descendant relationships among the Australopiths. White (1994) contended that *A. ramidus* was ancestral to *A. anamensis* and *A. anamensis* was then ancestral to *A. afarensis*. Others have argued that this scheme probably oversimplifies the actual relationships, especially because recent finds have significantly altered our understanding of the Australopiths and their relationship to the later *Homo* genus (Brunet et al., 1996). This criticism is well taken, because, as noted in chapter 4, more than a dozen different Australopith species probably existed, and we may never know the true ancestor/descent relationships among them (Fig. 5.1). With these cautions in mind, we can summarize the emergence of the Australopiths as follows:

1. By at least 5 million years ago the hominin branch separated from the common ancestor of humans and chimpanzees.
2. By about 4.5 million years ago a species had emerged along that branch called *A. ramidus*.
3. By about 4 million years ago another new species, *A. anamensis*, had emerged.
4. Soon thereafter *A. afarensis* emerged, and, over the next 2 million years or so, a number of forms evolved, including *A. africanus* (or gracile) and, later, *A. robustus*.
5. It is unclear which species were ancestral to which others or which species ultimately gave rise to the genus *Homo*. However, currently it seems more likely that the origins of *Homo* run through the gracile line rather than the robust.
6. By the time of *A. robustus*, a new genus had arisen called *Homo*, which was coexistent with *A. robustus* and probably other Australopiths.

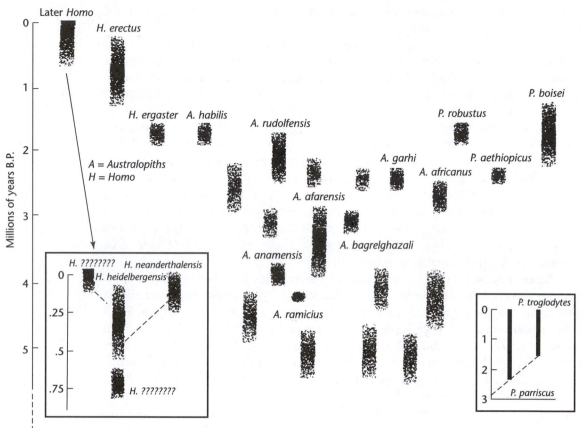

Figure 5.1 A graph depicting many of the known species of hominins and the approximate date when they appear in the fossil record. The horizontal dispersal of species is based on the comparative sizes of chewing teeth and brains. Species with larger chewing teeth span out to the right, and those with smaller teeth and larger brains are to the left. (Based on Wood & Richmond, 2000, p. 20.)

Body Type and Habitat

The anatomy of an animal can actually say quite a bit about where and how that animal lived. In warm climates, bodies need to dissipate heat effectively. Certain body structures are more advantageous for this than others. For instance, a body with a high ratio of surface area to mass will more effectively dissipate heat than one with the opposite configuration. A body with high surface area relative to mass is one that is long and lean in stature, so that the body, in effect, is more spread out to allow heat to dispel into the environment rather than being trapped close in. In cold climates, the opposite bodily configuration, short and stocky, would be advantageous in retaining heat. This is a simplified version of two rules introduced in the 19th century relating anatomic adaptations to climate. **Bergman's rule**, published in 1847, stated that people in warmer climates would be smaller bodied than people in colder climates, and **Allen's rule**, published in 1877, stated that people in warmer climates would have longer limbs than those in colder climates. These rules should be understood as broad generalizations subject to substantial local variation. However, in an extensive survey of global populations, Ruff (1994) found that the relationship of body type to climate held reasonably well. An important qualifier was the fact that in hot, humid, densely forested environments, body shape retained its high surface area to mass relationship, although body height remained small (the Pygmies of central Africa, for example).

This relationship becomes important because the extensive skeletal remains of the *A. afarensis* specimen called Lucy indicated a small-ape–like body. Although varying depending on the species, estimates for the size and weight of the Australopiths range from about 40–50 kg (88–110 lb) and 132–138 cm (4'4"–4'7") for males, and 30–34 kg (66–75 lb) and 100–124 cm (3'8"–4'1") for females (McHenry, 1992; McHenry & Berger, 1998). These dimensions suggest that Lucy and her species most likely lived in a closed, woodland habitat. One cannot assume from this evidence that all Australopiths inhabited dense tropical forests. Other evidence suggests that some species of *Australopithecus* inhabited more open woodland or savanna-type habitats. Lucy's body type, however, contrasts sharply with that of later hominins, indicating that the latter experienced a general shift in habitat.

Early Homo

The Olduvai Gorge is located at the very eastern edge of the Serengeti Plain in northern Tanzania. It is a massive cleft in the earth, 51 km (30 miles) long and 91 m (300 ft) deep, the result of millennia of earthquake and hydraulic activity. A seasonal river has helped to carve out its ancient 16-mile-diameter lake bed, which is more than 2 million years old. It seems fitting that a venue as impressive as Olduvai would be the place where evidence of the origins of the genus *Homo* would be discovered and even more fitting that the discovery would be made by the most renowned pair of fossil hunters, Louis and Mary Leakey.

By the early 1960s, the Leakeys had already made a number of significant finds from the Olduvai site, including *Australopithecus* remains and evidence of various ancient tools. Based on these discoveries, Louis Leakey, in fact, had pronounced *Australopithecus* a toolmaker. However, between 1960 and 1963 a series of perplexing discoveries forever complicated the picture of humanity's origins. Remains were unearthed of an ancient hominin who appeared to be older than some of the *Australopithecus* finds but was generally less robust, with smaller teeth and a larger brain. Louis Leakey became convinced that this was the true toolmaker of Olduvai and that it should be identified as a new species in the genus *Homo*, called **Homo habilis**, handy man.

Leakey's assertion that the toolmaker of Olduvai should be considered a member of the genus *Homo* was based on two distinguishing characteristics of the fossilized remains. First, the cranial capacity of the supposed toolmaker was substantially larger than that of the Australopiths. Brain sizes for Australopiths ranged from 450–500 cc, whereas Leakey's latest find had a brain size estimated at about 640 cc (still very small for a member of *Homo*). Second, the dentition of the new find was less robust than that of Australopiths with smaller molars and premolars. As might be predicted, the introduction of a new species did not come without a barrage of controversy. Critics argued that Leakey was dealing with either a large-brained Australopith or a smaller-than-usual *Homo erectus* (a later species of *Homo*). However, there was no consensus on which it might be.

In 1972, the Leakeys' son Richard, along with wife Meave and Alan Walker, described another puzzling find from the Koobi Fora of Kenya. They had uncovered skull fragments bearing many Australopith traits but with an astounding cranial capacity of 750 cc. Early attempts at dating the strange skull yielded an age greater than 2.5 million years, far older than any known *Homo* species. Although this dating later was called into question, other fossils associated with *Homo* were turning up with remarkably old dates, ranging from 2.5–2.3 million years (Hill, Ward, Deino, Curtis, & Drake, 1992; Schrenk, Bromage, Betzler, Ring, & Juwayeyi, 1993). The discoveries offered confusion but credibility to the contention that an early species of *Homo* existed somewhere between the later Australopiths and *H. erectus*. In fact, the variability in these discoveries led many to conclude that not one but two early *Homo* species emerged at this time.

In 1992, Bernard Wood formally proposed that early *Homo* was composed of two species: *H. habilis* and **Homo rudolfensis**. *H. rudolfensis* is distinguished from *habilis* by its flatter, broader face and more robust dentition (reminiscent of *Australopithecus*) but with a brain capacity that actually exceeds that of *habilis*. Although not everyone agrees with Wood's conclusions, a general consensus holds that at least two species of early *Homo* existed around 2 million years ago and that they were contemporaneous with at least two species of *Australopithecus*. It is unclear as to which species of *Australopithecus* might have been ancestral to *Homo* or which species of *Homo* might have given rise to the later *Homo ergaster* or *erectus*. It is on this last point that the two early *Homo* species are somewhat paradoxical, in that *H. rudolfensis* has the brain but not the face of a probable ancestor, whereas *H. habilis* has the face but not the brain.

In terms of body size and proportions, early *Homo* was not significantly different from *Australopithecus*. Males are estimated to have been about 52 kg (115 lbs) in weight and 157 cm (5'2") in height, and females were about 32 kg (71 lb) and 125 cm (4'1"). This represents a sexual size dimorphism comparable with *Australopithecus*, among whom female size was about 62% that of males. Early *Homo* is also characterized by variability in body proportions, so that some specimens appear generally more ape-like (with long arms and short legs) and others have more human-like form (Aiello, 1992; Hartwig-Scherer & Martin, 1991). In the later *H. erectus*, nearly all evidence of ape-like body proportions and shape would disappear.

Later Homo

As Roger Lewin (1998) pointed out in his text on human evolution, the story from this point ought to be simple. Somewhere in Africa, a new, even larger-brained species of *Homo*, *H. erectus*, emerged about 1.8 million years ago. After about 1 million years of puttering around Africa, *H. erectus* expanded out and colonized much of Europe and Asia. Then, either *H. erectus* slowly evolved into modern humans separately in each of its resident regions (anagenesis) or a dramatic speciation event occurred about 200,000 years ago in Africa that caused modern humans to emerge (cladogenesis). In rather quick order by evolutionary time scales, they set out across the globe replacing all resident earlier hominin forms. Unfortunately (or not, depending on one's perspective), the story has been complicated by many recent anthropological discoveries. Two scenes are crucial in this most recent act of hominin evolution: the first deals with the emergence and migration of *H. erectus*, and the second deals with the arrival of modern humans (*Homo sapiens sapiens*).

Scene 1: Homo erectus

History is full of tales of adventurous individuals, inspired by myth or money, setting off on perilous quests: Arthur's knights and the Grail, Ponce de Leon and the fountain of youth, Coronado and the cities of gold. Paleo-anthropology's contribution to this genre is the story of Eugene Dubois and his quest for *Pithecanthropus,* the missing link. In 1887, Dubois, a Dutch physician, secured a position as medical officer to the Dutch Army of the East Indies (now Indonesia). His real passion, however, was human evolution. *Pithecanthropus* was the name proposed by German biologist Ernst Haeckel for the so-called "missing link" between apes and humans. It was generally agreed that the transition from apes to humans took place somewhere in the tropics, and Haeckel, along with Darwin and Huxley, believed this missing link would most likely be found in Africa, not Asia. Dubois, however, was confident that the jungles of southeast Asia, with their populations of large apes, were a prime location (see Box 5.1).

For 2 years, Dubois hunted in vain on the island of Sumatra for evidence of Haeckel's ape-man. It was not until he concentrated his efforts along the Solo River on the neighboring island of Java that the search bore fruit. In October 1891, Dubois's prospecting team, which included a gang of convicts, unearthed a large skull cap near the village of Trinil. The cranium possessed a number of primitive features, including a prominent brow ridge, suggesting that its former owner might have been an ancient hominin. The following year, a femur that Dubois believed was part of the same specimen was found near the same location. The bones seemed to be those of an upright, bipedal human ancestor, but Dubois remained unconvinced that it was Haeckel's missing link until detailed measurements of the cranium revealed a brain capacity of 850 cc, far larger than would be expected for any ape. Thinking that he had at last uncovered his prize, Dubois dubbed his find **Pithecanthropus erectus**, erect ape-man. He had done it!

Instead of applause, however, Dubois's missing link was greeted with controversy and criticism. So bitter was the debate over exactly what he had found that Dubois eventually withdrew, specimens and all, from scientific circles. His skeptics were not entirely without foundation in their arguments. It now seems clear that the femur was not connected to the cranium but instead belonged to a much more modern *Homo*, possibly even *H. sapiens*. It was not until the 1920s that Dubois allowed his fossils to be re-examined by other scientists. At around this time and on into the next decade, other finds by Davidson Black and Franz Weidenreich in China and G.H.R. von Koenigswald in Java were re-igniting interest in *P. erectus*. Although similarities were apparent among the different finds, it was not until

EUGENE DUBOIS
The Search for Java Man

PROFILE *Born on January 28, 1858, in Eijsden, The Netherlands, Marie Eugene François Thomas Dubois, was a character as enigmatic as his name was long. In 1884, Dubois graduated with a degree in medicine and shortly thereafter was appointed lecturer in anatomy at Amsterdam University. Later that same year, he married and, to all outward appearances, was fully emersed in the congenial life of European academia. But appearances were deceiving.*

BOX 5.1

The Search Begins

Why would someone leave a good job and a comfortable life for the prospect of hunting fossils halfway around the world, risking disease and reputation in the process? For Dubois, a number of factors were at work. First, even as a youngster, Dubois had been interested in natural science, especially human evolution. Second, it took less than a year of teaching to convince him that he hated it. Finally, Dubois had developed a gnawing suspicion that his mentor, Max Furbringer, had been taking credit for some of his ideas. No evidence has ever surfaced to substantiate his fears on this matter, and this would not be the only time he would manifest what appears to be an excessive preoccupation with intellectual priority.

Dubois, along with his wife and baby, arrived in Sumatra (then part of the Dutch East Indies) in December 1887. As an army medical officer, he was forced to do his fossil hunting during his free time. After a few initial finds, the Dutch government agreed to provide him with two engineers and a crew of 50 forced laborers to help with the search for hominin remains. The difficult work and dense forests of Sumatra took their toll, however. One of his engineers died, the other proved incompetent and was transferred, and many of his crew took ill or took off. After hearing news that another fossil digger, van Rietschoten, had made important finds in the Wajak Mountains of East Java, Dubois moved his search from Sumatra to Java in 1890. The omens were better at this site. His engineers were competent and managed to stay alive, and a number of human fossil remains were found. In 1891, on the banks of the Solo River, he unearthed his first significant discovery: a skull cap and upper jaw molar of a hominin-like creature. In August of the next year, he found a femur at the same level as the earlier finds, which convinced him that the all the fossils were from the same species. For Dubois, these finds suggested the existence of a creature with an ape-like head set upon a bipedal body, exactly the ape/human combination one might expect of the missing link: *Pithecanthropus erectus*.

In 1894, Dubois published an article describing his finds and arguing that they belonged to a species intermediate between apes and humans. Having met with initial skepticism, Dubois traveled across Europe, displaying his fossils and vigorously defending his interpretation of their significance. A wide range of opinions emerged over what exactly Dubois had unearthed. To his dismay, nearly everyone agreed that the femur could not have come from the same species that produced the skullcap. Others concurred with Dubois that the skullcap was not that of a modern human, but many viewed it as simply belonging to a large ape. In the midst of this furor, Dubois realized that another scientist had obtained a cast of the skullcap and produced an extensive analysis of it. Livid that someone had trespassed on his intellectual property, Dubois withdrew his fossils from public scrutiny. Around 1900, he buried them under his home to ensure that no one could get to them. For decades, he refused to allow anyone access to his fossils until, in 1923, under intense pressure from fellow scientists, he relented. In the 1920s and 1930s, a number of fossil skulls similar to Dubois's specimen were found in Asia, lending credibility to his original argument. Despite what might have been affirmation, Dubois obstinately maintained that these other finds were in error and only *his* fossils represented the intermediate ape/human missing link.

Dubois officially retired in 1928 and died in 1940. In a eulogy, Arthur Keith provided this description of Dubois: "…his mind tended to bend facts rather than alter his ideas to fit them."

Source: By permission from **Theunissen, B. (1989).** *Eugene Dubois and the ape-man from Java.* Dordrecht, The Netherlands: Kluwer Academic Publishers. Photo © Museum Naturalis, Leiden.

1951 that a consensus was reached that the Chinese, Javan, and Dubois's original fossils represented a single *Homo* species called **Homo erectus**.

Since the 1950s, efforts to find *H. erectus* remains have continued in many regions throughout Asia. More attention has been directed at Africa, where a number of significant discoveries have been made. *H. erectus* fossils have been uncovered from a number of sites in northern, eastern, and southern Africa. Of special significance is the Lake Turkana region in northern Kenya. There, some of the oldest *H. erectus* remains have been found. For example, between 1973 and 1975, two nearly complete skulls were found, one of which (KNM-ER 3733) was dated at 1.8 million years old, making it one of the oldest *H. erectus* fossils on record (Leakey & Walker, 1976, 1985; Walker & Leakey, 1978). In 1984, a nearly complete erectus skeleton was found, dated at around 1.6 million years old (Brown, Harris, Leakey, & Walker, 1985). The **Turkana Boy**, as the skeleton became known, was more than 5 ft tall and about 12 years old (or 9, depending on how quickly one believes *H. erectus* matured; see Leakey & Lewin, 1992) when he died. The completeness of the skeleton allowed researchers to assess his overall body proportions, which revealed that he would have reached more than 6 ft in height, with a brain size greater than 900 cc had he survived to manhood. Furthermore, he would have been long and lean, typical of humans adapted to open, tropical environments. From Lucy to Turkana Boy, hominins had emerged from the forest to the savanna as taller, leaner, and brainier.

When it came to the dating of various *H. erectus* finds, an important pattern seemed to be emerging. The earlier discoveries from China and Southeast Asia were all relatively young. The Chinese fossils were variously dated between 250,000 and 800,000 years old. The Javan fossils were somewhat older, estimated at 750,000 to a little more than 1 million years old (see Klein, 1999, and Lewin, 1998, for discussions). None of the Asian fossils, however, were anywhere near the antiquity attributed to the African remains. This fit nicely with the scenario that *H. erectus* evolved in Africa around 2 million years ago, and then, after approximately 1 million years, expanded out of Africa and colonized Asia and Europe. Two recent developments have called this view into question. First, in the early 1990s a mandible was discovered in Dmanisi (in the Georgian Republic) that showed strong indications of being from *H. erectus* (Bräuer & Mbua, 1992; Bräuer & Schultz, 1996). The age of the mandible initially was put at between 1.6 and 1.8 million years, on par with some of the oldest *H. erectus* remains in Africa and obviously challenging the prevailing view of human origins. Some skepticism remained over the mandible until two partial crania were discovered at the same site, also showing strong *H. erectus* characteristics and dated at around 1.7 million years (Gabunia et al., 2000). Second, redatings for some of the Javan fossils have placed them at between 1.6 and 1.8 million years old, further confirming the presence of *H. erectus* outside of Africa very shortly after its emergence (Swisher et al., 1994).

How have the most recent finds changed the story of *H. erectus*? Although the issue is certainly not settled, most of the newer scenarios take the following plot line. Around 2 million years ago, a larger bodied, bigger brained hominin species evolved in Africa (exemplified by the Turkana Boy). This species is termed *Homo ergaster*. *H. ergaster* very quickly expanded from Africa to Asia. In Asia, *H. ergaster* eventually evolved into *H. erectus*, which then expanded its range throughout Asia, back into Africa, and into Europe. In time, *H. erectus* eventually gave rise to another species loosely known as **archaic Homo sapiens**, including the Neanderthals of Europe. Meanwhile back in Africa, *H. ergaster* either: (1) eventually gave rise to modern humans (*H. sapiens sapiens*) or (2) went extinct, leaving the African-dwelling *H. erectus* as the stock that eventually gave rise to modern humans (Fig. 5.2).

The emergence of erectus (for our purposes, I will simply refer to both ergaster and erectus as "erectus") crossed a significant Rubicon in the evolution of humanity. Many of the physical and behavioral attributes of erectus are recognizable as distinctly "human." Physically, erectus was larger than the early *Homo* species but with a marked decrease in sexual dimorphism. Males weighed in at about 63 kg (139 lb) and were about 180 cm (5'11") tall, and females were about 52 kg (115 lb) in weight and about 160 cm (5'3") tall. Note that females were about 83% as large as males, a substantial gain over the 60%–70% range observed for the Australopiths and early *Homo*, and about equal with modern standards. One possible reason for the decrease in sexual dimorphism could have been the adoption of a more cooperative lifestyle. Concomitant with the increase in body size was a significant increase in brain size. Erectus's cranial capacity ranged from 850 cc to 1,100 cc, approaching the modern human average of about 1,350 cc. Of even more significance are the behavioral/social characteristics associated with erectus, many of which will be explored in more detail in later chapters. Erectus presented the first evidence of hominins capable of wide-ranging migration, cooperative and systematic hunting, and the use of fire for cooking and warmth. Erectus also made significant advances in tool technology compared with earlier *Homo*.

THE HUNTING AND GATHERING LIFESTYLE. *H. erectus* sites and other hominin sites from the Olduvai Gorge in Africa and the caves of Zhoukoudian, China, include the fossilized bones of large animals, presumably butchered for their meat, bones, skins, and other products (Aigner, 1978; Bunn, 1986; Bunn & Kroll, 1986; Wolpoff, 1980). These sites provided some of the first evidence of hominin game

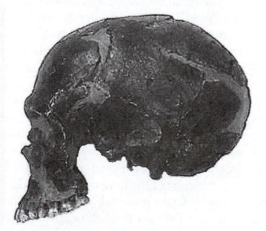

Figure 5.2 An early modern human skull (see p. 94).

hunting, with the transporting of the kill to a "home base" butchering site, where meat was shared and nearly all of the remaining carcass was processed and used in some fashion (Wu & Lin, 1983). Whether *H. erectus* or other hominins were proficient hunters or relied more on scavenging or a combination of both is a point of controversy (see Klein, 1999, pp. 243–248, 357–360 for discussions). What is clear is that meat was a component of *H. erectus*'s diet, and its procurement, processing, and distribution were important elements in their lifestyle. It is unlikely, however, that it was the only or even largest source of nutrition. Evidence from modern **hunter–gatherers** indicates that 75%–80% of the diet consists of locally gathered items, such as nuts, fruits, vegetables, and other foods (Lee & DeVore, 1968). The local environment of African *H. erectus* and key features of its anatomy made gathering an effective means of subsistence (O'Connell, Hawkes, & Blurton Jones, 1999). This evidence, coupled with the previously mentioned decrease in sexual dimorphism, suggests that with *H. erectus* a more cooperative, hunting–gathering lifestyle had taken form. Because the hunting–gathering lifestyle is assumed to have been an integral part of the human ancestral environment of evolutionary adaptedness (EEA), it is important to identify some of its critical aspects.

To gain insight into what life might have been like in human prehistory, researchers have generally relied on studies of modern hunter–gatherer tribes such as the **!Kung** of southern Africa. These studies are highly valuable, but caution is necessary when generalizing from modern hunter–gatherers to the hominin past, because today's hunter–gatherers must contend with the effects of the modern societies around them. The !Kung live in mobile, kin-based groups or bands of anywhere from 20–60 individuals. These bands will remain in place until local resources are exhausted (usually 3–4 weeks). Hunter–gatherers usually have a clear division of labor. Women have the responsibility of maintaining the base camp, including child care and gathering wood for fire and water for cooking. In addition, they gather local edibles from within a few-mile radius of the camp and may occasionally kill small animals for food (Shostak, 1981). When off gathering, mothers will leave their children in the care of relatives remaining at the camp. If the mothers are still nursing, the infants must be carried along. Men are the hunters, often ranging many miles from camp in search of game. When a kill is made, the meat is shared with all. In addition, men are responsible for constructing household tools and hunting gear, including bows, arrows, snares, and spears. At various times, the bands may break into constituent family units and temporarily subsist separately. At other times, several bands will gather together and renew old acquaintances, engage in ritual dance, trade goods, and arrange marriages. Among the !Kung, families are usually monogamous units, but polygyny is not unheard of. Bands are reasonably egalitarian in governance and have no chiefs, but older members often have more influence in decision making than others. Because of their nomadic lifestyle, hunter–gatherer societies rarely fall victim to epidemics of infectious disease. Instead, parasitic infections and infections transmitted from animal to humans are more common (Armelagos & Dewey, 1970). Life expectancy for hunter–gatherers is relatively short, between 20 and 40 years, reflecting a high infant morality rate and the fact that accidents and childbirth are common causes of death (Cohen, 1989; Dunn, 1968).

Many of the characteristics associated with the hunting–gathering lifestyle are believed to have been critical in the evolution of human nature. Gender differences in spatial abilities and social sensitivities are often attributed to the sexual division of labor common in hunter–gatherers. Preferences in mate choice and subjective aesthetic judgments often are linked to the visible indicators of parasitic infection (or lack thereof) and potential landscape productivity and security. Many of these issues will be developed further in upcoming chapters.

It is unclear to what extent the cultural characteristics of modern hunter–gatherers can be projected back on to *H. erectus* or other hominins. That hominin groups were kin based, like modern hunter–gatherers, and that infection from parasites and high infant mortality were constant threats seem relatively uncontroversial. Of a much more speculative nature is how far back in history one can extend the social and cultural elements, such as the presence of marriage, religion, and ritual noted in modern hunter–gatherers.

Without question, the physical and behavioral characteristics of *H. erectus* represent a significant departure from those of earlier *Homo*. However, the record of erectus's roughly 1 million years of history is one of relatively little change. The rather static existence of erectus was abruptly brought to an end with the advent of modern humans, and it is to that part of our story that we now turn.

Scene 2: Homo sapiens

If an omniscient Martian were to have surveyed earth about 300,000 years ago in search of hominin life forms, it would have documented their existence in various regions throughout Africa, Asia, Europe, and the Middle East. It would have noted that many of these creatures possessed physical features different from the *H. erectus* species present a million years earlier, such as even larger brains set on somewhat less robust bodies. Even so, our all-knowing alien would have recognized that these hominins were still obviously distinguishable from the modern humans who would come to dominate Earth centuries hence. In most regions of the world, our Martian would have labeled these hominins as *archaic H. sapiens*. However, in Europe and the Middle East, it would have been apparent to our Martian that a distinctive variety of hominin was taking shape and was especially adapted for the harsh, cold climate of Europe in the Ice Age. These, the Martian would call **Neanderthals**. The last scene of our epic involves the disappearance of these archaics into the shadows of evolutionary history, leaving only one *Homo* species to roam the earth: us.

Currently the most contentious debate in anthropology centers on the arrival of *H. sapiens*. On one side are those who espouse the **multiregional** evolution hypothesis, which argues that erectus populations in different regions of the globe slowly evolved into an anatomically modern human form. Thus the emergence of modern humans followed an anagenetic pattern throughout the world. The multiregional hypothesis is probably best exemplified in the work of Milford Wolpoff, an anthropologists at the University of Michigan (Wolpoff, 1980, 1996; Wolpoff, Thorne, Smith, Frayer, & Pope, 1994). On the opposite side of the ledger is the **single origin** or "**Out of Africa**" hypothesis, which contends that anatomically modern humans emerged via a relatively recent African speciation event. This view has been defended in the writings of Christopher Stringer of the Natural History

Museum in London (Stringer, 1990; Stringer & McKie, 1996). The two hypotheses can be distinguished clearly by a number of competing positions on issues dealing with the *place*, the *timing*, and the *process* of the arrival of modern humans.

1. Place: Because the multiregional hypothesis argues that the erectus-to-sapiens transition occurred in different regions across the globe, fossil evidence of this transition should be found in those different regions. By contrast, the single origin model argues that modern humans arose in one place, Africa, and it is only there that transitional fossil evidence should be found.

2. Timing: According to the multiregional hypothesis, modern humans arose at roughly the same time in different regions, so evidence of that emergence should date to about the same time period. By contrast, the "Out of Africa" hypothesis claims that modern humans arose first in Africa, so evidence of modern humans in Africa should be older than that found in other regions.

3. Process: Because the multiregional hypothesis argues for a gradual transition from erectus-to-sapiens, the evidence should show a continuity of change over time. By contrast, the "Out of Africa" hypothesis argues for a more abrupt speciation event, with replacement of archaic hominins by modern humans. Thus the evidence should show a discontinuous change from one population to another.

Although the issue certainly is not settled, recent evidence has tended to favor the single origin hypothesis more than the multiregional hypothesis. The details of all the lines of evidence that have been brought to bear on this issue are complex and beyond the scope of our discussion. Included here is a brief summary of a few of the areas of research that have been relevant in evaluating these hypotheses.

FOSSIL EVIDENCE. When comparing the fossils of anatomically modern humans from different parts of the globe, it does appear that the oldest specimens are found in Africa and the Middle East. For example, in 1967, a partial skull and other fragments judged to be from modern humans were found in southern Ethiopia and dated at around 100,000–130,000 years old (Bräuer, 1984; Day, 1972; Day & Stringer, 1982). Other anatomically modern and near-modern remains dated from 60,000–120,000 years old were found in the Klasies River Cave in South Africa and the Skhul and Qafzeh sites in Israel (Tchernov, 1992; see Klein, 1999, for summary). The oldest modern remains found in Asia and Europe have been dated at between 40,000 and 70,000 years. Moreover, modern humans arrived very late in Java, where evidence of archaics persists until somewhere between 50,000 and 30,000 years ago (Swisher et al., 1996; see Lewin, 1998, for discussion). The oldest fossil evidence thus far for the appearance of modern humans is found in Africa, as the single origin hypothesis predicts.

The issue of regional continuity is complicated, and some of the evidence from Asia can be argued in support of the multiregional view (see Lewin, 1998, for discussion). However, two findings are particularly difficult to incorporate into the multiregional model. Evidence found in the Middle East suggests successive occupation by Neanderthals and *H. sapiens*. Three sites, Tabun, Kebara, and Amud, contain Neanderthal remains, and two others, Skhul and Qafzeh, contain modern and near-modern remains. It was believed originally that the Neanderthal sites predated the other sites, leaving open the possibility that the Neanderthals were ancestral to (and therefore could have evolved into) modern humans. However, more recent datings have put the remains at the Skhul and Qafzeh sites at around 100,000 years, whereas two of the Neanderthal sites, Kebara and Amud, were found to be 60,000 years old. This calls into serious question the idea that the Neanderthals could have evolved gradually into modern humans. Instead, it suggests a pattern of extended coexistence of two different populations, with one (the Neanderthals) eventually giving way to the other (*H. sapiens*).

The evidence from Europe also seems consistent with idea of one population replacing another. The evidence of the presence of modern humans in Europe tends to follow a general east-to-west temporal progression, with older remains (dated at a little more than 40,000 years) found in the east and newer remains accumulating westward (Lewin, 1998; Mellars, 1996; Shreeve, 1995). Although this is generally true, reality is not so simple, because some "older" modern human remains have been found at sites in northern Spain (Bischoff, Soler, Marot, & Julia, 1989; Cabrera Valdés & Bischoff, 1989; Straus, 1994, 1997). The last evidence of Neanderthal occupation is found in southern Spain and dated at around 30,000 years old. The scenario of one species moving in and another moving out until there was no place left to go is hard to resist. Even more important is the fact that this pattern, although conforming to the "Out of Africa"/replacement model, provides little on which to build a case for a continuous process of one species evolving into another.

GENETIC EVIDENCE. Genetics-based evidence also has tended to be damaging to the multiregional model. Whenever genetic material is passed from parent to offspring, a certain degree of mutation within the genome is transmitted as well. As these mutations accumulate, genetic variability within a population increases. The rate and extent of these mutations can be used by research geneticists to determine the relatedness of populations and to explore evolutionary histories. Most human deoxyribonucleic acid (DNA) is found within the nucleus of cells, but a much smaller package of genetic material is also contained within the cell's mitochondria. Mitochondrial DNA (mtDNA) can be helpful in reconstructing evolutionary histories, because mutations tend to build up more quickly in nuclear DNA. Moreover, mtDNA is passed directly from mother to offspring and does not go through the process of sexual recombination, thus avoiding potential complications introduced by gene shuffling. A number of important conclusions have been drawn by examining the variability present in human and other species' mtDNA.

1. Humans have a far smaller degree of genetic variability compared with many other species (for example, only a tenth of the amount of variability present in chimpanzees).
2. The highest degree of variability is found in human populations of African descent, indicating that African populations are genetically the oldest.
3. Calculations based on the rate of mutation indicate a time of origin for the human population around 200,000 years ago (Cann, Stoneking, & Wilson, 1987; Ruvolo et al., 1994; Stoneking, 1993; Wilson & Cann, 1992).

Much of this work was interpreted initially as strong evidence for the single origin/"Out of Africa" model. However, questions about methodology have seriously undermined some of its conclusions, especially the African origin of the modern human population (Templeton, 1992; 1993). A study focusing on the Y chromosome has produced evidence for an Asian as well as an African origin for modern human populations (Hammer et al., 1997). Other studies of genetic variability, however, continued to support the "Out of Africa" model, indicating heightened genetic variability among African populations (Cavalli-Sforza, Menozzi, & Piazza, 1994; Jorde, Bamshad, & Rodgers, 1998; Relethford, 1998). Ruvolo (1996), using a different method involving the distribution of coalescence times for specific genes, found evidence of human origins around 200,000 years, reinforcing earlier mtDNA results. Another bit of relevant data comes from DNA sequencing studies, in which the similarity of different species' DNA can be compared. In 1997, researches successfully extracted DNA from fossilized Neanderthal bones and compared it with human DNA. The results showed that the Neanderthal DNA sequence differed on average by 27 nucleotide positions from the human DNA. By contrast, humans tend to differ by an average of 8 positions from each other. This degree of genetic distance argues against the notion of Neanderthals being ancestral to humans and, instead, implies that they were separate species with little or no intermingling (Krings et al., 1997; see Relethford, 1998, for an alternative view). In general, the genetic evidence is more in line with the expectations of the single origin model than the multiregional one. The results are far from conclusive, however, and may suggest an Asian as well as African population dispersal. Additional evidence and more sophisticated testing procedures will be necessary to sort out these controversies.

THE ONGOING CONTROVERSY. On balance, these various lines of evidence converge more favorably on the "Out of Africa" model than the multiregional one. It is important to re-emphasize, however, that the issue of human origins is far from settled and disagreement among experts persists. More sophisticated genetic studies on both mtDNA and Y chromosome markers have continued to find strong support for the single origin model (Ingman, Kaessmann, Paabo, & Gyllensten, 2000; Ke et al., 2001). A recent analysis of fossil skulls by Wolpoff and his colleagues (Wolpoff, Hawkes, Frayer, & Hunley, 2001), however, found evidence of anatomical continuity between modern human populations in Australia and Central Europe and more ancient *Homo* populations from the same local region. This finding supports the notion of local archaic populations evolving into modern *H. sapiens* in different regions of the world (Box 5.2). Although some attempts have been made to reconcile these competing positions (e.g., Treisman, 1995), continued spirited debate between these camps is likely to continue into the future.

The multiregional versus single origin debate could have direct significance for issues in evolutionary psychology. Although the multiregional view does not argue that regional erectus populations evolved into modern humans *in isolation* from one another (i.e., there would have been some gene flow among different regional populations to ensure certain universal sapiens traits), a greater degree of biological variability among different regional populations is envisioned in this model than in the single origin model. Klein (1999, p. 504), for example, questioned how substantial gene flow could have occurred among "small populations

"Out of Africa" Versus Multiregionalism

BOX 5.2

Recent Fossil Evidence

The "Out of Africa" hypothesis of human origins has enjoyed widespread acceptance among both researchers and the popular media. The story that humans arrived as the result of a sudden, dramatic event followed by a global conquest displacing all other hominins has mythic appeal. That this tale includes an "Eve"-like ancestral mother only adds to its allure. The popularity of this account overshadows the true controversy that exists over human origins. Probably no one has been a more ardent defender of the less heroic multiregional hypothesis than University of Michigan anthropologist Milford Wolpoff. He and his colleagues have

published a study of fossil skulls, calling into question the idea of a global replacement of hominin species.

The logic of the study was straightforward: Take a 20,000-year-old fossil skull from Australia or Eastern Europe that is known to be from an anatomically modern human and compare it with two older skulls, the skull of an ancient hominin species from the same region and the skull of a *Homo sapiens sapiens* from Africa. To which skull is the modern human skull more similar? Figure 5.A shows one of the comparison sets. If "Out of Africa" is correct, then the center skull from Australia should have more in common with the skull on the right from Africa than the skull on the left from Indonesia (which is regionally proximate to Australia). Why? According to the "Out of Africa" model, modern humans arose exclusively in Africa and subsequently fanned out across the globe replacing all resident hominin species. The older skull from Africa should represent a relatively close ancestor to the Australian skull, and the older Indonesia skull

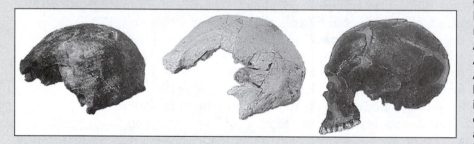

Figure 5.A A set of comparison skulls. The skull in the middle is WLH-50, a modern human skull from Australia. It is dated at anywhere from 13,000–30,000 years old. The skull on the left is a Ngandong specimen of an archaic *Homo sapiens* or late *Homo erectus* from Java (Indonesia). The skull on the right is a Qafzeh specimen of an earlier modern human from the Middle East. If humans emerged from Africa and spread globally (thus first appearing in the Middle East before Indonesia), then the center skull should be more like the right skull than the left. In fact, the opposite appears to be true.

that were thinly scattered across three continents." Foley (1995, p. 92) agreed, arguing that "by about 200,000 years ago there were probably distinct [hominin] populations, with their own evolutionary trajectories on each of the major Old World continents. They may not have been full species, but contact between them appears to have been limited." If multiregionalism is correct, then the critical elements of the EEAs for different evolving human populations in different regions could have varied substantially from one another. The predators, diseases, and survival problems to be solved on the African plain were not the same as those of the Javan rainforest or the Asian steppe, and, indeed, evidence of unique divergent characteristics in Asian erectus populations has been found (Andrews, 1984; Foley, 1995; Wood, 1992). Evolutionary psychologists envision a universal human nature as a function of our common evolutionary history. It seems that a much stronger case for this can be made with a single origin model than with a multiregional one.

Specimen	Number of differences from WLH 50
Ngandong 5	2
Ngandong 9	3
Ngandong 10	3
Ngandong 11	3
Ngandong 4	4
Ngandong 1	5
Skhul	5
Ngandong 6	6
Jebel Irhoud 2	6
Omo 1	6
Qafzeh 6	7
Qafzeh 9	7
Skhul 5	7
Omo 2	8
Jebel Irhoud 1	10
Laetoli 18	10
Singa	12

Table 5.A The table displays the number of pairwise differences between each comparison specimen and the WLH-50 skull. Note that the Ngandong specimens (from Indonesia) group to the top of the table and have the fewest differences relative to the African and Middle Eastern skulls. (Adapted from *Science* Magazine.)

should represent a separate, unrelated species that was displaced by the Africans when they advanced on that region.

Table 5.A shows the number of differences out of 16 traits examined between the Australian skull (WLH-50) and skulls from Indonesia (Ngandong) and others from Africa and the Middle East (Skhul, Qafzeh, Omo, Jebel, etc.). The Indonesia skulls congregate at the top of the table, showing the fewest differences from the Australian skull. The mean numbers of differences for each group were: Ngandong 3.7; African skulls 9.3; and Middle Eastern skulls 7.3. The average number of differences for the African and Middle Eastern skulls was significantly higher than that of the Indonesian skulls. Thus, the human skull from Australia was most similar to the ancient hominin skull from the same region and most dissimilar with the *Homo sapiens sapiens* skull from Africa, a finding in direct opposition to the predictions of the "Out of Africa" model. Wolpoff and his colleagues performed similar comparisons on other skulls from Eastern Europe and found the same general pattern: the skulls were either more or equally similar to older skulls from their own regions than they were to older African ones. These findings support the notion that regional populations of archaic hominins gradually evolved into modern humans, rather than being replaced globally by a small group of African humans.

Wolpoff's findings certainly do not settle the human origins debate. However, they do highlight the fact that some evidence is difficult to reconcile with the popular "Out of Africa" story. The evolutionary origin of humanity continues to be an unsettled and unsettling issue.

Source: **Wolpoff, M.H., Hawks, J., Frayer, D.W., & Hunley, K. (2001)**. Modern human ancestry at the peripheries: A test of the replacement theory. *Science, 291*, 293–297. Reprinted with permission of the American Association for the Advancement of Science and Milford H. Wolpoff.

The Evolution of the Brain

Being soft tissue, brains do not fossilize. To assess the size and character of the brains of extinct species, researchers use brain endocasts, impressions of the brain's convolutions as it pressed itself on the inner surface of the skull. Skull fossils and their endocasts have provided researchers with information about the brains of our hominin ancestors. As with so many issues in human evolution, the story of the evolution of the hominin brain has both a simple and a complicated version.

The simple version can be sketched out as follows. As one moves along the hominin branch from the common ancestor to the present, there is a general tendency for brain size to increase. The brain of the common ancestor was probably smaller than that of the average chimpanzee, which is about 400 cc. The common ancestor, however, was probably smaller bodied than a modern chimpanzee, so its brain size relative to body size was most likely comparable. The brain of *Australopithecus* was not significantly larger than an ape brain, in the range of 400–545 cc, and showed little change over the 2 million years or so of its existence. *H. habilis/rudolfensis* had a larger brain, ranging in size from 500 to 750 cc. With a brain ranging in size from 800–1,100 cc, the endowment of *H. erectus* was about 80% that of modern humans. Archaic *H. sapiens* had brains within modern standards, ranging from 1,100–1,400 cc, with the Neanderthal brain breaking 1,700 cc as an upper limit. With modern humans, the range of brain sizes falls somewhere between 1,200–1,400 cc. An interesting slight downward trend in brain size has occurred over approximately the last 40,000 years.

As part of the "simple" story, a number of behavioral changes initially were assumed to be connected with increasing brain size. For example, the arrival of *H. habilis*, with its much-larger-than-*Australopithecus* brain, coincided with some of the first evidence of tools. The arrival of *H. erectus*, which represented another substantial increase in brain size, corresponded with a number of important "firsts" in the evolutionary story, such as cooperative hunting, use of fire, expansion out of Africa, etc. With the emergence of modern humans have come other firsts, such as language, art, colonization of the globe, civilization, etc. The problem with the simple story is that, upon close examination, the importance of increasing brain size in any of these evolutionary "firsts" can be seriously questioned. One is left wondering exactly what a big brain is for, anyway?

Problems with the Simple Story

Although *H. habilis* is often credited with being the first hominin toolmaker, discoveries of some very old stone tools (ranging in age from 2.35–2.7 million years old), coupled with the fact that the hand bones of *A. robustus* suggest that it would have been capable of the precision and power grips necessary for tool manufacture, have led some researchers to suspect that it may have been creating tools before *Homo* (Feibel, Brown, & McDougall, 1989; Harris, 1983; Susman, 1988, 1994). Deacon (1997), in fact, argued that it may have been toolmaking in *Australopithecus* that created the context for the expanded brains of the *Homo* genus. The important point for our discussion is that *Australopithecus* may very well have been making tools despite its ape-sized brain. Furthermore, the increase in brain size from *H. erectus* to archaic sapiens was not marked by any significant change in behavior. Even more confounding is the fact the modern human brain was largely in place by about 150,000 years ago, yet for tens of thousands of years the behavior of modern humans was largely indistinguishable from that of their archaic counterparts (Bar-Yosef et al., 1992; Stringer & McKie, 1996). All of this suggests that brain size per se may not be the most critical factor in intelligence. If it were, elephants and whales would be considerably smarter than humans. Therefore, we now turn to the more complicated story, in which the brain must be understood in terms of the body within which it resides and the complexities of its organization.

Brain and Body Size

To put hominin brain expansion into proper perspective, two other factors should be addressed. First, one must disentangle increases in brain size from increases in body size. The brain grew over the course of hominin evolution, but so did the hominin body. Is the increase in brain size simply an artifact of increasing body size? The answer is no. Hominin bodies did generally increase in size from the Australopiths to *H. erectus*, but from *H. erectus* to modern humans the increase in body size has been negligible (McHenry, 1992). From erectus to sapiens, however, the brain continued to increase substantially in size. Another way to elucidate this is to use what is called the **encephalization quotient** (EQ), which is the ratio of brain size to body size. An EQ of 1 means that the observed brain size is what would be expected given an animal's body size (Jerison, 1973). Australopiths ranged in EQ from 2.2–2.9. This range is not that different from the EQ observed for chimpanzees (2.4). The EQ for the early species of *Homo* is about 3.5 and that for later *Homo* is more than 4.0. Turkana Boy, for example, had an estimated EQ of 4.5 (Begun & Walker, 1993). In about the last 300,000 years, however, the EQ has jumped dramatically to around 7, about what the EQ is for modern humans (7.4). Thus, the very recent increase in brain size cannot be accounted for entirely on the basis of increases in body size (Aiello & Dean, 1990; Martin, 1989). In fact, it is estimated that the human brain is about three times larger than would be expected for an ape our size (Passingham, 1982).

Brain Organization

A second important factor is the organization of the brain or how brain structure and circuitry has changed over the course of evolution. Often we get fixated on brain size, without recognizing that changes in size may be a byproduct of the brain's changing organizational structure. For example, humans have larger brains than monkeys, but the two brains differ in aspects of their wiring as well. Both human and monkey brains have two bundles of fibers, the corpus callosum and the much smaller anterior commissure, that connect the two hemispheres. If the corpus callosum is severed and the anterior commissure is left intact, monkeys have little disruption in the transfer of visual information from one hemisphere to the other. In humans, this transfer would be seriously impaired (see Gazzaniga, Ivry, & Mangun, 1998, for discussion). Thus, as species evolve, their brains do not just grow, they reorganize in adaptive ways. Scientists recently have devised a way of charting the evolution of brain organization based on **cerebrotype** or the relative sizes of 11 brain structures (Clark, Mitra, & Wang, 2001). Using this measure, significant shifts in cerebrotype can be observed with the emergence of apes and hominins. These cerebrotype shifts involve dramatic relative increases in the size of the neocortex, the very top wrinkled layer of brain, to the extent that in humans this structure comprises 80% of the total brain (Fig. 5.3).

Analyzing brain organization using cerebrotypes takes advantage of the fact that one can make direct comparisons of the brains of existing species. However, attempting to chart the evolutionary course of hominin brain organization is a far dicier proposition, given that one must work with the fossilized skulls and endocasts of extinct species. After an examination of endocasts, Holloway (1981a, 1984) argued that a move from an ape-like to a more human-like brain structure had occurred very early in hominin evolutionary history. A major part of his argument was based on the position of the **lunate sulcus**, a groove lying between the occipital, temporal, and parietal lobes (Fig. 5.4). In humans, this groove is located farther

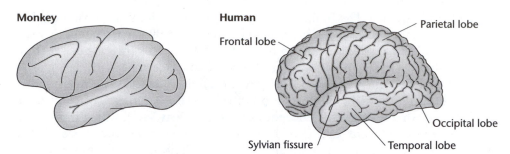

Figure 5.3 A comparison of brains. In different species the brain not only differs in overall size but in its organization and the relative sizes of various structures. For example, the frontal lobe in humans is greatly enlarged compared with that of the monkey, whereas the occipital lobe is only modestly different. (Adapted from Bownds, p. 49.)

back than in apes, allowing expansion of the parietal lobe. Holloway claimed that the back-shifting of the lunate sulcus was already present in *Australopithecus*. Falk (1980, 1991) took strong issue with Holloway's conclusion and argued instead that a more human-like organization was not present until the emergence of *Homo*.

Another aspect of the debate over the evolution of brain organization has focused on language. Brain endocasts of *H. habilis* show evidence of the presence of Broca's and Wernicke's areas, which are important in the expression and perception of language, respectively (Tobias, 1987, 1991). Some researchers have taken this to mean that a primitive form of language may have been present in *Homo* nearly 2 million years ago (Falk, 1987; Wilkins & Wakefield, 1995; Tobias, 1987). Others have contested this, arguing that the case for language that early in hominin evolution is highly speculative and not well established by the available evidence (Donald, 1991; Lieberman, 1984; Noble & Davidson, 1996).

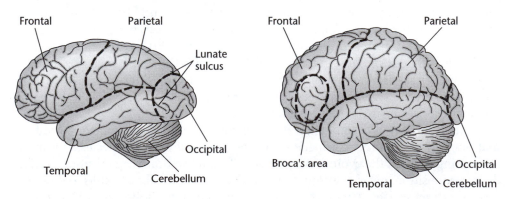

Figure 5.4 The back-shifting of the lunate sulcus. A comparison of the chimpanzee brain (left) and the human brain (right) shows that the parietal lobe has expanded in humans as a result, in part, of the back-shifting of the lunate sulcus. Researchers disagree on when during the course of human evolution this change in brain architecture occurred. (Adapted from Lewin, 1988, p. 446.)

Perhaps the most significant aspect of the evolution of human brain organization is the relative enlargement of the prefrontal cortex. The human brain has not only enlarged over the course of evolution, but it has enlarged in a specific way. Not all parts of the cerebral cortex have grown equally over the course of hominin evolution. For example, although humans retain the basic primate adaptation of being highly visually dependent, the human occipital lobe is actually smaller than would be predicted for a primate with a brain our size (Holloway, 1979; see Fig. 5.4). By contrast, the prefrontal cortex (at the very front part of the frontal lobe, see Fig. 5.4) is more than twice as large as would be expected (Deacon, 1988). Deacon (1997) argued that the sensory cortices (such as the primary visual cortex of the occipital lobe) are constrained by the limits of their input sources. These same limits are not present for association cortices that do not receive direct peripheral inputs but, instead, manage information flow within the brain. This is especially true for the prefrontal cortex, which largely lacks these natural limiting forces and, as a result, has expanded generously over the course of hominin evolution.

According to Deacon, the impact of this "frontalization" is profound. The frontal lobe appears to be involved in many higher order "executive" mental functions, such as working memory function, abstract and moralistic reasoning, control and direction of attention, and planning and coordinating complex behaviors (Gazzaniga et al., 1998, see pp. 423–464 for discussion). As the brain develops, a neural Darwinism takes place, in which connections within the brain are pruned so that only the more active and stable connections remain intact into adulthood. Because of the colossal size of the prefrontal cortex, it is able to extend its connections and dominate regions of the nervous system that are regulated by other structures in other species. So humans, for example, have conscious control over much of the vocal apparatus, whereas automatic subcortical control is more common among nonhuman primates.

Why Did the Brain Grow?

A number of factors have been implicated in the expansion of the hominin brain. Foley (1990) summarized the factors that have been shown to correlate positively with primate brain size. Briefly, the factors cluster into three broad categories:

1. **life history parameters:** such as the helplessness and immaturity of hominin newborns and their extended childhoods;
2. **ecological parameters:** such as expanded home ranges and increased meat consumption in the hominin diet; and
3. **social factors:** including the increasing size and complexity of hominin social groups.

Falk (1986; 1990) added to these factors another involving a unique blood-flow adaptation resulting from bipedalism whereby radiant heat was dispelled efficiently so as to keep the brain cool. Hominins that gave rise to humans found a way to keep their heads cool while standing upright in the sun, so that extended childhoods (allowing for increased learning), improved diet, and the memory and reasoning requirements of social living could "push" brain expansion without overheating the system. Tomasello and Call (1997) pointed out that the studies looking at brain size and ecological factors such as diet and home ranges have typically measured the entire brain size, whereas studies addressing social factors have concentrated on the evolutionarily newer neocortex. Both ecological and social factors could be important in the expansion of the hominin brain but at different times in evolutionary history and for different parts of the brain (such as ecological factors affecting subcortical structures and social factors affecting the neocortex). Many of the factors mentioned as important in hominin brain growth will be explored in more detail in later chapters.

The Evolution of Tool Technologies

Although brains do not fossilize, some products of the brain do. The tools hominins used for various tasks, such as hunting, butchering, and food preparation, are among such products. The types of tools that hominins used over the course of history have shown some potentially important evolutionary patterns and may provide us with insight into the cognitive capacities of different hominin species.

The oldest stone tools are associated with early *Homo* and possibly later forms of *Australopithecus* and date from about 2.6–1.5 million years old (Semaw et al., 1997; Wood, 1997). These tools are primarily small stone implements used for cutting, slicing, and chopping at flesh or for breaking bones to get access to marrow. These tools are referred to collectively as the **Oldowan** tool kit or industry, in reference to the Olduvai Gorge. Tools apparently were made by taking a rock (today known as a hammer stone) and striking it against another (the core) to produce a sharpened flake from the core that could be used as a tool (Toth, 1985). Toth contended that the flakes were the intended tools and the cores were an incidental byproduct. However, it appears that early hominins employed both flakes and cores, the former being useful not only for cutting meat but also grass stems and other vegetation and the latter being used more for chopping and cutting on carcasses (Keeley & Toth, 1981). A skillful toolmaker (called a knapper by anthropologists) would have to judiciously choose the right core and use the correct striking technique to reliably produce the type of edge necessary for the task at hand. Intriguing studies have looked at the cognitive requirements of Oldowan tool manufacture and have shed some light on the intellectual level of early *Homo*. These will be discussed in detail in chapter 16.

A second type of tool technology appeared about 1.4 million years ago and is generally associated with *H. erectus*. This is referred to as the **Acheulean** tool kit or industry. The name is derived from a site in France, St. Acheul, where many examples of the new technology were discovered. The major advance of the Acheulean industry was the production of larger, bifacial tools, especially handaxes. The Acheulean toolmaker created a more symmetrical implement than his/her Oldowan counterpart, which required more flakes to be properly "trimmed" off the surface to produce a two-sided edge (Isaac, 1986). Moreover, the Acheulean tool kit featured a wider range of artifacts, each more specifically designed for certain tasks, for example, scrapers for cleaning flesh and cleavers for breaking bones. A cursory comparison of an Oldowan with an Acheulean tool kit would reveal the fact that the latter contained many larger tools (Fig. 5.5). However, some researchers have argued that this difference is relatively minor compared with the cognitive advance underlying it. The Acheulean tradition represented an intellectual advance, in the sense that the toolmaker was fashioning a tool in accordance with a conceptualized end product (Gowlett, 1984; Wynn, 1979, 1993). Around 300,000 years ago, in later stages of the Acheulean tradition, the **Levallois** technique emerged, whereby the toolmaker would carefully prepare the core so that a specific shape of flake could be produced efficiently. The use of this technique seems to reinforce the notion that a preplanned concept was being brought to fruition through the actions of the toolmaker.

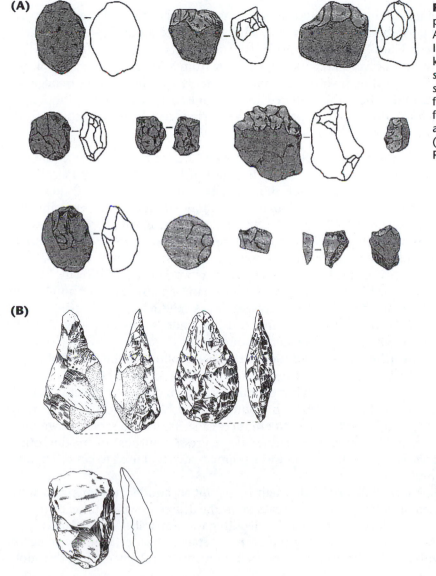

Figure 5.5 Representative samples from the Oldowan **(A)** and Acheulean **(B)** tool assemblies. In the top row of the Oldowan kit are examples of a hammerstone (far left), choppers, and scrapers. The bottom row shows flaked edges. The Acheulean kit features handaxes (top row) and cleavers (bottom row). (Reprinted, with permission of Roger Lewin, 1998.)

It is important to recognize that the Oldowan and Acheulean traditions are distinctions created by anthropologists to highlight important differences in the tools that are discovered. The two traditions did overlap, and an Acheulean tool kit might very well contain Oldowan-like tools. Moreover, some researchers have been critical of these distinctions, arguing that the differences are not well established and speculations concerning the mental capacity of the toolmakers are unfounded (see Noble & Davidson, 1996, for discussion). Less controversial is the observation that about 40,000 years ago a significant transition occurred in hominin toolmaking and in artifact production in general. This transition has been referred to as the **Upper Paleolithic revolution**.

The Upper Paleolithic Revolution

"Perhaps the most intriguing and enigmatic aspect of the Middle Palæolithic period is how and why it came to an end, after a period of around 200,000 years of remarkable stability." So began archeologist Paul Mellars's (1996, p. 392) discussion of the cultural upheaval that marked the change from Middle to Upper Paleolithic. Although the transition involved far more than tools, we will use these to begin to understand the changes that ushered in the modern human mind. The Upper Paleolithic tool industry in Europe, called the **Aurignacian**, is distinguishable from earlier tool traditions in a number of ways.

1. **Blade production.** A blade is defined as a flake that is twice as long as wide. Though blades were not unheard of before the Upper Paleolithic, their production increased dramatically both in quantity and quality at this time. Blade production became more sophisticated, requiring the toolmaker to indirectly strike the blade flake from the core (Kozlowski, 1990; see Mellars, 1996, chapter 13, for discussion). To do this, the toolmaker struck a hard hammerstone against a softer antler or bone that was positioned against the core. Thus, the core was not struck directly, but the force of the hammerstone was conducted through the antler or bone to the core, from which the blade flake was cut. A skillful toolmaker using such a technique could produce a high-quality blade, sometimes with a single blow or with a few subsequent retouches.

2. **Proliferation of new tool forms.** Upper Paleolithic toolmakers fashioned specifically designed tools for explicit functions, often by taking a standard tool design and modifying or altering it to increase its effectiveness. A scraper might be honed with a fluted end, or blades might be extensively retouched in various ways to produce bladelets, each to serve its own purpose. Tools were also created for the expressed purpose of making other tools. For example, a burin was a pointed-edge tool used to cut or engrave bone.

3. **Raw materials used.** Although bone, antler, and ivory sometimes were used in earlier periods to create tools, the degree to which these resources were employed in the Upper Paleolithic was unparalleled (Mellars, 1989). Moreover, the complexity and degree of standardization that was achieved with these materials had no equal in previous eras. Upper Paleolithic tool-

makers created an impressive range of antler, bone, and ivory artifacts, such as biconical pointed implements, antler batons, perforated bows, and bone tubes. The construction of these tools required multistep production processes often involving cutting, grooving, grinding, and polishing. It seems undeniable that the toolmaker had in mind a well-formed concept or image of the final product to guide the entire production process (Mellars, 1996).

In addition to advances in tool manufacture, the Upper Paleolithic provides evidence of a general cultural shift to a more identifiably "human-like" pattern. Along with tools, Upper Paleolithic humans also created an array of personal ornaments, such as beads and necklaces made from shells, ivory, and bone. Symbolic expression emerged and mushroomed in the form of bone and stone carvings, statuettes, and animal figurines (Fig. 5.6). Extensive trading networks for the exchange of raw materials also developed at this time. Seashells from the Atlantic and Mediterranean coasts have been found at Upper Paleolithic sites hundreds of miles inland (Taborin, 1993). Unquestionable evidence of ritualized burial with strong indications of religious significance also date from the period (White,

Figure 5.6 An exquisite example of art in the Upper Paleolithic. The famous lion-headed human figure carved in mammoth ivory, from the Höhlenstein-Stadel cave in southern Germany. At more than 30,000 years old, it is one of the oldest and most striking emblems of the cultural advance of the Upper Paleolithic.

1993). Coincident with these profound changes in human culture was the sudden disappearance of any evidence of archaic human forms, most especially the Neanderthals. Although many explanations are possible, from violent extermination to peaceful assimilation, there can be no doubt that the Upper Paleolithic marks the end of variable hominin species.

By about 30,000 years ago, the Upper Paleolithic revolution was complete and *H. sapiens sapiens* had brushed aside their cousins to stand alone as the sole species of *Homo*. Five million years of evolutionary sifting and sorting, along with a hefty dose of serendipity, had produced this uniquely self-aware and symbolic-thinking species, poised to have its turn atop the heap, its glorious hour upon the stage (Kauffman, 1995). How long will that shining moment last and to what end? This remains to be seen. What will be said of us when our light grows dim and we exit to join the dinosaurs and Neanderthals? What was it that distinguished this species from the others? This question will guide us in the next chapter.

SUMMARY

The first major transition marking the evolution of hominins was the commitment to a largely terrestrial existence with bipedal locomotion. This was established in large measure (although not entirely) in the earliest hominins, the Australopiths. Many species of *Australopithecus* emerged from 4.5–1.5 million years ago. The genus *Homo* emerged about 2 million years ago, with *H. habilis* and *H. rudolfensis* being two of its earliest representatives. *H. erectus/ergaster* emerged about 1.8 million years ago and trekked out of Africa to colonize parts of Europe and Asia. Two models have been proposed for the emergence of modern humans: the single origin model and the multiregional model. The single origin model claims that *H. sapiens sapiens* first emerged in Africa around 200,000 years ago and subsequently spread to other continents displacing more archaic hominin species. The multiregional model argues that *H. sapiens sapiens* evolved from separate archaic populations across the globe. Supportive evidence has been gathered for both models, but the balance of current evidence leans in favor the single origin model.

Hominin brains and tools also have shown important evolutionary patterns over the past 5 million years. A marked expansion in brain size coincided with the emergence of the genus *Homo*, with an even more dramatic increase occurring in the last .5 million years, with the emergence of archaic and modern sapiens. Brain size increases have not been uniform across different structures of the brain, with the neocortex and especially the frontal lobes becoming disproportionally enlarged relative to other brain structures. Hominin tools also have tended to grow larger and more sophisticated over time, beginning with the relatively small and simple Oldowan tools and advancing through Archeulean and Aurignacian stages. Aurignacian tools are associated with the remarkable cultural advance known as the Upper Paleolithic revolution, which commenced about 40,000 years ago and featured the production of body ornaments, art, and other aesthetic cultural artifacts.

KEY TERMS

Acheulean tools

archaic Homo sapiens

Aurignacian tools

Australopiths

cerebrotype

encephalization quotient (EQ)

hominid

hominin

Homo erectus

Homo habilis

Homo rudolfensis

Homo sapiens sapiens

hunter–gatherers

!Kung

Levallois technique

lunate sulcus

multiregional model

Neanderthals

Oldowan tools

Out of Africa model

Pithecanthropus erectus

single origin model

Upper Paleolithic revolution

REVIEW QUESTIONS

1. Discuss the important physical characteristics of the Australopiths, such as brain size, body type, sexual dimorphism, etc., and what these might indicate concerning lifestyle and habitat.

2. Who are Lucy and Turkana Boy? What do the differences between them suggest about the evolutionary changes that occurred between their two species?

3. Compare the single origin and multiregional hypotheses concerning the origins of modern humans. What evidence has been gathered to support each model?

4. Describe the course of brain evolution from *Australopithecus* to modern humans. Has there been a steady increase in size over this time period? How has brain organization varied?

5. In what ways do the tools of the Upper Paleolithic differ from their earlier counterparts? What might this indicate about their makers?

SUGGESTED READINGS

Klein, R.G. (1999). *The human career.* Chicago: University of Chicago Press.

Lewin, R. (1987). *Bones of contention.* New York: Simon & Schuster.

Lewin, R. (1998). *Principles of human evolution.* London: Blackwell Science.

Stringer, C., & McKie, R. (1996). *African exodus.* New York: Henry Holt.

Wolpoff, M. (1996). *Human evolution.* New York: McGraw-Hill.

WEB SITES

www.becominghuman.org/ on-line documentary about human evolution from the Institute of Human Origins.

www.anth.ucsb.edu/projects/human/ gallery depicting three-dimensional rotatable views of hominin fossils from the Anthropology Department at the University of California, Santa Barbara.

www.geocities.com/SoHo/Atrium/1381/index.html provides an overview of various hominin species, with descriptions of important physical features.

6

The Physical Human and the Control of Movement

> "The entire output of our thinking machine consists of nothing but patterns of motor coordination."
>
> —ROGER SPERRY (1952, PP. 297–98)

Deliberate Play

A WELL-WORN QUIP IS THAT FISH will be the last to discover water. The point, of course, is that sometimes we are blind to what is all around us. The mundane, the common, and the everyday are so familiar that we often fail to appreciate their significance. Consider the following scenario: a child approaches a small puddle of water and jumps over but slightly contacts the water's edge, causing a small splash. Disappointed, the child turns and tries again, adjusting the jump slightly but still failing to cleanly clear the puddle. Next, the child methodically paces back and gets a running start, which results in an easy float over the now rippling waters. The child repeats this success, using a shorter run-up. This may continue for quite a time, with the child eventually deciding that various ways of splashing *in* the puddle are eminently more rewarding than trying to leap over it. Anyone who has been around kids will find nothing startling in this behavior. It's just a kid being a kid. But the familiar nature of this behavior obscures its significance.

Pet owners occasionally witness the embarrassing spectacle of Fido jumping short of a narrow creek and sliding pathetically back into it, or Kitty missing a tree branch and scrambling desperately, claws extended, to keep from falling. But has anyone ever seen a dog, cat, or any other animal for that matter, having failed once, deliberately go back and repeat the act over and over, adjusting and modifying its component elements until they get it right? It was not only that our puddle-jumping kid was playing; animals play. Nor was it that the child was practicing; some animals may practice certain behaviors (although this very much depends on one's definition of practice). Our child was consciously decomposing a motor act into its component elements, adjusting and honing those elements, and recombining them to create a more effective novel action. "Our closest relatives the great apes just don't do that," stated psychologist Merlin Donald. "They do not rehearse and refine action. Nor do other advanced animals like dogs and cats" (Donald, 1993, p. 152).

That the play of human children can possess characteristics unique to our species should give us reason to pause appreciatively when next we are privileged to gaze upon such activity. It should spur our inquisitiveness as well. How is it that humans have achieved a level of motor control that allows for our unique physical capabilities? True, we do not swim with the sleek efficiency of sharks or dolphins, nor do our aerial acrobatics compare with those of gibbons or orangutans. But we march, dance, thread needles, caress lovers, and contort our faces in ways unrivaled by our animal comrades. The extent to which our humanity results from our embodiment often goes unrecognized. In this chapter, we will explore the evolution of our physical and biomechanical natures and the ways in which this has affected our psychology.

Getting Upright: The Structural Aspects of Bipedalism

One reason that humans have always thought ourselves categorically distinct from other animals is that from a physical standpoint we look so different. There are many facets to this "appearance gap," including our naked skin, small faces, lack of a tail, lean skeletal structure, and others. The most salient cue to identifying the human is our upright, two-legged posture and locomotion—in short, our bipedalism. Our cousins, the chimpanzees and bonobos, are capable of bipedal locomotion, but it is not their typical form of movement. Humans literally stand alone as the committed bipedal apes. The effects of this change on stature and movement are hard to overestimate. It is not a stretch to say that humanity owes much of what it considers to be its most precious and unique attributes to the fact that, millions of years ago, a bold group of primates abandoned the trees and cast their lots vertically on the ground. In its wake, this "decision" has left an array of structural adaptations distinctive to the biped.

To understand the structural adaptations of bidpedalism, we will start in the middle and work our way down and up the body. When a human pelvis is compared with that of a chimpanzee, differences in size and shape are obvious (Fig. 6.1). The human pelvis is short and broad, and the chimp's pelvis is long and nar-

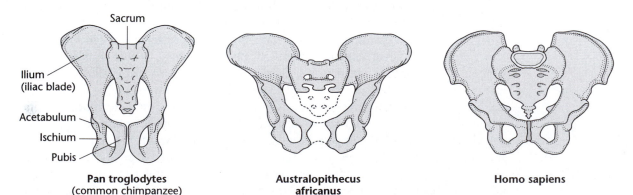

Figure 6.1 A comparison of the pelvis of the common chimpanzee (left), *Australopithecus africanus* (middle) and the human pelvis (right). Note that the chimpanzee pelvis is vertically longer and narrower than the human pelvis, which is short and broad. Note also the differences in the shapes of the iliac blades. (Adapted from Klein, 1999, p. 209.)

row. The iliac blade of the human pelvis extends back, centering the trunk over the hips. This difference helps the human maintain an upright posture with less strain and fatigue than the chimp experiences in such a position. In addition, the human femur (thighbone) is attached to the pelvis by strong, well-developed gluteal muscles, which help support and shift body weight during the walking stride. These same muscles are not as well developed in chimpanzees. Of even greater importance is the fact that the human femur angles inward on its way down to the knee, whereas the chimp femur runs nearly perpendicular to the knee on its way down from the pelvis (Fig. 6.2). This inward angling of the femur, the **valgus angle**, is critical to efficient bipedal movement, in that it positions the feet under the body's center of gravity with each step. By contrast, when a chimpanzee stands and walks, its center of gravity is higher and more frontally placed than that of a human. It must constantly shift its upper body laterally to stay centered over the weight-bearing leg, resulting in the rather amusing chimpanzee waddle. Amusing as it may be, it also represents an energy expenditure that makes bipedal locomotion too costly

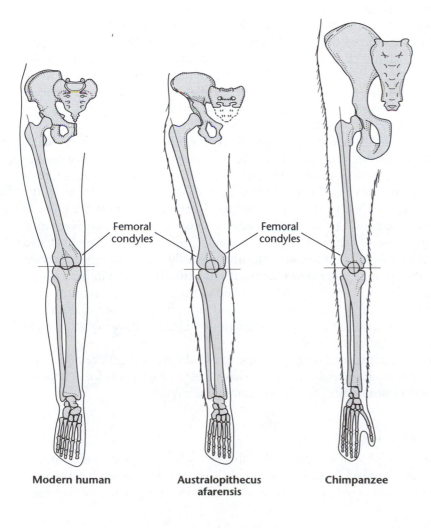

Figure 6.2 The valgus angle in humans and other primates. A comparison of the leg anatomy of humans (left), *Australopithecus afarensis* (middle), and chimpanzees (right), shows how the femur in the human angles inward as it connects from the pelvis to the knee, whereas the chimpanzee femur ascends nearly vertically. (Adapted from Klein, 1999, Figure 4.31.)

Femoral condyles

Femoral condyles

Modern human

Australopithecus afarensis

Chimpanzee

for chimps to endure for extended periods. Humans, on the other hand, are built for the two-legged long haul.

The walk itself is an interesting study in motion dynamics. It is composed of two phases, a **swing phase** and a **stance phase**. The swing phase begins with the push-off, in which power generated by the big toe helps to propel the leg forward in a slightly flexed position. The moving leg swings forward under the body and extends outward with the ball of the foot raised so that the heel strikes down first, initiating the stance phase. In the stance phase, the knee locks to provide support for the body as the other leg begins its swing. Take a stroll for a moment and concentrate on the intricacies involved in the biomechanics of the everyday walk. Herein lies another important anatomical difference between humans and chimpanzees. The chimpanzee cannot fully extend the knee in the stance phase as a human does, thus forcing the lower musculature to bear far more of the body weight load than does the human lower musculature. To get an idea of what this might be like, try standing and walking for a while with your knees constantly bent. Your legs quickly become sore. Bipedal adaptations extend to the very limits of the human anatomy, as evidenced by the fact that even the big toe has not escaped evolutionary modifications. Unlike the ape big toe, which angles outward from the other toes (similar to the human thumb in relation to the other fingers), the human big toe is adducted or pulled in line with the others. This, along with the general platform shape of the foot, aids in balance and in providing power for locomotion. In addition, the arches of the foot provide a stable, springy base for the body. Unlike the ape foot, the human foot has abandoned all pretense of being a grasping instrument and, instead, has fully embraced its role as the crucial bottom rung of the walking system.

Working upward from the pelvis, the effects of bipedalism are no less evident. The lower, lumbar region of the spine is curved and strengthened. The five lumbar vertebrae are larger and broader than their cervical and thoracic counterparts higher on the spine, allowing them to support more weight. The curvature of the human spine contrasts with that of quadrudpedal animals in which the spine is horizontal and straighter. Although the human lower limbs are relatively long compared with those of other primates, our upper limbs (arms) have shortened over time as their role in locomotion diminished. Finally, where the spine adjoins the cranium, the opening (**foramen magnum**) has shifted forward in humans. In the chimpanzee, the foramen magnum is located at the back of the cranium. This allows the chimp to more easily hold the head upright when on all fours. In humans, the vertical spine enters the cranium more centrally, allowing the head to be held in line with the upright body.

The physical adaptations corresponding to bipedal movement are distinctive to the human species. These adaptations also allow researchers to use fossil remains to assess the locomotor capabilities of our hominin ancestors.

Origins of Bipedalism

Why walk on two legs? Without doubt this ability has been a boon to us, but, if it were such a great adaptive innovation, one might suspect that it would have evolved in many other animals as well. For eons, most other living things have managed just fine on four limbs, more, or none at all. If by chance, humanity's tenure should end in the next few thousand years, one might rightly conclude that bipedalism wasn't all that it was cracked up to be. For the time being, however, our uprightness has served us well. We should consider carefully how such an adaptation could have arisen in the first place. A number of ideas have been proposed.

INCREASED FIELD OF VISION. The seeds of human origins were sown in the ecological ferment of East Africa that caused the forests to recede and give way to more open, savanna-type environments. In this context, it is argued, an adaptive advantage would accrue to those primates who could get upright and take in a more panoramic, long-distance view of the environment. This might have been aesthetically pleasing, but it was predators, not inspirational vistas, that our ancestors were standing up to see (Kortlandt, 1972). Away from the relative safety of the trees, a 3–4-ft primate was vulnerable to a range of large predators. Those primates that could see danger from farther away (by being upright) would be more likely to survive and reproduce. Although not unreasonable, this idea has serious problems. First, it ignores the fact that many primates can stand erect and walk bipedally when the need arises. An individual does not need to be a committed biped to gain the advantages of upright posture. Second, the earliest Australopiths probably spent a good deal of their time in dense woodland settings rather than the open savanna, yet bipedalism was well established among them. For these reasons, increased access to distant information seems more like a consequence of bipedalism than a cause.

FREEING THE HANDS. A number of researchers have focused on the various advantages of freeing the hands from locomotion to engage other activities. One of the most heartwarming versions of this approach was proposed by Owen Lovejoy (1981), who argued that the ecological conditions of the early hominins would have forced them into a nomadic lifestyle. Constantly moving to secure resources would have put great stress on their reproductive patterns. To survive, early hominins would have had to increase their birth rates and reduce infant mortality as much as possible. This could be accomplished if males actively provisioned females and offspring, so as to increase the viability of the infant and more quickly allow the female to regain reproductive potential. Among birds, monogamy (at least *social* monogamy) is widespread, and it is typically the male that provisions the nestlings by carrying food in his mouth and regurgitating it. The male hornbill, for example, will fill his cavernous beak with up to 250 figs per load to feed his mate and their chicks. Early hominins were not equipped with a hornbill-type transport implement, but they could carry provisions by hand. Over time there would be selection pressure for the best provisioning hominins, those who could carry the most, farthest. Bipedal adaptations would accumulate as a result of using the hands as provisioning tools. Although Lovejoy's image of the monogamous, faithfully provisioning ancestral male is touching, the degree of sexual dimorphism present in early hominins suggests that males were spending the lion's share of their time competing for females rather than supporting and caring for their one true love and her babies.

Lovejoy envisioned early hominins carrying provisions, but Mary Leakey and her colleagues imagined early hominins carrying their infants (Sinclair, Leakey, &

Norton-Griffiths, 1986). Primarily scavengers, early hominins would have followed herds of large grazers to get access to carcasses. As they moved along, hominin upper limbs would be occupied holding infants, and locomotion would increasingly depend exclusively on the lower extremities. Ardrey (1976) disagreed, claiming that bipedal adaptations, by and large, were a masculine affair resulting from the necessity to carry weapons for fighting and hunting. Some support for this view can be found in the fact that certain properties of human legs, such as their relative massiveness and the manner in which the knees lock, seem specifically designed as throwing adaptations (Fifer, 1987). One of the criticisms of both of these ideas is that there is little evidence that early hominins were either hunters or carnivores to any significant degree.

ENERGY EFFICIENCY. Going for a run with your dog can be a very depressing activity. At high speeds, human bipedalism is far less energy efficient than quadrupedalism. A sprint down the road wears you out, but Fido is barely winded. The situation changes, however, at slower speeds, where the two-legged trot can be as or more efficient than its four-legged counterpart. Thus begins the logic for the energy efficiency hypothesis proposed by Rodman and McHenry (1980). As the African forests receded and resources became more widely dispersed, those primates that could more efficiently get from one clump of resources to another would have a serious advantage over their competitors. Chimpanzees are woefully inefficient walkers, expending 50% more energy compared with other quadrupeds whether they knuckle walk or walk bipedally. By contrast, humans are less efficient runners but more efficient walkers than quadrupedal primates. A knuckle-walking chimpanzee can travel about 11 km (a little less than 7 miles) in day. Expending the same amount of energy, a bipedal hominin can cover up to 16 km (10 miles; Rodman, 1984). If bipedalism offered our primate ancestor an energy-efficient means of exploiting increasingly scarce resources, then selection would act in its favor. However, there is some question as to how large an efficiency gain would have been reaped. Some researchers have directly challenged Rodman and McHenry's assertion that bipedalism offers a significant energy savings (Jablonski & Chaplin, 1993; Mahoney, 1980; Taylor & Rountree, 1973; Taylor, Heglund, & Maloiy, 1982). Moreover, the hypothesis seems to assume that the common ancestor was a knuckle walker similar to a chimpanzee, an assumption not without controversy.

The energy advantage of bipedalism, however, may not be only in the movement but also in the upright stature. When standing upright in the equatorial midday, far less of the body is directly exposed to the sun than when hunched over quadrupedally. Wheeler (1994) has calculated that a 77-lb hominin would need to replace 3.3 pints of water a day as a result of heat stress, compared with 5.5 pints for a quadruped of the same size. The drastic reduction in body hair for hominins also may be part of a constellation of thermoregulatory adaptations that allowed hominins to remain cool while foraging in the tropical heat.

THREATENING RIVALS. A proposal by Jablonski and Chaplin (1993) focused on the intense competition that patchy forests and dwindling resources would have placed on prehominin groups. They noted that bipedal threat displays are nearly universal among primates and therefore were probably part of the behavioral repertoire of the common ancestor. As competition for resources escalated, those prehominins with the most impressive displays would have had a distinct advantage over others. Females with better displays could effectively secure more resources, whereas males with the best displays could more easily get access to females. Effective upright threat displays would help in the establishment of stable social hierarchies, thereby offering the advantage of decreased intragroup violence. Although speculative, it seems hard to resist the notion that once the bipedal threat display secured a selective advantage, the possibility of energy savings from bipedal locomotion may have stepped in to further the evolutionary path toward full bipedalism.

It is probably the case that a number of factors combined to make bipedalism advantageous for early hominins. Threat displays and locomotor energy savings may have kick-started the process, after which thermoregulatory advantages and all the benefits of freed hands may have helped to increase the momentum toward a vertically committed way of life. If so, when might this adaptation have taken hold in our evolutionary history? Were we upright before we had big brains, or did our big brains help us get upright?

The Evolution of Bipedalism

Boys will be boys—even when they inhabit the bodies of grown-up scientists. When, in a moment of puckish playfulness, ecologist David Western tossed a clump of elephant dung at paleontologist Andrew Hill, he had no inkling that Hill's tumbling attempt to escape being "turd bombed" would result in one of the great discoveries about humanity's past. With his nose unexpectedly to the floor of a dry riverbed near Laetoli, Tanzania, Hill caught a glimpse of some strange looking dimple marks in the rocks. The dimples, it turned out, were impact marks from a rainstorm some 3.6 million years ago. The rain had come shortly after a new layer of volcanic ash blanketed the surface, timing its descent perfectly so its delicate impressions would be preserved for the ages. The rain, however, was not alone in unknowingly painting itself upon this evolutionary canvas. Shortly after Hill reported his findings, Mary Leakey, the chief researcher at Laetoli, uncovered the ancient footprints of a small group of hominins whose ordinary trek across the African landscape had taken them across the same rain-stained ash (Leakey & Hay, 1979; Reader, 1981).

The footprints tell the story of two adult-size hominins, one larger than the other, walking close together stride for stride, perhaps hand in hand or with the larger's arm around the smaller's shoulder. The larger hominin may have slipped a bit in the ash, or he (?) may have paused to look eastward at the erupting volcano responsible for the volcanic soot below them. A smaller hominin (their child?) may have been walking behind the two, tracking in their prints. Although there are other fossilized tracks, no other limb prints are attributable to our small "family" of hominins. They unquestionably walked on twos, not fours, and their stride was hauntingly human. The big toe, which pointed forward and did not angle outward as in apes, pushed off to begin the swing phase. The foot landed heel first, then rolled onto the ball of the foot, where another big-toe push-off was initiated, cycling through the process again (Feibel et al., 1995; Tuttle, 1990; Tuttle, Webb, Weidl, & Baksh, 1990). By 3.5–4 million years ago, hominins already were upright and strutting about not all that differently from the way we do today. The prints have been attributed to *Australopithecus afarensis*, the same species to which the famous "Lucy" skeleton belongs. Because so much of Lucy was preserved, we have been able to infer quite a bit about the bipedal capacities of *A. afarensis*. The Laetoli prints suggest that *A. afarensis's* bipedal status was similar to that of humans today, but the anatomical evidence tells a more complicated tale.

The Bipedalism of Australopithecus

A number of anatomical features indicate that *A. afarensis* was a committed biped. Although much of the cranium is ape-like, the foramen magnum is positioned centrally as in humans, not dorsally as in apes. As we saw earlier, the central positioning of the foramen magnum is a sign of bipedalism. The pelvis and lower limb structure of *A. afarensis* provide further confirmation of bipedalism. The pelvis was human-like, broad and short in its structure, and the valgus angle of the knee was similar to that of humans (Fig. 6.2). Based on his analysis of the lower limb structure, Lovejoy (1988) concluded that *A. afarensis* was a fully committed terrestrial biped: "Lucy's ancestors must have left the trees and risen from four limbs onto two well before her time, probably from the very beginning of human evolution" (1988, p. 89).

Although there is little question that *A. afarensis* was bipedal, the degree of that commitment has been questioned. These doubts stem from both the general character of *A. afarensis* and from its specific bipedal attributes. On the general level, *A. afarensis* in many respects was more ape-like than human. It had an ape-sized brain, many of its cranial and facial features were quite ape-like, and its diet of fruits, leaves, bugs, and scant meat had more in common with that of chimps and gorillas than with humans. Even its specific bipedal adaptations were distinctive from those of modern humans. For example, although the pelvis was for the most part human-like, the iliac blades did not flare backward in the manner of the human pelvis, suggesting that *A. afarensis* did not balance itself in the same way that humans do. Lovejoy contended that this and other anatomical differences would not have had any significant functional effect on *A. afarensis's* stride and gait, which, although different in some details, would have been essentially the same as modern humans.

Lovejoy's view is not shared by others, who point to the fact that *A. afarensis's* lower limbs were shorter than modern humans, with curved feet and hand bones. Furthermore, the wrist and ankles were more flexible and mobile than those of modern humans, and the shoulder joints were oriented more toward the head (Jungers, 1988; Susman, Stern, & Jungers, 1984; Senut & Tardieu, 1985; Tuttle, 1981). Taken together, these anatomical features indicate a substantial degree of arborality in *A. afarensis*. Lucy and her kin may have spent as much time climbing trees, presumably to escape predators and to forage for food, as they did on the ground. Even when on the ground, *A. afarensis* would not have achieved the same striding gait as humans, according to Susman, Stern, and Jungers (1984). The legs of *A. afarensis* were relatively short, and the feet were rather large. These features, coupled with the fact that *A. afarensis* may have had to balance itself as a chimpanzee does, suggests that it may have had a bent-knee, bent-hip type of bipedal posture. Although Lucy undoubtedly walked, she walked differently and probably less efficiently than later hominins. Moreover, although Lucy *did* walk, it appears that she did not run. Schmid (1983) analyzed Lucy's upper body and concluded that *A. afarensis* would have had considerable balancing and breathing problems if she attempted to run any significant distance. The high position of the shoulders and the funnel-shaped chest would have made arm swinging difficult, and the abdomen had very little space to allow swiveling of the hips. These movements are critical to maintaining balance while running. Furthermore, Lucy would have had great difficulty lifting the thorax to allow the deep breathing necessary while running. Before getting very far, she would likely have toppled over or passed out, not desirable results for either chasing a meal or avoiding becoming one.

Another rather ingenious way of measuring ancestral bipedality involves the semicircular canals of the inner ear. These three canals, the anterior, posterior, and lateral, are part of the vestibular system, which is important for maintaining balance. Compared with apes, the anterior and posterior canals in humans are larger, but the lateral canal is smaller. It has been argued that these differences reflect part of the human adaptation to bipedalism and the balancing demands it makes on the body. Using computerized tomography to estimate the sizes of these canals in early hominins, Fred Spoor and his colleagues (Spoor, Wood, & Zonneveld, 1996) found that in Australopiths the canals were ape-like. Not until the genus *Homo* does the pattern of semicircular canal sizes attain the human pattern. Spoor concluded that the Australopiths did not move bipedally in the same manner as either modern humans or later hominins.

This evidence reviewed so far converges on the conclusion that the bipedalism of the Australopiths was not the same as that of modern humans, or even of later hominins. Instead, it was a bipedalism that coexisted with arboreal adaptations, suggesting that *Australopithecus* was not entirely committed to a terrestrial lifestyle but divided its time between the trees and the ground. Furthermore, different species of *Australopithecus* may have achieved a different balance between these environmental niches. For example, although *Australopithecus africanus* emerged .5–1 million years after *A. afarensis*, some evidence suggests that it may have been an even more arboreally adapted species than its predecessor. Studies focusing on the forelimbs and forelimb joints of *A. africanus* found them to be more robust than both modern humans and *A. afarensis* (McHenry & Berger, 1996; 1998). The robustness of the upper limbs often indicates the extent to which they are employed in locomotion, which in this case appears to be greater for *A. africanus* than *A. afarensis*. Recently discovered foot bones show the *A. africanus* big toe angled out from the other toes in a manner similar to but not as pronounced as modern apes (Clark & Tobias, 1995). The divergent big toe is another arboreal adaptation that proves to be quite functional in climbing trees and grasping limbs.

Researchers continue to debate the extent of *Australopithecus's* bipedal lifestyle, and some of the evidence is complicated and contradictory. For example, McHenry's (1986) analysis of the *A. afarensis* wrist concluded that there was no evidence of the features necessary for knuckle walking. However, a recent study (Richmond & Strait, 2000) claimed that Lucy's wrists were stiffened in a manner similar to knuckle-walking apes. In addition, the Laetoli prints suggest a human-like bipedal stride, but (as we saw) some analyses of Lucy's anatomy suggest that this was not the case. Additional evidence will be needed to sort out these issues. Currently, it seems clear that although the Australopiths were bipedal, they also possessed a number of tree-climbing adaptations and were probably as comfortable in trees as on the ground.

The Stature and Walk of Homo

With the advent of the genus *Homo*, any commitment to the trees was abandoned. Although the overall body proportions of *Australopithecus* retained the ape-like characteristic of elongated forelimbs and relatively shorter hindlimbs, *Homo erectus* sported more human-like body proportions, with shortened upper limbs, longer legs, and relatively low body-bulk-to-stature ratio (Aiello, 1992). The nearly complete "Turkana Boy" skeleton reveals that *H. erectus* had a narrower pelvic region than the Australopiths and a longer, thinner femur. The chest and rib cage of *H. erectus* had a more barrel-shaped appearance, contrasting with the more funnel-shaped chest of *Australopithecus*. These structural changes would have improved the energy efficiency of bipedal movement by increasing the power of the muscles of the pelvic region and allowing more effective breathing (Jellema, Latimer, & Walker, 1993). These adaptations leave little doubt that with *H. erectus* a bipedal, terrestrial lifestyle was fully in place.

Other aspects of *H. erectus*'s anatomy are also informative about the degree of motor control in this species and its evolutionary implications. Although the spine of Turkana Boy was, in many ways similar to that of modern humans, it differed in at least one potentially crucial aspect. The diameter of the internal canal through which the spinal cord passed was significantly smaller than that of modern humans. This suggests that the demand for neural input to the muscles of the thorax was far smaller in *H. erectus* than in modern humans, thus reducing the degree of conscious control of the breathing apparatus. Lacking the ability to make fine, voluntary adjustments of breathing patterns, *H. erectus* may not have been able to produce spoken language (MacLarnon, 1993; Walker, 1996). This conclusion is speculative, and the possibility of spoken language in *H. erectus* and other hominins is a controversial issue. However, it does show how our understanding of anatomical structure can provide potential insights into the behavioral capacities of extinct hominins and help formulate hypotheses for future research (Box 6.1).

The Hands and Toolmaking

Another trait that distinguishes humans from other animals is the precise, manipulative skill of the human hand. Human manipulative skill co-evolved with bipedalism, and, as we saw earlier, some have argued that the freeing of the hands was actually the evolutionary catalyst of upright walking. What makes human hands different from ape hands? Comparing a chimpanzee hand to a human's reveals the following differences: chimps' hands have curved phalanges (finger bones) with thinner fingertip pads. In addition, the thumbs are proportionally much shorter than human thumbs. These characteristics are not surprising, given that the chimpanzee hand is adapted to tree climbing and knuckle walking and that its physical make-up serves those functions quite well. The human hand, by

How Smart the Neanderthals?

BOX 6.1

What Bones Might Say about Intellect
The reputation of Neanderthals has ebbed and flowed over the years. They have been variously portrayed as everything from dim-witted, nonhuman brutes to compassionate ancestral humans who cared for their sick and elderly and lovingly buried their dead. Each new bit of evidence seems to recast our image of this extinct hominin species. Some researchers have compared the bones of humans and Neanderthals, searching for clues about the Neanderthal lifestyle and intellect. Some structural differences have been uncovered that may (may!) have important behavioral and cognitive implications.

The human pelvis and that of the Neanderthal are not all that different, but the pubic inlet, at the very bottom of the pelvis, was more forwardly placed in Neanderthals. At first, it was thought that this might have implications for Neanderthal reproduction. That idea now seems unlikely, but this difference may have implications for Neanderthal posture and locomotion (Rak, 1990; Rak & Arensburg, 1987). When walking, the Neanderthal's center of gravity would have been more directly placed on the hip joints, whereas in humans more of the upper body weight is distributed onto the thigh and gluteal muscles. Over time, the body load pushing down on the hip joints would have taken its toll, making Neanderthals less suited for long-distance travel.

Neanderthal walking may have been not only less efficient but also less goal directed. To understand the evidence relevant to this issue, one first needs to know that repeated stress causes bones to thicken. For example, the left and right arm bones of profes-sional tennis players can differ by as much as 60%, whereas for most people the effects of handedness produce only about a 5% difference in thickness (Gibbons, 1996). Trinkhaus (1992) examined cross-sections of Neanderthal leg bones and found (as expected) that they were thickened from use. However, the thickening was also symmetrical. This was in contrast to the leg bones of human hunter–gatherers, in which the thickening was more asymmetrical, reflecting a lifestyle of fairly consistent straight-ahead walking. The implication was that the Neanderthals spent a considerable amount of time walking in circles or shuffling side to side. Moreover, Trinkhaus also found that the necks of Neanderthal thigh bones were more sharply bent than those of humans, suggesting that as children the Neanderthals spent a significantly greater amount of time following the group in pursuit of food (Gibbons, 1996). All of this evidence suggests that Neanderthal movement was both mechanically and possibly cognitively less efficient.

Speculating on how Neanderthals walked and whether they walked with much purpose in mind is all very dicey business. Indeed, Klein (1999) claimed that the postural and locomotor differences between humans and Neanderthals would have been "minor." A pair of recent studies provided evidence that Neanderthals, in all likelihood, were quite efficient hunters and foragers (Richards et al., 2000; Sorensen & Leonard, 2001). As more fossil evidence accumulates and our ability to infer action from structure becomes more sophisticated, more light will be shed on the physical capacities of our hominin ancestors and the intellectual implications of those capacities.

contrast, is adapted for grasping and manipulating objects and has features that serve those activities. For example, both humans and chimps can bring the thumb over to contact the index finger, but only humans can extend the thumb completely across the hand to contact the fourth and fifth fingers. Humans, but not chimps, can go the other direction as well, folding the last two fingers over the hand to the base of the thumb in a position known as "ulnar opposition" (Marzke, 1996; Wilson, 1998). These structural and functional differences provide humans an arsenal of grips and a manipulative capacity superior to that of any of our primate cousins (Fig. 6.3).

Examining the evolutionary origins of the human hand is difficult, given the scarcity of the fossil record, especially for such species as *A. africanus*. Hand remains are more abundant, however, for *A. afarensis* and the much later *A. robus-*

Pongo

Figure 6.3 Primate hand—the hand of *Pongo* (orangutans). Note especially the proportionally small thumbs of the nonhuman primates. (Adapted from Wilson, 1998, p. 22.)

tus species. The hand of *A. afarensis* shows many ape-like characteristics, such as thin, curved figures and short thumbs. This fits nicely with the evidence reviewed earlier indicating the arboreal adaptations of the Australopiths. Although she agreed that the hands of *A. afarensis* were ape-like, Marzke (1996) concluded that they still would have had gripping and manipulative capabilities exceeding that of chimps or gorillas. Lucy could position the thumb against the side of the index finger, producing what Marzke calls the **pad-to-side grip**, useful for tightly grasping

Figure 6.4 Lucy's left hand. The left hand bones of *Australopithecus afarensis* are shown with palm-side up. (Reprinted by permission of Mary Marzke, Anthropology Department, Arizona State University, Phoenix.)

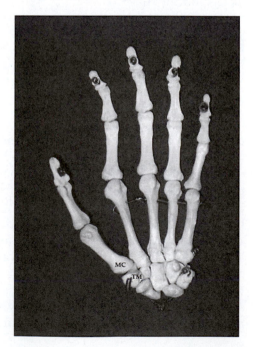

a small sharp stone when scraping or cutting. She could also use the **three-jawed chuck grip**, in which an object is secured by surrounding it with the thumb, index, and middle fingers, much the way one normally holds a baseball. Finally, with palm facing up, Lucy could hold and manipulate an object with the thumb on one side and the four fingers on the other in a grip called the **five-jawed cradle**. With this manual repertoire, *A. afarensis* could have used stones for pounding, digging, and throwing with a degree of skill and accuracy beyond that of great apes (Marzke, 1994, 1997). What Lucy and her kin could not do was bring the fourth and fifth fingers across in the ulnar opposition (just as chimpanzees cannot) to form the **oblique power grip** needed for holding and swinging clubs or manipulating tools such as hammers. The oblique grip also may have been important in giving *Homo sapiens* an advantage over the Neanderthals in tool manufacture and use. A recent analysis comparing *H. sapiens'* hands with those of Neanderthals suggests that, like Lucy, the Neanderthals would have had difficulty forming the subtle grips required to skillfully use tools for carving or painting (Niewoehner, 2001).

Compared with *A. afarensis*, the hands of *Australopithecus robustus* were more human-like. This species, which existed some 1–2 million years after *A. afarensis*, had hands with broader fingers and a longer, more dexterous thumb (Susman, 1994). Some researchers conclude, not without controversy, that *A. robustus* would have been capable of both the precision and power grips necessary for stone tool manufacture. The more manipulative hand of *A. robustus* opens up the possibility that the earliest stone tools may have been products of the later Australopiths rather than an innovation unique to the genus *Homo*.

Whether the first toolmaking hands were those of *Australopithecus* or *Homo*, were those hands engaging in acts unique in evolutionary history? By constructing the first stone tools some 2 million years ago, were ancient hominins exhibiting a manipulative and motor capacity beyond the capabilities of their primate brethren? Making stone tools in the manner of the Oldowan tool kit was not a haphazard affair. To produce the types of flakes and edges that qualify as Oldowan, Stone Age knappers would most likely have used a flaking technique called **percussion**. In the percussion technique, a hammerstone is struck against the core about 1 cm from the edge, using a strong, glancing blow that impacts the core at an acute angle. One should not underestimate the level of skill necessary for proficient stone tool manufacture. Modern anthropologists attempting to create their own Oldowan tool kits often have found the process challenging, and misstrikes not only waste time and resources but can lead to serious injury (Schick & Toth, 1993).

In 1993, Nicholas Toth and others set out to determine if the skill of the Oldowan toolmakers was beyond that of modern apes. They trained Kanzi, a pygmy chimpanzee (or bonobo), in the ways of Oldowan tool manufacture (Toth, Schick, Savage-Rumbaugh, Sevick, & Rumbaugh, 1993). Kanzi, as we will see in later chapters, is no ordinary ape. He is an extensively tested and studied subject in the area of language learning, and his extraordinary proficiency at symbolic communication ranks him as one of the smartest, if not *the* smartest, simian around. Kanzi was trained to construct Oldowan-type stone implements to receive a favored food reward. Although he was shown the percussion technique, Kanzi never used it when he created his stone tools. Instead, he energetically banged cobbles together, smashed a stone core against another hard object, or simply threw them on the floor to knock flakes from them. At one point, carpet was laid on the laboratory floor to prevent him from applying the "smash-it-on-the-floor" technique to create his flakes. Kanzi, however, was persistent, pulling up parts of carpet to expose the hard floor below. The experimenters concluded that Kanzi could make stone tools similar to those of the Oldowan tool kit. However, his tools were not as precise and well formed as those of the early hominins. Moreover, Kanzi did not create them in the same way as did human ancestors. What is unclear from this study is whether the difference between Kanzi's and early hominin's technical skills are rooted in cognitive or manipulative abilities or both (for more on the evolution of hands and toolmaking see Box 6.2).

KEY CONTRIBUTIONS

MARY MARZKE
The Evolution of the Hand

PROFILE: *Dr. Mary Marzke is a professor of anthropology at Arizona State University. She received her undergraduate degree (1959) and Ph.D. (1964) from the University of California, Berkeley. Her research focuses on the evolution of the human hand and bipedality. Most recently she and her students have been using three-dimensional imaging techniques to compare human hands with those of extinct hominins and other living primates.*

BOX 6.2 **The Cost of Human Hands**

Adaptations are not perfectly engineered natural products. Instead, they are compromises that balance necessary strengths with acceptable weaknesses. The human hand is no exception. The hands of most other primates are adapted for climbing and other locomotive functions. Over the course of hominin evolution, hands became superfluous to movement and more specialized as gripping, grasping object manipulators. However, being a manipulative tool instead of a means of locomotion has its disadvantages. Mary Marzke and undergraduate Alexandra de Sousa studied the differences among primate and hominin hands to understand how their design features solved adaptive problems and at the same time produced structural pathologies.

One of the reasons the human hand has more manipulative capacity than a chimpanzee hand is the increased flexibility and opposability of the thumb. Part of this increased flexibility results from the construction of the **trapezial-metacarpal** (TMC) joint. The contacting surfaces of the bones are broader and flatter in the human, whereas in the chimp they are narrower and more angular. The design of the chimpanzee joint effectively locks the chimp's thumb into place, reducing its freedom of movement.

It is thought that the broader and flatter design of the human TMC joint reflects an adaptation to object manipulation and tool manufacture over the course of hominin evolution. Although this change was advantageous for those purposes, it may have a downside as well: the incidence of osteoarthritis has been associated with the make-up of the human TMC joint. A comparison of the trapezial surface of the TMC joints of humans, *Homo habilis*, and chimpanzees shows that in habilis the surface was even flatter than in humans. Thus, ancient hominins may have had even more built-in flexibility than modern humans. This may have reduced the risk for oestoarthritis but increased the risk of another debilitating condition: thumb slippage.

As is so often true with adaptive structures, the modern human hand may reflect a compromise among competing interests. A thumb joint flexible enough to allow a high degree of manipulative skill becomes prone to arthritis, but, if made too flexible (to reduce the arthritis risk), it may too easily slip out of joint.

Source: **de Sousa, A.A., & Marzke, M.W. (1999).** Osteoarthritis in the thumb: An evolutionary compromise for prehistoric tool making? Retrieved February 1, 2002, from: http://lsvl.la.asu.edu/ubep99/abstracts/abst13/index.html. Go to the Web site to view figures of the hand.

A study by Wynn and McGrew (1989) suggested that the differences were not cognitive in nature, although this is still an open question. These researchers assessed the intellectual demands of Oldowan tool manufacture and concluded that the spatial/conceptual knowledge necessary for early hominin stone tool manufacture was no more demanding than that required of chimpanzees in their use of twigs and stones as tools for obtaining food. "Oldowan tools did not require a particularly sophisticated intelligence," concluded Wynn (1996, p. 267). However, the requirement that did appear to be beyond the capacity of apes was the ability to plan the proper sequence of motor actions and the ability to regulate the correct angle and force of impact on the core (Locke, 1999; Toth & Schick, 1993; Wynn, 1996). These findings suggest that by about 2 million years ago, hominins had achieved a level of technical skill exceeding that of apes. An important element of the skill (indeed, perhaps the most important element) was a level of motor control and manipulative capacity that permitted stones to be fashioned and shaped into sharpened and functional cores and flakes. Louis Leakey once proclaimed that toolmaking was what separated humans from other creatures. We now know this to be an overstatement. Other animals make tools. However, as early as 2 million years ago, hominins were demonstrating a nascent capacity for elevating the precision and skillfulness of tool manufacture beyond that which had ever been achieved before. With their newly freed and dexterous hands, hominins began exploring the limits of how the environment around them could be reshaped to suit their needs.

Which Hand to Use?

In humans, the skillful use of the hands almost always implies the use of the right hand. One of the characteristic traits of the human species is handedness—the fact that approximately 90% of humans display some degree of right hand preference for a variety of manual tasks. Corballis (1991) pointed out that for most animals it is symmetry rather than asymmetry that is of adaptive value: "Any asymmetry in legs or wings would be likely to cause an animal or bird to proceed in fruitless (and perhaps meatless) circles" (p. 81). The senses also need to be roughly symmetrical to detect prey or predator from either side of the animal's environment. In this context, asymmetry of motor control and coordination would have to offer some advantage beyond those already present in a symmetrical system. Corballis suggested that the advantage of asymmetry for a bipedal animal might be that it allows for planned, manipulative acts, with one hand specializing in the fine details of the act while the other supports and assists the act. In fact, this is exactly how the two hands interrelate to one another in the execution of a skilled bimanual behavior. The dominant hand engages in precise "micrometric" movements while the non-dominant hand plays a complementary role by framing and stabilizing the entire arena of operation using more "macrometric" movements (Guiard, 1987).

How far back in our evolutionary history can handedness be traced? Microwear analysis indicates the presence of a right hand preference in tool use as far back as .5 million years ago (Keeley, 1977; Semenov, 1964), but it is possible that handedness extends further back to the days of the Oldowan tool industry. Hominin skeletal remains dating from around 1.5 million years ago show evidence of structural asymmetries indicative of right handedness (Walker & Leakey, 1993). Toth (1985) studied the orientation angle of the Oldowan flakes dated from 1.4–1.9 million years old and found the proportion of right-oriented flakes exceeded the left-oriented ones by 57 to 43, a ratio nearly identical to that produced when modern right handers set about creating Oldowan tools. In more recent tool samples (approximately 300,000 years old), the ratio was even more pronounced at 61 to 39. These data do not prove that the Oldowan toolmakers were right handed, but they are consistent with the notion that early hominin toolmakers preferentially used their right hands when making tools and that preference may have been growing in strength over time.

Handedness very well may have offered hominins an advantage in manipulative skill that exceeds those of other primates. However, some researchers have gone even further with this line of reasoning, claiming that species-wide right hand preference is a trait unique to humans (Corballis, 1991; MacNeilage, Studdert-Kennedy, & Lindblom, 1987; Wilson, 1998). Indeed, early studies and observations of other animals, including nonhuman primates, tended to confirm this notion. For example, Steklis and Marchant (1987) reported no hand preferences in chimpanzees tested on seven different categories of hand-use tasks. Other studies and observations have shown that primates and other animals often show individual preferences for using a certain hand for a certain task but little evidence of a species-wide trend toward consistently using one hand (Annett, 1985; Annett & Annett, 1991; Bresard & Bresson, 1987; Byrne & Byrne, 1991; Lancaster, 1973). This conclusion has been called into serious question. A series of studies by William Hopkins and colleagues found that chimpanzees often do show a consistent right hand bias in gestural communicative acts, haptic search tasks, and coordinated bimanual manipulative tasks (Hopkins & Leavens, 1998; Hopkins & Rabinowitz, 1997; Lacreuse, Parr, Smith, & Hopkins, 1999). On haptic tasks, a clear evolutionary trend from strong left hand preference in New World Monkeys (spider monkeys and capuchins) to weaker left hand preference in Old World macaques (rhesus) to a clear right hand preference in apes (chimpanzees and humans; Lacreuse et al., 1999) has been observed. In his review of chimpanzee handedness, Hopkins (1996) estimated the ratio of right to left handers at about 2:1, far less than the roughly 8:1 ratio present in humans. Do these results, coupled with Toth's data suggestive of increasing right handedness in hominin toolmaking, indicate an evolutionary trend in handedness and cerebral asymmetry as we move along the primate branch from monkeys to apes to hominids? This is unclear, especially because questions remain as to whether laboratory findings necessarily generalize to hand use or preference in the wild (Marchant & McGrew, 1996). This does suggest, however, that manual asymmetry extends farther back in primate evolution than just the toolmaking hominins and that it has undergone significant alterations over evolutionary time. Like bipedalism, human manual asymmetry may be unique in commitment and degree rather than in mere presence.

Building Meaning Out of Movement

During the 1999 season, the National Football League banned a certain gesture some players engaged in after making a big hit or sacking the quarterback. The gesture involved "slashing" the hand across the throat, as if slitting the neck. Centuries earlier, at the battle of Agincourt (legend has it), the French promised that when their victory was complete they would cut off the fingers of the English bowmen. The French, of course, lost, and the English took great delight in prominently displaying their middle fingers to their vanquished foes, a sign of contempt that persists today among more that just the English. Why would these acts stir such emotion and controversy? The reason is that acts can be more than just motor behaviors, they can be meaningful representations. Human motor control involves not just being able to willfully manipulate the body in ways unmatched by other species but the ability to endow those acts with referential meaning. The acts refer to something else. Somewhere in the course of hominin evolution, some motor behaviors became signs and symbols that others could interpret. It is difficult, if not impossible, to verify exactly when and how this happened. Our accounts may be speculative, but there is no doubt that hominins traveled an evolutionary distance from simple motor reactions to gestural signs distinctive of our species. The ideas that have been proposed to try to fill in that gap may be the first step toward developing testable hypotheses in this area.

Praxis

Gorillas live in harem arrangements in which a single dominant male (silverback) controls a group of females. Because of their large size and energy requirements, the harem spends hour after uneventful hour peacefully munching on leaves as tense primatologists scrutinize and document their every act. So placid and laconic is the gorilla lifestyle that they undeservingly gained a reputation as being slow witted. Gorillas are anything but stupid, however, as anyone who has tried to mimic their food-processing rituals can attest (Byrne, 1996). A favorite gorilla treat are the leaves of giant nettles, the edges of which have sharp stingers that can quickly raise painful welts on the unwary. With relaxed confidence, the average adult gorilla will execute a sequence of maneuvers that separates leaf from plant, folds in its stinging edges, and plops it harmlessly into the mouth. Because nearly everything the gorilla eats requires overcoming piercing, hooking, stinging, or stabbing defenses, different sequences of actions are needed to handle different foods (Byrne, 1993). What is impressive about the gorilla intelligence is not just that they manage to avoid poking themselves while eating, but that they do so by *organizing a sequence of purposeful motor actions*, or by engaging is what is often called **praxis**. Corballis (1991) defined praxis as "internally generated, purposive skills that are unconstrained by the spatial features of the environment....Praxis [involves] the organization of purposeful, sequential actions in which spatial constraints imposed by the environment are minimal" (pp. 197, 213). By this he meant that when one engages in praxis, one's actions are not bound to the spatial features of the environment, as, for example, when one reacts to an oncoming stimulus by blocking it with the hands (Watson & Kimura, 1989). Instead, praxic actions are planned, intentional acts, composed of an ordered sequence of elements and designed to achieve some goal or have some effect on the environment, such as throwing a dart, catching a Frisbee between the legs, or (as with the gorilla) getting at a tasty morsel while avoiding its prickers.

Along with primates, a number of other animals probably also possess praxic skills, including birds with songs that entail a highly complex ordered sequence of motor behaviors. Praxis, therefore, is not a uniquely human trait but one that was likely present in our common ancestors at the commencement of hominin evolution. What is different about praxis in humans is that we are able to use it *generatively*. That is, humans have evolved the ability to not only purposefully order a sequence of motor actions but to deconstruct the sequence into its elements, refine the elements singly, and recombine them in novel ways. It was **generative praxis** that our puddle-hopping child at the beginning of the chapter was expressing. Corballis (1991) argued that it is this generative ability that is unique to humans and forms the foundation of our distinctive motor capabilities, including language. It is this generative capacity that allows humans to practice and refine motor routines, making them more efficient and making us more skillful. With generative praxis, our hominin ancestors could refine their toolmaking, hunting, and communicative skills, and pass these along to others.

Corballis saw the evolution of generative praxic skill proceeding slowly over the course of hominin evolution, punctuated by two important events involving the "freeing" of the hands. First, with bipedalism, the hands were freed from locomotion and could be applied to toolmaking and gestural communication. This, he believed, accounts for the tool technologies and cooperative social system of *H. erectus*. With *H. sapiens*, the hands were freed from primary communicative responsibility as largely gestural language gave way to largely vocal language, an event that helped precipitate the Upper Paleolithic "leap" (Corballis, 1999). From an evolutionary feedback loop, involving the expanding manipulative capacities of the hands and the inflating hominin brain, emerged a generative mind capable of analytically decomposing representations, refining and manipulating elemental components, and synthetically recombining components to form novel (and often improved) structures. A modern chimpanzee is probably no better at fashioning a termite-dipping stick than its ancestors a million years ago, but hominin technical skills did progress (often excruciatingly slowly, to be sure) over the course of our evolution. The gleeful splish-splashing of a child is one of the reasons why.

Throwing

Praxis represents a level of intentional motor control that goes beyond simply reacting to the environment. Instead, a sequence of actions is planned to affect the environment in some way. Calvin (1983, 1993) argued that with the advent of hominin bipedalism, the praxic act of throwing took on important evolutionary significance. Calvin began his argument by noting the fact that throwing is not easy, as evidenced by the lack of skill demonstrated by our primate cousins. Chimpanzees will sometimes throw rocks or branches as part of their aggressive displays. They rarely employ throwing as part of their hunting repertoire and for good reason: they're lousy at it (Lawick-Goodall, 1968; Plooij, 1978). Jane Goodall reported that on only 4 of 55 occasions did a thrown object actually hit an intended target (another animal), and all the hits were from distances of 6 ft or less (for more on primate/human throwing, see Box 6.3). In addition, no evidence suggests that apes or other primates practice their throwing skills to increase their accuracy (Donald, 1999). From the vast array of ancient spears and other hurled weapons and hunting implements, it is evident that our hominin ancestors achieved an unparalleled level of throwing prowess—one that probably exceeded that of cur-

Comparing Throwing in the Human and Monkey

BOX 6.3 Despite the emphasis placed on the importance of throwing in human evolution, few studies have actually performed cross-species comparisons of human and nonhuman primate throwing. One recent study, however, directly compared human throwing with that of capuchin monkeys (Westergaard, Liv, Haynie, & Suomi, 2000). Capuchin monkeys were chosen because of their highly developed manipulative skill. Moreover, unlike many apes (including chimpanzees), capuchins are full-time tree-dwellers, which means that they have a high degree of shoulder and arm rotation, useful both for swinging from branches and making a throwing motion. Of interest in this study was how accurate capuchins would be compared with humans, as well as the degree to which the monkeys would (1) throw overhand compared with underhand, (2) throw using a bipedal posture, (3) and show sex differences in throwing accuracy.

Twenty-five capuchins (17 males, 8 females) were allowed to throw stones at a bucket that was placed either 30 or 60 cm away. The bucket was filled with sweet syrup, and, if the monkey threw the stone into the bucket, he or she was allowed to lick the syrup from the stone as a reward. Twenty-five humans (13 males, 12 females) were tested in a similar manner; however, they threw a tennis ball into an empty bucket.

The results showed a number of important differences between the monkeys and humans. First, to equate general accuracy of throwing, humans were required to throw at buckets that were 300 or 600 cm away, 10 times farther in distance than the monkeys. Figure 6.A shows the handedness index calculated for both monkeys and humans, with positive scores indicating a tendency to use the right hand for throwing, whereas negative scores indicate a tendency to use the left hand. Humans showed a high positive score (indicating a strong right hand preference) and monkeys scored zero (no preference). Figure 6.B shows scores for the bipedal index or the tendency to assume a bipedal posture when throwing. Note again the significantly higher score for humans compared with monkeys. Figure 6.C shows scores for the overhand throwing index, which shows significantly higher scores for monkeys compared with humans.

A significant sex difference in throwing accuracy also was found for humans, with males having an accuracy index of .58 compared with a .44 for females (higher scores indicate more accurate throwing). Monkeys showed no significant difference in throwing accuracy between males and females.

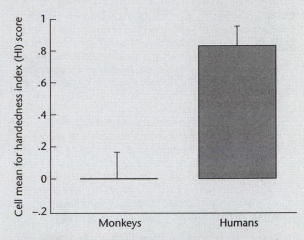

Figure 6.A Mean handedness index scores for monkeys and humans. Higher scores indicate right hand preference. Note how monkeys show virtually no handedness preference in throwing. (Adapted from Westergaard et al., 2000.)

The authors pointed to both the sex difference finding and the differences in overarm throwing as potentially significant in understanding the evolution of human throwing and motor control:

> The finding of a sex difference for throwing accuracy in humans but not in monkeys is noteworthy in view of research which has shown consistently that human males throw more accurately than do human females, independent of throwing or sporting experience, differences in strength or physique, or gender identity,

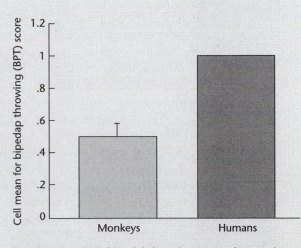

Figure 6.B Mean bipedal throwing scores for monkeys and humans. (Adapted from Westergaard et al., 2000.)

continued

Comparing Throwing in the Human and Monkey (continued)

BOX 6.3 suggesting that biology accounts for a greater percentage of variance in this realm than do differences in environment. A similar sex difference in throwing accuracy has been noted in research on boys and girls between 3 and 5 years of age, indicating that male superiority for throwing emerges early in life, although it must be noted that this sex difference was not found for perceptual tasks with less motor involvement. Our data suggest that the advantage for throwing accuracy in human males over human females does not extend to our nonhuman primate relations....The finding of interspecific differences in rates of overhand throwing vs. underarm throwing suggests that shoulder and arm rotation may have played an important role in evolutionary divergence of controlled ballistic movements among primates. (Westergaard et al., 2000, p. 1516)

The authors point to their findings to stress two points. (1) Over the course of hominin evolution there most likely was selection pressure on males to develop throwing skills. This same pressure was not present for hominin females. This supports the notion that hominin males and females were dividing up the labors of life, with men hunting (thus throwing rocks and spears at prey) and women gathering. Because this same division of labor is not present in monkeys, differences in throwing ability would not be expected. (2) Differences in throwing ability among different primate species (monkeys,

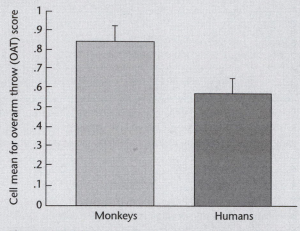

Figure 6.C Mean overarm throwing index scores. Note that monkeys show significantly higher tendency to throw overarm compared with humans.

apes, humans) also appear to be related to the rotational capacities of the shoulders and arms, which also differ among primate species by virtue of their lifestyles.

Studies such as these will continue to help to determine the viability of the throwing hypothesis and its significance in human evolution.

Source: **Westergaard, G.C., Liv, C., Haynie, M.K., Suomi, S.J. (2000)**. A comparative study of aimed throwing by monkeys and humans. Neuropsychologia, 38, 1511–1517.

---

rent humans (Isaac, 1987; Calvin even argued that the Acheulean hand axe may have been used as a "Frisbee-type" hunting instrument). Assuming our common ancestor possessed a gross threat throwing ability similar to that of modern chimps, then, over the course of hominin evolution, the move from unrefined and inaccurate threat throwing to a more precise predatory throwing ability was an important evolutionary achievement in motor control (Plooij, 1978).

This change was not simple. Calvin has shown that to hit an object such as a rabbit from a distance of 4 m (about 13 ft), the **"launch window"** is a mere 11 ms (11 thousandths of a second). The launch window refers to the point in the throwing motion at which the thrower must release the projectile for its trajectory to intersect with the target. Releasing too soon causes the projectile to sail over the target, and releasing too late leaves the projectile short of the target (see Calvin, 1983, for details). Increasing the target distance to 8 m shrinks the launch window to a mere 1.4 ms. This represents a serious problem for the mammalian nervous system, in that the degree of timing accuracy necessary to execute the throw is beyond the capacity of individual motor neurons. Moreover, the sequence of actions is executed too quickly for feedback mechanisms to make any adjustments once the action is initiated. The entire throwing plan must be mapped out ahead of time and run off ballistically. However, these problems can be overcome by using a large population of neurons and averaging their timing estimates. The timing error or jitter associated with spinal motor neurons is about equal to the 11-ms launch window when a target is at 4 m. Doubling the distance requires an eightfold decrease in jitter, which requires 64 times as many neurons working together. To obtain the timing accuracy necessary when the target distance is tripled requires 729 times as many neurons. Throwing stones to hunt down small animals may have been one of the catalysts in hominin brain expansion. However, it would not have been a bigger brain per se that was critical in developing throwing skills but the ability to temporarily recruit a large population of nerve cells for a specific task, similar to the passages on which the audience joins in on the Hallelujah Chorus. This "recruiting" may be accomplished more easily by a brain that goes through a prolonged period of postnatal development (Calvin, 1990).

In a series of experiments, Hammond (1990) demonstrated the importance of timing control in manual tapping and aiming tasks. Marzke's (1986, 1996) analysis of the hand of *A. afarensis* shows that it was capable of the grips necessary for potentially accurate, lethal throwing. Spears dating back 400,000 years confirm the long history of projectile use in hominin hunting (Thieme, 1997). Although these findings offer some support for Calvin's view linking throwing to hominin brain evolution, they by no means provide empirical validation for his scenario. In fact, it is unclear whether Calvin's evolutionary story can be tested in any satisfactory fashion.

Nevertheless, other researchers have found the throwing hypothesis useful in understanding other aspects of human motor and social behavior. In a far-reaching theory of human uniqueness, Paul Bingham (1999) cited the evolution of accurate throwing as a pivotal and foundational moment in the history of our species. Other animals can form cooperative groups, but their size and effectiveness are sorely limited by the group's inability to restrain the uncooperative, selfish tendencies of individual members. Accurate throwing, however, gave hominins the capacity for inflicting injury or death at a distance, thus greatly decreasing the risk to group members bent on punishing a noncooperator. Put simply, when "stoning" emerged as an effective group strategy for curbing destabilizing individualism, hominins began to reap unprecedented benefits from expanded group cooperation. This event, according to Bingham, was the launching pad for all the uniquely human abilities in language, adaptability, social organization, and technical skill. Bingham's intriguing theory will be discussed more thoroughly in a later chapter.

Noble and Davidson (1996) contended that the throwing act could have provided the link between motor behaviors and informative gestures or signs. The end posture of the throwing motion leaves the thrower's arm (and possibly finger) oriented toward the target. To another hominin observing the thrower, the end posture could constitute gestural information about the location of the target. This pointing posture could then be reproduced in other contexts with its meaning still attached, indicating the location of a tool, a predator, or a half-buried root. Natural selection may first have favored the motor abilities associated with accurate throwing, but it may not have been long before similar motor skills put in the service of communication also came under selection pressure.

Pointing

Another factor that has served to focus attention on the throwing/pointing act is the fact that humans are unique among primates in their use of this behavior. Although humans and apes share many motor acts in common, pointing is not one of them. No incidents have been reported of wild apes pointing to distant objects to draw the attention of conspecifics to that object (Tomasello & Call, 1997). Apes raised with humans, however, show a more sophisticated understanding of pointing and can use it to manipulate attention in a fashion similar to humans (Call & Tomasello, 1994a; Miles, 1990; Savage-Rumbaugh, 1984; Savage-Rumbaugh, McDonald, Sevcik, Hopkins, & Rupert, 1986). Even so, a number of differences between human and ape pointing have been identified. First, the ape pointing gesture is not the same as the human's. Humans extend the arm and index finger toward the target, whereas apes engage in a more gross arm–hand extension. Second, although apes interact effectively with other humans using pointing, other apes tend not to respond to such pointing. Savage-Rumbaugh (1984) reported that Kanzi's wild-born foster parents did not react to his pointing, but humans did. Third, evidence suggests that, when trained to point, apes fail to generalize the pointing gesture much beyond the training context. They fail to appreciate the attentional status of the human to whom they directed the act (i.e., the ape may point equally whether the human witnessing the pointing has his or her eyes open or closed). These problems, however, were absent in an ape who learned to point not by specific training but by being raised in a human culture (Call & Tomasello, 1994). Finally, Povinelli (Povinelli, Reaux, Bierschwale, Allain, & Simon, 1997; see also Povinelli, 2000, pp. 50–54) presented experimental data suggesting that chimpanzees fail to appreciate the referential aspect of pointing and, instead, rely on distance cues when determining how to respond to a pointing act. For example, when an experimenter pointed to a more distant goal but his pointing finger was physically closer to another goal, the chimps consistently went to the goal closer to the experimenter's finger.

Collectively, these differences suggest that apes and humans do not regard the pointing gesture in the same way and that the social context of each plays an important role in this difference. Apes may be capable of producing the act (or an approximation of it), but they do not live in a society that endows the act with representational meaning. In the course of hominin evolution, motor control evolved not just as a means of producing ever-more sophisticated and flexible behaviors but as a means of social communication and information exchange. The external, social context was as important in the evolutionary process as the internal, biomechanical one.

Mimesis

Praxic acts are intentionally ordered sequences, but they need not be representational. Mimetic acts are different in this respect; they are representational. Throwing is praxic. Pointing is mimetic in that it represents location or conveys meaning to another about location. The throwing movement could be mimetic if it were used to represent something, such as a child pretending to be baseball pitcher. Mimesis is also holistic and supramodal in its representational nature. What this means is that the entire act carries the meaning, and the meaning of that act could be embodied in a variety of different ways or modes. For example, imagine that you wish to convey a rhythmic pattern to another. That rhythm would be captured by the entire sequence of movements in which you engage, and it could be embodied in many different modes, such as drumming the fingers, bobbing the head, swinging and swaying the hips, or tapping the toes (Donald, 1999).

Merlin Donald (1991) contended that mimesis constitutes an autonomous cognitive system upon which other high-level systems, such as linguistics and symbolism, are based. In support of this view, he pointed to empirical evidence, such as the fact that some epileptic patients can lose all linguistic capacity and yet retain a remarkable degree of conscious awareness, problem-solving skills, and communicative and social abilities, all of which are rooted in the still-functional memetic system (Lecours & Joanette, 1980). Shaller (1991) confirmed these findings in her studies of deaf subjects who, despite not having acquired sign language or other linguistic capacities, demonstrated proficiency in social skills, mechanical repair, spatial cognition, and money handling. In addition, for centuries deaf–mutes have managed to function (sometimes quite well) in the complete absence of any linguistic ability or training (Lane, 1984). Finally, studies with brain-damaged individuals confirmed that mimetic gestures, such as pantomiming, are neurologically separable from linguistic gestures, such as sign language (Hickok, Bellugi, & Klima, 1996). Thus, Donald concluded, before language and symbolic thought there was mimesis, and it was the evolution of mimesis that started hominins on the path to becoming human.

Once integrated into an organism's motor repertoire, mimesis could be extraordinarily powerful. Because mimesis subsumes generative praxic ability, it can be used as a vehicle for perfecting and elaborating motor routines and transmitting those skills to others. Of even greater significance is that mimesis, because of its representational nature, would have been a powerful tool for social and cultural cohesion. Mimesis allows for such activities as group ritual, dance, and ceremony, and it enriches these by enhancing their intentional and emotional content. Donald (1991) believed that the evolution of mimetic skill explains a nagging paradox associated with *H. erectus*. This hominin possessed a brain about 80% as large as the modern human brain. Moreover, erectus fashioned tools, hunted, used fire, lived cooperatively in groups, embarked on the first hominin global migration in history, and successfully adapted for nearly 1 million years to a myriad of different environments. It seems implausible that these achievements could have come in the absence of language. Yet, as we discussed earlier, the anatomy of Turkana Boy militates against the presence of (at least spoken) language. Therein lies the paradox. According to Donald, this paradox dissolves if we accept that the culture of erectus was not linguistic but mimetic. It was with mimeses that erectus formed socially coherent communities, communicated intentions and desires, learned and passed on technical skills, and constructed the intellect necessary for global mobility and long-term success. Mimeses is still with us today in the meaning-enhancing gestures that accompany speech, in pantomime, and in the role-assuming play of children. The next time you "read" someone's body language, remember that you may be accessing a million-year-old form of intelligence that at one time was the organizing force of hominin life.

The Frontal Lobes and Free Will

One of the hallmarks of hominin brain evolution was the massive expansion of the frontal lobes. Deacon (1997) termed this "frontalization," highlighting the fact that, in humans, connections from the frontal lobe have invaded and established themselves in parts of the nervous system that are under subcortical control in other primates. For example, in most mammals, connections from the cerebral cortex to the brainstem motor nuclei controlling the muscles of the face, tongue, and larynx are relatively sparse and restricted to indirect access via the reticular premotor region. This means that, for most mammals, control of vocalizations is subcortical and involuntary. In nonhuman primates, because of the expanded frontal cortex, cortical connections to the brainstem are significantly greater and allow for conscious control of the face, mouth, and tongue. However, this control does not appear to extend to the vocal apparatus. Cortical damage does not disrupt vocalizations in monkeys, although in humans it can produce muteness (Jurgens, Kirzinger, & von Cramon, 1982). Observations of chimpanzee vocalizations indicate that they are bound to and triggered by emotional states. Goodall reported: "Chimpanzee vocalizations are closely bound to emotions. The production of a sound in the *absence* of the appropriate emotional state seems to be an almost impossible task for a chimpanzee" (Goodall, 1986, p. 125). There is some indication that food calls may be under more direct voluntary control. The exceptional bonobo Kanzi apparently can produce some distinctive vocalizations voluntarily (Hauser, Teixidor, Field, & Flaherty, 1993; Hopkins & Savage-Rumbaugh, 1991). However, no other primate exerts the degree of conscious, voluntary control over the vocal structures that humans do, a fact that Deacon attributed to the massive degree of cortical imposition on the brainstem nuclei regulating larynx and breathing function.

Mounting evidence suggests that our frontal lobes may be responsible for more than just an increased capacity to consciously control vocalizations. They may be the very seat of our ability to act according to goals and intentions rather than just reacting to environmental stimuli. MacKay (1987) developed a hierarchical model of motor control, at the highest level of which we conceptualize the action we wish to carry out. This concept reflects our intention, the result we wish to obtain from the motor routines that are implemented. Empirical evidence supports the notion that this highest level of motor control depends on activity in the frontal lobe. Studies monitoring cerebral blood flow indicate that, as a motor task becomes more complex, more areas of the frontal lobe become active, reflecting the activation of an abstract motor plan or a possible series of different plans vying for implementation. Moreover, if one is required to simply imagine a motor act, parts of the supplementary motor area of the frontal lobe become active (Roland, 1993). A recent analysis of the evolution of mammalian brain organization has shown that in primates a significant relative expansion occurred in those frontal lobe structures at the very "top" of the motor control hierarchy (Winter & Oxnard, 2001). Thus, in primates and especially humans, the capacity to voluntarily regulate and execute *intentional* (rather than reflexive) motor behaviors is highly developed.

Even more intriguing are findings by Lhermitte (Lhermitte, 1983; Lhermitte, Pillon, & Serdaru, 1986) that suggest that free will itself may have evolved over the course of primate frontal lobe expansion. His studies indicated that patients with prefrontal lobe damage would engage almost robotically in imitative and sometimes socially inappropriate motor behaviors. For example, if Lhermitte placed a hammer and nails on a table, the patient would spontaneously pick up the hammer and begin pounding the nails into the wall. In another instance, Lhermitte placed a hypodermic needle on a table and turned his back on the patient, who dutifully got up and gave the doctor a shot in his backside! Lhermitte argued that many complex motor routines may be stored in the brain and are simply "run off" in the presence of the right environmental context. It is not uncommon for the average person to do this. An example would be the act of putting the milk carton back in the refrigerator *before* pouring it in a glass. The sight of the milk carton on the counter triggered the stored motor routine. If we are capable of simply executing mindless motor patterns when a triggering stimulus is present, then why don't we do it all the time? Lhermitte claimed that it is the frontal lobe that holds stored motor patterns in reserve until we can determine whether the behaviors are appropriate to the social situation or are in accordance with our goals and intentions. In essence, the frontal lobe "frees" one from being a robot and allows conscious awareness and deliberation to affect how we behave.

The point is not that most other animals are robots and only humans have the capacity to freely choose our actions. Instead, it is that the frontal lobe may be critical to the conscious control of behavior. Over the course of hominin evolution, the frontal lobe has enlarged dramatically, allowing humans a degree of "free will" unparalleled in history. We probably will never know exactly when hominins achieved the motor capacity that allowed them to dance, march, and sing or when they realized they could choose not to act. Most likely it was a long, slow progression from stereotyped, reflexive action to the first accusatory finger point or the first tentative handshake. The hominins who breached those frontiers are long gone, but the rewards of that journey are with us in the form of a top-heavy brain that affords the capacity to think before we act, sculpt the way we act, and endow our actions with profound meaning.

The Freedom to Act

It was the summer of 1965, and Commander Jeremiah "Jerry" Denton was leading a group of 28 aircraft from the USS *Independence* on a mission attacking enemy installations near the North Vietnamese city of Thanh Hoa. Commander Denton was shot down and taken prisoner by the North Vietnamese. He spent the next 7.5 years as a prisoner of war, suffering humiliation, deprivation, and torture, including a nightmarish 4 years of solitary confinement.

On May 17, 1966, prisoner Denton was paraded before news cameras by his captors and instructed to answer questions "properly and politely," which he did. But as his mouth droned, "I don't know what is happening now in Vietnam....my only news sources are North Vietnamese....," his eyes blinked out the message "torture" in Morse code. It was a startling demonstration of courage, as well as an impressive display of motor control. Only a human can do that! Then again, only humans can wage the wars and forge the tools of torture that put Commander Denton in that situation in the first place. The freedom to act cuts both ways. Compassion's tender touch is matched act for act by anger's smashing fist in the full sweep of human willfulness.

SUMMARY

The most salient cue to identifying the human is our upright, two-legged posture and locomotion—our bipedalism. Humans literally stand alone as the committed bipedal apes. Human-evolved anatomical structures, such as the adducted big toe, the curving of the lumbar region of the spine, and the more centrally oriented positioning of the foramen magnum, are only a few qualities contributing to the bipedalism of modern humans. It is probably the case that a number of different factors combined to make bipedalism advantageous for early hominins, including energy efficiency, the ability to threaten rivals, and the freeing of the hands.

Another significant advance in motor control occurred in the evolution of the precise, manipulative skill of the human hand. Loosed from the contraints of locomotion, hominin hands became committed manipulative tools with a range of grips exceeding those of our primate cousins. As hominins used their hands and bodies, praxic skill, or the voluntary sequencing of goal-directed acts, evolved to unparalleled heights, and the ability to endow movement with meaning (mimesis) emerged. With the dramatic enlargement of the frontal lobe, conscious control of movement and "free will" were greatly enhanced in humans.

KEY TERMS

five-jawed cradle	oblique power grip	stance phase
foramen magnum	pad-to-side grip	swing phase
generative praxis	percussion technique	three-jawed chuck grip
mimesis	praxis	valgus angle

REVIEW QUESTIONS

1. What are some of the different factors that may have contributed to modern man's committed bipedalism?

2. What types of evidence have been found in Australopiths to refute Lovejoy's contention that they were committed terrestrial bipeds? What type of locomotion does this evidence point to?

3. How is praxis behavior different in humans and animals? What type of behavior was the puddle-jumping child involved in?

4. Explain the differences between praxic and mimetic behavior.

5. According to Dr. Lhermitte, free will evolved with the expansion of the frontal lobe. What does he believe occurs when a stored motor routine is present?

SUGGESTED READINGS

Corballis, M. (1991). *The lopsided ape.* Oxford: Oxford University Press.

Donald, M. (1991). *Origins of the modern mind.* Cambridge MA: Harvard University Press.

Wilson, F. (1998). *The hand: How its use shapes the brain, language, and human culture.* NY: Pantheon Books.

WEB SITES

www.handprint.com/LS/ANC/evol.html deals with human evolution with links to the hominin brain, hominin tools, and others.

www.janegoodall.org/chimps/index.html in depth look at chimpanzees' physical characteristics, habitat, communication, and social structure.

www.eatonhand.com/hom/hom033.htm the international hand library, a complete hand

7

The Function and Evolution of Emotions

Revisiting the Rational Soul

PHILOSOPHERS IN ANCIENT TIMES attributed human uniqueness to our rational souls. Rationality kept the animal passions in check. Without the rational soul, humans reverted to nothing more than primitive, callous beasts. These philosophers saw a clear distinction between rationality and passion and between thought and emotion and clearly viewed one (rationality) as superior to the other (emotion). Modern society, for the most part, has accepted this traditional dichotomy. For example, cognitive psychology defines itself as the study of thought. Of the 12 cognitive psychology texts on my shelf published from 1995 on, only one has a chapter on emotion. We tend to hold in high regard those who write books on physics and mathematics but look down our noses at those who pen romance novels. When science fiction envisions "advanced" life forms, these are typically broad-headed, intellectualized creatures who have evolved beyond the need for emotional expression (think *Star Trek*!). Like the philosophers before us, we continue to draw a firm distinction between the emotional and the rational, confidently trusting the latter, suspicious of the former. But is the emotional/rational distinction warranted? Could it be that emotions are just as responsible as rational thought for our uniquely human qualities? Even more provocative, is it possible that human intellect, in fact, is based upon emotion and cannot function properly without it? Consider the following examples.

1. Neuroscientist Antonio Damasio (1994) described the case of Elliot, a patient who suffered from a frontal lobe brain tumor that required surgical removal. Before the surgery, Elliot was a devoted husband and father, a responsible professional, and a well-respected community member and role model. The surgery had no direct negative effects on his intellectual functioning; he performed at levels above average to superior on measures of intelligence, working memory, and long-term memory. But the surgery left his intellect strangely disassociated from his emotions. This, in turn, left him unable to function adaptively in his social world. Elliot had no motivation to get up and go to work. He was entirely unable to keep to any schedule. When at work, he became easily distracted, often losing hours on meaningless tasks and failing to progress on important goals. After losing

137

his job, he embarked on a series of unwise, risky ventures that ultimately left him bankrupt, divorced, and isolated. Although Elliot was fully aware of the ways in which his actions (and inactions) had led to destructive consequences and of the suffering he caused himself and others, he seemed utterly incapable of changing. He would dispassionately discuss his failings with no hint of personal involvement, as if he were describing someone else's misfortunes. His detached rationality made him completely dysfunctional and left his life and the lives of those who cared for him in shambles.

2. In experiments assessing the decision-making abilities of patients with frontal lobe damage similar that of Elliot, both healthy and brain-damaged subjects were presented with different decks of cards that described either a payoff sum (e.g., "win $50") or a payment sum (e.g., "lose $100"). The point of the game was to maximize one's accumulated money (Bechara, Damasio, Damasio, & Anderson, 1994; Bechara, Tranel, Damasio, & Damasio, 1993; Damasio, 1994). Some decks of cards contained large payoff and payment sums (risky decks), and others had smaller quantities (conservative decks). Through trial and error, normal subjects adopted a successful strategy of avoiding the riskier decks and concentrating on the conservative ones. These subjects also produced an anticipatory galvanic skin response (GSR; sweaty palms) to the mere thought of picking from the risky deck. Thus, their emotional response guided their decision making even before they were fully conscious of why they were doing what they did. In the brain-damaged subjects, whose emotions and intellect were more disassociated, the more successful conservative strategy was never adopted (even after subjects were made aware of it), and the anticipatory GSR responses were not produced. Again, this "freeing" of thought from emotion proved to be more of an impairment than an advantage.

3. Emotion may play a critical role in moral as well as intellectual functioning. When presented with slides depicting disturbing images of suffering and murder, normal subjects and subjects with nonfrontal lobe brain damage showed large GSR responses, indicating emotional arousal. Patients with frontal lobe damage showed no GSR changes and remained troublingly undisturbed by the images. One subject even commented afterwards that he knew he *should* feel something, but he just did not (Damasio, 1994; Damasio, Tranel, & Damasio, 1991).

It often goes unappreciated that one of Western culture's most well known moral parables is an *emotional* appeal to ethical behavior, not an intellectual one. In the story of the Good Samaritan, a priest and a Levite first pass by the wounded stranger and offer no aid. As highly respected members of the religious establishment, they would have been fully versed in Judaism's various laws. In fact, it was most likely the laws requiring one to remain ritually pure that helped them justify their nonintervention. Knowledge of laws played very little into the reaction of the Samaritan, however, for we are told that he was "moved to pity" at the sight of the beaten, naked man.

The moral of all this may be that cold rationality is strangely *soulless*. Even Thomas Aquinas, one of the foremost proponents of the rational soul, recognized that our attraction to the good is a yearning, not a calculation. Intellectual understanding of moral codes is useless without the compassion to animate them. These examples are presented to dispel the idea of emotions as nothing but primal energies bent on vice and destruction unless restrained by the higher, more rational angels of our nature. Instead, we should view emotions as working in concert with our "higher intellect" to facilitate adaptive functioning. Rather than being animalistic relics worthy only of suppression, our emotions should be understood as a form of evolved, adaptive knowledge, honed by thousands of years of evolution. It may seem strange to speak of emotions as knowledge or as a type of intelligence, but as we'll see in this chapter and the next, emotions inform us about how to fit and function within the environment, just as our eyes, hands, and memories do (Plotkin, 1994).

Emotions as Evolved Knowledge

We can define knowledge from an evolutionary perspective as any physical state of the organism that allows it to adaptively relate to its environment (Plotkin, 1994, p. 117). How then do creatures come to adaptively "know" about their environments? One of the earliest means of gaining some practical knowledge about the external world arose in single-celled organisms more than 3 billion years ago in the form of **chemotaxis**. This involved simply sensing the presence of certain chemicals and moving either toward or away from them. A very primitive and highly restricted form of knowledge, to be sure, but still quite functional, given the needs of the organism. What about organisms with far more broad-ranging needs?

Monkeys have highly developed visual systems that are similar in many respects to those of humans. When the part of the temporal lobe involved in form and pattern recognition is disconnected from the brain's emotional center (the amygdala), an interesting form of "psychic blindness" occurs (Jones & Mishkin, 1972). Although the monkey's visual acuity is largely unaffected, it nevertheless fails to appreciate the affective quality of what it sees. Previously threatening stimuli, such as snakes or the handler's net, now elicit little or no reaction. Bad-tasting and inedible objects are placed into the mouth as readily as sweet-tasting treats. The monkey can see quite well, but the adaptive significance of what it sees has been stripped away. The monkey has lost its "street smarts" (or jungle smarts), which come in the form of the *emotion* associated with each visual pattern. This example shows clearly that emotions inform the organism about how to adaptively relate to the environment.

As an evolved form of knowledge about the environment, emotions perform four important functions: (1) they filter and amplify the fitness-relevant information from the environment; (2) they serve as honest signals about an organism's internal state; (3) they regulate social interactions; and (4) they act as superordinate regulatory programs for directing behaviors. We will look at each of these in more detail.

Emotions as Filters and Amplifiers

Our sensory systems are being bombarded constantly with more environmental signals than can be processed. To function effectively in the environment, we must be able to filter incoming information, attending to and processing the most relevant and discarding the rest. The emotional significance of an incoming signal is an important factor in determining if (or how deeply) it penetrates into the cognitive system. A dramatic example comes from studies of eyewitness accounts of crimes, in which recollections are often narrowly limited to the assailant's weapon. This phenomena, known as weapon focus, has been observed in both naturalistic and laboratory settings and often results in highly detailed recall of the weapon used to commit a crime but poor recall of the individual responsible for the act (Burke, Heuer, & Reisberg, 1992; Christianson, 1992; Steblay, 1992). This is just one instance of a way in which emotional arousal can cause a "narrowing" of attention so that mental energy is concentrated on only a few aspects of the environment (Easterbrook, 1959).

One study has shed light on the physiological mechanism behind the process of emotional filtering (Anderson & Phelps, 2001). In this study, subjects were shown a series of rapidly presented words in black ink, with a few appearing in green. Subjects were told to be on the lookout for the green words. In this type of situation, subjects usually are "keyed up" to detect the target (in this case, green) words. Once a target is found, the subject often relaxes momentarily. Thus, if two target words appear in succession, processing of the second is often impaired (this is referred to as "attentional blink"). As expected, when a pair of green words appeared sequentially, processing of the second was impaired. However, this attentional blink effect was overcome if the second word was an emotionally charged word, such as "rape" or "cancer." Thus, the emotional content of the word seemed to re-energize the subject's attentional focus in a way that emotionally neutral words did not. In addition, this study found that patients with lesions in the brain's amygdala, especially the left amygdala, continued to show the attentional blink effect even when highly emotional words were presented. The amygdala is an important emotion-generating center in the brain. These results demonstrate that emotional responding (via the amygdala) serves to energize and focus attention on relevant aspects of the environment, leaving other aspects of the environment "in the dark."

Emotion not only serves to filter the environment for relevant information but also to enhance or amplify the experience of that information. As an example, take pigs and truffles. Those who make their living by gathering truffles from the countryside and selling them to expensive restaurants often use trained pigs to help in their search. Certain female pigs are not only sensitive to the presence of truffles but show such a degree of hypersensitivity that they can locate a truffle even when it is buried up to a meter deep in the ground. It turns out that the truffles have a chemical similar to that emitted by male pigs when mating. What goes unnoticed by the rest of us is as loud as a siren's song to a passionate sow (Claus, Hoppen, & Karg, 1981). Similar effects can also be found in humans. Psychophysical experiments show that when making emotionally neutral judgments, such as estimating the length of a line, humans are pretty accurate. However, when the stimulus causes an emotional reaction, such as pain, our experience of the stimulus expands exponentially. For example, the discomfort we experience from electric shock increases more rapidly than the actual physical increases in shock intensity. Thus, doubling the intensity of a shock from say, 5 to 10 volts, would more than double the perceived pain (Stevens, 1961). Victor Johnston (1999) used the term **discriminative hedonic amplifiers** to describe the filtering and amplifying functions of feelings. He summarized it this way:

> ...qualitatively different feelings arise from environmental contingencies that fore-shadow fluctuations in different aspects of reproductive success....In this manner our feelings act like active filters, or what I call discriminant hedonic amplifiers, that define and exaggerate the reproductive consequences of environmental or social events associated with relatively minor fluctuations in reproductive potential.
>
> (Johnston, 1999; p. 83)

Emotions as Honest Signals

It is difficult *not* to express emotions. This is Jane Goodall's account of Figan, an adolescent male chimpanzee, whose difficulty in containing his emotions proved disadvantageous:

> On one occasion, when Figan was an adolescent, he waited in camp until the senior males had left and we were able to give him some bananas (he had had none before). His excited food calls quickly brought the big males racing back and Figan lost his fruit. A few days later he waited behind again, and once more received his bananas. He made no loud sounds, but the calls could be heard deep in his throat, almost causing him to gag.
>
> (Goodall, 1986, p. 125)

Humans are no different. Although we struggle mightily to contain and conceal our emotions, they often present themselves involuntarily in the form of a quiver in the voice, a blush of the face, or a dilation of the pupils (the reason that some professional card players wear sunglasses indoors). When we tell a lie, microexpressions in the face and voice escape to the surface, threatening to expose our deception (Ekman, 1992). Our smile to the camera never looks quite right, because it is a voluntary smile, not the involuntary smile elicited by an unexpected pleasure or a friendly joke (or, as the 19th-century scientist Guillaume-Benjamin Duchenne put it, the smile of politeness versus the sweet smile of the soul). In fact, Gazzaniga and Smylie (1990) showed that different parts of the brain are used to create these two expressions. Evolutionary psychologist Steven Pinker (1997) argued that it is by evolutionary design that our intellects abdicate their hegemony to the emotions so they can serve as authentic and reliable indicators of our intentions. This is a rather complicated way of saying that emotions serve as **honest signals** about one's internal state (for more about emotions as honest signals, see Box 7.1).

Honest signaling could hold fitness advantages for both the signaler and those close to the signaler, who, over the course of our evolutionary history, were likely to be genetic relatives. Because emotional displays provide a window into one's thoughts and intentions, they make it more difficult to practice deception, such as cheating on one's mate. A hominin of the ancient past would have been smart, then, to choose a mate who easily displayed emotion rather than one who was stoic and whose internal state rarely showed itself. Turning this around, it means that over the course of our evolution, those hominins who blushed easily, whose voices quivered when they lied, or who in other ways could not help but "give themselves away" would have been in great demand as mates. Their uncontrollable "emotional" honesty would have bought them individual fitness advantages.

PAUL EKMAN
Human Emotions

PROFILE *Dr. Paul Ekman is currently a professor of psychology in the Department of Psychiatry at the University of California Medical School in San Francisco. He earned his Ph.D. from Adelphi University in 1958 and shortly thereafter was drafted into the Army. From 1958 to 1960, he served as the chief psychologist at Fort Dix, New Jersey. After his discharge, he took a postdoctoral position at the University of California that eventually led to a full-time position. In 1972, he was appointed professor.*

BOX 7.1

Emotions as Honest Signals

In more than three decades of studying human emotions and emotional expressions, Paul Ekman has made a number of significant contributions to our understanding of the nature and importance of emotions. In the 1970s, he explored the universality of emotional expressions. His studies showed that the expressions used to convey such emotions as anger, fear, disgust, and happiness were the same across a wide variety of cultures. This finding supported the notion that human emotional expressions serve as species-specific signals about another's internal state.

More recently, Ekman's research has looked closely at the *honesty* part of the honest signaling element in human emotions. Although humans have evolved a potent capacity for deception, our emotions retain much of their honest signaling function as well. This means that even among those who are skilled liars, evidence of their deception (no matter how subtle) should be present in their unconscious emotional expressions. In his book *Telling Lies*, Ekman reviewed considerable research showing that when we lie, we often provide faint (and sometimes not so faint) cues to our deception. One such cue is a **microexpression**. A microexpression is a brief, often incomplete emotional expression that manifests itself before a person's conscious processing can extinguish it. J.J. Newberry of the Institute for Analytical Interviewing trains police officers to detect and use microexpressions when interacting with suspects. "Sometimes these microexpressions can save an agent's life," says Newberry (Hockenberry, 2001). For example, suppose an under-cover officer is setting up a drug buy with a suspect. A suspect may say, "I like you. I'm gonna do right by you," but if a quick flash of contempt comes over his face, then watch out. It may be a setup. Ekman has shown that microexpressions can be fairly reliable cues to deception. In one study, he found that 90% of deceivers produced detectable microexpressions. The cue, however, is not perfect. Thirty percent of truth tellers also were found to produce microexpressions (Frank & Ekman, 1997).

Liars produce other sorts of cues as well. Changes in normal voice tone, such as elevation in pitch, can signal deception. Deviations from normal eye contact may also be giveaways. Liars often depersonalize their speech (recall President Clinton's famous "I did not have sexual relations with *that woman*..."). To pick up on these signals, however, often requires familiarity with another's typical mode of conversation and communication. One cannot expect to be an effective lie detector in the course of a single interview. Newberry counsels police interviewers always to take the "good cop" approach with suspects. Get to know them and establish a rapport, he advises. Once you know how a person behaves when telling the truth about small matters, it becomes easier to detect changes in their normal pattern when dealing with more serious issues. A famous anecdotal story confirms this. As he interrogated Nazi war criminal Adolf Eichmann, Avner Less began to notice some revealing behavioral patterns. Eventually he came to realize that whenever Eichmann began a phrase with "Never! Never!" or "At no time! At no time!" he was about to lie (Less, 1983).

Sources:
Ekman, P. (1992). *Telling lies.* New York: W.W. Norton.
Frank, M.G., & Ekman, P. (1997). The ability to detect deceit generalizes across different types of high-stakes lies. *Journal of Personality and Social Psychology, 72,* 1429–1439.
Hockenberry, J. (2001). *The infinite mind: lies, lies, lies.* New York: Lichtenstein Creative Media, Inc. Accessed on February 1, 2002, at: www.theinfinitemind.com/mind161.htm.
Less, A. (1983). Introduction. In J. Von Lang & C. Cibyll (Eds.), *Eichmann interrogated* (pp. v–xxii). New York: Farrar, Strauss, Giroux.
Photo: Courtesy of Paul Ekman, © Fred Hodder.

Emotional displays provide not only information about internal states but also about external circumstances that brought on the internal states. If little Thor can see fear written on his mother's face, then he knows that something threatening is nearby and might affect him as well. Because Thor has his mother's genes, it is actually to her advantage to provide him with an advanced warning of imminent danger. In a group-living species in which individual fortunes are closely bound with the group's fate, it would be to everyone's advantage if critical information about the immediate environment could be broadcast quickly and efficiently, especially if the group's situation called for a uniform and hasty response. Excitement on the face of one hunter, for example, would quietly inform the rest about the presence of prey. Forthright communication of emotions among family or tribe members would hold advantages for all in terms of group cohesion, stability, and survival. Thus, it does not seem unreasonable that natural selection would favor automatic, involuntary expression and that those expressions would be stereotyped for easy recognition by conspecifics.

But this also raises an interesting issue: why would humans have evolved both the inability to entirely stifle real emotional expressions and the capacity to fake emotions to some extent (e.g., the polite smile). Cosmides and Tooby (2000) claimed that it all depends on the person or persons that are the object of emotional expressions. In our evolutionary past, emotional honesty would not have been advantageous in all situations. One must always keep in mind that natural selection is no moralist; whatever strategy works is likely to emerge. A selective advantage was likely accrued to those hominins who displayed emotions, but an advantage (maybe even a greater advantage) also might have been reaped by those who could display the right emotions without being compelled to act on them. A male, for example, capable of displaying concern for his mate, but not really feeling or acting on it, might have stumbled upon the best of all worlds in terms of fitness. His outward emotional expressions would make him highly competitive in the mating marketplace, but his lack of any real internal feeling would free him to a life of endless philandering (and wide distribution of his genes), rather than monogamous commitment. In this instance, being able to fake the emotion would have a fitness payoff. However, the fact that humans are quite adept at distinguishing authentic emotional expressions from faked ones suggests that there was also selection pressure for the ability to detect emotional "cheats" (Ekman & Davidson, 1993). Faking or masking emotions also might have been advantageous when confronting rivals or nongroup members. Defeating an adversary may require intimidating or deceiving him or her, in which case, masking fear with an expression of anger or hubris would likely increase one's chances of success. Although it is surely speculative and perhaps impossible to test, it seems that deception about one's emotions would require some conscious awareness of emotion. Could it be that those first hominins who gained some measure of voluntary control over their emotional expressions (for good or for ill) were also slowly, incrementally opening up the conscious awareness of their own minds?

Emotions as Social Regulators

The link between an animal's social life and its emotional life can be observed clearly in different primate species. Prosimians are small primates who are generally nocturnal and solitary. Compared with other primates, such as monkeys and apes, prosimians are also lacking in facial expressiveness. Their facial muscles are primarily designed for biting and chewing functions, and they display distinct expressions for only a few emotions, including fear, anger, and affection. Monkeys and apes, by contrast, generally have a larger, more complex musculature around the mouth and lips and show a far wider range of facial expressions (Chevalier-Skolnikoff, 1973). Monkeys and apes, in general, also are far more social than prosimians. This suggests that emotions serve another important function, that of helping to organize and regulate social relationships. Indeed, among group-dwelling monkeys and apes, specific emotional displays help to establish dominant–submissive relationships, repair damaged relationships, and convey the intent behind actions, such as indicating whether a smack on the head is intended as punishment or play.

In humans, one of the first and most noteworthy examinations of the social function of emotions was John Bowlby's work on **attachment** in infants. Bowlby (1969, 1988) proposed that the attachment system in human infants represented an evolved adaptation that kept an infant in close proximity to its caregiver, thus enhancing its chances of survival. The system was automatically activated whenever indicators of environmental threat reached some critical level. Once activated, the system would engage a number of behaviors, including crying, flailing arms, proximity seeking, etc., aimed at re-establishing contact with the caregiver. The critical thrust of Bowlby's argument was that these behaviors and emotional expressions had been organized as an adaptive system by natural selection because of the survival advantage they offered. In a primate species (especially humans) in which development is characterized by an extended period of infant and childhood dependency, the social bond between caregiver and infant is critical and the emotions inherent in the attachment system serve to reinforce that important relationship. Empirical work by Mary Ainsworth (e.g., Ainsworth, 1967; Ainsworth, Blehar, Waters, & Wall, 1978) in both naturalistic and laboratory settings provided convincing evidence to support Bowlby's theory.

The attachment system serves an important function in the caring and protecting of offspring. This system, however, can be observed in many species and can operate effectively based predominately on emotions such as fear and anxiety. The complex interdependency of human familial and social relationships necessitates even more sophisticated emotional systems that involve more than fear and anxiety (MacDonald, 1992). Emotional bonding systems based on affection and intimacy have evolved in humans to help cement the long-term, highly interdependent relationships that characterize families. The warmth and affection associated with close social relationships serve as social reinforcers that motivate people to establish and nurture close relationships. These relationships, in turn, facilitate the investment needed to raise dependent offspring and to help promote the reciprocal cooperation that can have fitness-enhancing qualities for individuals. The evolution of warm, affectionate relationships may also have served an important enculturating function. In other words, when caregivers and children have warm, affectionate relationships, cultural norms and group behavioral standards tend to be more readily accepted by the young.

Emotions as Superordinate, Regulatory Programs

Domain specificity is a basic assumption of evolutionary psychologists. Briefly, domain specificity refers to the idea that the mind is composed of separate problem-solving specialists, each designed to address a specific adaptive problem faced in the environment of evolutionary adaptedness (EEA). For example, to solve the problem of choosing a good mate, human minds were designed to be especially attuned to information about the appearance, health, and reliability of members of the opposite sex (a "mate attraction" module). To solve the problem of finding a good place to call home, our perceptual and cognitive systems were geared to process relevant information about landscape layout, resource availability, escape routes, and safe havens (a "home, sweet home" module). Specialized mental programs, however, are susceptible to internal conflicts, as happens with the visual system when its specialized systems for processing motion, form, and color, conflict to produce illusions (Hoffman, 1998; Rock, 1983). What happens when conflicts among the mind's domain-specific problem-solving programs arise?

Envision a hungry hominin of past ages who has successfully stalked, killed, and consumed a small antelope. The exertion followed by satiation easily puts the hominin into the "preserve energy" program with all of its requisite outputs: slowed movement and reactions, blood rushing to the stomach and away from the muscles, thoughts of sleep, contented disposition, lack of focused attention, etc. Then the faint, but unmistakable sound of an approaching saber-tooth tiger is heard. The "escape from danger" program stirs. However, its outputs will be in direct conflict with those of the currently engaged "preserve energy" program. The conflicting demands of these two mental specialists could leave our hominin frozen in indecision and, all too quickly, the reason for another creature's satisfied dozing. Those who could not adequately prioritize and regulate their various mental programs were unlikely to have lived long enough to become anyone's ancestors. Instead, a selective advantage went to those hominins who had a mechanism that acted as a superordinate programmer, activating certain subsystems and giving them priority and deactivating others so that conflicts could be averted. Cosmides and Tooby (2000) argued that another critical function of the emotions is to act as superordinate, regulatory programs, designed to override and settle conflicts among evolved problem-solving systems, so as to keep the organism functioning in adaptive ways.

Our ancestral environments would have presented recurrent situations in which the inability to properly coordinate specialized mental programs would have been catastrophic in terms of fitness. Furthermore, these situations would have had reliable and detectable signs indicating their presence. In these situations, selection would favor an emotional state that functioned as a subsystem orchestrator, coordinating subprograms so that the highest priority would be given to the program (or programs) that enhanced the detection of signals relevant to the situation and then activated the mental and physical systems needed to direct a response. For example, suppose our antelope-stalking hominin hunter was engaged in full pursuit of his prey. In the heat of the chase, he became separated from the rest of the hunting party and rushed headlong into unfamiliar territory. Being caught alone in unfamiliar territory was, in all likelihood, a recurrent situation over the course of hominin evolution. From a fitness standpoint, being alone in unfamiliar territory could have dire negative consequences. Without one's group, the probability of starvation, predation, or death at the hands of another hominin tribe were increased. The sooner one could identify the presence of this situation the more likely one could deal with it successfully. Unfamiliar territory would be signaled by a certain category of reliable cues: novel environmental patterns, unexpected perceptions (strange sounds, different-looking trees, etc.), a sense of disorientation (mistaking direction of movement), and so forth. What might have been the very first indicator of the cues associated with unfamiliar territory? A logically deduced, conscious awareness of being in strange terrain? Probably not. Long before this conscious awareness, a "gut feeling" that something was wrong probably indicated that a reordering of priorities might be needed. As our hominin continued his chase, he might have eventually reached a point at which this "gut feeling" caused him to break off the chase and take a good look around.

A recent study confirmed that people can use their gut feelings as reliable predictors of environmental events (Katkin, Wiens, & Ohman, 2001). Subjects were shown images of spiders and snakes, presented too quickly to be registered consciously. Electric shocks were associated with some of the images. Later, the images were shown again and subjects were asked to predict if a shock would occur (i.e., was this an image that was earlier paired with shock?). Those subjects who were highly sensitive to their own bodily states were found to be significantly better at predicting the occurrence of the shocks. These results indicate that environmental cues that cannot be recalled consciously may still manifest themselves in the form of vague bodily sensations (gut feelings) and that those most attuned to those gut feelings can use them as a means of predicting events. In our ancestral past, these vague feelings may have been essential in detecting situations in which a reordering of mental and behavioral priorities was necessary for survival.

As a superordinate program, emotions would have had far-ranging effects, causing changes in all aspects of an organism's functioning, including perceptual, motor, and memory systems. If we go back to our hominin hunter, we can see how this would play out. The moment before the chase was abandoned, our friend was in the throes of an emotional state we might call "predatory excitement." In that state, all of his mental and behavioral subprograms were adjusted to accommodate the demands of that emotional condition. The perceptual systems were keenly sensitive to information about the movements of the antelope but relatively insensitive to information about the look of the trees (while in predatory excitement, our hunter would avoid running into trees but would not study them in detail) The memory system was cued to recall past hunts and used that information to help inform the current chase. The motivational system was directed toward the capture of the prey. Concerns such as itchy feet or yesterday's disagreement with mother were pushed to the background, whereas thoughts of satisfying one's hunger and elevating one's reputation as a skillful hunter rose prominently to the fore. The physiological system commanded changes in blood flow, respiration, and hormonal release, all to maintain and enhance the actions necessary for the chase. The behavioral programs that maximized speed and quick reactivity were allowed highest priority. Thus, predatory excitement ordered the functioning of all other subprograms to productively coordinate their various effects.

However, as the feeling of predatory excitement gave way to "fear of the unfamiliar," all the subprograms began to recalibrate. Suddenly, the perceptual systems became sensitive to the layout of the immediate landscape and tracking the antelope became irrelevant. Thoughts of doom, death, and loneliness replaced concerns about hunger and reputation enhancement. The memory system searched frantically for any hint of environmental recognition. Behavioral priorities changed to actions geared to securing safety (should I climb that tree?) rather than those designed to capture prey. Notice that this wholesale reordering of subprogram priorities would be adaptive in the sense that continuing to have subprogram priorities set by predatory excitement would only plunge one deeper into unfamiliar territory, and a confusing jumble of uncoordinated subprogram activities would leave the organism frozen in indecision. Under the new order, our lost hominin has the best chance of dealing adaptively with the situation. The new emotion reset the hominin's entire functioning, settling any subsystem conflicts and directing all available energies toward solving the current problem.

The Evolution of Emotions

From Sensation to Perception

Going all the way back to Thomas Aquinas, scholars interested in emotions have categorized them into two types. For Aquinas, emotions were either affective or spirited (Kemp, 1990). Today, emotions tend to be grouped either as primary or secondary (Damasio, 1994; Plutchik, 1980), fundamental or complex (Izard, 1977), self-conscious or non-self-conscious (Parker, 1998; Tangney & Fischer, 1995), or as affects and emotions (Johnston, 1999). Although they differ in details, most of these dichotomies break along the line of whether an emotion is viewed as more innate and directly tied to a stimulus or as requiring more cognitive reflection and appraisal.

At the most fundamental level, an organism needs to be able to distinguish between beneficial and harmful stimuli. Distinct feelings of pleasure and discomfort directly tied to beneficial and harmful stimuli, respectively, would thus constitute the most basic level of emotional responding (Humphrey 1992; Johnston, 1999). Humphrey (1992) referred to feelings arising from direct contact with the environment simply as **sensations**. For example, if one encounters a fire, the infrared energy from the fire will contact the skin, setting in motion a series of physical events in the nervous system resulting in the feeling of pain. This feeling-laden sensation leads to the very adaptive behavior of withdrawing from the fire. Although sensations laden with feelings serve an important adaptive function, they have the disadvantage of requiring physical contact with external stimuli. As nervous systems evolved greater complexity, the capacity to indirectly experience stimuli and the feelings associated with them emerged. Thus, the mere sight of a distant fire evokes the memory of a past encounter, giving rise to an emotional state (fear) that produces the same withdrawal behaviors. Humphrey (1992) referred to this process as **perception** and noted that this has the added advantage of not requiring direct contact with the potentially damaging stimulus. One of the first important steps in the evolution of emotions was simply separating the experienced "feeling" from direct physical contact with the environmental stimuli.

The Brain and the Social World of Mammals

The evolution of the brain, coupled with increasing complex social relations, added to the emergence of more sophisticated emotions. MacLean (1990, 1993) argued for a triune model of the brain, consisting of three gross evolutionary divisions:(1) the **reptilian brain**, (2) the **old mammalian brain**, and (3) the **neomammalian brain** (Fig. 7.1). The reptilian brain was composed of the brainstem, including the pons, medulla, and reticular formation. Instinctual and survival-based drives emanate from the reptilian brain, including states of arousal, fear, and aggression. There is little, however, in the reptilian brain to support emotions of attachment or commitment, and this is reflected in reptilian behavior. Reptiles are largely asocial creatures and offer virtually no parental care to their offspring. In fact, some reptile young, lizards for example, do well to stay clear of their parents or they might get eaten.

The social situation changes dramatically with mammals. Encapsulating the reptilian brain is the old mammalian brain, including such structures as the cingulate gyrus, the septum, and the amygdala, all part of the limbic system—a central player in the evolution of emotions. MacLean's (1990) analysis revealed three broad patterns of behavior that distinguish mammals from reptiles: vocal signaling, juvenile play, and attachment. All of these distinctively mammalian characteristics play an important role in the relatively more sophisticated social lives of mammals. The mammalian limbic brain provides the neural substrate for the emotions that organize and regulate this more "advanced" social lifestyle. A critical part of this social lifestyle was the evolutionary change that occurred in parental care. For mammalian parents (generally mothers) to offer prolonged and careful postnatal nurturance, strong feelings of attachment needed to arise. MacLean contended that it was with the emergence of the limbic system and the old mammalian brain that the pleasurable feelings associated with the care and nurturance of offspring first arose.

Figure 7.1 Paul McLean's triune brain. A very general model for understanding the evolution of increasing complexity of the brain. The deepest, oldest layer of brain is the reptilian brain, with primary functions involving self-preservation and reproduction. Encompassing it is the old mammalian brain including the limbic system. This layer contributes emotional responses, including those involving parent–offspring attachment. The third layer is the neocortex or neomammalian brain, in which the highest cognitive functions reside. (Adapted from Bounds, 1999, p. 47.)

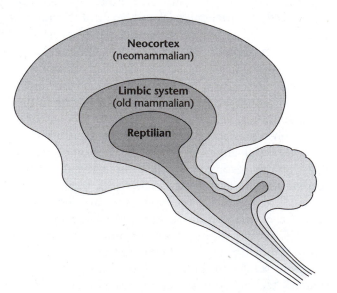

Surrounding the old mammalian brain is the neomammalian brain, the evolutionarily newest brain structure. This brain is composed of the neocortex. Its expansion in primates, especially humans, appears to be related to the increasing complexities of social living. The **neocortex** allows animals to process and construct an ever-increasing number of finely distinguished emotional responses. Complex social situations often require the discernment of subtle distinctions in emotional displays, as when determining whether an ape is fighting or play fighting.

LeDoux (1996) demonstrated this discriminative function nicely in his studies of the neural circuitry of emotions. He studied two brain pathways important in emotional responding. One pathway connects the thalamus (a structure important for processing sensory information) directly with the amygdala. This "fast" pathway was found to be capable of directing quick, automatic reactions to threatening stimuli. The other pathway also connects the thalamus to the amygdala but runs through the cerebral cortex on the way (Fig. 7.2). This "slower" pathway was found to be important when making emotional discriminations among stimuli. Rats were presented two auditory tones, only one of which they were trained to fear. The results showed that the fear response persisted even after the thalamus-to-cortex-to-amygdala connection was severed, indicating that the thalamus-to-amygdala connection alone was capable of mediating this response. However, rats with a severed thalamus-to-cortex-to-amygdala pathway showed fear to **both** tones, indicating that they could not discriminate the feared from the nonfeared tone. Rats with this pathway intact could discriminate between the two tones. Thus, it appears that the cortex is capable of making emotional distinctions among different stimuli, even stimuli of a similar nature. An analogous effect may occur in humans when we are victims of the old "snake in the can" gag. Remember removing the twist-off top of a can marked "peanut brittle" only to be startled witless when a coiled fake snake jumped furiously at you? The initial fear response was most likely the result of the thalamus-to-amygdala connection directing an automatic reaction to a (supposed) threatening stimulus. As the slower thalamus-to-cortex-to-amygdala connection processed the "joke" aspect of this situation, a dif-

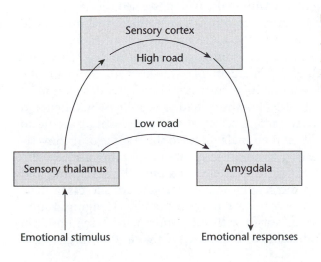

Figure 7.2 The two pathways of emotion. The low road is a direct connection between the thalamus and the amygdala, where automatic emotional responses are generated. The higher road runs through the cortex and allows cognitive mediation of emotional responses. (Adapted from LeFreniere, p. 63)

ferent emotional reaction emerged. The two systems function in tandem, using a "better safe than sorry" principle that, at times, can be exploited for fun. The critical point, however, is that with the evolution of the neocortex, more sophisticated emotional distinctions can be generated.

As animals evolved to live in more complex social arrangements, increased brainpower was needed to monitor and maintain a vast array of relationships (Dunbar, 1996). Within social groups, the cues associated with potential positive or negative fluctuations in reproductive potential would become more subtle. The expanding neocortex, especially the frontal lobes, allowed for increasing interactions between emotion and cognition, leading to more sophisticated emotions (Davidson, 1993). For example, in humans many emotional states are based on the anticipation of future outcomes, such as how another *will react* to some news or to a certain action. Moreover, emotional reactions can be based on how our own or another's behavior compares with some abstract code of conduct. Given the complexity of our social relations and the size of our neocortex, we might expect certain emotions to be unique to our species. Johnston (1999) for example, saw some emotions, such as happiness, sadness, fear, disgust, anger, and surprise, as primary and more widespread among animals. Many of these are essential for survival and for establishing parent–infant bonds. Other emotions, however, are more restricted to complex social situations and may be unique to humans. These he calls secondary emotions. They include guilt, pride, and envy.

Emotions and Hominin Evolution

If uniquely human emotions do exist, what factors forged their evolution? Over the 5 million years of hominin evolution, the complexity of the hominin social world increased enormously. In addition, hominins faced pressing challenges in raising highly dependent offspring and in securing adequate resources for their enlarging brains and bodies. How might all of this have affected their emotional evolution?

Miller (2000) presented a compelling case that many present-day human mental traits were the product of the preferences male and female hominins demonstrated in selecting their mates. Over the long course of hominin evolution, if females tended to mate preferentially with males who possessed certain attributes (such as the tendency to display certain emotions), then those attributes would tend to spread in the population (Parker, 1998). Around the time of *Homo erectus*, hominin infants were being born in an alarmingly altricial (helpless) state. This was, in no small measure, a result of the enlargement of the hominin brain and the fact that developing a brain of around 1000 cc required an extended period of postnatal dependency. To raise a healthy hominin child to viability would demand a staggering cost in parental investment. A selective advantage would accrue to those hominin females who could get their male mates to share some of the investment burden. But how would a hominin female go about selecting a mate who would be willing to hang around and help raise a child after the sexual fun and games had ended? After all, from the standpoint of reproductive success, a male hominin might do well to inseminate as many females as possible. Hanging around to help raise the kids certainly does not fit with that game plan. Some hominin males, however, might display **indicators of domesticity**, that is, they might show signs that they would be willing to hang around. One of these signs might be evidence of an emotional attachment, a sense of caring. If, over the course of hundreds of thousands of years, hominin females preferentially mated with those males who showed outward signs of a caring and a kind attitude, then the genes associated with the capacity to display and ultimately to feel a caring, kind emotion would emerge in the species (Krebs, 1998; MacDonald, 1992).

What's good for the goose works for the gander as well. Male hominins also played the mate preference game. If a male hominin is going to hang around and help raise a kid, he ought to be sure the kid has his genes. He would be wise to mate preferentially with females who displayed indicators of fidelity. Such females might be ones who feel guilty at having been deceitful. This would have been an especially urgent concern for hominin males, because they would have been spending quite a bit of time away from home on hunting excursions. A female whose guilty conscience would not allow her to fool around while her mate was out hunting and who showed obvious outward signs of fidelity would be a highly prized mate. Given the male's selection preferences, genes associated with feeling and displaying guilt or shame also would be widely propagated in the species.

If there is any validity to the notion that mate preferences played a potent role in the evolution of human emotions, we might expect to find some evidence of it in human mate selection today. Indeed, some evidence seems to exist. For example, Buss (1989) reported that, across 37 different societies, kindness was one of the most important attributes that both males and females looked for in a mate. Buss and Schmitt (1993) found that when males were considering long-term relationships, evidence of faithfulness was highly valued, and women who showed signs of promiscuity were eschewed. In other species, these same rules tend to apply. Male ringdoves will engage in extensive courtship rituals with females. Females generally will not mate with a male who refuses to go through all the required preliminaries. After all, if he does not have the patience and discipline to court properly, then he may not invest properly in the offspring. Likewise, males will generally not mate with a female who appears too eager. Her willingness may indicate that she has already had her hormones primed by another (Erikson & Zenone, 1976). As with birds, it appears that kind, reliable human males and modest human females have an evolutionary advantage in the matrimonial arts.

Not only would mate selections have affected the evolution of emotions, but selection pressures from the larger group also could have played an important role. Simon (1990) has shown how the trait of **docility** could have spread over the course of hominin evolution and that it would have had implications for the evolution of emotions. Docility refers to the tendency to uncritically accept social teachings, much the way young children unquestioningly emulate the behavior of parents and older siblings, or even the way in which adults can be compelled into certain beliefs and behaviors by social forces. Possessing docility would have individual fitness advantages as long as what the individual gains in knowledge and social acceptance is greater than the sacrifices one is required to make on behalf of the group. For example, by being docile (rather than obstinate) one may get taken advantage of or be compelled to make personal sacrifices. On the positive side, one also may learn important survival skills, gain social status, and make important friends and allies. If the latter outweigh the former, then the individual has enhanced his or her probability of harvesting an overall fitness gain. The presence of docility in an individual might be cued to others by the display of certain emotions, especially shame and guilt. These emotions could signal to others a desire to be "right" with the group and to accept the group's rules, standards, and teachings.

Another characteristic of *H. erectus* was the presence of larger, more cooperative tribal groups. A family living within an extended-family erectus clan would have both its own internal social dynamic and the larger group culture circulating around it. A selective advantage would be had for those docile children who could be most easily assimilated into these social structures. Within the family, those children capable of feeling shame or guilt when they had violated parental rules or feeling pride when they had upheld them would be capable of self-regulating rather than requiring constant parental oversight. Not only would this enhance their survival because many parental rules would be safety relevant ("Don't wander too far from camp, little Thor!"), but it also would reduce parental energy expenditure on current offspring so that more offspring could be produced. Enculturation of the young could be facilitated further by the presence of warm, affectionate relationships with parents and other care givers. A role model who is perceived as warm and caring is more readily imitated by children, and parental control of children and adolescents is enhanced when the parent/child relationship is marked by high levels of warmth and affection (Bandura, 1969; Jessor & Jessor, 1974; Mischel, 1976).

As with male–female pair bonds, one of the great advantages that group living holds for individuals is the ability to share burdens. However, for a group to maintain cohesion, burdens must be roughly equally distributed across group members. If not, resentments and disagreements can tear the group asunder. Again, advantages would accrue to group members who had the capacity to feel guilty when they let others take on their responsibilities or when they failed to "pay back" another who had done them a favor. In addition, those displaying the capacity to feel shame or guilt would be preferred by others when forming cooperative relationships, because group members could have more confidence that they would not be taken advantage of.

Although this scenario is reasonable enough, testable hypotheses still need to flow from it to offer more empirical support. Johnston (1999), for example, has used computer simulations to show that a system of cooperative reciprocity ("you scratch my back, I'll scratch yours") can evolve when individuals approach instrumental interpersonal relationships with emotion-based strategies. In other words, if two individuals enter into a cooperative arrangement in which they are both looking to make some kind of gain and both adopt the attitude that they will take advantage of the other if possible but also punish the other if they themselves are taken advantage of, then eventually the two settle into a reasonably balanced, nonexploitive, cooperative relationship. Thus, at least in theory, emotion can lead to cohesive, productive group arrangements.

Uniquely Human Emotions?

Darwin (1872/1965) was one of the first to appreciate the commonalities of emotional expression in animals and humans. When afraid or displaying subordination, monkeys and apes will lower the head, avert the gaze, and generally "shrink"

Figure 7.3 Dominant and submissive displays among primates. Note that the dominant male baboon strides in front of the females and younger baboons. (Photo © Guido Alberto Rossi/Brand X Pictures/PictureQuest.)

their posture. Humans show a similar pattern when ashamed or feeling guilty. Dominance displays in monkeys and apes take on the opposite character, with chest puffed out, the body upright and enlarged, the head held high and the gaze direct (de Waal, 1982) (Fig. 7.3). Prideful human primates display similarly. Goodall (1968) observed that both humans and chimpanzees express joy with a relaxed, open-mouth facial expression, short grunts, and laughter. It has been speculated that human laughing and smiling evolved from primate expressions of friendliness (bare teeth display) and play (open-mouth display; see van Hooff, 1972). Humans and chimpanzees also share similar expressions of anger and frustration, with both producing glaring eyes, compressed lips, and the annoying practice of pouting. From these accounts, it seems clear that there may be many emotions common to humans and other primates. But in the 5 million years since the hominin and chimpanzee lines diverged, the complexity of the hominin social world has increased substantially. Might that not suggest that certain emotions would be unique to our species' social environment? Are there uniquely human emotions?

Self-Conscious and Non-Self-Conscious Emotions

We have seen a number of different schemes to categorize emotions, such as primary versus secondary and sensations versus perceptions. A somewhat different and more distinctly evolutionary scheme was proposed by primatologist Sue Taylor Parker (1998). Parker divided emotions into non-self-conscious (NSCEs) and self-conscious emotions (SCEs). NSCEs are those shared by humans and most other mammalian species and are typically elicited by some environmental stimulus, including social stimuli. The list of NSCEs include many that occur on Johnston's list of primary emotions: happiness, sadness, anger, fear, surprise, and disgust. In many species, including primates, the expression of the NSCEs is ritualized and stereotyped for effective communication. For example, a chimp roughhousing with another sporting an open-mouth, no-exposed-teeth, play face is signaling "I want to play," not "I want to fight." Because misinterpreting the chimp's actions could have serious ramifications, natural selection has seen to it that this signal is more-or-less "standardized" within the species. In humans, certain emotions are also made manifest in species-typical stereotyped ways. Ekman (1972) found that emotions such as anger, fear, surprise, disgust, sadness, happiness, and interest (all NSCEs) were identifiable by a characteristic facial configuration across a variety of different cultures.

SCEs differ from NSCEs in that they are not directly elicited by external stimulation or events. Instead, their experience and expression requires cognitive reflection. Moreover, SCEs are largely unique to humans, and their expression varies in form (Barrett, 1995). SCEs include pride, envy, hubris, embarrassment, shame, guilt, jealously, and empathy (again notice the similarity to Johnston's secondary emotions). Parker contended that SCEs require the capacity to evaluate one's actions relative to a social standard. This requires a certain degree of self-awareness, a capacity lacking in most other species except, possibly, the great apes. In experiencing an SCE, one must reflect upon an act and weigh that act relative to the social norms of one's community or group. One must also have a conceptual understanding of "good," "bad," "competent," and "incompetent," as defined by social standards. Thus, if one evaluates an act as having upheld or even exceeded social standards, one might feel pride. However, if one evaluates an act as having violated social standards, one might feel shame or guilt. There is some disagreement over whether apes show evidence of SCEs. Patterson and Cohen (1994) reported that their gorilla, Koko, exhibited embarrassment, and de Waal (1996) provided accounts of chimpanzees expressing what seemed to be empathy. Tomasello and Call (1997), however, are unimpressed with these accounts and remain skeptical that apes have the self-awareness necessary for SCEs. They also claimed that "There have been no reports of nonhuman primates showing anything resembling embarrassment in connection with the mirror (test) or any other contexts...." (Tomasello & Call, 1997, p. 337). Even Parker conceded that if SCEs do exist in apes they would be "incipient" (underdeveloped) forms. Thus, we are left with the possibility of SCEs being largely, if not entirely, unique to humans, having evolved sometime after the phylogenetic split between hominins and chimpanzees. The next time you feel guilty or ashamed, you might remind yourself that you are (likely) having a uniquely human experience.

One to two million years ago, as the first global migrations of hominins commenced, a process was set in motion that forever changed the face of the earth. But it was more than just the physical environment that was irretrievably altered. The internal experience of life was revolutionized as well. *H. erectus* elevated community living to a standard never before witnessed in evolutionary history. Having a brain nearly within modern human range, this species hunted together, raised young together, shared food with one another, pushed across continents, and no doubt engaged in bloody battle with one another. By virtue of the demands of their community life, they also may have been the first to experience the real *feel* of life: not just *having* an emotion but *knowing* that one has an emotion. What must it have been like to be the first to stand before one's enemy experiencing fear but *consciously* suppressing it and forcing oneself to display confidence? To know "I am afraid" but to chose to think "I will not be"? Or for a new mother to gaze into her infant's eyes with an unprecedented awareness of the swelling love within her?

With an evolving, enriching capacity to feel, the gates to life's grandeur were opening before our unsuspecting ancestors.

SUMMARY

We should view emotions as working in concert with our "higher intellect" to facilitate adaptive functioning. Rather than being animalistic relics worthy only of suppression, our emotions should be understood as a form of evolved, adaptive knowledge, honed by thousands of years of evolution. Emotions inform the organism about how to adaptively relate to the environment. As a form of adaptive knowledge, emotions serve four important functions: they filter and amplify incoming stimuli for fitness-relevant information, they provide honest signals about another's internal state, they regulate social relationships, and they act as superordinate programs that minimize conflicts among mental modules.

The evolution of emotions has progressed from simplicity to increasing complexity. At the most fundamental level, an organism needs to be able to distinguish between beneficial and harmful stimuli. Positive emotions (pleasures) served to attract an organism to beneficial stimuli and negative emotions (discomforts, pains) repelled an organism away from damaging ones. Eventually, sensations (emotional responses tied to external stimuli) became distinct from perceptions (emotions detached from external stimuli). The increased complexity of the mammalian brain allowed for more sophisticated emotions, especially those associated with parent/infant bonding. Finally, with the expanded neocortex of primates and especially humans, social emotions and self-conscious emotions reached their highest level.

KEY TERMS

attachment	honest signals	old mammalian brain
chemotaxis	indicators of domesticity	perception
discriminative hedonic amplifiers	neocortex	reptilian brain
docility	neomammalian brain	sensations

REVIEW QUESTIONS

1. What are the four ways that our emotions may provide us knowledge about our environment?

2. What is attentional blink, and when does it occur? How can emotion affect it, and how does this provide evidence of one of the important evolutionary functions of emotions?

3. How do emotions serve as honest signals?

4. What are the anatomical aspects of the brain in MacLean's triune model, and what emotions are associated with them?

5. How are the views on emotion of Johnston and Parker similar?

6. What is meant by the fast and slow emotion pathways? How do they differ in terms of the emotional reactions they mediate?

SUGGESTED READINGS

Damasio, A.R. (1994). *Decartes' error: Emotion, reason, and the human brain.* New York: Putnam.

Johnston, V.S. (1999). *Why we feel: The science of human emotion.* Reading, MA: Perseus Books.

LeDoux, J. (1996). *The emotional brain.* New York: Simon & Schuster.

WEB SITES

www.brainchannels.com/evolution/physicalbrain.html for an inside view of the reptilian and mammalian brains; with links to the evolution of civilization and to the home site of the Evolution Channel.

www.kheper.auz.com/gaia/intelligence/MacLean.htm for an in-depth explanation of MacLean's triune model of the brain.

www.nmsu.edu/~ucomm/Releases/2001jan2001/johnston.html an informative page discussing Victor Johnston's work on facial attraction.

8

The Adaptive and Maladaptive Significance of Emotions

Emotions: Then and Now

IN THE PREVIOUS CHAPTER, WE LOOKED at the function of emotions as evolved adaptations and at some of the current theories about their evolution. In this chapter, we will concentrate on specific emotions and their adaptive significance. If we understand adaptations to be evolved solutions to recurrent problems encountered by hominins in the environment of evolutionary adaptedness (EEA), then we can ask: What problems do specific emotions address? For which evolutionary problem, for example, is jealousy an adaptation? Moreover, by viewing emotions as solutions to evolutionary problems we can gain an entirely new perspective on pathology.

The modern world differs in significant ways from that of our ancestral past. Emotional expressions that were adaptive then may not be adaptive now. Evolved emotional expressions may take on extreme, debilitating forms, similar to the way in which the immune system can become overactive and cause pathologies such as rheumatoid arthritis. A currently dysfunctional expression of an evolutionarily adaptive emotional response is sometimes referred to as **pseudopathology**. An example of this might be the male tendency toward aggressive behavior. In our evolutionary past, male aggressiveness served the important adaptive functions of facilitating the acquisition and holding of resources and of challenging other males for dominance and access to females. In today's world, however, criminality among males often stems from this same tendency toward aggressive behavior. From an evolutionary perspective, then, the goal of treatment is not necessarily one of trying to eliminate an emotional response but of attempting to return it to a more moderate, adaptive form.

In the following chapter, emotions will be grouped in two general categories: (1) **common emotions**, those that are part of nearly everyone's experience and remain largely adaptive even in our current context; and (2) **pathological** and **pseudopathological emotions,** those that are less common and often dysfunctional, either because of the contrast between the present and ancestral environments or because of the exaggerated forms taken.

Common Emotions

Shame and Guilt

Parker (1998) and Simon (1990) proposed that shame and guilt were sexually and socially selected emotions that facilitated parental control of juveniles, marital fidelity, and individual acceptance of group enculturation. In brief, these researchers argued that a selective advantage would be had by those children capable of feeling shame and guilt. They would be more easily assimilated into the culture of the family and tribe and, therefore, would reap more effectively the survival and reproductive benefits of group membership. Parker also argued that selection pressures within the group would have been especially strong in favor of daughters with the capacity to feel and display guilt for the purpose of enforcing virginity before marriage. Let's expand on this a moment.

Over the course of human evolution, parents had an interest in making sure that their daughters secured reliable, high-status mates to help in the provisioning of their grandchildren. An eligible, high-status male with a choice of mates would find a sexually naive female of greater value than a more experienced one, given his concerns about certainty of paternity. Thus, for parents to ensure a high-quality mate for their daughter and a good provider for their grandchildren, they had to find a way of controlling their daughter's sexuality. Over generations, daughters inhibited by feelings of guilt (or at least those who could give the external appearance of inhibition) from engaging in socially unacceptable sexual expression would have had a selective advantage over their more brazen competitors.

Although Parker's theory is plausible, it is difficult to verify empirically. The fact that women (and men) often feel guilty over sexual impropriety could be attributed to social and cultural factors as easily as evolutionary history. A bit more convincing is the fact that nearly every human culture has placed a high priority on female chastity (especially among those women who seek to marry high-status men), often using laws, divine dictates, and extreme punishments to ensure it (see Dickemann, 1981, for a review). For example, the code of Hammurabi imposed the death penalty for a girl who was found to be unchaste while still living in her father's home. Women in cultures as diverse as those of ancient Egypt, ancient Greece, medieval Europe, the medieval Islamic Empire, the Buddhist Asian subcontinent, ancient China, and even Samoa (contrary to the now questionable assessment by Margaret Mead) have had various restrictions on their movement, education, associations, and clothing, all aimed directly or indirectly at ensuring their sexual purity (Freeman, 1983). These customs might simply reflect the cultural norms of each locale, but evolutionary psychologists would argue that their universality reflects a deeper motivation stemming from our common evolutionary background.

The evolutionary utility of guilt and shame extend beyond the sexual realm. As hominin groups became larger, expanding out from family units to include extended kin and nonrelatives, the problem of maintaining group stability and cohesion became more pressing. The individual benefits garnered by group living would be lost if infighting and animosities fractured a group's cooperative spirit. When hominin groups competed and clashed, an advantage surely would go to the more cohesive, well-organized tribes. The ties of blood can help build cooperation among family members, but how does cooperation take root and thrive in larger groups among whom genetic relationships are weak or nonexistent? For cooperation to exist among nonrelative parties, consent to what is called **reciprocity** or **reciprocal altruism** must be present. Put simply, reciprocity refers to a relationship based on a "you scratch my back and I'll scratch yours" philosophy.

By at least 2 million years ago, life history and social factors would have been in place for the evolution of reciprocity in hominins (Trivers, 1985). The existence of reciprocity already has been documented in other species, such as vampire bats and chimpanzees (deWaal, 1989; deWaal & Luttrel, 1988; Wilkinson, 1984). In vampire bats, for example, one bat that has successfully procured a night's worth of blood will often return to the cave and share her load with another who has not been so successful. The favor then will be returned at a later date. Both bats benefit from this arrangement, because securing a night's blood supply is by no means guaranteed (most victims do not willingly or easily part with their own blood) and going for a few nights straight without nourishment can be fatal. Reciprocal arrangements, however, can be fragile. They are vulnerable to cheaters, those who greedily snatch the benefits of cooperation without rendering any of the payments. From a standpoint of individual fitness, cheaters have hit upon a highly advantageous strategy. They accumulate resources for themselves without having to dispense any to others, who, under some circumstances, might become competitors. However, cheating can be highly destructive to the group. The resentments, vendettas, and indignations spawned by this zealous individualism can quickly squelch the cooperative spirit needed to hold a large tribe or clan together. As the group fractures, its ability to compete with neighboring groups for scarce resources deteriorates. Thus, the problem of building cooperative relationships and, thereby, cohesive groups becomes one of making cooperation more beneficial to the individual than cheating.

Robert Frank (1988) used the example of a business venture between two individuals, Smith and Jones, to demonstrate that cooperation can actually serve individual interests better than cheating. Suppose Smith is a superb cook but lacks people and business skills. Jones, on the other hand, is as business-wise as he is charming. Together, they open a restaurant. Smith's culinary prowess and Jones's good sense make for a potentially highly profitable establishment. However, either one could cheat the other. Jones could skim from the register, or Smith could extract kickbacks from the food suppliers. In either case, the cheater would have an immediate payoff. Over the long term, however, cheating would be exceedingly foolish. Both the reduction in profits from the cheating or the discovery of the cheating could lead to the closure of the restaurant, in which case the few extra dollars made by cheating would be a paltry sum compared with the years of profits forfeited from the loss of the business. Moreover, if word got out that one of the partners was dishonest, starting up any new businesses in the future would be difficult. In the end, both Smith and Jones benefit more individually by cooperating honestly to make the restaurant a success. Therein lies the lesson of Frank's example: to make cooperating more individually beneficial than cheating, *do not cooperate with those looking for short-term gains.* Instead, only cooperate with those willing to make a long-term commitment. This is what Frank calls the **commitment problem**, the task of identifying those willing to make extended commitments.

This brings us back to guilt and shame. One of the functions of emotions is honest communication about the state of the environment and the internal state of the organism. If, in a group setting, I notice that your head is hanging, your face is downcast, your eyes are tearful, and your body is limp, one possible inference might be that you are feeling ashamed or guilty. Because emotional expressions are typically automatic and difficult to fake or conceal, I can be reasonably assured that your expression tells me something about your internal state (you're feeling really lousy). I will know that something in the immediate past brought this about (you have done something shameful, such as cheating). More important, it allows me to make predictions about your future behavior (one capable of feeling guilt or shame is less likely in the future to do shameful or guilt-worthy acts than one incapable of feeling these emotions). Expressing guilt and shame communicates to others the fact that you possess internal regulatory mechanisms against cheating. A guilty or shameful display says to the community, "I don't want to be excluded from future long-term reciprocal relationships; see, I punish myself when I cheat!" (Frank, 1988; Hirshleifer, 1987). Trivers (1985) contended that an array of emotions, including guilt, sympathy, affection, and gratitude, evolved as mechanisms for regulating reciprocal relationships. Those capable of feeling and expressing these emotions were more likely to be good reciprocators and thus reap the fitness benefits of long-term cooperative interactions. Those looking to establish reciprocal relationships sought out others who were capable of feeling and expressing these emotions, because the presence of these emotions signaled an individual's interest in long-term commitments rather than short-term gains.

Goleman (1998) found a strong link between individual success and what he called "emotional intelligence." In reviewing data from nearly 200 corporations and organizations, he found that a key attribute of top executives was not their capacity to compete against others but their ability to cooperate with others by reading their emotional signals. Goleman estimated that 85%–90% of the success of top executives was attributable to their expertise in building and maintaining good relationships. If successful humans today reflect strategies used by successful hominins of the past, then the role of emotions in establishing and regulating healthy long-term cooperative relationships is one with a deep evolutionary history.

So far in this discussion, shame and guilt have been assumed to be nearly interchangeable concepts. There is a distinction, however, that some scholars believe has evolutionary significance. Both emotions involve the realization that one has violated a social norm, but shame occurs as a result of group rejection, whereas guilt can be present even when others are unaware of the violation. Although closely related, the two are separable and can be measured independently (Tangney, 1990). Studies of preliterate societies suggest that individuals in these societies often possess a much more collective sense of self. In other words, the self is often defined relative to the group and one's role within it. For example, when Luria (1976) asked illiterate Uzbek peasants to describe their personal attributes, they either failed to understand the nature of the task or described themselves in terms of their relationship to others or the tasks they performed. In these individuals, he concluded, "self-awareness is a secondary and socially shaped phenomenon" (Luria, 1976, p. 145). Studies of ancient literature and oral cultures tend to confirm this collective rather than individualized sense of self (Ong, 1982). Anthropologists would agree that the group would have been essential to hominin existence. For our ancestors tens and hundreds of thousands of years ago, "there would have been no room for individual iconoclasts," commented Clive Gamble of Southhampton University. "Lack of cooperation meant death" (quoted in Stringer & McKie, 1996, p. 214). With this in mind, it becomes clear that shame would have been the evolutionarily older emotion. Guilt would have emerged later, as a more individualized sense of existence emerged. In our evolutionary history, one could not have violated a social norm unless the group was aware of the act and overtly condemned it, leading to shame. Guilt may have come into existence only with the advent of literacy, which allowed for the analytical deconstruction of knowledge, including knowledge of the self (Ong, 1982; Lewis, 1971; Luebbert, 1999; Payne, 1991). If these speculations are correct, then guilt, instead of being a useless, debilitating emotion as often described in pop psychology accounts, may be a relatively recent, uniquely human emotion calling us to reassess our actions and mend our relationships.

Love

There are only four questions of value in life, Don Octavio. What is sacred? Of what is the spirit made? What is worth living for, and what is worth dying for? The answer to each is the same: only love.
    JOHNNY DEPP TO MARLON BRANDO IN DON JUAN DEMARCO (1994).

One can expect to make few friends by arguing that love, the most revered of all human emotions, is but another adaptive response in service of our survival and reproductive needs. But (deep sigh), it is. Recognizing this, however, does not diminish its significance or value. Indeed, it may even deepen our appreciation of this most celebrated state to know that its presence is necessary, not miraculous. That which we call love actually has a number of different aspects. First is what might be termed **genetic concern**, that is, the parental (especially maternal) nurturing bestowed on offspring. Second is **attraction**, the recognition of reproductive potential in a breeding partner. Last is **friendship**, the development of an ongoing, sometimes longstanding relationship between conspecifics (not necessarily restricted to members of the opposite sex) and often based on reciprocity. In the great tradition of the gestalt psychologists, it may be that love is something that emerges as the combination of these factors but, in itself, is greater than the sum of these parts. With that in mind, let's look at each of the parts, highlighting their evolutionary history and value.

GENETIC CONCERN (MOTHERLY LOVE). Human infants are a solution to a deeply vexing evolutionary question. How do you create a large-brained, bipedal primate? This may not appear at first to be such a big problem. On close inspection, however, the conflicting demands of a swelled cranium and an upright posture become clear. The large brain requires a big head. Upright posture places constraints on the birth canal, so that birthing the big-headed baby becomes a near-fatal proposition. The problem is exacerbated by the fact that our primate heritage is one of **precocial** newborns; that is, many primates come into the world with their faculties at a reasonably well-developed stage. A comparison of a new-born ape's sensory, locomotor, and body temperature regulatory faculties reveals it to be far more capable than the relatively helpless human newborn. However, for a human baby to be born at a level of development comparable to that of a newborn ape, at least a 20-month gestation period would be required (Jolley, 1999). Imagine giving birth to a baby the size of a 1-year-old child! How is it, then, that *Homo sapiens* have not gone the way of the dodo bird? The answer is to be born **altricial**, that is, at a very early, helpless stage in development. Human infants are largely immobile, with immature, only partially functional sensory systems and a complete dependency on their caregivers for survival. Human infants, in effect, are born too early and wind up spending nearly a year of their gestation outside the womb. The upside of this, however, is that they are exposed to a year of external sensory stimulation, social interaction, and linguistic communication at a stage of brain development when other primates are still snugly wrapped within the womb (Martin, 1990).

Altricial infants are not an easy fit with primate lifestyles. Other mammals, such as mice and cats, are born altricial. Typically, however, altricial newborns are kept nested, safe, and hidden while the mother goes about the business of catching food. Primates are not nesting animals, and the primate infant must move along with the group, clinging to his or her mother's underside as she forages. For a precocial infant ape, hanging on as the mother scales a tree or picks a berry is no problem. For a human infant, it's out of the question. Not only does the human infant lack the requisite strength, but human mothers have no fur to which an infant can cling. Nor can human infants be nested and left alone for hours at a time while the mother attends to other business. Natural selection has conferred on human mothers the most demanding of situations: they have completely helpless offspring that require nearly constant attention.

Biology, however, gives as well as takes. Natural selection has seen to it that human mothers also possess biologically based bonding mechanisms that support and facilitate the strong emotional union of mother and child. Shortly after birth, most human mothers are subject to a rush of endorphins that help both to relieve discomfort and set the stage for maternal bonding (Trevathan, 1987). Moreover, the suckling of the infant stimulates the maternal release of oxytocin, which causes the uterus to contract, helps to expel the placenta, and reduces bleeding. It is quite possible that, in centuries past, the suckling of a newborn helped save more than one new mother's life (Trevathan, 1987). Oxytocin also has been associated with the strong emotional bonding of mother to infant and sometimes has been referred to as the chemical basis of love (Insel, 2000; Janov, 2000). In addition, biology sees to it that infants play a strong hand in the game of emotional attachments. The mother's voice affects the developing fetus while in utero. Within hours after birth, a newborn can recognize his or her mother's voice and prefers it to other female voices (DeCasper & Fifer, 1980; DeCasper & Spence, 1986). Only hours after birth, a newborn can recognize his or her mother's face and prefers to look at it more than at other female faces (Bushnell, Sai, & Mullin, 1989; Walton, Bower, & Bower, 1992). Within a week, a newborn can distinguish his or her mother's milk from that of others and shows a preference for it (Meltzoff & Moore, 1977). Within a few weeks, the newborn can distinguish his or her mother's smell and prefers it to that of others (MacFarlane, 1977). In a relatively short time, an infant's sleep cycle adjusts to roughly synchronize with that of mother, so that breastfeeding can take place without either one emerging fully from sleep (Small, 1998). Nature provides a foundation on which to build the emotions that will keep mother attentive to and concerned about baby. The deck is stacked. Mother's biology and baby's natural dispositions have evolved to make the very difficult not only possible but rewarding.

Biologically based systems of emotional attachment are not uncommon in the animal world. Kevin MacDonald (1992) pointed out that effective attachment mechanisms can operate simply using the emotions of fear and anxiety, without any real feelings of affection. When in the presence of a threat, the distressed infant will seek out its mother to ease psychological discomfort. This can be observed readily in many species, including apes, and can be seen in cross-cultural studies of humans (e.g., Ainsworth 1967; Hrdy, 1981). The high investment required by human infants, however, necessitated the evolution of a more elaborate emotional bonding system based not just on fear but on affection, in which close family relationships (especially mother and child) are inherently rewarding because of their positive psychological effects. MacDonald contended that the psychological construct of **warmth** represents an evolved emotional system designed to facilitate rewarding family relationships. Thus, love between mother and infant serves a critical and straightforward adaptive purpose: nature had to find a way to impel mothers to make the sacrifices necessary to nurture their highly altricial offspring. If not, their future would have been in serious doubt. Over generations of evolutionary time, those mothers whose chemistries best supported the development of powerful emotional ties with their infants were more likely to see their genes (in the form of healthy, viable offspring) safely into the next generation. Loving mothers were naturally favored.

Fathers love as well. However, translating concern for genes into love for offspring was not as straightforward an evolutionary process in males as in females. Because males do none of the gestating, birthing, or nursing of young, their biological (and, hence, emotional) attachment to offspring is far more tenuous than that of females. Moreover, the male contribution to reproduction (sperm) can be produced in such great abundance and spread with such relative ease (in terms of male energy expenditure) that developing too strong an attachment to a mate or offspring might work to a male's reproductive disadvantage. The fact that most men actually do love their children is a testament to the creative power of selection in overcoming the obstacles to paternal genetic concern. We have discussed the way in which sexual selection most likely played an important role in molding men. Hominin males had help in learning to love their children—from hominin women, who themselves needed help in provisioning, protecting, and raising their altricial offspring. Motivated by the need to care adequately for their helpless infants, hominin women differentially selected caring, devoted mates as fathers for those infants (Krebs, 1998; Parker, 1998; Miller, 2000). By giving preferential sexual access to males who showed evidence of caring (including caring for offspring), the genes responsible for a caring demeanor spread in males.

This explanation may be fine as far as it goes, but the question about male caring can be pushed back another level. Where did it originate? To say that females were selecting males who cared implies that males (some at least) already possessed the capacity to care about others and that females were directing and enhancing that already-present trait. A clue to the origins of male caring may come from observations of chimpanzee societies, in which the most important relationships are those among males. Male alliances and coalitions provide the basis for both the peaceful stability and the shifting power structure of the group. Often, the males who form these alliances have some genetic relationship, such as brothers or half brothers. There are some reasons to suspect that the social environment of the Australopiths and early *Homo* shared many characteristics in common with that of chimpanzee societies, with small collections of genetically related males jockeying for territorial dominance and access to females (Foley & Lee, 1989). Wright (1994) speculated that males first cared for their genetically related male comrades. Only later, under feminine persuasion, did male love of brother get coaxed into love of wife and child. Consistent with this view is the fact that male primates have been known to use parenting behavior as a mating strategy (Smuts, 1985; Smuts & Gubernick, 1992). Although most male primates are absent fathers, when they do offer some care or protection to a youngster it often results in greater sexual access to the mother. This suggests the very realistic possibility that, early on in our evolution, male hominins were nice to kids because it bought them sexual favors from mom. Over time, however, as females continued to favor ever more parentally minded males, genuine male love of children and family began to emerge.

ATTRACTION. Cross-cultural studies of male mate preferences have shown a remarkable consistency. Men prefer women who are somewhat younger than they and who are physically attractive (Buss, 1989). Put simply, men the world over want young and pretty women. But how does one define "pretty"? What is it exactly that constitutes a physically attractive woman? Although cultural variability plays a role in what is considered beautiful, a number of consistencies also have emerged. For example, Singh (1993) found that a female waist-to-hip ratio of about .7 is optimally "beautiful" across a number of different cultures. Of even greater significance is the fact that the waist-to-hip ratio in females is more than just skin deep. It is an indicator of fertility. Decreases in fertility have been linked to deviations from the .7 waist-to-hip ratio, which in turn has correlated with a relatively high proportion of free androgens to estrogens in the bloodstream. The waist-to-hip ratio serves as an observable sign of the unobservable internal hormonal state—and therefore fertility—of the female. Over the course of hominin evolution, those men who mated with females with a roughly .7 waist-to-hip ratio were more likely to have selected a highly fertile mate who would successfully conceive an offspring.

The hormonal variables that affect waist-to-hip ratio also affect other physically observable traits, such as certain facial features. On average, females tend to have fuller lips and smaller jaws than males. Both the fullness of the lips and the size of the jaw are affected by hormonal fluctuations at puberty, with fuller lips and smaller jaws associated with relatively greater exposure to estrogens than androgens (Johnston, 1999). Moreover, those female faces that are considered optimally "beautiful" tend to have fuller-than-average lips and smaller-than-average lower jaws (Johnston & Franklin, 1993). Across cultures, men also consider women with smooth and clear skin to be beautiful (Cunningham, Roberts, Barbee, Druen, & Wu, 1995). Blemishes, lumps, and discolorations of the skin often result from parasitic infections, a constant concern of our hominin ancestors. Gangestad and Buss (1993) found that among 29 different cultures a strong correlation (.72) existed between the prevalence of parasites and the importance placed on beauty in mates. Thus, as parasitic infection became a greater concern, a beautiful mate was increasingly valued.

Females also have been shown to use a number of consistent appearance factors when judging male beauty. A male face with high cheekbones, well-defined lower jaw and chin, and large (proportionally speaking) nose tends to be considered attractive. As in females, all of these male facial characteristics are influenced hormonally, in this case by the amount of testosterone in the body (Thornhill & Gangestad, 1993). Interestingly, increases in testosterone can have detrimental effects on immune system function. A prominent chin, strong jaw, and high cheekbones can be a man's way of displaying his robustness: "Look, I'm so healthy I can afford the extra testosterone it takes to grow a pretty face." Bilateral symmetry also has been found to be an important factor in judging the beauty of a male face. Symmetry has been found to be an indicator of robust health, resistance to disease, and a general sign of "good" genes (Moller & Pomiankowski, 1993; Symons, 1979). Humans are not the only species that values symmetry. Moller and Thornhill found a strong relationship between reproductive success and symmetry across 42 different species, including humans (Moller & Thornhill, 1998). Barn swallows are particularly fastidious along these lines, having been shown to be able to make discriminations of only a few millimeters in the symmetry of tailfeathers (Moller, 1992). The value of symmetry may lie in the fact that it requires a pretty effective set of genes to regulate growth on different parts of the body in spite of varying environmental influences. Human females are only continuing a longstanding traditional preference when they apply this criterion to their potential mates.

Looks are not the only feature that spurs attraction. Scent can be important as well. Both males and females find certain scent cues more attractive than others. In one study, males were asked to rate the sexiness of T-shirts that had been worn by females either during the fertile or the nonfertile stages of their menstrual cycles. The shirts worn during the fertile stage were rated as significantly sexier (Singh & Bronstad, 2001). In another study, females rated T-shirts worn by males. The female ratings of attractiveness were affected most strongly by the concentration of certain chemical cues related to the male's immune system function (Wedekind & Furi, 1997; Wedekind, Seebeck, Bettens, & Paepke, 1995). A recent study showed that these chemical scent signals cause arousal in specific regions of the brain. When men are exposed to estrogen-like compounds, increases in blood flow to the hypothalamus have been found. For females the same brain area is subject to increased blood flow, but testosterone-like compounds produce the effect (Savic, Berglund, Gulyas, & Roland, 2001). The hypothalamus is an important brain structure in regulation of emotions and reproductive behavior. Looking good and smelling right can produce powerful brain-based attraction effects.

The point of this biological dissection of attractiveness is this: what we consider attractive in members of the opposite sex are those characteristics that in our evolutionary history served as reliable indicators of reproductive potential. We are emotionally drawn to and become infatuated with those physical characteristics that informed our hominin ancestors about who had good genes, was healthy, and could produce strong, viable offspring. Our hominin ancestors could not carry out tests of androgen-to-estrogen proportions, testosterone levels, or parasitic presence in their potential mates (nor, as a routine practice, do we). However, this information was critical to reproductive success. What individual hominins could not do, natural selection accomplished over long periods of time and across large populations. In time, those hominins who selected as mates other hominins who had physical characteristics associated with fertility, viability, and health, were more likely to pass along the genes associated with that selective bias. We long for and lust after certain physical features because those features are good for the propagation of our genes today, just as they were thousands of years ago for our ancestors. Part of love seems to be an inexplicable pull of one to another—an attractive, romantic power that seems to overwhelm the intellect. It is that way because it evolved to be that way. It's not supposed to be easy to resist the genetic call of 2 million years of natural selection!

FRIENDSHIP. Among our ancestors, males and females likely chose mates who demonstrated a capacity for certain emotions. In males, this involved choosing females who could feel guilty about sexual deception. Females chose males who demonstrated a capacity for caring. The capacity for caring is certainly part of the complex of emotions that we call love, but the effects of sexual selection on emotions go further. Studies with primates show that both males and females exercise discriminative selection when choosing mates. This "choosiness" operates using a number of different criteria. Among group-living primates (such as chimpanzees and baboons), males tend to prefer females who are higher ranking and have proven skills in raising offspring. Females tend to prefer males who are higher ranking and possibly ones who come from outside the group, presumably as a guard against inbreeding (Hrdy, 1979; Small, 1993; Smuts, 1987). Both male and female primates have been found to have a preference for those opposite-sex individuals with whom they have developed a "special" long-term relationship (Smuts, 1985). This special relationship usually has been cultivated over an extended period of time during which the two have engaged in mutual grooming and preferential food sharing and the male has aided in protecting the female's offspring (which do not necessarily have any genetic relationship to him). If two humans shared an analogous type of relationship, we would probably consider them to be friends. Thus in our closest animal cousins, we find evidence of a pattern common among present-day humans, that is, mate preference as an extension of compatibility. The emergence of romance, sometimes unexpectedly, from friendship should not be considered a uniquely human process but should be understood as a human form of a long-standing evolutionary pattern.

We can now provide an evolutionary answer to the age-old question: What is this thing called love? It is not a single thing but an intricately textured mosaic. Like the diamond that often symbolizes it, love shows stunningly different forms as it is viewed from different perspectives. Like the diamond, love did not arrive suddenly, fully formed in the human species but evolved slowly, under pressure with the passing of the ages. Love is the passion and lust of the genes wanting nothing more than another body in which to see another day. Love is the self-sacrificing of the parent for the child, not because of desired martyrdom, but because of the deep, rewarding feeling of rightness it engenders. Love is the constant concern of long-time companions, sculpted in men by women over evolutionary time and in women by their burdensome infants. In humans especially and uniquely, love is knowing that it is right to love even when biology fails us and the feeling eludes us. Acting as love dictates even when our more primal passions push us in other directions may be when love has reached its highest form and humanity its highest peak.

Jealousy

Families should be a source of love and support and many are. Sadly, however, too many families are marked by violence and even murder. In their research on familial homicides, Daly and Wilson (1982) found that murder within the family is not indiscriminate. Family murder is overwhelmingly spousal murder, often involving a husband killing his wife (Fig. 8.1). In these instances, the most important and most frequently cited motive for wife killing was what Daly and Wilson termed "male sexual proprietariness" (Wilson & Daly, 1992, 1993). This refers to the fact that for men one of the most salient and critical elements of marriage is sexual exclusivity. The husband alone is to have sexual rights to his wife, and any hint of infidelity is cause for a severe reaction. In a substantial majority of cases of spousal homicide, the primary motivation behind the violence was the husband's discovery of or suspicion of his wife's infidelity or of her intention to leave him (Campbell, 1992; Chimbos, 1978; Daly & Wilson, 1998; Polk, 1994). This type of lethal assault is not confined to marriage. In fact, studies have found that women have a higher risk of murder in "nonregistered" unions such as cohabitation and common law marriages, presumably because of the increased instability of these arrangements and the increased likelihood of "adulterous" behavior (Daly & Wilson, 1988a, 1998; Wilson, Daly & Wright, 1993). Daly and Wilson (1998) reported that a chilling recurrent refrain of murderous men was the vow, "If I can't have her, no one will."

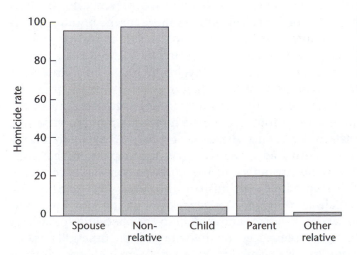

Figure 8.1 Homicide rates (per million) for household members based on their relationship status within the household. Note that the homicide rate for spouses is equal to that of nonrelatives, whereas the rate for genetic relatives (child, parent, others) is significantly lower. (Adapted from Daly & Wilson, 1998, p. 439.)

What lies behind this often fatal and particularly masculine emotional response? Individual and cultural factors certainly play an important role in male jealousy, but the universality of this response across varying cultures and throughout history argues for an even deeper level of explanation (Daly & Wilson, 1988; Wilson & Daly, 1992). In contrast to females, who tend to regard infidelity in terms of commitment and emotion, for males, infidelity is focused principally on the sexual act itself (Buss, Larsen, Westen, & Semmelroth, 1992; Daly, Wilson, & Weghorst, 1982). Put crudely, men don't care if their wives love someone else, as long as they don't have sex with anyone else. It is sexual infidelity that enrages men and, from an evolutionary perspective, this makes sense. An old adage says that, when it comes to children, women have knowledge and men have faith. That is, women know who the father is and men believe they know. Paternity certainty or the assurance that the child a man is raising does in fact carry his genes represented an acute problem for males throughout our evolutionary history. Imagine for a moment the predicament of a typical male hominin a few hundred thousand years ago. He has forsaken the unattached life for a (relatively) monogamous relationship with a female. Given the environment and circumstances of his tribe, this is probably the best course of action in terms of reproductive success. He will now hunt, protect, and provide for his wife and their offspring, ensuring that his genes will be passed on to the next generation. However, all his time, energy, and resources will go for naught if, while he is away on one of his frequent and extended hunting excursions, his wife has a temporary liaison with a local male. If this occurs, he will have been **cuckolded**—duped into raising another's offspring, incurring all of the labor and expense with none of the genetic payoff. It is not difficult to see that over evolutionary time those males who took an indifferent attitude toward cuckoldry would have been less likely to pass along their genes than those males for whom cuckoldry was an intolerable outrage. For our hominin ancestors, paternity certainty would have been enhanced for those males who were exquisitely sensitive to indicators of potential infidelity, tended to "guard" their females from other males, and were known to react strongly, even violently, to any evidence of extramarital shenanigans.

Although jealousy's most potent form is usually associated with males, females are not immune from this emotion. With females, however, jealousy is less focused on the sexual privileges of a relationship and more on the resource privileges. Men tend to feel more threatened by their wives' sexual infidelity; women tend to feel more threatened by a husband's emotional infidelity (Buss, Larsen, Westen, & Semmelroth, 1992; Daly, Wilson, & Weghorst, 1982). If a husband's emotional concern strays from his wife and their mutual offspring, then the resources necessary for raising the children could be in jeopardy. Turn our previous scenario around and imagine it from the female hominin's point of view. She has no concerns about maternity certainty, she knows precisely what children carry her genes. Her problem is ensuring adequate resources for shepherding her children to maturity. Without the contribution of her husband, her ability to secure those resources is seriously jeopardized. The husband, however, should he become enamored of another, can always propagate his genes through the "other woman" and, in the process, transfer his resources and energy to the alternative offspring. This could have devastating consequences for the wife and her fitness. Thus, we can expect natural selection to have favored women who were highly sensitive to indicators of their husband's emotional infidelity and who reacted strongly in the face of such circumstances.

Disgust

If one needed any convincing that different creatures have evolved very different views of the world, then stop for a moment and consider the members of the family *Scarabaeidae*, also known as dung beetles. Nothing could be more delightful to these bugs than to happen upon a 3-lb blop of elephant defecation: a wonderful place to settle down and raise the family—and good eating to boot! Why is it that the human reaction to elephant dung is one of disgust but for the dung beetle it is unmitigated rapture? What is it that we just don't get? The answer, of course, is that we did not evolve to be dung beetles, so dung does not serve the same function in our ecological niche as it does for the these insects. For humans, excrement is a source of contamination and infection, not nutrition. Therefore, it would hardly be in our survival and reproductive interests to have any special attraction to it. In fact, over evolutionary time, those of our ancestors who had an affinity for such things as dung, rotted meat, or vomit were far less likely to survive and reproduce than were those who avoided such things. Those objects and events that cause revulsion and disgust in us are those that in our evolutionary past represented some sort of danger, in this case danger from microbial contamination or parasitic infection. The obnoxious odor and nauseated feeling associated with disgusting objects strongly discourages ingestion and compels us to put distance between ourselves and such objects to lower the probability of potentially harmful contact.

Hart (1990) observed that in many species ritualistic behaviors are used to help reduce the threat of infection. For example, cats lick and groom themselves incessantly, and birds preen. In primates, grooming helps to clean the fur and remove ticks and other foreign particles. Marks and Nesse (1994) drew a connection between the ritualistic behaviors used to avoid contamination in other species and the behaviors used by humans, especially those with obsessive compulsive disorder (OCD). Individuals with OCD often wash and groom themselves endlessly to avoid or remove some (largely imagined) contamination. In OCD, normally adaptive responses, such as washing the hands or combing the hair, become exaggerated and excessive to the point of debilitation. From an evolutionary standpoint, this can be understood as an extreme form of an otherwise adaptive, functional response.

Fear

Fear usually is regarded as an emotional response to a specific threatening object. The response involves sympathetic nervous system activity resulting in rapid breathing, sweaty palms, pupil dilation, increased heart rate, changes in blood flow and other physiological effects often described as the "fight or flight" response. Upon encountering the threatening stimulus, the fearful individual goes into a highly aroused emotional and physiological state that facilitates escape behaviors. The adaptive function of fear is not difficult to fathom. Those who blithely wandered into the jaws of mortal danger ran the very probable risk of never returning and reproducing. Over the course of our evolutionary history, mortal dangers of many types were a repeated occurrence. These may have included predatory animals, threatening situations (such as being lost or trapped), exposure to elements (cold, heat, storms), poisons, and other hominins. Those of our ancestors who successfully avoided or fled from these dangers were more likely to leave progeny then those who did not. Over long spans of time, we would expect that the genetic disposition to feel afraid under the appropriate circumstances would spread in the population.

That modern-day humans have fears is not surprising. What *is* surprising, however (especially if one lacks an evolutionary perspective), are the objects and situations that are the sources of most people's fears. When surveyed about what causes discomfort or fear, the highest-rated responses were enclosed or high exposed places, mice, flying, spiders, and thunder and lightning (survey in *Public Opinion*, 1984). Marks (1987) reported similar findings, adding such items as social scrutiny, separation, and leaving the home to the short list of common fears. What is remarkable about this list of fears is how poorly it matches with the list of actual mortal threats common in our society. Far more people today are killed in auto accidents or by gun violence than by snakes, spiders, mice, lightning strikes, or from getting lost. Yet cars, guns, and other recent dangers, such as cigarettes, alcohol, and high-fat foods, provoke little if any fear in most people (Cook, Hodes, & Lang, 1986). Rare is the patient who seeks clinical help for a gun- or car-based phobia, whereas snake, spider, and unfamiliar territory phobias are quite common. Why are humans so deathly afraid of things that really are not all that threatening but intrepid in the face of those that are?

A large part of the answer, of course, lies in our evolution. We fear those objects, events, and circumstances that posed life-threatening dangers not in our current environment but in our EEA. Imagine what life must have been like for the millions of years that hominins roamed the forests and savannas of Africa. Snake venom, poisonous spider bites, and diseases carried by rats and mice would have been recurrent and potentially lethal dangers. Moreover, because these threats usually would have been recognized only at close contact, a strong, immediate response would have been required to escape. By contrast, a threat from a large predator could be identified from a greater distance and handled better with a more calculated, less automatic response. Antelope on the African plain attend to the presence of a lioness but do not show a fear response until she shows evidence of a charge.

Two important biological principles help establish fear reactions to certain stimuli. The first is called **prepotency** and refers to the fact that specific sensory stimuli attract our attention and elicit more powerful responses than others. For example, snake patterns and eye-like patterns tend to cause inordinate arousal in our nervous system (Marks, 1969; Ohman & Dimberg, 1984). One study provided a nice example of prepotency in action. Subjects were shown arrays of pictures containing both fear-inducing objects (spiders, snakes) and non-fear-inducing objects (mushrooms, flowers). Sometimes subjects were required to search for and identify the feared objects, and sometimes they had to search for the nonfeared objects. Subjects were significantly faster at identifying the feared objects, which appeared to "pop" out at the subjects and could be found easily, regardless of the number of distracting objects present in the array (Ohman, Flykt, & Esteves, 2001; also, see Box 8.1 for more on the detection of threatening stimuli).

Elaine Fox
The Detection of Threatening Faces

PROFILE: *Dr. Elaine Fox studied psychology at University College Dublin, where she completed her Ph.D. in 1988 on the psychopharmacological mechanisms underlying anxiety and cognitive processes. She was appointed Lecturer in Psychology at Victoria University of Wellington, New Zealand. In 1993, she returned to lecture in psychology at University College Dublin before going to the University of Essex (UK) in 1994. She has been appointed Associate Editor of the journal* Cognition and Emotion. *Her research spans many issues, including the evolutionary mechanisms behind the perception of threatening stimuli such as faces.*

BOX 8.1

The "Face in the Crowd" Effect

Our perceptual systems may have been selected to be especially sensitive to certain stimuli, especially those that might represent potential threats to our survival and/or reproductive success. This hypersensitivity and hyper-responsiveness has sometimes been referred to as **prepotency**. As a social species, human perceptual systems might be predicted to have evolved to be especially attuned to threatening facial expressions. One study seemed to provide evidence for this prediction (Hansen & Hansen, 1988). Subjects were required to search for a happy face within groups of either three or eight angry faces or to search for an angry face within group of either three or eight happy faces. The subjects took longer to find the happy face among eight angry faces than among three. However, finding the angry face took about the same amount of time, regardless of whether it was among eight or three happy faces. This finding suggests that angry faces "pop out" of a display, regardless of how many other patterns are present, but happy faces must be searched for in a controlled, purposeful manner. This

study, however, came under strong criticism for methodological reasons. A number of subsequent studies failed to replicate its findings. The question remained open: are humans especially attuned to threatening faces?

To address this question, Dr. Elaine Fox and her colleagues at Essex University had subjects view seven different types of displays, all involving schematic faces such as the ones seen in Figure 8.A. Three of the displays were "same" displays, meaning that all the faces had the same expression (either happy, angry, or neutral). Four other displays were "different" displays, in which one of the faces varied from the rest. These included: (1) an angry face among happy faces, (2) an angry face among neutral faces, (3) a happy face among angry faces, and (4) a happy face among neutral faces. Subjects were shown all seven types of displays and were required to determine (as quickly as possible) if one of the faces in the display was different from the rest (with a yes or no response).

Fox and her colleagues hypothesized that if evolution had designed the human visual system to be

Figure 8.A Examples of the displays used in the Fox et al. experiment on facial perception. (A) an angry face among happy faces in a four-face display. (B) An angry/sad face among neutral faces in an 8-face display. (Adapted from Fox et al., 2000, p. 66.)

continued

The Detection of Threatening Faces (continued)

BOX 8.1 especially sensitive to threatening faces (the threat hypothesis) then subjects' reaction times (rt) should show the following patterns. (1) Subjects should show longer reaction times on angry "same" displays than on happy "same" displays. In other words, subjects should linger longer over a display of all angry faces before responding "no" (no different face here) than on a display of all happy faces. This should be true because angry faces ought to exert a stronger "hold" on one's visual attention than happy faces. (2) Subjects should be significantly faster at finding an angry face among

neutral faces than at finding a happy face among neutral faces. (3) Increasing the number of faces in the display should not affect the reaction time for finding an angry face but should cause longer reaction times for a happy face. The last two hypotheses stem from the idea that our attentional systems have evolved to be especially efficient at detecting and processing a threatening face.

Figure 8.B shows the average reaction times for angry, happy, and neutral "same" displays (left graph). The average rt for angry displays (981 ms) was significantly slower than that for happy display

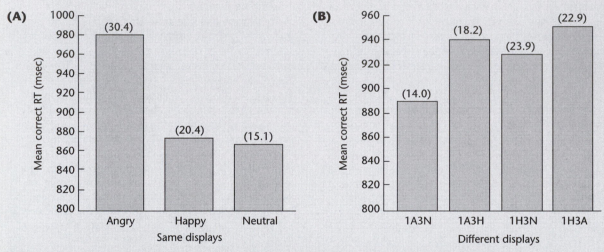

Figure 8.B Average reaction times (rt) for "same" (a) and "different" (b) displays, with percentage of errors in parentheses. (A) As predicted, the rt for the angry display is significantly slower than that for the happy display. (B) As predicted, the rt for finding an angry face among neutral faces (1A3N) was significantly faster than for finding a happy face among neutral faces (1H3N). (Adapted from Fox et al., 2000, p. 71.)

The second important principle is called **preparedness**, which refers to the fact that we are naturally inclined to develop certain responses to specific stimuli. For example, we naturally develop a nauseated reaction to bad food and a fearful reaction to snakes, not vice versa (Seligman, 1970). Just as water running down a hillside follows the path of least resistance, prepotency and preparedness provide the biologically preconditioned route to the establishment of certain fears. In normal humans, it is far easier to condition a fear response to pictures of snakes and spiders than to pictures of flowers and mushrooms (Ohman, Eriksson, & Olofsson, 1975; Ohman, Dimberg, & Ost, 1985). Even in individuals (such as alcoholics under treatment) who might be motivated to fear something, inducing fear to the target stimulus (in this case, alcohol) is often difficult (Gelder & Marks, 1970). Other primates show similar effects. Although they are not born fearing snakes, a young rhesus monkey need only see an occasion or two of another monkey responding fearfully to a snake to develop such a fear. The same, however, does not

(870 ms). The difference between the average number of errors (shown in parentheses above each bar graph) also was significant. The right graph shows the average rt data for the "different" displays, in which one face varied from the rest. The average rt for finding an angry face among three neutral faces (1A3N) was significantly faster and produced significantly fewer errors than finding a happy face among neutral faces (1H3N). These findings provide strong support for the first two hypotheses.

Figure 8.C shows rt data when subjects were required to search for an angry or happy face in a display of either four or eight total faces. Note that the rt increases with display size when subjects are searching for either an angry or happy face. However, the amount of increase is significantly less for angry faces than happy faces, or, put another way, increasing the total number of faces in the display has a far greater impact on a search for a single happy face than on a search for a single angry face. Angry faces do not automatically "pop out" of a crowd, but they are located much more efficiently than a happy face, a finding that offers support for hypothesis three.

The results of this experiment support the notion that the human visual system is especially tuned to the presence of a threatening face. An angry face appears to exert a powerful attractive pull on our attentional mechanisms, and, once detected, we seem to dwell on the face for an extended amount of time, unable to disengage and move on to other patterns. These are exactly the sort of characteristics one might expect if our perceptual systems had been honed by natural selection for hypersensitivity to threatening social stimuli.

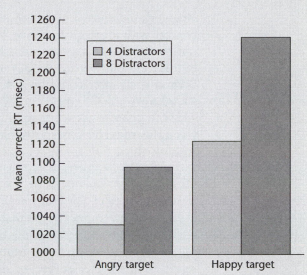

Figure 8.C Average rt data for finding an angry (left) or happy face (right) in either a four- or eight-face display. Note that in both cases the rt increases with the display size increase. However, the amount of the increase for the angry face is less. (Adapted from Fox et al., 2000, p. 85.)

Sources:
Fox, E., Lester, V., Russo, R., Bowles, R.J., Pichler, A., & Dutton, K. (2000). Facial expressions of emotion: Are angry faces detected more efficiently? *Cognition and Emotion*, 14, 61–92.
Hansen, C.H., & Hansen, R.D. (1988). Finding the face in the crowd: An anger superiority effect. *Journal of Personality and Social Psychology*, 54, 917–924.

apply to other stimuli such as flowers (Cook & Mineka, 1989; Mineka, Davidson, Cook, & Keir, 1984).

The development of fear in human infants has also provided strong evidence for naturally selected adaptations that govern *what* we fear and *when* we fear it. The emergence of certain fears, such as the fear of strangers (stranger anxiety), fear of separation from a caregiver (separation anxiety), fear of heights, and fear of collision, all show consistent patterns based on the physical maturation of the infant (see LaFreniere, 2000, pp. 121–129 for discussion). For example, the first evidence of stranger anxiety can be found in 4–5-month-olds in the form of a delayed negative reaction to the prolonged presence of a strange face. A stranger staring in silence at an infant will elicit little reaction at first. After about 30 seconds, however, the infant will begin to cry (Bronson, 1972). This reaction has been attributed to the infant's failure to assimilate the strange face into a familiar schema. Four to five months later, infants will demonstrate a strong and immediate negative reaction to a stranger's presence or approach, usually involving crying and attempts to establish contact with a caregiver (Spitz, 1965). Cross-cultural and twin studies have supported the notion of a consistent, biologically mediated timetable for the emergence of this fear (Ainsworth, 1963; Dennis, 1940; Plomin & DeFries, 1985; Sroufe, 1977). Because a stranger could be a threat, the adaptive value of this response is fairly straightforward. Of equal significance is that the timing of the response coincides with the infant's increasing mobility in the second half of the first year of life. Just when the infant becomes most likely to encounter strangers, a negative (and loud) emotional reaction emerges to alert his or her mother of possible danger.

The development of our fears, however, is not a biologically closed, predetermined process. The intensity of an infant's fear reaction is often influenced by environmental factors. For example, in cultures such as Japan, in which nearly constant mother–infant contact in the first years of life is the norm, infants tend to demonstrate more intense separation anxiety reactions (Miyake, Chen, & Campos, 1985). Moreover, infants often use others as a basis for learning the "right" emotional response to an object, event, or situation. This is referred to as **social referencing**. Infants will carefully monitor their mothers' reaction to strangers or to novel objects and use these as models for their own response (Feinman & Lewis, 1983; Marks, 1987). By monitoring a caregiver's facial and vocal signals, infants can be conditioned to fear a variety of objects or events. This suggests that our fear system is one designed with both innate predispositions and flexibility based on certain environmental cues. It is as if nature has provided us with the dual message of "fear these" (a naturally selected set stock of feared items based on recurrent threats in the EEA, such as snakes) and "if there are other things to fear, learn them based on critical relevant environmental cues, such as mom's facial reaction."

Emotional Pathologies and Pseudopathologies

Anxiety and Anxiety Disorders

The distinction between fear and anxiety is subtle. Subjectively, the two emotions are nearly identical, but two important differences separate them: (1) fear and anxiety have different effects on the body, and (2) the stimuli that trigger them are dissimilar. Let's look first at the physical effects. In one experiment (Rhudy & Meagher, 2000), subjects were exposed to either three brief electric shocks (fear condition) or the threat of electric shocks (anxiety condition). Subjective and physiological indices were used to verify that the condition induced the targeted emotion (either fear or anxiety). Pain thresholds were tested both before and after exposure to the emotion-inducing experiences for all subjects. Fear was found to increase one's pain threshold, whereas anxiety decreased one's pain threshold, a result that replicated previous studies using animals. In other words, fear makes one more tolerant of pain, but anxiety has the opposite effect. We will soon see why this makes sense from an evolutionary perspective, but first we'll look at the stimuli that trigger fear and anxiety.

The second difference between fear and anxiety is the objectiveness of the triggering stimulus. For fear, that which causes the onset of the emotion is generally clear, but, for anxiety, that which causes the reaction is often more amorphous. Humans have evolved the capacity to react similarly to both specific life-threatening stimuli (with fear) and veiled innuendoes of threat (with anxiety). Why would natural selection equip us with the capacity to become uptight at the mere hint of trouble (hints that are not always consciously recognized)?

If we put the two distinctive features of anxiety together, we begin to get some clues as to its adaptive function. Anxiety is: (1) a sensitizing emotion, especially with regard to pain, that (2) often occurs in the face of vague, imprecise triggering stimuli. Fear means that one is *in* a dangerous situation and must focus energy on escaping, thus an increased tolerance to pain would be helpful. Anxiety, however, means that one *might be entering into* a threatening situation and, therefore, an increased sensitivity to indicators of danger (such as pain) would be useful. It appears that our nervous system operates using the **smoke detector principle**: false alarms, although annoying, are still less costly than failing to react to a real crisis. The cues to a threatening situation may not always be obvious. If one's reaction is delayed until danger is a certainty, it may already be too late. When dealing with life-threatening situations, only one failure is enough to incur an enormous fitness cost. Thus, a selective advantage would go to those who gear up the fear response and become more responsive and vigilant at the slightest evidence of danger—even evidence that might fall below the level of conscious processing. Anxiety may alert us to the fact that there is something in our current context to be concerned about, despite the fact that at the moment it may be unclear exactly what should be feared.

Nesse and Williams (1994) provided an example of how anxiety might serve adaptive purposes. After being placed on an antianxiety medication, a female patient was emboldened to demand that her husband leave the house. He did, leaving her with three children, a mortgage, no income, and no friends or family to help out. In the long run, ending her marriage may not have been a bad course of action. A bit more anxiety about the transition, however, actually might have been beneficial.

If anxiety is something of an evolved "early warning" system, then its current prevalence as an emotional disorder may stem, at least in part, from the quickened, sometimes frenzied pace of modern life. Although the hunting–gathering lifestyle may lack much in terms of material comforts, the daily stress load is minimal. It often takes only a few hours of actual labor to ensure the day's supply of food (Sahlins, 1972). If this was true for our hominin ancestors, then another characteristic unique to modern *H. sapiens* is our tendency to scurry frantically from one place to another, finally hitting the bed harried and bedraggled. Natural selection may not have prepared us for an environment in which our anxiety response is continuously activated but in which potential threats and dangers are never examined closely enough to narrow down the potential source of the response. If this were to occur repeatedly, without ever resolving the cause of the response, the mounting ambiguities might become overwhelming.

PANIC ATTACKS. A panic attack refers to an overwhelming onset of anxiety that seems to have no discernible trigger. Usually an individual is away from home and, for no obvious reason, is overcome by a powerful sense of imminent danger. The attack usually consists of such symptoms as shortness of breath, sweating, flushing, dizziness, chest pain, and an irresistible need to "get out of here" (Nesse, 1987). The disorder affects about 6 of 1,000 men and 10 of 1,000 women. A single episode usually lasts about 30 minutes, followed by a prolonged period of exhaustion. Days may go by before the next attack. However, very often the frequency of attacks increases over time. Numerous theories have been attempted to explain panic attacks but none fully accounts for all of the symptoms. For example, Freud initially claimed that panic attacks were the result of sexual deprivation. One has to be extraordinarily creative, however, to connect sexual deprivation with such symptoms as chest and abdominal pain and a need to flee. Learning theories have argued that panic attacks result from an unconditioned response that spreads via stimulus generalization (Marks, Boulougouris, & Marset, 1971; Jansson & Lars-Govan, 1982). This, however, does not explain how patients with substantially different past histories end up with very similar symptoms. Even the success that physiological approaches have enjoyed with pharmacological treatments does not definitively demonstrate that organic defects are the ultimate cause of panic attacks (see Nesse, 1987, for discussion).

Nesse (1987) argued that an evolutionary view on panic attacks provides the best explanation for its symptomatology. He pointed out that of the 12 symptoms used to define panic attacks in the third edition of the *Diagnostic and Statistical Manual of Mental Disorders* (DSM-III), eight are either directly or indirectly involved in facilitating an escape response. In his view, the panic attack represents an extreme form of an otherwise normal, evolved response. In the case of the patient suffering from panic attacks, the normal anxiety response has become hypersensitive. Just as variability occurs in other evolved, genetically inherited traits, such as metabolic rate, body proportions, visual acuity, etc., there is variability in the anxiety response. A small proportion of individuals will fall at the extreme end of that variability. The problem of those with panic disorder is not that the response itself is dysfunctional but that it is triggered too easily and too often.

AGORAPHOBIA. Although agoraphobia is regarded as a distinct syndrome, it is closely related to panic disorder. In agoraphobia, the panic symptoms occur under circumstances in which the individual is in unfamiliar territory, wide-open spaces, or crowds of strangers. As with panic disorder, a variety of theoretical explanations have been proposed, but none adequately accounts for all of the factors associated with the problem. From an evolutionary perspective, the situations that spark anxiety in the agoraphobic are not difficult to understand. Open spaces with little in the way of shelter, hiding places, or escape routes would have exposed a modest-size hominin to an array of dangers, including large predators, weather, and other potentially hostile hominins. Unfamiliar territory would have meant isolation from one's tribe and all of the serious dangers entailed therein. Finally, given humanity's long history of tribal and ethnic conflict, it is hard to expect that our hominin ancestors were anything but fiercely xenophobic, thus being among strangers would never have been a promising predicament for our ancestors (Alexander, 1987; Wrangham, 1987). In healthy individuals, situations such as these elicit reactions ranging from mild concern to manageable anxiety. In agoraphobics, the response has simply gone to an uncontrollable extreme. Some aspects of agoraphobia seem well suited to an evolutionary explanation. For example, the fact that agoraphobics typically seek home and kin to relieve their symptoms is in perfect harmony with the character of an escape response. In addition, the fact that agoraphobia is more common in women than men also would make evolutionary sense. In our evolutionary past, women probably had more to fear from an unfamiliar setting, given the difficulties of trying to escape or hide with a child in tow.

Nesse (1987) offered a number of testable hypotheses stemming from an evolutionary approach to panic and agoraphobic disorders, empirically strengthening this new perspective. First, if escape reactions have been naturally selected for in humans and disorders of escape reactions represent extreme forms of this adaptation, then we would expect panic disorder and agoraphobia to show similar patterns across variations in human cultures. Already, he claims, there is some confirmation of this. Second, thresholds for panic responses should be normally distributed in the population, with those suffering from disorders representing the tail of the distribution. Finally, medications that block panic attacks also should block normal, adaptive anxiety responses and thus could be harmful in some situations. Medications that reset the anxiety response should be more effective in returning a patient to optimal functioning. Evolutionary medicine, as outlined in Nesse and Williams (1994) provides an emerging and insightful new perspective on physical and mental illness. These hypotheses provide a concrete way for evolutionary ideas to contribute to our understanding of pathology.

Cheaters: The Evolution of the Sociopath and Psychopath

Cooperative relationships are vulnerable to cheaters, those who take without giving. Emotions such as guilt and shame have evolved to curb cheating and promote cooperative interactions. However, it should be kept in mind that natural selection is no moralist. Cheating can be an effective strategy for enhancing fitness. It should be no surprise that cheating, too, has evolved and that an extreme form is embodied in the sociopath. To be an effective cheater, one must be able to display the outward signs of commitment but with none of the subjective emotional experience. Displaying concern, compassion, guilt, and shame can attract others who seek reciprocal relationships. Failing to actually "feel" any of these emotions frees the cheater to exploit the relationship to the fullest without suffering any sentimental consequences. In short, cheaters need to be able to "fake it," and the really vicious cheaters, sociopaths, fake it very well indeed. Because, we all occasionally "cheat" to various degrees in relationships, Mealey (1995) argued that the genetic predisposition to cheat remains in the population (and probably always will). Like all evolved traits, the tendency to cheat occurs in varying degrees, with a small minority of people having inherited an extreme form of the trait. By most outward indicators, these individuals seem normal, but they are utterly bereft of any capacity to experience the social regulatory emotions of guilt, empathy, remorse, or shame. They usually are quite sociable and have the ability to exhibit a range of emotions, but their expressions are empty of any genuine, internal feeling. In addition, their intellectual and reasoning skills are often first-rate, as evidenced by the sophistication of some of the scams they successfully execute. In describing one sociopathic subject, Widom (1976) remarked, "[he is] aware of the discrepancy between his behavior and societal expectations, but he seems to be neither guided by the possibility of such a discrepancy nor disturbed by its occurrence" (p. 614).

In supporting her theory that sociopathy represents an evolved, inherited trait, Mealey (1995) pointed to cross-cultural studies showing a strong genetic component to criminal behavior (e.g., Christiansen, 1977; Cloninger & Gottesman, 1987; Eysenck & Gudjonsson, 1989; Raine, 1993; Wilson & Herrnstein, 1985). In addition, the sociopath cannot be explained in terms of an intellectual or cognitive deficit, because these typically are not present in these subjects. Moreover, although environment plays a role in criminality and sociopathy, environmental effects are inconsistent and most children reared under "at risk" environmental conditions do not end up as sociopaths. Instead, Mealey argued that the environment interacts with genetic predispositions in such a way that those already genetically susceptible to cheating are increasingly prone to adopting that strategy under certain conditions. For example, males who are socially competitively disadvantaged would be expected to fall disproportionately into the ranks of the sociopathic. Males have evolved to compete for access to females (often through status), and when "legitimate" avenues of competition seem unavailable, a cheating strategy becomes more attractive, especially in those already predisposed to do so. In fact, empirical evidence tends to support this. Males are 3–4 times more likely to be sociopaths than are females (Robins, Tipp, & Przybeck, 1991). Among the cross-cultural risk factors for criminality, including sociopathy, nearly all either directly or indirectly relate to resource competition and acquisition, for example: youth, low economic status, large number of siblings, single-parent or disrupted family upbringing, and racial minority status (Cohen & Machalek, 1988; Ellis, 1988; Kenrick, Dantchik, & MacFarlane, 1983; Wilson & Herrnstein, 1985). The gene–environment interaction argument is also supported by studies showing that the biological contribution to criminality is stronger in upper-class subjects than in lower-class subjects (Satterfield, 1987; Raine & Dunkin, 1990; Raine & Venables, 1984). Because upper-class subjects occupy a more socially competitive station, only those with a very strong genetic tendency toward cheating would risk engaging in criminal or sociopathic behaviors. Among the lower classes, even relatively weak genetic tendencies toward cheating might be adequate for the manifestation of sociopathic behaviors, given their competitively disadvantaged circumstances.

The evolutionary approach to understanding criminal pathology also has been extended to psychopaths. Psychopaths are similar to sociopaths in that they seem incapable of empathizing with others or feeling guilty or remorseful about their transgressions. They are different, however, in that they are antisocial and often aggressive and violent. In most social species, mechanisms have evolved for regulating violence among conspecifics. Distress calls and submissive acts, such as whimpering or cowering, usually will result in the cessation of an aggressive attack. These same signals operate in humans as well. Crying, fleeing, or going limp often signal the aggressor that his or her opponent has "had enough."

Blair (1995) proposed that humans possess an evolved mechanism called a **violence inhibition mechanism** (VIM), which responds to signs of distress in others by activating withdrawal behaviors. Activation of the VIM is subjectively experienced as a moral emotion, such as empathy, sympathy, or compassion. Recent physiological studies support the notion that in some individuals the VIM fails to develop properly or is damaged, leaving these individuals less able or unable to experience moral emotions (Blair, Jones, Clark, & Smith, 1997). Without these emotions, a critical internal mechanism for regulating violent or aggressive behavior is lost. In comparing healthy individuals with psychopaths, Blair (1995) found that healthy individuals make a distinction between moral transgressions (those resulting in harm to a victim) and conventional ones (rule violations that do not result in victims, i.e., stealing from the cookie jar), but psychopaths do not. Moreover, when asked to explain why they believed a certain act was either right or wrong, psychopaths made significantly fewer references to a victim's welfare as a reason for judging an act as a transgression. This tends to support Blair's contention that it is the experience of moral emotions resulting from activation of the VIM that alerts individuals to a moral transgression and compels them to inhibit aggressive acts. The fact that psychopaths fail to make the moral/conventional distinction puts them into a unique category. People of different ages and cultures have been found capable of making this distinction, as have autistic children and abused children (Nucci, 1981; Song, Smetana, & Kim, 1987; Smetana, Kelly, & Twentyman, 1984). This tends to support Blair's argument for an an evolved, genetic factor in the making of a psychopath.

Depression

Depression is another emotional disorder that has attracted the attention of evolutionary-minded theorists and practitioners. Nesse (1990; 1999), for example, argued that some forms of depression could represent an evolved strategy for **disengaging from unattainable goals**. He pointed to examples in which antidepressive medications have been ineffectual but changes in life goals, careers, or personal ambitions have brought about dramatic improvement. Our moods, according to Nesse, help to regulate our investment in different activities or goals. Enthusiasm and optimism promote investment, whereas malaise and indifference reduce it. In our evolutionary past, those with internal mechanisms for telling them when to quit expending energy on an unrealistic objective would have had a fitness advantage over those who depleted themselves. As with other pathologies, the chronic depressive may be one in whom this mechanism has taken an extreme form, becoming active too quickly and relenting too slowly (Gut, 1989; Nesse, 1999).

The **social competition hypothesis** of depression also emphasizes the adaptiveness of knowing when to quit. According to the proponents of this hypothesis, depression would have evolved as a mechanism for compelling an organism to yield in competition to avoid the costs of continued conflict (Price, Sloman, Gardner, Gilbert, & Rohde, 1994). In the social and hierarchical context of primate life, mechanisms have evolved for regulating competition and maintaining group cohesion. Those who lose out in social competition must find a way of accepting (at least temporarily) their "one down" status. An "involuntary subordination strategy," in which the individual is inhibited from challenging those of higher status, affords a number of adaptive advantages: (1) it signals to others the non-threatening status of the individual; (2) it allows for reconciliation with former competitors; and (3) it serves as an important mechanism in preserving energy and resources by withdrawing the individual from additional, costly competition. As memory and cognitive capacity increase in more complex creatures, isolated judgments of when to engage or disengage from competition can become generalized into a more stable assessment of one's capabilities. **Resource holding potential** (RHP) is the term used by evolutionary theorists to describe an animal's assessment of its own prospects in competition. RHP may represent a primordial form of what is called "self-esteem" in humans (Archer, 1988; Parker, 1974). From an evolutionary point of view, low self-esteem may prevent individuals from participating in hopeless competitive engagements.

Price and his colleagues (Price et al., 1994) argued that the social competition hypothesis of depression provides a more complete explanation of the symptomatology of depression than do alternative models. For example, most other approaches

Robert Wright
The Evolution of Despair

BOX 8.2
The following are excerpted, with permission, from Robert Wright's article "The evolution of despair," which appeared in the August 28, 1995, issue of *Time Magazine*.

...The exact series of social contexts that shaped the human mind over the past couple of million years is, of course, lost in the mists of prehistory. In trying to reconstruct the "ancestral environment," evolutionary psychologists analyze the nearest approximations available—the sort of technologically primitive societies that the Unabomber extols. The most prized examples are the various hunter–gatherer societies that anthropologists have studied this century, such as the Ainu of Japan, the !Kung San of southern Africa, and the Ache of South America. Also valuable are societies with primitive agriculture in the few cases where—as with some Yanomamo villages in Venezuela—they lack the contaminating contact with moderners that reduces the anthropological value of some hunter–gatherer societies

...The past usefulness of unpleasant feelings is the reason periodic unhappiness is a natural condition, found in every culture, impossible to escape. What isn't natural is going crazy—for sadness to linger on into debilitating depression, for anxiety to grow chronic and paralyzing. These are largely diseases of modernity. When researchers examined rural villagers in Samoa, they discovered what were by Western standards extraordinarily low levels of cortisol, a biochemical by-product of anxiety. And when a Western anthropologist tried to study depression among the Kaluli of New Guinea, he couldn't find any.

One thing that helps turn the perfectly natural feeling of sadness or dejection into the pathology known as depression is social isolation. Today one-fourth of American households consist of a single person. That's up from 8% in 1940—and, apparently, from roughly zero percent in the ancestral environment. Hunter–gatherer societies, for all their diversity, typically feature intimacy and stability: people live in close contact with roughly the same array of several dozen friends and relatives for decades. They may move to another village, but usually either to join a new family network (as upon marriage) or to return to an old one (as upon separation). The evolutionary psychologists John Tooby and Leda Cosmides see in the mammoth popularity of the TV show *Cheers* during the 1980s a visceral yearning for the world of our ancestors—a place where life brought regular, random encounters with friends and not just occasional, carefully scheduled lunches with them; where there were spats and rivalries, yes, but where grievances were usually heard in short order and tensions thus resolved.

As anyone who has lived in a small town can attest, social intimacy comes at the price of privacy: everybody knows your business. And that's true in spades when next-door neighbors live not in Norman Rockwell clapboard homes but in thatched huts. Still, social transparency has its virtues. The anthropologist Phillip Walker has studied the bones of more than 5,000 children from hundreds of preindustrial cultures, dating back to 4,000 B.C. He has yet to find the scattered bone bruises that are the skeletal hallmark of "battered-child syndrome." In some modern societies, Walker estimates, such bruises would be found on more than 1 in 20 children who die between the ages of one and four. Walker accounts for

adequately explain the dysphoric mood associated with depression, but only the evolutionary model provides a compelling explanation for the distorted value assessment common in depression. In other words, most depressives find that previously rewarding activities and valued goal pursuits hold little interest or importance when in the depressive state. As an adaptation designed to disengage one from social competition, this aspect of depression makes sense. Organisms fight harder for more valued or rewarding resources; lowering the perceived value of an object or activity promotes cessation of activity designed to attain it (Parker, 1974). An evolutionary model also explains why depression is more prevalent among older subjects. It is the older generation that must cede power and resources to the younger, often a painful process (witness the battles between aging alpha male chimpanzees and their "young and hungry" competitors).

Some aspects of depression may not be attributable to a social competition hypothesis and may have other evolutionary origins. For example, the differing mating strategies of men and women may contribute to the increased incidence of depression in women (McGuire, Troisi, & Raleigh, 1997). Men tend to be more

this contrast with several factors, including a grim reminder of Hobbesian barbarism: unwanted children in primitive societies were often killed at birth, rather than resented and brutalized for years. But another factor, he believes, is the public nature of primitive child rearing, notably the watchful eye of a child's aunts, uncles, grandparents, or friends. In the ancestral environment, there was little mystery about what went on behind closed doors, because there weren't any.

In that sense, Tooby and Cosmides have noted, nostalgia for the suburban nuclear family of the 1950s—which often accompanies current enthusiasm for "family values"—is ironic. The insular coziness of Ozzie and Harriet's home is less like our natural habitat than, say, the more diffuse social integration of Andy Griffith's Mayberry. Andy's son Opie is motherless, but he has a dutiful great-aunt to watch over him—and, anyway, can barely sit on the front porch without seeing a family friend.

To be sure, keeping nuclear families intact has virtues that are underscored by evolutionary psychology, notably in keeping children away from stepfathers, who, as the evolutionary psychologists Martin Daly and Margo Wilson predicted and then documented, are much more prone to child abuse than biological fathers. But to worship the suburban household of the 1950s is to miss much of the trouble with contemporary life.

Though people talk about "urbanization" as the process that ushered in modern ills, many urban neighborhoods at mid-century were in fact fairly communal; it's hard to walk into a Brooklyn brownstone day after day without bumping into neighbors. It was suburbanization that brought the combination of transience and residential isolation that leaves many people feeling a bit alone in their own neighborhoods. (These days, thanks to electric garage-door openers, you can drive straight into your house, never risking contact with a neighbor.)

The suburbs have been particularly hard on women with young children. In the typical hunter–gatherer village, mothers can reconcile a home life with a work life fairly gracefully, and in a richly social context. When they gather food, their children stay either with them or with aunts, uncles, grandparents, cousins, or lifelong friends. When they're back at the village, child care is a mostly public task—extensively social, even communal. The anthropologist Marjorie Shostak wrote of life in an African hunter–gatherer village, "The isolated mother burdened with bored small children is not a scene that has parallels in !Kung daily life."

Evolutionary psychology thus helps explain why modern feminism got its start after the suburbanization of the 1950s. The landmark 1963 book *The Feminine Mystique* by Betty Friedan grew out of her 1959 conversation with a suburban mother who spoke with "quiet desperation" about the anger and despair that Friedan came to call "the problem with no name" and a doctor dubbed "the housewife's syndrome." It is only natural that modern mothers rearing children at home are more prone to depression than working mothers and that they should rebel.

But even working mothers suffer depression more often than working men. And that shouldn't shock us either. To judge by hunter–gatherer societies, it is unnatural for a mother to get up each day, hand her child over to someone she barely knows and then head off for 10 hours of work—not as unnatural as staying home alone with a child, maybe, but still a likely source of guilt and anxiety. Finding a middle ground, enabling women to be workers and mothers, is one of the great social challenges of our day.

inclined toward short-term sexual liaisons that can conflict with female strategies and lead to profound disappointment in women who seek longer-term commitments. Moreover, given the male tendency toward possessiveness and a preference for submissive females, an inclination toward depression in women resulting from interpersonal conflicts also would not be unexpected. These factors suggest not only a greater incidence of depression in women than men but indicate that, generally speaking, the antecedent circumstances leading to depressive episodes in men and women ought to be different. In women, deterioration in interpersonal relationships should often anticipate depression, whereas in men, the deterioration of social standing would be a more likely precursor. In fact, studies have tended to support this difference (Kessler et al., 1994; McGuire et al., 1997). Depression is a complex emotional disorder. A single model, whether from an evolutionary perspective or not, may not adequately explain all the manifestations. However, an evolutionary perspective on depression does provide some unique insights into its possible causes and new perspectives on its treatment (see Box 8.2 for more on depression, despair, and evolution).

The Evolution of Happiness

While many emotions have evolutionary significance, no other emotion is as sought after, satisfying, and possibly as elusive as happiness. In this final section, we will try to understand the evolution of happiness: what it is to be happy, why it evolved, and why it can be so difficult to truly achieve in our modern world.

Why be happy? It feels good to be happy, but the entire message of this chapter has been that emotions evolved because they served some adaptive function, not because they provided comfort or satisfaction to the individual. Psychologist Barbara Fredrickson (1998; 2000) argued that positive emotions, such as joy and contentment, act as catalysts that broaden one's thought and behavior. Joy, for example, produces social and intellectual playfulness, which can result in an extension and deepening of social relationships and enhancement of physical and creative skills. Contentment heightens awareness and appreciation of current circumstances and encourages the integration of present experience more fully into one's thinking. Fredrickson noted that these positive emotions generally occur in situations of perceived **security, acceptance,** and **satiation**. Over the course of our evolution, these circumstances would have been the optimal times for expanding social and intellectual resources. This led her to propose that positive emotions serve the adaptive function of facilitating the building up or "banking" of social, physical, and intellectual resources that could be accessed later when threats emerge. Happiness may alert us to potential opportunities for resource enhancement and energize us to take advantage of them. When should I make a new friend or learn a new skill? The gregarious playfulness brought on by positive emotions may provide the answer.

This leads us to a perplexing dilemma. On the surface, the modern world appears to provide many of the circumstances necessary for the generation of positive emotions. People in technologically advanced societies enjoy unprecedented levels of security and satiation. Never before have so many lived so well in terms of material comforts and expected life span. We are better fed, educated, and housed than at any time in history. Modern societies offer conveniences of travel, communication, and entertainment unimaginable in centuries past. In spite of this plenty, depression ranks as one of the most common of all emotional disorders, and rates of depression tend to be higher in more economically privileged countries (see Nesse & Williams, 1994, for discussion). In America, it is the materially self-denying Amish whose incidence of depression is about half the national average, not the lavish-living inhabitants of Manhattan or Malibu (Egeland & Hostetter, 1983). Although it is true that those struggling in poverty tend to be less happy than those who live more comfortably, no evidence suggests that increased wealth or material comfort produces greater happiness once basic needs are met (Inglehart, 1990; Lykken, 1999; Myers, 2000, see Fig. 8.2).

Why aren't we all deliriously happy? Two reasons: (1) humans possess certain adaptations that actually operate against feeling positive emotions; and (2) although the modern world provides much in terms of security and satiation (two important factors in eliciting positive emotions), it lacks a third crucial factor—acceptance. Let's look at each of these in turn.

Although it is true that happiness may serve an important adaptive function, it is also true (paradoxically) that humans are naturally designed against feeling

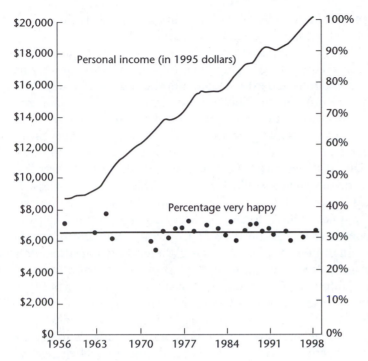

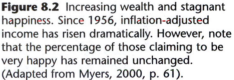

Figure 8.2 Increasing wealth and stagnant happiness. Since 1956, inflation-adjusted income has risen dramatically. However, note that the percentage of those claiming to be very happy has remained unchanged. (Adapted from Myers, 2000, p. 61).

abundant happiness. We adapt quickly to new environmental circumstances, and, although this holds many fitness advantages, it also means that the pleasures of our current situation quickly grow tedious. This has often been referred to as the **hedonic treadmill effect**. Despite larger houses, fancier cars, and a plethora of shiny new gadgets, Americans today report being no happier than their counterparts decades ago who went without (Diener, Suh, Lucas, & Smith, 1999; Myers & Diener, 1995). Happiness often is not achieved by elevating our material condition, because we quickly adjust to that condition and consider it mundane. Moreover, research has uncovered a second finding, **asymmetry of affective experience effect**, which also erodes our experience of happiness. This effect refers to the fact that bad experiences cause greater increases in unhappiness than comparable good experiences cause increases in happiness. For example, the degree to which people feel bad when they lose $100 is greater than the degree to which they feel good when they find $100 (Kahneman & Tversky, 1984). We have evolved to feel pain more intensely than pleasure and for good reason: feeling bad alerts us to situations that could have high fitness costs and compels us to react, but feeling too good can lead to complacency, which may have negative fitness consequences. Thus, the modern world offers us ample means to find *material* security and satiation. But these are circumstances to which we are naturally designed to adapt quickly and view as commonplace. The positive emotions we draw from our material comforts are short-lived and easily vanquished by the negative emotions that stem from perceived material losses. From this, one might conclude that we humans simply cannot be happy. But this is not true. Instead, the more accurate interpretation is that the world provides "happiness" in a form that is simply not enduring, given our evolved natures. Therein lies the problem.

Consider the world of our evolutionary past. For thousands, perhaps millions of years, hominin existence consisted of being born into, living with, and dying among, a close-knit band of family and extended kin numbering 20–150 members. Privacy was neither valued nor sought. The constant embrace of intimacy and familiarity were as commonplace as the breeze on one's cheek or the dirt between one's toes. Within this group one would grow to maturity, take up his or her proper role, compete for status, cooperate for mutual gain, and share food in equal measure with the burdens, diseases, and dances that marked hunter–gatherer life. The material nature of this existence would have been meager. One "possessed" only what one could carry along. Status would have been achieved not by possessions but by social and physical skills. If today's hunter–gatherers are any indicator, the amount of time spent in the actual business of acquiring "daily bread" would have been far less then than now. Modern hunter–gatherers often accumulate a day's worth of provisions in a few hours, leaving the rest of the day for other pursuits, including leisure (Sahlins, 1972). From this, we can see that the core of life in our ancestral environment was relational, not material. Our interpersonal connections were deep and enveloping, almost smothering by today's standards. It was from within this social web that we evolved our understanding of life's purpose, an understanding that remains entrenched in our psyches despite radical changes in the way we live our lives.

Consider the world of today. Although its many conveniences and technologies offer us longer and healthier lives, the modern world does not necessarily offer happier lives than those of our ancestors. Most of us live in sprawling, urban metropolitan areas, surrounded daily by thousands of disinterested strangers, passing us silently on the street, standing impassively beside us in the grocery store or at the bus stop. It has been estimated that on a 10-minute walk through midtown Manhattan one encounters more than 200,000 unresponsive strangers (Milgram, 1970). As evening descends, we encase ourselves in our cars and aim them toward our detached homes, where walls successfully hide us from neighbors who hardly know us and speak to us only rarely. With immediate families whose members are often too busy to dine together and extended kin who are often too far off to be of much service, people today often feel they have no group within which they are fully accepted. Yet in another uniquely modern paradox, the mass media have made us part of a global tribe in which our lives are measured against the standards of beauty, success, and physical prowess of the world's elite. Modern life has made us dual citizens of a largely empty familial group on the one hand and a vast geographically dispersed crowd on the other. This has had devastating effects on the human pursuit of happiness. By wrenching us from our clans, modern life often deprives us of the intimate social networks that nurture and strengthen the spirit. At the same time, the idealized images of beauty, success, competence, and self-assuredness that regularly inundate us from television and magazines force us to compete against a standard that all but assures ultimate failure.

Evolutionary psychologist Doug Kenrick has studied extensively the effect of media images on attitudes and relationships. When men are repeatedly exposed to images of beautiful models, they report a decrement in commitment to their wives or girlfriends compared with that reported by men exposed to images of average-looking women (Kenrick, Gutierres, Goldberg, 1989; Kenrick, Neuberg, Zierk, & Krones, 1994). Women show a similar effect when presented repeatedly with images of dominant, high-status men. They report a decline in love and commitment to their husbands or boyfriends. We evolved in small groups in which competition for mates was restricted to roughly 10–20 others. Today our competition includes not only those few in our immediate social context but the slickly retouched images of Hollywood filmmaker and New York fashion studios. These images affect our assessment of ourselves as well as our mates. Both men and women show a decline in their assessment of their own value and attractiveness after repeated exposures to media images of successful, attractive models (Gutierres, Kenrick, & Partch, 1999). Using a mathematical model, physicists Guido Caldarelli and Andrea Capocci showed that, as increasing numbers of individuals demanded mates meeting the attractiveness standard set by Hollywood stars, the overall satisfaction of the society declined. In other words, as more and more people expect to get mates looking like fashion models or movie stars, fewer and fewer people find happiness and satisfaction in their own relationships. "When the concept of 'most beautiful' in the world tends to be the same for everyone it becomes more and more difficult to make more people happy," laments Caldarelli (quoted in Brooks, 2000, p. 40).

We have created a world that offers much materially but is relationally impoverished. Our evolved natures lead us to quickly become accustomed to and bored with material acquisitions and to judge increments in material status with decreasing degrees of satisfaction. No matter how much we accumulate, it can never match up to the standards of the media image makers. At the same time, the rich interpersonal relationships that are so central to human happiness have become more elusive. Evolutionary psychologist David Buss (2000) offered guidelines for increasing one's happiness, nearly all of which involve enriching our experience of personal relationships. Noting that happiness and successful marriage are closely connected, Buss advised selecting a long-term mate who shares one's interests, values, and personality characteristics. This can increase the likelihood of long-term stability in the relationship and reduce the potential for infidelity, jealousy, divorce, and step-family arrangements, all of which increase personal stress and interpersonal tension. Maintaining ties with extended kin, either by keeping in close geographical proximity or by taking advantage of technology such as e-mail and direct video links, can help keep one enmeshed within a nurturing social network and reduce the crippling effects of isolation. Developing deep friendships, according to Buss, can have a similar vitalizing effect on one's life and outlook. This, he argued, can be fostered by cultivating a good reputation for oneself as a reciprocator and by seeking out groups in which one's unique talents are appreciated (an art teacher, for example, volunteering to teach evenings at a nursing home). One who offers critical, irreplaceable skills to various groups or organizations will find themselves highly valued and will elevate their own status and sense of self-worth, counseled Buss. Being the only one capable of programming the investor club's computer, fixing the church bus, or baking the marshmallow chocolate cookies for the scouting retreat make one an important link in the social community, not all that different from the important roles that members played in our ancestral bands.

It is more than a little ironic that at the beginning of the 21st century, the best advice science can offer on the creation of happiness differs little from that given by the author of *Ecclesiastes* more that 2000 years ago:

> Here again, I saw emptiness under the sun: a lonely man without a friend, without a son or brother, toiling endlessly yet never satisfied with his wealth. Two are better than one; they receive a good reward for their toil, because, if one falls, the other can help his companion up again; but alas for the man who falls with no partner to help him up.

> (ECCLES. 4:7–10)

SUMMARY

Understanding emotions as adaptations leads us to ask which problems specific emotions address. Some emotions deal directly with problems of survival. For example, fear compels us to avoid life-threatening circumstances. Disgust motivates us to put distance between ourselves and potential sources of contamination. Other emotions solve problems associated with group living and social functioning. Shame and guilt help to regulate social relationships and ensure healthy reciprocity. Love helps to ensure a strong bonding of parent to child and long-term mates to each other. Positive emotions serve the adaptive function of facilitating the building up or "banking" of social, physical, and intellectual resources that can be accessed later when threats emerge. The fact that many people today find it difficult to achieve happiness may be the result of a sense of interpersonal alienation, something almost unheard of in our ancestral past.

The evolutionary approach to emotions also provides interesting insights into pathology. Many pathological or pseudopathological emotional states may result from an extreme, exaggerated form of an otherwise adaptive emotional response. For example, depressive states may serve an important adaptive function in compelling people to disengage from unproductive activities or refrain from social competition. In an exaggerated form, however, the depressive state can be maladaptive and destructive. Anxiety also may have adaptive value in altering someone's behavior when he or she might be entering into a threatening situation. Elevated or continuous anxiety, however, can be debilitating. Finally, evolutionary explanations may prove useful in understanding the most dangerous and destructive members of our society: sociopaths and psychopaths. Because social cheating can have fitness advantages, we would expect everyone to have some evolved cheating tendencies. These tendencies will be extreme in some individuals. When accentuated by certain environmental circumstances, moral emotions may be stunted so that these individuals are unable to regulate social conduct.

KEY TERMS

acceptance	cuckolded	paternity certainty
altricial	disengaging from	precocial
asymmetry of affective	unattainable goals	preparedness
experience effect	friendship	prepotency
attraction	genetic concern	pseudopathology
commitment problem	hedonic treadmill effect	reciprocity

reciprocal altruism
resource holding
   potential
satiation

security
smoke detector principle
social competition
   hypothesis

social referencing
violence inhibition
   mechanism
warmth

REVIEW QUESTIONS

1. How are shame and guilt different? How did each contribute to our survival?

2. Explain each of the three different aspects of love.

3. Although human males do not partake in an infant's gestation, birth, or nursing, how did their ability to love and care for their offspring evolve?

4. Why are women in "nonregistered" unions at greater risk of being murdered by their male companions? What explanations for this might evolutionary theory provide?

5. In what ways does jealousy differ between women and men?

6. If anxiety is something of an evolved "early warning" system, what may be the cause of its current prevalence as an emotional disorder?

7. What is the reasoning behind our evolution to feel pain more intensely than pleasure?

8. How does the lack of acceptance devastate the human pursuit of happiness?

SUGGESTED READINGS

Gilbert, P., & Bailey, K.G. (2000). *Genes on the couch: Explorations into evolutionary psychotherapy.* London: Taylor & Francis.

Baron-Cohen, S. (1997). *The maladapted mind: Classic readings in evolutionary psychopathology.* East Sussex, UK: The Psychology Press.

Nesse, R., & Williams, G.C. (1994). *Why we get sick: The new science of Darwinian medicine.* New York: Random House.

WEB SITES

www.nytimes.com/books/first/b/buss-passion.html the first chapter of David Buss's book, *The dangerous passion: Why jealousy is as necessary as love and sex.*

www.umkc.edu/sites/hsw/other/evolution.html read more about the evolution of attraction in Jan Norman's Web article "The evolutionary theory of sexual attraction."

COOPERATION

The Evolution of Cooperation

The Wasp and the Slime

"SURVIVAL OF THE FITTEST" is the phrase by which most people understand evolution. It brings to mind images of a mean, pitiless world where the strong trample the weak and the mighty exploit the lowly. Indeed, the natural world can be an ugly place, and its brutality can lead the thoughtful to ponder unsettling questions about cosmic purpose, justice, and hope.

Even the untrained eye can sense something menacing about the wasps of the *Ichnemonidae* family with their conspicuously long antennae and ovipositor. These insects are emblematic of just how deep the roots of evolutionary cruelty run. Having spotted an orb-weaving spider, the wasp descends and stings it—not a lethal sting but a paralyzing one. The wasp then lays an egg on the spider, which recovers and unsuspectingly continues about its business. For a week or so, the spider seems unaffected by the wasp larva which, all the while, is slowly consuming its host. Then, one evening (the spider's last), instead of weaving its usual web, the orb spider weaves a web of an entirely different design, one suited not for its usual purposes of capturing prey but for its parasitoid's use as a cocoon support. Once the web is complete, the wasp larva finishes the job of killing and consuming the spider and settles into its custom-built cocoon. So sinister was this manner of manipulation that it left Darwin doubting all notions of a benevolent presence pervading the universe.

The evolutionary coin, however, has another side. The roots of cooperation, it turns out, run just as deep in nature's character as do those of competitiveness and conflict. Take the slime mold, for example. The separate cells that form the slime mold can, and under some conditions, do exist separately. However, when conditions are not conducive to individualism, the cells unite to form a unit of up to 100,000 slime cells. The mold forms a stalk with spores projecting from the end. These spores wait patiently to be transported to a more fertile locale by latching onto a nearby bug. The cells that form the stalk eventually die, sacrificing themselves for the good of the spores (and slime in general). However, because slime cells are clones, their sacrifice is not in vain; their genes live on in the dispatched spores (Kessin & Van Lookeren Campagne, 1992; Matsuda & Harada, 1990). (In fact, it appears that the relatedness of cells may not entirely explain the cooperativeness of the cellular slime mold, but the details need not concern us here.)

191

Cooperativeness can be found not just among cells but within the cell itself. The cell's mitochondria were most likely once free-living bacteria that abandoned (or more accurately were ingested away from) the single lifestyle for a life of cellular domesticity. Within the cell, they scavenge for potentially damaging free oxygen molecules while providing energy for the cell. In return, they benefit from the stability and protection available to those that live behind rather than beyond the lipid version of Hadrian's wall (Margulis, 1981; Margulis & Sagan, 1986).

So which is it? Is evolution, as the philosopher Thomas Hobbes might have said, a bloody battle of all against all, or is it an ever-expanding feast of cooperative sharing in which all benefit from mutual give and take? The answer, of course, is that it is a bit of both. Tweaking Richard Dawkins's famous description of the "selfish gene," primatologist Frans de Waal has recast evolution in terms of the "self-promoting gene":

> To say "selfish gene" is misleading. Self-promoting gene would be better. They do promote themselves, in many different ways through many different kinds of behavior….Some animals survive through cooperation, kindness and supportive behavior, not just by aggression and selfishness.
>
> (QUOTED IN FLOYD, 2000)

Genes do what they have to do to promote themselves and that may mean compelling their organisms to behave selfishly or brutally. Often, however, it can mean directing the organism down a more altruistic path.

If cooperation can be as self-promoting for a gene as competition, the question then becomes with whom should one cooperate? For a gene, the first answer to that question is "another gene like me." Working cooperatively with another or others with genes that are the same or similar has proven to be an effective strategy for gene promotion, because the common genetic interest of all parties involved benefits. Where does one find others whose genes are "like mine"? Among kin, of course.

Kin Selection and Cooperative Behavior

The concept of kin selection was discussed in chapter 1 but will be revisited here. Recall that the impetus that spurred the development of kin selection theory was the presence of seemingly altruistic behaviors in many animals. For example, a ground squirrel may stand on its hind legs and emit a loud alarm call when a predator is present. Although this alerts other squirrels in the area and gives them time to seek shelter; it also directs the predator's attention to the call, exposing the squirrel to mortal risk. The squirrel's alarm call appears to be the very antithesis of what natural selection is all about: it lowers the squirrel's own probability of survival and reproduction and enhances the survival and reproductive probabilities of others. Genes associated with those sorts of behaviors would appear sorely handicapped in the evolutionary race.

The important contribution of Hamilton (1964) was to direct attention away from organisms themselves and, instead, focus on the genes. The question should not be what good is the behavior for the individual organism but what good is the behavior for the genes the organism carries? Upon close inspection, the ground squirrel alarm call is not indiscriminate. It occurs more often when relatives are nearby (Trivers, 1985). De Waal's self-promoting gene is back again. Because parents and siblings share about half their genes with the "alarmist" squirrel, saving a few family members can be as genetically profitable (or even more so) as saving oneself. Cooperative behavior need not involve this level of self-sacrifice to be genetically beneficial. The important point of kin selection is that by virtue of their shared genetic interests, cooperation among family members could easily find favor with natural selection.

Consider for a moment the potential power of reciprocity between kin versus reciprocity between strangers. If A does B a favor that enhances B's fitness, then certainly B (and B's genes) benefit. However, if B is kin, then A also benefits, because B shares many of A's genes. If, at a later time, B reciprocates, then A has a dual gain: once by virtue of increasing B's fitness and again by having its own fitness enhanced. The same logic holds for B. Thus cooperation among kin can be a non-zero-sum game: everybody wins. (It is more complicated then this, of course, as one must consider the cost borne by the helper relative to the benefit bestowed upon the recipient weighted by the relatedness of both.) The same logic, however, does not hold for unrelated strangers. If A helps B and B never returns the favor, then B wins, hands down. A has sacrificed some of his effort and resources (thus lowering his fitness) to elevate B (who is now more fit), and, because the degree of genetic relatedness between the two is minimal, A has nothing to show for his loss. He is simply in a weakened position when it comes to competing against B for reproductive success. The important lesson is this: the risks of reciprocity are greatest when dealing with strangers and minimized when dealing with kin. By minimizing the risks of reciprocity, kin selection acts as the thin end of the wedge, giving cooperation the meager advantage it needs to pry its way into the ecosystem.

Primates are among the creatures that have elevated the cooperative approach to survival to its most sophisticated form. The highly social monkeys and apes thrive within a well-orchestrated web of communal relationships, ranks, and unarticulated rules of exchange. It was from this type of primate milieu that human social instincts and collaborative tendencies emerged. Although human cooperativeness has its unique elements, much of what we see in our ape cousins is a reflection of ourselves.

Cooperation Among Nonhuman Primates

Cooperative behaviors have been observed among monkeys and apes, both in natural settings and in laboratory studies. We will look first at cooperation in naturalistic settings, where in many instances helping and fighting go hand in hand.

Naturalistic Observation

Savanna baboons are big, ground-dwelling monkeys who live in large social groups numbering anywhere from 20–200 members. A dominant male will control a group of females, thus making the reproductive prospects of subordinate males rather bleak. However, lower ranking males sometimes work together to dethrone the reigning patriarch (Bercovitch, 1988; Packer, 1977; Noe, 1992). Once their cooperative assault is over, however, any *esprit de corps* quickly dissipates as partners become adversaries in the race to claim the spoils (the female baboons, in this case). Male colobus monkeys operate similarly, joining forces to "liberate" groups of females from rival owners (van Hooff & van Schaik, 1992). Baboons and colobus monkeys typify the way in which cooperation manifests itself in monkey societies; that is, it is almost always found in connection with aggressiveness and competition. Cooperation in battle is also present in apes but extends well past that context.

Probably the most celebrated case study of chimpanzees' cooperation in competing was described by Frans de Waal in his book *Chimpanzee Politics* (1982), in which the shifting sands of power and intrigue among Luit, Yeroen, and Nikkie were laid out in detail. The melodrama opened with Yeroen as the alpha male. Behind the scenes, Luit had been cultivating relationships with other ambitious males, including Nikkie. Together, Luit and Nikkie undermined Yeroen's base of support, particularly among the females, whom they punished for associating with Yeroen. Because Yeroen failed for the most part to protect his female allies from Luit and Nikkie's assaults, he eventually found himself isolated and deposed from power. As the new alpha male, Luit sought to establish a relatively stable and harmonious kingdom. When hostilities erupted among other chimps, he often intervened and encouraged reconciliation. When Luit did take sides in a dispute, he typically supported the party who appeared to be losing, elevating the weaker chimp's status as a hedge against other more threatening rivals—including Nikkie, whose unsatisfied thirst for power became an increasing menace to Luit's rule. In an attempt to outflank Nikkie, Luit made overtures toward Yeroen, who was initially warm toward an alliance with Luit. In the end, however, Yeroen joined forces with Nikkie to topple Luit. Nikkie and Yeroen seemed to have worked out a deal. Nikkie could have the power, but Yeroen got the sex. Alone, Nikkie was no match for Luit, but with Yeroen behind him, he could keep Luit at bay. The price for Yeroen's support, however, was that Yeroen had more frequent sex with the females in the troop. This cooperative arrangement eventually came crashing down when Nikkie seemed no longer willing to yield sexual dominance over the females to Yeroen. The two clashed in a ferocious battle that left both of them injured, with Luit back in power. The story of these three chimps is fairly representative of the way in which cooperative arrangements among male chimpanzees are formed, broken, and re-formed. Male chimps will assist one another in fights, mutually groom, and share food to establish relationships in which both participants seek an individual payoff in resources and status within the group (Fig. 9.1).

Apparently cooperative behavior also has been observed among the male chimpanzees of the Tai forest of West Africa as they hunt colobus monkeys (Boesch & Boesch, 1989). Monkey hunts usually involve 2–6 chimps and often begin when one chimp spots potential prey in nearby trees and alerts his companions with a characteristic "hunting bark." As the chase commences, the chimps will coordinate with one another so that different hunters take different roles in pursuing the quarry. One chimp may climb the tree in which the monkey sits, while others climb adjacent trees and still others stay on the ground below in anticipation of the monkey's attempt to escape. Behaviorally, the chimpanzees undoubtedly are working together effectively to capture the monkey. What is unclear is the extent to which this behavioral coordination demonstrates a conscious understanding of roles and goals. Their cooperation may simply represent an ability to maximize hunting effi-

Figure 9.1 Chimpanzee cooperation. Chimpanzees share food, mutually groom, and often form coalitions to help one another. (© T. Davis/PhotoResearchers.)

ciency based on past experience; that is, from observing past chimp and monkey chases, a chimp may realize that climbing an adjacent tree or staying on the ground is a good way to get first access to the monkey as it tries to escape (see Byrne, 1995; or Tomasello & Call, 1997, for discussions of chimpanzee hunting).

Once the catch is made, a "capture call" is sounded and the entire hunting party gathers to share the meat. The meat often is shared primarily with other hunters and secondarily with members of the troop who did not participate in the hunt (Boesch, 1994). Other factors can also affect how meat is shared among chimpanzees and bonobos (pygmy chimpanzees). For example, dominant males tend to share meat with others who have groomed them more in the past or with females whose sexual favors they wish to curry (de Waal, 1987; Nishida, Hasegawa, Hayaki, Takahata, & Uehara, 1992). The connection between grooming and food sharing has been observed also in more controlled settings. For example, de Waal (1989) found that a chimp was more likely to receive food from another if a few hours earlier the chimp had groomed the giver. Moreover, a chimp was less likely to share food if he or she was the one who had rendered rather than received the earlier grooming. In other words, the chimps seemed to be keeping track of who owed whom. de Waal (1982) reported another instance of cooperative food sharing in which Nikkie broke off a large tree branch and held it in place to allow Luit to climb over an electric fence to get at some tasty, leafy branches. Luit tossed down branches for all members of the group but preferential portions went to Nikkie.

These examples provide us with evidence of two types of cooperative arrangements in primates. First is **mutualism**, in which two or more parties work together to accomplish a goal that neither could achieve singly and in which the rewards of such cooperation are usually realized immediately. Such was the case for the baboons that ousted the dominant male and for the chimpanzee monkey hunters. The second is **reciprocity**, in which one party aids another with no immediate return, but a return of the favor likely will be granted in the future. Reciprocity was evident in the grooming and food-sharing behavior of chimpanzees and in the various "political" arrangements among Yeroen, Nikkie, and Luit. Observational data have shown us quite a bit about how our primate cousins cooperate with each other in their natural world. Laboratory studies have shed some light on how deeply they understand what they are doing.

Laboratory Studies of Primate Cooperation

Determining whether behavior is truly cooperative can be difficult. If two animals simultaneously pursue a prey, are they working together to achieve a common goal or have the self-interests of the two simply overlapped coincidentally? To address this problem, researchers looked closely at primate cooperative problem solving, with an emphasis on two important issues: (1) the capacity of monkeys and apes to modify their own behavior based on the actions of another to achieve a common end, and (2) their ability to engage in "role reversals," in which partners switch responsibilities in a cooperative task. In a very early set of studies, Crawford (1937, 1941) trained individual chimpanzees to pull a rope attached to a box of food until the box was within their reach. Pairs of chimpanzees were then presented with a box that was too heavy to be pulled by only one chimp. Crawford was interested in whether the chimpanzees could figure out how to work together to pull the box. At first, the chimps failed to effectively coordinate their pulling. It was not until Crawford taught both the chimps to pull when a verbal command was issued that their behavior was sufficiently coordinated to succeed in the task. Later, Crawford found that these same subjects were able to coordinate their actions on a different cooperative task, in which a sequence of four buttons on a control panel was pressed for a food reward. When the correct button sequence required a chimp in one cage to press two buttons and another chimp in an adjacent cage to press two other buttons, the chimps quickly learned how to coordinate their actions properly. Chimps that did not have experience with the first task, however, were not as successful in cooperating on the second.

Chalmeau (1994) and Chalmeau and Gallo (1996) used a similar paradigm in which a food-dispensing machine was attached to the side of a cage. The machine dispensed a favorite chimpanzee food item but only when two widely separated handles were pulled simultaneously (Fig. 9.2). Experimenters found that chimps could learn to work together, but the apparatus was heavily dominated by the alpha male, who claimed more than 95% of the food rewards. This chimp would wait by one of the handles until another chimp neared the other handle or sometimes he would physically lead another chimp over to one handle, then go over to the second handle and begin pulling. Although these studies indicate that chimpanzees do have some capacity for adjusting their actions in light of the actions of others to achieve a goal, they also point out some of the limitations of their cooperative abilities. Their cooperativeness was not spontaneous, often requiring much training and human intervention, and social ranking sometimes inhibited cooperation, with dominant individuals amassing most of the benefits and leaving subordinates little incentive to cooperate.

When chimpanzees have been trained extensively in symbolic communication, their ability to coordinate their actions has been found to be quite impressive. Savage-Rumbaugh, Rumbaugh, and Boysen (1978) used two language-trained chimpanzees in a task that required one chimp to "tell" the other what type of tool was needed to open a box containing a food treat. The chimps were placed in adjacent cages where one had access to the locked box containing the food treat and the

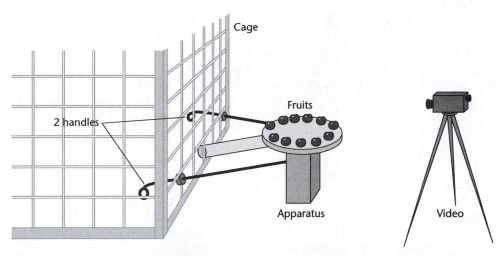

Figure 9.2 A depiction of the apparatus used in Chalmeau's studies of chimpanzee cooperative problem solving. Two widely separated handles extend from the food dispenser into the cage. The handles must be pulled simultaneously for the food to be released down the tube into the cage. (Adapted from Tomasello & Call, 1997, p. 222.)

other had access to a set of tools that could be used to open the box. Using a keyboard with lexigram symbols, the chimp in the cage with the box informed the chimp in the adjacent cage which tool was needed to open the box. Thus informed, the "tool" chimp then fetched the appropriate tool and handed it to the other chimp, who would open the box and (sometimes) share the food reward. The chimps cooperated effectively when the lexigram keyboard was available, but when it was removed and the chimps were forced to work with only their natural gestures and vocalizations, their cooperation broke down.

Chimpanzees have shown some ability to adjust their actions based on the responses of others, but studies with monkeys have been less definitive. Two separate experiments used the same procedure to test cooperativeness in baboons and macaque monkeys (Fady, 1972; Petit, Desportes, & Thierry, 1992). In both cases, food was hidden under rocks that were too large for a single animal to move. Both the baboons and the macaques showed little evidence of being able to coordinate their actions to remove the stones. However, a different task used by both Mason and Hollis (1962) and Povinelli, Parks, and Novak (1992) showed evidence of cooperative behavior among monkeys. These experiments used an apparatus that permitted a subject on one side to see which two of four cups contained food rewards. On the other side of the apparatus were four handles corresponding to the cups. The trick was to pull the correct handles on one side to give access to the food cups on the other. Two subjects working together could obtain the food if the one on the cup side (the informer) could successfully communicate to the other on the handle side (the operator) which handles to pull. Rhesus macaque monkeys successfully coordinated their actions both in monkey–monkey pairs and monkey–human pairs. (For more on monkey cooperation or lack thereof, see Box 9.1).

The Povinelli et al. (1992) study and Povinelli, Nelson, and Boysen (1992) addressed the issue of role reversals in cooperative tasks. Using the previously

Dr. Elisabetta Visalberghi

Capuchin Monkeys: Working Together Without Cooperating

PROFILE: *Dr. Elisabetta Visalberghi graduated in Biology at the Institute of Genetics, University of Rome, in 1975. Since 1982, she has worked at the Institute of Psychology (CNR) in Rome, where she has built a unique research program on the cognitive capabilities of capuchin monkeys. Since 1994, she has served as the head of the Comparative Psychology Section of the CNR. Dr. Visalberghi has been a visiting scientist at several well-known research groups and institutions across the United States, including the Yerkes Primate Center in Atlanta, GA.*

"Cooperation" Among Capuchin Monkeys

Capuchin monkeys are a species of New World monkey known for their intelligence and manipulative abilities. Like chimpanzees, capuchins sometimes engage in group hunting and appear to pursue prey (often squirrels) in a coordinated fashion. But how can one be sure if their hunting behavior represents a *real* cooperative effort and not the result of individuals coincidentally chasing the same prey? One of the hallmarks of cooperation is the ability to take into account another's behavior and adjust one's own actions accordingly. To see if capuchins, in fact, could cooperate in this fashion Visalberghi and colleagues Benedetta Pellegrini Quarantotti and Flaminia Tranchida used a task in which two handles must be pulled simultaneously for monkeys to receive a food reward. The handles were set far enough apart so that a single monkey could not reach them both, but instead, had to rely on another monkey to pull one handle while he or she pulled the other. Before testing, pairs of monkeys were trained on using the handles to receive food rewards.

The experimenters hypothesized that if the monkeys could truly cooperate with one another, then their handle-pulling behavior ought to show evidence of adjustment based on the actions of their partner. Therefore, monkeys should: (1) pull the handle more often when their partner was on the platform where the other handle was located, (2) pull the handle more often when their partner was within reach of the other handle, and (3) pull the handle more often when their partner was pulling his or her handle. The results showed that in time all the pairs of monkeys successfully obtained rewards from the apparatus. However, the data provide little evidence

described cup-and-handle task, the experimenters trained both chimpanzees and rhesus macaque monkeys to be either informers or operators. After the subjects had successfully cooperated in their trained roles, the roles were reversed. The point was to see whether, without explicit training, the primates understood the task from their partner's perspective and could spontaneously adopt the other role. Three of the four chimpanzees quickly adjusted to the new role and performed effectively. The monkeys, however, showed no evidence of being able to spontaneously reverse roles. Although this study seems to show clearly an ape/monkey difference in ability to understand a cooperative task from another's perspective, Tomasello and Call (1997) expressed some skepticism about this conclusion. They pointed out that one of the chimpanzees that showed spontaneous role reversal was Sheba, an extensively trained, human-encultured ape who may not be representative of apes in general. They also questioned whether the other two chimps that showed role reversal might not have benefited from human partners who were overly generous in their interpretation of the chimpanzees' behavior.

A number of conclusions can be drawn from these studies of nonhuman primate cooperative problem solving. First, these studies generally confirm what already was apparent from naturalistic observations: monkeys and apes are capable of cooperative behavior. Apes may be somewhat more capable, but this conclusion is not universally accepted (see Tomasello & Call, 1997, for a discussion).

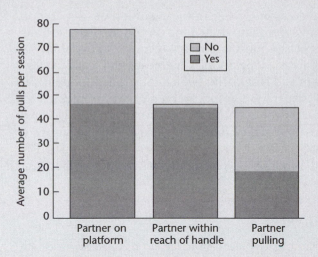

of cooperation. The graph shows the proportion of times a handle was pulled (yes) or not (no) under the three conditions. It is important to note that the monkeys pulled the handle when their partner was off the platform nearly as often as when he or she was on it (left). Furthermore, they actually pulled the handle less frequently when their partner was pulling the other handle than when he or she was not pulling the other handle (right). Only when their partner was within reach of the other handle did the monkeys show a significant increase in handle pulling (middle). Thus, on two of the three measures assessing whether one monkey was taking another monkey's behavior into account and adjusting his or her own behavior accordingly, the data showed a null effect.

Visalberghi et al. (2000) concluded that capuchins do not take into account the actions of others when engaging in a cooperative task. Furthermore, they argue that these results contrast with findings that have shown stronger evidence of truly cooperative behavior among chimpanzees and also among 3-year-old children. When chimpanzees hunt, they must coordinate their actions in both time and space, a feat that requires extensive experience in working together. This skill is generally lacking in monkeys. It may be that the most sophisticated forms of primate cooperation are restricted to the great apes, with humans having achieved the very highest levels to date.

Source: **Visalberghi, E., Quarantotti, B.P., & Tranchida, F. (2000).** Solving a cooperative task without taking into account the partner's behavior: The case with capuchin monkeys *(Cebus apella). Journal of Comparative Psychology*, 114, 297–301.

Second, extensive human contact and training appears to elevate the cooperative abilities of nonhuman primates, especially apes. For example, in Crawford's (1937, 1941) studies, apes initially failed to cooperate and only succeeded after additional human intervention. Afterward, only apes with human training managed to show cooperation on a second, different, collaborative task. In the Savage-Rumbaugh et al. (1978) study, note the extent to which cooperation was dependent upon symbolic communication and, in its absence, how the cooperation broke down. Finally, in the Povinelli et al. (1992) study, evidence for role-reversal ability was found for three apes, all of whom had extensive backgrounds of human contact, with the most convincing evidence being found for the most extensively human-trained subject.

None of this belittles ape cooperative capabilities. The fact that they can learn the tasks presented to them and master symbolic communication is a testament to their intelligence. The point is that an important aspect of cooperative behavior lies in the culture around an individual as well as the capabilities within that individual. That apes became more capable of sophisticated forms of cooperation when extensively exposed to human culture is evidence of the power of the social environment to actualize internal potential. Understanding the evolution of human cooperative abilities involves recognizing that critical elements of this process went on outside as well as inside individual hominins. Hominin social organization and culture played an essential role in the evolution of cooperation. This evolving culture created pressures that selected for certain intellectual traits, such as memory, empathy, and, perhaps most important, communicative ability. In their review of studies of primate cooperation, Chalmeau and Gallo (1996) observed that for both mutualism and reciprocity (which they called spontaneous and nonspontaneous forms of cooperation, respectively) a critical element is the ability to communicate with another about one's role and level of knowledge. Over the course of evolution, humans have achieved the ability to effectively engage in this type of communication, and it has enhanced our cooperative capacities. This achievement is best understood as both an evolved internal mental attribute and an external social phenomenon.

The Evolution of Mutualism

Cooperation based on mutualism can be found in a variety of species, especially those involved in predator–prey dynamics. A prey that is too large to be killed by a single lioness may be chased toward other pride members, so that they can use their numbers to fell it. Musk oxen may join together to fend off a predatory assault that could prove lethal if faced alone. Where animals face an environment that is hostile because of weather conditions, scarcity of resources, presence of predators, or the difficulty of capturing prey, the evolution of mutualism may be favored (Scheel & Packer, 1991).

Mutualism is fairly common among primates. Most primates live in social groups that offer relative security from predators (as do smaller primates) and defense against other hostile same-species groups (as do chimpanzees). In addition, some primates, such as chimpanzees and baboons, may engage in group hunting. We would expect the tendency toward mutualism to have been present in the common ancestor from which hominins and chimpanzees emerged. Moreover, as hominin evolution proceeded, the environment faced by our ancestors would have easily qualified as hostile. The receding forests of East Africa would have exposed the diminutive *Australopithecus* to a host of unfriendly neighbors, including large predatory felines. The enlarged body and brain of *Homo erectus* meant that increasing amounts of meat had to be scavenged or hunted, activities that were dangerous for individuals but less so for groups. Although *H. erectus* had less to fear from nonhuman predators than did his or her predecessors, mortal threats from other bands of hominins would have made intragroup cohesion a survival necessity (Alexander, 1987). These factors highlight the way in which the success of hominins depended in large measure on natural selection's ability to take those incipient mutualistic proclivities and elaborate them into more sophisticated forms, making our ancestors better cooperators.

Hominin mutualism diverged from that of other primates in two important ways (Tooby & Devore, 1987). First, hominin coalitions became larger and more structured than those of other primates. This permitted hominin groups to tackle tasks far beyond any individual's capability and beyond that of any other primate. For example, organized hominin hunting groups were capable of bringing down mammoth and other large prey that no hunter on his own would have had any hope of killing. Contrast this with chimpanzee hunting parties, in which the prey is never larger than what an individual could secure by himself (Byrne, 1995). Second, hominin coalitions featured (and continue to feature) a uniquely high degree of male intergroup aggression. In other words, hominin males waged war on one another with a frequency and skill never before seen among primates (or any other species for that matter). Jane Goodall (1986) described in chilling detail the "war" that broke out between two rival groups of male chimpanzees in the Gombe reserve of Tanzania. When a group of six males broke away from the main troop and established their own territory in the southern (Kahama) part of the reserve, they were hunted down systematically, savagely beaten, and killed by the more numerous males of the north. As well orchestrated as this butchery might have been, it pales in insignificance beside the vast scope and mechanical efficiency of the Roman legions, the Mongol hordes, or even the likely capabilities of *H. erectus* fighters. As hominin evolution unfolded, our ancestors managed to organize themselves into increasingly more effective mutualistic cooperative groups that greatly broadened the range of challenges that could be met and benefits that could be enjoyed. As with so many of our unique human qualities, our expansive mutualism conferred upon us a constructive as well as destructive power unapproached by other animals.

The Evolution of Reciprocity

Robert Trivers (1971) cited a number of conditions favorable to the evolution of reciprocity. These include: (1) long life span, (2) low rate of dispersal, (3) high degree of mutual dependence, (4) long parental care, (5) ability to assist conspecifics in combat, (6) flexible dominance hierarchies, and (7) good memories and recognition abilities. Close examination of these conditions reveals two major themes. Conditions 1–4 and 7 lay the groundwork for an intelligent species that lives a relatively long life in a fairly stable social setting. Conditions 5 and 6 provide the basis for the ability to form cooperative arrangements and the incentive to do so.

These conditions can be highlighted using chimpanzees as an example (although reciprocity is not unique to chimpanzees in the animal world, see Box 9.2). Chimpanzees live in social groups that range in number from 30–100 members. Subgroups often will form, with members freely shifting from one subgroup to another (called fission–fusion communities). Males typically remain in the community of their birth, whereas females often will migrate to other communities when they reach sexual maturity. Chimpanzee infants will continue to nurse for about 3 years and remain in close proximity to their mothers for their first 5–7 years. Maturity for both sexes is not reached until about 8 years, and females usually give birth initially at around 10 years. Chimpanzees can sometimes live 50 years or more, depending on local conditions. Social ranking exists for both males and females in chimpanzee communities, but ranking can be fluid, especially for males, who often form coalitions and compete for dominance. An alpha male may remain in power for a number of years but, eventually, will be ousted by another, often younger, male, usually in concert with a circle of supporters.

In the chimpanzee lifestyle, then, we see the basic conditions in place for reciprocity. They live long lives surrounded by a reasonably stable group of con-

GERALD WILKINSON
Reciprocity Among Vampire Bats

PROFILE *Gerald S. Wilkinson is a professor in the Biology Department at the University of Maryland. Although he is probably best known for his work on cooperative behavior among vampire bats, he also has been actively involved in research dealing with the mechanisms of sexual selection and the evolution of communication and language. Communication and cooperation are closely linked, and, working with colleagues in computer science and linguistics, Wilkinson has developed computer-simulated models of the origins of language. For his innovative research and quality teaching, Wilkinson has earned a number of honors and awards, including the Distinguished Scholar Teacher Award in 1997 and the Faculty Research Award in 2001.*

BOX 9.2

Altruistic Vampires

Chimpanzees are not the only animals in which the conditions necessary for reciprocity are present. Another and rather unexpected candidate is the vampire bat (*Desmodus rotundus*). These bats roost communally in groups of about 12 females in the hollows of trees or in small caves. Female bat communities are fairly stable in their make-up. Wilkinson noted that a female may remain in her same roost community for anywhere from 2 to more than 10 years. Vampire bats are smart, in that they can discriminate old friends from newcomers and keep tabs on who owes whom a favor.

In the evening, bats depart the roost in search of night's supply of blood, usually procured from local livestock. However, the nightly blood-sucking business is not a sure deal. Wilkinson's observations showed that on any given night nearly 20% of the bats failed to find food (success varied greatly with age, with older bats generally being far more successful than younger bats). Vampire bats cannot survive long without blood sustenance, but starvation among the bats is rather rare. Vampire bats, it turns out, are more than willing to share their blood with others in need. Their generosity, however, is not charity. Wilkinson found that two factors explained blood sharing among the bats: **relatedness and association**. Relatedness refers to genetic relatedness (parents/offspring, sisters, half-sisters, nieces, etc.). Association refers to the degree to which two bats shared time together, thus allowing for opportunities for reciprocity.

Of 110 cases in which one bat (the donor) regurgitated blood to another (the recipient), 77 involved a mother and her nursing offspring. Of the 33 remaining cases, Wilkinson was able to measure both genetic relatedness and degree of association in 21 of the blood-sharing pairs. For each of these pairs, Wilkinson calculated an association index, or the amount of time two bats spent together taken as a proportion of the total time any single bat was observed (varying from 0 to 1). He also calculated a relatedness index ranging from .5 (parents/offspring, full sisters, etc.) to 0 (total strangers). Graphs 9.B and 9.C show these measures for the 21 blood-sharing pairs. Note that for all 21 pairs the association index is .6 or greater, and for 16 of 21 pairs (76%) the relatedness index is .25 or greater. Thus, bats do not share indiscriminately but overwhelmingly favor

---

specifics. They have good visual and memory capabilities and thus can recognize and remember other group members. This means that the phrase "I know who you are and I know what you did," has meaning if not expression among chimps. In addition, given that chimpanzee hierarchies allow some measure of upward mobility, which, in turn, has substantial fitness consequences, the incentive for building coalitions and cooperative arrangements is strong.

So what's missing with chimpanzees? Why don't they negotiate trade deals and settle border disputes by, say, relinquishing a few females in estrus for a couple of hectares of prime range land? Or, put another way, what has been added to reciprocity over the course of hominin evolution that has allowed it to take on more sophisticated forms in us?

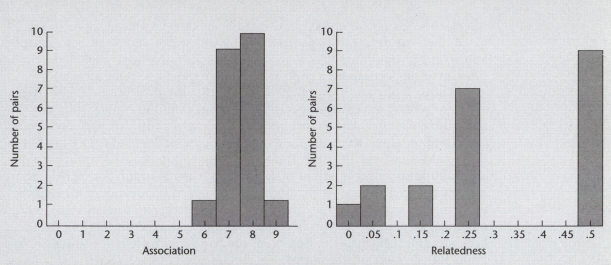

The association and relatedness index for the 21 pairs. Note that most pairs (16 of 21) had relatedness scores of .25 or .5. (Adapted from Wilkinson, 1984, p. 182.)

those who are related and with whom they spend a great deal of time.

The fitness logic of sharing with kin is straightforward enough: given the large percentage of shared genes between kin, helping kin is helping one's own genes. But helping another who has little or no genetic overlap is far riskier, which explains why vampire bats do not share blood with a complete stranger. In the second part of Wilkinson's study, he captured bats from two separate roosts and housed them together in a lab setting. Each evening, he pulled out one bat and prevented it from obtaining blood. The others were allowed a night's ration of blood. Wilkinson waited to see which bats (if any) would offer aid to the starved bat. In 12 of 13 cases in which a blood sharing occurred, it involved a donor–recipient pair from the same original roost group. In addition, Wilkinson noted that those bats that received a blood donation were significantly more likely to reciprocate later when another bat (from their group) needed aid. This suggests that bats tend to recognize "old friends" and keep track of who owes whom within their communities.

As with chimpanzees and humans, all the necessary conditions for reciprocity seem to be in place with vampire bats. They are an intelligent, long-living species and live in stable communities with dependent offspring and powerful mechanisms for recognizing others and keeping track of others' behavior. Although they probably will always be undeservingly associated with Dracula, the kindness of these vampires may help soften their reputation.

Source: **Wilkinson, G.S. (1984)**. Reciprocal food sharing in the vampire bat. *Nature*, 308, 181–184.
Photo: Courtesy of Gerald S. Wilkinson.

Trivers (1985) contended that by about 2 million years ago, all the conditions favorable for the evolution of reciprocity would have been present in hominins. This means that by about the time of *H. erectus* or slightly before, hominin social and lifestyle conditions were roughly comparable to that of chimpanzees. Hominins, however, began elevating reciprocity to never-before-seen levels of sophistication. Tooby and Devore (1987) counted four ways in which hominin reciprocity reached unique status. First was the frequency, degree, and variety of reciprocal arrangements made by our ancestors. As hominins began to create tools, weapons, and clothing, they had more that could be bartered and traded. Chimpanzees, by contrast, have only a limited range of exchangeable resources (i.e., food, sex, grooming, and social support) on which to construct reciprocal agreements. Second, if one has more "building blocks" on which reciprocity can be based, then the degree of negotiation, contingency, and complexity of exchange also is upped significantly. Is a good stone scraper worth a rabbit hide and a promise of support against a rival, or does that require two stone scrapers?

Third, Tooby and Devore (1987) noted that the division of labor between the sexes became increasingly specialized among hominins. Among chimpanzees, males are the hunters and sometimes share their spoils with females in return for sex. However, when the panting and hooting is over, males tend to lose interest in the females and their offspring. Humans are not chimpanzees. Somewhere along the evolutionary line, hominin males began "hanging around" and helping to raise offspring. This arrangement provided increased opportunities for reciprocity between the sexes. To the extent that hunter–gatherer societies today reflect our ancestral past, we can conclude that hominin males did the hunting, bringing back meat for their mates and children, and females gathered more local edibles. From this division others flowed, for example, males constructed the hunting tools and females produced digging sticks. Males butchered and cut the meat, and women cleaned and cooked the food. Amongst the !Kung of southern Africa, for example, men hunt and fashion the tools for hunting and for the household. Women gather wood and water for the home and for the preparation of food (Shostak, 1981). By specializing in certain skills and then sharing the fruits of their labor, males and females created an advanced form of economic exchange by which both accrued benefits that neither could have realized alone (Berndt, 1970; Ridley, 1996). Researchers do not agree about the timing of the emergence of this gender-based form of reciprocity. At one extreme is Lovejoy (1981), who argued that the conditions for a largely monogamous social system were in place as far back as the Australopiths. At the other end are Steele and Shennen (1995), who did not see such cooperation emerging until the arrival of *Homo sapiens* about 100,000 years ago.

Finally, Tooby and Devore (1987) pointed to mate exchange between groups as another way that hominins elevated reciprocity to unique levels. All primates have some means of avoiding incestuous matings. In monkeys, it is the male who usually wanders among troops. In gorillas, females may abandon one harem for another. Chimpanzee females typically will leave their natal group at maturity to join another. As descendants from the same primate stock, hominins inherited this same practice of exogamy; that is, members of one sex leaving their native group as a means of avoiding incestuous sex. With humans, however, there is a big difference. We do not just wander off and join a new group. Hunter–gatherers will set aside certain times when wandering bands reunite in a large festive gathering. On these occasions, old acquaintances are renewed, goods exchanged, dances danced, and rituals enacted. Most important, marriages are arranged. The arrangement of a marriage was a formal way of establishing or solidifying an ongoing connection between two groups. In 1889, the "father" of anthropology, Edward Tylor, recognized the crucial role that marriage played in early human societies: "...there is but one means known of keeping up a permanent alliance," he wrote, "and that means is intermarriage." Intermarriage, in his view, was the "practical alternative" to warfare and possible annihilation (Tylor, 1889, p. 267). Sometime during the course of hominin evolution, our ancestors hit upon that practical alternative and began using it as a means of building reciprocal relationships, thus enlarging the power of cooperation beyond individuals to entire groups.

A final point should be stressed about the unique qualities that emerged in reciprocity over the course of hominin evolution. Recall that Chalmeau and Gallo (1996) emphasized the role of communication in the formation of mutalistic and reciprocal arrangements. The limitation of chimpanzee communication constitutes one of the factors that constrains cooperative potential. For hominins to extend cooperation as they did almost certainly required possession of a means of communicating with one another about roles they would play in cooperative arrangements. Does this mean that hominins such as *H. erectus* must have possessed spoken language? Maybe. Some researchers, such as Deacon (1997) and Bickerton (1990), argued that *H. erectus* would have had a primitive form of spoken language. This language would not have been as sophisticated as modern human language but would have been a significant step above chimpanzee hoots and grunts. Others, such as Donald (1991), disagree, arguing that erectus would have been restricted to a gestural form of communication based on mimesis. In either case, it seems clear that to cooperate with one another our ancestors had to communicate with one another as well.

Reciprocity and Game Theory

Imagine for a moment that you are a petty thief. You and your partner Frank recently pulled off a heist. Unfortunately, things did not go well and you were both arrested. You and Frank have always had a standing agreement: neither rats on the other. The police, however, offer a tempting deal. If you rat out (testify against) Frank, you can go free and Frank will get 10 years. If you do not, then the prosecutor has enough evidence to convict both you and Frank of a lesser offense that carries a 2-year sentence. So far, the choice may not seem all that tough, but, to complicate matters, the prosecutor offers Frank the same deal. If he turns on you, he walks and you do 10 years. If both of you talk, then you both get 5 years. The choices and the outcomes can be diagrammed in a matrix so that each course of action and its consequence can be seen clearly (Fig. 9.3).

This scenario is known as the **prisoner's dilemma** and has been used in a branch of mathematics called game theory as a means of investigating the conditions under which cooperation may emerge. Let's look closely at your options. You cannot control what Frank does, only what you do. You have two options. You can either cooperate with Frank by sticking to your original deal and not talking, or you can defect, in which case you break your deal with Frank and sing like a canary. If you choose to cooperate (not talk), it can be seen from the matrix that you restrict your outcomes to two possibilities: you get either 10 or 2 years, depending on what Frank does. If you choose to defect (talk), then your outcomes are either 5 or 0 years, depending on what Frank does. If only the police would allow you to discuss the matter with Frank, you could point out to him that the best course of action for both of you is to cooperate and stick to the original deal. If you do this, you both will end up with only a 2-year sentence. However, because the police have no intention of allowing you and Frank to confer, the cooperative route becomes very risky. It is only by being honorable and sticking to the origi-

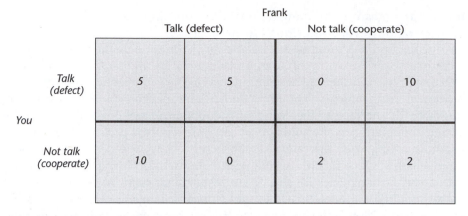

Figure 9.3 Prisoner's dilemma matrix. Frank's options are shown at the top. He can either talk (defect) or not talk (cooperate; in this case cooperate means cooperate with you not the police). Your options are listed on the side in italics. Outcomes for both you and Frank are shown within the matrix. For example, if you and Frank both talk, then you get 5 years in jail (in italics) and so does Frank. If you talk, but Frank does not, then you get 0 years in jail and Frank gets 10.

nal agreement that one runs the biggest risk of being suckered and ending up with a 10-year sentence. The only sure way to avoid this possibility is to defect and hope that your partner is the sucker. The prisoner's dilemma really boils down to a decision about your partner: can he or she be trusted? If so, cooperate by not talking. If not, defect.

It turns out that the prisoner's dilemma provides a realistic model for the challenge of reciprocity (also called reciprocal altruism) in the natural world. Animals cannot make promises of future behavior to one another or outline terms of payment and repayment. Explicit contractual obligations in relationships are beyond the animal intellect and communicative abilities. Lacking these abilities, reciprocity would seem doomed before it ever got started in the natural world. Yet it has evolved. We have seen how vampire bats share blood and how primates trade favors. Reciprocity even occurs across species, such as the small fish and shrimp that run "cleaning stations" on coral reefs and cater to larger predatory fish that are often plagued by parasites in their mouths and gills. The client fish, which, under other circumstances would readily eat their cleaners, arrive at a designated station, open their mouths, and wait patiently for a good oral scouring. The cleaners get a meal, the clients rid themselves of harmful parasites, and nobody eats the hired help (Trivers, 1971). But how does all this get started in a silent world in which the little fish can't tell the big fish, "Don't eat me. I'm trying to do you a favor"?

The problem of getting reciprocity going in hominins seems at first to be daunting. In a single encounter between self-interested organisms, the cooperative strategy turns out to be an evolutionary loser. The risk of being a sucker forces both participants to adopt a noncooperative posture. However, when researchers set up the prisoner's dilemma as an ongoing game in which participants played each other in repeated sequences, the situation changed. Under these conditions, participants learned to work together to minimize defections to the mutual benefit of both. Not until the game neared its end did players look to take advantage of each other and try to score a big "killing" (Poundstone, 1992).

In 1979, Robert Axelrod, a political scientist, set up a computerized tournament to see what strategies would prove most effective for players caught in the prisoner's dilemma. By converting the possible years of prison in our earlier example to points, Axelrod could quantify the success of different strategies in a series of 200 iterations of the prisoner's dilemma. He invited colleagues to submit programs that modeled different strategies that organisms might adopt when encountering other organisms in the natural world (actually Axelrod's original interests were not in evolution, but his study provided a nice model of an evolutionary process). For example, an "always defect" program would never cooperate and always would look to take advantage of another player, whereas a "random" program would sometimes cooperate and sometimes defect. The winning program was called Tit For Tat (TFT) and was submitted by Anatol Rapoport. Only five lines long, TFT was one of the simplest of the original 14 programs. In a second round of the tournament, another 62 programs attempted, without success, to oust TFT. The rules for Rapoport's program were simple: (1) start by cooperating, (2) then do whatever your partner did last. If your partner cooperates, you keep cooperating. If your partner defects, then punish him or her by defecting the next time. The sheer simplicity of TFT suggests that its emergence as random mutation in the natural world might not be all that implausible. The logic of TFT was as straightforward as it was powerful. When encountering a new partner, try to establish a mutually beneficial relationship (cooperate). In this fashion, TFT could reap the gains of reciprocity and could continue to do so indefinitely, partner willing. By meeting defection with defection, TFT guarded against losses from being suckered. If there were cooperators out there, TFT would find them and work with them. When it encountered a cheater, it minimized its losses by refusing to be repeatedly victimized. The sacrifice TFT made for adopting this strategy was to waive big payoffs of a one-time "suckering" of another. In later computer simulations designed to more closely model natural selection, TFT continued its stellar performance. Nasty strategies thrived early on as they bled big gains from unwary partners, but, as they proliferated, they forced a decline in the number of victims left to exploit. This was when TFT began its surge, eventually dominating the cyber ecosystem (Axelrod, 1984).

Later research has shown that even TFT can be bested under some circumstances. For example, an environment dominated by TFT may become vulnerable to other strategies if TFT becomes bogged down in endless cycles of retaliatory defections. An even more generous program, called (aptly enough) Generous TFT, which occasionally forgives defections and keeps cooperating rather than retaliating against them, can overtake TFT (Lomborg, 1993; Nowak, May, & Sigmund, 1995). Other programs, such as Pavlov and Firm But Fair, also can outdo a simple TFT approach under certain conditions, but the moral of the story remains intact. All of these programs primarily seek cooperation and not exploitation (see Ridley, 1996, for discussion).

Let's try to summarize the important points that this approach makes about the evolution of reciprocity. (1) A simple cooperative strategy such as TFT could arise by chance and establish itself as the dominant mode of interaction among a community of organisms. (2) Its proliferation would not necessarily require communicative ability among the organisms using the strategy. (3) For TFT to thrive, however, repeated interactions among organisms must occur, as more exploitative strategies will dominate in one-off encounters.

All of this seems too wonderful to be true. Computer models indicate that cooperative behavior can simply emerge naturally and proliferate in an ecosystem without guidance, deep intellectual reflection, or symbolic communication. The nasty get pushed aside and the nice rule. Evolution really is a pussycat after all. Of course, it is all too wonderful to be true. To get a more realistic perspective, we must examine the criticisms of the game theory approach to understanding reciprocal altruism.

Criticisms of the Game Theory Approach

Three major criticisms have been aimed at the **game theory approach** to understanding the origins of reciprocity. One criticism is that it relies too heavily on computer models and has not had sufficient empirical validation in the natural world. The problem, of course, is that trying to understand the evolution of cooperation forces one to speculate about what happened millions of years ago. It is impossible to go back and observe the process. We are left with explanatory models that try to account for how we ended up where we are today. This, however, is fair game in science. The point is not that game theory claims to have irrefutable empirical evidence of what happened in the past but that it currently provides the best account—*in comparison with other possible models*—of how we ended up with the phenomena we observe today. Some critics jab at game theorists by asking, "Yeah, but you weren't there, so how do you know that's what happened?" Game theorists can respond, "OK, have you got a better idea?" The power and elegance of game theory is that it provides a way of understanding how cooperative relationships could evolve in the absence of sophisticated rationality and communicative skills, something that obviously *did* happen and cries out for an explanation. Ultimately, the game theory approach will probably be superseded by more potent theories, but it currently provides the best framework for understanding the evolution of cooperation and building the newer, better models that will replace it. (See Wright, 1994, for an excellent discussion of this criticism of game theory.)

A second criticism is that Axelrod's computer simulations stacked the evolutionary deck in favor of cooperation. TFT did not emerge in a void but among many players, some of whom had cooperative tendencies built into their programs. Thus, from the get-go, TFT had something to work with to establish a community of cooperators who eventually could overwhelm their more uncooperative counterparts. In the natural world, however, the first cooperator would have been just that—the first (and only) cooperator. As such, its fate in a world of self-absorbed gene machines would have been sealed. Finding no one to cooperate with and being cheated at every turn, Señor Reciprocity would have been stomped into a fine powder and whisked away by the first gentle zephyr. The presence of a single cooperator is inadequate to get cooperation going in the ecosystem.

To solve this conundrum we need to unsheathe the fine edge of kin selection. Hamilton and Axelrod (Axelrod, 1984) argued that kin selection most likely acted as the vehicle that gave cooperation access to the natural world. A potential community of cooperators already exists among genetic relatives. It is not difficult to understand the evolutionary logic behind genes that impel altruistic behavior on the part of parents toward offspring. Concern for one's own genes also could explain why older siblings, aunts, uncles, and grandparents also tend to be kind and cooperative toward their younger sibs, nieces, nephews, and grandchildren. In each case, the genetic self-interest of organisms provides a bridge toward behaving cooperatively with another. How does the younger relative, however, who up until now has been receiving all the benefits of reciprocity, learn to pay back some of the niceness that he or she has been receiving? Genes that instruct juvenile organisms to reciprocate to those who treat him or her nicely would do the trick. Because those who treat the juvenile nicely are most likely to be older genetic relatives, then the "be nice to the nice" genes in the youngster would still tend to enhance his or her overall fitness, because most of the reciprocity would be directed toward relatives. However, notice that the "be nice to the nice" gene is general. It will more than likely render aid to relatives but does not restrict itself to that. As the youngster gets older, the tendency of the gene to reach past relatives is likely to increase.

A final criticism focuses on the fact that game theory approaches tend to concentrate on reciprocity between pairs of individuals and reveal little about how reciprocity might expand from pairs to larger groups. The critics rightly point out that when the same two individuals play the prisoner's dilemma repeatedly the short-term gains from defection fade in comparison with the longer-term gains of cooperation. However, as group size increases, the number of members who are strangers to each other also grows. Thus the opportunities for one-off encounters between strangers increase. One could make a profitable living by exploiting strangers once for big gain and then quickly moving on (the con artist strategy). Kitcher (1993) showed that one way to foil this strategy was to have a collection of discriminating altruists (DAs) in the group. DAs operate using the TFT strategy, except that they simply refuse to play with anyone who defected on them in the past. As DAs expand in the population, those trying to survive through one-shot exploitations have an increasingly difficult time finding anyone to play with. Similarly, Nowak and Sigmund (1998) found that when players had "reputations" based on their past history of either cooperation or defection and information about those reputations freely flowed among group members, other players tended to avoid those with bad reputations. The result in both cases was **social ostracism:** the isolation of noncooperators.

Ostracism and banishment have been commonly used tools for enforcing social stability in human communities. The effectiveness of these tools is amplified by the fact that humans make predictive rather than merely retrospective judgments about who to partner with. Based on looks, behaviors, companions, habits, hobbies, interests, affiliations, etc., we construct a rough sketch of another's character and make decisions about whether or not we want involvement with that individual. Although one can certainly fret about the fairness of all of this, it turns out that our predictive judgments are reasonably accurate. Frank, Gilovich, and Regan (1993) allowed a roomful of strangers to interact for 30 minutes. Then, each person made judgments about who he or she thought would cooperate or defect in a one-time prisoner's dilemma encounter. Their accuracy was considerably better than chance. The lesson seems to be that what happens in a one-off encounter is not forgotten. Reputations are established and used by other group members as a basis to shun or marginalize those who represent a threat to the group's cooperative spirit. In addition, certain detectable traits appear to be associated with one-off exploiters and cue others to stay clear.

Social Hierarchies and Human Cooperation

We saw earlier that chimpanzee societies are hierarchical in nature, with both males and females possessing social rank that translates into certain privileges, including increased probability of reproductive success. All social primates live in variably hierarchical societies in which ranking can be fairly rigid (rhesus monkeys) or more supple (bonobos). Given the generality of this characteristic, it is likely that early hominins inherited this social tendency as part of the primate legacy of the common ancestor. Human hunter–gatherer tribes, however, are marked by a high degree of egalitarianism (Erdal & Whiten, 1994; Knauft, 1991; Woodburn, 1982). Over the course of hominin evolution, then, a transition from a more hierarchical to a more egalitarian social order seems to have occurred.

Hunter–gatherer tribes, such as the Ache of South America and the Hazda and Aka pygmies of Africa, are strikingly egalitarian. Such tribes typically have no chiefs, decisions usually are based on consensus, and hunted spoils are shared freely with all. This does not mean, however, that social status does not exist. Among the Ache, the best hunters generously share their kills—and their genes. The public display of hunting prowess, accomplished in part by bountiful sharing, earns the hunter a respect that yields dividends in an abundance of extramarital affairs (Hill & Kaplan, 1988, 1994). The same is true for the Hazda men, who, from a rational standpoint ought to just hunt small game and fowl to feed their families, but instead insist on stalking the more conspicuous giraffe (Hawkes, 1993). Finally, although the Aka pygmies have no true chief or headman, a skillful hunter can became a kombeti, a man of great respect or influence in the tribe. Not surprisingly, a kombeti usually has more wives and children than a regular blue-collar pygmy male (Hewlett, 1988). Social status has not been eliminated in most hunter–gatherer tribes. Its manifestations are less egregious and more fundamental. A man of status earns his rank not by clothes, vocal eloquence, or birthright, but by skills directly related to survival, and his payback is more carnal than material in nature.

It is crucial to recognize that human cooperativeness evolved within an ever-present context of social hierarchy. This has left an imprint on the ways we interact with one another. In our evolutionary past, social standing was critical to reproductive success, especially for men. Even today, our reciprocal arrangements are not just about the direct exchange of one favor for another but also the subtle (and sometimes not so subtle) strategic maneuverings designed to raise our social status. As we cooperate, we also jockey for position. Our jockeying involves two (often unconscious) characteristics: a **self-serving bias** and **deference to higher status**.

The self-serving bias refers to the fact that people tend to attribute their successes to internal factors (such as skill) and blame their failures on external circumstances (such as bad luck). In addition, an opposite pattern of attribution tends to occur when accounting for the success and failure of others. The self-serving bias is a strategy of self-enhancement by which we try to elevate our own standing and denigrate that of others. This self-aggrandizing tendency shows itself in many ways. For example, when husbands and wives are asked how often they perform certain household chores, such as doing the dishes, taking out the garbage, or cleaning the house, both spouses often claim to perform the tasks more than half of the time (a mathematical impossibility, of course; Ross & Sicoly, 1979). Likewise, when asked who was more responsible in caring for elderly parents, each of two siblings claimed to do the majority of the work (Lerner, Somers, Reid, Chiriboga, & Tierney, 1991). When we are involved in group efforts that succeed, we tend to attribute that success to our own contribution to the group. If the effort fails, however, we tend to attribute the failure to the influence or inadequacies of other group members (Miller & Ross, 1975). Anthropologist Bronislaw Malinowski was pleasantly surprised by the Trobriand Islanders' penchant for gift giving but a little dismayed when he found that they spent an inordinate amount of energy boasting about the gifts they had given and griping about gifts they had received (Malinowski, 1929). The pervasiveness of the self-serving bias indicates that when we give we are not just out to help others but are trying to enhance our own status by putting others in our debt, fostering a reputation as a "good group member," and reminding others of everyone else's deficiencies.

What effect does the self-serving bias have on our cooperative relationships? It means that we tend to be egocentrically biased in our assessments of what we owe relative to what is owed us. We will always try to get just a shade more than we give. This is hardly shocking news, but it does add a pinch more cynicism to our understanding of human relationships. It does not mean, however, that human relationships are nothing more than a heartless game of one-up-manship. If I do two favors for Frank and he repays me with three, Frank is still better off (by two favors) than if we had never formed a relationship. It is not that we humans are naturally exploitative in relationships. It is that we are not naturally equitable. From an evolutionary perspective, this makes sense. Imagine two hominin females who are happily "married" to their respective mates. Each of the females is generally upholding her end of the marital bargain. If one, however, can convince her mate to provide a little more meat, a little better shelter, and a bit more protection, resources, and attention to her and her offspring, then she will have achieved a fitness advantage over Mrs. Jones in the cave next door. The same would hold for males as they spar among themselves for whatever slight advantage they can muster to elevate their stature and therefore their access to females. Like good portfolio managers, our ancestors were the ones who, over the long span of evolutionary time, were the most deft at optimizing the return (what they got back) on their investments (what they gave). The hominins of the past who approached cooperative relationships with a strictly equitable strategy instead of an optimizing one were less likely to leave offspring and, therefore, less likely to be our ancestors. In this light, the self-serving bias can be seen as an evolutionarily ingrained approach to reciprocal relationships that ensures that we will always look to maximize the yield on relationships.

Deference to higher status represents the one exception to our generally self-centered approach to cooperative relationships. In general, we will always tend to overestimate what we have given and underestimate what we have gained, but we will forego this rule when dealing with those of higher status. When those of equal or lesser status owe us, we are quick to demand repayment, usually requiring a little more than what they actually owe. With those of higher status, we are more than willing to give excessive favors with only a minimal tangible return. Put baldly, we tend to "kiss up" to those above us. In a sense, however, there is an equity to this. When a person of high status agrees to a cooperative arrangement, one of the assets he or she brings to the party is the high status itself. One who associates with high status has his or her own status elevated simply by virtue of the association. Being seen walking through the halls with the company president can be its own reward. It is the status that is being "paid for" by the favors flowing freely from subordinate to superior. Although most of us could readily supply anecdotal evidence to support our deference-to-status tendency, experimental evidence has accumulated as well. For example, when stuck in traffic, drivers are more likely to honk if they are behind a low-status vehicle, say, an Oldsmobile, than if they are behind a high-status vehicle, such as a Mercedes (Doob & Gross, 1968). Moreover, drivers of low-status cars are slower to honk at other vehicles than are drivers of high-status vehicles (Diekmann, Jungbauer-Gans, Krassig, & Lorenz, 1996). Humans are not the only ones who show these sorts of status effects. Recall that once he became the alpha male, Luit tended to support lower status males, cultivating them as a base of support against more threats from higher ranking males. Simply by associating with them he elevated their status and put them in his debt.

The Evolution of Human Relationships: Deception and Complication

By virtue of our primate heritage and evolutionary history, we humans are naturally social creatures, destined to form mutually beneficial cooperative relationships. We are not a solitary species, but a gregarious one that finds its greatest rewards in community with others. However, the same evolutionary process that has fashioned us to reach out cooperatively to others has designed us to snatch from others as much personal gain as our relationships can tolerate. The evolutionary approach to understanding human nature has provided us with yet another unsurprising conclusion: human relationships can be complicated. It is the depth of that complication that is evolutionary psychology's real surprise. We approach our relationships with an evolved eye, seeking our own status gain. This means that we naturally try to give enough to others so that they will want a relationship with us but not so much that we fail to net a profit from the whole affair. Others approach their relationships with us in the same manner. Moreover, the status that each of us brings to our relationships becomes part of the currency we trade, coloring our evaluations of fairness and balance.

These factors, however, are only the iceberg's tip when it comes to the potential messiness of human relationships. Very few of us would opt for a relationship with someone who openly concedes that personal status gain is what he or she is after. The best person with whom to form a cooperative relationship is one who seems to have our best interests at heart, rather than their own. The important point is not whether one actually has another's best interests at heart but whether one is effective in convincing another that this is true. Remember that evolution is no moralist. **Deception** is widespread in the ecosystem. Certain female fireflies mimic the flashing of another type of firefly so that they can lure the interloping males close enough to eat them. The viceroy butterfly cloaks itself in monarch-looking colors, fooling birds into thinking that it tastes equally bad. The king snake looks like the poisonous coral snake, but this is a self-protective sham. Even more impressive are snakes of the genus *Pliocerus*, which sport different surface patterns to match those of a more dangerous type of snake found in their region.

Natural selection favors the deceiver as well as the honest organism, and a good deceiver stands to reap a generous reward from reciprocal relationships if he or she is capable of convincing many others to engage in cooperative arrangements. Simply imagine for a moment a hominin we'll call "Slick Cooperator." Everyone wants to be friends or lovers with Slick. He is intelligent, compassionate, empathetic, hardworking, charming, and all the other qualities that one looks for in a close companion. In fact, so friendly and decent is Slick that we don't mind doing him an extra favor or two here and there, because, well…he's such a nice guy. That, of course, is the secret his success. His warm smile and heartfelt handshake earn him a modest profit from his numerous relationships and even a rare "big kill" now and then. Whether Slick really *cares* about others is irrelevant. His success is based on his ability to convincingly project the outward signs of caring, signs that attract others to him. It may be distasteful to admit, but Slick Cooperator is our ancestor. To varying degrees, we all pretend to care so that we will get something we want or need from another. For some this is a consistent lifestyle, for others it is an infrequent moral lapse, but for all it is a possibility.

Alexander (1975, 1987) argued that deceptive cooperators would create selection pressure for the ability to detect deception, which would in turn create pressure for even more effective deception. The ultimate in effective deception would be **self-deception**, in which deep down a person is really out for his or her own best interest but is not aware of it. When such a person is truly convinced that he or she really does care and is motivated only out of genuine concern, then he or she can be most effective at deceiving and taking advantage in a relationship. Let's step through this slowly, using a smile as an example. Suppose the first step toward forming a cooperative relationship is a smile that signals, "I'm a good guy. Get involved with me." Over evolutionary time, those who smile more get involved in more relationships and increase their fitness, until you have a population of smilers. Later, some smilers arise who can smile both when they mean it and when they don't (deceptive smilers). Because they smile more often, they get involved in more relationships, reap more rewards, and increase their fitness, until you have a population that can smile both sincerely and deceptively. Deceptive smilers gain part of their advantage by subtly exploiting those who are susceptible to being duped, thus reducing the fitness of those susceptible to duping. Over time, then, the proportion of those who can be duped declines and the proportion of those capable of detecting deception increases, thereby making the deception business more difficult. When we lie, veiled cues to our insincerity are present in our facial expression and vocal patterns (Ekman, 1985). Others can detect these cues and become aware of the deception.

Motor Control, Violence, and Hominin Cooperation

BOX 9.3

Game theory called attention to one of the serious obstacles to the evolution of cooperation: corralling the noncooperators (cheaters). Game theory's solution to this, social ostracism, can be a powerful force. Paul Bingham (1999), however, argued that the cheating problem required a more assertive suppression in the form of active punishment. It was only when cooperative groups could unleash a low-cost, highly effective punishment on cheaters that cooperation was freed to evolve into the uniquely human forms present today. Bingham's theory is significant because it integrates evidence from hominin physical, technical, and social evolution into a single model that purports to explain not only human cooperative capacities but all uniquely human capacities, including language, adaptability, higher cognitive functions, and technical and scientific skill.

Bingham began by noting that in all large-bodied, social animals a heavy cost is associated with punishing cheaters. Suppose chimpanzee A has consistently shared meat with chimpanzee B. When a battle for alpha status is staged, however, B abandons A, allowing him to be beaten and bruised. For A to punish this act of noncooperation, he must actively deny B access to future food resources, attack B's kin (not an uncommon strategy among chimps), or directly assault B. Any of these retaliations involve a potentially high cost, because A must physically place himself at risk against B or B's kin. The high cost of punishment means that cheaters often get away with their exploitative acts, thus reaping fitness rewards and

placing severe limitations on the benefits that can be achieved through cooperation.

The "cost of punishment" problem has proven insurmountable for all primates except hominins, who, about 2 million years ago, began to expand cooperation into uncharted waters. The evolutionary event responsible for this remarkable achievement, according to Bingham, was the emergence of accurate throwing. The ancestors of *Homo* evolved the capacity to use projectile weapons to reliably and accurately inflict injury or death at a distance. This permitted what Bingham calls **coalitional enforcement**; that is, the ability of group members to inflict injurious or lethal punishment on noncooperators at relatively little risk to themselves. With coalitional enforcement, keeping cheaters in line no longer involved risky direct physical confrontations. Instead, a cheater could be "stoned" from a distance of 20 m or more. Hominins, quite serendipitously, stumbled upon a way to exponentially elevate the cost of cheating. When cheating no longer paid evolutionary rewards, a sudden onset of cooperative spirit ensued.

Bingham (1999) pointed to the following evidence to support his claim. First, accurate throwing is a unique human trait. In addition, humans are also unique in the size and sophistication of their cooperative groups. This, of course, does not mean that one causes the other, but the possibility of a link between the two cannot be dismissed summarily. Second, the fossil record supports the co-occurrence of the emergence of hominin throwing ability and increased

---

An audience that is increasingly difficult to deceive pressures a deceiver to find ways to eliminate the cues that reveal deception. The best way to eliminate these cues is to not lie. But how can someone not lie and still continue to deceive? The answer is for the deceiver to be unaware that he or she is lying. Thus, the evolutionary arms race between deceivers and those trying to detect deception would inevitably lead to self-deception. The tendency to seek advantage in relationships continues unabated but operates below our level of conscious awareness. My smile looks sincere, because I really believe that it is, but my genes know better. I smile and say (sincerely) that your well-being is my utmost concern, but, genetically, I just want to insure that my investment in our relationship has a payoff. Of course, you do the same to me. Relationships can be complicated.

At this point, it seems painfully naive to ask if there is evidence that people engage in self-deception. Most of us probably suspect that we do—and we do. In a study by Epley and Dunning (2001), subjects were asked to make predictions about

social competence. For example, skeletal adaptations in *Australopithecus* and early *Homo*, along with fossil remains of tools and projectiles, strongly indicate that accurate throwing ability was present in these species. Coincident with this was an expansion in cranial capacity and reorganization in cortical structures supportive of increased communicative ability and social proficiency (Holloway, 1996; Falk, 1985; Wilkins & Wakefield, 1995). This pattern is further confirmed in *Homo ergaster/erectus*, in whom advancements in tool/weapon technologies, skeletal adaptations important for throwing, brain size, and social organization have been documented.

Third, although hominins were creating throwing implements and weapons for hundreds of thousands of years, the fossil record shows no evidence of substantial intergroup warfare before about 40,000 years ago. The evidence for extensive hunting during this time is equivocal (Keeley, 1996). This raises the question of what hominins were doing with all their projectiles and weapons. Moreover, the thickening of the hominin crania and the pattern of wounds observed on some skeletal remains suggests that a noteworthy proportion of hominin deaths were violent (Klein, 1999; Lieberman, 1991; Trinkaus, 1986). In Bingham's view, these observations make sense if one considers the possibility that hominins were engaging in extensive intragroup violence (coalitional enforcement) with a goal of punishing noncooperators. This hypothesis becomes even more plausible in light of the fact that throughout recorded history, significant proportions of people have been killed by their own states or societies. Scully's (1997) study of sanctioned violence showed that across the centuries the propor-

tion of people killed by their own social groups ranged from nearly 9% (in the 13th century) to slightly less than 4% (in the 19th century). In the 20th century, it has been estimated that anywhere from 170–360 million people have been killed by their own governments, substantially more than those killed in the century's notorious wars (42 million). Although the intragroup murder rate is relatively low among hunter–gatherers (1% in the !Kung), it is still a nontrivial proportion of the total population (Lee, 1979).

Finally, Bingham also contended that the notion of coalitional enforcement helps to explain one of the most perplexing issues in human prehistory, the origins of the Upper Paleolithic "leap." About 40,000 years ago, a dramatic stride in hominin cultural and social evolution took place, marking the beginning of the modern human mentality. Bingham pointed out that this event was coevolutionary with the development of a new generation of thrown weapons, including light-weight, long-distance spears. These new weapons allowed for multigroup coalitional enforcement, whereby an alliance of groups could band together to punish a renegade band. Cooperation and information exchange could thereby extend across groups and regions, laying the groundwork for the cultural and social advances associated only with the Upper Paleolithic. Although Bingham marshaled an impressive array of arguments and evidence in defense of his theory, only time and additional testing will determine the viability of his model. There is, nevertheless, a bizarre irony in the notion that our unique cooperative capacities have an intimate evolutionary connection to our unique capacities for violence.

their own and others' generosity in a series of hypothetical situations. When actually confronted with a situation requiring generosity, subjects' predictions about others proved fairly accurate. Their predictions about themselves, however, were far too charitable. For example, when asked how much of their $5 participation payment they would donate to a charity, most subjects said that they would give about half but that others would give only about $1.80. When actually given the chance to donate, subjects averaged about $1.50. This indicates that we are pretty accurate at assessing how nice others will be but tend to delude ourselves about our own benevolence.

How should one react to all this supposed deception going on in human relationships? One response is outright rejection. For philosopher Holmes Rolston III (1999), it all is a bit much to swallow. In his view, it is tortured logic in the extreme to propose a double negative to explain a positive. To understand why someone does a good deed for another (the positive), proponents of the evolutionary approach must argue that the doer deceives both him- or herself and the recipient of the good deed (the double negative). It is certainly more parsimonious to contend that on occasion we do nice things simply because we want to be nice. To read self-interested deception into every nice act is to force the data to conform to a theory, rather than using data to test a theory. For Rolston, proponents of the evolutionary view approach human nature with the attitude:

> Always look for the subtler self-interested motive. If you do not find it, look again. It must be there because the theory demands it. If you cannot find it, there must be a mistake, either yours in not detecting where the genetic self-interest is present, or a mistake of the actors, who fail in acting in their self-interest.
>
> (ROLSTON, 1999, P. 257)

Rolston rightly points out that the logic of deception and self-deception can be convoluted and difficult, if not impossible, to test. That does not mean that the evolutionary view is wrong, only that at the moment there is reason not to accept it uncritically as correct.

A second response to all of this is one of cautious acceptance. Let's assume that at least some of what the evolutionary psychologists say is true and that at least some deception plays into our relationships. This response asks us to develop a healthy skepticism about our own motives and desires in our relationships with others. This might do us all some good. The next time we point the finger of moral indignation at another we might ask ourselves if we are truly defending a universal moral principle or simply seizing an opportunity to guard our self-interests. The next time we demand retribution from another, we might ask if we would be so bold if the one in our debt was of higher status or whether our insistence on "justice" applies only to those below us in the social hierarchy. Finally, when we do a good deed, we might question whether we really do expect something in return and whether our generosity represents not gifts freely given but loans to be recovered later (with interest). Perhaps the answer to self-deception is a more vigorous form of self-scrutiny and honesty. There is nothing uniquely human about reciprocity, self-serving biases, or deferring to higher status. Monkeys and apes do as much. But a life deeply examined—now there's something only a human can do.

SUMMARY

Genes use both cooperation and competition as means for promoting themselves. To work cooperatively with each other, genes look for genes similar to themselves (i.e., kin). Because kin share genetic interest, cooperation among family members could have been easily favored with natural selection. Comparisons across species have proven valuable in understanding the evolution of cooperation in humans. At least two types of cooperative arrangements have been documented in primates: mutualism and reciprocity. Where animals (including early hominins) face a hostile environment as a result of weather, scarcity of resources, presence of predators, or the difficulty of capturing prey, the evolution of mutualism may have been favored. Conditions favorable to the evolution of reciprocity include an intelligent species, long lives, and fairly stable social settings. These conditions are present in many primate species and most likely would have been present by about 2 million years ago in our hominin ancestors. Hominins elevated reciprocity in a number of ways, including sophisticated exchanges involving tools, labor, and other products; cooperative arrangements between the sexes involving specialization of labor and skill with mutual exchange; and cooperative arrangements between groups through marriage.

One very useful approach to modeling the evolution of cooperative systems has come from game theory. Game theory models have shown how reciprocal arrangements based on a TFT strategy evolve and become stabilized in a population, even when each member of the population is acting in his or her own self-interest. Despite criticisms, game theory seems to provide a very promising means of studying the evolution of cooperation.

Human cooperativeness evolved within a context of social hierarchy, a factor that continues to influence us today. Human relationships exhibit evidence of self-serving biases, deference to higher status, and deceptive and self-deceptive qualities, all in keeping with evolutionary expectations. To varying degrees, we all deceive others to get what we want or need. Monkeys and apes use these types of behaviors, too, but the human is the only species capable of personal insight.

KEY TERMS

coalitional enforcement	mutualism	self-serving bias
deception	prisoner's dilemma	social ostracism
deference to higher status	reciprocity	
game theory approach	self-deception	

REVIEW QUESTIONS

1. Why might the risks of reciprocity represent a threat to one's fitness?

2. Describe the four ways in which early hominins' reciprocity reached a unique status.

3. Explain how TFT provides a logical explanation for the evolution of cooperation among self-interested organisms.

4. What is the difference between mutualism and reciprocity? Give evidence of both from primate studies.

5. According to Bingham, how was the behavior of cheating punished by our ancestors in a manner that avoided serious personal injury?

6. Explain the benefits of a self-serving bias and deference to higher status.

7. Why did Rolston criticize the evolutionary explanation for "nice" behaviors?

SUGGESTED READINGS

de Waal, F. (1996). *Good natured*. Cambridge, MA: Harvard University Press.

Wright, R. (1994). *The moral animal*. New York: Vintage Press.

Wright, R. (2000). *Non-zero: The logic of human destiny*. New York: Vintage Books.

Ridley, M. (1996). *The origins of virtue*. New York: Viking Books.

WEB SITES

http://pespmc1.vub.ac.be/COOPEVOL.html read more about the *Evolution of Cooperation* by F. Heylighen, with links to the history of evolution, social evolution/conflicts between levels, and other articles.

www.taumoda.com/web/PD/setup.html this site takes the visitor through steps that work out different models related to the evolution of cooperation, with access to a library containing relevant information.

10

Cooperation Between the Sexes I: Evolution

"An old acquaintance of his once remarked: 'A woman might have tempered his character.'"

KARNOW, 1983, P. 215

What Genes Have Wrought

WHY HAVE SEX? FOR HUMANS, the answer seems simple enough: because it's fun! The point of evolutionary psychology, however, is to keep pushing back the questions until we reach the most fundamental level of inquiry. Why is it fun? Because it feels good. Why does it feel good? Because feelings are indicators of fitness consequences, and sex has positive fitness consequences. To ensure that one's genes are propagated into the next generation it helps to have offspring, and to have offspring one has to engage in sex. Our genes "want" us to have lots of sex to raise their probability of immortality. To encourage this, natural selection has seen to it that sex feels really good. Sex feels good for the body because it is good for the genes.

The quote that opens this chapter, however, casts a complicating shadow on this seemingly lucid logic. The character in question was Ngo Dinh Diem, the intense, authoritarian president of South Vietnam, who was murdered by his own people in November 1963 (only weeks before John F. Kennedy's assassination). Diem's acrid disposition, obstinacy, and outright cruelty contributed in no small way to the tragedy known as the Vietnam War. To suggest, as the quote does, that history might have been different (whether slightly or significantly) if Diem had a wife, is to acknowledge that male–female relationships among humans have far more ramifications than genes ever intended. One can hardly overestimate the impact of gender interactions. Of the 282 articles of Hammurabi's code, nearly a quarter (68) deal with family and sexual relations (Darlington, 1969). The quality of one's personal life and the quality of life in an entire community are often influenced in major ways by the state of male–female relationships. With so much riding on the way that men and women relate to one another, the central function of simply propagating genes becomes obscured. With the complications, pressures, and conflicts inherent in opposite-sex relationships, some of us actually forget to have sex or even consciously opt against it (Abbott, 2000).

This brings us full circle, back to the original question: why have sex? If sex brings with it a bargeload of interpersonal baggage that can at times sabotage the

219

entire purpose of gene propagation, then why bother? Why would the genes take such a risk, especially when it is far simpler and more reliable to replicate asexually. So perplexing was this question that, in 1975, prominent evolutionary biologist George Williams called the ubiquitous presence of sex something of a crisis in evolutionary biology. "Sexuality is a maladaptive feature," he complained, yet most creatures lack the preadaptations for ridding themselves of it (Williams, 1975, pp. 102–103). What have the genes wrought, and why have they wrought it?

The Case Against Sex

From a genetic point of view, the case against sex is straightforward. The genetic recombination inherent in sexual reproduction means that about 50% of an individual's genome will not be passed on to the offspring. Giving up half of one's genetic code seems like an odd waste given the fact that it is difficult for a set of genes even to reach the point of potential reproduction. Of the few million egg cells that a woman has, only about 400 will ripen and be released for possible fertilization. In today's industrialized society, of those 400, fewer than 10 (on average) eventually will be fertilized. Of these, only about one fourth will result in successful pregnancies. About half of all fertilizations fail to implant properly in the uterus. Of those that do implant, another half spontaneously abort, usually because of genetic defects (Adler & Carey, 1982; Avise, 1998; Roberts & Lowe, 1975; Sutton & Wagner, 1985). In the struggle for life, the genes that succeed in shepherding an organism to adulthood have run a hazardous gauntlet indeed, proving their adaptive worthiness. Ripping this winning team asunder and tossing away half seems foolish.

Other circumstances indicate that sex ought to be a losing evolutionary strategy. First, it is mechanically more complicated and thus takes more time and energy than asexual reproduction. Under optimal circumstances, the *E. coli* bacterium can divide every 20 minutes, thereby begetting about 4 generations in only 90 minutes. If it reproduced sexually, only one generation could be produced in that same amount of time (Gould & Gould, 1997; Stearns, 1987). Second, various diseases, such as AIDS, syphilis, and gonorrhea, can exploit sex as an effective means of transmission. Infection with one of these can lead to sterility and even death, hardly beneficial to the propagation of the genes. Finally, the time, energy, and resources necessary to find a mate can sometimes be prohibitively costly. If mates are rare or widely dispersed, one may have to travel long distances, risking life and limb. If mates are more abundant, one often must compete with others or expend time and energy evaluating the suitability of the competitors. For some animals the sexual act itself can be dangerous, in that it leads to vulnerability to predation (it's hard to run away with your pants down, so to speak). This is why in many animals, such as antelope, the time spent in the sexual act is minimized to only a few seconds (Jolly, 1999). With all this going against it, it is rather baffling that 99.9% of animal species reproduce sexually (White, 1978). Where's the payoff?

The Case for Sex

Two powerful arguments for sexual reproduction are known by cryptic names: **Müller's ratchet** and the **Red Queen**. Müller's ratchet (named for geneticist Hermann Müller) refers to the fact that damaging genetic mutations can quickly accumulate to intolerable levels in asexually reproducing species. In humans, the rate of mutation is such that it is estimated that anywhere from 1–3 new mutations are added with each generation (Crow, 1999; Eyre-Walker & Keightley, 1999; Lerner & Libby, 1975). In an organism such as *E. coli* that can sprout three or four generations in the time it takes to watch the average horror movie, a similar mutation rate would quickly load up the genome with enough defects to produce disastrous consequences. In fact, one of the reasons why asexually reproducing organisms produce such an abundance of offspring may be because only a relatively few are truly fit for their environments (Gould, 1999; cited in Jolly, 1999, p. 53). By virtue of sexual recombination, deleterious mutations can be dispersed among offspring or even excised out of the genome entirely. Margulis and Sagan (1986) referred to DNA recombination as a massive cellular health care system in which repairs on defects can be carried out, helping to maintain the advantageous stability of the genome. The shuffling and sorting of sexual recombination helps to counteract Müller's ratchet, an especially important trait for species such as *Homo sapiens* who produce few but long-lived offspring. Although Müller's ratchet undoubtedly has played an important role in the evolution of sex, one study questions whether this theory alone could account for the evolution and maintenance of sex, given the relatively low mutation rates in many species (Keightley & Eyre-Walker, 2000). Other explanations are needed.

The **Red Queen** argument takes its name from the character in Lewis Carroll's *Through the Looking Glass* who tells Alice that it takes all the running you can do just to stay in the same place. The name is an oblique reference to the fact that in an ever-changing environment successful organisms must, like the Red Queen, keep moving, changing, and evolving to remain adapted. Thus, the argument goes, sexual recombination provides the variability and flexibility needed for organisms to cope with rapidly changing environments. But this oversimplified view quickly runs up against a major problem: it is in relatively stable ecosystems, such as rain forests, that sex is most prevalent. In more transient, unstable environments, such as freshwater ponds or Arctic tundras, asexual species are found more often (Ridley, 1996). Why bother with sex if your environment is fairly predictable from one generation to the next? The answer is that what appears stable and predictable often is a deceptive guise for a raging dynamo of evolution. The forests and grasslands where our primate and hominid ancestors lived were and continue to be hotbeds of parasite activity. Parasitic organisms can evolve with frightening alacrity. The *E. coli* bacterium, happily living in our guts, can produce 10,000 generations in a matter of months. That's about as many generations as humans have engendered since the appearance of *H. sapiens* 150,000 years ago. This rapid turnover allows parasites and pathogenic microbes to evolve quickly to foil the host's defenses. Over the course of evolution, longer living, larger bodied organisms faced an increasingly serious challenge from rapidly adapting parasites that could very quickly evolve into strains too formidable for their immune systems. The host organisms responded by having sex. By shuffling their genomes with each generation, they became "moving targets," presenting their parasitic competitors with novel immune responses in each generation.

The power of sex to outwit dangerous parasites was nicely demonstrated in an experiment using a little fish called the topminnow (Lively, 1987). Topminnows come in both sexual and asexual varieties, both of which can become infested with a parasitic worm that causes black spot disease. When both types were present in a common pool, the asexuals were afflicted far more severely by the discoloring black spots than the sexuals. Of even greater interest was the fact that when a small group of sexually reproducing topminnows was isolated and forced to interbreed, they became as susceptible to the disease as their asexual compatriots. Only after a few "strangers" were added to the pool did the incidence of the disease fall back to its usual low level. The lesson of the experiment was clear. It was not sex per se that offered protection against parasites. It was the genetic recombination that occurred as a result of sex. Because of their fast rate of reproduction, it took only a few generations for a strain of worm to arise that was able to outmaneuver the asexual topminnows' defenses. Each subsequent generation of asexual topminnow was a virtual clone of the previous generation, so they were "sitting ducks" (or fish) for the worms, which had already evolved to evade the immune response of the fish. The same was true for the interbred sexual topminnows, in which genetic variability had been severely compromised. The sexual topminnows, however, were the epitome of the Red Queen. Their genomes and immune systems constantly shifted and shuffled about so that the worms could never quite figure out how to counter them effectively. Despite all its disadvantages, sexual recombination has evolved as a remarkable tool for the genes to have their cake and eat it, too. By virtue of sex, the genome can conserve its adaptive stability against the build-up of damaging mutations (Müller's ratchet) and at the same time introduce enough variability (the Red Queen) to thwart the malicious intent of fast-paced parasites.

The Meaning of Sex

Reproducing sexually is inherently more complicated than reproducing asexually. First, you generally need two sexes rather than one. Second, you have to get the two sexes together somehow to take care of the recombination business. To appreciate the complexities and challenges of sexual reproduction, one first needs to understand the very nature of being male or female.

Parental Investment and Reproductive Strategies

From a biological point of view, the difference between the sexes has nothing to do with body size, hair length, aggressiveness, analytical thinking, emotional sensitivity, or the zest with which one wields the remote control. At the most basic level, what makes one male or female is the size of one's gametes (sex cells). Females have bigger gametes. Females produce large eggs, whereas males produce tiny sperm. But (stealing a phrase from Darwin), from so simple a beginning, the most amazing things can evolve. Producing large eggs takes greater metabolic resources than producing tiny sperm. Over time, the proportion of sperm to eggs can become exceedingly large. In other words, there are a lot more sperm out there than eggs. This imbalance becomes even more exaggerated with mammals, in which the female's eggs are fertilized internally, gestated internally for an extended period of time, and postnatal suckling of the young is required. Because the time a mammalian female spends in gestation and nursing takes her out of the egg-producing business, this further reduces the total number of "available" eggs in the marketplace. Meanwhile, mammalian males go right on producing profuse amounts of sperm, the vast majority of which will have no evolutionarily satisfying place to call home. This "gamete imbalance" has two important ramifications when it comes to understanding the meaning of sex: (1) differential parental investment and (2) divergent reproductive strategies.

Parental investment refers to any effort a parent makes on behalf of one offspring that increases that offspring's chances of survival and at the same time reduces the parent's ability to expend effort on other offspring (Trivers, 1972). The tired mother's lament, "I can't have more kids because I'm too drained [physically, financially, emotionally, whatever] raising this one," captures the essence of parental investment. **Differential parental investment** refers to the fact that the two sexes do not invest equally in the care and raising of offspring. Females almost always invest more. Mammalian females not only expend relatively more energy producing their eggs, but they continue expending resources in the form of weeks or months of internal gestation, postpartum nursing, and nurturing. In some species, such as primates, female care of young in the form of protection and feeding can extend for years. Mammalian males, by contrast, typically contribute only a few moments of time and a tablespoon or so of semen to the next generation. More than 95% of mammalian males offer no parental care whatsoever in the raising of their young. In his usual candid fashion, George Williams was uncompromisingly blunt about the difference:

> [A mammalian male's] essential role may end with copulation, which involves a negligible expenditure of energy and materials on his part, and only a momentary lapse of attention from matters of direct concern to his safety and well-being.....[For females, however] copulation may mean a commitment to a prolonged burden, in both the mechanical and physiological sense, and its many attendant stresses and dangers.
>
> (WILLIAMS, 1966, PP. 183–184)

The fact that males and females differ vastly in the amount of investment they make in their offspring leads to **divergent reproductive strategies**. Although it is something of an oversimplification, this divergence can be characterized as one of quantity versus quality. Males want quantity. The average male's reproductive interests are best served by impregnating as many females as possible. Overloaded with cheaply produced and easily disseminated sperm, a male's fitness usually is limited only by the number of females to whom he can gain access. In a classic experiment, A. J. Bateman (1948) closely monitored the reproductive patterns of fruit flies. Females tended to have the same number of offspring, regardless of how many males they mated with. The same was not true of the males. A male's reproductive success followed a simple dictum: the more they mated, the more they procreated. Males with voracious appetites for frequent sex are widespread throughout the animal kingdom, producing some interesting and amusing phenomena. In some species of frogs, males mount other males so often that a distinctive "don't bother" release call has evolved. Coaxing out the amorous side of a male turkey can be easily accomplished with a primitive replica of female turkey's head suspended about 15 inches off the ground (Trivers, 1985). The indiscriminate eagerness of some snakes is even more embarrassing, because, as Darwin (1871) noted, they sometimes work up a pretty respectable lust before realizing their partner is dead!

It is hardly a mystery why Williams (1966) concluded that the male reproductive strategy is best understood as "an aggressive and immediate willingness to mate with as many females as may be available." If along the way a few of those females happen to be unreceptive, dead, or not female, then no great loss, just move on and try again!

Females, on the other hand, want quality. Because they possess the scarce and valuable eggs and must devote a considerable proportion of their lives tending to what emerges from those eggs, females' reproductive interests are best served by securing high-quality genetic material from the males. A female who mates with a weak, diseased, or dim-witted male is more likely to have defective genes passed to her offspring, which might mean wasting her precious time, eggs, and energy on offspring unlikely to survive to viability. For females it is not *frequent* sex that holds the most profitable fitness payoff but *worthwhile* sex. In fact, in some species' adaptations have evolved to actively discourage females from extraneous copulations. The male bean weevil, for example, has a penis equipped with slashing spines that cause internal lacerations to the female when mating. Mating only twice can reduce a female's life span by nearly two thirds compared with that of virgin weevils (Crudgington & Shiva-Jothy, 2000). When the copulatory unit price is that high, a female bean weevil had best choose wisely the first time around. Bean weevils may be a bit extreme, but finicky females—like overeager males—occur throughout the animal world. Many female species demand "gifts" before sex and withhold sexual favors if the gifts fall short of expectations. For example, the female hanging fly refuses sex unless she is fed a dead insect during the act. Even then, if the meal is so skimpy that she can finish it before he finishes with her, she simply moves on to another. She apparently does not want the genes of someone who does not have the wherewithal to scrounge up at least one decent dinner (Thornhill, 1976). Male African weaverbirds hang upside down from the nests they have built and vigorously flap their wings to invite a quality inspection from the females. While the male serenades her, the she-weaver pokes, prods, and pulls at the nest, critiquing its value with a skepticism worthy of fastidious building inspector. If everything is up to snuff, she stays; if not, she moves on to the next nest (Buss, 1998). Even cosmopolitan female bonobos show a distinct sexual preference for males who provide them with meat (de Waal, 1995). Requiring males to provide gifts or build sturdy nests gives females some information about the genes of a potential mate. If he can produce quality (gifts, nests, etc.), it is more likely that he possesses quality (genes).

Female Choice and Male Competition

Parental investment differences lead to differences in reproductive strategies that, in turn, lead to two other important effects: **female choice** and **male competition**. Female choice refers to the fact that females have a certain power to select which males will provide the genetic material to fertilize their eggs. A female's fitness is enhanced if she can secure high-quality genes for her offspring, thus making it more likely that her sons and daughters will be healthy, strong, smart, and able to produce grandchildren. A wide array of indicators of male worthiness exists across a variety of species and includes various display behaviors (the orangutan mating call), structural ornaments (a stag's antlers), courtship rituals, and outright male-on-male violence. The information these indicators provide can be used by females to assess whose genes may be best suited for propagation in her offspring (Fig. 10.1). For example, a male who can produce a loud, intimidating call is likely to be healthy, energetic, and in possession of good lungs and vocal apparatus. The genes that produced those traits in him could provide similar advantages to her offspring. Furthermore, the intimidating call also might keep away predators and ensure a large, secure, resource-rich territory for the raising of her young. Over long spans of evolutionary time, those females who assessed male attributes with a keen, critical eye and chose their mates wisely were the ones most likely to leave descendants.

If females choose, then males are the chosen. As Alison Jolly (1999) pointed out, it is almost universal in the animal kingdom that the chosen are more violent than the choosers. In the pursuit of females, males run into one ever-present obstacle: each other. A male eager to display his powerful mating call (and thus prove his genetic worthiness), quickly finds a chorus of other males intent on doing the same. Male competition can take many forms, some more direct and violent than others. Male lions often exchange roars at a distance, with the "weaker" roarer simply moving on to another territory rather than risking an actual fight. Two bighorn sheep will ram horns until one has had enough and moves on, leaving the other with the territory and local females. Male chimpanzees engage in aggressive displays that involve loud vocalizations, dragging and throwing branches, daring

Figure 10.1 Males use a number of display behaviors to advertise their genetic worthiness. A long tail, a loud call, a show of strength, bright colors, or an impressive set of antlers could all serve as indicators of good genes to females sizing up mates. (© Martin Ruegner/Pictor International Ltd./PictureQuest.)

swings and charges, and sometimes violent clashes that can result in injury or death. Although ultimately the males are competing for access to females, that access comes as a byproduct of securing more proximate goals. The more proximate goal is usually control of a territory and its resources (the goal, for example, for lions or orangutans) or establishing status within a group hierarchy (the goal, for example, for wolves or chimpanzees). Where male-on-male competition is intense, selection pressures emerge that usually lead to certain male traits being advantageous and therefore highly represented in the male population. Such traits as large body size, aggressiveness, and weaponry (like large canine teeth and sharp claws) are common in species in which males battle with one another for females. These traits are often sexually dimorphic; that is, they occur in a more exaggerated form in males than in females (for example, male gorillas are about twice the size of females).

Female choice and male competition are not independent processes. The two operate together and place limits on each other. For example, female choice can be limited by male competition. If a male has secured a territory and successfully banished all competitors, a female in that territory has little choice of mates. On the other hand, because the winner's genes probably had something to do with his victory, he is probably not such a bad choice after all. Even so, a male's success in competition is no guarantee that females will submissively accept his genes. Among primates there is a correlation between alpha male status and reproductive success (i.e., alphas tend to have more offspring), but the correlation is not perfect (Berard, Nurnberg, Epplen, & Schmidtke, 1993; Bercovitch, 1995). A female gorilla may choose another mate by simply running off to another harem. Female chimpanzees are notoriously promiscuous and, despite the best efforts of the alpha male, often "sneak" copulations with lower status males. Female chimps may even copulate with males outside of their community, although the extent of this activity is a subject of debate. One study showed that more than half of the newborns in one wild chimpanzee community were fathered by males outside of the group, and, despite more than 10 years of alpha status shared between two males, neither managed to leave a single viable offspring (Gagneux, Boesch, & Woodruff, 1999). This study was sharply criticized on methodological grounds for overestimating the number of offspring fathered by males outside of the group, and follow-up analyses suggest that extragroup paternity actually may be very rare (Pusey, Constable, Ashley, & Goodall, 2001). Nevertheless, it is clear that males and females actively thrust and parry with one another to further their genetic interests. Females choose, but the choices may be limited. Males compete, but their competition does not necessarily settle the issue.

Maleness and Femaleness

It is important to recognize that the traits we usually think of as distinguishing male and female are not *inherent* to maleness or femaleness but, instead, are the results of differing degrees of parental investment. In other words, human females tend to be more nurturing, not because they are female but because they have an evolutionary history as heavy parental investors. Human males tend to be more aggressive, not because they are male but because they have an evolutionary history of relatively less parental investment and relatively more competition. The critical test of this logic comes in the form of a few species in which the parental roles are reversed. One of the most well-known examples is the phalarope. Male phalarope birds patiently sit and incubate the eggs while the females chase about looking for more mates. Female phalaropes are larger, more colorful, and aggressive than males because they compete amongst each other for mates. The males fastidiously choose from the best of the lot (West-Eberhard, 1991). A similar pattern is found among Mormon crickets, with females battling over a male's packet of edible sperm. The Mormon cricket males are modest and deliberative, rejecting about half of their potential copulations (Trivers, 1985). Male pipefish take the females' eggs and chauffeur them around in saclike structures that provide nutrients to the eggs. Meanwhile, the females pursue other males, initiating mating rituals in an attempt to spread their eggs about as widely as possible (Clutton-Brock & Vincent, 1991).

These examples reinforce the biologist's conviction that maleness and femaleness are ultimately a matter of gamete size and not much else. From there, natural selection can take a variety of directions in working out how the sexes will contribute to the genesis of the next generation. For mammals and primates, that direction has involved relatively greater female parental investment with varying degrees of female choice and male competition. It is precisely here that we find the meaning of sex for *H. sapiens*. As primates, our evolutionary history has fashioned males and females differently. It is by evolutionary design that male and female human primates approach sex and opposite-sex relationships with diverging interests and varying priorities. Sex means that human males and females have to find some mutually acceptable arrangement whereby our discordant interests can harmonize long enough to assure another generation of *H. sapiens*. We are, however, not alone. Within the parameters of relatively greater female parental investment, female choice, and male competition, countless other species have had to work out their male–female conflicts and complications. The variety of systems that have emerged is truly impressive.

Primate Social Systems

Sexual reproduction requires that males and females get together to engage in the copulatory act. As a result of differences in their parental investments, however, males and females have somewhat conflicting interests when it comes to maximizing fitness. Natural selection is faced with a formidable challenge: how to create a system that successfully knits together the dissimilar fitness interests of males and females of a particular species. If males and females cannot find enough common ground on which to bring forth the next generation, then the genes of both are destined for oblivion. It is instructive for us to examine how natural selection has managed this challenge in our primate cousins so that we can better appreciate the intricacies of the human situation.

As highly social creatures, primates have evolved entire social systems around mating and the care of offspring. Most male primates contribute only minimally to nurturing the young. Therefore, it is not surprising that primate social systems tend to revolve around females and their relationships and circumstances. In most Old World monkeys, female kin groups are the core of social life. A female monkey usually spends her entire life in her natal group, with a social rank inherited from her mother. Together with her female kin, she will raise her own offspring and assist in raising her relatives' offspring. A male monkey usually leaves his native group to live a solitary life on the periphery of the female society. He will lurk in the shadows, waiting for a chance to invade and control a group long enough to sire viable offspring. Soon enough he will be run off by another male or by the collective action of the group's females as they grow weary of his presence.

Social systems vary among Old World monkeys but, generally speaking, are more uniform than those found among apes, where the diversity is quite remarkable. As with monkeys, however, at the heart of this diversity are the females, the ways in which they have evolved to cope with the distribution of food resources, and the demands this places on caring for themselves and their young (Wrangham, 1980, 1987). A kernel of truth exists in the idea that among apes, females adapt to the environment and males adapt to the females.

Gibbons: Monogamy

Gibbons are small, acrobatic apes (one of the so-called "lesser" apes) that live in monogamous pairs. In their rain forest habitats of southeast Asia, food is widely distributed in discrete patches, making the most efficient foraging strategy one in which a lone gibbon establishes a modest-size territory and moves about exploiting the local resources. When they reach maturity, gibbon females set out alone, with males dispersing singly in pursuit of them. Opposite-sex pairs link up, establish a joint territory, and commence to raise their offspring. The male offers a substantial amount of parental assistance. This monogamous arrangement means that there is very little male-on-male competition for females. This lack of male competition is reflected in the absence of size dimorphism between male and female gibbons. Both male and female gibbons will aggressively defend their territory. In this instance, the female is every bit as dangerous a foe as her male partner.

Orangutans: Exploded Harems

The term orangutan means "old man of the forest" and reflects the fact that the natives of Borneo considered them to be members of another (human) tribe. In their dense forest homes of Borneo and Sumatra, orangs feed largely on widely dispersed fruits and other vegetation. Given its large size, one orang can easily consume the few ripe fruits that might be present on a single tree, leading to the necessity of constant foraging in the rain forest canopy, a task best accomplished alone. Orang females stake out moderate-size territories within which they search tree to tree for ripe fruit and other edibles. Males compete with one another to establish large territories encompassing those held by a number of females. The male will mate with the females within his territory and, although offering little in the way of parental care, will defend the territory against threats to the infant, such as other male orangs. This system is a form of **unimale polygyny**, in which a single male simultaneously controls the reproductive destinies of many females, also called a "harem." However, despite the fact that females' territories often overlap slightly, they prefer to remain apart from one another and so do not form the single concentrated group that is more typical of a harem. Orang males are forced to patrol a very large area within which the females are scattered, hence the term "exploded harem" (Galdikas, 1995). Moreover, the intensity of male competition for territory is evidenced by the size dimorphism between males and females. Tipping the scales at more than 90 kg (200 lb), the average male is more than twice the weight of the average female.

Given the similarities of diet, habitat, and foraging behavior between orangs and gibbons, one might ask why they have such different social systems. Why are gibbon males monogamists and not polygynists? It's hard to say, but one must consider the fact that it takes a great deal of time and energy to control the vast territory required of an orang male in securing his harem. The gibbon male, by contrast, exerts less energy establishing a territory and more on direct maintenance of offspring. This is not such a bad strategy, because gibbon females have much shorter birth intervals (about 3 years) than orangutan females (nearly 8 years). A male gibbon's fitness interests are well served by hanging around a single female for an extended period of time, whereas a male orangutan is better served by trolling about in a large territory where at least one of the resident females is likely to be receptive. Given the huge size difference between orangs and gibbons, orangs will necessarily have to forage more widely to satisfy their nutritional needs. For a male orang, then, establishing a large territory serves both subsistence and reproductive purposes.

Gorillas: True Harems

Gorillas are the largest of the apes, and their diet consists of enormous amounts of leaves, foliage, and other low-quality vegetation. In contrast to orangs, gorilla food resources tend to occur in dense clumps or patches rather than widely distributed "spots." Female gorillas often forage in groups and jointly defend their patch of resources from others. They tend to roam about in groups of anywhere from 4 to 20 members. Gorilla males then compete to control a group of females, **the harem**, to which a single male (the silverback) will have sole reproductive access. Female group members generally will remain for years with a single silverback. However, females do exercise some degree of choice in the form of occasionally transferring from one group to another (Fossey, 1983; Watts, 1990). Male group members are tolerated when they are juveniles, and occasionally an elder silverback will bequeath his harem to his son. More often, males leave their native groups and attempt to establish their own harems. Within the group, the female and her young benefit from the silverback's protection from predators and from other male gorillas that can be infanticidal (Watts, 1989). As with orangutans, competitiveness for harems has produced male gorillas that are twice the size of their female counterparts.

Chimpanzees: Multimale Polygyny or the "Boys Club"

Chimpanzees come in two varieties: common chimpanzees and bonobos (also called pygmy chimpanzees). Common chimpanzees are probably the best-known apes. They live in social groups of about 50 individuals, but these groups are highly flexible, often breaking into smaller subgroups and then reuniting in a variety of arrangements (fission–fusion communities). Chimps are omnivores, feeding on various fruits, leaves, bugs, and some meat. Chimpanzee females often forage alone or in the company of their dependent offspring. Because the females tend to distribute themselves widely over a large range when foraging, a single chimpanzee male has a difficult time trying to exert control over them. Moreover, unlike gorillas and orangutans, chimpanzee females are only slightly smaller than the males. High-ranking females occasionally dominate younger, lower-ranking males. This has produced an interesting arrangement among chimpanzees: the males form the most enduring social relationships. Males, rather than females, are the ones that tend to remain in their natal groups, forming themselves into coalitions to establish enough territorial control to ensure access to the females. A single male will assume alpha status, but his dominance is achieved only through the cooperation of a circle of supporters. They assist him in patrolling and securing the territory, and he rewards them with a certain degree of access to the resident females—hence the term **multimale polygyny**. The females are not entirely passive in this process, because their support or lack thereof also can play a role in determining which chimp retains alpha status. Moreover, despite the best efforts of the dominant male, female chimps tend to mate promiscuously, often consorting with several males while in estrus (de Waal, 1982; Goodall, 1986).

In many respects, bonobos are quite similar to their "common" cousins. One difference lies in the bonobos well-deserved reputation for sexiness. For most primates and, indeed, just about all animals, sex seems to entail no special pleasure and is often dispensed with in a few seconds. Bonobos are an exception of which Hugh Hefner might noddingly approve. Just about any occasion is suitable for bonobos to engage in some form of sex play, whether it is old friends renewing an acquaintance, new friends establishing a bond, one chimp trying to calm another, or the unexpected discovery of a rich cache of fruit (de Waal & Lanting, 1997; Furuichi, 1992; Takahata, Ihobe, & Idani, 1996; Wilson, 1980). More significant, evidence indicates that female bonobos may use sex as a means of extracting resources from males and that sex may serve as a tension-reduction strategy and an alternative to aggression within the bonobo community. If so, bonobos may be one of the few (or only) animals outside of humans who use sex as a utilitarian tool apart from procreation (de Waal, 1995). Might some of the tendencies we observe in humans be related to such a use of sex as a utilitarian tool? An additional difference between common chimps and bonobos is that for bonobos, stronger associative bonds appear to exist among females than males. This often results in female groups dominating individual males within the bonobo community.

What lesson do we take from this excursion into the social systems of our primate cousins? The lesson is one of appreciating diversity. With the exception of polyandry (one female sharing many males), just about every possible male–female arrangement is represented among the apes (Fig. 10.2). Natural selection will try just about anything to get males and females together long enough to successfully sprout the next generation. We may rail against the gorilla's exploitative machismo and smile sweetly at the gibbon's honorable monogamy, but our stamp of approval is of little concern to natural selection. It simply wants adaptation, not equity or moral integrity. Neither the gorilla nor the gibbon represents some "natural state" for *H. sapiens*. They, along with the other apes, simply represent some of the ways natural selection has solved the problem of weaving together the divergent reproductive interests of males and females. That *H. sapiens* are also primates, sharing many characteristics in common with our animal cousins, tells us

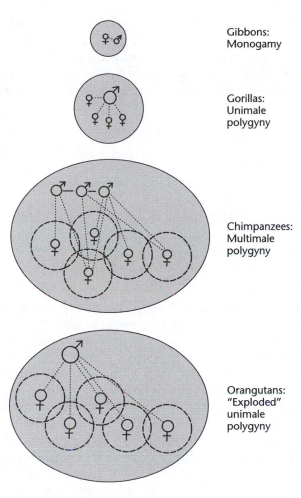

Figure 10.2 A summary of nonhuman primate social systems. Gibbons establish joint male–female territories and practice monogamy. Gorilla females jointly defend a resource patch, and males compete to control the female group, thus producing unimale polygyny or a harem. Chimpanzee females forage alone or in small groups across a wide territory, making it difficult for a single male to corral them. Thus, groups of related males work together to control a wide territory containing many females, producing multimale polygyny. Finally, orangutan females establish separate territories across a wide range, forcing a single male to establish an even broader territory encompassing that of many females, producing an exploded harem. (Adapted from Lewin, 1998, p. 158.)

that some of what we find in other apes may generalize to us as well. By the same token, however, given the wide diversity that exists among our cousins, we can, with equal assurance, expect profound differences between ourselves and nonhuman primates.

The Evolution of Hominid Social Systems

The social customs of extinct species do not fossilize with their bones. Any recounting of the evolution of hominid social systems and male/female relations necessarily involves a certain degree of speculation. This does not mean, however, that our speculations are reduced to wild imaginings. Along with using animal and primate models, such as the ones discussed previously in this chapter, researchers have at least two other approaches for trying to reconstruct the course of our ancestral past. One approach is to look for the common characteristics across related species in an effort to identify the properties most likely to have been present in the common ancestor of those species. This is referred to as a **phylogenetic approach**. Humans are most closely related to chimpanzees and gorillas. Richard

Wrangham (1987) examined 14 behavioral traits of humans, gorillas, common chimpanzees, and bonobos in an attempt to isolate the shared traits. From the traits common to these species, he constructed a profile of what the social world of the common ancestor might have been like. In Wrangham's view, the species from which humans, gorillas, and chimpanzees emerged was one with the following characteristics:

1. Closed social networks (i.e., ingroup members were readily distinguished from outgroup members);
2. Males dominated in-group relations;
3. Males occasionally existed singly away from the group;
4. Intergroup relations were generally antagonistic;
5. Males sometimes engaged in preemptive stalk-and-attack encounters with males of other groups;
6. Females left their natal groups for reproductive purposes (exogamy);
7. Social bonds among females were weak but usually tolerant; and
8. Males practiced polygyny.

Ghiglieri (1989) used a similar comparison to conclude that the ape/hominin common ancestor also would have had only a minimal amount of male parental investment in raising offspring. Noble and Davidson (1996, p. 142) generally concurred with these assessments, arguing that "females associated with each other but did not form alliances, and males were sometimes solitary, and little involved in rearing offspring." The important contribution of the phylogenetic approach is that it helps us to understand the possible starting point from which the evolution of hominin social systems proceeded.

The second approach to reconstructing the processes of hominin evolution is called the **behavioral ecological approach**. This approach combines the characteristics and constraints enumerated in the phylogenetic approach with the ecological context of the species. Put more simply, behavioral ecology asks how a species with particular characteristics responds to the demands of a changing environment. Thus, if our common ancestor was a group-living species with hostile intergroup relations, weak female social bonds, female exogamy, male aggression, minimal male parental investment, etc., and the habitat of this species began to change in certain ways, what would result?

Robert Foley (Foley, 1995; Foley & Lee, 1989) has been one of the foremost advocates of this approach in trying to reconstruct hominin evolution. Foley and Lee (1989) contended that the social structure of the common ancestor would have been roughly gorilla-like about 10 million years ago, when the East African ecology underwent a prolonged cooling and drying transition. As dense forests gave way to a patchwork of woodland and open grassland, the social world of our ancestors changed to one more resembling that of the chimpanzee. With food resources in widely dispersed patches, females would be forced to forage as small groups over increasingly large territories. Males would respond by banding together in kin groups to control the territory within which the females and their offspring were resident. Predation and threats from other groups would make larger group sizes advantageous, with male kin-based alliances forming the nucleus of the group. This would have been roughly the condition of *Australopithecus*. Jolly (1999) drew a similar conclusion based on evidence of the Australopith diet and the strong tendency of primate males to be territorial and aggressive (Sponheimer & Lee-Thorp, 1999; Wrangham & Peterson, 1996). In her view, *Australopithecus* existed in chimplike fission–fusion communities with male-bonded groups and promiscuously mating females. As in chimps, female promiscuity may have helped protect offspring from infanticidal males. In such a situation, the males might be inclined to spare an infant's life because of the possibility that it might be his offspring.

We should pause here, however, and consider a controversy that could have a profound impact on our understanding of the social situation of *Australopithecus*. In their original assessment of *Australopithecus afarensis* (Lucy), Johanson and White (1979) interpreted the fossil evidence as indicating a species with extreme size dimorphism, males being considerably larger than females. However, later analyses cast this interpretation into turmoil, with some researchers agreeing with Johanson and White (e.g., Aiello, 1994), others arguing that the fossil evidence was inconclusive (e.g., Richmond & Jungers, 1995), and still others strenuously asserting that Lucy was male, not female, and that what looked like one species with large males and small females was actually two distinct species with almost equal-size sexes (e.g., Hausler & Schmid, 1995; Zihlman, 1997).

Thus we have two very different images of *Australopithecus afarensis*: (1) a single species with extreme size dimorphism between males and females or (2) at least two distinct species with males and females of about equal size. If the first image is correct, then the size dimorphism in *Australopithecus* would suggest a substantial degree of male competition and polygyny, factors that would tend to limit whatever degree of male cooperativeness was present in our early history. If male kin groups were patrolling and controlling territories, as Foley, Lee, and Jolly envision, there was probably as much competitiveness within these groups as cooperativeness. High degrees of intragroup competitiveness would have made it difficult for these groups to grow very large or become well coordinated. If the second image is correct, then competitiveness among males may have been quite limited, and the more peaceful and monogamous portraits of *Australopithecus* painted by some (e.g., Lovejoy, 1981) may be plausible. The controversy is not settled, but for our purposes we will assume the Australopiths to have had big males and small females and to have existed in a chimp-like social setting similar to that suggested by Foley and Lee (1989) and Jolly (1999).

Transitioning from *Australopithecus* to *Homo*, Foley and Lee (1989) again saw important ecological factors at work that altered social structures. As seasonal changes affected food supply distributions and availabilities and increases in body size demanded greater intake of protein-rich foods, *Homo* was adapted to consuming more meat. Acquiring meat necessitated expanding home ranges, which pressured males into forming larger, more cooperative kin-based groups to secure the expanded territories needed for an adequate supply of hunted or scavenged meat. At the same time, females also were confronted by pressures, including increasingly dependent and burdensome offspring, that required aggregation into larger cooperative groups. Although assistance from other females certainly played an important role in the care and raising of these altricial and slowly maturing young, paternal care also entered the picture. With *Homo,* ecological and life history factors conspired to force increases in both intra- and intersex cooperation and group sizes. It is not surprising, then, to find fossil evidence indicating that *H. erectus* lived in larger, more cooperative groups with a significant decrease in size dimorphism between the sexes (Klein, 1999; Lewin, 1998; McHenry, 1991).

Speculations on the Social Life of Homo erectus *and Neanderthals*

Once we get past the phylogenetic and behavioral ecological approaches to reconstructing hominin evolution, our scientific footing becomes increasingly treacherous. A few ideas, however, have been put forward concerning the social lives of *H. erectus* and Neanderthals that merit mention, although it must be acknowledged that the challenge of gathering convincing evidence still awaits. Terrence Deacon (1997) argued that marriage may have been an invention of *H. erectus* that was brought on by the conflicting demands of group living and male provisioning. The fossil evidence indicates that *H. erectus* lived in larger, more cooperative groups than earlier hominin species. It is also with *H. erectus* that we have evidence of more human-like physical and life history factors, such as large brains, more extended childhoods, and substantial consumption of meat. *H. erectus*, therefore, was a group-living species in which males contributed significantly to the provisioning of offspring by procuring and sharing meat. Deacon, however, pointed out that coexistence of group living and male provisioning represents an evolutionarily unstable situation that cannot long persist. No species can unite group living with male provisioning unless it deals with the problem of **paternity certainty**. A male will not provision an offspring unless he can be reasonably certain that the offspring is his. In a group setting, with many males jousting for sexual access to females, this sort of certainty is not readily forthcoming. To better highlight this problem, take wolves and chimpanzees as examples. Both are group-living animals, but wolf males actively provision offspring and chimpanzee males do not. Why the difference? Because chimpanzee females mate promiscuously, and no male can be certain that any provisioning effort will benefit his genes. In wolf packs, however, only the dominant male and female are allowed to reproduce. The males who assist in provisioning are usually related to the offspring, either as father or older brothers, and thus can be certain that the pups they care for are their genetic legacy. Deacon stated the situation succinctly:

> Group living and male provisioning can occur together only in instances where reproductive access is completely limited and unambiguous, as in the case of social carnivores. There can be no stable compromise pattern unless this principle is somehow maintained. (1997, p. 392).

If *H. erectus* males actively provisioned offspring, as we are confident they did, then some social mechanism had to ensure paternity certainty. A wolf-like system in which only dominant tribe members were allowed to reproduce appears incredible. The most likely solution, according to Deacon, would have been something utterly unprecedented in evolutionary history: a "symbolic solution." Using ritual and ceremony, *H. erectus* began to symbolically and publicly "mark" individuals as having exclusive sexual privileges with one another. By doing so, the individuals and the entire tribe would be unambiguously aware of the special status endowed upon the couple. Others would know that these individuals were "off limits," and group harmony could be maintained and paternity certainty assured.

Group living and male provisioning could coexist. Deacon contended that this symbolic solution was a critical step in the evolution of language.

Deacon's scenario is not unreasonable, and some observations lend it credibility. For example, work by Hans Kummer and others with hamadryas baboons indicated that the males tend to respect one another's sexual "rights" to certain females. This suggests that the incipient codes of sexual privilege and conduct present in the primate mind came to full flower as the hominin brain expanded to be nearly human in size (Kummer, 1995; Kummer, Gotz, & Angst, 1974; Sigg & Falett, 1985). Moreover, male primates exhibit a clear preference for older, higher-ranking females who have already proven their reproductive and mothering capacities (Smuts, 1987). Human males clearly do not share this same preference, with younger, sexually naive women universally seen as more desirable as long-term mates (Buss, 1989). An evolved preference for younger, untested females might be expected if, in our ancestral past, social restrictions (marriage arrangements) made older, experienced women unavailable (Buss, 1994; Symons, 1979). On the other hand, if *H. erectus* did invent marriage, abundant evidence suggestions that the form was polygamous and not monogamous. In any case, Deacon provided an interesting and provocative image of our past that will surely stimulate debate and research as its validity is assessed. Deacon's image of *H. erectus* also stands in stark contrast to the rather dark picture that other researchers have painted of the social world of another hominin species, the Neanderthals (Box 10.1).

Sexual Selection and the Shaping of Homo sapiens Men and Women

An interesting thing happened over the course of hominin evolution. Out of pure self-interest, males and females actively shaped and molded one another. They did this through the power of what is called **sexual selection**. Up to this point, for simplicity, we have attributed all responsibility for the evolution of primate and hominin social systems to natural selection. This is not entirely accurate. Another type of selection, sexual selection, also has contributed to this evolution. In fact, a strong argument can be made that sexual selection has been as important as natural selection in weaving together the divergent fitness interests of hominin males and females (Miller, 2000). To understand the important role of sexual selection in shaping the hominin social world and in fashioning *H. sapiens* men and women, we first must define what sexual selection is and how it works.

Natural selection makes creatures more adapted to their environments. Sexual selection makes creatures more proficient in securing potential mates. In sexually reproducing species, males and females must get together to reproduce. As we have already seen, this getting together typically involves males competing and females choosing. Certain traits, such as longer teeth, stronger antlers, bigger vocal cords, or sharper claws, give some males competitive advantages over others. In addition, some traits make members of one sex (usually males) more attractive to the other. Brightly colored feathers, for example, often signal good health and good genes to potential mates. None of these traits necessarily makes an animal more adapted to its environment. Bigger antlers and longer teeth require more metabolic resources to grow and can subtract from the immune response. Bright colors can

Neanderthal Fathers...Absent Fathers?

BOX 10.1 In stark contrast to Deacon's image of *H. erectus* is the portrait of the Neanderthal social world painted by Lew Binford and Olga Soffer. Based on his studies of Neanderthal dwellings in Combe Grenal (in Southern France), Binford (1992) argued for the presence of two distinct and separate home base sites. The more centrally located sites were characterized by the presence of small tools for smashing and bone marrow extraction, along with skull and teeth fragments. Here, he contended, the females and children lived, primarily existing on locally gathered, low-quality edibles, along with some protein extracted from bone fragments and skulls. At the periphery was a second class of sites, where larger butchery tools and evidence of extensive fire use were present. Here the Neanderthal males lived, primarily existing on hunted meat. Neanderthal males and females, according to Binford, lived separate lives, coming together only for reproductive purposes and with little or no male protection or provisioning of the young ("visiting fireman" was Binford's term; see also Shreeve, 1995). In sympathy with this rather pessimistic view is Olga Soffer (1994), who claimed that although mother–child bonds among Neanderthals were strong, wider family bonds were nonexistent. She pointed to the fact that both Neanderthal males and females were extraordinarily strong and robustly built, in contrast to early *Homo sapiens*, among whom females were more slender and lighter than their male counterparts (Frayer, 1986). Male *H. sapiens* were taking some of the foraging and provisioning burdens from females and thus were selected for relatively greater size and strength. No evidence is available to suggest that this same process occurred in Neanderthals, Soffer contended. Her studies show that nutritional stress was more acute among Neanderthal juveniles than among *H. sapiens*, and a higher proportion of Neanderthals died before adulthood than their human counterparts. All of this, she argued, supports the notion that Neanderthal fathers were absent fathers, species wide.

These claims have not gone unchallenged and, indeed, have stirred quite a controversy among archaeologists and anthropologists. Mellars (1996) argued that the evidence cited in support of the Binford/Soffer model is open to many other interpretations and that a substantial amount of contradictory evidence exists as well. Moreover, whatever supposed deficiencies Neanderthal social life might have entailed, they survived for more than 200,000 years under often very adverse conditions—a claim *H. sapiens* cannot echo. Even so, Mellars and others (e.g., Gamble, 1986) agreed that the social universe changed dramatically about 40,000 years ago as the Neanderthals were dying out and *H. sapiens* were expanding. At this time, semipermanent "villages" were being established, kin networks were swelling, and dwelling sites were growing more expansive. The Neanderthal social world may not have been as stilted and segregated as Binford and Soffer believe, but it does appear to have been dramatically less inclusive and sophisticated than the emerging human society of the Upper Paleolithic.

make one more obvious to a predator. Thus, sexually selected traits are simply those traits that provide advantages in reproduction, not necessarily in survival. In the game of evolution, winners do not have to live long lives. They simply have to live long enough to pass on a lot of genes.

Darwin first recognized the significance of sexual selection when he contemplated the origin of the many male peculiarities found in the natural world, such as peacocks' tails and insect gift giving (Darwin, 1859, 1871). He identified two forms of sexual selection: **intrasexual** and **intersexual**. Intrasexual refers to competition within a sex (usually among males) for access to the other sex. It is from intrasexual selection that male weaponry such as antlers, large canine teeth, loud intimidating roars, and long sharp claws most likely emerged. Intersexual selection refers to ways in which the choice preferences of one sex (usually females) affect the other sex (usually males). It was from female choice that such adornments as prominent, brightly colored feathers (peacock tails) and courtship behaviors (insect gift giving) most likely emerged.

The importance of intrasexual selection (male-on-male competition) was readily accepted by Darwin's contemporaries and later generations of researchers, but the importance of intersexual selection (female choice) was largely ignored (Cronin, 1991). Recently, however, the power of female choice in driving evolution has been accepted more widely, and two mechanisms explaining how that choice works have been proposed: the **handicap principle** and **runaway selection**. The handicap principle claims that some male physical and behavioral traits act as indicators of quality genes (Zahavi, 1975). The peacock's tail, for example, requires great metabolic resources to grow and hampers escape from predators. Only an exceptional bird could afford the burden of such an adornment. Male guppies will sometimes swim right up "in the face" of larger predatory fish in what seems to be a stupid suicidal display of bravado. Female guppies, however, realize that only a fish with a superb set of genes could venture such a hazard and live to tell the tale. Likewise, only a genetically well-endowed male gray tree frog could risk exhausting himself producing the loud, long, high-pitched mating call that leaves the females weak-kneed. The call, which, given the frog's small size, requires more energy per minute than running a marathon, turns out to be truthful advertising: the offspring of the longest callers have been shown to grow more quickly and reach a larger size than those of shorter callers (Welch, Semlitsch, & Gerhardt, 1998). The essence of the handicap principle is that if females are looking for quality, then an advantage can be gained by males who evolve the most obvious and ostentatious way of displaying the potency of what they're packing.

Runaway selection refers to the fact that certain traits may become predominant in males simply because females prefer them (Fisher, 1930). These traits need not have important genetic ramifications, and the preference for these traits need not be overwhelmingly strong to get the process going. Imagine for a moment a population of female rats in which a certain percentage of them by chance happen to prefer mating with male rats with tan-colored fur. Over time, this preference gets amplified, as those with the preference mate with tan-colored males, produce more tan-colored sons and more tan-preferring daughters. Those without the preference mate randomly with males (at least with regard to fur color), so a few tan-colored males and tan-preferring daughters pop up among their offspring as well. Eventually, as the population of tan-preferring females grows, selection pressure develops for all females to prefer tan-colored males, because a tan-colored son would be likely to have more offspring than a non-tan-colored son (the "sexy son" strategy).

Once initiated, this process, in theory, could get out of hand (hence, the term "runaway"). If females have a preference for bushy hair, would it not be the case that the bushiness of hair would continue to increase over many generations, ultimately leaving males blinded and stumbling beneath their overgrown locks? Such "supernormal" traits have been produced in experimental settings (e.g., Andersson, 1982). In reality, threats of predation, survival disadvantages, and metabolic constraints serve to regulate runaway selection. Within these limits, however, females appear to be free to follow their whims when it comes to what they like in their mates. In one experiment, male finches' legs were banded with black, red, green, or blue plastic rings. The females showed a distinct preference for the males with either black or red bands and rejected the blue- and green-banded males (Burley, 1988). This suggests that in some instances female mate preferences can be affected simply by aesthetics, leading some to speculate that this may have provided the evolutionary origins of a human sense of artistic beauty.

Although the handicap principle and runaway selection are not the same thing, they are not entirely independent of one another. Female preferences often have genetic implications. Let's go back to guppies for a second. In streams where guppies have many predators, they tend to be nondescript in color. However, in other streams where parasites and not predators are the problem, females show a distinct preference for brightly colored males (Houde, 1997). The greater the parasite load, the brighter the guppies. Females may find fancy hues aesthetically pleasing and may continually "push" that trait to extremes, but a male's bright colors also signify robust health and parasite resistance. We must keep in mind that these two mechanisms often work in concert to produce some of the most unique and charming traits observed in the natural world.

Sexual Selection and Hominin Evolution

If sexual selection is capable of producing gaudy displays in other animals, such as overgrown tails and blowhorn mating calls, then could it possibly have left similar marks on humans? The answer is yes, it may have left its imprint in numerous ways. In humans, however, the most significant ornament of sexual selection may be the one most sequestered from public admiration. Encased within the skull, the human brain makes no direct display of its presence but is the source of all other displays. Its inflated proportions in the hominin body may have had more to do with the dating game than the surviving game. Is it possible that our most prized possession, our big brain, is the product of the same process that gave the world pompous bird-tails and blaring frog croaks?

As can be seen in Figure 10.3, in a little more than 2 million years, the hominin brain has expanded three-fold. This rapid growth has been interpreted by some as the result of a runaway selection process (see Byrne & Whiten, 1988; Miller, 1998. Note: not all researchers are convinced that the expansion of the hominin brain is all that unusual; see, for example, Williams, 1992). For millions of years *Australopithecus* survived in the forests and grasslands of Africa with a brain no larger than that of an ape. Then, suddenly, for reasons as yet unclear, an explosion of brain growth commenced in the *Homo* lineage but not in the contemporaneous *Australopithecus robustus*, a closely related species sharing the same habitat. This dramatic brain expansion continued over the next 2 million years, then stopped about 100,000 years ago.

For some researchers, the most cogent explanation for such an event is sexual selection. Byrne and Whiten (1988) and Whiten (1991) emphasized social intelligence and male-on-male competition for mates as the prime movers in the evolution of the brain. As hominin communities became larger, reproductive success became less dependent on brawn and more on the ability to cooperate, cajole, deceive, and socially manipulate others to advance in the social hierarchy. This produced an evolutionary "arms race" in social intelligence. Miller (1998) did not dispute this possibility but placed more emphasis on female choice in selecting those mates who demonstrated ever higher levels of social intellect. High levels of social and communicative skills indicated not only the male's good genes but also emo-

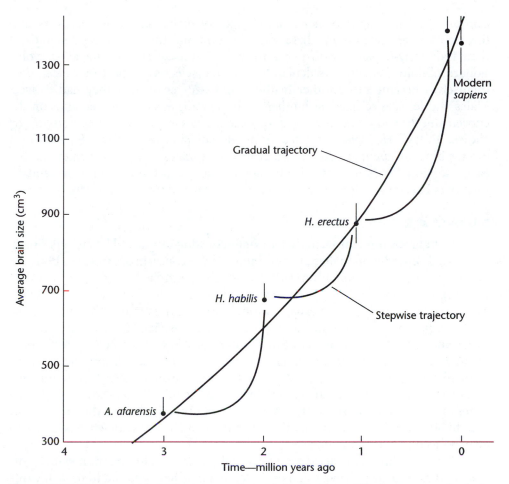

Figure 10.3 The increase in brain size over the past 4 million years. The increase accelerated dramatically over the past 2 million years. (Adapted from Lewin, 1998, p. 449.

tional sensitivity, reliability, ingenuity, industriousness, and the ability to acquire resources, all traits of great benefit to a female and her offspring.

The vast multitudes of bacteria, microbes, insects, and other creepy-crawly "bugs" bear witness to the fact that a big brain (or any brain at all) is hardly a necessity for survival. Should it be any real surprise if it turns out that our big brains owe their existence more to our interactions with each other than to our interaction with the environment? The prominent role of sexual selection in hominin evolution means that not only were our ancestors being adapted to the environment, but they were also being adapted to each other. When we wonder why it is that men are the way they are and women are the way they are, one inescapable conclusion emerges: because women selected men to be that way, and men did likewise to women.

Contemplate for a moment the array of adversarial forces deployed over the countless millennia on our unsuspecting ancestors. They struggled to adapt and survive against immediate and long-term climatic variations. Their bodies and immune systems fought for health and longevity against predators, parasites, and diseases. Under the constant threat of starvation and the increasing demands of their frail, long-dependent offspring, their communities struggled against evolutionary oblivion. Finally, the demands of sexual selection meant that *H. sapiens* themselves became just another in the long list of challenges they had to face. Males and females selected each other, with the choosers placing demands on the chosen and the chosen competing among themselves to constrain the liberty of the choice. Today's *H. sapiens* resulted from the collision of all these forces. Put a brainy, bipedal, ape in an environment in which males compete, females choose, each individual tries to maximize fitness and adapt to the environment, and all members have to get along in the process, and you end up with something like us.

SUMMARY

At first glance, it might seem that asexual reproduction would be far superior to sexual reproduction where fitness interests are concerned. However, both the build-up of dangerous mutations (Müller's ratchet) and the harmful effects of fast-evolving parasites (the Red Queen) provide powerful selection pressure for sexual over asexual reproduction. Sexual reproduction requires that males and female "get together," for purposes of exchanging genetic material. However, in doing so, males and females have divergent fitness interests. These divergent interests come about as a result of differential parental investments: females almost always invest more resources in the raising of offspring. For this reason, females tend to look for quality in their mates. Indicators of quality could include displays advertising good genes and the ability to secure territory and resources. Males, on the other hand, tend to be more interested in quantity, given the relative ease with which sperm can be produced and disseminated.

Among primates, a varied array of social systems, including monogamy, unimale and multimale polygyny, and exploded harems, have evolved to serve the different fitness interests of males and females. Using phylogenetic and behavioral ecological approaches, researchers have attempted to map out the evolutionary course of hominin social systems, moving from unimale polygyny, to multimale polygyny, to more monogamous systems that feature high levels of male investment in offspring. Over the course of this evolution, sexual selection most likely played an important role in the evolution of some uniquely human characteristics, including our large brains.

KEY TERMS

behavioral ecological
  approach
female choice
handicap principle
harem
intra- and intersexual
  selection

male competition
monogamy
Müller's ratchet
multimale polygyny
parental investment
phylogenetic approach

Red Queen
reproductive strategies
runaway selection
sexual selection
unimale polygyny

REVIEW QUESTIONS

1. Explain how differential parental investment leads to divergent reproductive strategies in males and females.

2. What is meant by the statement that maleness and femaleness have nothing to do with being male and female but with one's evolutionary history of parental investment?

3. Describe different primate social systems. What factors brought these systems about? Why can't they be viewed as a "natural state" for human male–female relationships?

4. Define runaway selection and the handicap principle. Give an example of each.

5. What are the different approaches that can be used to try to reconstruct the evolution of social systems in hominins? What do these approaches say about the evolution of male–female relationships in humans?

SUGGESTED READINGS

Cronin, H. (1991). *The ant and the peacock: Altruism and sexual selection from Darwin to today.* Cambridge: Cambridge University Press.

Deacon, T. (1997). *The symbolic species.* New York: W.W. Norton.

Miller, G. (2000). *The mating mind: How sexual selection shaped the evolution of human nature.* New York: Anchor Books.

Ridley, M. (1993). *The Red Queen: Sex and the evolution of human nature.* New York: Viking.

WEB SITES

www.pbs.org/wgbh/evolution/sex/advantage/index.html good discussion and resources relating to the evolution of sex.

www.grungyape.com/new/information.html a good beginning source for learning about primate behavior and social systems.

www.zoology.ubc.ca/~otto/PopGen500/Discussion2/Overheads.html an excellent page describing the various hypotheses regarding the evolution of sex.

11

Cooperation Between the Sexes II: The Male Perspective

Flies, Mice, and the War Between the Sexes

IT IS HARDLY A NEWS FLASH from the frontiers of science to say that men often fail to understand women and vice versa. The evolutionary perspective discussed in the previous chapter shed light on the origin of some of these misunderstandings. *Homo sapiens* males and females have evolved with different, frequently conflicting fitness interests. If any of their fitness needs are to be satisfied, however, they must reach some measure of cooperation ("can't live with 'em..."). The popular media seldom miss an opportunity to label this situation as the "war between the sexes," a pessimistic and dangerously unconstructive characterization. If it were a war and each side were trying to win, a rude bit of enlightenment would await the victor. Consider the following.

Male competition can take many forms. Instead of physical combat with all its bleeding and bruising, males of some species let their sperm do the fighting for them. That's the muriqui way! Primatologist Alison Jolly (1999) provided a rather colorful description of these large and woolly New World monkeys:

> New World muriqui are amazing—they have virtually no aggression between adults and no possessiveness about sexual partners. Males essentially queue up to mate with an estrous female;....There is competition, of course—at the level of the sperm. Katie Milton wrote that when she first saw her study group of muriqui, she thought they had some fearful elephantiasis; their huge scrota just could not be normal. Well, they are normal—for males who are willing to stand in line to flood the female with semen, while laying a reassuring blond arm across a comrade's furry shoulders. (p. 174)

This strategy may have advantages for males in that it reduces levels of intrasex violence, but a chemical battle going on inside a female's body is not always the healthiest thing. Normally, however, females evolve to meet this challenge. Those who are least detrimentally impacted by the sperm wars leave the most offspring, with the daughters inheriting their mother's tolerance capacity. What if the females do not evolve? Like muriqui monkeys, fruit flies also use sperm competition as a means of determining paternity. The sperm of male fruit flies contains toxins deadly to other sperm. William Rice (1996) bred fruit flies in such a manner as to allow the males to evolve over generations but not the females. Once a female had mated, she and her daughters were removed from the experimental sample and replaced by flies from another population. The males, however, were always descendants of the original experimental group. This meant that the sperm wars could go on unabated but with the females held in evolutionary stagnation. Eventually, the sperm-killing toxin became lethal not only to other sperm but to the females as well. This one-sided evolution proved fatal for all.

American deermice come in both monogamous and polygamous varieties. Because a polygamous female deermouse mates with many males, her litter typically contains half siblings who share a common mother but have different fathers. In this competitive environment, it pays for the male deermouse to have aggressive genes that are ready to take full advantage of any successful impregnation. Genes of the polygamous male deermouse have evolved to "push" the developing fetus to be as large as possible to maximize its potential for survival at the expense of its litter mates (the fetus's siblings, after all, are not necessarily related to it's father). The polygamous female deermouse has evolved to deal with these aggressive male genes and has ways of curbing the resource-grabbing tendencies of each developing fetus. None of this evolutionary history, however, is true for monogamous deermice. As a monogamist, the female's entire litter contains true siblings with a common genetic interest that minimizes in utero resource competition. What happens if monogamous and polygamous deermice interbreed? If a monogamous male mates with a polygamous female, his offspring turn out to be puny and weak, because the paternal genes did not fight for every scrap of resource while in utero. If a polygamous male mates with a monogamous female, his aggressive genes overwhelm her meek system, diverting every bit of resources to his developing offspring and ultimately killing her (Vrana, Guan, Ingram, & Tilghman, 1998).

The lesson of these examples is clear: if the species is to have a future, males and females must evolve together, reacting and adjusting to one another. If the genetic interests of either are allowed to run roughshod over those of the other, disaster could be in the offing. The winner in the battle of the sexes is a loser in the evolutionary long run. Although their genetic interests may be different, males and females must find a cooperative common ground for the good of both. Nobody (or nobody's genes) can get everything he or she wants. Nor should they. But what if they did? What if *H. sapiens* males or females triumphed in the battle of the sexes and achieved everything their little genes desired? What would it be like?

The World According to XY

If men's genes were allowed to run wild, unchecked by female choice or other evolutionary constraints, how would the world look? Some might argue that it would look pretty much the way it does now. (The whole history of civilization is simply an example of men's genes run amok, they might contend.) Well, maybe or maybe not, but to explore this, we must first define exactly what it is that men's genes are after. That, it turns out, is fairly easy: *if given free reign, men (men's genes, that is) would want a harem filled with young, pretty, sexually naive women who would be kind, coy, faithful, healthy, and ready to bear and nurture for him (and only him) many children.* From here we must tear apart this definition and see why men's genes are after these things. Then we must figure out why men cannot have them (at least not all of them).

Why a Harem? Polygyny Not Monogamy

As mammals, human males share many characteristics with the multitude of other mammalian males running about. Most notably, they possess copious amounts of cheaply produced and easily disseminated sperm. From this perspective, it is in a man's fitness interests to gain sexual access to as many women as possible. "But wait," protests the avowed "promise-keeper" husband, "humans are also primates and we have already seen that at least one primate (the gibbon) has adopted (relatively) faithful monogamy as a lifestyle. Who is to say that humans have not evolved as faithful monogamists?" Well...we do—our bodies do, that is. The evidence of our **polygyny** is contained, in part, in our sexual size dimorphism (Alexander, Hoogland, Howard, Noonan, & Sherman, 1979). Recall that gibbons have about equal-size males and females, because monogamy leads to little male mate competition. Human males, on the other hand, are an average of about 12% bigger than females. The fossil record suggests that this dimorphism was even greater in our evolutionary past. Males are not just larger but hairier, stronger, taller, have deeper and more threatening voices, riskier life history patterns, and die at earlier ages than females (Daly & Wilson, 1983, 1988; Ghesquiere, Martin, & Newcombe, 1985; Short & Balaban, 1994). This suite of sexually dimorphic characteristics is consistent with evolution under a polygynous mating system with male-on-male competition for mates (Fleagle, Kay, & Simons, 1980; Martin, Willner, & Dettling, 1994).

Additional evidence for male polygyny can be found in the prevalence of this practice across cultures and time. According to Murdock's *Ethnographic Atlas*, 85% (980 of 1,154) of past or present societies, including most hunter–gatherer societies, allow (or allowed) men to have multiple wives. Daly and Wilson (1983) reported a similar breakdown in their survey of 849 different societies, with 83% classified as polygynous, 16% as monogamous, and only .5% as polyandrous. Because it is a fair assumption that in most of these societies men have a disproportional influence on public policies, then it is not unreasonable to conclude that in most places throughout history men have simply followed their natural tendencies and taken multiple wives, usually with the backing of some religious or cultural tradition.

Even in modern Western societies in which monogamy is the norm, men continue to find ways to follow their ambivalent genes. In most marriages, it is the husband's—not the wife's—dissatisfaction that more reliably predicts the breakup of the marriage (Buehlman, Gottman, & Katz, 1992). In other words, men, not women, are more often the driving force breaking up a marriage. And why not? It is far more likely that men will improve their financial standing and remarry after divorce, whereas women are more likely to remain single and to be more impoverished (Charmie & Nsuly, 1981; Wright, 1994). The net result is **serial monogamy**, whereby a man can remain married to a women long enough to dominate her reproductive years and then move on to another. In most industrialized countries today, men of wealth and high status cannot hold harems replete with dozens of young and pretty women. Instead, they must distribute their harems over longer periods of time. The end result, however, is not all that different. Serial monogamy translates into a temporally extended version of polygyny, a single male dominating the reproductive destinies of several women. Because widespread serial monogamy would tend to increase the number of males left without mates, evolutionists would predict that its presence would lead to increases in male violence and rape. A recent study, in fact, demonstrated a relationship (correlational not necessarily causational) between the practice of serial monogamy and increases in incidences of rape in the United States (Starks & Blackie, 2000).

Polygyny has been fairly widespread, but very, very few men obtain the vast hedonistic harem their genes desire. This is because other evolutionary pressures have moderated polygyny. It is in these pressures that we find the reason that men's genes cannot have all of what they want. ("Want" is used metaphorically; genes, of course, do not really want anything!) Although men are bigger than women, the difference is rather modest, not at all approaching orangutan or gorilla proportions. This indicates that men have been selected for more than just brawn and size. Female choice has selected men for other traits, including intelligence, social competence, kindness, and devotion (Buss, 1989; Chance, 1962; Krebs, 1998; Miller, 1998). In an intelligent primate species in which the male size advantage is only slight, a lone male could find a well-coordinated group of females as threatening as another male. Recall that it is not uncommon for a male bonobo to be dominated by a coalition of females (de Waal, 1997). The first reason, then, why most men fail to establish a harem of any notable size is that they simply lack the gorilla-like capacity to physically intimidate and monopolize a respectable collection of females. Most reconstructions of our ancestral past strongly suggest that controlling a group of females would have required not a lone male but a relatively cooperative group of males. Herein lies the second problem with establishing large harems: other males. The genes of meekly compliant males willing to help a comrade command a female-rich territory and ask for nothing in return were long ago culled from the population. Male groups undoubtedly would have required sharing of the females, and, although the sharing may not always have been entirely equal, it must have been equitable enough to avoid destructive in-fighting. The notable degree of egalitarianism in hunter–gatherer societies would tend to support this view (Erdal & Whiten, 1996). It is interesting to note that when polygyny has reached exaggerated proportions for the (lucky?) few, it often existed in concert with political authoritarianism (Betzig, 1982, 1986, 1992; MacDonald, 1990). For example, a Zulu king might have had more than 100 women in his possession. The harem of King Moulay Ismail the Bloodthirsty of Morocco had around 500 women, all younger than 30. Similar numbers have been reported for some Chinese emperors. Historically, for one man to amass a harem of which his genes would be proud, it was first necessary to attain the power to subdue the objections of other men (Bingham, 1999).

Why Young and Pretty? The Importance of Reproductive Value

Saying that men desire women who are young and pretty does little more than state the obvious. Obviousness, however, is not an explanation as to why it should be so. Why should men exhibit this specific preference? After all, it is an inclination at variance with other primate males. Most male primates bypass young, untested females for older, experienced ones who have a proven track record of successful mothering (Smuts, 1987). This makes great evolutionary sense. Why risk your genes with an unproven youngster when competent veterans are available? This simple, powerful logic, so readily accepted by other primates, has been thoroughly lost on human males. Contrary to what some women may think, men are *not* apes—at least when it comes to long-term mate preferences.

Evolutionary psychologist David Buss undertook one of the most extensive studies of human mate preferences (Buss, 1989; Buss & Schmitt, 1993). With the help of more than 50 collaborators and spanning 37 different cultures, six continents, and five islands, Buss's work qualifies as one of the most ambitious and inclusive cross-cultural studies to date. All major religions, races, ethnic groups, and education levels were represented. The sample stretched from the mighty metropolises of Sao Paulo and Shanghai to the rural villages of the Gujarati Indians and the South African Zulus. The total sample had more than 10,000 subjects, ranging in ages from 14–70. His findings uncovered some important universals in human mate preferences. For example, both males and females placed a high priority on good health, kindness, and intelligence in long-term mates, but men placed a much greater emphasis on youth, beauty, and sexual conservatism (Figs. 11.1 and 11.2). Put another way, men, much more than women, desire a mate who is young, pretty, and with no history of sexual promiscuity. Buss's work confirmed and broadened similar findings in primarily U.S. samples (Feingold, 1990, 1992;

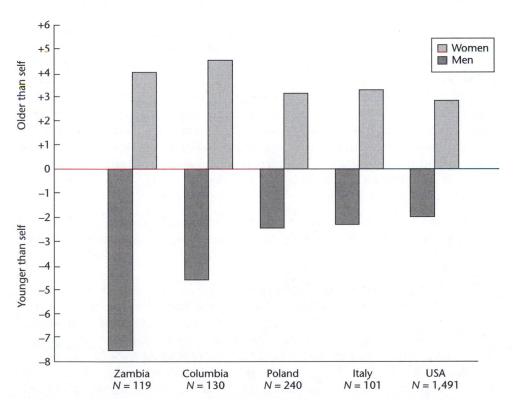

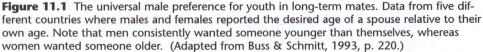

Figure 11.1 The universal male preference for youth in long-term mates. Data from five different countries where males and females reported the desired age of a spouse relative to their own age. Note that men consistently wanted someone younger than themselves, whereas women wanted someone older. (Adapted from Buss & Schmitt, 1993, p. 220.)

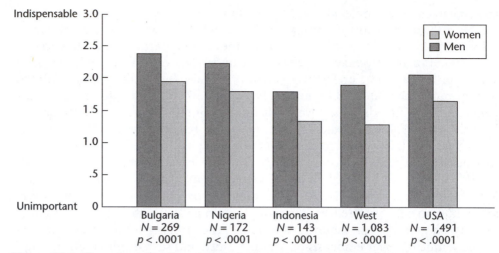

Figure 11.2 The universal male preference for beauty. Males and females in six different countries rated the importance of physical attractiveness in long-term mates. Note that in every case males rated physical attractiveness significantly higher than did females. (Adapted from Buss, 1998, p. 423.)

Powers, 1971). As boorish and crude as some men might occasionally be, it is nevertheless quite clear that their mate preferences are not those of the average ape.

Somewhere along the hominin evolutionary road, male mate preference diverged in significant ways from that of our closely related cousins. Why? Over the course of hominin evolution, males quit behaving like chimpanzees toward females and their offspring and slowly began to behave more like human dads. That is, they began to invest heavily in the care, provisioning, and upbringing of their young. Humans are almost unique among mammals in that we are high in **male parental investment** (MPI). Like gibbons and many bird species, males who hung around to help raise the kids reaped an increasing fitness payoff over the course of hominin evolution. Many of the reasons for this have already been touched on in other contexts:

1. Hominin offspring became increasingly demanding and dependent. It is of little benefit to one's genes to practice a "love 'em and leave 'em" strategy if one's offspring die of starvation or end up as tiger bait for lack of adequate care.

2. The rising proportion of meat in the hominin diet meant that males were engaging in more hunting and scavenging, leading to the acquisition of food resources that were often too large to be consumed individually. Sharing the carcass with one's immediate family made far more genetic sense than letting the rest rot after having consumed one's fill.

3. Sexual selection also affected males, as females actively chose better providers and helpers for mates, thus increasing the genes associated with those behaviors in subsequent generations. These factors enticed hominin males into a lifestyle of relatively heavy parental investment. It is important to note that when we say "relatively high parental investment" we are

comparing males with the males of other species, not with human females. Human males care for their children quite a bit more than other mammalian or primate males, but even that level of investment is typically dwarfed by the care given by human females.

So—young and pretty females are preferred because human males are high parental investors. This simply pushes the question back a level. Why do heavily parental-investing males prefer young and pretty females? The answer is simple: in our ancestral past those males who maximized their investment were more likely to leave copies of their genes. In maximizing their investment, two factors were critical: (1) **reproductive value**, and (2) **paternity certainty**. We will defer a discussion of paternity certainty, because, in fact, the male emphasis on "young and pretty" is more directly geared toward reproductive value. Reproductive value refers to the criterion used in selecting females who have the greatest capacity to produce many viable offspring. A male who selects a female capable of producing six healthy children has provided more richly for his genes than one whose mate can produce only three. In our evolutionary past, males with a keen eye for selecting females who could produce an abundance of viable offspring had an evolutionary advantage over their less discriminating buddies.

The relationship between youth and reproductive value is fairly straightforward. Younger females have the majority of their reproductive lives before them. The average 18-year-old woman has more years of reproduction to offer than a woman who is 26. Not only do males prefer youthful brides, but they act on this preference as well. Across 27 different countries, grooms have been found to be, on average, older than brides by anywhere from a little more than 2 years to almost 5 years (Buss, 1989). As men age, their desire for youth increases. Thirty-year-old men want wives who are, on average, about 5 years younger than they, whereas 50-year-old men want wives who are 10–20 years younger (Kendrick & Keefe, 1992). As men acquire more status and power, their desire for youth becomes more pronounced. When advertising for mates, relatively wealthy German men expressed interest in women who were up to 15 years their junior, whereas less wealthy men only asked for women who were 5 years younger, at the most (Grammer, 1992). Historical studies have also confirmed that, in centuries past, men of wealth and status usually had younger brides than their less prosperous counterparts (Roskaft, Wara, & Viken, 1992; Voland & Engel, 1990).

The male preference for youth has one important exception. Teenage males (ages 12–18) have been shown to prefer females who are a few years their senior (Kendrick, Keefe, Gabrielidis, & Cornelius, 1996). This finding is important, because it reinforces the notion that it is reproductive value and not relative age per se that motivates male mate preferences. A 15-year-old male would have no evolutionary reason for preferring a 12-year-old female over an 18-year-old, because, despite her youth, the 12-year-old's reproductive value is more ambiguous. Moreover, the preference for a slightly older female contradicts an alternative explanation that men desire youth because younger mates are more easily dominated.

Beauty, in the language of male genetics, corresponds to health, and a healthy woman has more reproductive value than an unhealthy one. Males universally view clear, smooth skin and featural symmetry as important factors in judging a woman's beauty. These indicators of comeliness also serve as outward signs of freedom from parasitic infection, a constant concern in our ancestral environment (Cunningham, Roberts, Barbee, Druen, & Wu, 1995; Gangestad & Buss, 1993; Gangestad, Thornhill, & Yeo, 1994). A beautiful female face is usually characterized by a generally symmetrical look combined with specific features, such as a small nose and jaw, delicate chin, large eyes, and full lips. Collectively these factors produce a healthy, youthful face (symmetry, large eyes), with overt signs of fertility expressed in the size of the lips, chin, and jaw, all of which are affected by estrogen levels at puberty (Johnston, 1999; Johnston & Franklin, 1993; Moller & Pomiankowski, 1993; Symons, 1979; Thornhill & Gangestad, 1993).

Moving from the face to the body, males around the globe judge a waist-to-hip ratio of about .7 as optimally attractive, and, in keeping with evolutionary expectations, this ratio also has been found to be indicative of hormonal levels conducive to fertility (Singh, 1993). The conspicuousness of female breasts also (predictably) has attracted much attention (Singh & Young, 1995). Even the most casual comparison between ourselves and our primate cousins reveals the obvious evolutionary distance traveled "from hairy, flat-chested ape to modern buxom women" (Margulis & Sagan, 1991, p. 96). Zoologist Desmond Morris in his classic *The Naked Ape* (1967) was one of the first to propose that female breasts serve an important pair-bonding function. Humans are very unusual, in that the sex act is typically performed face to face. According to Morris, the physical and emotional enhancement of the act brought about by the female's swollen, frontally placed breasts helped to cement an extended pair bond between the couple. In his view, breasts acted as **pair bond enhancers**. Others have debated the merits of this idea (e.g., Lovejoy, 1981; Morgan, 1985), but there is little question that enlarged, symmetrical breasts were a sexually selected characteristic. As fat storage devices, they helped to indicate the presence of resource reserves ready to support the rigors of pregnancy (Low, Alexander, & Noonan, 1987; Miller, 1998; Szalay & Costello, 1991). Red swellings on a female chimpanzee's backside attract males and signal that it is time for serious competition for sexual access. The curvaceous shape of a young human female may serve a similar signaling function, in that full symmetrical breasts and an optimal waist-to-hip ratio indicate robust health and fertility, whereas the small waist indicates youth and a nonpregnant status (Jolly, 1999). Anyone who suggests that men do not respond to such signals with attraction and competition needs to peep out of the cave a bit more often.

Why Coy, Kind, and Sexually Naive?
The Importance of Paternity Certainty

Imagine a male hominin of the distant past (call him Fred) contemplating the marital plunge. Shall he forsake all others (more or less) for Wilma or Betty? Betty is sexually assertive, makes it abundantly clear that she wants him in the worst way, and, lo and behold, they have enjoyed numerous rousing sessions of Stone Age sex long before any nuptials have been pronounced. Wilma is shy and modest and shows cautious interest in Fred but little interest in sex. Over the past few weeks, their only physical contact has been a few playful kisses. Betty has offered and undoubtedly will continue to offer ample reproductive opportunities.

But if she so readily offers those opportunities to Fred, who is to say that she wouldn't offer them to others? Or that she hasn't already done so? Might she continue to do so after they are married? What about those long hunting trips when he's away with the boys getting meat for the family? And what about Wilma? As shy as she is, she certainly must be a virgin. No doubt she will avoid other men while *her* hubby's away. Fred's dilemma was faced recurrently by male hominins over the course of our evolutionary history. Did Fred or the countless male hominins before and after him sit down and consciously think through all the contingencies and ramifications of this conundrum? Probably not. Once the initial sexual thrill had past, Fred, like most men today, probably just had an indifferent, ambiguous gut feeling that Betty was not Miss Right. His genes, honed by eons of evolution, had done the thinking for him. Those who risked their genetic legacies on the Bettys of our past were less likely to pass on their genes and the associated desire for sexually bold females as long-term mates.

It turns out that Fred's gut feeling about Betty was well founded. The single best predictor of postmartial infidelity is premarital sexual permissiveness (Thompson, 1983; Weiss & Slosnerick, 1981). Old habits are hard to break, apparently, and long before sex researchers documented this fact, genes were encoding it and ingraining it on the male psyche. Around the world, it is men, more than women, who place a high value on virginity. Buss's work revealed that, in more than 60% of the 37 cultures studied, males were significantly more interested in virgins as long-term mates than were females (Buss, 1989; Buss & Schmitt, 1993; Fig. 11.3). Even in cultures in which premarital sex is not discouraged, female promiscuity is a turn-off for males looking for wives. Although Swedish men take a generally laissez faire attitude toward sex, they continue to find highly promiscu-

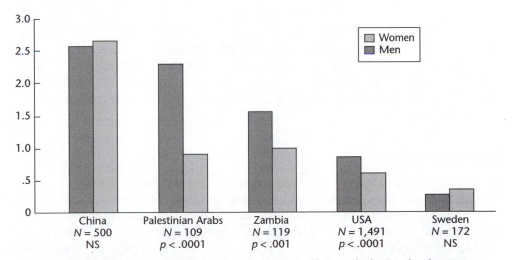

Figure 11.3 The desire for chastity in a long-term mate. The graph depicts the degree to which males and females in different countries believed chastity (no sex before marriage) was an important attribute in a long-term mate. Note that the desire for a chaste mate varied greatly across cultures, being very important to Chinese men and women and Palestinian men but relatively unimportant to Swedes. Note also that it is men more often then women who place a high value on chastity. (Adapted from Buss & Schmitt, 1993.)

ous women to be poor candidates as wives (Buss, 1994). Trobriand Islanders, who encourage their adolescents to have active sex lives, nevertheless disapprove of young females who are too overt in their sex-seeking behavior (Malinowski, 1929). The same genetic call that prodded Fred away from the free-loving Betty and toward the more inhibited Wilma is present universally in men today.

Why so? It goes back to the fact that hominin males evolved into high parental investors whose genes sought to maximize this investment by increasing **paternity certainty**. As the name indicates, paternity certainty refers to ensuring that the offspring one invests in do, in fact, carry one's genes. A man with a sexually impulsive wife is at greater risk for becoming an "adoptive" father. As laudable as it might be, adopting and raising an unrelated child does a man's genes absolutely no good. Thus, our male ancestors were those who most vigilantly ensured that their investments went to their own offspring. Selecting coy, sexually naive women as brides helped to ensure paternity certainty. Moreover, the preference for youth also played indirectly into this, because younger females were likely to be sexually inexperienced and thus less likely to cheat or to arrive at the nuptials already pregnant.

With this information we can paint an evolutionary picture of how human males ended up as they are now. As evolutionary pressures steadily elbowed men out of their chimp-like mating patterns into a higher parental investment pattern, males responded by (more accurately: were adapted by) demanding a monopoly over the reproductive output of a single mate. Some have encapsulated this evolutionary sexual give-and-take as the **meat-for-sex deal**. Males agreed to be reliable providers for wife and family (meat) in return for young females who agreed to have the full measure of their reproductive lives dominated by a single man (sex). To many, this may sound reasonable enough, and perhaps the world would be better place if everyone could just live with this evolutionary deal and let it be. The world, however, is an imperfect place. We already saw that most men could not obtain the harems for which their genes yearn. The world's imperfections also leave many men's genes unsatisfied with the specific meat-for-sex deal they wind up with. There are, after all, only so many beautiful, coy, kind, intelligent, robust, 18-year-olds to go around. Even if one happens to obtain such a prize, she is bound to age, and, with each passing year, a man's desire for her is likely to decline as her youth dissipates. How have male genes evolved to cope with the disappointing realities of the world?

The Mixed Strategy

Trivers (1972) noted that for males who are high in parental investment the optimal reproductive course would not be a complete abandonment of a low-investment strategy but a mix of the two. Consider two hominin males both willing and ready to take the meat-for-sex deal and contribute heavily to the care and raising of their offspring. One remains utterly faithful and, with his wife, produces a number of viable offspring. The other is similarly faithful (pretty much) to his wife but also keeps his options open for any short-term no-strings-attached copulations that might just happen to pass his way. If he is successful at identifying short-term mating opportunities in which no investment demand will be required and a few of the offspring from those encounters manage to survive despite his abandonment, then he will have achieved a fitness advantage over his unwaveringly monogamous compatriot. Yes, from a moral perspective we might see this as pretty lousy, but remember that natural selection is no moralist. If a selective advantage is to be had by sexual opportunism, then we might well expect our male ancestors to have engaged in such a strategy. Is there any evidence to suggest such a thing?

A number of converging lines of evidence support the notion of mixed reproductive strategies in men. First, mixed reproductive strategies among males are not uncommon in the natural world. Bluegill sunfish, for example, have two types of males: domestics and drifters. Domestics dutifully build nests, await females who deposit eggs in the nests, then fertilize and guard the eggs. Drifters prowl around looking for opportunities to surreptitiously fertilize eggs, then swiftly disappear, leaving the domestics holding the bag (Maynard-Smith, 1982). Likewise, North American tree swallows are generally monogamous, but many males will take brief "sabbaticals" away from their home nests looking for whatever extramarital mating opportunities might be available (Kempenaers, Everding, Bishop, Boag, & Robertson, 2000). Even gibbons will cheat if the opportunity presents itself. Second, recall that other studies have shown a direct link between male reproductive success and the number of sex partners (e.g., Bateman, 1948). Based on historical data, this same pattern appears to be true with human males. Men historically have increased their fitness by increasing their number of partners rather than by increasing the number of offspring from a single partner (Betzig, 1986). Third, empirical studies confirm that men typically have more sex partners than women (except for prostitutes; see Brewer et al., 2000). For example, a recent study showed that although only one tenth of women had two to four sex partners during a year's period of time, the figure was nearly one fifth for men. Furthermore, the number of subjects reporting five or more partners over a year's time was nearly 5 times greater for men than women (Laumann, Michael, Gagnon, & Michaels, 1994; Fig. 11.4).

Fourth, although most men marry, for a substantial proportion this does not end their quest for additional sex partners. Married men tend to have more extramarital affairs than do married women, although the reported incidence has var-

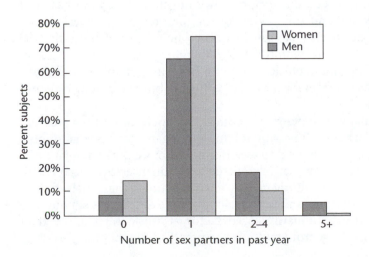

Figure 11.4 Over the course of a single year, most people remain monogamous. However, when people do report having more than one sex partner in 1 year, it is men more often than women who indulge themselves. Of those reporting having two or more sex partners in a year, twice as many were male (more than 23%) than female (less than 12%). (Adapted from *USA Today*, 1994, October 7.)

ied greatly from study to study. For example, in his groundbreaking work on human sexuality, Kinsey found that nearly twice as many men (50%) as women (26%) had affairs (Kinsey, Pomeroy, & Martin, 1948, 1953). Decades later, another large-scale survey confirmed this vast difference, showing that only 18% of married women reported extramarital affairs compared with 41% for men (Hunt, 1974). Other studies confirm the higher incidence of extramarital affairs in men but with a much smaller difference between the sexes. For example, Athanasiou, Shaver, and Tarvis (1970) found that 40% of men and 36% of women reported having affairs. Laumann and his colleagues (Laumann et al., 1994) reported much lower figures, with about 25% of men and 20% of women reporting infidelity. In addition, there is the ubiquitous presence of prostitution, a practice found in every society studied, past and present, and in which the consumers are overwhelmingly male. Kinsey reported that nearly 70% of men reported having some experience with prostitutes, but the number of women reporting such experience was so low as to not warrant mention (Kinsey et al., 1948, 1953). To support all this extracurricular sex, a man had better be able to lie with conviction. Sure enough, there is empirical support for the notion that men are more deceptive than women when it comes to representing how kind, sincere, and trustworthy they are (Tooke & Camire, 1990). So not only do men tend to cheat more, but they are better liars as well.

A final bit of evidence attesting to men's naturally philandering nature is physiologically based and far more controversial. Work by Baker and Bellis (e.g., Baker, 1996; Baker & Bellis, 1995) indicated that the type of sperm a man produces can vary, depending upon whether he is with his regular partner or having a one-night stand. When having sex with his regular partner, a man's ejaculate typically will produce about 200 million sperm, only about 10% of which are actually fertilizing sperm. The rest, blockers and killers, are designed to thwart fertilization by any "foreign" sperm that might somehow find its way into his partner's body. If, per chance, the man should have a sexual rendezvous with a strange woman, his ejaculate will contain up to 600 million sperm, with a much higher than normal percentage being fertilizing sperm. In other words, the male body is by nature designed to optimize any opportunistic copulations that might come down the road, while at the same time guarding priority over his mate. This work has been sharply criticized, however, and solid evidence for the presence of sperm other than fertilizing sperm has been established in only one species of butterfly (the *Lepidoptera*; Birkhead, Moore, & Bedford, 1997; Silberglied, Shepard, & Dickinson, 1984). The presence of killer and blocker sperm in humans certainly would signify a highly functional mechanism for maximizing fitness, but compelling evidence for this remains to be gathered.

These data cumulatively support the notion that men, more than women, have evolved to maximize their fitness by mixing monogamy with sexual opportunism. Men, more than women, tend to seek out numerous extracurricular partners, and men, more than women, actively misrepresent themselves to accomplish that goal. One cannot discount cultural factors when explaining these male–female differences, but the pervasiveness and universality of these differences support the contention of a deeper, evolutionarily based factor at work. Men, more than women, gain a fitness advantage from multiple partners. Culture may serve to exaggerate or mollify the varying evolved reproductive strategies that men and women are inclined to pursue.

The Madonna/Whore Dichotomy

If men have evolved to pursue a mixed reproductive strategy, then we would expect that to affect not just behavior but cognition as well. The male mind should have evolved a categorical mode of thinking that reflects and supports their mixed strategy of reproduction. Before laying out the details of how the male mind facilitates fitness strategies, we first need to define what is meant by "categorical thinking" and its general adaptive function.

Decades of psychological research have demonstrated the pervasive tendency of humans to perceive and understand the world in categorical terms (see Medin & Ross, 1997, pp. 368–395; Smith & Medin, 1981, for discussions). Rarely is a new stimulus perceived as something entirely novel, even though it may be something never before seen by an individual. Upon being told that we will eat our lunch beneath the moringa tree, I know pretty much what to look for, even though I may never have seen a moringa before. That's because I understand the general properties of the category "tree." Because the moringa is a member of that category, I can be pretty sure that I'm looking for something taller than me, with branches and leaves that provide shading from the sun. By relating the "technically" new stimulus to a familiar category, I am much more efficient in responding to and functioning within my environment. Therein lies the great adaptive value of categorical thinking. It saves energy and resources because one need not learn each new stimulus from scratch but simply tag it as a certain category member and react accordingly. Our facility with language has allowed us to take categorical thinking to new heights, but it is not a capacity unique to humans. Most animals have mechanisms for distinguishing kin from non-kin and readily treat members of the two categories differently. Vervet monkeys have distinctive alarm calls signifying whether a predator approaches from the ground (such as a leopard) or from the air (an eagle). After hearing the call, other vervets will either run to trees or hide beneath the bushes. What is most telling, however, is that young vervets will emit the air predator call to falling leaves or when other, nonpredatory birds are present. Moreover, vervets raised in environments where there is no threat from predatory cats continue to use the land predator call when encountering a pet dog (Cheney & Seyfarth, 1990; Hauser, 2000). This suggests that the categories "air predator" and "land predator" are present early on in a vervet monkey's head and that experience adaptively refines the category and tags the call to the specifics of the environment.

What type of evolved categorical thinking would we expect to find in men, given their mixed reproductive strategies? We would expect categories reflective of the two distinct types of reproductive situations that men perceive, committed long-term and uncommitted short-term situations, and the distinct types of partner for each situation. Women have long suspected that men have a rather simple-minded approach to sexual matters. For men, there are two types of women: the matrimonial kind you take home to mother and the other kind you just have fun with. Evolutionary psychologist Donald Symons dubbed this particularly masculine form of thinking as the **Madonna/whore dichotomy** (Symons, 1979). One can raise a righteous wail about the unfairness of it all, but, from the point of view of man's genes, it makes perfect sense.

Recall Fred and the difficult choice he faced between Betty and Wilma. Actually, his choice was not all that difficult because, after a few sweaty sessions with Betty, a palpable indifference toward her was already setting in. From an evolutionary perspective, we would expect this indifference to steadily magnify to such a degree that he would be inclined to start thinking of her in almost contemptuous terms ("whore"). This would serve the adaptive benefit of helping Fred to minimize any emotional ties to Betty that might compel him to expend resources on her or any of her offspring. Just as chimpanzee males do not bother helping to raise the offspring of their promiscuous female partners, we would expect Fred to have mental mechanisms for guarding his resources from offspring of uncertain paternity. Meanwhile, we would also expect that Fred's somewhat delusional image of Wilma would grow only more pristine over time ("Madonna"), along with his desire for her. By placing Wilma on a virtuous pedestal, the idea that her offspring could be anything but his would never enter his mind, thus freeing him to provide slavishly and unquestioningly to his (assumed) genetic descendants. Fred's "Madonna" image of Wilma may be one of the factors that helps sustain a longstanding relationship between them. Of course, no one can say for certain whether Betty will prove to be the insatiable whore Fred expects or whether Wilma will be the gracious Madonna of his dreams. The critical point is that on average and over thousands of generations, Betty-like past histories more often preceded unfaithfulness than Wilma-like ones, and the Madonna/Whore mentality helped men successfully play those odds.

Other than informal anecdotes and popular common knowledge, what evidence is there that men really think this way? The evidence takes two forms: anthropological and psychological. Anthropologically, the consistent theme of highly prized female purity juxtaposed with despised female corruption is not difficult to find. In his book on Samoan culture, Derek Freeman (1983) described the way adolescent girls were often guarded and intimidated by their older brothers to preserve their virginity. Any questionable behavior would be met with a verbal abuse and sometimes physical beating. A virgin bride was highly valued by the influential families of the village. Moreover, a women found not be a virgin on her wedding day was subject to public denunciation as a "whore." The Samoans were hardly unique. The good girl/bad girl dichotomy is a recurrent theme in the oral and folk traditions of such diverse cultures as those of southeast Asia, the Islamic world, Europe, and indigenous Americans. (Wright, 1994). Many cultures, both past and present, have developed laws, customs, and traditions aimed at preserving female virginity and punishing its illicit loss (Dickmann, 1981). From the code of Hammurabi to foot-binding practices in China to female circumcision in parts of Africa, the range of (usually male-instituted) social traditions and practices aimed at restricting female freedoms and thus preserving virtue stand as testament to the importance males place on this commodity. The great value of female purity is typically mirrored by the devastating disgrace occasioned by its loss.

Psychologically, an almost qualitative shift occurs in men's attitudes about women when considering long-term versus short-term mating prospects. Intelligence, kindness, coyness (or other indicators of sexual reserve), youth, and beauty all rate as high priorities when men consider wives. For a short-term fling, however, priorities shift dramatically. When considering a casual sex partner, a man's concerns about such traits as intelligence, honesty, loyalty, kindness, and even emotional stability decline significantly, whereas overt sexiness becomes highly salient (Buss & Schmitt, 1993; Hill, Nocks, & Gardner, 1987). Evidence of promiscuity is highly unsuitable in a potential wife, but it is actually desirable in a short-term sex partner. When considering a potential wife, only the most obtuse male would find "already being married" to be a desirable trait. For a brief liaison, however, this status is positive. This contrasts sharply with females, who consistently view such factors as intelligence, looks, and resources as important in both long- and short-term mates.

The substantial turnaround that men do when considering long- versus short-term relationships makes evolutionary sense, because concerns over paternity become irrelevant with short-term mates. Instead, priority shifts to maximizing sexual access (finding someone willing to do it and do it now) and minimizing commitment or potential resource extraction. In other words, men do not want to have their time, energy, or other resources (in the past, meat; today, money) diminished by the short-term female mate or any of her offspring. Thus, for a quick sexual fling, men's genes compel them to look for just about anything female that shows signs of sexual interest. It's all the better if she has her own pool of resources (hers or her husband's) and therefore will not be requiring any from her transient partner. Moreover, if she happens to be dull intellectually, dishonest, or unkind, it only makes it easier to think of her in derisive terms ("whore") and make it easier to break any emotional bond that might entail providing her with resources. Not necessarily a pretty picture, but natural selection is not always pretty. It is, however, quite effective. In this instance, it has effectively shaped men's minds to think in very distinct ways about long- and short-term matings and the women who might be partners in those relationships.

Social Status and Reproductive Success

> Power is the ultimate aphrodisiac.
> HENRY KISSINGER (ALTHOUGH HE WAS BY NO MEANS THE ORIGINATOR
> OF THE PHRASE), *NEW YORK TIMES*, JANUARY 19, 1971.

We have seen that men's fondest genetic desires are thwarted at every turn by a world filled with other men trying to satisfy their genes, females exercising meticulous selectivity, and the indifferent laws of supply and demand. Under such circumstances, what are male genes to do? The answer is that they have evolved to do the best they can. To the extent that it is genetically advantageous, men have evolved proclivities toward honorable, responsible monogamy. On the other hand, when it is advantageous to be exploitative and philandering, men also have the genetic propensity in that direction. When it comes to attracting mates, men have evolved tendencies both to compete and cooperate with each other. The complexities of the world have been roughly matched by the evolved flexibilities of male fitness strategies. Having a flexible array of strategies could lead to paralyzing confusion ("Do I cheat now or not? Should I compete or cooperate?"). Genes, however, do not direct specific behaviors. Instead, they merely give rise to vague dispositional urges (gut feelings). Wouldn't the most advantageous state of affairs be one in which all the varying male reproductive tactics were reduced to a single, elementary gut urge? Such an urge would energize men to try to put themselves in the most favorable position possible for satisfying their fitness interests: a position of **status** and power. From a position of status and power, a man would be a formidable competitor for other men. He would have his pick of the most desirable long-term mates, not to mention ample opportunities for short-term liaisons. Evolving over the countless millennia in a highly social, group-living context, all the convoluted male fitness schemes have been reduced to this simple genetic call: do what you must to rise in status in your group. That is the best strategy you can take.

Among hunter–gatherers, possessions are few, clothes are simple, and life offers few of the amenities and luxuries that most of us take for granted. In this environment, achieving status takes on its most unadorned form. A man proves himself through hunting skill. He shares the spoils with his fellow tribe members and simultaneously earns their respect and puts them in his debt. He thereby achieves status, and status buys him sex. Studies of both the Ache of South America and the Hazda of Africa confirm that better hunters have more extramarital affairs and more offspring (Hawkes, 1993; Hill & Kaplan, 1988, 1994). Among the pastoral Kipsigis of southwestern Kenya, status is judged by land (Borgerhoff Mulder, 1987, 1988). Men with more land have more wives and offspring. The same was true of 19th-century Swedes, among whom rich landholders consistently married younger, more fertile wives than did their poorer, landless countrymen (Clarke & Low, 1992). From the African Mukogodo to Trinidadian and Micronesian islanders, male wealth and status have consistently translated into greater reproductive success (Cronk, 1991; Flinn, 1986; Turke & Betzig, 1985). We have already encountered the grand and prolific harems of Morocco and China (Betzig, 1986). Even in more modern times, either through the practice of serial monogamy (J.S. Bach, Johnny Carson) or simply via multiple affairs (Pablo Picasso, Jimi Hendrix), males of prominence continue to reap sexual and reproductive rewards. (Note: it is important to remember that genes cannot ensure that one will have numerous offspring, they can only motivate one to engage in the behaviors that have been associated in the past with more offspring. With today's contraceptive technology, a man of high status may not have more children than a man of low status, but evolutionary psychologists would expect him to have *greater sexual access* to females. This is apparently the case [Perusse, 1993, 1994]).

Evolved Paths to Status

Men seek status in different ways, and the paths they take in their pursuit of prominence provide another example of evolved gene–environment interaction at work. Studies assessing the way a boy's home environment affects his social and intellectual development have shown a consistent pattern: boys raised in father-absent households tend to be more aggressive, more exploitative, and denigrating toward females, and they display more exaggerated "masculine" behaviors (see Draper & Harpending, 1982, for review). Of even greater interest is the fact that boys raised in father-absent households show a reversal of the usual male pattern on tests of cognitive ability. Boys usually score higher on spatial and mathematical skills than on verbal skills, but boys raised in father-absent households score higher in verbal abilities and lower on spatial and mathematical skills (Carlsmith, 1964).

Draper and Harpending (1982) interpreted this as an example of the way in which early environmental experiences, especially at ages 1–5 years, serve to direct boys to adopt specific fitness strategies as they grow up. A boy without a father learns that male investment in family and child rearing is nonessential and, therefore, that reproductive success is more dependent upon obtaining a high number of low-investment sexual partners. To succeed with this strategy, he must have a potent arsenal of manipulative and domineering interpersonal skills. The collection of traits common to these boys (aggressiveness, verbal skills, and a bad attitude toward women) is actually very adaptive for one who engages in direct male-on-male competition for a high number of low-investment mates. Boys raised in father-present households, however, learn that male investment is essential to reproductive success and, therefore, tend to adopt a strategy of high investment in a single mate (or a few mates) and their mutual offspring. They dedicate their energy toward the manipulation of *things* rather than *people*. Thus, they have reduced verbal skills, but better spatial and mathematical abilities. Moreover, because they engage in more cooperative behaviors and their competitiveness with other males is more indirect, they tend to be less aggressive and confrontational and have a reduced desire to dominate. Their status would tend to be a byproduct of professional achievement as opposed to direct domination of opponents. Although males seem designed for status seeking and competition, the *way* they compete and the *type* of status they seek appear to be functions of their early experiences with the male social role.

Reproductive Variance and Cultural Dimorphism

Competing for status produces winners and losers. In this way, human males are no different from most mammalian males, in that they play for high stakes in the reproduction game. Males, in general, have much higher **reproductive variance** than females. That is, females are fairly similar to each other in terms of the number of offspring they produce, whereas males tend to either produce many, many offspring or almost none at all. For example, among elephant seals, the most productive females have about 10 offspring. For males, 80% leave no offspring, but the most successful bulls can leave more than 90 (LeBoeuf & Reiter, 1988). Among the Kipsigis, the most successful men had 20 or more children, with one individual having more than 80. Others had only a few or no children at all (Borgerhoff Mulder, 1988). Both historically and evolutionarily, winners in the male status game could amass a huge fitness payoff and losers might very well see their genes trounced into oblivion.

In an evolutionary environment in which winners reap huge fitness rewards and losers suffer possible genetic extinction, one would expect intense competition. The fact, then, that males are generally more aggressive, far more prone to violence, have riskier life history patterns and higher juvenile mortality rates, and die sooner than females fits with an organism that emerged from a winner-take-(nearly)-all evolutionary past (Daly & Wilson, 1983, 1988; Ghesquiere, Martin, & Newcombe, 1985; Short & Balaban, 1994; see also Box 11.1 for more about men and warfare). In addition, Geoffrey Miller (1995, 1998) called attention to what he

Why Men Fight

BOX 11.1

Two facts become obvious when studying the history of human warfare: (1) War has always been with us, and (2) it is and always has been largely a male affair. Is the question of why humans wage war really a question of why men fight with each other?

For more than 20 years, anthropologist Napoleon Chagnon lived and worked among the Yanomamo people of the rain forest regions of southern Venezuela and northern Brazil. The Yanomamo are hunter–gatherers who commonly engage in intervillage warfare. Chagnon (1988, 1997) noted that the primary motivators for the formation of a war party involved: avenging the death of kin from an earlier conflict, retrieving or kidnapping women, avenging stolen goods or property, or because of a mystical experience, such as a prophetic dream. Although the proximate causes for war may have varied, what the the Yanomamo men were really fighting about, according to Chagnon, was reproductive success. The proximate motivators were either directly (e.g., capturing or retrieving women) or indirectly (e.g., vengeance for kin or stolen goods) related to this

goal. Among the Yanomamo, a man who proved himself as a successful warrior (or unokai) was allowed to marry earlier and more often and thus produced more children (Fig. 11.A).

Studies of other traditional societies echo the patterns found in the Yanomamo. For example, the Blackfoot Indians of North America engaged in frequent raids to obtain horses, which were then used as payment for brides (Denig, 1961). The Meru of Kenya use livestock as their currency for purchasing a bride, and raiding parties regularly ambush other villages to steal livestock holdings. In addition, a successful raiding party also may steal women and girls to be held as wives, concubines, or "daughters" to be sold in exchange for more livestock (Fadiman, 1982). Manson and Wrangham (1991) studied the causes of warfare across 75 traditional societies and concluded that reproductive issues were at the core of most of the violence. In more than 80% of the societies studied, the causes of intergroup violence were either access to females or access to the resources necessary for attracting or purchasing a bride. It is important to note that when men fight in traditional societies, they

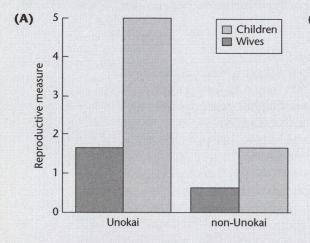

(A)

Figure 11.A The average number of wives (dark bars) and children (light bar) for Yanomamo men who either distinguished themselves as brave warriors (unokai) or did not (non-unokai). Unokai roughly translates as revenge killer.

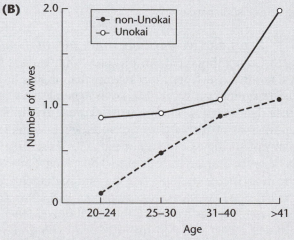

(B)

Figure 11.B The number of wives for men of different ages who either achieved unokai status (open dot) or did not (black dots). Note that unokai men always had more wives and married them earlier in life. (Adapted from Low, 2000, p. 226.)

termed the **cultural dimorphism** between the sexes. This refers to the fact that throughout recorded history males have dominated the cultural, political, and economic life of every society ever studied. Along with producing immensely more murder, violence, and indiscriminate mayhem than women, men throughout

usually are fighting along with family and extended kin. Thus, kin selection also may play a role in male warfare, in that even if a man is not fighting directly for his own reproductive interests, he may be helping kin secure theirs, which benefits his genes as well.

But hasn't all of this changed with modern warfare? We no longer live in extended tribal kin groups, and wars today are fought by nation-states with huge, mechanized armies. True, war has changed, but the motivation behind those involved in war has not. During the Middle Ages, most wars in Europe continued to be small-scale conflicts, usually waged by powerful men attempting to expand or defend their property (see Low, 2000, chapters 13 and 14, for a discussion). Property, of course, would have been a critical resource for one's status and reproductive success. With the Renaissance, the scale of war enlarged, with nations battling nations using more sophisticated weaponry. The fitness benefits of war also shifted from the warriors themselves to those who sponsored the warfare, such as weapons makers and political leaders. Entrepreneurs, industrialists, politicians, and generals (all mostly males) continued to reap the rewards of higher status, huge profits, and greater resources from the activity of war, whereas soldiers themselves saw their direct reproductive benefits fade. However, given the prospects of many economically disadvantaged men, the potential rewards of military service were usually sufficient to fill the ranks.

Despite the changes in war, the evolutionary factors that made men warriors continue to be seen today. Although the large-scale wars of the 20th century attracted considerable (and deserved) attention, the vast majority of wars in the 20th century were local, small-scale conflicts, usually involving ethnic or tribal disputes over resources. Since 1945, at least 80 small-scale conflicts of this type have claimed any-where from 15–30 million lives (Brogan, 1990). Military training continues to emphasis the "brotherhood" of those who serve, mimicking the kin basis of ancient war parties. The honor and status accorded those in uniform continues to be a critical element in recruiting and retaining those who serve. Hackworth (1989) argued that it is when these primal fundamentals breakdown that military endeavors are most likely to fail, as in the U.S. effort in Vietnam. In that conflict, the "familial" bonding of units often was short-circuited by poor training and dissatisfied superiors. Moreover, the society at large bestowed little or no honor or status upon those who fought. The evolutionary warrior motives were undermined, and the effort ultimately collapsed.

Shakespeare best articulated the primitive yearnings that have always inspired the warrior. In *King Henry V*, before the battle of Agincourt, young King Henry exhorts his men with a rousing speech. He calls them all "brothers," not just to each other but to him as well (what better status enhancement could there be than to be kin to the king?). Moreover, he appeals directly to their manhood and promises them that theirs will be of greater value than that of those comfortably asleep in England. No indirect appeals here—the bard went right to the heart of manly fitness:

> We few, we happy few, we band of brothers;
> For he to-day that sheds his blood with me,
> Shall be my brother; be he ne'er so vile
> This day shall gentle his condition:
> And gentlemen in England now a-bed
> Shall think themselves accurs'd, they were not here,
> And hold their manhoods cheap whiles any speaks
> That fought with us upon Saint Crispin's day.
>
> (King Henry V,
> Act IV, Scene III)

Sources:
Brogman, P. (1990). *The fighting never stopped: A comprehensive guide to world conflict since 1945.* New York: Vintage Press.
Chagnon, N. (1988). Life histories, blood revenge, and warfare in a tribal population. *Science, 239,* 985–992.
Chagnon, N. (1997). *Yanomamo: The fierce people.* 5th ed. Fort Worth, TX: Harcourt Brace.
Denig, E.T. (1961). *Five Indian tribes of the upper Missouri: Sioux, Arickaras, Assiniboines, Cree, Crows.* Norman, OK: University of Oklahoma Press.
Fadiman, J.A. (1982). *An oral history of tribal warfare: The Meru of Mt. Kenya.* Athens, OH: Ohio University Press.
Hackworth, D.H. (1989). *About face: The odyssey of an American warrior.* New York: Simon & Schuster.
Low, B. (2000). *Why Sex Matters.* Princeton, NJ: Princeton University Press; chapters 13 and 14.
Mason, J., & Wrangham, R. (1991). Intergroup aggression in chimpanzees and humans. *Current Anthropology, 32,* 369–390.

recorded history have also produced much more art, music, and literature. For Miller, male cultural productivity amounts to nothing less than display behavior, similar to that of a peacock strutting about with its tail unfurled. Some evidence supports Miller's theory. For example, jazz musicians are overwhelmingly male, and their peak productivity tends to occur in their 20s and early 30s, prime ages for attracting mates (see Miller, 1999). Similar trends have been found in poetry, mathematics, and theoretical physics (see Simonton, 1988, for review). However, other professions, such as novelist, historian, and physician, show productivity peaks in later years than evolutionists might predict. Still, as Miller (2000) pointed out, the car beside you from which that loud, booming noise emanates is mostly likely occupied by a young male. His throbbing vehicle is a modern testament to the masculine tendency to display. Evolutionarily speaking, this tendency is predictable, given that men, more than women, stood to collect exorbitant fitness gains from the accumulation and public exhibition of resources, power, and status.

Some scholars object to this reasoning, arguing that this dimorphism reflects the historical persistence of **patriarchy**. In nearly all societies, men wield more power and control more resources than women, thus effectively restricting women to traditional, subordinate social roles (Lerner, 1986; Sanday, 1981). But evolutionists would contend that citing patriarchy as the cause of these differences only begs the question of identifying the origins of patriarchy. As we have seen before, one of the strengths of the evolutionary approach is its willingness to tackle ultimate questions. In this instance, the evolutionist would contend that patriarchy arises from the fact that the differential parental investments made by males and females have resulted in females evolving as the choosers and males as the chosen. As the chosen, males have powerful evolutionary incentives or evolved motives for engaging in competitive and cooperative economic exchanges to acquire the resources necessary to attract and provision mates. In addition, males have evolved motives to joust for political and social power to better their own status and influence within their social groups. Finally, males have evolved motives for publicly displaying their genetic value, whether through risky behaviors, best-selling novels, or Olympic gold medals. Societies, evolutionists argue, almost always have existed as patriarchal because, over our evolutionary history, it was males, more than females, who realized vast reproductive profits from winning social, economic, political, and cultural games and have therefore evolved to play those games as if their lives (no, their genes!) depended on it (for more on the patriarchy/evolution issue, see Box 11.2).

SUMMARY

Over the course of human evolution, male genes were selected to solve a number of adaptive problems. As mammalian males with an abundance of cheaply produced sperm, human males have evolved with generally energetic sexual appetites. However, given the extended dependency of hominin offspring, males also were selected for their ability to form pair bonds and to provision offspring for extended periods of time. To maximize fitness under these circumstances, male genes were further selected for the ability to select mates who were young, pretty, and sexually naive. These factors tended to correlate with maximal fertility, reproductive value, and assurance of paternity certainty. In other words, by being attracted to young, pretty, and sexually naive mates, males could maximize reproductive output from one or a select few mates and could increase the probability that the offspring of that (or those) mate(s) carried his genes.

Patriarchy, Evolution, and Culture: The Swedish Experience

BOX 11.2 The problem of disentangling patriarchy from evolution is complex and may never be entirely resolved. Although certainly not definitive, one case study that sheds light on this issue can be found in Sweden, a society that, over the last half century, has almost entirely dismantled the social and economic infrastructures supporting patriarchy. Does the disintegration of patriarchy leave in its wake an absence of cultural dimorphism?

Beginning in the 1930s and then accelerating dramatically in the postwar years, Sweden developed one of the world's most comprehensive social welfare systems. The Swedish system featured extraordinarily aggressive efforts aimed at abolishing inequalities between the sexes. In pursuit of this goal, generous benefits in health care, child care, parental insurance, taxation, and economic incentives for working women and mothers were adopted. Parental insurance, for example, allows women, both married and single, to take off work for childbirth and child care without the threat of job loss. Health care for mothers and children is provided at no charge, as are day care services. Social and educational programs have been adopted to facilitate women's active participation in all aspects of the workforce, and strong unions bolstered by government policies have prevented large pay differentials from arising across different sectors of the job market. The result has been the near elimination of any economic dependence women might have on individual men (husbands). In stark contrast to most other cultures, Swedish women gain very little economically from husbands, making a man's status or resources largely irrelevant to a woman's fitness interests (Posner, 1992).

By many measures, Sweden has been quite successful in generating equality between men and women. In 1998, the proportion of women in the workplace was nearly equal to that of men, with 74% of women ages 20–64 employed outside the home compared with 79% of men (unless otherwise noted, all statistics from Swedish Institute, 2000). In higher education, the percentage of women earning terminal degrees (27%) was slightly higher than that of men (24%). In government, the gains of women have been most striking. Nearly 44% of the members of the Swedish parliament are women. The current ruling party has 11 female and 9 male cabinet ministers. At the local level, this equality of representation continues: 41% of municipal council members are

women, as are 48% of county council members. This provides support for the notion that patriarchy is really a social construct and that when this construct is deconstructed through social change, equality emerges.

The Swedish story, however, is not that simple and, in many respects, provides aid and comfort to evolutionists. Although the state now provides women the economic benefits once offered by husbands, Swedish women continue to place a high value on a man's financial prospects when considering long-term mates (Buss, 1989; Buss & Schmitt, 1993). This preference is weaker in Sweden than in other cultures in which husbands are more economically valuable, but it is noteworthy that the preference has not vanished. Furthermore, evolutionists would point out that despite decades of the most invasive gender-equity-based social engineering in human history, much of Swedish society remains highly sex segregated and cultural dimorphism at the highest levels is alive and well.

In higher education, three of four engineering students are male, and three of four education students are female (Swedish Institute, 2000). The Swedish labor force, like those of all Nordic countries, has clear gender divisions: more than three fourths of women work primarily in public-sector, female-dominated occupations, whereas two thirds of men work in the higher-paying private sector (Core, 1994; Persson, 1990; see also *The Economist*, March 5, 1994, p. 80–81). At the highest reaches of Swedish society, the disparities continue. Although 40% of postgraduate students are women, only 22% of university instructors and only 8% of full professors are women. A 1988 study reported that women accounted for only 1% of the board members of Swedish companies, and more recent analyses have continued to find very low percentages of women in positions of senior management in the private sector (Persson, 1990; Swedish Institute, 2000). On average, women continue to earn less then men, and the wealthiest top-level private- and public-sector executives are almost exclusively male (Vogel, 1990). Even that paragon of Swedish equality, the government, has admitted recently that "women tend to be allotted fewer influential appointments," and "men still dominate nearly all policy-making bodies" (Swedish Institute, 2000, p. 2).

Some of this difference certainly can be attributed to discrimination, but a government study published in

continued

Patriarchy, Evolution, and Culture: The Swedish Experience (continued)

BOX 11.2

1993 attributed most of the income difference between men and women to the increased incidence of part-time work by women and to differences in occupational and education choices (Swedish Institute, 2000). For example, a 1997 study found that 27% of women ages 20–64 were working part-time, compared with only 7% of men. This reflects the fact that the parental insurance program allows for part-time work for parents, and it is mothers, far more than fathers, who take advantage of these benefits. Sweden's parental insurance also provides time off for child care, which, once again, is used far more by mothers than fathers. A study by Sweden's National Insurance Board concluded that 95% of the insured days off were used by mothers (Persson, 1990). Studies of Sweden's adult and vocational education programs show that women continue to make generally "traditional" (often lower paying) choices when it comes to education and job training (Swedish Institute, 2000).

These data suggest that Swedish women and men set different priorities and make different choices, which have ramifications for pay and career advancement. Because Swedish law provides equal benefits regardless of one's profession and prohibits large pay differentials between upper- and lower-level salaries, there is only modest economic incentive for pursuing a nontraditional career or for ambitiously trying to climb the corporate ladder (Persson, 1990). Why put in all that work if the financial reward is meager? These disincentives seem to have less effect on men, whose desire to reach the highest pinnacles of status appear to be as strong in Sweden as anywhere else.

Cultural dimorphism, of course, has a cultural component, but it may also reflect something deeper about human nature. Perhaps humans, like every other creature on earth, have *evolved natures* that manifest themselves at least partially in the varying ways that males and females approach life. It may be that men and women tend to organize life's myriad experiences using somewhat different value systems. These different approaches, in turn, produce the phenomenon of men and women generally assuming different social roles in dissimilar spheres of society. Most men and women probably strive for some satisfying combination of the material and personal spheres, but

it may be by evolutionary design that the balance of these is not the same (generally) for them. Indeed, one recent study has shown exactly this. In assessing the personalities and life goals of nearly 700 male and female college students, Roberts and Robins (2000) found that both males and females put a high priority on having good relationships and living exciting lives. Males, however, tended to place a higher value on the achievement of economic goals, whereas females sought more socially enriching ones.

Having said all this, two important cautions are in order. The assertion that, generally speaking, men and women may have different evolved natures really says very little about the potential of individuals. A hallmark of evolution is variability; thus, there always will be (and indeed always have been) men and women whose predispositions lead them in nontraditional directions. An enlightened society should give these folks their fair shot to fulfill their potential and make their contributions just like everyone else.

Second, it is important not to confuse evolved tendencies with inherent value. One contribution of the feminist movement may have been in accurately pointing out that throughout most of history humans have mistakenly viewed the male approach and contribution to life as somehow "better." The Greek philosophers and those who followed them often were quite explicit in claiming that men were more rational than women and therefore higher on the Great Chain of Being. The future challenge may be in getting people to realize the folly of this belief. It was through partnership that male and female hominins managed to elevate cooperation to unprecedented heights over the course of our evolution. By specializing in certain social and economic realms and then sharing the fruits of their efforts, male and female hominins eased their mutual burdens and reaped rewards neither could realize alone. The benefits of this partnership continue today, as numerous studies have demonstrated that married people live longer, happier, healthier lives than do the unmarried, even in Sweden (Myers, 2000; Weitoft, Haglund, & Rosén, 2000). Our future challenge may be in finding ways for this partnership to continue to evolve and productively serve us and our communities.

Over the course of evolution, human males seeking to maximize their fitness did so within a competitive social context. This context created selection pressure for males with effective competitive and status-seeking skills. Many evolutionists today contend that male traits, such as competitiveness, the desire to dominate and achieve high status, risk taking, and the tendency to engage in excessive display behaviors, stem from the high reproductive variance that occurred between the winners and losers in the ongoing evolutionary contest for mates. Although controversial, it may well be the such phenomena as cultural dimorphism and patriarchy are byproducts of evolutionary selection pressures on human males.

KEY TERMS

cultural dimorphism
Madonna/whore
   dichotomy
male parental investment
meat-for-sex deal

pair bond enhancers
paternity certainty
patriarchy
polygyny
reproductive value

reproductive variance
serial monogamy
status

REVIEW QUESTIONS

1. Define paternity certainty and reproductive value. How has each played a role in the evolution of male reproductive strategies?

2. What is meant by reproductive variance, and why has it affected the evolution of human males more than females?

3. Identify the different strategies that men might use to achieve status, and describe the environmental factors that tend to "push" males toward one strategy or another.

4. What is categorical thinking? What type of categorical thinking might have evolved to support a mixed male reproductive strategy.

5. What is cultural dimorphism? What are the evolutionary and nonevolutionary forces that might be important in explaining it?

SUGGESTED READINGS

Miller, G. (2000). *The mating mind.* New York: Basic Books.

Tiger, L. (1999). *The decline of males.* New York: Golden Books.

Wrangham, R., & Peterson, D. (1996). *Demonic males: Apes and the origins of human violence.* New York: Houghton Mifflin.

WEB SITES

www.evoyage.com/ a rather informal evolutionary psychology site dealing with many issues including the evolution of human males.

http://biomed.brown.edu/Courses/BIO48/19.Evol.of.Sex.HTML provides succinct notes on the evolution of sex.

www.human-nature.com/books/geary1.html provides chapter 1 of David Geary's book on the evolution of sex differences.

12

Cooperation Between the Sexes III: The Female Perspective

The World According to XX

LET'S GO THE OTHER WAY NOW and see what the world would be like if females' genes were permitted unrestricted domination. Unconstrained by male choice or any other limiting selective pressures, how would female genes direct behavior so as to maximize their fitness? At first blush, the answer seems easy: Wouldn't they, like their male counterparts, want a harem of young, muscular studs for maximum breeding purposes? Actually, no. Females, unlike males, do not gain a great fitness advantage by having more sex partners. Instead, a female's reproductive success is far more dependent upon her physical stamina and that of her offspring and the resources available for raising her young. *Paradise, then, for female genes would be the presence of two male partners: one high-quality gene provider and one high-quality resource provider.* Once again, we need to look more closely to understand why females' genes are after these things and why they cannot have them (at least not all of them).

Why Two Partners? Not Polyandry, But Not Quite Monogamy Either

Polyandry refers to a single woman with multiple husbands, the female version of a harem. This practice is nearly nonexistent throughout the world. Where it does exist, it tends to do so in concert with polygyny, with both men and women permitted multiple spouses. The polyandrous arrangements, however, almost never take the form of a harem. Instead, a variant of serial monogamy allows husbands (often brothers) some measure of paternity certainty (Daly & Wilson, 1983). The absence of polyandry is unsurprising to evolutionists, because it holds little fitness benefit for either men or women. The fact that even in the most sexually liberal societies, such as Sweden, there is no groundswell for legitimizing the practice further suggests that there is scant interest in it on the part of women. If women have little interest in polyandry, does that mean that they are naturally monogamous? No. As we saw earlier, the optimal fitness strategy for men was a mixed one, with monogamy supplemented by opportunistic philandering. Women have evolved to play a similar game, but they play it differently and with different goals. However, before we get into these differences, we should examine the evidence that indicates that women have evolved not as exclusively faithful monogamists but as clever "mixers."

The evidence for mixed reproductive strategies in women takes a number of forms. Females with mixed reproductive strategies can be found throughout the animal kingdom. Occasionally, the ostensibly monogamous male North American tree swallow slips away from home in search of "alternative" mating opportunities. Often, his extra-pair copulation (as biologists refer to it) is with a nested female swallow whose mate happens to be away at the most (in)opportune moment (Kempenaers, Everding, Bishop, Boag, & Robertson, 2001). Thus, the female can be viewed as an equal participant in the "extramarital" breeding strategy. Among gibbons, too, it not just the males who will cheat if the opportunity presents itself. Of even more significance is the fact that among chimpanzees, our closest primate relatives, females typically mate promiscuously, which suggests that our primate heritage is one of something less than unflagging female faithfulness. The most compelling evidence of female infidelity, however, is not found in our animal relatives but in ourselves. To understand this evidence, however, we must make some (rather intimate) cross-species comparisons.

When his harem is threatened, the male gorilla puts on one of nature's most awesome displays. With nostrils flaring and massive canine teeth exposed, the chest-thumping gorilla is a terrible sight to behold—an intimidating exhibition of raw, primate masculinity. But in one aspect (the one that really counts), *Homo sapiens* males can accuse the gorilla of being downright wimpy. Despite his enormous bulk and power, the male gorilla is pathetically undersized when it comes to testicles. The testes of the average gorilla weigh only about 30 g. Compare that with the chimpanzee, who, despite being only about one third the gorilla's size, sports an enviable 120-g set of testes. Why all this concern with male genitalia? The reason is that a species' mating behavior is one of the factors affecting **testes size** (Harcourt, Harvey, Larson, & Short, 1981). Gorillas live in harems in which the silverback can use his physical prowess to impose faithfulness on the resident females. Chimpanzees live in large social groups in which even the alpha male cannot prevent females from mating with other males. Thus, unlike gorillas, male competition among chimpanzees extends all the way to the sperm level. If a female is mating promiscuously, then an advantage will go the male who can pump the most sperm into her when he gets his chance (remember the muriqui monkeys from chapter 11). Because larger testes produce more sperm, natural selection favored well-endowed chimps. Gorillas, on the other hand, have no need for advanced hydraulics, because the silverback can effectively prohibit illicit matings. The lesson is clear: unfaithful females tend to produce larger testes in males. So, what about humans? The average man has testes that weigh about 41 g, slightly smaller than would be expected based on body size and obviously much smaller than the chimpanzee's. However, it is significant that human testes are larger than both gorillas and orangutans, two primate species in which faithful females are best assured. Human testes size strongly suggests that there was at least mild selection pressure for sperm-level competition. Hominin females were not as promiscuous as chimps, but they seem not to have been entirely monogamous, either.

Not only do men's testes give a clue about past female infidelity, but the factors that affect sperm production further confirm this conclusion. Baker and Bellis (1989, 1993a, 1993b) analyzed ejaculate samples from couples who had been sexually active immediately after varying durations of separation. The quantity of sperm in the samples was found to vary depending upon how long the couple had been physically apart, and this variance was independent of the amount of time since the man's last ejaculation. Put another way, regardless of when he last had sex, a man seems programmed to produce more sperm, depending on how much opportunity his mate has had to gather sperm from competitors. The greater that opportunity, the more he retaliates by increasing sperm production upon his return home—a cagey adaptation to help safeguard paternity no doubt, but such a mechanism would most likely only evolve if the threat of infidelity was real. Evidence suggests that it was, both in the past and today. Paternity tests in some urban areas have shown that nearly one fourth of children were not sired by the fathers of record. Even among hunter–gatherers, among whom the opportunities for infidelity are far fewer, a small but nontrivial proportion of children are biologically unrelated to their presumed fathers (Betzig, 1993).

It is not only male but female genitalia that indicate a less-than-Puritan feminine past history. Human females are unique among primates in that they show almost no outward signs of ovulation. Prominent red swellings highlight female chimpanzee and bonobo fertile periods, and, although visual cues are not as obvious for gorillas and orangutans, pheromones effectively tell males when it's time to "get busy." In humans, however, ovulation is most often so covert that females, as well as males, are left in the dark. A number of theories have been advanced to explain concealed ovulation in humans, most of which involve some degree of sexual adventurousness on the part of our foremothers. The **resource extraction** theory argues that concealed ovulation served as an effective tool for eliciting resources from males (Symons, 1979). Proponents of this theory point out that among common chimpanzees and bonobos the meat-for-sex exchange is not uncommon. Smart males, however, would be less likely to make the exchange if it were obvious that the female was not sexually receptive. Concealed ovulation makes this determination impossible, thereby enhancing the ability of the hominin female to use sex as a means of getting males to provide important resources for her and her offspring. Other evidence supporting this theory is found in the fact that among hunter–gatherers the sex-for-resources exchange is not unheard of, sometimes netting a women a healthy cache of material rewards and gifts (Shostak, 1981). Moreover, although women consider a man's personal resources important when assessing a long-term mate, this concern is even more exaggerated when assessing short-term mates (Buss & Schmitt, 1993).

A second explanation for concealed ovulation is aptly called the **seeds of confusion** theory (Hrdy, 1981). This theory extends from the fact that among primates promiscuous mating can actually serve a protective function by confusing paternity. Infanticidal males are not uncommon in the natural world. When a new alpha male takes over among langur monkeys, he is likely to kill the troop's infants in an effort to bring the females more quickly into estrus and thereby populate his new group exclusively with his offspring (Hrdy, 1977). This same grisly strategy has been observed among lions and gorillas (Shaller, 1972; Watts, 1989). Given this, one might wonder why a new alpha male chimpanzee does not engage in the same infanticidal slaughter. One of the reasons might be that because he (along with his mates, to be sure) has probably mated with at least some of the resident females, there is a chance that some of his victims could be his own. The paternity confusion created by promiscuous mating serves as a protective device against the shifting sands of male primate power. Concealed ovulation enhances the efficacy of this protective device by prohibiting males from knowing whether their specific copulatory event was fruitful or not. Put more simply, because a man can never be certain that he is *not* the father, he has reason to leave the kid alone. Like chimpanzees, our foremothers evolved in a social context of competitive, jealous, and potentially violent males in which the "seeds of confusion" strategy might fill a necessary niche. In fact, evidence suggests that male infanticide of nonrelated children was not a trivial issue for females and their offspring in our evolutionary past. In some societies, including hunter–gatherers, men have had the right to demand the death of fatherless children, especially when issues of marriage were being considered (Daly & Wilson, 1988; Hill & Kaplan, 1988).

Seeds of confusion and resource extraction need not have been mutually exclusive strategies in our evolutionary past. Both may have had a hand in accounting for the evolution of concealed ovulation. In fact, Morris (1967) and Diamond (1997) pointed out that concealed ovulation might also serve the more honorable function of pair bond enhancer. Because a husband can never be sure exactly when his wife is fertile, he has incentive to hang around and keep the amorous fires burning over an extended period of time. In truth, concealed ovulation probably evolved in service to many purposes and thereby effectively increased the range of strategies that a female might use to forward her fitness interests.

CONCEALED OVULATION AND CUCKOLDRY. A reproductive strategy that might have directly benefited from concealed ovulation and might also have been very useful over the course of hominin evolution was **cuckoldry**. Suppose you were a female a million years ago, with a mate who was a reliable provider but rather lacking in the genetics department. To ensure robust as well as aptly provisioned offspring, you might surreptitiously obtain the genetic material from a more desirable source but at the same time feign fidelity to your mate. This tidy bit of deception would be greatly facilitated by concealed ovulation, in that hubby would never know that his sexual sorties were wholly unproductive. Moreover, female orgasm also acts as a mechanism for regulating conception by favoring stimulating lovers over lethargic ones. Thus, although you may have continued to have routine, not-so-exciting-anymore sessions of sex with your husband, every now and then, when the coast was clear and the mood was right, you slipped out for a few raucous cave-shaking encounters with the sexy stud next door. Ultimately, this could have produced the desired state of affairs. You kept the good provider unsuspecting and happy, and you did not waste your reproductive time with weak, sickly offspring.

The story sounds plausible, but does any evidence suggest that the women of our past actually behaved this way? We have already cited evidence showing that a notable proportion of children are biologically unrelated to the man who believes himself to be their father. Furthermore, women show cyclical changes in sexual desire and attraction to certain masculine features supportive of a cuckoldry mating strategy. Women report the strongest sexual desire during the fertile phase of their menstrual cycle (Regan, 1996). Women in the fertile phase of their menstrual cycle (follicular phase) show a significantly stronger attraction to masculine facial features (e.g., larger, squarer jaws, high cheekbones, more prominent brow-ridges, etc.) than do women in nonfertile phases (Penton-Voak & Perrett, 2000; Penton-Voak et al., 1999; see Box 12.1). In addition, women in the fertile phase of

Ovulation and Facial Attractiveness

BOX 12.1 If you were designing a creature whose job it was to obtain the best genetic material possible for her offspring and at the same time ensure that the offspring would have the advantages of a reliable resource provider, what sort of emotional desires would you implant in her head? One possibility would be to design her emotions so that, when the chances of becoming pregnant are the highest, she would be attracted to those features that indicate "good genes" in a partner and, when chances of becoming pregnant are lower, she would find indicators of kindness, faithfulness, and loyalty most attractive. This emotional combination would enhance the probability of obtaining genetic material from a genetically high-quality short-term mate and obtaining resources from a more dependable long-term partner. Researchers Penton-Voak and Perrett (2000) set out to test this possibility by measuring women's attractedness to different male facial features at different times during their menstrual cycles.

Women were identified as in either the follicular phase of their cycle (high conception risk group) or the menses or luteal phase (low conception risk group). These women were then asked to select the "most attractive" male face from a set of computer-generated composite faces with either exaggerated masculine or feminine features.

Results of the experiment are shown in Figure 12.A. The graph shows the percentage of subjects who selected a specific face as being "most attractive." The percentages along the horizontal axis represent the degree of feminization versus masculinization of the facial features, with negative values indicating increased feminization and positive values indicating increased masculinization. Women in the high conception risk group (light bars) showed a significant preference for the face with 30% masculinization of features. These women were found to be significantly more likely to choose a masculinized face than were women in the low conception risk group. Although there was a clear preference for the feminized faces (especially the 30% feminized face) among the low conception risk group (dark bars), the difference proved nonsignificant. A previous study, however, showed a significant preference for feminized faces among women in the nonfertile phase of their cycle (Penton-Voak et al., 1999).

This variability in attractiveness tends to support the idea that in our evolutionary past females engaged in a cuckoldry mating strategy in which genes were obtained from one source and resources were obtained from another. Women, like men, seem to have evolved using a mix of reproductive strategies.

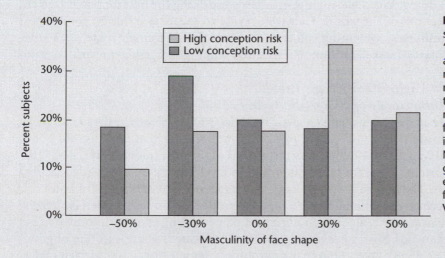

Figure 12.A The percentage of subjects who rated a face as "most attractive." The percentages at the bottom of the graph represent the degree of femininization or masculinization of the facial features, with negative numbers indicating increasing femininity and positive numbers indicating increasing masculinity. Note that the high conception group showed a significant preference for the 30% masculinized face. (Adapted from Penton-Voak, 2000, p. 45.)

Sources:
Penton-Voak, I.S., & Perrett, D.I. (2000). Female preference for male faces changes cyclically: Further evidence. *Evolution and Human Behavior,* 21, 39–48.
Penton-Voak, I.S., Perrett, D.I., Castles, D., Burt, M., Kobayoshi, T., & Murray, L.K. (1999). Female preferences for male faces change cyclically. *Nature,* 399, 741–742.

their cycles also find scent cues associated with more symmetrically built men more attractive than those associated with men who are less symmetrical (Thornhill & Gangestad, 1999). Women in nonfertile phases make no distinction between the scents of symmetrical and asymmetrical men. Symmetry and masculinized facial features are associated with high testosterone levels and thus are indicators of good genes. Moreover, these masculine attributes also have been associated with lower levels of investment in romantic partners and higher levels of marital instability and divorce (Gangestad & Thornhill, 1997; Mazur & Booth, 1998). The attraction that peaks when the probability of conception is highest, then, is most likely an attraction to genetic quality not to reliability, trustworthiness, or prolonged investment. Women's emotions seem to have equipped them with a regular "pull" toward a studly, no-commitment, he-man when the chances of conception are greatest—a sly tactic for getting genes from one source and investment from another.

But do women actually act on these emotions? A study of more than 3,000 women in Britain revealed that those who were having extramarital affairs consistently timed their illicit copulations to correspond with the fertile phase of their menstrual cycles (Baker & Bellis, 1995). Were they consciously trying to get pregnant by their lovers? Probably not. They just had sex when they felt most "sexy." But their genes had evolved under conditions in which this sort of behavior represented a "genetic" opportunity to be maximized, and their behavior followed accordingly.

Concealed ovulation (and the various strategies it entails), male testes size, and sperm production all point to a single inescapable conclusion about our ancestral females: they were not exclusively monogamous. Their genes were unsatisfied with a single mate, but they were not yearning for harems either. What exactly were these genes doing? Well...like male genes, they were doing the best they could, given the imperfections of the world. They were trying to secure two things: good genes and good resources, something you cannot always find in a single mate. Let's look at the next part of our definition to see exactly what "good genes" means.

Why a High-Quality Gene Provider?
The Importance of a Good Body and Mind

The desire for high-quality genetic material is fairly easy to understand: quality genes produce more robust offspring. The importance that selection for good genes has played in our evolutionary history has often gone underappreciated. One of the important themes of hominin evolution has been the increasing dependency of infants. The altriciality (helplessness) and extended development of hominin infants placed an exceptional burden on their mothers. This factor often is cited as a critical reason why male provisioning and pair bonding evolved in our species. Infant dependency, however, also creates intense pressure for the selection of good genes (Miller, 1998). Over the course of evolution, female hominins selected males who could provision and care for their infants, but there is evidence to suggest that, first and foremost, female hominins selected males with high-quality genes. In our ancestral past, regardless of how devoted a father might have been, a sickly, undersized newborn almost always meant a waste of valuable time and energy on the part of the female. In addition, Foley (1992) showed that the per month energetic and nutritional requirements of hominin infants are no greater than those of ape infants who are provisioned almost exclusively by their mothers. This suggests that although male provisioning would have been advantageous, it may not have been an irreplaceable necessity for the survival of the infant. Male provisioning in the environment of evolutionary adaptedness (EEA) would have been less reliable than genetics (as it is today). Once a female had acquired quality genetic material, it was hers (or, more accurately, her offspring's) for good. The male from which it emanated may turn out to be a deceptive louse or may get eaten by a sabertooth tiger on the way home one day. For these reasons, Miller (1998) contended that the most pressing concern of ancestral females was gene quality, with provisioning capacity as a secondary worry.

The desire for good genes is straightforward, but assessing and acquiring them is more complicated and represented a major challenge in our evolutionary past. Judging genetic quality involves evaluating not only perceivable physical traits but also more subtle behavioral and mental qualities. Good genetics includes body and mind, and ancestral females had to evolve a highly discerning eye for both. If not, their genetic legacies were in peril.

THE GOOD BODY. How did hominin females judge gene quality? As is true of nearly all "choosing" females in the animal kingdom, they looked for outward displays of quality, some of which are as obvious to a woman's genes as the nose on man's face. Studies assessing male beauty show that females consistently find certain facial features, such as high cheekbones, a well-defined jaw and chin, and (proportionally) large noses as attractive (see chapter 8). These features have been found to be associated with higher testosterone levels in the body, a physiological factor associated with virility and with immune system function. Thus, the same facial features that draw women's ardor serve as displays of potency and immune system vigor. Bilateral symmetry is also consistently found to be attractive in male faces and bodies (Langlois & Roggman, 1990; Gangestad, Thornhill, & Yeo, 1994). Symmetry also has been found to be linked to robustness, health, and freedom from parasitic infection. Thus the masculine features that women find desirable appear to serve the same function as the peacock's tail: they publicly announce one's genetic quality.

One aspect of looking good goes beyond objective qualities like symmetry and jaw definition. Looking good also means looking similar to oneself. Just as good looks correlate with good genes, similar looks correspond to similar genes. Studies of married couples show that they tend to be highly similar to each other on a variety of measures. For example, significant positive correlations have been found for age, socioeconomic factors, intellectual measures, and some personality and physical attributes (Jensen, 1978; Lykken & Tellegen, 1993; Mascie-Taylor & Vandenberg, 1988; Spuhler, 1968; Susanne & Lepage, 1988). In other words, smart, rich, tall, type A women tend to marry smart, rich, tall, type A men, and not-so-smart, not-so-rich, short, type B women tend to marry not-so-smart, not-so-rich, short, type B men. Given that modern societies are far more mobile and diverse than those of our ancestral past, one can reasonably conclude that these same effects would have been at least as strong then as they are now. This has often been referred to as **assortative mating**, the idea that mating selections are not necessarily random but, instead, are based on a restricted sample. A number of theories have been proposed for these assortative mating effects. For example, it has been suggested that these correlations are a function of geographic propinquity (people marry people who live close to them) or comfortableness (people marry others with whom they feel comfortable). Studies support both ideas. People who live close together are more likely to marry, and the farther apart an engaged couple live from one another, the more likely their engagement will be broken (Berscheid, 1985; Berscheid & Walster, 1978; Clarke, 1952). The comfortableness hypothesis finds support in the fact that people of the same race, religion, ethnicity, family background, and with similar drinking and smoking habits tend to marry and remain married longer than those who differ on these factors (Burgess & Wallin, 1943; Hill, Rubin, & Paplau, 1976). Although propinquity and comfortableness provide proximate explanations for why similar people marry, it leaves unexplained the reason that similar people tend to live close to each other and are comfortable with each other. As we have seen so many times, the ultimate explanation appears to require a deeper, evolutionary-based perspective.

It turns out that physical and behavioral similarities can be used as indicators of genetic similarity, or, put more scientifically, phenotypic similarity predicts genotypic similarity (Dawkins, 1976; Thiessen, 1999). Biologist Richard Dawkins (1976) has called this the "**green beard**" effect. If I have a green beard, I am likely to be positively predisposed to another with a green beard, because our phenotypic (physical) similarity strongly suggests a commonality of genes. Marrying another with similar genes appears to hold great fitness advantages for the couple. Couples with similar genotypes tend to have longer, more stable relationships and more children than those with more dissimilar genes (Bereczkei & Csanaky, 1996; Thiessen & Gregg, 1980). In addition, because assortative mating increases the number of similar genes in each parent, offspring are actually related to each parent by slightly more than the 50% (Thiessen, 1999). Thus, an assortative strategy would have a strong selective advantage, in that there is an increased probability of producing more offspring and each offspring is marginally more genetically related to the parents.

Other studies also have demonstrated a community element to assortative mating. When shown individual photographs of men and women and asked to pair them up as dating couples, subjects have been found to construct dating pairs that are assorted or composed of highly similar individuals (Thiessen, Young, & Delgado, 1997). Moreover, assorted couples were rated higher in terms of their long-term compatibility, number of children they might have, and the extent to which others would want to interact with them. These findings suggest that when two similar people marry, the community around them has higher fitness expectations for them and is more willing to offer social support (Theissen, 1999). It seems reasonable to assume that in our ancestral past these social pressures would have been even more acute and that when females made mating choices, their feelings of attraction or nonattraction were powerfully affected by the perceived degree of support they might expect from friends and family.

THE GOOD MIND. It is not only *looking* sharp that can indicate something about genetic quality. One may have to *be* sharp as well. Geoffrey Miller (2000) has argued that outward signs of intelligence, such as communicative ability, creativity, empathy, and resourcefulness, are just as much displays of genetic quality as strong jaws and broad shoulders. Our female ancestors, he contended, went more than just skin deep when it came to judging quality. An intelligent mate was likely to produce an intelligent child, whose chances of survival would be enhanced by his or her brain power. To bolster his idea, Miller pointed out that many human intellectual functions, such as wit, verbal eloquence, higher mathematical ability, and music, have little if any direct survival function and, thus, are inadequately explained by natural selection. However, sexual selection, especially female choice, can produce runaway effects (see chapter 10), like the peacock's tail, that have no direct survival function but act as effective quality displays. The massive human brain, with all its attendant powers, is a prime candidate as a sexually selected ornament. Some support for Miller's view can be found in Buss's (1989) cross-cultural study of mate preferences, in which males and females across the globe identified intelligence as one of the most important factors in a long-term mate. In addition, Kenrick, Sadalla, Groth, and Trost (1990) showed that, when it comes to sexual relations, females are far more selective about the intelligence level of their partner than are males. If our ancestors had dispositions similar to modern men and (especially) women, then selection for intelligence may indeed be plausible.

Another factor that may add even more credibility to Miller's hypothesis is that of **mate copying**: the idea that females use the preferences of other females as a basis for making their own judgments about attractiveness. Put more simply, another's mate suddenly looks very sexy simply because he is already the mate of another. This phenomenon has been shown in a number of animals, including deer, birds, and fish (Clutton-Brock & McComb, 1993; Dugatkin, 1992; Gibson, Bradbury & Vehrencamp, 1991). Take a female guppy, for example, and allow her to watch as another female chooses between two courting males. When given her opportunity to pick between the same two males, she reliably picks the one chosen earlier by the first female. Dugatkin (1992) found that he could even get female guppies to "change their minds." After having chosen male guppy A (and rejected B), if a female is then allowed to witness another female choosing B rather than A, on a second chance choice she will reverse herself and go with B (it's a female's prerogative, no?). Dugatkin and colleagues (Dugatkin, 2001; Cunningham, Dugatkin, & Lundy, 2001) also showed that this effect can generalize to human females as well. The point is that mate copying provides a mechanism for magnifying the already potent effects of runaway sexual selection. If female hominins did start to select mates based on intelligence and that preference was copied by others, the resultant "snowballing" effect could provide a feasible explanation for the almost alarming rate of hominin brain expansion over the last 2 million years.

One criticism of Miller's thesis might be that among modern *H. sapiens* judgments of intelligence are greatly facilitated by the presence of spoken language. If, as many researchers contend, spoken language was absent or vastly limited through much of our ancestral past, then upon what basis could females make intellectual discriminations? One notion is **neophilia**, the love of novelty. Among many birds, a male capable of producing the most varied and diverse song repertoires is assured of copious amounts of female attention (Catchpole, 1980, 1987; Podos, Peter, Rudnicky, Marler, & Nowicki, 1992). Female humpback whales seem similarly affected by the "latest thing" in male humpback songs. When a few male humpbacks from Australia's west coast emigrated to the east coast, the resident east coasters wasted no time in switching their tune to that of the new immigrants (Noad, Cato, Bryden, Jenner, & Jenner, 2000). Apparently, there was no sense sticking to the same old song when the market gave the new one rave reviews! Small (1993) documented this same effect in primates, noting that "the only consistent interest seen among the general primate population is an interest in novelty and variety" (p. 153). It has been demonstrated, too, that the detection of novelty in the environment actually causes discharges from the brain's own opioid system, a self-reinforcing experience (Izquierdo & McGaugh, 1985; Siegfried, Netto, & Izquierdo, 1987). This opens up the possibility that, in our evolutionary past, females with an eye for creativity, possibly in courtship behavior, communication, toolmaking, or even lovemaking, may have helped to launch the intelligence spiral leading to humanity.

Why a Good Resource Provider?
The Complexities of Female Relationships

The same evolutionary theme that we cited in the previous section seems to offer a straightforward answer to the question that heads this section. As hominin infants became more altricial, females needed increasing amounts of help to care and raise their offspring. Females needed a partner who was a good resource provider to help ensure the survival of a helpless, slowly maturing infant, and, as a consequence, male–female pair bonds evolved. Once again, however, this oversimplifies the situation. Yes, female hominins were undoubtedly selecting males who could be more helpful around the cave (or campsite), so that longer-term intersex cooperative relationships emerged slowly over time. The oversimplification is that it was not only relationships with males that were evolving. Relationships with other females were also evolving in rather intricate and sophisticated ways. Just like the male–male relationships discussed in chapter 11, female–female relationships became increasingly cooperative and competitive.

Like males, females evolved in an imperfect, disappointing world in which one's genes did not always get everything they wanted. Sperm may have been in great abundance in our evolutionary past, but capable, resource-providing males were not (and are not). Although our species is high in male parental investment (MPI), that investment varies widely in quantity and quality. Some males are not interested in investing at all. Just as males compete for relatively scarce female eggs, hominin females evolved to compete for relatively scarce male investment. It has been popularly assumed that cultural restrictions, arranged marriages, and the generally low status of women in strict patriarchal societies would have offered our ancestral females little choice in mates (and therefore little opportunity for competition). However, there is good reason to believe that these conditions only arose in the last 10,000 years or so, with the advent of settled agriculture (Fisher, 1992). Thus, over the course of much of our evolution, females were actively choosing and competing for the best of the male lot. This competition may not have been as intense as its male counterpart, but it was not insignificant. The feminine conflict over high-status, high-investing males has left its mark.

COMPETING FOR RESOURCES.   Sara Hrdy (1981) was one of the first to suggest that our primate heritage bequeathed to women a competitive as much as a cooperative nature (and she drew fire from some quarters for voicing the thought). The idea, however, is hardly farfetched. Female primates establish and exist within their own hierarchical systems and can be just as unabashed as males when it comes to using rank for their own betterment and that of their kin. If you are a male bonobo, for example, having a powerful mom willing to use her influence can be a great advantage. When the females are in estrus, male competition in the bonobo community becomes acute. A dominant bonobo female sometimes will help her son get access to the best mates by making the initial sexual overtures to a prime female candidate and then simply handing over her over to junior (Furuichi, 1992; Takahata, Ihobe, & Idani, 1996). Bonobo females may be subtle, but competition among other female primates is more direct. Among some harem-living primates, dominant females will sometimes harass subordinates and aggressively prevent them from mating with the alpha male (Small, 1988). In multimale polygynous primates, such as chimps and some monkeys, females actively compete to establish relationships with the highest ranking males. Female competition can even get lethal. Dominant female ring-tail lemurs may prevent a rival or subordinate female from retrieving a fallen infant and returning it to safety, and infanticidal females are not unheard of in chimpanzee communities (Jolly, 1998; Goodall, 1986). By establishing themselves in rank, female primates actively gather and guard the resources they need for themselves and their kin, often by excluding other females from the same resources. The details of our evolutionary past are always sketchy, but at least two factors suggest that a similar form of female competition would have been present during hominin evolution.

First, given the relatively high infant mortality rates among hunter–gatherers and the well-known infanticidal nature of many male primates, one can only conclude that raising infants was an extremely high-risk venture for hominin females (Cohen, 1989; Dunn, 1968). They undoubtedly did whatever was necessary to secure resources for their infants, including engaging in fierce competition (when necessary) against other females. Second, evidence from our evolutionary past supports the practice of female exogamy, that is, it was females, more than males, who left their natal groups for reproductive purposes (Seielstad, Minch, & Cavalli-Sforza, 1998; Wrangham, 1987). Thus, hominin social groups probably often featured numbers of unrelated females of reproductive age among a network of male kin. Cooperative relationships among non-kin females within these groups emerged and were critically important, but the lack of female blood ties also strongly hints at a social environment conducive to competition. We have good reason to expect female competitiveness to have been an important part of our evolutionary history and for that to evidence itself in women today.

One way that females might compete would be through sexual signaling, much like the male displays discussed earlier. There is some suggestion that this, in fact, occurs. Figure 12.1 shows the results of a study in which men and women from 138 different cultures were assessed on the kind of information that they signaled about themselves with their dress and ornamentation (Low, 1979; see also Low, 2000 pp. 84–88). Men and women showed opposite display patterns when it came to signaling marital status and wealth/power. In less than 10% of the cultures studied, men signaled their marital status, whereas in more than 70% women did. Men signaled wealth/power in more than 60% of the cultures, whereas less than 40% of women did so (and often the wealth/power the women signaled was that of their husband or father). The results are fairly clear: men use their dress and ornamentation to signal their *social status*, and women use these to signal their *marital status*. Even more interesting is the fact that, in societies in which women can and do hold positions of real social and political power, the tendency to signal that power is actually less than in those societies in which a woman's wealth and power is the result of male family relations. Thus, even when women have real power to display, they tend not to do so—in sharp contrast to men. Instead, women use their displays to signal their sexual availability (or unavailablity). There is even some indication that the degree of this signaling varies with a woman's menstrual cycle. Two studies found that women who frequent singles bars tend to wear more make-up and jewelry around ovulation than at other times and that their "display" attracts more male attention (Hill & Wenzl, 1981; Grammer, Ditta-

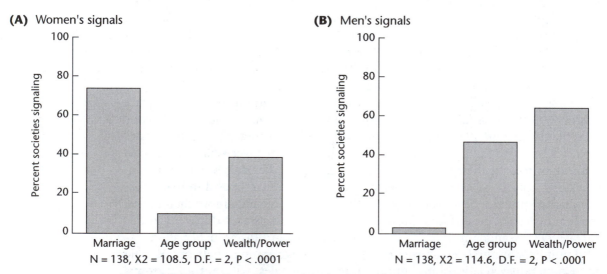

(A) Women's signals

Percent societies signaling

Marriage   Age group   Wealth/Power
N = 138, X2 = 108.5, D.F. = 2, P < .0001

(B) Men's signals

Percent societies signaling

Marriage   Age group   Wealth/Power
N = 138, X2 = 114.6, D.F. = 2, P < .0001

Figure 12.1 What kind of information do men and women signal using their dress and ornamentation? Across 138 different cultures, men and women were assessed for three different types of signaling: marital status, age group, and wealth/power. The graphs show the percentage of cultures in which women **(A)** and men **(B)** used dress and ornamentation to signal these three types of information. Note the reverse relationship between men and women on marital status and wealth/power. In the majority of cultures, women signal marital status but men rarely do. In the majority of cultures men signal wealth/status but women do not, and, in the cultures where they do, this is often the wealth/status of male relations (fathers, husbands, etc.). (Adapted from Low, 2000, p. 89.)

mini, & Fischmann, 1993. Note: both studies were presented as papers and, as of yet, are unpublished. These findings should be regarded as tentative).

Deceptive displays also appear to be part of the female arsenal of competitive weapons for mate attraction. Tooke and Camire (1991) found that women, more than men, employed deceptive physical displays such as dyed hair, false fingernails, padded clothing, etc., as a means of sex appeal. Just as with our primate relatives, female competition can take more direct forms. Women, more than men, have been found to use verbal derogation and insult as a means of devaluing a female rival in the mind of a desired male. As evolutionists would predict, these verbal assaults tended to focus on the rival's physical appearance or sexual past history, both highly sensitive areas in terms of a male's fitness interests (Buss & Dedden, 1990).

Given the crucial importance of securing the necessary resources for herself and her offspring in our ancestral past, one should not be surprised to find evolved competitive mechanisms in women today. A good man was hard to find in the EEA, and finding one could mean the difference between life and death for the genes. Once found, one's prize had to be claimed and defended, and those who did that best survived to be our ancestors. Competing for resources, however, is only half the story. Knowing that the velvet touch can often be more self-serving than the hammer, female genes also have evolved to make fast friends and charm reluctant lovers. Female hominins were truly the community builders of our past. This was not because they were vying for the Stone Age equivalent of the Ladies Auxiliary Service Award, but because it was in their fitness interests to have a strong social network.

COOPERATING FOR RESOURCES. The helpless, slowly maturing hominin infant all but guaranteed tragic doom for the solitary hominin mother. Imagine a teenage girl in the Stone Age who has just been transferred from her father's clan to that of a distant cousin. Very quickly, she will be paired up, pregnant, and struggling to keep herself and her baby fed, warm, and alive. She cannot really fight for what she needs, but she may be able to bargain, coax, and smile her way to reproductive success. After all, she came from a long, long line of females who did exactly that and passed their winning ways on to their daughters. In our evolutionary past, it was females, more than males, who benefited from a rich social network of cooperative relationships. A strong web of caring kin and non-kin relationships can be the sturdiest bulwark against potentially fatal deprivation. Our foremothers were the ones most facile at weaving that social web so essential for their protection and that of their children. That web included female friends, extended family, cousins, sisters, and others, but it typically started with a male mate.

COOPERATING FOR RESOURCES: THE PAIR BOND. To establish the necessary supportive social web, a hominin female would first need to identify a desirable mate. If a Stone Age "sexy" man bore some resemblance to his modern counterpart, then one highly desirable male trait that hominin females looked for was the capacity to provide resources. In his international study of mate preferences, Buss (1989) found that a universal concern of females in judging a long-term mate was "good financial prospects" (Fig. 12.2). In all cultures studied, women placed significantly more value on this factor than did men. A similar result was found for the factor "high social status." Across the globe, women see a highly respected, financially

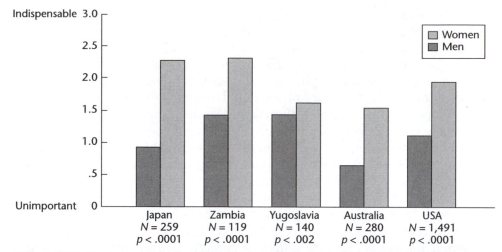

Figure 12.2 The female desire for a mate with good financial prospects. The graph shows how strongly men and women in five different cultures expressed the desire for a mate with good financial prospects. Note that in every culture women rated this attribute significantly higher than did men. (Adapted from Buss & Schmitt, 1993; also Buss, 1998, p. 421.)

successful man as prime husband material. These characteristics of modern women make sense in light of the evolutionary challenges that faced their female ancestors. In terms of a female's fitness, a good husband is one who has or can acquire ample resources. In our past, that meant a man who was a good hunter or toolmaker. Today, that means someone who has good job prospects, can earn a decent wage, and has the capacity for advancement. Some females may actually sit around and rationally contemplate a man's education and future prospects, but, far more often, a man's erudition, profession, and success just become part of his general sex appeal in a way that has no parallel in men's perceptions of women.

It is one thing to find a mate with resources to invest but another to actually secure the investment. A dependent, slowly maturing infant not only needs adequate resources but also needs those resources to be invested continuously over an extended period of time. A good husband, therefore, not only must have resources to give but must be willing to make a long-term commitment to giving. A second important step in building the social network is the establishment of the extended pair bond. The truly remarkable accomplishment of our female ancestors was their ability to literally domesticate the male of the species. Over a few million years, females transformed males from wild, violent ape-men into more-or-less responsible, provisioning husbands and fathers. They sent them out to hunt and, even more significantly, compelled them to return and share. This metamorphosis certainly was not accomplished using eons of lecturing on moral philosophy. It was done in way that hairy ape-men could relate to: with sex.

We have already explored one of the adaptations that may have helped cement the male–female pair bond, concealed ovulation. Males may have continued to hang around with a single female to ensure the paternity of the offspring, or, as Lovejoy (1981) has unromantically termed it, they practiced **copulatory vigilance.** Unlike most ape females, which are sexually receptive only when in estrus, hominin females evolved to be nearly constantly receptive, which in turn provided incentive for hominin males to stay in close proximity to their mates. Sex may have evolved as an instrument of pair bonding precisely because hominins were having more frequent sex.

Humans are unique in that sex tends to involve such things as extended foreplay, face-to-face copulation, and conspicuously announced female orgasm. Musings over the potential function of orgasm in females have been going on for decades. However, recent studies have illuminated the evolutionary significance of this response. Orgasmic contractions actually serve to pull sperm further up the reproductive tract, thereby enhancing the probability of conception (Baker & Bellis, 1993b). This is inelegantly referred to as the **upsuck hypothesis**, and the lesson of it is fairly clear: exhilarating sex is more likely to produce pregnancy. Screaming-good sex, however, is not always easy to come by, especially for women. Nearly 30% of women (compared with only 5% of men) report never or only sometimes having an orgasm with their partners (Laumann, Michael, Gagnon, & Michaels, 1994). Because orgasm is not easy, it is more likely the product of a steady relationship rather than a one-off encounter. The overt nature of the orgasm also may serve as a signal to the male of both his sexual flair and a heightened probability of impregnation, thus reinforcing his loyalty, continued investment, and sexual interest.

Closely connected (literally and figuratively) to orgasm, of course, is the male penis. Another notable effect of female hominins seeking hedonistic pleasure has been the evolutionary growth of the male sex organ. Once again, thanks to women, human males have it all over gorillas and chimps when it comes to what's "down under." Averaging more than 5 inches in length and 1.25 inches in diameter, the *H. sapiens* penis towers over the less-than-3-inch members of its ape competitors. In addition, unlike other ape penises, which utilize a bone when achieving erection, the human penis swells with blood, giving it a pleasure-enhancing flexibility unheard of among other animals. Little wonder that Eberhard (1985) dubbed male genitals "internal courtship devices." Is there wisdom to be found in the fact that it was by pleasing hominin females that hominin males slowly evolved from brutes into men? Of course, female hominins did not realize they were shaping the husbands and fathers of the future. They were simply selecting those males who gave them the best sexual thrill. But then, as now, a good sexual thrill often required effort, empathy, and commitment, and those traits were evolving right along with the groans and moans.

COOPERATING FOR RESOURCES: THE EXTENDED SOCIAL NETWORK. Identifying a mate with resources and then establishing and maintaining an extended cooperative relationship with him goes a long way toward solving the dependent-infant investment challenge. However, as we have seen repeatedly, having a mixed array of fitness strategies at one's disposal can be more advantageous than doggedly pursuing a single one. Our female ancestors had back-up plans should their male mates prove inadequate, unreliable, or unexpectedly short lived. An important final step in the weaving of the social web was the development of a network of supportive relationships that extended beyond the immediate home to include neighbors, friends, and kin.

In hunter–gatherer communities, a solitary female bearing the burden of caring for and raising an infant is simply unheard of. Surrounded by female friends, sisters, and extended family, mothers have access to a rich, supportive social network. After living with the !Kung of Southern Africa, Marjorie Shostak (1981) concluded that there was no "working mother/child care" issue among these hunter–gatherers. All moms were working moms, and all moms and other females shared in the care of the young. As the women worked, their children accompanied them or were left with older sisters or other relatives or friends until mom's return. "The isolated mother burdened with bored small children is not a scene that has parallels in !Kung daily life," reported Shostak (1981, p. 238). Do today's hunter–gatherers reflect the feminine social world of our evolutionary past? There is reason to suspect so. Although ape moms can literally drop babies without great effort, our earliest ancestors would have found the birthing process a stressful ordeal. With bipedalism came a narrowing of the birth canal, which left Australopith females only scant room to pass a newborn's shoulders (Rosenberg & Travathan, 1995; Trevathan, 1987). The situation became even worse with the great cranial expansion of *Homo*. This evidence led Alison Jolly (1999) to offer midwifery as a candidate for "at least the second oldest profession" (p. 325). Very early on in hominin evolution, females were probably helping other females in birth and that help most likely continued as the baby grew. Females helping other females formed the basis of a network of reciprocal relationships in which the tending of infants and children was traded, similar to the way males exchanged tools and weapons.

Given the importance that a strong social network would have played in the lives of ancestral females, evolutionists would predict that it is women, more than men, who place a high value on interpersonal relationship. Modern social science research confirms this prediction. Females have been shown to be more empathetic and to place a higher value on helping and sacrificing for others (Hoffman, 1977). Gilligan's (1982, 1993) work on male–female differences in moral development has reinforced this point. Gilligan criticized the well-known framework developed by Lawrence Kohlberg (1969), who contended that moral development progresses through a series of stages moving ultimately toward an abstract set of ethical principles. According to Gilligan, Kohlberg's emphasis on ethical codes and justice represented morality from a male-biased perspective. Her research demonstrated that females tended to approach moral issues from a perspective of attachment and affection rather than from a perspective of rules and justice. Gilligan was quick to point out that her research does not mean that women cannot or do not form and use moral codes but that their ethical orientation is more focused on the relationships and interdependencies of life. "Women's sense of integrity appears to be intertwined with an ethic of care, so that to see themselves as women is to see themselves in a relationship of connection…." (Gilligan, 1997, p. 137). The important point is that when assessing what is right or wrong, moral or immoral, males tend to concentrate on whether or not rules have been violated, whereas females tend to concentrate more on relationships and how they will be affected. One approach cannot be thought of as better than the other. Indeed, most studies of moral development fail to find significant gender differences (Walker, 1984). Thus, it cannot be argued that the male or the female approach consistently produces more ethical behavior. Instead, they are simply different approaches, with each offering valuable insights on moral issues. Recall that the golden rule takes two forms in the New Testament, one insisting on justice, "Do unto others as you would have them do unto you," and another emphasizing relational care, "Love thy neighbor as thyself" (Kohlberg & Candee, 1984).

Females and the Mixed Strategy

As we saw with males in the previous chapter, the best way that genes can deal with the world's imperfections is to be ready to use a mix of reproductive strategies. A female's genes are no different; they play the odds as well as they can, doing their best to maximize fitness and obtain the resources they need to get by. When it is to their advantage, females have the capacity for faithful monogamy. If one's mate is inadequate genetically or proves to be an unreliable provisioner, a female's genes stand ready to cheat and get the sperm or the provisions from other sources. If the mate has skipped town, a female's genes stand ready to cultivate a network of female friends and relatives to provide aid and support—whatever it takes to get the job done. Two million years of collective wisdom in making do has been passed along to modern women. With an array of strategies at one's disposal, however, how does one decide which course to follow? The answer is that the choice of strategy hinges on three important factors: (1) the degree of future uncertainty or instability, (2) the perceived availability of investing males, and (3) a female's perception of her own mate value. Let's examine each one in turn.

Future Stability or Certainty

A general reproductive pattern is present across various species. Smaller species tend to mature more quickly and reproduce sooner than larger ones. A number of factors play into this pattern, but an important one is simply the certainty of living another day. Smaller creatures tend to have less certain futures than larger ones, and it makes sense to mature quickly and reproduce as soon as possible (Low, 1998). Humans, especially females, are also responsive to cues that foreshadow **future uncertainty**, and it is becoming increasing clear that our response to these cues may be the result of evolutionary mechanisms at work. High stress levels typically have detrimental effects on health and immune system function. However, a number of studies have shown that stress actually accelerates reproductive maturity in human females. Girls growing up under more stressful conditions and without a biological father present in the home have been found to reach menarche earlier than girls growing up with low stress levels and fathers present (Ellis & Garber, 2000; Graber, Brooks-Gunn, & Warren, 1995; Moffitt, Caspi, Belsky & Silva, 1992; Surbey, 1990). Even when a biological father *is* present in the home, reduced levels of father–daughter interaction also have been associated with earlier onset of puberty (Ellis, McFayden-Ketchum, Dodge, Pettit, & Bates, 1999). These findings may seem counterintuitive from a general health standpoint, but they are predictable from an evolutionary perspective. Stress, and the absence of (or little interaction with) a biological father may serve as potent cues to an uncertain future, which may in turn activate genetic mechanisms for speeding up reproductive potential (Surbey, 1998).

In line with evolutionary expectations, teenage mothers come disproportionally from economically deprived urban areas where indicators of future uncertainty and instability are most salient (Chisholm, 1993; Geronimus, 1987, 1991). A recent study examining the rate of teenage pregnancies in Scotland found that from the early 1980s to the mid 1990s the rates of teenage pregnancy remained steady or decreased in affluent areas but increased in more economically deprived ones (McLeod, 2001). A range of factors contribute to high rates of teenage pregnancy, and one must be careful not to dwell exclusively on those rooted in our evolutionary heritage. However, evolutionary factors should not be dismissed summarily when confronting this issue. Burton (1990) examined the reproductive "timetable" considered desirable by black women living in impoverished conditions. For these women, childbearing in the teenage years and the achievement of

KEY CONTRIBUTIONS

WILSON AND DALY
Rational Reactions to Difficult Environments

PROFILE: *Drs. Margo Wilson and Martin Daly are professors in the Psychology Department at McMaster University, Hamilton, Ontario, Canada. For many years, they have been interested in the application of Darwinian principles in understanding interpersonal conflict and violence. They have focused especially on family violence and parent–offspring conflicts. In addition, they also have actively researched a variety of ecological issues, ranging from the behavior of desert rodents to the perception of coastal ecosystems.*

The Evolved Mind in a Bad Neighborhood

Two problems commonly associated with poor inner city neighborhoods are violence and teenage pregnancy. Politicians, sociologists, and pundits of one stripe or another provide varying explanations for the root cause of these problems: the lack of economic opportunities, moral deficiencies, family decay, etc. From an evolutionary perspective, however, higher rates of violence and teenage pregnancy may be the "rational" reactions of males and females when they perceive a shortened life expectancy. Evolution may have designed human youngsters to be especially sensitive to environmental indicators of shortened life expectancy, such as: (1) the absence of grandparents, especially grandfathers; (2) the death of peers and age-mates; and (3) routinely encountered images (either real life or fictionalized) that reinforce the precariousness of life in the neighborhood. In the face of such cues, how would a primate mind that is evolved to maximize reproductive success respond? Wilson and Daly hypothesized that males and females would respond with varying strategies designed to enhance "short-time horizon" fitness. Males, for example, would be more prone to

heightened levels of risk taking, including acts of violence, that might help to elevate their short-term status. Females would accelerate their reproductive timetables, to ensure reproduction while their youthful energy and health are still intact. From the perspective of middle-class values, these responses might be deemed "reckless." However, from the point of view of the genes, they are perfectly rational, given that more long-term strategies, such as getting a college diploma to enhance one's status or delaying childbirth until one has greater resources, might lead to no reproduction at all.

To test this hypothesis, Wilson and Daly analyzed life expectancy data (how long people live) along with birth rate and homicide data in 77 different Chicago neighborhoods from 1988–1993. First, they looked at the relationship between "cause deleted" male life expectancy and homicide rates across the different neighborhoods (Fig. 12.B). "Cause deleted" life expectancy means that the effects of homicide were removed from the life expectancy data. Even with that effect removed, a highly significant relationship ($r = -.88$; $P < .0001$) was found between male life expectancy and homicide rates across the neighborhoods. Thus, as neighborhoods have males in them

grandmotherhood in the 30s was considered desirable, given the uncertainties of finding a suitable husband and of living to an age more typical of grandmothers. This finding suggests that future uncertainty not only manifests itself physically in the form of early maturation but also psychologically in the urgency with which one views the timing of reproduction (for more on reproductive strategies in difficult environments see Box 12.2.)

Availability of Investing Males

Evidence indicates that a girl's maturation rate is affected by the presence or absence of a father in the household. It has been suggested that father-absence may

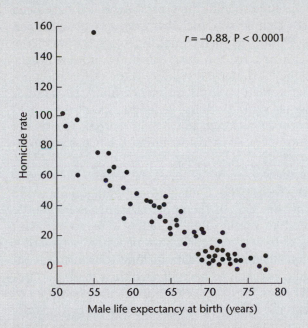

Table 12.A shows birth rate data for mothers of varying ages in neighborhoods of high, low, and median life expectancy. Note that there were 2.5–4 times as many births to mothers between the ages of 15 and 24 in the neighborhoods with the shortest life expectancy as in the ones with the longest life expectancy. This is what one would expect if females were accelerating their reproductive timetable under conditions in which life expectancy was relatively short.

More work from a number of different perspectives is necessary to fully understand the problems encountered by those growing up and living in violent, impoverished conditions. But these data, along with many other studies by Wilson and Daly, have demonstrated the value of including an evolutionary perspective in our understanding of urban social ills.

Age specific birth rates (per 1000 women per year) in 10 neighborhoods with longest life expectancy, 10 with shortest life expectancy, and 10 nearest median life expectancy in Chicago, 1988–93.

with increasingly short life spans (shortened life spans that are *not* the result of murders), they also tend to have more homicides. This offers support to the notion that males are engaging in more violent behavior (homicides) as they perceive their environments to be ones in which lives are short. Although this finding supports Wilson and Daly's hypothesis about males' reactions to shortened life expectancy, additional work needs to be done to link these violent behaviors to status seeking and resource holding, additional important components of the evolutionary view.

	Birth rate in neighborhoods		
Age of mother (years)	Shortest life expectancy	Median life expectancy	Longest life expectancy
10–14	9	2	1
15–19	190	86	45
20–24	224	128	90
25–29	129	103	103
30–34	83	84	89
35–39	39	43	42
40–44	9	10	7

Source: **Wilson, M., & Daly, M. (1997).** Life expectancy, economic inequality, homicide, and reproductive timing in Chicago neighborhoods. *British Medical Journal, 314,* 1271–1274.

signal to the maturing girl that there is a paucity of investing males in the environment, thus swaying her to adopt a more promiscuous short-term mating strategy rather than one that is more sexually reserved and long term (Draper & Harpending, 1982). Although the evidence for a direct link between father-absence and a more promiscuous mating strategy has been equivocal, it does seem that female reproductive strategies vary depending on a female's perception of the **availability of investing males** in the environment.

The Hiwi and the Ache are two hunter–gatherer tribes living in similar ecological circumstances in South America. One major difference in the two tribes is the ratio of men to women. The Hiwi tribe has an oversupply of men, and the Ache has an undersupply (Hill & Hurtado, 1996). In pursuit of only a few available men, Ache women tend to adopt short-term mating strategies, getting what they can from a man before he plunges back into the well-stocked pond. Marriages among the Ache are notoriously unstable, and extramarital affairs are common. By the time he or she is 40 years old, the typical Ache will have been married and divorced 12 times. By comparison, the Hiwi form a virtual Norman Rockwell vision of family values. With many men contesting for each woman, the women have the power to extract long-term commitments and continual investments from their mates. Among the Hiwi, marital stability is the norm, and illicit affairs are infrequent. Are Hiwi women radically different from Ache women? Absolutely not. They are radically the same. Each has genes that have been honed by hundreds of thousands of years of evolution to adjust their reproductive strategies to the environmental circumstances. Each is just doing the best she can to maximize fitness.

In Victorian England, it was the women of the lower classes who had a reputation for loose morals (Barret-Ducrocq, 1989). Some of this reputation may have been the result of exaggeration by members of the upper class, but there is little doubt that the sexual mores of the 19th-century English gentry were more conservative than those of the working classes. Working class women, however, faced a more challenging time finding quality mates capable of long-term investment. Evolutionary psychologists would expect this to have affected their mating strategies. It makes perfect evolutionary sense for a female to evaluate the availability of investing men in her environment and adjust her reproductive strategies accordingly. The women discussed earlier in the Burton study (1990) seem to be doing exactly this. Moreover, Cashdan (1993) found that women who perceive a scarcity of males interested in long-term investment tend to dress more provocatively and engage in more sex than women who perceive an abundance of quality mates. Given the economic deprivation, uncertainty, and lack of investing males in some run-down urban settings, it is not surprising to find an alarmingly high proportion of single, young moms.

Perception of One's Own Mate Value

Trivers (1972) was one of the first to suggest a relationship between a young woman's attractiveness and her number of sex partners. Interestingly, based on evolutionary theory, the relationship ought to be an inverse one; that is, young women who see themselves as attractive—that is, as having a high **perceived mate**

value—should have fewer sex partners. Why? In terms of fitness, the female's beauty is a commodity that can be bartered for the greatest amount of resources, which would most likely come from a high-status, high-resources-holding, high-investing male. The highly prized male will undoubtedly find a Madonna-ish female more attractive then a promiscuous one. Thus, the pretty girl has incentive to practice sexual restraint. Because the very best males may be unavailable to the not-so-pretty girl, her best bet for acquiring vast resources may be to extract a little out of many sex partners. (In all of this discussion, it is important to reiterate that no one is claiming that any young women sit down and consciously think through these options. Like the males, they just follow their gut feelings. When asked why they did or did not fool around, the responses are likely to be quite similar: "because it made me feel good" or "because it just didn't feel right.")

Trivers's predictions have been supported by at least one other study. Walsh (1993) found that female self ratings of attractiveness were negatively correlated with their sexual practices. Those who rated themselves as less attractive tended to have more sex partners. Also in line with this reasoning is the fact that when considering short-term mates, women showed an exaggerated preference for men who have immediate material rewards to lavish on them (Buss & Schmitt, 1993).

Far from being hard-wired, female genes display a remarkable degree of fluidity in adjusting reproductive behaviors to best fit with the relevant aspects of environmental context (Fig. 12.4). A healthy, pretty girl growing up in a stable, secure environment with an abundance of reliable males about would not be expected to behave in the same manner as one whose personal and environmental situation was vastly different. This only serves to reinforce an important principle of the evolutionary approach: humans have evolved to respond in adaptive ways to their circumstances. (See Box 12.3 for more on the social implications of evolutionary psychology.)

Figure 12.4 Evolution appears to have fashioned female reproductive strategies to be responsive to many environmental factors, such as future certainty (or uncertainty), the availability of investing males, and the perception of one's own mate value. It is by genetic design that the course of a girl's life history is strongly affected by how she views herself and the world around her. (Photo of Anya; courtesy of Joyce Weiner.)

Evolutionary Psychology and the Good Society

BOX 12.3

For decades, researchers have argued back and forth about genetic versus environmental determinism, secretly knowing the whole while that neither of these simplistic approaches could fully explain the diversity of human behavior. Psychology textbooks routinely set up the radical nativist and empiricist straw men only to knock them down to draw an emotionally satisfying if scientifically vague compromise of genetic–environment interaction. We always knew that had to be the answer, but exactly how it worked—how precisely the genes and the environment combined to produce Mozart or Mengele or your neighbor Joe—was never quite clear. One of the strengths of evolutionary psychology is that it begins to provide the outline for the way in which these genetic–environmental interactions might function.

Genetically, individuals may be very much the same in their capacity for flexibility. Put more specifically, females are born with genes that allow for different reproductive strategies to be realized. They may differ in their genetic propensity to follow one path or the other. For example, it is known that genetic factors play a role in the tendency to be shy or gregarious, to be thrill seeking or risk avoidant. A girl with genetic tendencies toward shyness and risk avoidance is probably already genetically biased toward a more Madonna-ish reproductive strategy. Genetics, however, is not the entire story. The home,

community, culture, and society send messages to girls about future stability and the availability and willingness of males to commit to long-term investment. The frequency and strength of these messages combine with the genetic predispositions of individuals to produce outcomes. Research on these issues from an evolutionary perspective is still in its infancy, but clear predictions can be formulated. A society or community that clearly and forcefully tells young women that the future is foreboding and that males are irresponsible, unreliable bums can expect those young women to disproportionally adopt promiscuous, short-term mating strategies. This should be especially acute in those already genetically predisposed to that strategy.

It is here that another strength of the evolutionary approach becomes apparent. By clarifying our understanding of gene–environment interactions, the evolutionary approach also leads to some rather specific and highly thought-provoking implications. For example, suppose that it is agreed that a society could be improved by making marriages more stable, divorce less frequent, and males less violent. By putting a few findings together, we can begin to see a possible course for pursuing this agenda. (1) From Cashdan's (1993) study and the Hiwi and Ache comparison a lesson can be drawn: a healthy supply of males willing to make long-term investments leads to increasing numbers of females adopting long-term,

SUMMARY

A number of lines of evidence support the notion that ancestral hominin females practiced a less than monogamous reproductive strategy. Male testes size suggests some sperm-level competition, which is common among species in which females mate promiscuously. In addition, female attractedness to various masculine "good gene" indicators varies cyclically, peaking when chances of conception are highest. This suggests that females have been designed by evolution to seek quality genes from one source and quality investment from another.

The indicators that women use to assess good genes include male facial and other physical characteristics. Moreover, females often are attracted to physical and behavioral features that are similar to their own, thus elevating the chances of similar genes being shared between partners (assortative mating). Some evidence suggests that females may also have been selecting males based on intellectual capacities, such as communicative skills, problem solving, and originality (neophilia).

rather than short-term, mating strategies. This tends to enhance the power of female choice in directing males to be more responsible and faithful husbands and fathers. (2) It appears to be good for both society and males if females can achieve this power. Divorce and extramarital affairs were far less common among the Hiwi, and studies have shown that married men live longer, are happier, and engage in far less violence and criminal behavior than unmarried men (Daly & Wilson, 1988, 1990; Myers, 2000). (3) The world at large, however, is far more like the Ache situation then the Hiwi; that is, there tends to be an undersupply of investing males, thus producing greater female competition for desirable mates and weakening the power of female choice to curb male tendencies toward deception, dishonesty, and infidelity. Thus, an evolutionary suggestion derived from these findings might be to make a concerted effort to increase the supply of males who are sincerely interested in long-term investment. In theory at least, this would accentuate the power of female choice, reduce female competition, and potentially lead to rewards of increased stability, fidelity, and peacefulness. How could this be done? Again, recommendations based on an evolutionary understanding are available. The answer might lie in harnessing the strong male tendency toward competition and status seeking.

One approach might be to base male status on such qualities as faithfulness, honesty, loyalty, and monogamy. What if a concentrated effort was made to teach young boys that the highest virtue was to be faithful to one's wife and family? What if men who lived up to such standards were rewarded with status and respect? "A man stands by his clan!" might be the credo of this effort. Magazine covers and corner offices could be dispensed as liberally to good husbands and fathers as they are now to sports heroes and rich investment bankers. At the same time, an effort could be made to strongly encourage girls to use their evolved powers of selectivity and discrimination when contemplating mates with whom they will share their sexual favors. "No sex for low-quality males!" could be their slogan. This would create ever more fierce competition among the males to be good husbands and fathers, because only the best of them would be selected by choosy females.

The point here is not that these evolutionarily based social initiatives could successfully engineer a utopian society of peace and moral goodness. No, there would always be cheating, deception, violence, and selfishness. The more critical point is that the forces that can increase virtue in a society are already a part of the evolutionary process. Goodness and virtue and the processes that animate them are not other-worldly in origin. They are as much a part of our nature and ecology as are our proclivities toward violence, self-indulgence, and exploitation. The difficult challenge is that of harnessing and applying the forces that can serve to magnify our more commendable natural traits while minimizing our less savory ones. The evolutionary perspective can give us a clearer view of some potential options, but it is still up to us to muster the fortitude to put whatever options are deemed most suitable into practice.

As is the case with males, females seem to have a mixed set of reproductive strategies that vary depending on different factors, including the perception of their own mate value, the availability of investing males, and the degree of future certainty or uncertainty. When perceived mate value is low, the number of investing males is low, and the future appears uncertain, females seem more likely to adopt a more promiscuous, short-term mating strategy.

KEY TERMS

assortative mating	future (un)certainty	resource extraction
availability of investing males	green beard	seeds of confusion
copulatory vigilance	mate copying	testes size
cuckoldry	neophilia	upsuck hypothesis
	perceived mate value	

REVIEW QUESIONS

1. What is meant by a cuckoldry mating strategy? What evidence suggests ancestral females practiced this strategy?

2. Discuss the resource extraction and the seeds of confusion theories for the origins of concealed ovulation. Are they mutually exclusive?

3. What physical features might a women assess when judging good genes?

4. Discuss why an extended social network would have been more advantageous to a female's fitness interest than to a male's over the course of our evolutionary past.

5 What factors tend to influence the mating strategies that a woman might adopt?

SUGGESTED READINGS

Buss, D. (1998). The psychology of human mate selection. In C. Crawford & D.L. Krebs (Eds.), *Handbook of evolutionary psychology* (pp. 405–430). Mahwah, NJ: L. Erlbaum.

Geary, D. (1998). *Male/female.* Washington, DC: American Psychological Association.

Low, B. (2000). *Why sex matters: A Darwinian look at human behavior.* Princeton, NJ: Princeton University Press.

WEB SITES

ftp://ftp.princeton.edu/pub/harnad/BBS/.WWW/bbs.campbell.html copy of a paper on the evolutionary origins of female aggression by Anne Campbell from Behavioral and Brain Sciences.

http://evolution.humb.univie.ac.at/institutes/urbanethology/beauty/beauty.html neat site dealing with the latest research on the evolution of beauty.

www.beautyworlds.com/theoryofbeauty.htm another site dealing with the evolutionary and biological basis of beauty.

http://news.bbc.co.uk/hi/english/sci/tech/newsid_376000/376321.stm#top news article discussing the cyclical changes in women's attraction to male features.

DEVELOPMENT AND FAMILY DYNAMICS

13

Parent/Offspring Conflicts: Prenatal and Postnatal

The Golden Age of Rome

THEY SHOULD HAVE BEEN THE BEST OF TIMES for Gaius Julius Caesar Octavianus, also known as Augustus Caesar. Two thousand years ago, Augustus was the undisputed leader of the world's most celebrated empire. All the world Rome cared to own, from Gibraltar to the Black Sea, from the English Channel to the African Red Sea coast, was under Augustus's imperial thumb. The vast Mediterranean Sea was a Roman pond. Just the hushed whispering of Caesar's name could send armies marching, villagers scurrying, and enemies trembling across three continents. With Augustus's reign, Rome ushered in its Golden Age, the *Pax Romana*, two centuries of unprecedented peace and stability in which Roman order and ingenuity flourished. It would not be long before Romans would elevate Augustus to god-like status.

Despite his sterling reputation and worldly magnificence, Caesar's family life was in enough disarray to make a barbarian weep. Having recently divorced his wife, Scribonia, for not being tolerant enough of his infidelities, Caesar quickly found himself smitten with Livia. She had the virtue of being far more understanding of Caesar's sexual wanderings (even encouraging them at times) but was inconveniently already married. Being emperor, however, had its advantages. Caesar simply ordered Livia's husband to grant a divorce so that he and Livia could marry. But although he could deftly manipulate adults, dealing with his own daughter, Julia, was an ordeal even mighty Caesar could not manage. While still an infant, Augustus betrothed his daughter Julia to Mark Antony's son. When the boy and his family ran afoul of Augustus, the engagement was broken and the fiance killed. At age 14, Julia was wedded to Augustus's nephew, Marcellus, who died soon thereafter. After a second and then a third marriage, all at the behest of her domineering father, Julia's patience ran out. She staged a most unseemly rebellion. Deserted by her third husband, Tiberias, she struck out on her own, taking on countless lovers and offering herself as a prostitute at numerous drunken orgies. Embarrassed and outraged, Augustus banished his now 37-year-old child to a lonely island in the Tyrrhenian Sea.

From an evolutionary perspective, the scandals of Caesar's family represent some of the more notorious manifestations of the tensions and struggles inherent in human kinship. Common genetic interests provide incentive for family members to build common cause. However, their often diverging individual fitness desires can, at the same time, become a source of conflict and strain. This is why it is often within families that we witness the most loving, self-sacrificial acts as well as the most bitter feuds and rivalries. In this chapter and the next, we will explore how our evolutionary history has left its imprint on child development and family relations. We will see that evolution has locked family members together in a mutual dance: a tense, passionate tango of complementing and contesting roles in which each must find ways of satisfying self-interest without jeopardizing necessary kinship links. It is interesting to note that Caesar's banishment of Julia came only after she had already provided him with four grandchildren and that her defiance of him came only after she no longer needed his influence or protection for herself or her offspring. As we shall see, the way we relate to our family members is often influenced by the value those individuals possess in helping us achieve our fitness goals.

The Microscopic Tango

To adults, children often can seem quite selfish and whiny. If brother or sister gets a chocolate kiss, everybody had better get a chocolate kiss or the interminable moan of "that's not fair" will most certainly arise. From a genetic point of view, the source of this sort of sibling conflict is fairly straightforward: with the exception of identical twins, siblings are related to each other by only 50% of the genome. Therefore, genetically speaking, a child sees him- or herself as twice as valuable as his or her brothers or sisters. Put another way, a child is twice as related to him- or herself as to his or her sibs. This is not the case, however, from the parents' perspective. Mom, for example, is equally related to all her offspring (by 50%) and, therefore, sees her children as being (generally) of equal value (Trivers, 1974). Herein lies one of the first sources of familial conflict: each child is genetically motivated to secure more resources from mom (chocolate kisses, real kisses, whatever) than that obtained by other siblings, whereas mom is genetically motivated to dispense resources roughly equally. What mom sees as fair is almost never going to be judged fair by any of her children. (In this instance evolutionary psychologists are not saying anything that mothers have not already been painfully aware of for centuries!)

When Robert Trivers (1974) first expounded on the evolutionary origins of **parent–offspring conflict**, he suggested that the seeds of this struggle might be sown long before birth. Contemporary research has shown his prediction to be correct. From the first moments after fertilization, a microscopic tension is present between the genetic ambitions of the fast-developing zygote and the resolutely conservative environment in which it grows. The tension begins in the very exchange of genetic information between sperm and ovum. In the sexual recombination of genes, normally it does not matter if a trait is coded by a gene from the mother or father. A dominant trait for say, brown eyes, results in a brown-eyed child regardless of whether it was mom or dad who supplied the gene. Recently, however, a startling exception to this basic rule of Mendelian genetics has been found. Certain genes, called **imprinted genes**, express their associated traits only if inherited from one parent or another. Currently about 40 imprinted genes have been identified. At least one, **Igf2**, has been found to be a central player in par-ent–offspring conflict. *Igf2* stands for insulin-like growth factor 2 and is only effec-tive if it is paternally inherited (i.e., comes from dad, not mom). As its name implies, this gene facilitates fetal growth and is present in a variety of animals, including mice, opossums, and humans. In mice, paternally inherited *Igf2* can lead to offspring that are significantly larger than they otherwise would be (Haig, 1993). This is unquestionably advantageous for the mouse pup and for its father who gave it the "get big" gene, but it comes at a price to the mother, who bears the big baby, and to its litter mates, who lose out in the in utero competition for maternal resources. Why would dad push for a big baby, especially if that entails risks for mom and her other offspring? The answer is quite simple: neither mom nor mom's other offspring are (necessarily) related to dad, but the baby inheriting his growth gene most assuredly is.

Females confront the *Igf2* challenge with an imprinted gene of their own, **M6p**, which serves to blunt the resource-demanding effects of *Igf2*. Thus, evolu-tion has produced something of genetic gender balance that maximizes fetal growth without undo strain on mom or siblings. But what if this balance is upset? Biologists Wolf Reik and Miguel Constancia genetically engineered and bred male mice who were incapable of producing the *Igf2* gene. The results were dramatic. Without dad's genes pushing for every bit of growth possible, resultant offspring were 30% smaller than normal (Melton, 2000). The extent to which these findings apply to humans is unclear. While these genes are present in humans, they do not appear to be imprinted by gender. Futhermore, in a strict-ly monogamous species, intersexual genetic conflicts are minimal (Holland & Rice, 1999). But, as we saw earlier, our heritage was not one of strict monogamy (nor is it currently). Thus, it would be surprising if some degree of genetic gen-der conflicts are not part of human gestation, as they are in many other species. The edgy in utero tango of power, however, does not end with a maternal–pater-nal genetic staredown. As pregnancy proceeds, the evolutionary balancing acts go on.

Embryonic Trials and Tribulations

The speedily dividing and growing fertilized ovum has a strange and unique status within the mother's body. Because its genetic complement is only half derived from the mother, it is not recognized as her own tissue. It runs the risk of being branded an invading organism and prompting a potentially fatal immune system response. On the other hand, if internally gestating organisms routinely rejected their zygotes as invaders, then they probably would have gone extinct eons ago—no mammals, no us. Most oviparous (egg-laying) species do not face this problem. The mother produces a shell that serves to protect the developing embryo from both external hazards (after ejection) and the mother's own immune system (before ejection) (Sharman, 1976). One of the monumental accomplish-ments in the evolution of internal gestation was overcoming the maternal immune response, which was naturally inclined toward eliminating offspring. It turns out that a fair amount of the burden in overcoming mom's immune response is placed on the tiny, tiny "shoulders" of the developing embryo. An early test of its fitness may be its ability to manipulate the mother's internal environment so that its very presence is accepted.

One of the first milestones in achieving pregnancy is the successful implantation of the fertilized egg in the lining of the uterus. As it approaches the implantation site, the busily dividing ovum secretes an enzyme that alters the uterine cells, making them amenable to attachment (Begley, Firth, & Hoult, 1980). Once attached, the conceptus then emits hormones that suppress local immune system response, making the immediate environment safe for the time being (Smart, Roberts, Clancy & Cripps, 1981). It is not enough, however, just to suppress immune system response. The attached ovum will be swept away quickly unless it can also stifle menstruation. This it accomplishes by secreting the hormone human chorionic gonadotropin, which has the effect of inducing the mother's body to maintain adequate levels of the hormones progesterone and estradiol. It is when levels of these hormones drop that menstruation commences. In later stages of pregnancy, the placenta will continue to secrete various steroids to prevent the breakdown of the endometrial tissue and to maintain healthy support of the pregnancy (Begley et al., 1980). It is important to note how highly active the fertilized ovum is in promoting the pregnancy. If it fails to send the right signals to the mother's body, spontaneous abortion typically follows. Nearly three fourths of all fertilizations fail to result in successful pregnancies, usually because of some genetic deficiency in the zygote. Evolution seems to have erected a series of tests or hurdles that the potential new being must first pass before it is allowed to place a 9-month drain on its mother's energy resources.

As the pregnancy progresses, the delicate balancing act between the developing fetus's tendency to secure as large a share of maternal resources as possible and the mother's tendency to preserve resources for herself and future offspring goes on unabated. Inevitably, this balancing act results in a variety of inconvenient and uncomfortable symptoms for the expectant mom. Occasionally, these symptoms can enlarge into genuinely threatening complications. Haig (1993) analyzed pregnancy complications from the perspective of maternal–offspring conflict. For example, diabetes and diabetes-like symptoms are not uncommon consequences of pregnancy for some women. Often, these symptoms can be traced to changes in pancreatic function and carbohydrate metabolism associated with the diversion of energy resources to the fetus. Unlike nonpregnant women, pregnant women depend extensively on fatty acid metabolism rather than carbohydrate metabolism for energy production. Carbohydrates tend to be preferentially diverted for use by the fetus. This change in metabolism can result in a diabetic-like state for some women. Here, it seems that natural selection has hit upon the fact that mothers can survive the diabetes-like complications more often than fetuses can survive low energy reserves. Other common symptoms associated with pregnancy, such as hyperventilation and anemia, also seem attributable to fetal resource demands (Hayashi, 1979). In each case, selection has managed to strike a balance between the conflicting interests of the fetus and mom by taxing the stronger (mom) with symptoms ranging from uncomfortable to potentially damaging (although usually survivable) to keep the weaker (fetus) viable.

Sometimes, however, the cost to mom becomes too high and the balance shifts in her favor. The incidence of spontaneous abortion or miscarriage has been shown to be higher in conditions of increased maternal stress, such as where there is physical trauma, a lack of adequate nutrition, or emotional strain (Bernds & Barash, 1979; Wasser & Barash, 1983). As a reproductive strategy, early termination of pregnancy under conditions in which the maternal investment would be too high makes evolutionary sense. Those females who cut their losses early, thereby preserving time and resources for use under more auspicious circumstances, stood a better chance of ultimate success than those who risked their energy and lives trying to reproduce when conditions were unfavorable. This is probably why fetal death rates are consistently higher than maternal death rates and probably always have been (Mackey, 1984). In line with evolutionary predictions, however, as a mother gets older, her body's tendency to abort a suspect pregnancy declines. Although a 40-year-old woman has 2–6 times more genetically abnormal eggs than a 20-year-old, this increase falls far short of explaining the 25–50-fold increase in genetic birth defects among offspring of older women (Forbes, 1997). Instead, it seems that mother's body becomes less discriminating as the reproductive years wane. With time running out, it's better to brave the perils of a questionable pregnancy than to chance leaving no legacy at all.

In assessing the causes of miscarriage, two distinct categories emerge. On the one hand are those terminations that involve a defective zygote within a healthy maternal environment. On the other are those that involve a healthy zygote but an unhealthy or suboptimal maternal context (Surbey, 1998). Many miscarriages, of course, are probably the result of some combination of both these factors. In any case, from the perspective of parent–offspring conflict, spontaneous abortion can be understood as a mechanism for settling this conflict in favor of mom when the burden of pregnancy is too heavy and future reproduction may be in jeopardy. One of the structures that appears to be playing a key role in balancing the risks between mother and fetus is the placenta (Mackey, 1984). Because the placenta is genetically an identical twin to the fetus, it normally should be biased in favor of the fetus's interests. Generally it is, diverting energy and resources to the fetus even when this places a strain on the mother's functioning. However, because mother's death would spell the end of both the placenta and the fetus, the placenta should have evolved so that there would be a limit to how much it indulges its developing twin. The high rate of fetal mortality cited earlier seems to confirm this reasoning. (For more on the way in which mom and fetus have adapted to one another, see Box 13.1.)

Choosing Babies and the Trivers-Willard Effect

The images that often tear most deeply at our hearts as we watch *National Geographic* or *Wild America* or any of the other countless "nature" shows on television are those that depict the deaths of baby animals: the frail, limping young antelope unable to keep up with the herd as it races headlong from the cheetah or the puny, injured leopard cub abandoned by its mother so that she can devote her precious energy more fully and successfully to her healthy offspring. Nature does its cold calculations: the greatest value of those with scant hope of survival is simply to provide a means of bettering the survival chances of others. Here is where we humans often puff out our chests in righteous pride: so much better are we

Is Morning Sickness an Adaptation?

BOX 13.1 Nearly all women experience some level of nausea and appetite change during pregnancy. For many, this results in bouts of vomiting, especially in the early stages of pregnancy. This is colloquially referred to as "morning sickness," although the symptoms are not necessarily more acute in the morning. The more exact term of **"pregnancy sickness"** is used in clinical circles. For some time, pregnancy sickness represented a bit of a conundrum for evolutionists. Nausea and vomiting would seem only to weaken the expectant mom, making her less able to successfully sustain the pregnancy. One might suspect that natural selection would operate against this tendency, yet its prevalence and persistence in the population suggest just the opposite. What possible benefit could be gained by tossing one's badly needed nutrients in the toilet or on the cave floor?

Freelance scientist and thinker Marjorie Profet (1992) argued that pregnancy sickness serves a protective function for the fetus by forcing mom to adopt a bland diet. This diet is low in the toxins and teratogenic chemicals that over the course of our evolutionary history would have had a harmful impact on the growing baby. She points out that the foods that most pregnant women find unappealing, such as cabbage, broccoli, mushrooms, basil, and cauliflower, are ones that contain a variety of plant hormones and naturally occurring chemicals that can cause birth defects and fetal organ abnormalities. Mushrooms, for example, contain a class of chemical known as hydrazines, an ingredient in rocket fuel, and basil has estragol, a hormone that can produce genetic defects.

Profet's theory sounded plausible, but it had little scientific support until recently. In a comprehensive review, Flaxman and Sherman (2000) found empirical evidence that both confirmed and broadened Profet's theory. First, they concluded that, as the theory predicted, pregnancy sickness symptoms peaked between weeks 6 and 18 of pregnancy, the time when embryonic organ development was in its most vulnerable stage. Second, they found that in every study to date, women who experienced pregnancy sickness were significantly less likely to miscarry than those who did not. Moreover, the more severe the symptoms (vomiting versus simple nausea) the less

likely a miscarriage would occur. Finally, as expected, most women's taste aversions included such things as caffeinated beverages, alcohol, and strong-tasting vegetables. One rather unexpected finding was that even stronger aversions were found to meat, fish, and poultry products. One proposed explanation for this was that in our evolutionary past these foods would have been a potential source of harmful microorganisms and parasites, an especially acute danger to an expectant mother's health, given her suppressed immune system.

Flaxman and Sherman (2000) concluded that the available evidence indicates that pregnancy sickness is an evolved adaptation that compels pregnant women to avoid foods that in our ancestral environments would have been potentially dangerous to themselves and their babies. Huxley (2000) agreed that pregnancy sickness serves as an adaptive function but pointed out that its symptoms also reduce levels of certain maternal anabolic and growth hormones, effectively shifting the nutrient and energy partitioning from the mother's body to the developing placenta. Put more simply, the nausea and vomiting of pregnancy sickness forces mom to slow down and eat less, and this has physiological effects that promote placental growth.

Despite this apparent support, the theory does have some unsightly wrinkles in it. Although it appears that those who experience pregnancy sickness are less likely to have miscarriages, no evidence has been produced to suggest that pregnancy sickness is linked to a reduced probability of fetal abnormalities (Flaxman & Sherman, 2000; Weigel & Weigel, 1989). In addition, studies assessing women's overall caloric intake during pregnancy have not found significant reductions in such foods as coffee, mustard, broccoli, pepper, or meat products as might be predicted by Profet's theory (Beal, 1971; Brown, Kahn, & Hartman, 1997). Thus, it seems that the issue of the adaptive value of pregnancy sickness is not settled and awaits further research before definitive conclusions can be drawn. Despite this, Profet's pregnancy sickness theory provides another example of the value of an evolutionary approach in helping to frame questions and motivate research.

compared to our beastly mates! *Homo sapiens* would never act so crudely, so indifferently toward our fellows, especially our children! But how we view ourselves often does not fit with reality. The same brutal life-and-death choices that confront antelopes and leopards certainly faced our ancestors as they fought to scratch out mere existence from their harsh world. It may not be pleasant to face, but the echoes of our species' particular set of cold calculations made over the course of a million years of hardscrabble living are still with us today.

Given the bleak realities of our ancestral past, natural selection no doubt favored those mothers who could make blunt assessments of their infants and circumstances. When the cost of investment was abnormally high and the perceived return was low, fitness was best enhanced by cutting one's losses early and trying again later. In the past, that most certainly meant killing or abandoning an infant. Infanticide, however, is not just something restricted to our ancient past. Throughout most of human history, it has been a rather common fact of life (and death). Roman law, for example, permitted a father to kill or abandon a newborn if it was female, sick, or economically unaffordable. In their groundbreaking work on infanticide, Daly and Wilson (1988a) examined 60 different societies, looking for the most common factors leading to the killing or abandonment of infants. The most common factors were related to: (1) questionable paternity, where an infant may not have been or almost certainly was not the husband's offspring; (2) questionable reproductive value of the infant, i.e., situations in which infant ill health or abnormality raised concerns about the viability of the infant; and (3) questionable maternal circumstances, in which the cost of raising the child might have outweighed the benefits, such as when the mother was unwed or had little familial or paternal support, or where economic hardship seemed inevitable. Note that these factors fall into line with evolutionary expectations: when the cost of investment is high (as a result of lack of support or difficult economic and environmental circumstances) and the perceived benefit is low (because of an unhealthy or abnormal infant), the probability of infanticide increases.

A similar pattern has been found in abortion rates. The prospect for male support appears to be an important factor in determining whether or not a woman terminates a pregnancy. A study tracking abortion rates from 1975 to 1981 found that 65% of unmarried women terminated their pregnancies, compared with only 10% of married women (Henshaw, Forrest, & Blaine, 1984). The promise of financial support from the baby's father, from family, or from the state also decreased the probability of abortion. Teenagers who expected financial help from external sources have been found to be significantly less likely to abort than those who do not (Leibowitz, Eisen, & Chow, 1985; Hill & Low, 1990). Historically, the decision about whether a child was allowed to live or die, was accepted or abandoned, or was closely related to mother's perception of her ability to invest in the infant and to the perception of the child's physical quality (Boswell, 1990). Like all other creatures, we humans have been making hard choices about life and death for a long, long time.

We have seen that humans sometimes "choose" babies by either investing or not investing in a current offspring. Our choices need not always be this cut and dried. Sometimes parental investment can be differentially dispensed rather than just rendered or withheld. Mann (1992) studied mothers who had low birthweight, at-risk twins, where the health status of one twin was clearly better than that of the other. In comparing the behavioral interactions between mom and the twins, she found that mom directed a greater amount of positive parental behaviors, such as holding, soothing, and mutual gazing, toward the healthy infant than the unhealthy one. This difference persisted even when overall rates of exposure and discharge dates were taken into consideration. Thus, mom appeared to be investing more in the healthier of the two infants. Similar findings have been documented in cases in which one infant, by virtue of its sex, was regarded as more valuable (in terms of fitness) than another. Suppose for a moment that you are a female Florida pack rat mom that has hit upon hard times. Would it make sense to allow your daughters to nurse more than your sons? Yes, and, in fact, that's exactly what pack rat moms do. If poorly fed, lactating female pack rats will force their sons off the teat prematurely, sometimes allowing them to starve to death, while giving preferential access to their daughters (Daly & Wilson, 1983). Why? Recall that males tend to have higher reproductive variance than females; in other words, a male either has loads of offspring or hardly any at all. If times are tough, then mom's boys are likely to turn out undersized and uncompetitive in the reproductive marketplace. Her girls, however, are a better bet for producing offspring, even if they come from a disadvantaged home. Therefore, when there is stress in the household, daughters become more valuable to the parents than sons.

It turns out that this logic can be stated in a more general way: parents should invest in the offspring sex that is more likely to produce a higher fitness payoff. This logic was first formalized by biologist Robert Trivers and mathematician Dan Willard and is referred to as the **Trivers-Willard effect** (Trivers & Willard, 1973). Generally speaking, this formal logic dictates that when conditions (in the broadest sense of the word) are good, have sons. When conditions are not so good, have daughters. A son who can be groomed into a strong, smart, high-status male has a decent chance at hitting the motherlode (fatherlode?) in terms of offspring. A weak, stupid, low-status male is likely to grow old—lonely and childless. Thus, under relatively impoverished conditions, it is better to put effort into daughters who are more likely to reproduce and may have the opportunity to attract a high-status male (or, in human terms, marry "up"). Support for the Trivers-Willard effect has been found in many species. Among red deer, for example, high-status females have mostly sons, whereas low-status females have mostly daughters (Clutton-Brock, Albon, & Guinness, 1984). In primates, despite the complications brought on by exogamy, the general rule of "invest in the sex with the higher potential payoff" still holds (Altmann, Hausfater, & Altmann, 1988; Dittus, 1998; van Schaik & Hrdy, 1991).

Humans, too, seem to follow the Trivers-Willard logic. Those for whom conditions are the best want sons, not daughters. In medieval Europe, as well as 19th-century India and China, the practice of female infanticide was most prevalent among the upper classes (Dickmann, 1979). In medieval Portugal, more boys were conceived in the years when rains and harvests were good than in not-so-good years (Jolly, 1999, p. 122). Usually, as couples get older, their material circumstances improve. Thus, one would expect that older women would tend to produce more boys and younger women more girls. That was certainly the case in 19th-century Sweden, where mothers older than 35 had disproportionately more boys, whereas those younger than 25 had more girls (Low, 1991). In Micronesia, anthropologists have observed that high-status parents spend more time with their sons, whereas low-status parents spend more time with their daughters (Betzig & Turke, 1986). Recent studies in the United States show the same pattern. As U.S. families become more affluent, they tend to dote more on sons than daughters. Low-income mothers breast-feed a somewhat higher percentage of daughters than sons. Among high-income mothers, however, about 90% of sons and only about 60% of daughters are breast-fed (Gaulin & Robbins, 1991). Low-income women wait longer to have another child after the birth of a daughter than of a son, whereas the opposite is true for high-income women. Genealogical records show that wives of high-status Mormon men, especially the youngest and most privileged women, tended to have more boys than girls (Mealey & Mackey, 1990). As if to put an exclamation point on all this, studies of American presidents have shown a clear preponderance of sons over daughters. There have been 90 sons of presidents but only 63 presidential daughters (Ridley, 1994). Are couples sitting around making rational calculations about environmental and economic conditions and the potential reproductive success of sons versus daughters and then jumping up and saying "Honey, we should have a girl [or boy]?" Probably not, but the evidence suggests that on a population-wide basis, the genes have played out these odds and have biased us toward certain sex offspring under different conditions. (For more on parental investment and reproductive success, see Box 13.2)

The Plight of Cinderella: Evolution and Nongenetic Offspring

In the previous chapter, we noted that male infanticide had been documented among monkeys, gorillas, and lions as a means of hastening estrus in females and therefore enhancing a dominant male's reproductive success (Hrdy, 1977; Shaller, 1972; Watts, 1989). The general scenario works something like this: a new male takes over a monkey troop or lion pride. If the females in the group already have young offspring, then it is to the new patriarch's reproductive advantage to kill the infants. Why? Two reasons: (1) the offspring are not his genetically, and (2) nursing offspring tends to suppress ovulation, thus delaying the new male's opportunities for impregnating resident females. A new alpha male cannot afford any delays, because the days of his dominance are numbered. Thus, in some species, stepchildren are an excess that natural selection simply cannot afford. What about humans?

As a highly social primate species, with an evolutionary history that includes hierarchical groups with male-on-male competition, we might expect selection against stepfatherhood to have been part of our heritage. Sadly, there is evidence to support this. The men of the Ache tribe of South America have been known to kill newly fatherless children. Even if these children are not put to death, their survival odds are far poorer than those with both biological parents. Ache children raised by stepfathers after the death of their natural father are half as likely to survive to age 15 as those raised by both biological parents (Hill & Kaplan, 1988). Similar increased risk to stepchildren has been reported in cultures as diverse as 17th–19th century Germany and contemporary Caribbean villages (Flinn, 1988b; Voland, 1988).

The heightened precariousness of stepchild life appears to be a universal phenomenon. Daly and Wilson (1988a, 1988b) found that having a step-parent constituted the single most important risk factor behind the severe maltreatment of children. According to 1976 data on child abuse in the United States, the risk of fatal abuse was about 100 times greater for a child living with one or more substitute parents than that for a child living with both natural parents. As expected, stepfathers perpetrated most of this abuse, with the youngest children being at

BOBBI LOW
Global Population and Reproductive Strategies

PROFILE: *Bobbi Low received her B.A. in biology in 1962 from the University of Louisville. In 1967 she earned a Ph.D. in evolutionary zoology from the University of Texas. She is a professor of natural resources and faculty associate in population studies at the University of Michigan. Her teaching and research interests are in the evolutionary and behavioral ecology of wildlife species and resource control and reproductive success in vertebrates, including humans. She is currently engaged in work using evolutionary theory to assist in understanding human activities, especially patterns of resource use.*

BOX 13.2

The Complexities of Global Population
In terms of reproductive success, the human species has been an unqualified triumph. Our population today is at an all-time high and, if current demographic trends prove accurate, will continue to expand for the next 50–100 years. Most scientists agree, however, that this expansion comes at a cost. To one degree or another, global warming, environmental degradation, dramatic declines in ocean fisheries, natural resource depletion, accelerating loss of species and species' habitats, and an array of other environmental concerns have been linked to increasing human population. For many scientists and nonscientists, the answer to this problem is straightforward: we must reduce human population growth. The method for doing this is also straightforward: education and economic development must be improved in developing countries. This conclusion is based on the fact that the wealthy, technologically advanced nations of North America and western Europe have birth rates that are currently at or below replacement levels. Birth rates in the more impoverished regions of Asia, Africa, and South America are well above replacement levels. According to this logic, we can expect birth rates to fall as economic conditions improve in the developing world.

But Dr. Low argues that this type of thinking vastly oversimplifies the situation. A number of studies have shown that within some cultures, wealth and fertility are often positively correlated, with wealthier families having more children than poorer families (Birdsall, 1980). Moreover, as families become wealthier, they consume more. Families in the developed world consume 15–20 times more resources per child than families in the developing world. Increased economic development may simply end up trading a numbers problem for a consumption problem. The reason for this may lie in our evolution.

Different species use different reproductive strategies to maximize their fitness. A tiny insect with a life span measured in weeks (such as a firefly) does best to mature quickly and produce many, many offspring that receive little or no parental care. Biologists refer to this type of species as an **r-selected** species. Humans, however, are just the opposite. We mature slowly, live long lives, and bestow quite a bit of costly care (or parental investment) on our offspring. Biologists call us a **K-selected** species. This is a pattern common in highly competitive environments. As a K-selected species, humans have evolved to be attuned to how much investment is necessary to successfully raise our offspring to maturity. It may be that parents in wealthy nations are not so much reducing their family size to save the earth (although they might tell themselves that) as much as they are simply adjusting their reproductive strategy to best fit with their circumstances. Economic development may serve as an environmental signal compelling parents to invest more heavily in fewer offspring. As part of a fitness-maximizing strategy, **consumption as parental investment** can become just as competitive as reproduction. If the Joneses down the street have two personal computers, a newly renovated activity room, and a new minivan to cart little Suzy to dance classes, soccer practice, and space camp, then won't my kid need at least as much (and probably more) to be successful? It may be that American and European consumption is just as much to blame for felling the rain forests as the poor Brazilian or Indonesian farmer who needs additional land to feed his six kids.

So what's the answer? There may be no easy answers to our global environmental problems, but a first step toward solving them is to recognize the ways in which our own evolved reproductive strategies complicate our situation.

Sources:
Birdsall, N. (1980). Population growth and poverty in the developing world. *Population Bulletin*, 35, 3–46.
Low, B. (2000). *Why sex matters: A Darwinian look at human behavior.* Princeton, NJ: Princeton University Press (see chapter 15).

greatest risk. Evolutionary theory would predict that stepfathers would target the youngest stepchildren for fatal violence, because the younger the child the longer the delay before the mother can be impregnated. Looking at more than 408 cases of child homicide in Canada, Daly and Wilson (1988b) found that stepchildren aged 2 and younger were nearly 70 times more likely to be murdered than children living with their natural parents (Fig. 13.1). After age 2, the relative risk dropped to about one sixth of what it was earlier. In collating abuse and homicide data from the United State, Canada, and Britain, Daly and Wilson (1994) concluded that stepchildren are 50–100 times more likely to suffer fatal abuse than children from intact homes, even after such factors as economic status, maternal youth, and individual proclivities toward violence among remarried and nonremarried populations had been factored out (Daly & Wilson, 1985; Wilson, Daly, & Weghorst, 1980). In addition, as evolutionary theory would predict, step-parents have been found to be discriminatory in their violent behavior, singling out nongenetically related children for abuse and death when both biological and stepchildren were present in the household (Daly & Wilson, 1985; Lightcap, Kurland, & Burgess, 1982). Stepchildren also were more likely to suffer nonfatal abuse than natural children. Wilson et al. (1980) reported that stepchildren under the age of 3 were nearly 7 times more likely to be abused than children living with both natural parents. Among preschoolers, stepchildren were 40 times more likely to be abused, and this increased risk could not be explained by other factors such as family size, socioeconomic status, or maternal age (Daly & Wilson, 1985).

Violent or abusive behavior directed at stepchildren can be understood as a type of negative parental investment that is largely perpetrated by males. Studies also indicate that positive investments on the part of step-parents are also reduced significantly in comparison with those made by natural parents and that females are more often the responsible parties. Economist Anne Case and her colleagues studied the amount of investment in health care, education, and food made by step-parents and natural parents and found significant differences that echo those noted by Daly and Wilson. Using economic data from 1968–1985, Case, Lin, and McLanahan (1999) found food expenditures decreased significantly when a non-

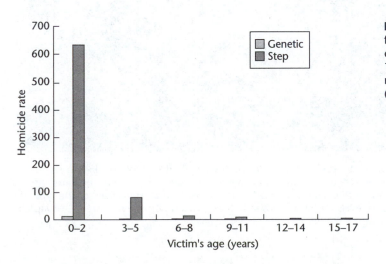

Figure 13.1 The murder rate (per million) for genetically related children and stepchildren of varying ages in Canada from 1974–1990. Note the huge differential in murder rates for the youngest children. (Adapted from Daly & Wilson, 1998.)

biological parent was present in the household. This effect was generally more pronounced when the nonbiological parent was the mother, and the effect was constant for step-, foster, and adoptive mothers, thus supporting the contention that it was the genetic mother–child connection that was critical in modulating food expenditures. In addition, consistent with Daly and Wilson's findings on child abuse, reductions in spending on food were greatest for the youngest children and were independent of the family's economic circumstances. Using data from South Africa, Case, Lin, and McLanahan (2000b) found that when a biological mother was present in the household, significantly more money was spent on such food items as milk, fruits, and vegetables and significantly less on alcohol and tobacco.

Children raised with a nonbiological mother also acquired significantly less education than children raised by natural parents (Case, Lin, & McClanahan, 2001). This effect could not be explained by positing that step-, foster, or adoptive mothers were less competent or generally de-emphasized the importance of education (Fig. 13.2). When biological children were present in a household also having step-, foster, or adoptive children, it was exclusively the nonbiological children whose education suffered, not the biological children. In assessing health care investments, Case and Paxson (2001) found that children with stepmothers had significantly fewer visits to the doctor and dentist for routine care and were less likely to have a consistent locale for health care services. They were also less likely to wear seat belts and more likely to live with a smoker. These effects persisted even when controlling for such factors as household income, parental occupations, and

Households with:	Mean education of the **birth** children in households of this type (Standard error of mean)	Mean education of the **step** (adopted, foster) children in households of this type (Standard error of mean)	Difference between the **birth** and **step** (adopted, foster) children's education (Col 1–Col 2) (Standard error of mean)
Step and birth children of the mother	12.70 (0.16)	11.95 (0.14)	0.75 (0.21)
Adopted and birth children of the mother	12.78 (0.23)	12.16 (0.27)	0.62 (0.35)
Foster and birth children of the mother	12.76 (0.18)	11.43 (0.24)	1.33 (0.30)
Only **birth** children of the present mother	12.81 (0.02)		

Figure 13.2 Mean education levels achieved for both birth children (column 1) and step-, adopted, or foster children (column 2), in various types of households listed at the left in which both birth and nonbirth children were being raised. Note that, regardless of the type of household, the education levels for birth children in these mixed homes were higher. (Adapted from Case, Lin, & McLanahan, 2000a.)

education levels. Significant differences in health care investments were not observed when the stepchild had regular contact (at least two visits a month) with his or her birth mother. Case and Paxson concluded that health care investments are largely mother controlled, and, although legal, emotional, and social factors unquestionably conspire to make stepchild investments more challenging, the role of genetics cannot be ignored in the way that (sometimes scarce) household resources are allocated.

All of this paints a rather dreary picture of step-parents and other nonbiological parenting arrangements. The point here is not that step-parents are evil individuals who abuse, neglect, and otherwise sabotage the happiness and success of their nongenetic children. In fact, on close inspection, one can see that the vast majority of step-parents are not violent or abusive toward their kids. Daly and Wilson (1988b) found that the murder rate among birth children who were less than 2 years old was under 10 per million, whereas it approached 700 per million among stepchildren. Yes, this is a 70-fold increase, but it also reveals that 99.93% of step-parents are not murdering their children. We must, therefore, understand that children raised in step-parent and other nonbiological parenting arrangements are at a greater risk for abuse, substandard health care, lower educational attainment, etc., than children raised by their natural parents. In an absolute sense, however, the level of that risk varies greatly and in many cases may be quite small.

Moreover, there are reasons (speculative to be sure) for suspecting that adopting or otherwise caring for nongenetically related minors might have had a functional place in our evolutionary history. Jolly (1999) pointed out that a family or clan that took in and raised nonrelated youngsters increased their numbers, making them more competitive against other groups. Among nonhuman primates, adopting orphaned youngsters is not unheard of, even among males (Goodall, 1986; Jolly, 1985). The critical point made by evolutionists such as Daly, Wilson, Case, and Trivers is that parental investment is a *resource*. In some circumstances, it is to the parents' advantage to distribute that resource equitably and widely, possibly even extending beyond the boundaries of genetics. However, when that resource is limited, it must be recognized that genetics play a key role in the way the investment will be dispensed among those contending for it.

SUMMARY

Although common genetic interests provide incentive for families to build a common cause, individual fitness can become a source of conflict and strain. This is why it is often *within* families that we witness loving, self-sacrificial acts as well as the most bitter feuds and rivalries. How has our evolutionary history left its imprint on families and child development?

An early source of familial conflict occurs because each child is genetically motivated to secure more resources from mom than those obtained by other siblings. Genetically, mom sees each child as being of equal value, but children see themselves as being more valuable than their siblings. Why? Siblings are related to each other by only 50% of the genome, but a child is related to him- or herself by 100% of the genome. Therefore, what the child sees as a fair distribution of resources within the family is not going to be the same as what mom sees as fair.

Parent–offspring conflict occurs in the first moments of fertilization. Each parent contributes certain genes, called imprinted genes, which tend to operate exclusively in their interests and not necessarily in the interests of the other partner. For example, paternally imprinted genes may tend to push the developing fetus to be as large as possible, even if this puts a burdensome strain on the mother's health. A microscopic tension begins with the exchange of genetic information between sperm and ovum. If the developing fetus is deemed too costly, a spontaneous abortion or miscarriage can sometimes settle a parent–offspring conflict in favor of mom.

Additional evidence supporting the importance of genetic interests within the family has been found in families with nonbiological children. Research has found that having a step-parent constitutes the single most important risk factor for severe maltreatment of children, with the risk of fatal abuse being up to 100 times greater than that for a child living with his or her biological parents. Stepfathers appear to present the greatest violent or abusive threat, especially to the youngest stepchild. Food, education, and health expenditures decrease significantly as well, especially when the nonbiological parent is the mother.

However, it must be noted that this is the case in every nonrelated family. Parental investment is a resource. There may be circumstances when it is to the parents' advantage to distribute that resource equitably and widely, possibly even extending beyond the boundaries of genetics.

KEY TERMS

consumption as parental
    investment
Igf2
imprinted genes

K-selected species
M6p
parent–infant conflict
pregnancy sickness

r-selected species
Trivers-Willard effect

REVIEW QUESTIONS

1. How do *Igf2* and *M6p* work together to maintain a balance between genetic tensions found moments after fertilization?

2. Why has evolution seen fit to tax the mother with stronger ailments or complications during pregnancy? Explain a possible evolutionary theory behind "morning sickness."

3. What is the Trivers-Willard effect and how might it explain the fact that low-income women wait longer to have other children if their first child is a daughter?

4. According to the theory of evolution, why do step-parents invest less in their nonbiological children?

5. Explain a possible reasoning behind adoption or caring for nongenetically related children.

6. Given the difficulties of our ancestral past, evolutionary psychologists might contend that family sizes larger than two or three were rare in our evolutionary history. How might this affect the population issues discussed in Box 13.2 and Bobbi Low's argument that consumption may serve as fitness-maximizing strategy?

SUGGESTED READINGS

Daly, M., & Wilson, M. (1998). The evolutionary social psychology of family violence. In C. Crawford and D.L. Krebs (Eds.), *Handbook of evolutionary psychology* (pp. 431–456). Mahwah, NJ: Erlbaum.

Hrdy, S.B. (1999). *Mother nature.* New York: Pantheon Books.

Jolly, A. (1999). *Lucy's legacy: sex and intelligence in human evolution.* Cambridge, MA: Harvard University Press (especially chapters 4 & 5 on families, parents, and children).

Surbey, M.K. (1998). Developmental psychology and modern Darwinism. In C. Crawford and D.L. Krebs (Eds.), *Handbook of evolutionary psychology* (pp. 369–404). Mahwah, NJ: Erlbaum.

WEB SITES

www.science.mcmaster.ca/Psychology/dalywilson/excerpts.html provides selected excerpts form Martin Daly and Margo Wilson's *The truth about Cinderella* (1998).

www.chass.utoronto.ca/ecipa/archive/UT-ECIPA-SIOW-99-03.pdf the article "Differential Fecundity and Gender Biased Parental Investments" re-examines the application of the Trivers-Willard effect on humans.

www.geneimprint.com good site to learn about the latest research on imprinted genes and their effects.

www.omnimag.com/archives/interviews/profet.html an interview with Marjorie Profet about her ideas on pregnancy sickness and other issues.

14

Childhood Development and Family Life

The Prepared Learner

CHICKENS ARE NOT AS DUMB as you think (or as movies portray them). A day-old chick already knows what's what in the visual world around it. It will peck at an object that is shaped like a sphere but not at one shaped like a pyramid. That's a good thing for a chicken, given that seeds are generally sphere shaped not pyramidal (Tinbergen, 1951). Even more impressive is that they will run for cover when a cross-shaped object moves across their visual field in the direction of its short end but will ignore the same cross-shaped pattern moving in the direction of its long end (Fig. 14.1). Again, this is a pretty smart thing, because one pattern is vaguely that of the harmless long-necked goose, but the other is like that of the very predatory hawk. The fact that chickens make these important discriminations without much visual experience indicates that nature has prepared them for the environments they will face. They are prepared learners. They have been given an evolutionary head start in acquiring the knowledge needed to deal successfully with their worlds. Evolution has been no less generous to human children. What's good for the chicken is good for the child as well!

Do nothing special to an infant and it will still manage to accomplish two of evolution's most stunning skills: walking and talking. It has become increasingly clear to developmentalists that the achievement of these competencies would be nearly impossible without the presence of evolutionary-based biases in learning. This means that infants do not arrive in the world as all-purpose learners who can

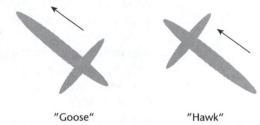

"Goose"   "Hawk"

Figure 14.1 (left) A chicken exposed to this visual image will give little if any response. The image is simply a cross-shaped object moving in the direction of its long end (arrow). (right) If this image is presented, however, the chicken will seek cover. This image is a cross-shaped object moving in the direction of its short end. The left object simulates a harmless goose, whereas the right object simulates the predatory hawk. (Adapted from Hoffman, 1998, p. 9.)

acquire *any* skill, competency, or manner of knowledge. Instead, they arrive as **prepared learners** who are biased toward the acquisition of *certain* abilities and forms of knowledge. These learning biases can be thought of as **evolved adaptive rules** or guidelines, honed by natural selection to direct the infant's learning and development in adaptive ways by structuring the way the infant interprets and interacts with the world. To explain this phenomenon, we will begin with an example from human language learning.

Adaptive Rules in Language Learning

Here's a fairly commonplace exchange between a mother and a very young child:

Mom: (pointing to Rover in back yard): That's doggie! Say hi to doggie! Isn't he a cute doggie?!
Kid: ahhhggg...ooowwweee...ooggg...haaaaa....
Mom: Doggie...yes....doggie! Isn't he pretty?...Doggie!
Kid: ahhhggg...ooowwweee...ooggg...haaaaa...
Mom: Ohhh, such a cute doggie!
(This could go on for quite a while!)

The point here is not that the child is suddenly going to burst out yelling: "OK, I got it. It's a dog, already!" The point is that, through exchanges such as this, in very short order the child will have figured out that the word "doggie" applies to that furry, four-legged, slobbering animal yapping about the backyard and will begin to use the word competently in conversation. This seems unremarkable enough until one realizes that the label "doggie" could have reasonably referred to an almost unlimited number of different aspects of the situation in which it was used. How did the child know that mom was referring to the animal itself and not the animal's fur, color, or legs or the fact that it was running about, sniffing, or fetching a bone or that it was bigger than a cat, ate out of bowl, or a multitude of other possible features that could have been present or in operation when "doggie" was uttered? When one contemplates all the possible attributes that could be tagged to a word each time it is used, it seems almost incomprehensible that children are able to pick up so easily on the correct meanings and usages of linguistic labels.

The ease with which children learn word meanings provides evidence that their learning is facilitated by adaptive rules. These rules direct the child's learning such that when determining what a word means they explore only a restricted subset of all the possible alternatives They are naturally biased toward learning some things and not others. In language learning, at least two important rules have been identified (Markman, 1989, 1990). First, children assume that any linguistic label applies to a whole object rather than a subpart or feature of the object (**whole object assumption**). When mom used the term "doggie" in reference to the animal in the back yard, the child's language learning biases automatically predisposed him or her to apply the label to the entire animal and not to a specific feature or subpart of it, such as its color or tail. Second, infants and children have been shown to operate using a **taxonomic constraint**, by which word labels are generalized on the basis of similarity in kind rather than function or theme. For example, having learned the word "doggie," the child tends to apply it to other dog-like creatures rather than to bones or cat chasing or other concepts associated with dogs. Markman and Hutchinson (1984) showed just how specific the taxonomic constraint is to the linguistic context. Under most circumstances, children group items according to common theme or function. However, when dealing with linguistic labels, their strategy changes dramatically. When Markman and Hutchinson showed children a picture of a cow and asked them to select another object that was the same, they only picked a taxonomically related object (such as a pig) 25% of the time, more often choosing a thematically related object (such as milk). However, when a linguistic label was used to name the object, taxonomic selections increased to 65%. Later studies showed that the taxonomic bias was present in children as young as 15 months (Waxman & Hall, 1993).

Recent studies by University of Oregon psychologist Dare Baldwin (Baldwin, 2000; Baldwin & Tomasello, 1998; Baldwin, Markman, Bill, Desjardins, & Irwin, 1996) have shed light on the processes behind these adaptive language learning rules. Infants as young as 12 months have been shown to be especially sensitive to social cues linking spoken words to objects. These cues include body posture, gestures, pointing, and, most critically, directional gaze. Infants are exquisitely attuned to the eyes of another person and follow eye gaze to locate the object to which a word refers. In one study, for example, as infants explored a novel object, an adult verbally announced the name of the object. Subsequent testing showed that it was only when the adult was clearly visually attending to the object that 18-month-old infants established a reliable connection between the label and the object (Baldwin et al., 1996). When mom says "doggie," the infant automatically zeroes in on the relevant environmental object by using mom's eye gaze as an attentional pointer connecting the verbal utterance to an external object.

Adult behaviors and facial expressions add to the process of tagging the right word to the right object. For example, consider an experiment in which 18-month-olds heard an adult say that she was searching for a "toma." Next, the adult extracted various objects out of a bag. Infants in these circumstances were found to tag the label "toma" only to an object to which an adult had reacted with a facial expression and behaviors indicating a satisfactory resolution to the search (Tomasello & Barton, 1994; Tomasello, Strosberg, & Akhtar, 1996). This led psychologist Michael Tomasello (2000) to argue that perceiving others as **intentional agents** is a uniquely human attribute that plays a fundamental role in children's language learning. Perceiving others as intentional agents means that one understands that others are capable of willfully deploying their attentional mechanisms in the environment around them. Put more simply, infants seem to naturally understand that attention is something controlled voluntarily, that looking at something indicates that a person is thinking about that object, and that a person's subsequent vocalizations are therefore directed at that thing. It is noteworthy that autistic children are far less skilled at using these same social cues to guide their language learning, which suggests that one of the major deficits in this disorder is in the ability to appreciate the information provided by the intentional behaviors of others (Baron-Cohen, Baldwin, & Crowson, 1997).

Adaptive Rules in Motor Behavior: Learning to Walk

Similar evidence of evolutionary preparedness can be found in the process of learning to walk. Children are not born knowing how to walk anymore than they are born knowing how to speak their native language. Given a normal environmental context, however, they are endowed by their evolutionary heritage with the ability to assemble both walking and speaking responses. Thelen and Smith (1994) and Thelen (1995) have shown that the child's acquisition of motor routines, such as learning to walk, can be understood in terms of the interaction between a dynamic, goal-oriented biomechanical system and its environment. To get a sense of what this means, imagine watching a horse gradually picking up momentum as it crosses a grassy field. One of the elegant beauties of equestrian movement is the graceful way in which the horse's gait smoothly shifts as it accelerates. The walk seems to mysteriously and suddenly shift into a trot, then the trot abruptly transforms into a gallop, and the horse is off at full speed. As it gains speed, does the horse consciously think, "OK, time to change to an alternate pattern of relative leg movements?" Probably not, because the horse does not need such thought processes. Given the horse's biomechanical structure, these different gaits simply emerge as the most efficient solutions to the problem of moving its four limbs effectively to generate greater speeds. Horses are not born knowing what gaits to adopt at what speeds. Instead, they discover them as they mature and gain greater locomotor experience. That is why a young foal can look awfully awkward as it tries to keep up with mom. But the fact that every horse tends to discover the same set of dynamic solutions indicates that there are physical constraints on the process. Under normal circumstances, the horse is virtually bound to develop the typical walk, trot, and gallop gaits.

Thelen (1995) and Thelen and Smith (1994) reviewed a considerable amount of data supporting the notion that these same principles apply to infants learning to walk. For example, the biomechanical structure of an infant's legs is such that even in early infancy the leg movements are not random but reasonably coordinated (Thelen & Fisher, 1983). As the infant grows, more differentiated control over the legs is gained. For example, movements can be directed from the knees as opposed to just generated from the hips. This allows the infant to explore a wider range of possible movement solutions to the various locomotor "problems" that are encountered. The "solutions" of rolling over, crawling, and eventually walking, tend to emerge naturally, based on infant biomechanics and their interaction with the surrounding environment. Certain constraints operate on this process at different levels. At one level, infant locomotion is often motivated by certain inborn goals, such as a desire to keep in close proximity to mom or to retrieve desired objects.

At the biomechanical level, the structure of the infant's legs, joints, and muscle attachments guides the manner in which the most efficient goal-attaining actions can be realized. Thus, a toddler could hop or crawl to solve the problem of keeping up with mom, but as different movement solutions to this problem are explored, the very nature of the infant's body almost inevitably leads him or her to the walking movement. Kids, like horses, are not born knowing how to do this, nor are they endowed with a preformed genetic program for it. Instead, they discover it. The fact that under normal circumstances nearly every kid discovers the same general movement patterns (rolling, crawling, walking) indicates how effectively adaptive "walking" rules guide the overall process.

Adaptive Rules and Understanding the Physical World

Language learning is facilitated by rules that attach words to whole objects rather than features or subparts of objects. This seems only to beg the question of how an infant acquires an understanding of what an object is. Here again, we find evidence of evolutionary biases in learning that guide the way in which the child interprets the physical world. For example, from a very early age, infants seem to understand that one solid object cannot magically pass through another. To test very young infants, researchers took advantage of the fact that unexpected events typically result in increased attentiveness on the part of infants, whereas highly familiar or expected events result in boredom and inattentiveness. In other words, if an infant stares intensely at something, we can be fairly sure that it violated the infant's expectations. Developmentalist Renee Baillargeon (1987) showed infants as young as 3 months a solid screen rotating through a 180° arc. Once the infants were accustomed to and rather bored with the moving screen, she placed a block in the pathway of the screen. As the screen moved toward the block, it obscured the infant's view of the block, thus forcing the infant to remember the presence of the block and its potential effects on the movement of the screen. Baillargeon wanted to find out what event the infants would then consider "unexpected." If the infants understood the block to be a solid object that remained present even when it could not be seen, then they would expect the screen to halt when it presumably came into contact with the block. They should therefore find that event rather boring, even though it was actually a novel perceptual event. What ought to surprise them would be the screen doing exactly what it had always done before, that is, completing its 180° arc as usual but, in doing so, "magically" passing through the block. Thus, if the infants had a basic understanding of the physical properties of solid objects, they should be surprised by an event that was perceptually familiar. That's exactly what happened. Infants looked longer when the screen moved uninhibited through its 180° arc. The remarkable finding here is that only a few months after birth infants are already able to evaluate the world based not just on perceptual aspects but by using a fundamental principle of physics: two solid objects cannot occupy the same space at the same time. Put another way, infants seem to have a natural bias against interpreting the world in "magical" ways that violate basic principles of physics.

A more recent study by Gergely and his colleagues provides further confirmation for the idea that infants use their rudimentary knowledge of physics to form expectations about events around them (Gergely, Nadasdy, Csibra, & Biro, 1995). In their study, 1-year-olds watched a video depicting two balls separated by a barrier. One ball rolled up to the barrier, went up and over the barrier, landed on the other side, then rolled to and made contact with the second ball. This sequence was repeated until the infants became bored. Then they were presented with one of two test sequences. Both test sequences presented the two balls without any separating barrier. In one, a ball rolled directly to the other and made contact. In the other, a ball rolled part way to the other, made an arching motion as if going over a barrier, then came down and rolled over to the other ball. The second sequence depicted the same motion that had been shown in the original sequence, and the infants might have been predicted to consider the first sequence as novel and pay more attention to it. The results, however, showed that infants paid relatively more attention to the second (familiar) motion. Although it was a familiar motion, it was unexpected, given the absence of the barrier. With no physical barrier separating the two balls, the infants appeared to expect a direct path of motion and found its occurrence uninteresting. As was the case in the Baillargeon study, infants' judgments of what was "novel" and what was "familiar" were affected by their understanding of physics. Impressive as this may be, it seems that an infant's knowledge of physics goes even further.

Place a newborn in front of a TV on which an image of a cube is displayed. Slowly the image of the cube grows larger, filling up more and more of the screen. How does the infant react to this? His eyes close, his head pulls back, and his arms come forward as he readies for an impending collision with the cube. The infant interprets the enlarging cube as a "**looming**" stimulus, an object with an increasing retinal image size that indicates it is getting (dangerously) closer and closer to the child's head. Schiff (1965) demonstrated that newborns who had never before been exposed to a looming stimulus reacted to it as if it were an advancing projectile. To appreciate the significance of this observation, ponder for a moment all of the other possible interpretations of such a visual scene. The stimulus could have been an object growing larger but remaining stationary. It could have been (what it was) a projected two-dimensional image of a stationary object getting larger. It could have been a stationary object to which the individual was moving closer. Or it could have been a stationary object remaining the same distance away while everything else in the visual scene was steadily becoming smaller. We again seem to have an example of adaptive rules that operate to restrict the range of possible interpretations that the infant uses to understand the physical nature of the environment. A similar example of adaptive rules can be seen in the way infants use movement as a cue to the presence of a single object. For example, show an infant a rod that is moved back and forth behind a block so that the block occludes the middle portion of the rod (see Fig. 14.2). By 2 months of age, infants understand the rod to be a single solid object, not two separate objects moving in synchrony (Johnson & Aslin, 1995).

The biases infants and children bring to their understanding of the physical world can even produce some startling errors. In one experiment, 2- and 3-year-old children were presented with an apparatus containing three tubes pointing

Figure 14.2 Infants exposed to a rod that is moved back and forth behind an obstruction interpret it as a single solid object, not as two objects somehow moving perfectly in tandem. (Adapted from Goldstein, 1999, p. 479.)

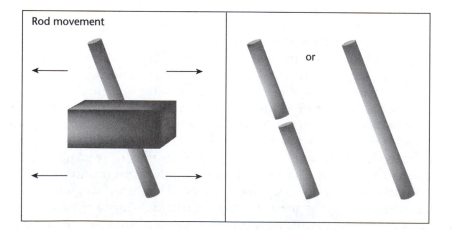

down toward three boxes (Hood, 1995). Tubes and boxes were lined up so that objects dropped into tubes A, B, and C would fall straight into boxes 1, 2, and 3, respectively. After showing children the apparatus, the experimenter introduced a twist, literally. An opaque S-shaped connector was used to attached tube A to box 3, so that an object dropped into A would no longer go straight down into box 1 but would instead fall into box 3. After an object was dropped into tube A, children were allowed to search for the object. Consistently, children search in box 1, not 3. This error persisted for more than 20 trials and even with feedback about the actual location of the object. Not until a transparent connector was used did the children's performance improve. When the path of the falling object was not visible, children assumed it would fall straight down in accordance with gravity, thus producing what is called the **gravity error**. Adult tamarin monkeys also committed this error, indicating that they too interpret their world using a gravity-based rule (Hood, Hauser, Anderson, & Santos, 1999). Experimenters can contrive circumstances in which the gravity rule is exploited, but under most natural circumstances this is clearly a sound rule for both monkeys and humans to apply when trying to understand how the world works.

Despite what seems to be a staggeringly difficult challenge, by the end of the first year of life infants have successfully (and rather easily) become experts on the physical nature of their world. The list of their accomplishments is truly impressive. By 2 months, infants can use movement to identify objects. By 4 months, they can distinguish biological movement (e.g., a person walking) from nonbiological movement (e.g., a toy rolling) (Fox & McDaniel, 1982). By 6 months, infants understand that an inanimate object, such as a block of wood or a billiard ball, must be contacted if it is to move and are surprised if it somehow moves on its own. However, they are not surprised to see a human move on his or her own (Baillargeon, 1995; Kotovsky & Baillargeon, 1998; Leslie, 1982; Leslie & Keeble, 1987). Infants this age also realize that an object cannot roll down two paths at once or emerge from one end of a screen without first having disappeared behind the opposite end. By 7 months, infants are able to use shading, perspective, and interposition (when a closer object blocks the view of a more distant one) to construct three-dimensional depth in the visual scene (Granrud & Yonas, 1984; Granrud, Yonas, & Opland, 1985; Oross, Francis, Mauk, & Fox, 1987; Yonas, Cleaves, & Petterson, 1978). By 1 year of age, children understand how their actions with an object can cause effects on other objects. For example, they appreciate the fact that pulling on a towel tied to a toy will bring the toy within reach (Willatts, 1984). By this age, they also show evidence of attributing emotions and intentions to various objects based on the "behavior" of those objects (Gergely et al., 1995; Premack & Premack, 1995, 1997). In explaining how infants manage to construct a functional understanding of the visual world around them, Donald Hoffman concluded:

> It is impossible. Unless, of course, kids come to the task with innate rules by which they learn to construct visual worlds. If they are born with rules which determine the visual worlds they can learn to construct, and if these rules are universal in the sense that all normal kids have the same rules, then although these rules blind them to many possibilities, these rules can also guide them to construct visual worlds about which they have consensus. Two toddlers, from

opposite ends of the earth, can both be shown the same novel image and see, in consequence, the same visual scene. (1998, p. 14)

John Locke was wrong; we are not born as tabulae rasae. We are born with a wealth of evolutionary history that has adaptively structured the ways we approach and understand the world around us. Evolution has stacked the deck. Our little ones learn what they need to know to function in the environment and summarily dismiss the countless nonadaptive possibilities.

Evolved Developmental Modules

One of evolutionary psychology's basic assumptions is that the human mind is composed of domain-specific modules—mental adaptations for solving certain problems posed by the environment of evolutionary adaptedness. Nowhere has the notion of mental modules been more prominent and aroused more spirited debate than in the area of childhood development. Two proposed **developmental modules** that have attracted considerable attention are those dealing with face recognition and theory of mind.

Face Recognition

"Debate about the nature of face recognition is unbelievably heated right now. It has polarized groups of researchers." That is the assessment of Charles Nelson, a developmental neuroscientist at the University of Minnesota (quoted in Bower, 2001). The polarized groups to which Nelson referred are those who see **face recognition** as an innately specified mental module and those who see it as an outgrowth of more general perceptual capacities. Evolutionists, of course, tend to see face recognition as one of the domain-specific mental capacities honed by natural selection to solve the problem of developing attachments to caregivers and of dealing with the complexities of social living. A number of lines of evidence can be cited in support of this view.

One type of evidence is the expertise that infants show when dealing with faces, a skill that emerges very early in life with little or no learning or experience. Only hours after birth, human infants fixate attention on and are able to imitate facial expressions (Meltzoff & Moore, 1995; Reissland, 1988). Within days, infants can remember faces to which they had only very brief exposure. For example, 3- and 4-day-old babies were given a single 40-second exposure to photographs of female faces. Two minutes later, they were allowed to look at those photographs along with photographs of other female faces. They showed a clear preference for the new photos (Pascalis & de Schonen, 1994). Other studies have shown that only hours after birth, neonates recognize and prefer their mothers' faces to those of other females (Bushnell, Sai, & Mullin, 1989; Walton, Bower, & Bower, 1992). Within just a few days of birth, infants show a greater preference for faces rated by adults as attractive rather than to those rated as unattractive (Slater et al., 1998).

Six-week-old infants are capable of imitating an atypical facial display, such as extending the tongue out of one side of the mouth. In one study, after seeing an adult display this expression, infants attempted to reproduce it and, over time, managed to improve their reproduction of the expression (Meltzoff & Moore, 1995). This suggests that these infants were attempting to match a stored representation of the facial expression. Infants can also remember and identify adults based on facial expressions. While sitting quietly sucking on a pacifier, infants in one study were exposed to two adult males, each of whom made a different facial expression. For example, "Joe" would protrude his tongue at the infant, and "Fred" would pucker his lips. Twenty-four hours later when re-exposed to "Joe" (who now remained expressionless), the infant would protrude his or her tongue. When re-exposed to "Fred," the infant would pucker his or her lips (Meltzoff & Moore, 1995). Although 3- and 4-month-old babies can distinguish among the silhouettes of different dog and cat heads, they nevertheless prefer human head silhouettes to those of dogs, cats, or other animals (Quinn, Eimas, & Tarr, 2001). Nelson (1993) found that infants are more discriminating than adults when it comes to identifying differences in the faces of both monkeys and humans. Collectively, this research suggests that human infants are born with an evolutionary head start when it comes to understanding and processing face information.

Neuropsychological studies have provided another line of evidence in favor of an evolved face recognition module. Damage to selected parts of the brain's right temporal lobe can produce a condition called **prosopagnosia**, or the inability to recognize faces. An individual with prosopagnosia usually can identify other objects or even parts of the body but is impaired in discriminating among faces and associating a face (even his or her own) with a specific person or name (Banich, 1997; Tranel, Damasio, & Damasio, 1988). Farah, Rabinowitz, Quinn, and Liu (2000) described the case of Adam, a prosopagnosia victim who suffered temporal lobe damage when he contracted meningitis only 1 day after birth. As a teenager, Adam continued to show very poor face recognition ability. Often, when brain damage occurs very early in life, other healthy parts of the brain assume the function of the injured area. This did not occur with Adam, which suggests that the face recognition area is genetically predetermined and that other areas cannot usurp its domain. Brain imaging studies have shown that a specific part of the right temporal lobe, the fusiform gyrus, may be the critical face recognition area (Kanwisher, 2000; Kanwisher, McDermott, & Chun, 1997). Significant increases in the neural activity of the fusiform gyrus have been recorded when healthy adults examine faces. These same increases in activity are not found when people look at other objects, letters, or even the backs of human heads.

Not all the evidence, however, is consistent with a genetically specified face module. For example, elevated levels of activity in the fusiform gyrus can be demonstrated as subjects gain increasing expertise in perceiving visual patterns other than faces (Gauthier & Nelson, 2001; Gauthier, Tarr, Anderson, Skudlarski, & Gore, 1999). This suggests that "face" processing per se may not be hard-wired to this particular brain region. Other research has suggested that an infant's early "expertise" may not be confined to faces but may be more generally directed toward certain geometric properties, some of which are found in faces. An infant's sensitivity to faces can be found within only days or even hours after birth, but a preference for curved over straight contours also can be found only a few days after birth. Some studies report that a newborn's visual preference for faces can be eliminated if the outer contour of the face is masked (Pascalis, de Schonen, Morton, Deruelle, Fabre-Grenet, 1995; Simion, Valenza, & Umilta, 1998). Young infants also show a marked preference for forms in which more elements are present in the top

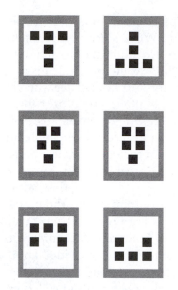

Figure 14.3 Three pairs of nonface stimuli in which one member of each pair has more elements in the top portion than the bottom. When these pairs are presented to newborns, they look longer at the one with more elements at the top. (Adapted from Simion et al., 2001, p. 62.)

half than in the bottom half. An infant will stare longer at a collection of squares forming a T pattern than at one forming an upside-down T (Simion, Cassia, Turati, & Valenza , 2001; Fig. 14.3). This could indicate that what newborns possess is not a specific preference for faces but a more general preference for curved, asymmetrical visual patterns that can easily become an effective face recognition device with some (maybe quite minimal) experience. No doubt the question of the existence of a special-purpose face recognition device in the human brain will continue to generate productive research in the future. (Note: Infants may be good at recognizing other faces, but they may practice deception with theirs! See Box 14.1.)

Theory of Mind

A **theory of mind** refers to an understanding of another's mental state. Based on external cues, we humans readily make assessments about the internal emotional, attitudinal, or motivational state of another. For example, if you spot a friend and wave "hi," only to have her ignore you and pass by without a word, you might instantly begin to wonder "what's wrong with her?" Is she mad at you for something? Did she lose her job? Did so-and-so tell her about what you were doing last night? In one way or another, all these are inferences about *her* mental state. Our attributions concerning others' mental states can get quite involved, but generally they are not quite this elaborate. If someone is staring at a magazine, we assume they are reading an interesting article. If someone rubs his or her eyes, we assume they are weary. A nod signifies understanding. A blank stare and glazed-over eyes mean boredom. These are simple, everyday mental state attributions that come naturally to humans. The ability to make these attributions seems to unfold naturally in children, starting with the ability to recognize intentions in actions.

From a very early age, infants seem to recognize that human actions are motivated by the intentions of the actor. Ponder for a moment what an infant perceives when witnessing an adult engaging in a continuous series of actions, such as turning on a faucet, splashing the face with water, grabbing a towel, and drying off.

John Whitfield
Deceptive Baby Faces?

DECEPTION FUELS DOMESTIC BLISS
Evolution May Make Men Ignorant and Gullible
21 November 2001

BOX 14.1 **Nature Science Update**

Gentlemen: ignorance is bliss and gullibility is the best policy. A new mathematical analysis suggests that evolution favours babies who don't much resemble their fathers, and males who believe their partner when she says a child looks just like him.

Anonymous-looking newborns make for uncertain fathers. But they also allow men to father children through undetected adultery, Paola Bressan of the University of Padova calculates. The assertion—common across many cultures—that babies are the spit of their dad, is a way to get men to care for their offspring despite their uncertainty, she adds.

Mummy, daddy and baby might look like a heart-warming scene of family togetherness. But evolutionary biologists have no truck with such sentimental nonsense: to them, each of the trio is pursuing its own, often competing, interests.

The wild card is adultery. A baby comes into the world unsure of whether the male providing for it is its biological father. Being rumbled could mean neglect, or worse—infanticide. It's easy to see how, in an evolutionary sense, babies might not want to resemble anyone in particular.

Whether fathers benefit from having recognizable babies is trickier. If dads pass on some genetic badge that allows them to identify their children, they could avoid raising another man's child. But they will not be able to sneak any offspring into other families.

Bressan proposes that these two forces cancel each other out. Having anonymous babies stops fathers mistakenly rejecting their own children, which, in a slowly reproducing species such as humans, is probably a cost greater than that of raising someone else's child. When the interests of babies and mothers are also taken into account, genes for anonymous babies should spread.

Human babies certainly seem to be masters of disguise. Neutral observers asked to match infants to their fathers do only slightly better than chance.

In fact, some of newborns' features seem designed to enhance anonymity, says evolutionary biologist Mark Pagel, of the University of Reading. He points to the blue eyes and blond hair of many newborn Europeans, which result from genes being switched off at birth.

Could evolution mark babies with their fathers' identity? Pagel thinks so: "There's a lot of genetic variation to play with, and all sorts of things that are very easy to produce developmentally," he says.

Mother's Instinct

So everybody's happy? Not quite: if all babies are anonymous and fathers are uncertain, males would invest less in kids whether they sired them or not.

A mother's strategy to counteract this, says Bressan, could be to remark on the baby's likeness to his father. Her mathematical model shows it can benefit a father to believe these assertions and increase his care for the child, as long as the chance that he is being deceived is slim enough.

Denson McLain, a behavioural ecologist at Georgia Southern University likes this idea. "The harm to a father of being sceptical towards his own children is greater than the cost of rearing someone else's child," he says.

McLain has found that mothers remark more on their babies' resemblance to their partner if he or his relatives are there to hear her than if he is absent.

Pagel, however, doubts that evolution would favour trusting males. The warm glow that dads get from hearing that junior has their nose might simply be "good old-fashioned vanity," he suggests.

Sources: **John Whitfield**, reprinted by permission from *Nature*, November 21, 2001. Copyright © 2001 by Macmillan.

Does the infant perceive this sequence as just an indistinguishable blur of activity, or does he or she realize that each is a separate, discrete act motivated by the actor's intention to accomplish some goal? Baldwin and her colleagues (Baldwin, Baird, Saylor, & Clark, 2001) showed infants videos of people engaged in a sequence of simple everyday activities. Later, infants saw these scenes replayed with the action frozen in different places. The infants' interest peaked in scenes in which a discrete act was frozen before its completion, whereas no increase in attention was noted when that action was frozen after its completion. It was as if the infant realized that the actor intended to accomplish some goal (such as drying the face) and was surprised when the act terminated before the goal was complete. The imitative behavior of somewhat older infants shows a similar sensitivity to the intentions of the model. Meltzoff (1995) had two groups of 18-month-old infants observe a model opening a jar. One group watched as the model grasped a jar, turned the lid, and successfully opened it. When given the opportunity, these infants readily reproduced the model's behavior. The second group watched as a model attempted to open the jar but failed because his hand kept slipping off the lid. When given their chance to reproduce the act, the infants in the second group did not reproduce the model's failed act but, instead, successfully opened the jar, thus reproducing the intended act. These experiments reveal that by around 1 year of age, a human infant is capable of thinking beyond the superficial structure of human actions to process them at a deeper, more cognitive level.

Penetrating into the minds of others takes an even more dramatic turn at around age 4. In what has become a classic study, Wimmer and Perner (1983) presented 3- and 4-year-olds with the following scenario. Puppet Sally and puppet Anne have been playing ball. Sally must leave, but before she does, she takes the ball and places it in a box. While she is gone, Anne removes the ball from the box and hides it under the bed. Sally returns. At this point, the child witnessing this bit of puppet intrigue is asked where Sally will look for the ball. It turns out that the child's answer hinges on his or her age. Three-year-olds generally say that Sally will look under the bed, but 4-year-olds say she will look in the box. Wimmer and Perner interpreted these results to mean that by age 4 children understand that people can entertain "false beliefs." In other words, the contents of one's mind do not necessarily have to conform to reality or the knowledge of other minds. Three-year-olds, on the other hand, have not yet recognized this radical independence of minds: the fact that minds can possess knowledge not in keeping with reality or with what others know. Three-year-olds seem to assume that because they know where the ball is, Sally must know, too. Thus, according to this research, it is not until about age 4 that children developed a full-blown, "theory of mind," in which they fully appreciate how the mental lives of others affect behaviors.

Subsequent research has indicated that the transition that children go through from age 3 to 4 may be more gradual then first suspected. Many 3-year-olds will pass the Sally–Anne test if, instead of witnessing Anne moving the ball from box to bed, the child herself is allowed to move the ball. Moreover, 3-year-olds often show implicit signs of understanding that the ball is not in the box, such as increased eye fixations on the box (Clements & Perner, 1994; Slaughter & Gopnick, 1997). Thus, it is possible that the 3-year-olds understand more about the Sally–Anne situation then they can express verbally.

The "theory of mind" issue has attracted considerable research attention for at least two important reasons: (1) it may be a uniquely human ability (this will be explored further in the last chapter), and (2) it may be based in a domain-specific mental adaptation. This second point has been bolstered by findings indicating that the ability to infer the mental states of others may be lacking in autistic children (Baron-Cohen, 1997). Autistic children typically fail the Sally–Anne test (i.e., they think Sally will look in the box; Baron-Cohen, Leslie, & Firth, 1985; Baron-Cohen, 1995). They also show an array of other symptoms indicative of failure to appreciate the mental states of other, including: a lack of spontaneous pretend play (Baron-Cohen, 1987), an absence of speech terms referring to mental states (Baron-Cohen, Leslie, & Frith, 1986; Tager-Flusberg, 1992), and an inability to use directional gaze as an indicator of linguistic reference (Baron-Cohen, Baldwin, & Crowson, 1997). However, their ability to comprehend nonmental representations, such as maps, graphs, or models, is generally unimpaired (Charman & Baron-Cohen, 1992; Leekam & Perner, 1991; Leslie & Thaiss, 1992). All of this suggests a specific "theory of mind" deficit as a major component of autism. The brain area(s) responsible for this capacity have yet to be clearly identified, but one study has indicated the right orbitofrontal cortex as an important center for theory of mind (Baron-Cohen et al., 1994). Much work remains to be done in understanding autism and its links to theory of mind, but the connection currently observed strongly suggests the presence of an evolved module for tapping into the mental lives of others, one that appears disabled in autistic individuals.

Growing Up Human

As youngsters mature through childhood into adolescence and adulthood, the evolutionary perspective continues to provide a useful framework for understanding the storm and stress of that passage. Two developmental domains have benefited especially from the application of evolutionary principles: (1) the presence of sexual dimorphism in maturation rates and (2) the developmental patterns in child/parent relationships.

Sexual Dimorphism in Maturation Rates

Boys and girls do not mature on the same schedule. The physical changes that transform the childhood body into that of an adult begin about 2 years earlier for females than males (Tanner, 1990). Although there has been much evolutionary-based speculation about why **sexual dimorphism in maturation rates** exists, only a modest amount of empirical data has addressed these ideas. The maturation rate differences between males and females is actually more complex than the simple fact that females start sooner than males. The sequence of events also varies between the sexes. For females, the onset of physical changes, such as increases in height and development of secondary sexual characteristics, typically precedes gametogenesis, that is, the production of ova. For males, the sequence is reversed. They typically produce some potent sperm cells before the onset of any dramatic physical changes (Surbey, 1998; Weisfeld & Billings, 1988). Thus, our evolutionary history seems to have been one in which selection acted in favor of physical maturation before reproductive maturation in females but vice versa in males. Why?

One argument is that this reflects varying reproductive strategies in males and females. Adolescent males must prepare themselves for mate competition in a hierarchically structured social system. Over the course of our evolutionary history, an advantage might have gone to those males whose physical maturation did not too greatly outpace their mental and emotional maturation. This may help explain why males generally mature later than females. Moreover, reproductive potency might be achieved early in this process to maximize lifetime fertility and the range of available reproductive strategies. A boy who matures early physically can rise quickly to the top of his social hierarchy and thus optimize his mating opportunities. Studies documenting the numerous advantages of early maturation for boys tend to support this reasoning. Early-maturing boys are perceived as more masculine and physically attractive (Jones & Bayley, 1950). They also tend to be more socially confident, athletic, and popular and are more often placed in positions of leadership by their peers (Duke et al., 1982; Livson & Peskin, 1980). An early-maturing boy, therefore, often has the physical prowess, emotional poise, and sexual potency to take full advantage of his prominent status in the male hierarchy.

It would be too hasty, however, to see this as casting males whose physical maturity comes later into the evolutionary abyss. The fact that boys achieve gametogenesis early means that even if a boy looks physically immature, he is likely to be sexually potent. Thus, it may be that the male maturation sequence allowed for late-maturing males to engage in a more "stealth" reproductive strategy, in which they could take advantage of whatever reproductive opportunities might arise, without being perceived as a direct threat by other males (Weisfeld & Billings, 1988). The fact that late-maturing males tend to be more creative, flexible, and innovative in problem solving might offer some support for this view (Jones, 1957, 1965). However, one might also expect that late-maturing males would be more socially skilled or intelligent than early maturers, which appears not be the case. Thus, it seems that the evolutionary view provides a reasonable story about why males mature as they do, but additional research in this area is still necessary.

The fact that girls mature physically before being fertile indicates that there was selection pressure for a "preparatory period" to allow girls to develop the skills necessary for good mate selection and effective child care. In most industrialized countries, girls reach menarche between ages 12 and 13. Studies of hunter–gatherers, however, indicate that this milestone probably was not reached until much later (around age 16) in our ancestral past (Howell, 1979). Thus, the lag between the ages at which a girl appears mature and when she is actually fertile was probably somewhat longer in our past than it is today. A mature-looking girl is more likely to attract male attention and be permitted child care responsibilities than an immature-looking one. Thus, in our ancestral past (and possibly to a slightly lesser extent today), early physical maturation would allow girls time to gain some degree of experience in assessing male worthiness and in developing child care skills before being capable of actually bearing children. This hypothesis may sound reasonable, but an adequate test of it has not been performed. It is true that older girls contribute considerably to the care of their younger siblings, both in hunter–gatherer societies and in modern cultures, and in so doing they gain useful skills (Shostak, 1981). However, proving that maturation rates evolved to allow this practice would appear to be a difficult challenge indeed. The data comparing early-maturing and late-maturing girls show a complex mix of effects, few of which are directly relevant to this evolutionary hypothesis (see Shaffer, 1993, pp. 181–182, for discussion). As with the boys, the evolutionary perspective on girls' maturation rates represents an open area for future research.

Developmental Patterns in Parent–Child Relationships

The ebb and flow of the parent–child relationship through the childhood and adolescent years also has come under scrutiny from evolutionary theorists. Slavin (1985) put an evolutionary spin on Freud by suggesting that repression evolved to maintain the critical kinship bond between parent and child. Because the child's fitness interests before adolescence are entirely intertwined with those of the parents, the child would be highly motivated to repress any thoughts or memories that might conflict with the goal of maintaining parental acceptance. Adolescence marks the onset of the child's independent fitness interests, so that this repression is lifted and increasing parent–child conflicts arise. Although one might question Slavin's explanation, there is little doubt that the parent–child relationship is often more stressful during adolescence than in the years before. A more straightforward evolutionary explanation is that the child's reproductive success directly affects the parents' fitness (Trivers, 1974). A child who fails to reproduce or who severely degrades his own reproductive value has not only placed his own genetic material in peril but also that of his parents. Adolescence is the time when an offspring's reproductive value is poised for realization, and one would expect parental mindfulness of their offspring's behavior and choices to peak at this time as well. One also would expect this parental mindfulness to be more intensely focused on daughters than on sons, because maternity certainty is absolute but paternity certainty is not. In other words, parents can be certain that a daughter's offspring is their genetic relative but can never have this same degree of certainty for any of their son's presumed offspring.

As expected, increased stress in the parent–daughter relationship has been documented to be coincident with menarche (Hill, Holmbeck, Marlow, Green, & Lynch, 1985). Within 6 months of menarche, daughters perceived their mothers as less accepting and both parents as more controlling and less egalitarian than before menarche. Flinn (1988a) conducted extensive studies on the phenomenon of "**daughter guarding**" among families in a Caribbean village. He found that fathers actively monitored and restricted their daughters' interactions with potential suitors. As one might expect, this did not always go over well with the daughters. A peak in argumentative and combative father–daughter interactions was found when daughters were between the ages of 11 and 15. Daughters with resident fathers were found to spend more time at home and to have more antagonistic interactions with nonrelated males than did daughters without resident dads. From an evolutionary perspective, this is exactly the sort of behavior that might be expected if dad were trying to ensure that his daughter landed a high-quality mate. Recall that a high-status male looking for a long-term mate would be most interested in a relatively young, sexually inexperienced female. Although it may have been overbearing and rancorous, "daughter guarding" seems to have paid off. In the end, Flinn (1988a) found that daughters with dads were more successful at achieving stable marriages than those without. A variety of reasons may explain why parent–child relationships can sour during adolescence, some having little to do with reproductive value or parental fitness concerns. However, one should not discount the fact that some elements of the parent–child relationship have deep evolutionary histories. This may help explain some of the motivations behind both the parents' and the child's actions and attitudes.

The role of reproductive value in the parent–child relationship evidences itself not only in parent–adolescent turbulence but also in feelings of grief. The degree of grief that parents experience at the loss of a child has been shown to be affected by the child's perceived reproductive value. Crawford, Salter, and Jang (1989) asked adults to imagine the deaths of variously aged children and the intensity of grief associated with each. Grief intensity grew in step with the child's age, peaking just before adolescence, just at the time when the parent's investment in the child's reproductive potential was about to pay off. Of course, one might argue that most offspring do not "pay off" with reproduction until well after adolescence, so why wouldn't grief peak closer to age 20 or so, when most of today's offspring are getting closer to marriage and family. The answer is that, in our ancestral past and, indeed, throughout most of our recorded history, the marriageable age was much younger than what it is today. In fact, Crawford et al. (1989) found that the curve describing imagined grief fit almost perfectly with the curve describing the life-history reproductive potential among !Kung hunter–gatherers (the correlation was .92). Parental grief also has been found to be affected by the child's health status and the degree of phenotypic similarity between the parents and the child (i.e., to what extent did the child look like the parent or parents) (Littlefield & Rushton, 1986). These findings add support to the notion that reproductive value plays an important role in the affective bond between parent and child. A healthy child is more likely to reproduce, and a phenotypically similar child is perceived to (and may, in fact) have more genetic overlap with one of the parents.

Postreproductive Kin Investment

Humans live relatively long lives compared with other mammals (and average life spans grew significantly in the past century in most modern societies). Our slow maturation rate means that children live many years before reaching sexual maturity and that their parents need to survive many years to see them through to that point. Still, the extended human lifespan is rather unusual. Studies of lions and baboons show that they generally do not live much past the point of viability for their last offspring (Packer, Tatar, & Collins, 1998). We humans, rather strangely, seem to greatly outlive our reproductive usefulness. In females, the reproductive potential is abruptly terminated decades before bodies cease to function. In the cold competitive world of natural selection, it seems odd that we are "allowed" to live longer than is necessary to reproduce or to protect and rear our children. What's the point?

It's possible that there is none. Remember that not all the products of evolution are adaptations. A lifespan that extends well past the reproductive and parenting years could simply be an incidental byproduct of other adaptive traits, such as slow maturation rates, bipedalism, big brains, or, most intriguingly, parental nurturance. Studies of primates have shown a connection between care bestowed on offspring and lifespan, for both males and females (see Fig. 14.4). Those who engage in more nurturance of offspring tend to live longer (Allman, 1999, see data summary, pp. 178–188).

For example, among chimpanzees, females almost exclusively care for offspring, getting little if any help from males. Among captive populations, females also live about 42% longer than males. Among monogamous apes, such as gibbons and siamangs, where males are far more active in caring for young, the differences

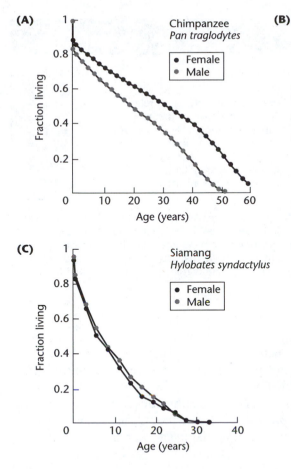

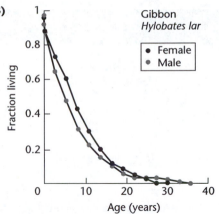

Figure 14.4 Lifespans in three primates species. **(A)** The relative proportion of male and female chimpanzees alive at various ages. Note that at every age females make up a larger proportion of the population than do males. **(B and C)** The relative proportion of male and female gibbons and siamangs alive at various ages. Note that in both species the proportion of males and females is nearly equal. In chimpanzees, males engage in almost no care of offspring, whereas, in gibbons and siamangs, males engage in extensive offspring care. (Adapted from Allman, 1999, pp. 178, 180.)

in lifespan are greatly reduced. In fact, siamangs are the only apes among which males carry infants and actually have slightly longer lifespans than females (Allman, Rosin, Kumar, & Hasenstaub, 1998; Fig. 14.5). Part of this is undoubtedly because those who care little for offspring (usually males) engage in more risk-taking behaviors. However, another relevant fact is that selection may favor genes in caregivers that protect them from the damaging effects of stress. Sapolsky (1992) found that among vervet monkeys that were subjected to chronic stress, only the males suffered substantial cell loss from the brain's hippocampus. Females' brains were protected by the hormone estrogen, which helps to maintain a healthy supply of the neurotransmitter serotonin in the hippocampus (Pecins-Thompson, Brown, & Bethea, 1998). Serotonin, in turn, aids in preventing the destructive effects of stress hormones on the brain. Selection seems to favor those caregivers who can better handle the stresses and strains of life, resulting in more resilient, longer-living caregivers. The fact that many of these same patterns are repeated in humans (e.g., females tend to live longer and care more for young; men tend to suffer more from the ill effects of stress; married men live longer than singles, etc.) suggests that similar effects may be present in us as well.

It is also possible, however, that long lifespans do have some direct adaptive value. From a gene's point of view, having extended kin around as a continual

Primate	Female/Male survival ratio	Male care	
Chimpanzee	1.418	Rare	
Spider monkey	1.272	Rare	
Orangutan	1.203	None	
Gibbon	1.199	Pair-living, but little direct role	Increasing male survival / Increasing male care
Gorilla	1.125	Protects, plays with offspring	
Human (Sweden, 1780–1991)	1.052–1.082	Supports economically, some care	
Goeldi's monkey	0.974	Both parents carry infant	
Siamang	0.915	Carries infant in second year	
Owl monkey	0.869	Carries infant from birth	
Titi monkey	0.828	Carries infant from birth	

Figure 14.5 The relationship between female/male survival ratio and the extent of male care of offspring in different species. Note that in those species in which male care is rare to nonexistent, such as chimpanzees, orangutans, and spider monkeys, there is a female-biased survival ratio (>1). However, in species in which there is extensive male care of offspring, such as siamangs and owl and titi monkeys, there is a modest male-biased ratio (>1). (Adapted from Allman, 1998, p. 184.)

source of investment could be highly advantageous, even (maybe *especially*) if those kin are not currently rearing their own direct offspring (Gaulin, 1980). This would help to explain the sexual dimorphism that exists in declining reproductive value with age. Although male fertility does decline with age, it does not go through the dramatic cessation that occurs in postmenopausal women. Gaulin hypothesized that given the heavy physiological investment that females make in their offspring, at some point in their lives it is adaptive to stop investment in new offspring and concentrate resources on the offspring of relatives (grandchildren, nieces, nephews, etc.). Males, on the other hand, invest far less physically in direct offspring and, therefore, can more viably split their investments between new direct offspring and kin offspring. An elder helping to provision grandchildren or other kin offspring is still (genetically speaking) helping him- or herself.

This idea has been advanced as the grandmother hypothesis—the idea that in our ancestral past those offspring with grandmothers around to aid in their provisioning would have been at a selective advantage over those without (Hawkes, O'Connell, Blurton-Jones, Alvarez, & Charnov, 1998). Some anthropological data tend to support the hypothesis. For example, among Hazda hunter–gatherers, Hawkes found that a woman's foraging activity was (not surprisingly) greatly reduced after having a baby (Hawkes, O'Connell, & Blurton-Jones, 1997). This often produced nutritional stress on the new mother and her other young children unless offset by the foraging activity of grandmothers. Children with grandmothers who helped out with foraging were found to have significantly enhanced growth and development compared with those receiving no grandmotherly aid. Despite this evidence, the grandmother hypothesis remains controversial and requires more testing before we can be confident that helpful grandmothers were an important selective advantage.

From an evolutionary perspective, one would expect that **grandparental investment** would follow a predictable pattern; that is, maternal grandmothers would invest the most whereas paternal grandfathers would invest the least in their grandchildren. Why? Because of the combination of two important factors: genetic certainty of offspring and the balance between investing in kin versus direct offspring. Because maternal grandparents have **maternity certainty** (they know their daughter's children have their genes) and paternal grandparents have **paternity uncertainty** (they must trust that their daughter-in-law's children are their son's as well), then we would expect maternal grandparents to be more investing then paternal grandparents. In addition, because postmenopausal women can no longer reproduce but older men can, women have nothing to gain by withholding any resources from grandchildren (or kin offspring), whereas men might. Smith (1988) surveyed nearly 600 grandparents using the amount of time spent with grandchildren as a measure of investment. He predicted the following pattern of time spent: maternal grandmothers > maternal grandfathers and paternal grandmothers > paternal grandfathers. His results generally conformed to the prediction, with maternal grandmothers spending nearly twice as much time with their grandchildren as paternal grandfathers, with the other groups in between. A similar pattern also has been found with maternal and paternal aunts and uncles (Gaulin, McBurney, & Brakeman-Wartell, 1997).

The End of the Dance: Death and Bequeathment

Over the course of the last two chapters, we have seen the shadow of our evolutionary heritage at nearly every stage of human development. From the microscopic balancing act within the womb, to morning sickness, to the parent–offspring struggles going on from childhood through adolescence, the contours of our evolutionary past reveal themselves in vague hints or bold relief. Very little of it, however, was especially unique to our species. Quite to the contrary, most of what we have reviewed so far evidences a profound commonality between humans and other animals. The Trivers-Willard effect, parent–offspring conflicts, and the presence of adaptive rules in learning—none of these respect the comforting but largely subjective boundaries we erect between ourselves and other species. At the end of life, however, we see clear signs of human uniqueness. The rites, rituals, and sentiments that attend human death are shared in common with none of earth's other inhabitants. One of those rituals, of course, is the inevitable reading of the will. Only humans amass material possessions and then bequeath them to their surviving loved ones. But, as if nature simply could not resist having the (very) last laugh, even this distinctly human practice has not escaped evolution's shroud.

Strongly polygynous societies tend to be male-biased in their inheritance practices (Cowlishaw & Mace, 1996; Hartung, 1982). In other words, where men are permitted multiple wives, families tend to leave a larger proportion of their wealth and resources to sons rather than daughters. Many factors may play into decisions about inheritance, but evolutionary principles would predict a male bias in inheritance in polygynous societies. We have already seen that males have higher reproductive variance than females (some men have many, many offspring and others have few or none). Polygyny would tend to exaggerate these differences, as men with more resources can acquire multiple wives. Thus, in a polygynous society, more so than in a monogamous one, it would be to a parent's reproductive advantage to provide ample resources to a son to raise his chances of siring multiple offspring. Daughters, whose reproductive output is already more limited, are less likely to require vast resources to attract mates and reproduce. As evolutionists would predict, male-biased inheritance tends to disappear as a society becomes more monogamous.

The evolutionary approach has also been fruitful when applied on a more personal level. In an analysis of more than 1,000 wills, Smith, Kish, and Crawford (1987) found that specific patterns of bequeathment fit an evolutionary model: (1) kin were bequeathed more goods and property than non-kin; (2) closer kin were bequeathed more than distant kin; (2) when heirs were equally related, more goods and property went to those of higher reproductive value; and (4) in accordance with the Trivers-Willard hypothesis, wealthier families left more to their sons, whereas poorer families left more to their daughters. You can't take it with you, but you can make sure it continues to serve your fitness interests even after the dance is done.

SUMMARY

Human infants and children show evidence of evolved adaptive constraints or rules in a variety of areas, such as language learning, learning to walk, and learning about the nature of the physical world. These constraints serve to narrow the range of possible alternatives infants entertain as they try to interpret information in the world around them. Some evidence has accumulated for specific mental modules in face recognition and theory of mind. In face recognition, the early infant preference for face-like stimuli and physiological evidence linking the fusiform gyrus with face recognition abilities argue for a specific face-recognition module. However, other evidence has not been so supportive. In theory of mind, the evidence seems stronger and suggests that a deficit in "mind-reading" abilities may be behind autism.

Boys and girls show dimorphism in maturation rates, with girls maturing earlier than boys. Girls also show a different pattern of maturation, with physical maturation preceding reproductive maturation. Boys show the opposite pattern. These patterns may be linked to varying reproductive strategies, but additional evidence seems necessary before drawing any firm conclusions. Reproductive value appears to affect parental attachment to children as well as the degree to which material goods and resources might be dispensed to offspring in the form of inheritance.

KEY TERMS

adaptive restraints

daughter guarding

developmental module

face recognition

grandparental investment

gravity error

looming stimulus

maternity certainty

paternity uncertainty

prepared learner

prosopagnosia

sexual dimorphism in
   maturation rates

taxonomic constraint

theory of mind

whole object assumption

REVIEW QUESTIONS

1. Describe some of the evidence that indicates that infants' learning about the physical nature of the world is guiding by adaptive constraints or rules.

2. What are the whole object assumption and the taxonomic constraint? How do they guide language learning?

3. Cite evidence that supports the presence of a face recognition module. What are the arguments against such a module?

4. Why would maternal grandparents be expected to invest more in their grandchildren than paternal grandparents? Is there evidence to support this?

5. Why would evolutionists expect to find a relationship between polygyny and male-biased inheritance? How does reproductive variance play into this relationship?

SUGGESTED READINGS

Bjorklund, D.F., & Pellegrini, A.D. (2002). *The origins of human nature: Evolutionary developmental psychology*. Washington, D.C.: American Psychological Assocation.

Low, B. (1998). The evolution of human life histories. In C. Crawford & D.L. Krebs, (Eds.), *Handbook of evolutionary psychology* (pp. 131–162). Mahwah, NJ: Erlbaum.

McDonald, K. (1988). *Sociobiological perspectives on human development*. New York: Springer-Verlag.

WEB SITES

www.socialpsychology.org/develop.htm Social Psychology Network's developmental page, with numerous links on many topics in developmental psychology.

www.oklahoma.net/~jnichols/dev.html MegaPsych developmental page, with many developmental links.

www.usc.uwo.ca/clubs/wpa/links5.html Western Psychological Association's developmental Web page, with many links and information on varied topics.

HIGHER COGNITION

15

Thought and Reasoning: Comparative

"For man, therefore, the life according to reason is best and most pleasant, since reason more than anything else is man."

ARISTOTLE, NICOMACHAEN ETHICS

"...reason is wholly instrumental. It cannot tell us where to go; at best it can tell us how to get there. It is a gun for hire that can be employed in the service of any goals we have, good or bad...."

HERBERT SIMON, REASON IN HUMAN AFFAIRS, (1983, PP. 7–8)

Whatever Happened to the Rational Soul?

SOPHOCLES CALLED REASON "the gods' crowning gift to man." Greek and medieval philosophers identified the rational soul as a unique human attribute of divine origin. This deeply respectful attitude toward our capacity for reason is reflected in the quote from Aristotle that opens this chapter. For him, reason was the very essence of humanity—the faculty that separated man from beast. In its absence, our animal nature, insatiable in its brutality, would rear up uninhibited and unashamed. However, as the second quote indicates, much of the Aristotelian-type reverence for reason has largely dissipated in modern times. What went wrong with our rational souls?

As an astute observer of human behavior and decision making, as well as a man who wrote with some of the 20th century's most horrific events in mind, Simon's sober assessment of rationality offers none of the poetic admiration of past thinkers. He was well aware of the fact that it was the intellectual class of Europe, more than the working class, that so enthusiastically embraced National Socialism (the Nazis). These intellectuals included such luminaries as scientist Konrad Lorenz and philosopher Martin Heidegger (Carey, 1992; Deichmann, 1966; Weindling, 1989). At a time when only 15% of the German population were members of the Nazi party, 45% of German physicians were members (Kater, 1989). Simon recognized that increased education and superior rational skill did not guarantee a more humane outlook on life. It may be that in the time since Aristotle we have come to realize that the human capacity for rational thought does not fundamentally alter our basic motives and desires. Evolution has bestowed on us the ability to think with more sophistication and power than any other creature on earth. We use that power, however, primarily to construct more effective means for achieving certain ends. The ends or goals are most often *not* the products of rational thought but of emotion and desire (Calne, 1999).

If our increased brain power has not necessarily made us "better" but simply "more able," then it is important for us to examine critically what it is about our minds and our thinking that has evolved. To do this we need to start by defining what is meant by rational thought. In cognitive science, definitions of rationality vary, but a common theme among them is the notion that rationality is a process whereby concepts are assembled, organized, or transformed to draw conclusions and guide actions (see for example, Calne, 1999; Clark, 2001; Halpern, 1989; Medin & Ross, 1997). Thus, when an organism is being rational, it is organizing or assembling its knowledge in ways that make it more able to interact effectively with its environment. With humans and possibly some other animals, this often means gaining a more sophisticated understanding of the regularities and patterns present in the environment and the causal forces that create those patterns. Reason is an aspect of intelligence that works in conjunction with other intellectual faculties, such as consciousness, memory, representation, and transformational operations. Neurologist Donald Calne (1999) provided an extensive discussion of rationality in his book *Within Reason: Rationality and Human Behavior*, arguing that reason can be thought of as a concept assembler that gives priority to empirical data and allows for flexibility in the face of changing environmental circumstances. This is in contrast to instinct, which is relatively inflexible. Support for this view can be found in studies of patients who suffer from frontal lobe damage and resulting dysexecutive syndrome, in which memory, language, and other general cognitive functions are unaffected but the ability to organize thoughts and concepts in an adaptive way is lost (Duffy & Campbell, 1994). For example, one patient concluded that money must grow on trees, because both money and trees were green. This patient also had difficulty constructing an appropriate sequence of motor actions, often putting the box of detergent into the washer with the dirty clothes rather than pouring the detergent into the machine. Over the course of evolution, humans have acquired an unprecedented proficiency at organizing thoughts and ideas in functional and insightful ways. This, in turn, has provided us with an unparalleled talent for figuring out how things work and, most recently, has elevated us to treacherous heights in our ability to control and manipulate the natural world.

Ape Thinking and Human Thinking

If rationality is the ability to assemble concepts in adaptive ways, then what evidence is there of this ability in our ape cousins and how does it compare with human rationality? Comparative studies allow us to more precisely identify those aspects of rationality that might be unique to our species. Do comparative studies reveal qualitatively different thought patterns in humans, or is human thinking simply a quantitative extension of that of chimpanzees? The hominin evolutionary line split from that of the chimpanzees' some 5 million years ago. What happened to thought over the course of those 5 million years?

Studying thinking in animals has never been an easy proposition. Field studies require researchers to spend months or years in an animal's natural environment documenting its lifestyle, habits, breeding activities, and, when possible, evidence of problem solving or other "intelligent" behaviors. Over the last half century, a wealth of data from field observations has shown apes to possess surprisingly well-developed abilities in social cognition, tool use, and recognition memory (see Byrne, 1995; Goodall, 1986; Tomasello & Call, 1997, for discussions). Field observations are important, but many questions about animal thinking can be adequately answered only through controlled experimental tests. Here again, there are significant challenges and difficulties. Finding appropriate tests that reveal something meaningful about an ape's mental powers is not easy. One test, however, that has proved quite useful is the **tube task**, originally developed by Haggerty (1913) but more recently modified and extensively employed by Elisabetta Visalberghi.

Visalberghi's Tube Task

Figure 15.1A shows a simplified representation of the basic tube problem. A desirable parcel of food, often a peanut, is placed in a clear, horizontally oriented tube. To extract the food, the subject must insert a smaller stick into the tube and push the food out one end. Initially, Visalberghi and Trinca (1989) presented the tube problem to capuchin (New World) monkeys. Within a relatively short period of time, most of the monkeys had figured out how to use the stick to extract the food. But did they understand the causal relations that produced the desired effect? That is, did they recognize that the location of the food within the tube and the diameter and length of the stick relative to the tube all played important roles in the ultimate extraction of the food? To examine this, the experimenters complicated the task by removing the single stick and replacing it with (1) a bundle of sticks that was too wide to be inserted and therefore had to be unbundled to be useful, (2) three short sticks that had to be inserted one after the other in the same end to push out the peanut, and (3) an H-shaped stick with two shorter sticks attached at right angles that had to be removed before the stick itself could be inserted (Fig. 15.1B).

The monkeys successfully solved each of these more demanding tasks, but their performance showed no evidence of understanding the underlying conceptual relations involved in each task. For example, in the bundle version of the test, the

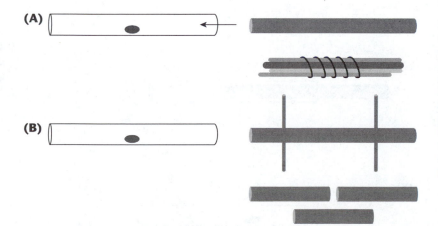

Figure 15.1 (A) A simplified schematic of the tube task. A desired food reward, such as a peanut, is placed inside a transparent tube. A stick must then be inserted into the tube to push the reward out of the tube. **(B)** In more demanding conditions, a bundle of sticks, an H-stick, or a set of smaller sticks must be used. (Adapted from Povinelli, 2000, p. 103.)

monkeys often attempted to insert the entire bundle of sticks or, after breaking the bundle, selected a broken piece that was too small to work and discarded more appropriate sticks. In addition, in the three (short) sticks version, they often failed to insert all three sticks into the same end, thus failing to make contact with the food. Finally, in the H-stick version of the test, they often removed the obstructive sticks from one end, only to attempt inserting the other end in the tube. The fact that these errors did not decrease over the course of the testing suggests that the monkeys' problem-solving abilities were based more on trial and error than on any real understanding of the causal nature of the task. The monkeys simply tried everything and anything to get at the food and eventually stumbled upon a solution.

To further explore what the monkeys understood about the tube problem, Visalberghi and Limongelli (1994) modified the tube task into a **trap tube task**. A trap was placed in the tube to catch the food and prevent it from being extracted (Fig. 15.2A). The monkeys now had the additional problem of trying to extract the food without letting it fall into the trap. The way to do this was to push the food to the side away from the trap by inserting the stick in the end farther from the food. Of the four monkeys tested, only one successfully solved the trap tube problem. To see if this monkey had acquired an understanding of the way the trap worked, Visalberghi and Limongelli (1994) rotated the tube 180° so that the trap was facing up rather than down and was therefore ineffectual (Fig. 15.2B). Despite the fact that the trap could no longer "trap" the food, the monkey continued to push the food out the end of tube away from the trap. He even continued this strategy when presented again with the original (trapless) tube! This behavior strongly suggests that the monkey was following a procedural rule ("always insert the stick in the far end of the tube") rather than operating on the basis of an understanding of how the trap worked.

What about apes? Might we expect their bigger brains to help them develop a more sophisticated understanding of the tube task? Visalberghi, Fragaszy, and Savage-Rumbaugh (1995) tested 10 apes (five chimpanzees, four bonobos, and one

Figure 15.2 (A) In the trap tube problem, a trap at the bottom of the tube must be avoided if the reward is to be successfully extracted. The solution is always to insert the stick at the end of the tube further from the reward (correct) instead of from the end closer to the reward (incorrect). **(B)** For the inverted tube condition, the end at which the stick is inserted is irrelevant. (Adapted from Povinelli, 2000, p. 105.)

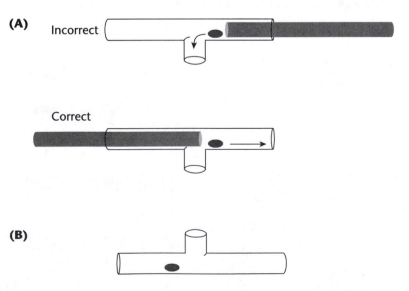

orangutan) on three versions of the tube task: (1) the basic tube task, (2) the bundled stick condition, and (3) the H-stick condition. All the apes quickly solved the basic tube and the bundled stick problems. However, their performance was more error prone on the H-stick condition, in which they committed many of the same errors as the monkeys. Limongelli, Boysen, and Visalberghi (1995) administered the trap tube problem to five chimpanzees, two of whom, after more than 70 trials, managed to successfully solve the task. To test if these two were simply following a procedural rule ("always insert the stick in far end of the tube"), the experimenters varied the location of the trap in the tube, thus sometimes requiring the chimps to put the stick in the end of the tube closer to the food to successfully retrieve it. The apes quickly adjusted their behavior to successfully retrieve the food every time. Based on this, the experimenters concluded that the apes had acquired an understanding of the causal nature of the task. A number of researchers, however, have expressed skepticism about this conclusion, noting that the apes could have been following a different procedural rule, such as "always push the food away from the trap," and that the critical inverted (trap at the top) condition was not administered (Povinelli, 2000; Tomasello & Call, 1997).

Povinelli (2000) tested four chimpanzees on the trap tube test and found that only one was able to solve the problem after 100 trials. The successful subject was then tested on the inverted tube condition to see whether she had acquired an understanding of the way the trap worked or was simply following a procedural rule. When the trap was facing upward, this subject continued to push the food out of the tube by placing the stick in the far end of the tube. This behavior persisted even when the stick was pre-inserted in the opposite end of the tube before the trial, thus requiring the ape to remove the stick from one end and transport it to the other (farther) end for insertion. Even when the trap was facing upward and extra effort was required, the ape persisted in inserting the stick in the far end. In addition to this finding, Bard, Fragaszy, and Visalberghi (1995) found that, when presented with the H-stick and three short sticks versions of the tube task, most of the apes committed more errors in later trials, thus showing no evidence of having gained a conceptual understanding of the nature of those tasks. These findings support the notion that apes may be more efficient learners than monkeys but, like monkeys, may fall short of comprehending the underlying causal attributes of the problems they confront.

Using Tools and Understanding the Physical World

In 1997, primatologist Rosalind Alp was following a group of chimpanzees through the West African forests of Sierra Leone. She watched as a female chimpanzee pondered the tantalizing fruits dangling from a heavily thorned kapok tree. The fruits were too much for any red-blooded chimp to resist, but the thorny branches promised to exact a heavy toll on any animal trying to pilfer them. To the jaw-dropping surprise of our primatologist, the chimpanzee broke off a couple of branches, positioned them under her feet and held them securely to her soles with her dexterous toes. With her feet protected, she ascended the tree unscathed and, having found a comfortable perch from which to munch kapok fruits, proceeded to break off another branch to sit on, sparing her delicate rear end from a thorny encounter (Alp, 1997).

Figure 15.3 The flimsy rake tool had a base made of a thin strip of rubber (left), whereas the rigid tool had a base made from plywood. When the flimsy tool was laid out horizontally on the table, with its base placed straight and perpendicular to the handle, its overall appearance was very similar to the rigid tool. However, it was not sturdy enough to serve as an effective rake. (Adapted from Povinelli, p. 165.)

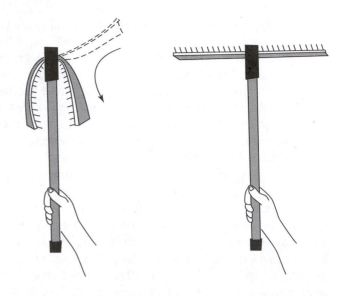

Seats and sandals are not the only tools that wild chimpanzee have invented. Sticks are often used to "dip" or "fish" in termite mounds or ant hills (Goodall, 1986). Chimpanzees can be quite meticulous about selecting the right size stick and have been observed modifying sticks for more effective use by removing extraneous twigs and leaves. Chimpanzees have also been observed using leaves as sponges to mop up blood or water and as makeshift umbrellas for protection from rain (Byrne, 1995; McGrew, 1992). They also employ stones in a hammer-and-anvil fashion to crack nuts (Boesch, 1991; Matsuzawa, 1994). Finally, and perhaps most impressively, chimps appear to be the only nonhuman animals to have ventured into the manufacture and use of dental equipment. McGrew and Tutin (1973; as described in Hauser, 2000) reported several instances in which one chimp fashioned a short stick and, in the course of grooming another chimp, used the stick as a dental probe for cleaning and picking the groomee's teeth. These reports are intriguing but leave unanswered the level of conceptual understanding that chimpanzees possess as they construct and utilize their various implements. Do they, for example, understand that such properties as the shape, rigidity, and length of a stick are integral to its functionality as a tool? Do they have a conceptual grasp of the basic causal relations between the nature of the tool, how it is used, and the end that it produces? To address these questions, we need more controlled studies.

A study involving David Premack's (1976) language-trained chimpanzee, Sarah, suggested that chimpanzees might indeed possess such an understanding. Sarah was shown a series of slides depicting various object transformations, such as a whole apple on the left and an apple cut in half on the right or a blank piece of paper on the left and a paper with writing on it on the right. Accompanying the slides were depictions of various tools, and Sarah was to pick the one that produced the represented transformation. For example, when presented with the slide showing the whole and sliced apples, she was given a choice of a pencil, a bowl of water, and a knife. In this case, of course, the knife would be the proper selection. Sarah consistently selected the proper tools for slides showing both familiar and unfamiliar items. This strongly suggested that she had acquired an understanding of the functional properties of tools and the kinds of effects they cause. Other language-trained apes also passed this test, but non-language-trained apes failed. Sarah also demonstrated that she could discriminate the proper tool based on the sequence in which items were presented. For example, when shown "paper→written-on paper," she selected a pencil. When shown "written-on paper→paper" she selected an eraser.

Sarah's performance was impressive, but critics have charged that Premack's methods may not have adequately eliminated the possibility that Sarah was basing her responses on associative strategies, such as recognizing that knives and certain states of apples (such as being in a cut-up state) go together (Povinelli, 2000; Tomsello & Call, 1997). Moreover, as a human-encultured, language-trained ape, Sarah may not have been representative of typical chimpanzee behavior or ability. Probably the most strenuous critic of the notion that chimpanzees' problem solving and tool use are based on an understanding of abstract physical principles is Dan Povinelli. He presented a series of more than two dozen experiments (Povinelli, 2000) in which he concluded that chimpanzees' understanding of the physical world was based on directly perceivable statistical and perceptual regularities and not on **abstract physical causes**, such as force, mass, or shape.

To understand how he drew this conclusion, we need to take a close look at an example of one of his experiments. One experiment involved teaching seven chimpanzees to use a rake-like tool to retrieve a desired food item. They then were given a choice between a sturdy rake tool and a flimsy one (Fig. 15.3). Before testing, the apes were allowed to use both the sturdy and flimsy rakes in free play so that they were familiar with the properties of each. When the test was administered, chimps were shown each rake and its sturdiness or flimsiness was clearly demonstrated. The two rakes were then placed before each chimp, with a food reward placed behind each. The chimp was allowed to choose a rake by pulling on one of the handles to "rake in" the food. It is important to realize that once the two rakes were set before the chimp, they looked similar perceptually (the experimenter straightened out the flimsy rake blades upon setting it in place). The key for the chimp was to recognize that one rake did not possess the physical property of rigidity and therefore was incapable of pushing the food reward. If this was understood, then the chimp should select the rigid rake. If the chimp based his or her selection on directly perceivable patterns, then selection should have been more or less random.

Six of the seven chimps selected randomly. The lone chimp who consistently selected the rigid rake was given a follow-up test to determine whether her performance was based on an understanding of the importance of rigidity or she was simply following a procedural rule ("avoid the flimsy rake"—a rule, incidentally, that Povinelli believed she might have adopted based on her fear of rubber snakes). The follow-up test supported the notion that she was following a procedural rule and not using an understanding of rigidity as a basis for her response. Other experiments designed to test the chimps' appreciation of such physical properties as shape, connectedness, and supportiveness produced a similar pattern of results (Povinelli, 2000). In every case, Povinelli found evidence that chimpanzees based their problem solving and tool use on their well-developed perceptual and pattern-recognition abilities, not on an abstract understanding of physical principles (for more on ape "folk physics," see Box 15.1).

DAN POVINELLI
Ape Folk Physics

PROFILE: *Dan Povinelli received his undergraduate degree in physical anthropology from the University of Massachusetts at Amherst in 1986 and his Ph.D. from Yale University in 1991. As a faculty member in the psychology department at the University of Louisiana, Lafayette, Povinelli has created something of a stir with his comparative work dealing with the mental lives of apes and children, often finding differences that cut against the grain of conventional wisdom.*

BOX
15.1

Do Apes Understand the Notion of "Connectedness?"

One aspect of Dan Povinelli's work has been to look at what apes understand about the nature of the physical world. For example, do they base their problem solving on salient perceptual patterns or on a deeper understanding of causal relations that are not always immediately obvious? In one experiment, chimpanzees were trained to use a stick to obtain an otherwise out-of-reach apple. Figure 15.A depicts the percentage of times that the apes selected the correct stick when given a choice between one capable of retrieving the apple and one that was not. For example, on the trials depicted by the open bars (bars 2 and 4 on Fig. 15.A), the apes were presented with a long and short stick (depicted below each bar). On almost 100% of the trials they selected the correct (long) stick. However, note that on the "aligned" conditions (dark bars 1, 5, and 6) the apes choose randomly between the two selections. Here they were presented with a long stick and three shorter sticks, lined up to appear equal in length to the long one. Before being placed in front of the apes, the short sticks where clearly shown to be three separate detached elements. Despite this, nearly half of the time the apes tried to use them to get the apple. When the three short sticks were staggered, rather than aligned (bar 3), the apes clearly knew not to choose them.

To confirm that the apes were using perceptual patterns as a basis for their judgments, a second experiment was conducted using connected/unconnected, staggered/aligned sticks (Fig. 15.B). In this way, the perceptual appearance of the stick could be separated from its physical connectedness.

On a given trial, an ape would be shown that a staggered/connected stick was clearly a single piece (the experimenter would wave it about before the ape) and that the aligned/unconnected stick was made of separate pieces (the experimenter would hold the pieces apart from one another before lining them up). Then the two were laid before the ape, and he or she was allowed to choose one for retriev-

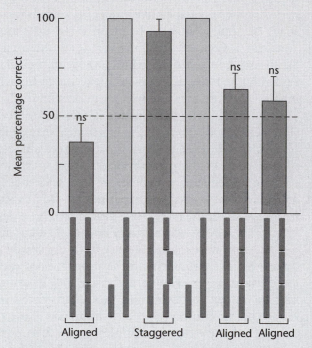

Figure 15.A Mean percentage of trials in which the apes first chose the correct tool for retrieving the apple. The dotted line indicates the 50% or chance level of performance. The stick icons below each graph represent the choices that were presented to the apes in each condition. (Adapted from Povinelli, 2000, p. 238.)

ing the apple. Figure 15.C shows that when given a choice between staggered/connected and aligned/unconnected (condition A), the apes almost always chose the wrong one (aligned/unconnected). Note that in condition B, when both sticks looked the same but only one was physically connected, the apes chose randomly. The results seemed clear: apes were basing their choices on perceptual patterns and not on an understanding of physical connectedness. The understanding of unseen physical causes may be a trait that evolved along the hominin line after its separation from the chimpanzee line.

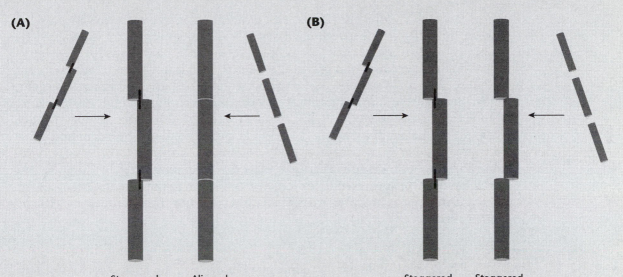

(A)

Staggered–
connected   Aligned–
                   unconnected

(B)

Staggered–
connected   Staggered–
                   unconnected

Figure 15.B Stick tools used in Povinelli experiment (experiment 18, Povinelli, 2000). Pair (a) consists of one in which three short sticks that have been connected into a single unit but are staggered so that the three elements can be seen easily (staggered/connected) and another in which the three elements are unconnected but aligned so that they give the appearance of a single unit (aligned/unconnected). Pair (b) consists of the staggered/connected stick and another that is staggered but unconnected. Note that for (b) both look the same but only one is a single solid unit. (Adapted from Povinelli, 2000, p. 241.)

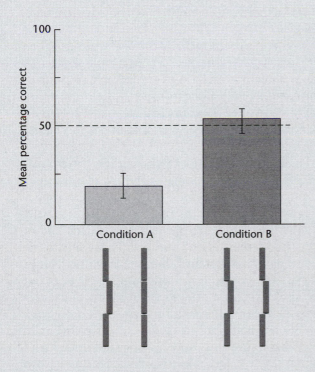

Figure 15.C Mean percentage of trials in which the ape chose the correct stick for retrieving the reward. Note that when presented with pair (a) (Fig. 15.B), the apes consistently chose the wrong one (the aligned/unconnected one). When presented with pair (b), they chose randomly. Thus, apes based their choices on the physical appearance of the stick, not its underlying physical nature. (Adapted from Povinelli, 2000, p. 243.)

Source: **Povinelli, D. (2000).** *Folk physics for apes: the chimpanzee's theory of how the world works.* Oxford: Oxford Univerisity Press.

Povinelli's findings are in line with archaeologist Steven Mithen's conclusions about the differences between chimpanzee and human tool use (Mithen, 1996). Chimps, Mithen argued, lack the "technical intelligence" that allows for the manipulation and transformation of physical objects. This leaves them unable to create sophisticated tools composed of distinct elements or parts and unable to create novel uses for the simple tools that they do construct. For example, a sharpened stone can be used to cut meat, but a human would readily recognize that it could also pry stones out of a crack in the sidewalk, punch a hole in leather, pound a nail in a tree, hold down papers on a windy day, and be thrown at birds to scare them from a berry bush. These alternative uses tend to go unrecognized by chimpanzees, which is unsurprising given that alternative uses often require an understanding of the underlying physical properties of an object and how those properties relate to other objects.

Numbers

That chimpanzees have a rudimentary understanding of numbers is not surprising. Many species assumed to be not nearly as "smart" as chimps have demonstrated numeric abilities. One of the most celebrated cases was Alex, Irene Pepperberg's gray parrot (Pepperberg, 1994). Daily training for more than 2 decades produced the avian world's foremost seed-crunching number cruncher. When presented with a tray containing keys and corks of different colors and quantities (e.g., one gray cork, two white corks, three gray keys, and four white keys), Alex proved capable of reporting the correct number of a specific set of items (e.g., Irene: "How many white corks, Alex?" Alex: "Two."). Lions also seem to have some basic understanding of numbers. When members of a lion pride heard a tape with one strange lion roaring on it, they reacted by boldly approaching the presumed intruder. When they heard a tape with three lions roaring, they backed off (McComb, Packer, & Pusey, 1994). In the wild, chimpanzees demonstrate a similar tendency. A group of males will usually only move against another male if the intruder is alone and if they have him outnumbered by at least three to one (Harcourt & deWaal, 1992; Hauser, 2000). But once again, we can ask how "deep" this understanding of numbers goes?

Numerical knowledge can exist at different levels. One of its simplest forms is **subitization**, which refers to an understanding of number based on pattern discrimination. We often can "read off" a quantity almost instantly, for example, when a die rolls up a two and a four or when someone tosses three coins onto a table. Without counting, the visual pattern formed in these examples is usually enough for us to determine instantly how many are present. At the deep end of numerical knowledge is **conceptual understanding of number.** This refers to the fact that a number represents a symbol with a certain value and meaning relative to an entire system of numerical symbols. For example, the number "5" does not only signify a certain quantity, it also specifies a unique value within the entire number system. It is, for example, a prime number, half of 10, 5 times more than 1, and what you get if you add two more to a pile of three items. A very young child may know enough to prefer five cookies to one but probably does not understand that five cookies is two less than seven and that 15 cookies would be required if two of her friends are also to receive the same amount. Where are chimpanzees when it comes to this scale of numerical knowledge?

The answer is that the most highly skilled, human-trained, chimpanzees do seem to have an understanding of numbers that approaches a number concept. The chimpanzee Sheba was given more than 3 years of training in associating Arabic numerals with quantities and, as a result, has developed some basic arithmetic skills. When she found a box containing one orange and later found another box containing two oranges, she successfully selected the number 3 from a set of cards depicting the numerals 1–4 (Boysen, 1996). Another chimp, Ai, demonstrated even more impressive abilities. Ai, too, has had years of numeric training and as a result has learned the count sequence from zero to 10. When presented with number sequences on a computer monitor, Ai can reliably pick out the correct sequence, regardless of the intervals involved. For example, Ai would know that 2,8,9 is a proper sequence but 4,6,1 is not (Matsuzawa, 1985). In these two chimpanzees, at least, a simple understanding of number concept appears to be present.

Another study, however, demonstrates how difficult it can be for even the most highly trained chimpanzees to use their numerical knowledge. Two of the world's smartest chimps, Sarah (the astute tool selector) and Sheba (of mathematical fame) were paired together in a game of give and take (Boysen, 1996; Boysen & Bernston, 1995). One chimp played the role of selector, and the other was the receiver. The selector was allowed to choose between two containers holding delicious treats. The trick, however, was that the container chosen by the selector always went to the receiver. Thus, if Sarah was the selector, then the container she chose went to Sheba, not to her. The two containers had different quantities of treats. Therefore, a numerically keen chimp ought to choose the one with fewer treats in it so that she would ultimately receive the more generous portion. Unfortunately, neither Sarah nor Sheba was able to master this task. When presented with the treats, it was simply impossible for either chimp to inhibit the urge to select the one with more in it. In a later test, however, the treats themselves were replaced by Arabic numerals. So instead of holding four treats, the container held a card with the number "4" on it. When numerical symbols replaced the actual food items, Sheba (the number-trained chimp) was able to choose the lesser symbol so as to receive the greater reward. This experiment, like Povinelli's work discussed previously, demonstrates how difficult it is for chimpanzees to "think past" their immediate perceptual inputs. The acquisition and use of symbols may aid in this ability (as it did for Sheba), but a symbol-using chimp is a rare specimen indeed and nonexistent in the wild.

Sherlock Holmes Reasoning

Premack and Premack (1994) dissected causal reasoning into three levels. At the most superficial level, an organism witnesses a series of events and must be capable of simply tagging the correct (also visible) cause to the events. For example, when witnessing one billiard ball strike and move another, one must realize that (at least superficially) the movement of the second ball was caused by the first. At the intermediate level, the organism must be capable of decomposing a series of events into constituent causal elements, such as differentiating and correctly labeling the actor, action, and instrument in a sequence of events. Thus, one must be able to recognize that John (actor) rolled (action) the ball (instrument) that struck and moved the second ball. At the deepest level, an organism must be capable of making inferences about unseen causal forces, such as seeing a dead body on the pool room floor and, from the available evidence, deducing that John must have murdered the hapless victim by throwing a billiard ball at his head (what the Premacks call **Sherlock Holmes reasoning**). In a series of studies, Premack and Premack (1994) provided evidence that chimpanzees were capable of all but the deepest level of causal reasoning.

The Premacks showed their star pupil, Sarah, a series of videos depicting someone using a tool to engage in an action, such as a character named John painting a wall with a paintbrush. Although her performance was less than stellar, Sarah was reasonably accurate in labeling the actor, action, and instruments present in each video. Sarah, however, failed when presented with a video that required her to infer an unseen cause. An example was a video of someone trying to stamp out a fire. After viewing the video, Sarah had to decide if matches, a bucket of water, or a pencil was the cause. Other studies reinforced this same general theme. For example, chimpanzees were trained to run down a pathway where a food reward awaited at the end. However, on some trials the food reward was replaced by a rubber snake (something very frightening to chimps). The Premacks wondered if one chimp could deduce what was at the end of the pathway based on the reaction of another chimp who had just completed a run. One chimp watched in an adjacent holding area as another ran down the pathway. Then the chimp who had just completed a run, and was consequently very happy or very agitated, was placed in the holding area along with the observing chimp. Could the observing chimp deduce what was at the end of the pathway based on the emotional status of the "just been there" chimp? Apparently not. No chimp ever altered its running behavior as a function of the emotional state of another. Once again, the chimpanzees seemed unable to link an unseen cause (what was at the end of the pathway) with a current event (the emotional state of the other chimp).

A final test in this series was particularly interesting, because it involved a cross-species comparison between chimpanzees and young children. Both children and chimps watched as an experimenter placed two different treats in two separate containers. The subjects' view of the scene was blocked momentarily, and, when their view was restored, they could see the experimenter eating one of the treats. The question being addressed was whether the subjects could figure out which treat was still available for them to retrieve and consume. For example, if a chimp watched an experimenter place an apple in the container on the left and a banana in the container on the right and next saw the experimenter eating the banana, would the chimp realize that the container on the right was now empty and that only the apple in the left container was still available to be eaten? Although 3- and 4-year-old children generally performed well on this test, only one of four chimpanzees was able to solve it. In a second test, the same procedures were followed with one exception: each treat was wrapped up in a rather elaborate, time-consuming fashion before being placed in its container. Thus, it had to be unwrapped before it could be eaten. However, no extra time was allotted between the blocking of the scene from the subjects' view and the moment when they saw the experimenter consuming one of the treats. Therefore, they should have been able to figure out that the treat that the experimenter was eating could not have come from either of the containers. Neither the chimps nor the younger children recognized this. Only the 4-year-olds realized that both treats were still in their respective containers.

What Has Evolved? Understanding the Unseen Causes

A common theme emerges as we look across these studies examining chimpanzees' abilities in solving the tube task, using tools and numbers, and making causal attributions. Chimpanzees are extraordinarily adept at pattern recognition and procedural learning but tend to struggle when required to organize abstract concepts. With the tube task, they could avoid the trap procedurally, but they failed to understand conceptually how it functioned. With tools and the statics and dynamics of the physical world, they proved quite capable in recognizing and reacting to meaningful patterns but failed when it came to understanding and using more abstract physical principles, such as rigidity or connectedness. With number, they gained some conceptual appreciation of value but had difficulty applying that knowledge when faced with tangible, sensory information. Finally, their ability to make cause-and-effect judgments faltered when they were required to make inferences about the ways in which unseen, abstract variables affected currently perceptible events.

Different researchers have attempted to characterize this human–ape cognitive distinction in different ways. Merlin Donald (1991) argued that apes have **episodic minds**, meaning that current perceptual patterns can cue associated patterns in memory but have difficulty consciously organizing and integrating separately stored episodic memories to create sophisticated schemata. Put more simply, apes live in the "here and now," supplemented by whatever memories happen to be cued by current sensory inputs. They do not integrate knowledge across time to create coherent "theories" about how the world works or to construct an enduring sense of self. This, he believes, is a key factor in their limited capacity for imitation, teaching behavior, and the invention and use of symbols (Donald, 1998). The Premacks, Povinelli, and Tomasello and Call all concur with this assessment to one degree or another but are generally more restrictive in their conclusions. As we have seen, the Premacks (Premack & Pemack, 1994) primarily concentrated on the ability to make causal inferences based on unseen factors (Sherlock Holmes reasoning) as an important dividing line between human and ape thinking. Povinelli (2000) contended that an ape's understanding of the physical world ("ape folk physics") is based upon directly perceivable patterns and not unseen, abstract forces. For example, to the chimp, when a billiard ball strikes and causes movement in another, it is the ball and only the ball that is the cause of movement. Humans, by contrast, understand that there is an unseen exchange of energy, a physical property of "force" that is the deeper, underlying cause of the movement. Tomasello and Call (1997) argued in a similar fashion, saying that apes fail to appreciate the myriad mediating factors that can serve as causes. For example, in their view, when a chimp sees a branch shaking, causing a fruit to fall, the chimp would not understand that "branch shaking" results from some force operating on the branch and that such a force could be generated in multiple ways (by the wind, by a hand shaking it, by another branch striking against it, etc.).

The distinction between Povinelli's view and that of Tomasello and Call is subtle but potentially important. In Tomasello and Call's view, a chimp seeing a

DARWIN AND WALLACE REVISITED
Is Human Thinking Different in Quantity or Quality?

BOX 15.2 Darwin provided considerable evidence for evolutionary continuity between animals and humans. His contemporary and fellow naturalist Alfred Wallace, however, concluded that human thinking represented a qualitative leap from that of other animals. The research reviewed in this chapter has highlighted both commonalities and differences in human and ape thinking. Is human thinking best understood as an extension of animal cognition, or is it a discrete, qualitative "advance" in thought? Although most scientists believe that Wallace vastly underestimated the power of selection, he was not the only prominent scientist to perceive a yawning gap between humans and other animals. Many contemporary scientists have wondered aloud about the seemingly gratuitous nature of human intelligence. Physicist Eugene Wigner penned one of the most memorable expressions of this puzzlement in his essay "The unreasonable effectiveness of mathematics in the natural sciences" (Wigner, 1960). Like Wallace, Wigner wondered why human mathematical prowess worked so well in allowing us to understand the natural world. Its penetrating efficacy seemed somehow "unreasonable." Nobel Prize-winning geneticist Max Delbruck commented similarly:

> ...our concrete mental operations are indeed adaptations to the mode of life in which we had to compete for survival a long, long time before science....Why, then, do the formal operations of the mind carry us so much further? Were those abilities not also matters of biological evolution? If they, too, evolved to let us get along in the cave, how can it be that they permit us to obtain deep insights into cosmology, elementary particles, molecular genetics, number theory? To this question I have no answer. (Delbruck, 1986, p. 280)

Astronomer John Barrow echoed these sentiments:

> Why should our cognitive processes have turned themselves to such an extravagant quest as the understanding of the entire universe? Why should it be us? None of the sophisticated ideas involved appear to offer any selective advantage to be exploited during the preconscious period of our evolution....How fortuitous that our minds (or at least the minds of some) should be poised to fathom the depths of Nature's secrets. (Barrow, 1991, p. 172)

Similarly, Reading University archaeologist Steven Mithen recalled his thoughts while dining with a group of colleagues:

> Could these surgeons, linguists, and theoretical physicists be expanding the boundaries of human knowledge in such diverse and complex fields by using minds which were adapted for no more than a hunter–gatherer existence? (Mithen, 1996, p. 47)

Is it possible that both Darwin and Wallace hit upon some elements of truth when it comes to understanding human intelligence? Darwin argued for continuity and quantitative differences between humans and animals. Wallace argued for discontinuity and qualitative differences. In some instances, however, quantitative differences can become qualitative. For example, the difference between a drop of water and the Pacific Ocean is strictly quantitative (one has more water). But by virtue of the difference in quantity, differences in kind exist: a drop dries in a second on a hot day, and the Pacific is a vast ecosystem critical to the earth's climate. It is unlikely that Wallace's mysticism is necessary to explain human evolution, but gradual change and continuity of evolution can themselves produce unpredictable and outwardly mysterious products. Contemporary research in complex systems informs us that continuously adding new elements to an interactive, dynamic system can produce phase transitions in which new, previously unpredicted patterns may emerge (Gell-Mann, 1994; Kauffman, 1995). The human brain and the social context within which it functions are highly interactive, dynamic systems. The course of human evolution has seen dramatic change both in size and in patterns of interactivity. These changes were likely incremental in nature and need not have involved any supernatural intervention (as Wallace believed). However, novel and qualitatively new patterns of thought could emerge from this gradual evolutionary process. Just as the evolution of flying need not have involved a "half a wing" intermediate stage, the plane at which human thought exists may not be perched upon easily discernible ascending increments from that of our animal cousins.

branch swaying in the wind would probably not realize that a vine hanging from the limb might also be used to cause the branch to sway. Povinelli likely would take issue with this, especially if the chimp has seen vines and swaying branches associated in the past. However, the chimp would not be able to make the distinction between a vine simply laying across a branch (which could not cause swaying) and one tightly twisted around a branch (that could be used to cause swaying). For Povinelli, it is not that chimpanzees are unable to deduce other ways of producing effects, it is that they do not understand what physical properties are prerequisites to creating effects (the vine must be physically connected to the branch to cause swaying, not just in contact with it).

Across all these researchers and studies we see a convergence of thought. What has evolved over the course of the 5 million years since the chimpanzee and hominin lines separated seems to be the ability to "think past" the sensory world to a level of abstract causal concepts. Somewhere along the evolutionary line, hominins started "seeing" the unseen world of abstract physical concepts and began using those concepts as a basis for their reasoning. Does this make human thinking qualitatively different from that of other animals or primates? (See Box 15.2 for more.)

SUMMARY

Comparing human and ape rational abilities allows us to formulate ideas about those aspects of thinking that evolved exclusively along the hominin line. One task that has been used extensively to assess nonhuman primate rationality and problem solving is the tube task. In this task, a subject must use a stick to remove a desired reward from a clear plastic tube. Studies using the tube task suggest that monkeys primarily engage in trial-and-error problem solving, with little conceptual understanding of the principles governing the task. Apes are more efficient learners than monkeys, but their knowledge of the underlying principles of the tube task also appears to be quite limited. Experiments assessing apes' comprehension of abstract physical causal properties, such as rigidity, connectedness, and force, have failed to find evidence that apes can use these principles to solve problems. Instead, these studies suggest that ape thinking is largely based on powerful pattern recognition abilities. Thus, an important mental ability that appears to have evolved along the hominin line is that of "thinking past" the immediate perceptual or episodic input to formulate abstract theories of how the world works.

KEY TERMS

abstract physical causes
conceptual understanding
    of number

episodic minds
Sherlock Holmes reasoning
    subitization

trap tube task
tube task

REVIEW QUESTIONS

1. Describe the tube and trap tube tasks. How might these tasks be solved simply using procedural rules rather than an understanding of underlying causal factors?

2. Give an example of what Premack meant by Sherlock Holmes reasoning. Describe an experiment design to test this level of reasoning in chimps.

3. How did Povinelli test chimpanzees' understanding of connectedness and rigidity? What did the findings indicate?

4. How does subitization differ from a conceptual understanding of number?

5. What is meant by an understanding of unseen, abstract physical causes? If this ability is unique to humans, then to what can we attribute chimpanzee problem-solving abilities?

SUGGESTED READINGS

Mithen, S. (1996). *A prehistory of the mind.* London: Thames and Hudson.

Povinelli, D. (2000). *Folk physics for apes: A chimpanzee's theory of how the world works.* Oxford: Oxford University Press.

Tomasello, M., & Call, J. (1997). *Primate cognition.* Oxford: Oxford University Press.

WEB SITES

www.learnlink.emory.edu/~npatel2/ Emory University site dealing with primate cognition. Has many useful links.

www.pri.kyoto-u.ac.jp/ Web site of the Primate Research Institute of Kyoto University in Japan.

http://veederandld.20m.com/primates.html A very impressive site with considerable information on primates and just about every possible link one could think of.

16

Thought and Reasoning: Evolution

Evolution of Human Thought: What Do Tools Tell Us?

ANYONE TRYING TO RECONSTRUCT the evolution of hominin thinking quickly runs into a very serious problem. How do you measure the thinking capacity of long-extinct species? Brains do not fossilize, nor do the thoughts contained within them. The products of brains, however, may fossilize, and this is where most researchers begin when they try to assess the cognitive capacity of our ancestors. One product of our hominin ancestors that has survived over the millennia are the tools they used in hunting and food preparation. A close analysis of these tools provides clues about the thought processes that went into creating them.

Oldowan Tools

The first hominin tools appear in the archeological record about 2.6 million years ago. These tools were simple stone "flakes" used for cutting and scraping meat from carcasses and were most likely produced by a later species of *Australopithecus* and/or an early species of *Homo* (see discussion in chapters 4 and 5). Collectively, these early tools are known as the **Oldowan** tool kit or industry. A number of studies have been carried out to assess the cognitive capacity needed to create Oldowan-type tools, the most well known of which involved training the bonobo Kanzi to create his own Oldowan tool kit (reviewed in chapter 6). The results suggest that Oldowan tool manufacture may have required an enhanced capacity for planning and executing motor sequences. However, it did not involve any significant advance in spatial or intellectual skill beyond that found in present-day apes (Toth, Schick, Savage-Rumbaugh, Sevcik, & Rumbaugh, 1993; Wynn & McGrew, 1989). Other research tends to support this conclusion. For example, simple observational learning appears sufficient for acquiring the skill needed to create Oldowan tools (Washburn & Moore, 1980; Wright, 1972). College students and even an orangutan were able to make their own Oldowan tools after watching someone else make them. (I'll leave it to the reader to decide which is the more impressive demonstration!) Moreover, Oldowan toolmakers tended to use and discard their implements on the spot, with little regard for storage or the possibility of future use. Clive Gamble (1993) described early hominins as engaging in "highly episodic behavior where stone tools were made to do the job in hand before being dropped and their makers moving on..." (p. 138).

Wynn (1979, 1985, 1993) applied a Piagetian framework to assess the cognitive demands of Oldowan tool manufacture. The developmentalist Jean Piaget described children's intellectual development as progressing through stages in which their thought became increasingly more sophisticated. Wynn concluded that the hominins responsible for the Oldowan tools were functioning at a level equivalent to Piaget's preoperational stage. The preoperational stage is marked by a high level of egocentrism in thought, in which future planning, appreciating another's perspective, and understanding such concepts as reversibility and symmetry are severely limited. Wynn (1996) went on to argue that, given the nature of the Oldowan tools, it was highly unlikely that the creator had any real design criteria in mind when tools were being produced. Thus, Oldowan tools provide very little evidence of cognitive sophistication beyond that of apes. Nothing about the tools suggests a deep appreciation of spatial relations or indicates that their creators were engaging in conscious design or were planning for future activities. With this in mind, it should be no great surprise that a few primatologists have claimed that the tool culture of some chimpanzees is comparable with that of the Oldowan industry (Boesch & Boesch, 1984).

Acheulean Tools

Oldowan tools showed little evidence of advanced cognition, but the situation changed with the later **Acheulean** (or Acheulian) industry. The Acheulean tool kit appeared about 1.4 million years ago and was generally associated with *Homo erectus/ergaster* and some other pre-sapiens species. The Acheulean industry endured for more than a million years across three continents and showed evidence of variability and slow evolutionary advance. Early Acheulean tools shared much in common with their Oldowan predecessors, although later Acheulean tools were obviously larger and better crafted. Probably the most representative member of the Acheulean tool kit was the bifacial hand axe. In its later form, this tool was substantially larger than anything found in the Oldowan kit, and it displayed a degree of symmetry and a "fit" with the hominin hand not found in earlier tools (Leakey, 1976). Oldowan tools could be manufactured with only a few blows, but far more time and retouching were required for creating the Acheulean hand axe (Holloway, 1981b; Isaac, 1986). Moreover, although humans (and apes) were able to learn Oldowan techniques from mere observation, this was mostly likely insufficient for learning how to make Acheulean tools. The same graduate students who successfully created Oldowan tools based on observation were unable to reproduce Acheulean tools in this manner (Washburn & Moore, 1980). This finding may be significant, in that it suggests that Acheulean tool culture could not be transmitted without some capacity for imitation and active teaching. The ability to imitate and to actively teach appear to be uniquely human characteristics.

Despite decades of observation and documentation, only two studies have presented accounts of what might be considered active teaching among apes. **Active teaching** refers to instances in which one ape appears sensitive to another ape's level of knowledge and attempts to guide the less "informed" ape to a new level of skill or understanding (Boesch, 1991; Matsuzawa, 1999). In these cases, a mother chimpanzee (apparently) was attempting to teach her offspring how to use stones to crack nuts. Whether or not these instances were truly examples of ape instruction is open to question, but their extreme rarity is itself informative (Tomasello & Call, 1997). One reason that active teaching may be so rare (or, indeed, nonexistent) among apes is the limited ability of apes to accurately reproduce the actions they observe. Nagell, Olguin, and Tomasello (1993) and Call and Tomasello (1994b) presented apes and children with a task in which a rake-like instrument was used to obtain an out-of-reach object. All subjects learned how to use the rake by watching a model. Children were found to be very sensitive to the precise details of the way in which the model used the rake. They reproduced the specific means the model employed to obtain the object. Apes, on the other hand, were insensitive to the details of the use of the rake and, instead, copied only the general procedural acts aimed at getting the object. This type of learning has been referred to as **emulation** learning, in which one learns that there is a functional relationship between objects (e.g., one object can be obtain, smashed, extracted, elevated, etc., by using another) but the specific details of how to accomplish this are not directly learned and usually must be acquired through trial and error. Although some evidence suggests that human-encultured apes (apes raised as human children, often with extensive language learning) can learn by imitating, this skill appears to be absent among wild apes (Tomasello, Savage-Rumbaugh, & Kruger, 1993).

Given that Oldowan tools are within apes' productive capabilities, it may be that emulation learning was sufficient for their construction and transmission. If so, then the early hominins who created these tools were probably not doing anything significantly more sophisticated in terms of teaching and learning than what apes can do today. However, given that the Acheulean tools are beyond ape capabilities and cannot be produced simply based on observational learning, then it seems logical that *H. erectus* was engaged in unprecedented forms of learning and instruction. Acheulean tools may indicate the emergence of the motor, cognitive, and communicative systems, including possibly imitative and pedagogical skills, that are unique to the hominin evolutionary branch.

The Acheulean toolmaker, unlike his Oldowan counterpart, may very well have had a distinct image in his or her head that guided the manufacturing process (Lewin, 1998). Gowlett (1992), for example, contended that the Acheulean hand axe clearly demonstrated that a "preconceived form was held in mind" and "impressed upon stone" (p. 342). This conclusion, however, has been questioned by others, who argued that the form of the hand axe can be more simply explained based on ecological factors, such as the availability of certain raw materials (McPherron, 2000). Other tools of this period reinforce the notion of a cognitive advance. Spears dated at around 400,000 years old suggest that hominins of this time were engaged in organized group hunting for large game, a collaborative skill beyond that of any ape (Thieme, 1997). The quality of the weapons themselves testify to a "depth of planning, sophistication of design, and patience in carving wood, all of which [until now] had only been attributed to modern humans" (Dennell, 1997, p. 768).

A number of researchers have identified a watershed point in hominin toolmaking and cognition at around 300,000 years ago. Ambrose (2001), for example, contended that the emergence of "composite" tools (tools assembled from a number of component elements) at around this time marked a significant cognitive advance. These tools required an unprecedented level of motor coordination, planning, and problem solving, which, he argued, ultimately set the stage for the evolution of spoken language in hominins. Wynn's (1985, 1996) Piagetian analysis of the Acheulean industry also pointed to a significant cognitive advance at around 300,000 years ago. The carefully retouched bifacial handaxes of this period show clear evidence of an appreciation for symmetry and reversibility, according to Wynn. The designer was following a mental template and attempting to recreate that image in stone. For Wynn, these artisans were functioning at least at the Piagetian level of concrete operations of later childhood and possibly even at the adult level of formal operations.

Significantly, Wynn saw no great cognitive advance in any of the tools produced after 300,000 years ago. It is on this point that Mellars (1996) and others have questioned Wynn's conclusion by pointing out that the tools produced about 40,000 years ago, during what has been termed the Upper Paleolithic revolution, show marked differences that suggest yet another intellectual step forward. For example, it is at around this time that we begin to see tools designed specifically for the purpose of creating other tools. Second, it is only with the advent of the Upper Paleolithic that evidence of tools designed specifically for aesthetic reasons is found. For example, objects referred to as the **Solutrean blades** are so long and thin that they would have had no practical value. However, their precise symmetry and elegance attest to the time and effort the toolmaker spent in creating them. The fact that they are preserved at all indicates that they were not used in day-to-day activities but were more ornamental, used for ritual purposes or simply to celebrate the toolmaker's skill. This suggests that with the Upper Paleolithic, hominins began to think about their tools in entirely new ways. Their tools became reflections of themselves and their skills. This, along with other evidence to be discussed shortly, makes a compelling case that, with the Upper Paleolithic, hominins had achieved the level of abstract thought that is the hallmark of human rationality.

Neanderthals and the Upper Paleolithic Revolution

Evidence of a more sophisticated tool culture emerges in the fossil record at around 40,000 years ago, along with other artifacts, ornaments, and primitive art that indicate that a radically novel form of hominin thinking had taken hold. In addition, in Europe and the Middle East at this same time, we also see the demise of *H. sapiens'* last counterpart *Homo* species, the Neanderthals. Considerable research energy has been expended trying to understand these two events and the possible connections between them. Were our ancestors the sole beneficiaries of a new and powerful mode of thought that animated their awareness, vitalized their spirits, and condemned their competitors to extinction? What was it that gave our minds the potential to understand and harness the very forces responsible for our existence? For many students of human evolution, the captivating art and artifacts of the Upper Paleolithic are the very foundation of the distinctly human mental life we experience today (Fig. 16.1). Gazing upon the stone record of our Upper Paleolithic past, we become transfixed by the materialized expression of a species becoming human. What on earth were they thinking?

Figure 16.1 Paleolithic sculpture of a woman carved into a cave wall in Dordogne Valley, France. (© Charles and Josette Lenars/CORBIS.)

Along with advances in tool production, including "ritual" or aesthetic tools, the Upper Paleolithic period provides us with the first evidence of symbolic ornaments and art. As is often the case, one of the most elegant examples of the primitive symbolism of this period was discovered quite by accident. For some time, the curators at the Museum der Stadt in Ulm, Germany, were serenely content with their 30,000-year-old statuette of a human figure carved in ivory. True, it was headless, but what is to be expected from so old an artifact? When a lion's head, also carved in ivory and from about the same time period, was presented to them, the connection went unnoticed—until someone just happened to position the lion's head atop the human figure. Imagine their amazement when the head was found to fit perfectly on the human form (Stringer & McKee, 1996; Fig. 16.4B). The half man, half lion ivory statuette is one of the oldest examples of the imaginative art of the Upper Paleolithic. A somewhat younger example is the combination human-bird-reindeer drawing (Fig. 16.4C) found among the famous cave "paintings" from Trois-Freres, France. Mithen (1996) pointed out that these primitive art forms represent something extraordinary in the evolution of the mind: **impossible entities**, objects that no mind could ever have encountered in nature. Baron-Cohen (1999) referred to these as evolution's **first fictions**, representations of the artist's mind and imagination, not the products of experience. Of equal importance is the fact that these artifacts demonstrate the mind's evolving capacity as a concept assembler or conceptual organizer, a process essential to rationality. The art and artifacts of the Upper Paleolithic provide the first evidence of the mental integration of widely differing concepts to form entirely abstract notions. For the first time in evolutionary history, we have evidence of hominins "thinking past" their tangible, sensory worlds and attempting to draw conclusions about an ill-defined, foggy world of pretense and supposition.

That presumptive world also may have been the basis for an emerging belief in a hoped-for afterlife. Evidence of burial is present before the Upper Paleolithic period. However, Upper Paleolithic burial sites are unique in the degree of ornamentation associated with bodies. For example, the Sungir burial site (about 100 miles east of Moscow) has been dated at around 28,000 years old and contained three bodies, an approximately 60-year-old male and two adolescents, one male and one female. Each was wrapped in thousands of ivory beads, necklaces, and bracelets. It is estimated that the hours of labor necessary to complete such an outfitting would have run into the thousands—per body (White, 1993). This strongly suggests that the beads represented a symbolic adornment, testifying to the deceased's status in life. The younger bodies were no less adorned than their older burial mate. Because the younger ones could not have earned their status, it must have been assumed or inherited from their connection to the elder. This suggests an understanding of social stratification based on kinship lines. The amount of care and effort expended on the manufacture and placement of the beads seems unlikely unless they held ritualized significance for those involved. The surviving friends and relatives of these individuals wanted to convey a message about their dead companions. To whom was the message directed? To the gods, perhaps, in hopes of a high station in the afterlife? To their dead companions, maybe, in the belief that they could somehow still recognize the message and its significance? If either, then we have evidence of the beginnings of organized religious belief, and a nascent concept of the immortal soul (Stringer & McKee, 1996).

Symbolic ornaments, abstract art, and ritualized burial provide evidence of our ancestors' emerging skills of mental representation, manipulation, and imagination. It seems unlikely that our hominin forebears could have afforded such elaborate cognitive activities if a more practical, natural reasoning had not already been in place to permit them a fairly effective mastery in meeting their basic survival needs. There is evidence that such a capacity was in place before the Upper Paleolithic revolution and that it may have given *H. sapiens* a competitive edge over their Neanderthal counterparts. From about 100,000–50,000 years ago, Neanderthals and *H. sapiens* shared space, if not time, in the Levantine region of present-day Israel. The most likely scenario was that this region was occupied alternately by one group and then the other, with little direct contact between the groups. Extensive excavations of the region have uncovered a number of ancient remains that have provided interesting insights into how the two groups lived. At first glance, it is hard to find any substantial differences between Neanderthal and *H. sapiens* remains. Their tools seem indistinguishable, suggesting that their minds also may have been. Upon close inspection, however, it becomes clear that, even if the tools were the same, the way in which they were employed was not.

Among the Levant's remains were the teeth of gazelle hunted by both humans and Neanderthals. Like the rings on trees, gazelle teeth contain internal alternating light and dark striping corresponding to seasonal variations in food sources. Darker stripes correspond to the winter season and lighter stripes to the summer season. By "reading" the teeth, one can determine the season in which the animal was killed. At Neanderthal sites, the gazelle teeth were a mix of light and dark stripes, indicating that at a single site gazelles were hunted year round. At human sites, gazelle teeth were exclusively either light or dark in striping, indicating that a single site was used for one season of hunting and no more (Lieberman & Shea, 1994; Lieberman, 1993). This implies that the humans were following the gazelle migration patterns, establishing camps near to seasonal feeding grounds, hunting the resident gazelle, and then moving on with the herd. The Neanderthals stayed put and were forced to venture farther and farther as the migrating gazelle moved to more fertile ground. Because they used a less efficient strategy in exploiting their environment, the Neanderthals ended up working much harder to sustain themselves. "They were more active. They had to work harder and hunt more, because they used the environment differently from the modern humans," contended Lieberman (quoted in Stringer & McKee, 1996, p. 105). This increased labor also was reflected in their skeletal morphology. Neanderthal bones were bigger and thicker than those of humans, further testifying to their labor-intensive lifestyle. Moreover, the Neanderthals created and discarded their hunting implements at a rate 10 times greater than humans, suggesting a relative lack of forethought.

Anthropologist Lew Binford characterized the intellectual difference between our *H. sapiens* ancestors and the Neanderthals as one of "**planning depth**" (Binford, 1985, 1992). Humans think ahead and perform actions with benefits that will be realized only at some future point in time. Neanderthals, by contrast, were somewhat wanting in this domain. Binford noted the way in which hunter–gatherers "curate" their tools, that is, leave them at a particular site for future use. The rate at which Neanderthals made and discarded tools suggests that "curating" was a foreign concept. After more than 75,000 years of occupancy at one cave site, Neanderthals left behind more than 17,000 tools and less than 7,000 bone fragments (Binford, 1989; see also Shreeve, 1995, pp. 154–156). Along with the inefficient use of tools, Neanderthals' lack of planning depth also left them unable to exploit larger patterns in the natural world. Binford's analysis of the Neanderthal site at Combe Grenal in southern France revealed that the Neanderthals almost never fed on the salmon from the nearby Dordogne River. Bear caves in the same area, however, show an abundance of salmon remains. It was the bear, not Neanderthals, who took advantage of the seasonal salmon runs, freely exploiting an easily accessible, protein-rich food source. This food source, however, required both recognition of and planning for a naturally occurring environmental pattern. Binford's ideas have not gone uncriticized. Mellars (1996), for example, expressed skepticism about Binford's rather unflattering assessment of the Neanderthals but conceded that an obvious cognitive advance dawned with the modern humans of the Upper Paleolithic:

> Many of Binford's conclusions could no doubt be contested from several aspects of the archaeological data....Nevertheless, the central point of Binford's argument is that whatever degree of forethought, prediction, long-term planning, etc. can be identified in the behavior of Middle Paleolithic groups, would seem to be greatly exceeded by patterns that one can document in the ensuing Upper Paleolithic. (Mellars, 1996, p. 386)

This discussion is not intended to cast the Neanderthals as hairy dimwits who deservedly lost out to their more svelte and savvy hominin cousins. Remember that the Neanderthals survived for more than 200,000 years under often very difficult circumstances. Modern humans have been around for 150,000 years or less. Moreover, the differences in Neanderthal and human intellect are controversial. Recent findings in Portugal suggest that Neanderthals may have had a capacity for symbolism and may have interbred with humans (Kunzig, 1999). More important, evidence suggests that *H. sapiens* were recognizing naturally occurring patterns and planning ahead to maximally exploit those patterns. The apparent thought patterns behind the ancient hominin remains of this time are recognizably human and show evidence of a familiar rationality.

The Great Puzzle

The stunning cultural and intellectual advance associated with the Upper Paleolithic period presents us with one of evolution's most vexing puzzles. The modern human brain emerged approximately 150,000 years ago and has undergone little obvious change since that time. Yet, the abstract thought, symbolic art, and cultural artifacts so distinctively associated with modern humans did not appear until about 40,000 years ago. For 100,000 years, hominins with bodies and brains for the most part indistinguishable from our own walked the earth but left scant evidence that their minds were different in any significant way from the other hominin species present at the time (Lindly & Clark, 1990). What was it that caused the sudden explosion of uniquely human mentality after tens of thousands of years of dormancy? There is no clear answer, but some intriguing clues point to an astonishing conclusion: the human mind is not in the head!

Other significant changes associated with the Upper Paleolithic are the increasing complexity of social life and the heightened degree of economic and social exchange. Upper Paleolithic residential sites are generally larger than those of earlier time periods, indicating that social groups had enlarged (Mellars, 1989). *H. sapiens* of the Upper Paleolithic apparently spent far more time in multifamily aggregated communities than did earlier hominins (David, 1973; Mellars, 1985). The personal adornments, such as jewelry, necklaces, and beads, so common in this period may have served an important function in helping to identify an individual's status and role within an increasingly complex social structure. In addition, it is only with the Upper Paleolithic that we begin to see evidence of longer-term village-type settlements in which relatively large groups of people congregated in more permanent "built" shelters (Gamble, 1986).

These larger, more complex social groups also engaged in more extensive trade with other groups, sometimes hundreds of miles away. Raw materials from the Atlantic and Mediterranean coasts have been found at Upper Paleolithic sites hundreds of miles inland (Taborin, 1993). The critical point is that the Upper Paleolithic ushered in a revolution in social life as well as one in tools and technology. The uniquely human aspects of mind may very well owe their existence as much to the social transformation of the Upper Paleolithic as to the physical transformation that brought about the *H. sapiens* species. Our minds are what make us human, but what makes our minds *human minds* are other humans!

> There is no extramodular capacity in humans, no general intelligence. Humans are nothing more than souped-up primates, chimpanzees with certain enhanced abilities. A naked human, without history and without society, is no more capable of

creating science or technology than is a naked chimp. But our special abilities allow for the accumulation and storage of information, and this makes it possible, over the course of many generations, for science and technology to emerge. This type of good design emerges not through natural selection, but out of the interaction of humans with other humans and with the external world. (Bloom, 1999, p. 306)

> …we are not suggesting that there are matters occurring in brains that get *translated* into 'understandings' among persons….We are asserting that 'understanding' describes an interpersonal achievement, full stop. Brains are needed for this, but they are not where understanding occurs. (Noble & Davidson, 1996, p. 105)

Somehow it was the interaction of humans with humans in complex social networks that worked the magic of the Upper Paleolithic revolution. Exactly how this happened is mere speculation. However, one possibility is that the evolving hominin social/environmental context, in fact, did physically change the brain, not in size or any other obvious characteristic, but in wiring. We have seen how the enlarged hominin frontal lobe produced what neuroscientist Terrence Deacon (1997) called a "leveraged takeover." That is, as different parts of the brain compete for connections within the brain's internal architecture, only the strong (typically the most active) survive, and those connections emanating from the frontal lobe may be the strongest. The frontal lobe is the seat of our most "advanced" cognitive operations, such as abstract thinking, future planning, goal-directed behaviors, and other **executive functions** that allow humans to organize and execute long-range strategies.

Coolidge and Wynn (2001) argued that these frontal lobe executive functions hold the key to modern human cognition. They cited evidence that executive functions, such as sequential memory, organizational thinking, and future planning, are heritable traits (Eaves et al., 1993; Pennington & Ozonoff, 1996; Stevenson, 1992) and that the first substantial evidence of these functions occurred around the time of the Upper Paleolithic in *H. sapiens* but not Neanderthal populations. It is around this time that complex tools requiring a multistage sequential construction process appeared (Klein, 2000; Knecht, 1993). Moreover, at this time we have the first evidence of the creation of watercraft for long-range excursions and the colonization of distant lands (such as Australia), both of which required a capacity for organizational thinking and foresight previously unheard of among hominins (Davidson & Noble, 1992). It may be that, as generation after generation raised their children in a social environment of ever-increasing complexity, a leveraged takeover took place inside the hominin brain, so that the frontal lobes and their executive functions came to dominate and drive the functioning of other brain centers. Even more intriguing is the possibility that this transformation was led by the play of children. Recent research has revealed a link between brain development and childhood play behavior. More "playful" animals tend to have proportionally larger brains, and play behavior in the young tends to peak at times of maximal synaptic brain growth and pruning (Bekoff & Byers, 1998; Iwaniuk, Nelson, & Pellis, 2001; Lewis, 2000). It possible (although at this point merely speculative) that the vanguard of the Upper Paleolithic revolution was of the most innocent variety: children at play, whose slow maturation and relatively stable circumstances afforded them phenomenal opportunities to reorganize their brains in a most amazing way. For more on play and the brain, see Box 16.1.

Play and the Brain

BOX 16.1 Two recent studies have examined the relationship between brain size and play behavior. Iwaniuk, Nelson, and Pellis (2001) assessed brain size and play across 15 different mammalian orders, including *Rodentia* (rodents), *Marsupialia* (marsupials), and primates. They measured a number of different types of play, including play fighting, locomotor play, wrestling, and sex play. For brain size, they used the **encephalization quotient** (EQ), discussed in chapter 5. Their results showed a significant relationship between brain size and play when looking across different orders but no consistent relationship when comparing the various species within an order. Thus, for example, primates played more and had bigger brains than rodents, but, among the different species of rodents, larger brains did not necessarily mean more play. The researchers concluded that the relationship between brain size and play was not linear but stepwise. For increases in play frequency and complexity to be observed, some threshold expansion in brain size must be achieved. By way of a vastly oversimplified example, suppose that a brain must increase 100 cc before any changes in play behavior can be detected. Then those creatures with brains between 100 and 190 cc will tend to play similarly. A creature with the 210-cc brain, however, will have more frequent and more sophisticated play. Between 190 and 210 cc, an important threshold of brain size was crossed, resulting in a significant change in play behavior. Because brains within an order tend to be more alike in size than brains across orders, the relationship between play and brain size is one best observed at a more macro level.

Another study, however, produced somewhat contradictory findings. Lewis (2000) studied play behavior and brain size specifically among various primate species. In this study, play was categorized as either solitary locomotor play (running, jumping, or climbing alone), object play (manipulating, throwing, waving, etc., an object), or *social play* (tickling, play fighting, chasing, wrestling, kicking, etc., with another). Furthermore, Lewis did not use the EQ as a measure of brain size but **neocortex ratio**, in which the neocortex is taken as a ratio of the remainder of the brain (neocortex/nonneocortex brain). Seven primate species were observed, including ring-tail lemurs (a prosimian), red-handed tamarins (New World Monkeys), owl-faced monkeys, diana monkeys, macaques (all Old World Monkeys), siamangs (a lesser ape), and chimpanzees (a great ape).

Figure 16.A shows the scores for the seven primate species on the three types of play and neocortex ratio. There is a general tendency for play scores to increase along with neocortex ratio. However, a significant relationship was found only for the measure of social play and neocortex ratio. Unlike the Iwaniuk et al. (2001) study, Lewis (2000) observed a significant relationship between at least one measure of play (social play) and an alternative measure of brain size (neocortex ratio) for species within an order. It may be that relatively fine-grained analyses are necessary to uncover the relationship between brain size and play when comparing species within the same order. This study suggests that for primates, it is a specific type of play, social play, that is most directly connected to brain size. This has led to an important hypothesis about the critical role of the social environment in the evolution of human intelligence and language (see chapter 17).

Species	Solitary locomotor	Object play	Social play	Neocortex ratio
Pan troglodytes	22.1	11.2	21.5	3.22
Hylobates syndactylus	15.0	0.5	21.0	1.58
Macaca sylvanus	5.2	4.1	17.0	1.50
Cereopithecus diana	12.5	1.7	5.3	1.44
Cereopithecus hamlyni	3.1	1.4	5.7	1.41[1]
Saguinus midas	4.2	0	3.2	0.97
Lemur catta	5.7	0	2.0	0.90

[1]As neocortex data for C. hamlyni is unavailable, the mean from all cereopithecines is used here.

Figure 16.A Play behavior measures of seven primate species as well as their neocortex ratios. Species are, from bottom to top: ring-tail lemur, red-handed tamarin, owl-faced monkey, diana monkey, barbary macaque, siamang, and chimpanzee. (Adapted from Lewis, 2000, p. 418.)

Sources:

Lewis, K.P. (2000). A comparative study of primate play behavior: Implications for the study of cognition. *Folia Primotologica*, 71, 417–421.

Iwaniuk, A.N., Nelson, J.E., & Pellis, S.M. (2001). Do big-brained animals play more? Comparative analyses of play and relative brain size in mammals. *Journal of Comparative Psychology*, 115, 29–41.

Evolved Human Reasoning

We tend to view human thinking as a cold, abstract process, detached from the realities of bodily existence. Our review of the evolutionary history of human thinking should remind us that rationality, like other human traits, evolved to serve our survival and reproductive needs. We are designed for "hot cognition" not "cold calculation." In other words, our rational processes work with our emotions to advance our fitness interests. How then might we expect our evolutionary history to affect our rationality?

Dominance and Agreeableness

Humans evolved in a highly social context in which issues of social status and cooperative/competitive relationships played a significant role in survival and reproductive success. Given this, we would expect human reasoning to be an **evolved social reasoning**, especially attuned to ramifications of social information and situations. Kenrick, Sadalla, and Keefe (1998) contended that, as a result of our evolutionary heritage, human reasoning should be highly sensitive to two important social dimensions: **dominance** and **agreeableness**. Dominance refers to interpreting our relations and interactions with others along a dominant–submissive continuum. Having evolved in hierarchically structured groups, we humans naturally and automatically use social status as a mechanism for understanding relationships. For example, being called by a nickname may be a welcome expression of informal acceptance when coming from one's boss but is considered disrespectful coming from one's child. Agreeableness and disagreeableness form the limits of the other continuum that humans use to understand their social relationships. In our hominin past, it was important to be able to identify potential competitors and coalition partners. Thus, we have a natural tendency to think about others in terms of the ways they help foster our fitness goals or the threats they might pose.

Some research has supported this idea. Evidence suggests that when we judge personalities, five factors are most salient: openness, conscientiousness, extroversion, neuroticism, and agreeableness. These have been referred to as the "Big Five" personality traits (Goldberg, 1990; McCrae & John, 1992). Considerable research has examined the evolutionary significance of these personality traits (Buss, 1992a, 1996; Hogan, 1983). Extroversion, for example, has been found to be related to one's ability to secure resources and attain positions of social prominence. Agreeableness has been found to be related to one's trustworthiness and suitability as a coalition partner. Extraversion and agreeableness also are the two personality traits that are most directly related to interpersonal relationships and are the most important in terms of the amount of variance in personality attribution that they explain. Additional support for the relevance of these factors has come from studies in social perception and cognition. Studies examining the attributes that spontaneously and consistently attract attention find that a person's age, gender, and status are often automatically encoded by others (Brewer & Lui, 1989; Hastie & Park, 1986). These factors very well may serve as cues to where another falls on the dominance–submission and agreeableness–disagreeableness continua. Thus, the themes of dominance and agreeableness appear to be most salient when it comes to how we think about others.

Evidence also suggests that humans may have specific mechanisms for perceiving indicators of cooperativeness (or the lack thereof) in others. In some visual scenes, certain features have been found to automatically "pop out" at the observer (Treisman & Gelade, 1980). For example, a tilted line set among a group of vertical lines will immediately attract our attention, regardless of how many vertical lines are present in the array. It just seems to jump or "pop out" of the visual scene. The fact that certain perceptual features stand out in this way has provided evidence for specially designed "feature detectors" in the visual system, such as specific receptors designed to encode lines at certain angles. Hansen and Hansen (1988) used this approach to show that an angry face set among happy faces would pop out and immediately attract the attention of the viewer, regardless of how many happy faces were present. This suggests the presence of perceptual mechanisms especially attuned to facial cues of noncooperation or threat. Other research has found that negative information about another tends to carry inordinate weight when we evaluate that individual (Pratto & John, 1991). These studies indicate that both our perception of the social world and our social thinking are not purely objective but excessively sensitive to signals about status, cooperativeness, and possible social threats.

Cheat Detection

Another way that the social evolutionary origin of human thought manifests itself is in the very process of logical reasoning. Our ability to be logical appears to be affected by the content to which we apply our reasoning power. The more social that content, the more logical we become. In the 1960s and 1970s, Peter Wason devised a logical reasoning task that seemed to show how blatantly irrational most people are (Wason, 1966; Wason & Evans, 1975; Wason & Johnson-Laird, 1972). The task has become known as the Wason selection task: A subject is presented with four cards. Each has a letter on one side and a number on the other. The cards are presented as shown in Figure 16.2, and the subject is asked which two cards should be turned over to accurately verify whether the following rule is being obeyed: "if a card has a vowel on one side, then there is an even number on the other." Try this yourself.

If you were like most of Wason's subjects, you selected E and 4, which is, of course, wrong (the correct selections are E and 7). Before explaining why it is wrong, let's try another similar logic problem framed in a slightly different way. Suppose your teenage daughter has cajoled you into allowing her to have a party at the house. You agree to the party but only if she promises that there will be no underage drinking. She agrees. You come home early the evening of the party to a

Figure 16.2 Four cards used in the Wason Selection Task. The cards have letters on one side and numbers on the other. The subject is told to turn over the minimal number of cards to verify whether the rule "if there is a vowel on one side then there is an even number on the other" is being followed. (Adapted from Medin & Ross, 1997, p. 407.)

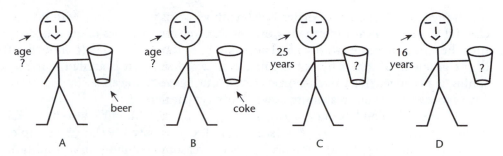

Figure 16.3 A modified version of the Wason Selection Task using a more realistic scenario. Evolutionary psychologists argue that this form of the task is easier because it involves cheat detection, a skill for which our evolved reasoning capacities are well adapted.

house ripe with the scent of beer. Figure 16.3 depicts four partygoers. For two of them (A and B), you know what they are drinking but not their age. For the other two (C and D), you know their age but not what they are drinking. Which two should you request additional information from (either age or content of drink) to determine if your daughter's promise ("if someone is drinking beer then he or she will be over 21 years of age") is being kept?

The answer here seems painfully obvious: you check the first partygoer who has beer (to make sure that he or she is over 21) and the last one who is only 16 to make sure that he or she is drinking a coke (or some other nonalcoholic beverage). If you look closely at this choice, you will see that it is really just the Wason selection task recast in a different form. When this alternate form was used, significantly more people correctly solved the task than when it was presented in its original form (Cosmides, 1989; Cosmides & Tooby, 1989). Why the difference? One argument is that when recast in a more concrete form, the problem relates better to everyday experience. In other words, its familiarity makes it easier. This argument fails, however, because studies that have used concrete but unfamiliar reasoning problems have found the same improvement in performance (Chen & Holyoak, 1985; Chen, Holyoak, Nisbett, & Oliver, 1986; Hoch & Tschirgi, 1983). Another hypothesis is that people are more adept at pragmatic reasoning (as opposed to abstract reasoning), especially when it involves situations in which permission is being granted based on fulfilling some obligation (if you do X you are allowed Y). Evolutionary psychologists Leda Cosmides and John Tooby (1992) refined this argument and provided an explanation as to why we are so skilled at evaluating permission situations. They contended that evolution has honed us to be expert **"cheat detectors."**

The second task, they claimed, is presented in the form of a social contract in which a very real potential for cheating on the contract is present. You and your daughter made a social arrangement. You agreed to do one thing (permit the use of your house for her party) in return for her commitment to do another (prohibit underage drinking). Now you are concerned that her end of the bargain is not being held up. This is exactly the type of reciprocal, tit-for-tat arrangement that would have been at the core of our social relationships throughout evolutionary history. Our ancestors survived by engaging in just such arrangements ("if you watch my kids, I'll share the berries I pick with you"; "if you have sex with no one else, I'll share the meat I hunt with you"; etc.). Over the vast ages of evolutionary time, hominins became awfully good at picking out those who tried to mooch off of the goodwill of others by not keeping their word. Thus, it is argued, our reasoning is not a generalized, all-purpose logic but, instead, a keen social logic. We have evolved to use our reasoning power to detect cheaters.

This conclusion has drawn criticism (e.g., Fodor, 2000), but it also has been replicated in a number of studies (see Cosmides & Tooby, 1992). For example, Gigerenzer and Hug (1992) compared subjects' reasoning abilities in a condition in which a social contract was merely present versus another in which cheating on a contract was being assessed. Performance was significantly better when subjects were attempting to detect cheating, demonstrating that it was specifically cheat detection that people excelled at and not just evaluating social contracts. Another recent study has found evidence of the cheater detection advantage in children as young as two (Cummins, 1999).

Frequencies, Not Probabilities

Imagine you are a physician presented with the following problem: Disease X is rare, occurring in only 1% of the population, but it is very often fatal. A new test has been devised to detect disease X. The new test has a 99% true–positive rate. In other words, 99% of those with the disease will generate a positive test result. It also has a 2% false–positive rate; that is, 2% of those who do not have the disease also will generate a positive test result. Patient A takes the new test and comes up positive. What is the probability that patient A actually has disease X? Without doing any high-power calculating, give a ballpark estimate as to what you think the probability might be.

When a problem similar to this was given to doctors, including physicians at the Harvard Medical School, they tended to vastly overestimate the probability of A actually having disease X (Eddy, 1982; Casscells, Schoenberger, & Grayboys, 1978). If you found this problem challenging and ended up guessing somewhere in the 70%–90% range, then you were not so different from the physicians who were tested. In fact, the probability is 33%. This raises two questions. How could the actual probability be that low? And why does it seem as if it ought to be much higher? The answer to both of these is found in the concept of **base rate neglect**. Base rate neglect refers to the fact that, when dealing with probabilities, we humans generally ignore the overall probability of some object or event occurring in the environment. The base rate information was provided when we were told that disease X occurs in only 1% of the population. That information drastically changes the meaningfulness of the true–positive and false–positive probabilities provided later. However, we tend to ignore or neglect the implications of the base rate when making our probabilistic judgments. Take a look at another version of the same problem expressed in a way that makes it seem much easier to take the base rate information into account.

Disease X is rare. In a group of 1000 people, only 10 are likely to have the disease. A new test has been devised to detect disease X. When it is given to the 10 who have the disease, all of them produce a positive test result. However, when the test is given to the remaining 990 who do not have the disease, 20 of them also produce a positive test. Thus, among 1000 people, a total of 30 are likely to produce a positive test result. A random sample of 1000 people have been given the new test, and subject A has come up positive. Subject A has a _____ out of _____ chance of actually having the disease (fill in the appropriate numbers).

Looked at it in this way, the answer seems easy. Out of 1000 people, we know that 30 will test positive, and, of those 30, 10 will have the disease. Thus, subject A's chances of having the disease are 10 out of 30 (or 1 out of 3, or 33%). When the disease X problem was presented in a form similar to the second way presented here, 76% of subjects got it right, compared with only 12% who responded to the problem in the first form (Cosmides & Tooby, 1996; see also Gigerenzer & Hoffrage, 1995). Why the difference? Cosmides and Tooby (1996) argued that because the second form presents the problem in terms of frequencies rather than probabilities, it is intuitively more understandable. Using frequencies one can easily see that the 1% base rate of disease X leaves a large pool of healthy subjects (990) and that even a small percentage of false positives (2%) among them can add up to a large number of healthy people who produce positive test results. This dramatically affects the way we interpret the seemingly "accurate" 99% true–positive information.

As with the cheater detection advantage, the advantage of using frequency data can be traced back to our evolutionary history (Comides & Tooby, 1996). Probability estimates are a relatively recent mathematical invention, but, for millions of years, hominins had to make judgments about the frequency with which events occurred together. For example, the number of times a certain grove of trees was visited and fruit was found, or certain tracks were spotted and game animals were nearby, or even how often a distinctive quality of eye contact led to sexual intercourse. Both animals and humans are sensitive to such information and store it almost automatically (Hasher & Zacks, 1984; Real, 1991). As was true with our logic processor, our mental calculator has evolved not as a general purpose number cruncher but as a specialist designed to address specific adaptive needs.

The Gambler's Fallacy

The fact that we tend to be more effective thinking in terms of frequencies than probabilities indicates that the natural context of thought is critical to its efficacy. We evolved to think about naturalistic problems that confronted us over the course of our evolution. Another well-known area in which this arises is in the common logical error known as the gambler's fallacy. A simple example is the tossing of a coin. If a coin is tossed 10 times and the first nine results are H-T-T-H-H-H-H-H-H, most people will contend that the tenth toss is more likely to be tails than heads. Why? Assuming the coin is fair, we expect that in a series of tosses the results should come out roughly even, about as many heads as tails. Because our coin has shown a recent run of heads, it must be due for a tail. Of course, a moment's reflection will reveal how illogical this reasoning is. The coin has no memory, so how could it possibly "know" that it just had a run of heads? The probability of a tail on the 10th toss is no different than on any of the other tosses: 1/2, or .50. This fallacious thinking also shows itself in sports, where both basketball players and fans have been shown to believe that a player's chance of making a basket is greater if he or she made a basket on the previous try as opposed to missing

(Gilovich, Vallone, & Tversky, 1985). Again, the probability of making a shot remains constant, a fact confirmed by analyses of actual game records.

Why does the gambler's fallacy persist? The reason seems to be that humans have a very difficult time *ignoring past history* when assessing the likelihood of current events. We evolved in a context in which past history *was* relevant to current events. For example, if one has been regularly exploiting the same berry patch, then the likelihood of finding berries there eventually will diminish to zero. If it has been raining consistently for an extended period of time, then the likelihood that the dry season will commence soon increases with each passing day. It has only been very recently that humans have invented games of chance and constructed other contexts in which events are truly independent of one another (Pinker, 1997). We did not evolve in these artificial, well-engineered environments of statistically isolated events but in naturalistic ones in which past events were often relevant and highly informative about current or future circumstances.

Evolved Sex Differences in Thought, Skill, and Perception

Another way in which our evolutionary history has affected our thinking is in the area of evolved sex differences in cognition and perception. As discussed in chapters 9 and 10, one of the unique attributes of hominin evolution was the degree of reciprocity and cooperation exhibited by the sexes. Hominin males and females assumed different, often complementary, social roles and benefited from the mutual exchange of products and skills. For example, hominin males were largely responsible for hunting, and females gathered local edibles and handled child care. As a result of engaging in divergent activities for perhaps a million years or more, hominin males and females would have been subject to somewhat different selection pressures. This notion is referred to as the **division of labor hypothesis**. It contends that these different selection pressures would have molded a set of sex-specific cognitive and behavioral skills of which we should find evidence today in modern men and women (Silverman & Eals, 1992).

Division of Labor: Males

It is, of course, impossible for us to know exactly how the older males of a long-ago hominin tribe transmitted their hunting knowledge and know-how to the next generation. Among the !Kung San of southern Africa, Lee (1979) reported that young boys receive little formal hunting instruction from older men until early adolescence. Around age 12, San boys accompany their elders on hunts and learn by watching and doing. Not for another 3–6 years, however, do most boys acquire the competence necessary to make a solo kill of a good-size prey. If this is any reflection of the way our ancient ancestors passed along hunting skills, then we can assume that much of the burden was on the learner. Those who failed to acquire sufficient expertise suffered the consequences. Because men today are the descendants of those hominin males who were the better hunters, what skills might we expect to see that reflect this evolutionary heritage? One proposal is that spatial abilities, especially in such areas as spatial orientation, three-dimensional visualization, and mental rotation, would have been critically important for successful hominin hunting and, therefore, should be relatively more developed in modern men than women. Indeed, a voluminous amount of research has demonstrated a distinct male spatial advantage.

Men tend to outperform women on tasks of spatial rotation, orientation, map reading, maze solving, speed estimates of moving objects, and the recognition of embedded shapes. Generally speaking, the male advantage tends to be greater on tasks requiring transformations in three-dimensional rather than two-dimensional space (see Halpern, 1992, for a review; also, Law et al., 1993; Linn & Peterson, 1986; McGee, 1979; Silverman & Phillips, 1998). The male spatial advantage also has been replicated extensively in cross-cultural studies in Japan (Mann, Sasanuma, Sakuma, & Masaki, 1990), England (Lynn, 1992), Scotland (Berry, 1966; Jahoda, 1980), Ghana (Jahoda, 1980), Sierra Leone (Berry, 1966), and India, South Africa, and Australia (Porteous, 1965). In addition to measured differences in ability, males and females also differ in the strategies they use to confront spatial challenges. For example, in way finding, men tend to use more global cardinal orientations, whereas women use more localized landmarks. A man might give directions to another by saying, "go straight a half mile and turn north," whereas a woman might say, "go straight five blocks and turn right at the courthouse" (Bever, 1992; Galea & Kimura, 1993; Ward, Newcombe, & Overton, 1986).

While the hominin men were out hunting (and honing their spatial orientation skills), hominin women were gathering closer to home. If the division of labor theory is correct, then modern women ought to possess skills that reflect their past history as well. McBurney, Gaulin, Devineni, and Adams (1997) tested males and females on both mental rotation and object location tasks. As expected, the men outperformed the women on the mental rotation test. The women, however, outperformed the men on the object location test. Other studies have confirmed female superiority at recalling object locations. Women outperform men on tests measuring the recall of locations within an array and object locations within an office space in both incidental and intentional learning conditions (Eals & Silverman, 1994; Silverman & Eals, 1992; Silverman & Phillips, 1998).

All of these data are in line with the notion that men and women divided up the workload in our evolutionary past, but some alternative hypotheses need to be addressed. Annett (1985), for example, proposed that these spatial differences might be attributable to differences in the development of hemispheric laterality between males and females. Because their left-hemisphere-based verbal skills mature more quickly than males, females may be prompted to adopt verbal-based strategies to solve spatial problems. Males' left-hemisphere verbal skills mature more slowly; thus, they are more likely to adopt nonverbal strategies (for example, mental imagery) when facing spatial challenges. In this case, not having verbal skills available for use on spatial tasks actually proves to be a benefit for males, because nonverbal strategies typically are more effective then verbal ones for spatial tasks. Annett's theory has gained some general support from a recent study using functional magnetic resonance imaging (fMRI) to determine which parts of the brain were active during a spatial task (Groen, Wunderlich, Spitzer, Tomczak, & Riepe, 2000). The study confirmed that men and women tend to use different strategies when solving spatial problems, but not necessarily the strategies predicted by Annett's model. A weakness of the theory is that females are not always inferior to males on spatial tasks (object locations, for example), nor do they always use verbal strategies for solving spatial problems. Eals and Silverman (1994), for example, found female superiority for an object location test even in incidental learning conditions in which verbal labels could not have been used.

Another alternative for explaining male–female spatial differences rests on the idea of male polygynous "wandering." Gaulin and Fitzgerald (1986) tested the spatial abilities of male meadow voles (which are polygynous) and pine voles (which are monogamous). Male meadow voles, but not pine voles, were found to have superior spatial abilities when compared with females. Moreover, male meadow voles had much larger ranging areas than male pine voles. The argument is that because they are wandering about looking for more mates, male meadow voles have been selected for a keen sense of space. As monogamous "homebodies," the male pine voles are under no such selection pressure. This theory works well for voles (and presumably many other species), but it runs into a problem when applied to humans. In our evolutionary history, it was females, more than males, who wandered from their native territories for mating purposes (Seielstad, Minch, & Cavalli-Sforza, 1998). It appears, then, that the division of labor hypothesis offers one of the best explanations for sex differences in human spatial functioning.

If, as the division of labor hypothesis envisions, hominin men were out doing the hunting, then we might also expect that certain physical skills, such as throwing, would also show a male advantage. Indeed, this appears to be the case. In a now classic study, Goodenough and Brian (1929) demonstrated that children as young as 4 years of age already show a significant sex difference in throwing accuracy, with boys being more accurate than girls. Geary (1998) reviewed more recent studies and concluded that a male advantage in both throwing velocity and distance is present in the preschool years, in some cases as early as 2 years of age. The fact that differences emerge so soon in life makes it unlikely that factors such as socialization or gender differences in parenting are responsible for their presence. Instead, it seems more probable that these differences are reflections of physical differences between boys' and girls' bodies, some of which can be traced back to the womb. For example, boys have relatively longer forearm bones (ulna and radius) than do girls. This difference is observable in utero (Gindhart, 1973; Tanner, 1990) and represents an important element in the structural basis of the throwing act. Geary (1998), however, pointed out that the male advantage in throwing is accompanied by other male advantages in tracking and blocking oncoming projectiles. To him, this indicates that division of labor (male hunting) alone does not explain all these differential abilities and that male-on-male competition for mates must also be considered an important factor in their evolution.

Division of Labor: Females

If a history of hunting and fighting has produced modern men who can now read maps and throw stones (or footballs), then what special skills have modern women inherited by virtue of their history? We have already touched upon one of these: the female superiority in object location attributable to their work as gatherers. Hominin women's work entailed more than just gathering local nuts and roots or keeping things tidy while breathlessly waiting for Bubba to bring home meat. Around the campsite, food required preparation and children required tending. Moreover, as one matured from childhood to adulthood, there were males to scrutinize and select among. Hominin women had no problems keeping busy. But what skills would be selected for on the basis of this sort of busy-ness? When comparing males and females on sensory-based tasks, females consistently outperform males in nearly all sense modalities except vision. In touch, smell, taste, and hearing, females are generally more sensitive and have better discriminative powers than males (Velle, 1987). In olfaction, for example, a number of large-scale studies have confirmed female superiority (e.g., Cain, 1982; Doty et al., 1984; Wysocki, Pierce, & Gilbert, 1991). In one study, females outperformed males on the identification of 64 of 80 (80%) different odorants (Cain, 1982). More research needs to be done to connect these abilities to our evolutionary past, but there are reasons to suspect that such connections are likely. For example, evidence of female superiority in olfaction has been found in neonates as young as 2 days old, which suggests that these differences are more biologically based than the result of enculturation or learning (Balogh & Porter, 1986). Breast-feeding infants can identify their mothers based on olfactory cues but cannot identify their fathers by such clues (Cernoch & Porter, 1985). Mothers, too, have been found to be highly accurate at identifying their newborns by smell, even after only very minimal contact with them (Porter, Cernoch, & McLaughlin, 1983). Mothers can distinguish among offspring on the basis of olfactory cues alone, and siblings can use olfaction to distinguish kin from strangers (Porter & Moore, 1981). All of this strongly suggests that olfaction has played an important role in the evolution of mother–infant emotional bonds and in kin recognition. Moreover, women, more than men, use scent cues as a basis for attraction and sexual interest (Franzoi & Herzog, 1987; Hertz & Cahill, 1997).

From an evolutionary perspective, one reason why we might expect female superiority in the use of olfactory cues is the important role smell plays in reproduction. In other species, the presence of certain pheromones (secreted chemicals) can trigger stereotypic responses. For example, estrus in some female apes is signaled by certain pheromones, which, in turn, cause a predictable male response. Human females have been found to be highly sensitive to certain olfactory cues. Female menstrual cycles are linked to chemicals released by both males and females who are nearby on a regular basis. Male underarm secretions can affect the regularity of women's cycles, whereas female underarm secretions can affect their mutual synchrony (Cutler et al., 1986; Preti, Cutler, Garcia, Huggins, & Lawley, 1986).

Females also have been found to be exquisitely sensitive to chemical cues signaling information about the human immune system. Recall that one of the main reasons for sexual reproduction (as opposed to asexual) has to do with keeping the immune system one step ahead of deadly parasites (see chapter 10). For the sake of fitness, it would be nice if females could select mates whose immune systems were optimally different from their own, thus ensuring that the offspring would be more difficult targets for parasites. Female mice have evolved so that they are naturally attracted to males with chemical cues that indicate that they have certain genes (major histocompatibility [MHC] genes) that vary from their own. MHC genes have an important impact on immune system function.

What about human females? Claus Wedekind and his colleagues (Wedekind & Furi, 1997; Wedekind, Seebeck, Bettens, & Paepke, 1995) had undeodorized male graduate students sleep in the same T-shirts for two nights straight. Female college students then smelled the shirts and rated them for the sexiness of the wearer. Females rated as most sexy the T-shirts worn by males whose MHC differed from their own. Although this effect was significant and reliable, it did have one very interesting exception. Women on birth-control pills rated men with similar MHC as being the most sexy. Evolutionarily, however, this all makes sense. If you are looking for a mate, look for someone different from yourself. If you are already mated and pregnant (birth control pills mimic pregnancy), then stay close to kith and kin. Thornhill and Gangestad (1999) also found that females in the fertile phase of their menstrual cycles find the scent cues of symmetrically built males more attractive than nonsymmetrically built males (Fig. 16.4; recall that bilateral symmetry is also related to immune system function). Males, however, showed no evidence of preference for the scent of symmetrically built women. It appears that it is females, more than males, who are especially attuned to scent cues that signal a mate's genetic quality and that this keen ability waxes and wanes with the probability of conception.

Their general level of olfactory sensitivity may be less than that of females, but males, too, have been shown to use scent cues in assessing female fertility and immune system compatibility. For example, Singh and Bronstad (2001) showed that men prefer the scent of a women in the fertile phase of her cycle to that of a woman in her nonfertile phase (see Box 16.2). Men also can discriminate among scent cues associated with a woman's MHC profile. This may be one of the factors driving female perfume preferences. Milinski and Wedekind (2001) have shown a connection between a female's MHC profile and her perfume preference. This leads to the intriguing possibility that when women choose a perfume they are not looking for a scent that masks their own odors as much as one that amplifies (and advertises) their own MHC-related scent cues.

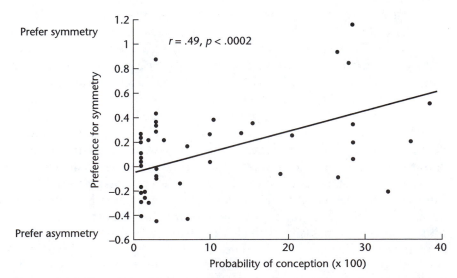

Figure 16.4 The relationship between females' preference for scent cues associated with male symmetry and their probability of conception. As indicated on the graph, the relationship was highly significant, with the preference for symmetry increasing as the probability of conception increased. (Adapted from Thornhill & Gangestad, 1999, p. 187.)

DEVENDRA SINGH
The Scent of an Ovulating Woman

PROFILE: *Dr. Devendra Singh received his Ph.D. from the Ohio State University and is a professor in the psychology department at the University of Texas at Austin. His research has contributed significantly to our understanding of the evolutionary significance of human physical attractiveness. His research interests include: (1) identifying morphological features that are universally judged to be attractive, (2) specifying hormonal and physiological correlates of physical attractiveness to determine whether attractiveness is a true signal of health and genetic quality, and (3) using such information to understand and explain eating disorders and body image dissatisfaction.*

BOX 16.2 | **Males prefer the scent of an ovulating female**

Concealed ovulation is one of the characteristics that uniquely mark the human species. But could it be that ovulation is not as "invisible" as we suspect? To investigate this possibility, Devendra Singh and Matthew Bronstad had each of a number of female college students wear a new, white, 100%-cotton T-shirt to bed for three nights during the fertile (follicular) phase of their menstrual cycle. During this time, they were prohibited from wearing perfume, using scented soaps or shampoos, eating spicy foods, engaging in sexual activity, or sharing their beds with anyone or anything (e.g., pets). A second T-shirt was worn for three days during the nonfertile, luteal phase of their cycle. Before bedding down with their clean T-shirts, participants were required to wash all their bed covers and sheets in unscented detergent. After each T-shirt was worn for the required three days, it was placed in a zip-lock bag and stored in a freezer. Male college students were then recruited to participate as raters. The raters were presented the defrosted T-shirts in pairs, with one member of the pair being the shirt worn by a female during her follicular phase and the second being the shirt worn by the same female during her luteal phase. Raters smelled each shirt one at a time and rated it for sexiness, pleasantness, and intensity on a scale of 1–10, with 10 indicating very sexy, pleasant, or intense. This procedure was continued until all pairs of shirts had been rated.

The analyses revealed that for 15 out of 21 pairs the average rating for pleasantness and sexiness was higher for the follicular T-shirt than the luteal T-shirt. Even after leaving the shirts at room temperature for a week and rerating them, the T-shirts worn during the follicular phase continued to have significantly higher sexiness and pleasantness ratings.

Singh and Bronstad (2001) concluded that ovulation in human females may not be as concealed as originally believed. These findings, along with others that have shown that during their fertile phase women tend to have more symmetrical breasts, lighter skin, and tend to wear more revealing clothing, suggest that detectable signs are present that signal fertility. The authors further speculate that, over time, a pair-bonded male may become insensitive to these cues (especially scent cues) but a non-pair-bonded male may not. This raises the possibility that these cues may serve to facilitate cheating as well as promote fertilization in a bonded pair.

Source: **Singh, D., & Bronstad, P.M. (2001).** Female body odour is a potential cue to ovulation. *Proceedings of the Royal Society of London B, 268,* 797–801.

The Loss of "Pure" Experience

What creature would not want to have the mental powers of *H. sapiens*? To us, the adaptive significance of being able to think rationally and symbolically seems unquestionable. Being able to "think past" the sensory data and grasp the underlying conceptual and theoretical properties responsible for the functioning of our world has permitted us power and control unmatched by any other species. There has been no "trade off" in the evolution of our minds. We have only *gained* in perceptual and cognitive power and have sacrificed nothing for it. Or have we?

A classic experiment in the human problem-solving literature was conducted by Karl Dünker more than a half a century ago (Dünker, 1945). A group of subjects was presented with a box, inside of which were a screen, a candle, some matches, and thumbtacks. They were told to use the materials to make a lamp. A second group was presented with the same materials, except that the screen, candle, matches, and thumbtacks were presented *with* the box, not in it. The second group had a much higher success rate in solving the problem. (To make a lamp: use the matches to drip some candle wax on the top of the box, mount the candle in the wax and thumbtack the whole thing to the screen). Often the subjects in the first group simply tossed the box aside once they had gotten the materials from it. It had served its purpose (so they thought).

Throughout this entire section on evolved human reasoning we have seen that the *form* of a problem's presentation often is more important than the *nature* of the problem itself. A box is not just a box. When presented with materials inside it, it becomes represented in the mind of the (human!) user as "something to put materials in." It takes on a conceptual life of its own, separate from the raw physical stimulus that the eyes perceive and the hands touch. Having evolved to "think past" the tangible world, we humans bring a virtual mountain of top-down symbolic, conceptual, and schematic baggage to every sensory event. This allows us to contact and contemplate the abstract, "invisible" physical forces and natural laws that drive the world. It provides us with the insight and empathy to understand the thoughts and feelings of other humans. But it also taints, embellishes, constrains, and even distorts every sensation, sapping them of their purity. Thus, when Henry V's 6,000 soldiers defeated more than 30,000 French knights at the battle of Agincourt, it had little to do with French military incompetence or the soggy terrain that bogged down the heavily armored French fighters. To Henry and all of England, it was a great sign of God's favor upon them and their righteous cause. (Never mind that a decade later God would apparently switch allegiances and begin fighting for Joan of Arc and the French!) Although our interpretations of reality may not be as grand as King Henry's, to some extent we are all like Dünker's subjects, unable to see things simply as they are. Chimpanzees do not have this problem; in fact, their visual memory may be superior to ours (Humphrey, 1998; Povinelli, 2000). Evolution gives no free gifts. In the 5 million years since our line split from the chimpanzees, *H. sapiens* have given up the innocent experience of life.

SUMMARY

One way to reconstruct the evolution of hominin thinking is by looking at handmade products, such as tools used in hunting, and assess the degree of cognitive ability required to construct those tools. Oldowan tools showed little evidence of advanced cognition. However, the later Acheulean tools were larger and better crafted, demonstrating a higher level of cognitive ability. The bifacial axe, perhaps the most representative element of the Acheulean tool kit, required considerable time, planning, and retouching for its creation. The ability to make this type of tool shows the emergence of motor, cognitive, and communication systems, including imitative skills unique to the hominin branch.

Advances in tool making during the Upper Paleolithic period provide the first evidence of symbolic ornaments and art. Artifacts produced in this era show evidence of the mind's evolving capacity for imaginative and abstract thinking. Evidence of a belief in the afterlife seems apparent with the practice of ritualized burial found at Upper Paleolithic sites.

Although the human brain is thought to have emerged 150,000 years ago, symbolic art, abstract art, and cultural artifacts did not appear until about 40,000 years ago. What caused this sudden use of human mentality after more than 100,000 years of dormancy? Clues found throughout history demonstrate that the human mind may not be in the head but in socialization with others. The Upper Paleolithic era appears to have ushered in a revolution in social life as well as one in tools and technology, and it may be this social context that is responsible for the relatively sudden emergence of human-like thinking.

Evidence of social context surrounding the evolution of human thinking can be found in our proficiency at social reasoning as opposed to abstract reasoning. Furthermore, modern men and women possess differential skills in thought and perception consistent with the notion that during the course of hominin evolution males and females were adapted to different social roles and engaged in different forms of labor.

KEY TERMS

Acheulean tools	dominance	Oldowan tools
active teaching	emulation	planning depth
agreeableness	evolved social reasoning	Solutrean blades
base rate neglect	executive functions	
cheat detection	first fictions	
division of labor hypothesis	impossible entities	
	neocortex ratio	

REVIEW QUESTIONS

1. Why might Acheulean tools be regarded as requiring more cognitive capacity than Oldowan tools?

2. Give two examples of primitive art in the form of impossible entities. What do these represent about hominin thinking?

3. Give an example that demonstrates how the Neanderthals and *Homo sapiens* were intellectually different from one another.

4. What is meant by evolved social reasoning, and why might it be that humans seem more capable of applying their reasoning skills in social rather than abstract settings?

5. Explain the evolutionary significance of the "Big Five" personality traits.

6. What is the division of labor hypothesis and what evidence is there to support it?

SUGGESTED READINGS

Byrne, R. (1995). *The thinking ape: Evolutionary origins of intelligence.* Oxford: Oxford University Press.

Corballis, M.C., & Lea, S.E.G. (1999). *The descent of mind.* Oxford: Oxford University Press.

Geary, D. (1998). *Male/female.* Washington, D.C.: APA Press.

WEB SITES

www.socialpsychology.org/wasona.htm to perform the Wason's Four Card Task.

www.handprint.com/LS/ANC/stones.html good site for information on the various hominin tool industries.

http://hebb.uoregon.edu/focus04/ University of Oregon's Web site for the evolution of cognition focus group.

http://ruccs.rutgers.edu/ArchiveFolder/Research%20Group/research.html the Web page of the Rutgers University Research Group on Evolution and Cognition.

The Evolution of Language

Why You Should Never Write a Chapter on the Evolution of Language

PERHAPS NOTHING IS MORE EMBLEMATIC of human uniqueness than language—truly nothing like it exists on earth. No other species has a system of communication that even approaches the creative potential, expressive power, and almost limitless flexibility of human language. But exactly *how* this prize made its way into our hands (minds, really) is an issue clouded in obscurity. Over the centuries, seemingly intelligent people have lapsed into wild, irrational speculation about the origins of language. For example, 17th-century writer John Webb claimed that Chinese was humanity's foundational language, preserved by Noah and his family on the ark during the great flood (Yaguello, 1991). In the 18th century, Scottsman James Burnett claimed that humans acquired language from birds, just as we had learned weaving and spinning from spiders (Burnett, 1773). With the publication of Darwin's *Origin* in 1859, one might suspect that theorizing on the pedigree of language would have adopted a more objective, temperate tone. This was not the case, however. In 1866, the Linguistic Society of Paris, the leading linguistic organization of the day, took the remarkable action of banning all papers dealing with language origins (Aitchison, 1998).

Although the situation has improved significantly and the ban (happily) has been lifted, we still do not know how language evolved. There is a good chance we may never know (for certain at least). This ignorance provides us with the first reason to think twice before writing a chapter on the evolution of language. This reason alone, however, rates less than a speed bump's worth of inhibition, because science often is energized by difficult questions. Moreover, saying that we do not know how language evolved is not the same as saying we know nothing about it or that we have no credible ideas. We have plenty of both. In fact, herein lies the second problem with writing a chapter on language evolution: entire books, too numerous to mention, have been written on the evolution of language and on specific aspects of language, such as phonology and syntax. No chapter, kept to a reasonable length, could hope to do justice to the vast abundance and broad diversity of ideas and theories that have been proposed or to the debates that have ensued on these issues. What follows, then, is an attempt to synthesize and organize the major themes in the evolution of language. It will, no doubt, prove inadequate in many respects. The aim, however, is to provide the reader with an appreciation for the complexity and significance of this topic and ignite a curiosity to probe deeper into this fascinating area by checking out some of the references cited here.

What Is Language?

A short answer or a long answer can be given to this question. The short answer is that language is a symbolic system of communication, which, in spoken form, utilizes basic elements called **phonemes** and **morphemes**. Phonemes are the basic units of sound in a language. For example, in English, /b/ refers to the "ba" sound associated with the letter b. English has about 45 basic sounds or phonemes. Ponder for a moment the fact that all you are doing when you speak English is simply combining and recombining 45 basic sounds. In the course of doing so, however, you have the power to incite a riot, inspire one to go on living or to lay down his or her life, move someone to tears, or bore another person to near insanity! Morphemes are the basic units of meaning in a language. A morpheme can be a word, such as "dog." A morpheme can also be a subword unit, such as "s," which, when attached to "dog" indicates plurality: "dogs."

The short answer provided in the preceding paragraph was fine as far as it went. However, it failed miserably to capture the important features that make language so evolutionarily significant. To truly appreciate language, we must press our definition further and recognize that language, as a symbolic system of communication, in the words of von Humbolt (1836), "makes infinite use of finite means." In others words, from out of the finite, language makes the infinite possible. Language does this because it possesses a number of indispensable characteristics that make it a communication system set apart from all others. Let's now lay out the long answer to the question of what language really is and see how it creates the infinite out of the finite.

"Infinite Use of Finite Means"

How can one create infinite communicative potential from finite communicative elements? To answer, we must begin by examining the state of the communicative arts in the absence of language, that is, with animal communication systems. By and large, animal communication systems are direct external expressions of internal states. Most animal communication involves a direct line between an animal's internal state and its auditory, gestural, and facial expressions, expressions usually designed to elicit some response from others. Thus, the animal is hungry, fearful, contented, sexually aroused, or whatever, and it signals this state to those around it for the purpose of eliciting some desired response. This leads us to the first important characteristic of language: **intervention**. Language is something that intervenes between the organism's internal state and its external expressions (Studdert-Kennedy, 1998). By breaking this link, language opens the possibility of expressing something other than the raw form of one's internal state. Communicative expression is thus permitted a certain freedom from the emotions, motives, and desires that drive the internal state of the organism. This freedom necessarily implies a second important characteristic of language: **conscious control**. Certain elements of language must be nonautomatic processes. The organism must be capable of exerting some form of voluntary control over the ultimate expressive message. Physiologically, humans have achieved this by bringing much of the vocal/articulatory structures under the control of the frontal lobe of the cerebral cortex, as opposed to the subcortical control more common in most other animals and primates.

The system described so far breaks the direct automatic linkage between internal state and external expression. However, for this system to achieve the infinite, it must possess a third characteristic: **generativity**. Generativity refers to the fact that a relatively small set of primitive elements can be arranged, rearranged, combined, ordered, and reordered to construct a nearly limitless set of more complex elements. Generativity was discussed in chapter 6 in the context of the evolution of motor movements, where complex motor routines could be constructed and refined from more basic elements, such as a throwing motion composed of shoulder rotation, forward striding, and wrist snapping, all set upon a bipedal posture. With language, generativity refers to the combining of a relatively small set of elemental sounds (phonemes and morphemes) to construct a limitless array of meaningful expressions (phrases and sentences). By itself, however, generativity does not ensure infinity of expression. For that, the fundamental elements upon which generativity operates must have two additional important characteristics: **arbitrariness** and **discreteness** (Hockett, 1963). Arbitrariness means that the fundamental elements of the system (in language, phonemes) have no inherent meaning. For example, the /b/ ("ba") sound associated with the letter b means nothing by itself. Its meaning emerges only from the way it is used in combination with other elements. This is critical, because if an elemental sound possesses inherent meaning, then it places constraints on the meaningfulness of the larger units of which it is a part. For example, suppose that among some creatures the /b/ sound means "I'm angry." Whenever "book," "hubub," "bad boy," "tbtzoba." or "bebopalubop" is uttered, the same response occurs in the listeners—they scram! Regardless of the accompanying sounds, the meaning of /b/ remains intact and therefore prejudices the interpretation of the larger units. Without arbitrariness, the meanings that a language can express are limited by the fundamental units available. With arbitrariness, meaning is allowed to emerge from the manner in which meaningless units are combined, and a small set of fundamental units can produce a dizzying variety of meanings.

Discreteness refers to the fact that elements in a system retain their integrity when combined and do not mix or blend with other elements. With language, one of the places in which the power of discreteness is most apparent is in the way morphemes combine to create novel words. Morphological units retain their integrity when combining to create novel words and ideas, they do not blend together to form some "averaged out" meaning. This quality of morphemes has been referred to as the **particulate principle** (Studdert-Kennedy, 1998). As an example, consider the word "singularities," which is a combination of two morphemes, "singularity" and "s." Singularity means "the quality of being singular, peculiar, uncommon." The "s" means "plurality, many, or more than one." By combining these morphemes, we create a new word that means "many singular, uncommon, qualities," as in the sentence: "He is a man of many singularities." If morphemes were blended together, so that word meanings occupied some average space between the morphological meanings, then singularities would simply mean "a few" (the average of single and many). Note that blending morphemes means that the resulting word will always have a meaning bounded by the limits set by the meanings of morphemes. Thus, language would be limited to the "idea space" found within the bounds of the available morphemes. Getting outside that space to explore novel, creative word meanings can only happen if morphologically intact units are combined, not blended. The infinite becomes possible when generativity is based on arbitrary, discrete units.

One critical element of language, then, is combining small sets of elements to create larger more meaningful ones. Another critical characteristic of language (number six, if you're counting) is that this combinatorial process must be rule based, not random or haphazard. **Syntax** refers to the system of rules used in the construction of "lawful" combinations of phonemes, morphemes, phrases, and sentences. Without an agreed-upon set of rules for what constitutes a meaningful message, language would lose all of its communicative power. For example, word order is a crucial element of syntax in English. Somewhere along the line, we English speakers all agreed that when making meaningful phrases we would put the subject first, the verb second, and the object last. Thus, we all understand that "Mary hit John" means something entirely different from "John hit Mary." If we all had our own rules for making phrases or if there were no rules, communication would break down. This leads us to a seventh important characteristic of language, it must be *shared by a community*. Because communication is an interpersonal act, language cannot exist within a single individual. Consider for a moment what I will call the Frenchman's nightmare. Imagine the last monolingual French speaker in an otherwise entirely monolingual English-speaking world. Does the Frenchman have language? It may sound strange, but the answer is most assuredly no. The Frenchman has a symbolic system, certainly, but not one that is capable of communicating. Language must be shared.

Finally, language is **referential**, that is, its symbols refer to other objects or events. When I utter the sound "dog," the sound is meant to refer to a specific object in the environment (one with fur and four legs and that barks and slobbers). In a sense, my sound is intended to direct the listener's attention or point the listener's mind toward a specific object or event. The referent in language may be a concrete object present in the here and now or it may be a displaced referent, with the object or event in the past or the future or perhaps even as an entirely hypothetical concept. It is this referential power that allows humans to use language to explore the past, theorize about the future, and weave imaginary worlds of supposition.

Now we are in a position to formulate a more complete definition of language. It is a generative system that intervenes between an organism's internal state and its external expression and that uses syntactical rules to combine a finite set of discrete and arbitrary elements to create an infinite set of communicative symbols that carry referential meaning to be shared with others. Now that we know what language is, we can begin to address the question of how it evolved. We begin by asking if animal communication shows any evidence of the important aforementioned properties of language.

Animal Syntax

Many animals produce long calls or songs that seem to involve the combining and recombining of discrete, separable elements. Whale and bird songs have been particularly attractive to researchers, because their productions appear to be rule based, hinting at the possibility of syntax. Researchers have spent untold hours recording and analyzing whale and bird songs to determine whether these animals, in fact, employ syntactical rules with discrete and arbitrary elements, the very foundations of language.

As they swim about in breeding waters, humpback whales will groan out a prolonged serenade designed to capture the attention and ardor of potential mates. Careful analysis reveals that these songs can be decomposed into subphrases, which combine to form phrases, which in turn combine to make themes, which combine to make songs, which are broadcast in sessions that may be repeated for hours on end (Payne & Payne, 1985; Payne, Tyack, & Payne, 1984). The combinations are not random and show evidence of an underlying system of rules at work guiding song construction. The rules, however, do not appear to be generative in nature. Once a whale acquires the song of a resident group, he continues to sing that song right along with all his mates. Any change in the song pattern will be reflected by the entire group. Whales appear to have no interest in singing unique songs. This contrasts sharply with human children, who will use their acquired syntactical rules to generate an almost embarrassing assortment of novel and creative utterances. Moreover, there is no evidence that the whale's phrases or songs carry any referential meaning beyond that of announcing group membership or displaying endurance to potential mates or rivals. Whale songs may provide an example of very elementary syntax, but that syntax appears to function on a restricted set of elements with meanings that are severely limited.

Bird songs show a similar pattern. A set of rules does seem to guide the combination of notes, syllables, and phrases to make extended (and sometimes quite beautiful) songs. For example, in their studies of the songs of black-capped chickadees, Jack Hailman and Millicent and Robert Ficken found that a strict four-note sequence is always observed (Hailman & Ficken, 1987; Hailman, Ficken, & Ficken, 1985, 1987). The rules seem to work as follows: the notes A,B,C, and D must always be sung in that order and a phrase must end on D. However, repetitions and omissions within the sequence are permissible. For example, AADD or BCDD are acceptable phrases (in fact, they are quite common). Although it is still an open question as to whether the different combinations convey different messages, there is no compelling evidence that they do. In other songbirds, such as sparrows, different song arrangements do seem to carry distinct messages, but the range of these messages is quite limited. Different songs are used to announce one's individual or group identity, defend territory, or attract mates (Marler & Peters, 1989; Marler & Pickert, 1984). This, however, seems to pretty much exhaust the conversational repertoire of most birds.

Many primates also produce long calls composed of distinct series of different vocalizations. A number of New World monkeys, including titis, tamarins, and capuchins, as well as gibbons (an Old World lesser ape) produce extended calls that show evidence of a rule-based system used in the combining of shorter, clearly distinguishable vocal units (Cleveland & Snowdon, 1981; Marshall & Marshall, 1976; Raemaekers, Raemaekers, & Haimoff, 1984; Robinson, 1979, 1984). Capuchin monkeys, for example, construct compound calls based on a system of (rather loose) rules specifying which vocalizations may precede and follow others. However, unlike English, in which word order strictly specifies the role an element can play in the meaning of a sentence (subject—verb—object), meaning and order do not appear to be intimately linked in capuchin calls. Instead, evidence suggests that capuchins combine calls in a "blending" fashion, in which the meaning of the compound call is a rough average of the elements (Robinson, 1984; Hauser, 2000). In apes, variations in long calls do seem to serve different functions. In gibbons, mated and unmated males produce different long calls, and other variations signal such things as sex, location, and territorial defense (Raemakers et al., 1984). Chimpanzee long calls generally serve social functions, such as maintaining group cohesion over long distances or reinforcing kinship and coalition bonds, especially among males who will sometimes chorus in unison (Mitani, 1994; Mitani & Brandt, 1994).

Taken as a whole, the picture with primates is not very different from that of birds and whales. Primate long calls display some evidence of very primitive syntax, but there is little evidence of generativity in their productions and the range of functions is quite limited (Ujhelyi, 1998). Syntax often has been regarded as a uniquely human attribute, and the syntactical ability shown by nonhuman primates, whales, and birds certainly appears paltry in comparison. However, as psychologist David Premack once speculated, perhaps the real reason that animals do not talk is *not* because they have no syntax but because they have nothing interesting to say (Premack, 1986).

Symbolic Reference

The most notable examples of what appear to be genuine referential content in animal communication are the alarm calls of vervet monkeys. It's not easy being a vervet. The habitats of these smallish Old World primates are teeming with every manner of predator attacking from high and low. From above, vervets must be on guard against hawks and eagles. From below, snakes are a lethal concern. And from somewhere in between, leopards, cheetahs, and other large predators can make life miserable (and short) for these little monkeys. Vervets, however, have evolved an elaborate alarm call system in which distinct calls signify the type of predator present. Upon hearing a particular call, another vervet will immediately respond in an appropriate manner. For instance, when an eagle call is sounded, nearby vervets will scan the sky and dart under the nearest bush. By contrast, a leopard call will send vervets scurrying to treetops (leopards can climb trees, but not to the highest, flimsiest branches). The important question raised is whether the vervet's distinctive calls function like words that act as referents for specific predators. In other words, when the vervet makes its leopard noise, is he or she doing basically the same thing I do when I make *my* leopard noise (the word "leopard")? One could argue that an alarm call simply attracts attention. Once attentive to their surroundings, monkeys may simply respond based on environmental cues, such the sight of circling birds above or the movement of vegetation nearby. To see if this was the case, Seyfarth, Cheney, and Marler (1980) played recorded vervet alarm calls to unsuspecting monkeys in out-of-context situations. Thus, the only basis for a response would be the nature of the call itself, because no relevant environmental information would be present to inform the monkeys about the kind of predator that was supposedly present. Despite this, monkeys dashed up trees when the leopard call was played, flung themselves under bushes to the eagle alarm, and stood erect staring groundward when the snake call sounded. It seemed as if the calls alone carried the meanings of "eagle," "leopard," and "snake."

Further studies and observations tend to confirm the notion that the communicative capacity of some animals does include an understanding of referential content. The sign-language-trained chimpanzee Washoe originally learned the sign for "open" in the context of doors. However, he quickly generalized this sign to other "closed" situations, such as when confronted with a container or faucet (Gardner, Gardner, & Van Cantfort, 1989). David Premack's language-trained chimp Sarah produced the symbol "same" when confronted with half an apple or a container half-filled with water (Premack & Premack, 1983). In these examples, the apes appear to understand that a particular linguistic symbol refers to specific and somewhat abstract conditions in the environment. The dances of honeybees can inform hive mates about the location and condition of a cache of nectar, a referent that is displaced in both time and space (Gould, 1990; Gould & Gould, 1988). Rhesus monkeys even understand that certain calls refer to the same thing and, therefore, should be treated similarly, even when the calls themselves are acoustically different. For example, both a "warble" and a "harmonic arch" are used by the monkeys to refer to a high-quality food source, and a "grunt" is used to refer to a low-quality food source. Hauser (1996) presented monkeys with repetitions of warbles until they were bored stiff and no longer responded to them. Then he played a harmonic arch. Although the harmonic arch sounded different, it failed to arouse any response in the monkeys. This suggests that the monkeys categorized the sounds based on their referent and not on acoustic qualities.

All of this suggests that some animals have a certain referential capacity in their communicative systems. But how do these referential abilities compare with humans? The answer seems to be that animal referential capacities are (once again) strictly limited compared with those of humans (Hauser, 2000). First, with only rare exceptions (such as honeybees), animal communication is restricted to here-and-now references. A vervet monkey does not make a leopard call to "discuss" yesterday's big cat incident. Even with honeybees, who do show some capacity for displaced reference, the range of topics is limited pretty much to food and where to find it. Second, the animal's communicative signals continue to be strongly tied to its emotional state. Nearly all chimpanzee utterances are linked to emotional states (Goodall, 1986). Monkey alarm calls also are not dispassionate statements of current events. The degree of threat is indicated by the frequency and intensity of the call, and the type is indicated by the manner (e.g., eagle versus snake) of the call itself. Even bees get excited and dance more vigorously when the food source is of especially high quality. The point here is that the animal's signal conveys not only referential information to the observer but also highly reliable information about the animal's (relatively) immediate experience and internal state. This is not necessarily the case with human language, in which the referent of an utterance might be reasonably clear, but the experience and internal state of the speaker may be equivocal at best. If we are walking along and I suddenly blurt out "chicken," then it's fairly clear what I'm referring to—but what exactly is going on in my head? Am I hungry? Am I shocked at seeing a chicken crossing the road? Did I suddenly realize which came first? Have I discovered the answer to my cholesterol problem?

Finally, unlike human words, the referential signals of animals are not entirely arbitrary with regard to their function in the environment. For example, the acoustic properties of the vervet's alarm calls vary in functionally significant ways depending on the predator. The big cat alarm is loud and multisyllabic, informing both the predator and other monkeys of the situation at hand. Nothing could be more disheartening to a famished feline hunting via stealth than to hear "we know you're out there!" broadcast far and wide around monkeyville. The eagle alarm, by contrast, is a loud, unisyllabic announcement that is difficult for an air predator to localize (Hauser, 2000). A similar pattern can be heard in squirrel alarm calls, in which a difficult-to-localize "whistle" warns others of an approaching hawk, whereas an easier-to-home-in-on "chatter" is used to announce the presence of a land-based threat such as a coyote (Owings, Hennessy, Leger, & Gladney, 1986; Leger, Owings, & Gelfand, 1980). The physical properties of human words are in a very real sense arbitrary in relation to the environment. If we all agreed tomorrow to warn of fire by yelling "doblath," we could do so and would still get out of the building with just as much efficiency as before. The same would not be true of squirrels and monkeys. Their calls refer, but the physical character of their calls also interacts in functional ways with the environment. Changing the acoustic properties of the signal would reduce that functionality.

Ape Language Studies

Thus far we have seen that in their natural settings some animals show evidence of a few basic properties of language: discrete elements, primitive syntax, and concrete and displaced reference. On its own, no nonhuman animal has managed to put all these elements together in a generative way. But the fact that we can find hints of language in many creatures has proved tantalizing to many researchers. Could human-assisted training do for them what natural selection did for us and expand their embryonic linguistic skills into full-blown language? And wouldn't the animals most likely to accomplish such a feat be our closest relatives, the great apes, who apparently have "linguistic" brain structures similar to those of humans (see Box 17.1)? The most intriguing and controversial chapter in the entire study of animal communication systems is the history of ape language studies.

The first noteworthy attempt to teach an ape language was made in the 1950s by Keith and Cathy Hayes, who raised the chimpanzee **Vicki** as, literally, a member of their family. In every way, Vickie was treated the same as the Hayes's infant son, including exposure to the rich linguistic environment typical of a human household. The purpose was to see whether Vicki would acquire spoken language in a manner similar to the way in which human children effortlessly pick up language from normal, daily stimulation. The results were a tremendous disappointment. Before Vicki's untimely death at age 7, she could say only four (not very intelligible) words, despite intensive speech training far exceeding anything typical for the average child (Hayes & Hayes, 1951).

Language and the Ape Brain

BOX 17.1

Ape Brains Show Linguistic Promise

Three members of the family of great apes have a crucial speech-related brain feature previously thought unique to humans. This is the finding of a pair of researchers in Atlanta, GA,

who carried out magnetic resonance imaging (MRI) scans on chimpanzees, bonobos, and gorillas. They say they were surprised no one had looked for the crucial lopsided structure in great apes before. The discovery could imply that evolution of brain structures linked to speech began before the ancestors of humans and apes parted ways.

Puzzling Discrepancy

Brodmann's area 44 is part of the Broca's area in the human brain. It is critical for speech production and is larger in the left hemisphere than in the right. Claudio Cantalupo and William Hopkins of Emory University and Georgia State University were puzzled by the fact that apes had a similar structure but obviously could not speak.

"The part possession by great apes of a homologue of Broca's area is puzzling, particularly considering the discrepancy between sophisticated human speech and the primitive vocalisations of great apes," they write in the journal *Nature*.

Right-Handed Apes

"This may be explained by the contribution that gestures have made to the evolution of human language and speech," they speculate. Captive great apes tend to gesture with their right hands, especially when making some kind of vocal noise, they note. Their theory is that, as the ancestors of humans and great apes learned to grunt and gesticulate, the left side of their area 44s grew larger. However, it appears that for some reason grunting and gesturing went on to become language in humans but not in the apes.

Source: **Cantalupo, C., & Hopkins, W.D. (2001).** Asymmetric Broca's area in great apes. *Nature, 414*, 505. Copyright © 2001 Macmillan Publishers Ltd. Reprinted by permission.

One serious problem with the Vicki experiment was the fact that the chimpanzee vocal apparatus does not permit articulate speech in the same manner that the human vocal system does. It was clear that no chimp could speak, but did that necessarily mean that no chimp could acquire language? In the 1960s and 1970s, a number of researchers embarked on projects designed to teach apes American Sign Language (ASL). Apes are highly dexterous, so the motor movements of signing were a much better fit with their behavioral proclivities. Beatrix and Allan Gardner used the same general approach as the Hayeses. They raised their chimp Washoe as though it were a human child, part of a household rich with sign language instead of speech (Gardner, Gardner, & Van Cantfort, 1989). Herbert Terrace and his colleagues at Columbia University used a more controlled setting to teach ASL to their chimp Nim Chimpsky, and Francine Patterson began teaching ASL to the gorilla Koko (Patterson & Linden, 1981; Terrace, Petitto, Sanders, & Bever, 1979).

The results of these projects have been mixed. Washoe, Nim, and other similarly trained apes have proved capable of acquiring vocabularies ranging from 100–150 signs. They may even be capable of using their "words" generatively. For example, when encountering a swan on a river, Washoe reportedly made the signs for "water" and "bird," (i.e., she called it a "water-bird"). Critics, however, point out that Washoe may simply have been using signs to describe two prominent aspects of the visual scene: the water and the bird. Furthermore, critics have argued that many of the signs in Washoe's and other apes' vocabularies are more in the minds of their trainers than they are in the minds of the apes. With the exception of Terrace's Nim project, much of the data attesting to apes' abilities has been anecdotal and not always well documented (Ristau & Robbins, 1982). Upon visiting Nim Chimsky, Jane Goodall commented that all of the signs he demonstrated were familiar to her from chimps in the wild (Pinker, 1994). Furthermore, the most spectacular claims from the Koko project (such as the highly developed syntax, spontaneous signing, and the production of puns, jokes, and even lies) have yet to be published in scientific journals in which they can be scrutinized critically (Lieberman, 1998, p. 45; Willingham, 2001, p. 527). Thus, the degree to which these projects can claim actual acquisition of language skills above and beyond instrumental learning and experimenter bias remains unclear.

A truly unique project in ape language learning is the ongoing Kanzi project of Sue Savage-Rambaugh at Georgia State University. The project is unique in at least two ways: (1) Kanzi is a bonobo (*Pan paniscus*) rather than a common chimpanzee (*Pan troglodytes*). Bonobos are a much rarer subspecies of chimpanzee and are thought to be somewhat more intelligent and socially more similar to humans than their common cousins. (2) Kanzi's language acquisition occurred via serendipity rather than concerted effort, which makes his learning more comparable to that of human children than other ape language learners. Originally, Savage-Rumbaugh set out to teach language to Kanzi's mother, Matata, using a system of computer-keyboard-based "words" called lexigrams. Kanzi was literally just hanging around while experimenters were busily trying to train Matata to use the lexigram keyboard to communicate with them. Matata was largely a disappointment, but Kanzi astounded the experimenters by spontaneously learning to use many of the symbols. The experimenters decided to allow Kanzi to continue learning simply through casual, everyday interaction rather than a strict training regiment. The results have been the most impressive to date in ape language learning.

Kanzi not only has acquired an extensive vocabulary of lexigram symbols, but his acquisition and subsequent use of those symbols has been very "human-like." Unlike most other language-trained apes, Kanzi was quick to generalize a symbol's meaning beyond its immediate context. Thus, he almost immediately understood that the symbol for "juice" could be used when he was thirsty, when there was a spill on the floor, when he wanted a reward for a job well done, or in numerous other appropriate situations. The symbol was not strictly tied to the specific context in which it was learned. In addition, Kanzi spontaneously acquired a bidirectional understanding of symbols, which contrasts sharply with the strictly one-directional manner more common with other ape language learners. After most apes have successfully learned to produce a certain symbol when presented with a certain object, often they later will fail when required to produce the object when presented with the symbol. Kanzi never had this problem (Tomasello & Call, 1997). Other aspects of Kanzi's language use are almost eerily human. He can be quite conversant and even unselfish in his use of language, such as when he makes requests on behalf of other apes. He has proved capable of applying his skills in entirely novel settings, such as "talking" a blind researcher around his enclosure.

Kanzi has even been known to take his keyboard along with him as he ventures through his forested enclosure, apparently talking to himself with the lexigram symbols (Savage-Rumbaugh & Lewin, 1994).

Even more impressive is Kanzi's ability to understand spoken English. Many animals can respond to commands, such as when a dog obligingly "sits" or "stays." Kanzi, however, is able to comprehend and respond appropriately to relatively complex sentences that require an understanding of the syntactical role of words being used. For example, Kanzi can successfully execute a verbal command such as "take the telephone outdoors" or "put the money in the mushrooms" (Savage-Rumbaugh et al., 1993). Note that in these examples the actions cannot necessarily be deduced from the knowledge of the objects. Kanzi also can reliably distinguish between commands such as "put the ball on the hat" and "put the hat on the ball." Tomasello (1994) scrutinized Kanzi's language comprehension performance and concluded that Kanzi understands that the object being acted on (that which is to be "put" in the preceding example) must come first in the command, whereas the placement of the object ("on the…") must occur afterward. This indicates some basic understanding of syntax, but it is more of the variety of recognizing that language marks such things as "giver" and "thing to be given," or "putter" and "thing to put," rather than the more general categories of "agent" and "action." It is noteworthy that Kanzi's language *production* trails somewhat behind his *comprehension*. His lexigram "utterances" tend to show a consistent, lawful ordering with action first and object second ("tickle Kanzi," "chase ball," etc.), but there is no evidence that he understands that producing words in varying orders could convey different meanings (Greenfield & Savage-Rumbaugh, 1990, 1991).

What can't Kanzi do? As impressive as his abilities are, some intriguing differences remain between Kanzi's comprehension and use of language and that of the average human. Kanzi, for instance, falters when commands involve acting upon more than one object. If asked to "give Sue the bottle and fork," Kanzi will hand over the bottle but not the fork. His linguistic productions are usually very short, two-word requests designed specifically to obtain something for himself. Greenfield and Savage-Rumbaugh (1990) analyzed Kanzi's utterances and concluded that 96% of what Kanzi produced were requests, leaving very little of his linguistic energy devoted to merely commenting or socializing. Contrast this with the linguistic behavior of human children (and some adults) who are more than content to rattle on and on about nothing in particular. Most researchers who have studied Kanzi's abilities have concluded that he operates at about the level of 2- or 3-year-old human child (Lieberman, 1998; Tomasello, 1994; Tomasello & Call, 1997). Quite impressive as apes go, but would anyone attempt to argue that the differences between a competent adult speaker and 2-year-old child are insignificant?

Lessons from Animal Language Studies

What does this survey of animal "language" teach us? First, we see incipient forms of many of the critical elements of language in many different species. A very primitive form of syntax may guide the calls of a number of different animals, including birds, whales, and some primates. The calls of these animals often are based upon smaller arbitrary and discrete units. In some species, evidence suggests that calls have a referential function, such as the alarm calls of vervet monkeys.

There is even evidence of displacement in reference in the dances of honeybees. The exploits of Kanzi demonstrate that, in apes at least, many of these incipient qualities can be expanded into a linguistic competence that is vaguely human in some respects. Taken together, these findings give the impression of a natural linguistic energy trembling just beneath the surface in the mental architectures of many creatures. Many of the basic elements seem to be out there, so that under the right circumstances they could develop and expand. Why, then, are there no talking apes or whales? With all its obvious advantages, why has language flowered on only one tiny twig of life's immense tree? Wouldn't a chimp with language be in a vastly more competitive position than one without? Thoughts such as this have crossed the mind of more than one prominent researcher, including Jane Goodall:

> Sometimes, when watching the chimpanzees, I have felt that, because they have no human-like language, they are trapped within themselves. Their calls, postures and gestures, together add up to a rich repertoire, a complex and sophisticated method of communication. But it is non-verbal. How much more they might accomplish if only they could talk to each other. (1990, p. 208)

Maybe so—but, then again, maybe not. It is quite possible that the reason that no other animals have language is simply because it would do them no good. Our dismay over the lack of language in other animals is entirely a result of the fact that we see language from an exclusively human-centered point of view. We see how useful and advantageous it is *for us*. This blinds us to the fact that language also has many disadvantages. It seems patently obvious to us that honeybees would do so much better if they could talk to each other in the hive, rather than having to do that "waggle" dance to inform others about a local food source. The only problem, of course, is that a talking honeybee would have a head so huge that it couldn't fly! Language has disadvantages. It is conceivable that in the 5 million years since the divergence of the hominin and chimpanzee evolutionary lines, talking chimps began to emerge along their line, just as talking hominins did along ours. Those prototalkers, however, were quickly outcompeted by the nontalkers and thus summarily dispensed to the dustbin of history (Knight, 1998). Only through the most unlikely confluence of circumstances has our lineage found language to be a strength rather than a weakness. In every other species throughout evolutionary history, language has been a loser. Studies of animal communication systems have helped to elucidate just how extraordinarily difficult it is to make language an asset to an organism's survival. Language just should not evolve, and animal studies and ape experiments have given us a clearer idea of why.

Why Language Should Not Evolve

In our extended definition, language is something that intervenes between the internal state of an organism and its outward auditory expression. Intervention requires a certain degree of conscious control over the vocal signal. Thus, if language is to evolve, the first major evolutionary challenge is *bringing the communicative signal under conscious control*. However, it is precisely at this point that we run into a conflict of interest between those sending messages (signalers) and those receiving messages (receivers), a conflict that has successfully blocked the evolution of language in all but our own species.

Evolution is a competitive business. Natural selection will favor both signalers and receivers who can use their skills to their own reproductive advantage (Krebs & Dawkins, 1984). Imagine for a moment that you are a squirrel that has gained a small measure of conscious control over your vocal calls. When you spot a hawk circling above, instead of automatically vocalizing "Hawk! Hawk!" (in Squirrelese, of course), you have the capacity to substitute that signal for a "Coyote! Coyote!" signal (note: this substitution need not imply an *intentional* act on the part of the squirrel. Initially it could have been just a lucky accident, sustained later by positive consequences). While you and your fellow squirrels are scurrying about collecting acorns, you notice a hawk above and shout out "Coyote!" Your comrades dash up to treetops, where they become easy targets for the hawk. Meanwhile, you take cover under a nearby bush until danger passes. Losing a few of your squirrel buddies suits you just fine, of course, because this means less competition for high-quality mates, more acorns for you to eat, and a higher likelihood of producing your own copious offspring. This would seem to be a good scenario for the evolution of ever-increasing conscious control of vocal signals. There is only one problem: at the same time that the trait of greater conscious control over vocal signals is spreading in the squirrel population, so is the trait of ignoring those consciously controlled vocalizations. To understand why this is so, revisit that first occasion when you made your deceptive "Coyote!" call. Not every squirrel immediately ran up a tree. A few hung around on the ground and, instead of heeding your warning, they copied your actions and dove for cover. They survived and spread their trait of skeptical listening. Thus, over the generations, as the more gullible squirrels were eaten up, the proportion of squirrels likely to follow the voluntary signal (the vocal call) would dwindle rapidly and be overwhelmed by those following the more reflexive action. One day a descendant of yours calls out "Coyote!" only to find that everybody is too smart to listen! As listeners evolve to disregard consciously controlled signals in favor of involuntary ones, conscious control over signals loses its fitness advantage.

This example highlights the fundamental conflict of interest between signalers and receivers that blocks the evolution of conscious control. Signalers are interested in conscious control, because they can use it deceptively to their advantage. But listeners are interested in reliable messages that offer useful information about the environment, and the most reliable messages are the *involuntary, automatic* ones. Smart listeners make voluntary signals useless. This is precisely why chimpanzees do not talk: they're too smart. Chimpanzee listeners have evolved to be highly discriminating and demanding. They simply will not allow vocal signals to be anything but truthful, reliable messages about another chimp's internal state. Thus, chimpanzee vocalizations have remained largely under the control of the emotional, limbic brain and are almost exclusively bound to emotional states (Goodall, 1986; Knight, 1998). Chimpanzees deceive in many ways but not with vocal signals. With great effort, they can suppress vocalizations when doing so is advantageous, but "there are no reported examples of apes of any species using vocalizations to actively mislead or deceive conspecifics" (Tomasello & Call, 1997, p. 258).

This evolutionary logjam between signalers and receivers has proved insurmountable for all but one rare species: us. For some strange reason, skeptical listeners failed to put a stop to the increasing voluntary control of hominin vocalizations. In fact, it is quite obvious that human listeners today are anything but skeptical. We assume honesty rather than deception. We search for reasons why someone would lie, not for reasons why someone would be truthful. We readily ask complete strangers for directions. Although we are the products of the same competitive process that created all other primates, we listen, not at all like skeptical chimpanzees, but as trusting humans. The penetrating question, then, concerning the evolution of language in humans, is why hominin listeners so readily believed everything they were told? The answer, of course, can only be that somehow the messages being sent enhanced the fitness of the listeners. This means that hominin signalers were sending honest messages. But why send honest messages when dishonest ones are far more advantageous to the sender? A splendid singularity occurred along the hominin branch that made honest talk advantageous to both senders and recipients. The insurmountable obstacle to the evolution of language had been surmounted: a trusting community had formed. In the trusting community, a signaler can trade off honest voluntary vocalizations for status within the group (Dessalles, 1998). The honest signals provide useful information to the listeners, and the status provides an advantage for the signaler. Everybody wins, and the evolutionary gateway opens wide to language and beckons it onward.

The Evolution of Language I: Getting Control of the Signal

We do not know how language evolved. Thus, the ideas sketched out in the next sections must be understood as reasonable scenarios, not scientific facts. Supportive evidence for these theoretical notions will be discussed, but in most cases conclusive tests of these theories still need to be formulated. Many ideas are controversial, and some may prove ultimately untestable. However, science begins with ideas, and we do have some plausible ideas about how language evolved and how hominins achieved control over their vocalizations within the context of a trusting community.

As far back as 4 million years ago, *Australopithecus* had achieved a level of unprecedented bipedalism among primates. With bipedalism, the hands became free from the responsibilities of locomotion and could be used for other purposes, such as making tools and throwing stones. William Calvin (1993) argued that accurate throwing may have provided the bridge between the involuntary signals of ancient primates and the conscious control of movement necessary for language. Calvin showed that accurate throwing cannot rely on neural feedback mechanisms but must be planned out in advanced. Thus, accurate throwers must be capable of organizing and executing a sequence of preplanned motor actions. Primates, as a rule, are dreadful throwers. Hominins, however, broke with this tradition and began honing their throwing skills to never-before-seen levels. If *Australopithecus* was able to significantly advance throwing skill beyond that of present-day apes, then the motor foundations of language may go back as far as 3 million years or more. Two lines of evidence suggest this possibility. First, analysis of the Australopith hand (see chapter 6) indicates that this species would have had the dexterity necessary for gripping and throwing stones. Second, Oldowan tools make their appearance in the archeological record about 2.6 million years ago, and although they do not necessarily represent a significant advance in intellectual prowess, they do seem to indicate a level of motor control and planning beyond that of apes. Later forms of *Australopithecus* may have been engaged in the creation of some of these tools. Thus, it is possible that a significant advance in sequentially planned, voluntarily executed motor routines was in place in later forms of *Australopithecus* and that this served as the foundation for the motor control necessary for the later evolution of speech.

Corballis (1991) and Deacon (1995) also pointed out that the advances in throwing and tool-making skills would have necessarily involved generativity. In other words, those species of *Australopithecus* and/or *Homo* who were accurate throwers and skillful tool makers would have had the ability to decompose their motor routines into more fundamental elements that could then be recombined in novel ways to produce new routines. This generative ability, first evolved and applied to motor actions, could have been co-opted later in the service of language, in which phonological and morphological elements must be combined to create meaningful utterances and sentences. This scenario is further bolstered by the fact that these functions share space in the left hemisphere of the brain. Analyses of Oldowan tools suggest that their creators were right handed, which means that the advances in motor control guiding tool manufacture and throwing were mediated largely in the left hemisphere. Dunbar (1996, pp. 136–139) marshaled evidence indicating that right-hemisphere dominance for emotional and facial information has a long evolutionary history, predating (and including) primates. Thus, as more controlled and generative motor capacity evolved, its cerebral representation was localized in the left hemisphere by virtue of the right's already established preoccupation with emotional information. Brain endocasts from early species of *Homo*, such as *habilis* and *rudolfensis*, show enlargements in left-hemisphere regions containing both Broca's and Wernicke's areas, leading some researchers to propose that linguistic ability may already have been present in these species (Tobias, 1987; Wilkins & Wakefield, 1995). It is also possible, however, that these areas represented a more general motor-generative capacity that language later co-opted (Corballis, 1991).

Merlin Donald (1991, 1999) incorporated many of these ideas into his more general theory of language evolution, which relies heavily on the concept of **mimesis**: the ability to represent and refine motor actions. Mimetic skill, according to Donald, involves the ability to mentally represent motor actions in the head and to voluntarily rehearse and refine them to increase their precision and effectiveness (Fig. 17.1). A human can mentally envision the perfect throw and then practice the action, often refining the basic elements and organizing them in more fluid ways. Apes throw stones and sticks, but they do not practice throwing stones and sticks. Only humans do that, and, according to Donald, it is mimesis that permits this. To engage in motor practice, one must have voluntary access to one's own mind, what Donald called **autocueing** (Donald, 1993). Apes have excellent memories, but there is no evidence that they can voluntarily retrieve information from their minds. Instead, their minds are cued from the environment. Hominins, by contrast, began to retrieve, at will, representations of motor routines in entirely out-of-context situations. They began to throw stones, just for the sake of bettering the act, not because there was something they wanted to kill or scare away. To support

Plan　　　　　　　**Execute**　　　　　　　**Review**

Figure 17.1 An important element of mimesis is the ability to consciously envision, plan, execute, and review motor actions. In this way, actions can be rehearsed and refined to progressively approach an idealized model of performance. (Adapted from Donald, 1999, p. 144.)

his argument, Donald pointed to evidence of a wide array of representational and intellectual skills present in the absence of language, based, according to him, on a largely autonomous and evolutionarily older mimetic system (see chapter 6; Donald, 1998). The critical point is that the advances in motor control presumably present in late *Australopithecus* and early *Homo* also may have entailed other foundational aspects of language, such as generativity, symbolic representational abilities, and autocues or voluntary access to the mind's contents.

Donald (1998) proposed a sequence of mimetic evolution in which the earliest forms include such abilities as throwing, toolmaking, and emotional displays. Only later do mimetic abilities dealing with the sharing of motor knowledge emerge, involving such significant skills as pedagogy and imitation, thereby allowing for the transmission of specific motor skills, such as those involved in toolmaking. This sequence fits well with the evidence about the transition from Oldowan to Acheulean tool cultures. As discussed in the previous chapter, the Acheulean culture emerged about 1.4 million years ago with *H. erectus*, involving larger, more sophisticated tools that demanded greater representational capacity on the part of the toolmaker. By about 300,000 years ago, the Acheulean industry had evolved from simple single-component tools to "composite" ones, in which a number of separate elements had to be joined or bound together (Ambrose, 2001). Constructing these tools required that *H. erectus* be capable of planning and executing a predetermined sequence of motor acts. This general motor-sequencing skill is also essential to the construction of grammatical phrases. Furthermore, experimental evidence demonstrates that Acheulean tools would have been difficult to make based on mere observation, which suggests that *H. erectus* may have engaged in some level of active teaching in order to transmit toolmaking skill to younger generations (Washburn & Moore, 1980). The presence of distinctive variations in Achulean tools based on locale and region supports the notion of cultural transmission of toolmaking skills (Foley, 1987; Mithen, 1994; Wynn & Tierson, 1990). Acheulean tools, therefore, may indicate that somewhere between 1 million and 300,000 years ago, *H. erectus* had elevated mimetic skill beyond accurate throwing to complex tool production and efficient teaching of motor skills in a relatively stable culture. If so, then not only do we have an example of the kind of consciously controlled motor skills necessary for spoken language, but also the use of those skills for the purpose of transmitting honest information. This runs us smack-dab into the question of why any hominin would voluntarily transmit honest information. He or she would have done so only as part of a community in which sharing honest information was rewarding for the sharer.

Evolution of Language II: The Trusting Community

We have seen thus far that hominins' expanding motor capacities may have laid the groundwork for the conscious control necessary for language. That conscious control could be used for communicative purposes (such as teaching another to make a tool), but the next step of actually voluntarily sharing honest information could only be accomplished through the simultaneous emergence of **trusting communities** of hominins.

Group Mimesis, Ritual, and Male Provisioning

According to Donald (1998), some of the last forms of mimesis to emerge would have been those involved in group activities such as dance, elaborate games, and rituals. In these activities, mimesis is not just used to share motor information but as a means of symbolic representation. With group dance or other forms of ritualized mimesis, a group can recreate a past event, collectively engage in ceremony, and reinforce tribal values and identity. In doing so, group cohesion is strengthened and relational bonds among members are established, renewed, and invigorated. A number of researchers have argued that the emergence of **ritual** might have been the key to the creation of trusting groups in our evolutionary heritage.

Terrence Deacon (1997) argued that ritual provides the solution to a vexing and potentially devastating problem that faced *H. erectus*. A variety of pressures, such as increasingly dependent offspring, the increasing need for meat in the diet, and competition from other hominin groups, conspired to force erectus into larger, more complex social groups for survival. Large social groups, however, do not coexist easily with male provisioning of offspring. As discussed in chapter 10, without a reasonable degree of paternity certainty, males generally will not bother to provision youngsters. For gibbons, the solution to this problem is for a mated pair to establish a wide territory and live relatively isolated from other gibbons, thereby minimizing opportunities for hanky panky (or what biologists call extra-pair copulations). Hominins, however, live more like chimpanzees, in large multimale, multifemale groups in which hanky panky is hard to avoid. Unlike chimpanzees, however, *H. erectus* could have used evolved mimetic skill as a ritual means of publically "marking" a mated couple. A mated pair could be symbolically rather than physically isolated. Once so marked and acknowledged by the entire community as a legitimate pair, the mated couple would be understood as "off limits" to other group members. This would reduce the detrimental effects of rampant mate competition and increase paternity certainty, thus allowing for male provisioning of offspring. Group living and male provisioning could coexist and *H. erectus* could avoid extinction.

Christopher Knight (1991, 1998) and Camilla Power (1998) concurred with Deacon about the important link between ritual and male provisioning in the establishment of a trusting community but contended that the original trusting community would have been largely female centered. In an almost bizarre evolutionary scenario, Knight and Power argued that the stress of highly dependent offspring would have forced hominin females to band together and deny sex to males unless the males consented to provision their offspring. The story goes as follows: About 1 million years ago, the burden of slowly maturing, highly dependent offspring placed extreme pressure on hominin females. Male provisioning would have been essential to care for their offspring. A constant threat to male provisioning for mothers and expectant mothers would have been present in the form of any adolescent girl maturing into fertility. The presence of fertile young women could have potentially induced (or seduced) resident males to switch from parental provisioning to mate provisioning. Moreover, by the time of late erectus and early archaic *Homo*, most, if not all, outward signs of ovulation were gone, except for the bleeding of menstruation. Hominin males would have been highly sensitive to the presence of menstrual blood on any female, as this would be the only reliable indicator of fertility. However, pregnant hominin females and hominin mothers would also have been highly sensitive to this sign, as it would be a reliable indicator of a threat to their survival and that of their offspring.

To control this threat, hominin females would have used ritual to establish strong communal bonds among themselves and to coerce into their group any maturing adolescent females who might otherwise divert the attention of resident males. In essence, hominin females formed a union that graciously shared material benefits and social support among members in good standing but mercilessly shunned and intimidated female outcasts. Upon reaching her first menstruation, an adolescent girl had two choices: join the female union and follow their rules (especially with regard to relations with males) or go it alone (completely alone). Joining the female club would have involved engaging in ritualized actions, symbolic dances, and having the body smeared with blood and painted with red ochre dye to show commitment to the group. Within the female community, there would be complete loyalty and trust; outside the group would be only isolation from one's friends and kin. It would have been within this tightly bonded female community that ritualized motor routines eventually could give way to spoken language. Within this group, honest information would have been highly valued. Those able to provide quality information about strategies for maintaining group solidarity or about the activities of in-group and out-group members who could affect group cohesion or effectiveness would enhance their community status. Those found to be undermining group unity by spreading lies or putting individual gain above those of their "sisters" would have risked ostracism or banishment. This trusting community could provide the ecological niche in which both signalers and receivers could gain from honest communication.

This is, unquestionably, an imaginative and exotic (if not erotic) evolutionary tale. But what possible evidence could support such an elaborative yarn? Power (1998) cited two lines of evidence: (1) archeological evidence indicating the use of red ochre as a pigment-altering substance, and (2) the near ubiquity of female rituals and alliances surrounding fertility and first menstruation among traditional societies and hunter–gatherer cultures. First let's deal with the archeological evidence of red ochre use in hominin evolution. The first evidence of ochre use dates back about 200,000 years to sub-Saharan Africa, where it is found only infrequently and sporadically in the archaeological record (Knight, Power, & Watts, 1995). However, by about 130,000 years ago, the use of red ochre escalated in both frequency and geographic spread. The use of ochre across Africa was widespread and exceeded that in other regions until the Upper Paleolithic, when evidence of its use in parts of Asia and Europe increased to similar levels. Although red ochre has practical applications, among traditional societies these uses have been outweighed by its symbolic and ritualistic functions (Power & Watts, 1996). This suggests that the increasing evidence of red ochre in the archeological record reflects increased ritual activity among our hominin ancestors.

Second, studies of traditional cultures have documented numerous examples of "coming of age" ceremonies that possess characteristics consistent with the Knight and Power model of female coalitions. First, these ceremonies tend to involve coercion of and sacrifice from the one being initiated into the group. For example, in societies such as the Khosian, !Kung, /Xam, Kua, Hazda, and others in south and central Africa, initiations often involve periods of strictly enforced seclusion, surgeries and bloodletting (sometimes from the genitals), and rigorous training in dances and ceremonies, all done under the constant threat that failure means ostracism and loss of marriageablity (Ardener, 1975; Blacking, 1985; Boddy, 1982; Parker, 1995; Valiente-Noailles, 1993; see Power, 1998, pp. 122–125, for summary). This would be expected if the young initiate is viewed as inherently threatening to the adult group and must therefore prove her commitment to them to gain acceptance.

These ceremonies also often involve overt and collective displays of female fertility, aimed directly at males in the community. The newly emergent fertility of individuals is subjugated to group fertility and linked to male provisioning. In many rituals, once an initiate's seclusion is ended, all the women smear themselves with blood, dyes (including red ochre), or animal fat to signify group menstruation or fertility and engage in sexually explicit dances enacting intercourse, pregnancy, labor, and childbirth. Themes of hunting and provisioning are also present in many of these ceremonies. Among the /Xam, many of the same pigments and decorations the women use on themselves are also used to adorn the men as they go out on hunting expeditions. Among the Kalahari San, the Eland Bull dance, which marks a girl's first menstruation, also serves as a motivational ceremony to send the men out to hunt (Knight, 1998). Furthermore, in some communities, initiates are schooled in a secret language shared only by members of the female in-group (Ardener, 1956). Thus, in hunter–gatherer societies today we see widespread evidence of ritual ceremonies surrounding female fertility and coming of age. These ceremonies possess the characteristics expected if they evolved to serve the function of uniting females in collective sexual regulation so as to compel males to provision their offspring. Although these stories and the evidences cited in their support certainly cannot be argued to have definitively established the way in which trusting communities evolved, they do provide a viable framework for future research in this area.

But Why Talk?

We have thus far explored the possible basis for both the conscious control and the trusting communities necessary for the evolution of language. Still missing, however, is a possible explanation for why language necessarily took the spoken form in hominins. Why not evolve some form of gestural or sign language? Why talk? To answer this question, we must first address another one: why have a big brain that allows for talking in the first place?

What is a big brain for anyway? Dinosaurs had bigger brains than cockroaches, but it is the latter who are still with us and the former perished long ago. By far the most common and enduring form of life on earth are bacteria, which have no brains at all. It is easy to see that a brain is not necessary for survival and that a big one does not necessarily ensure a species of greater longevity than less endowed competitors. One set of skills, however, does seem to benefit from more gray matter, namely, social skills. Dunbar (1992) examined the link between a primate's brain size and a wide range of ecological factors, such as territorial range, diet, daily travel distance, etc. He concluded that social group size was the single best predictor of a primate's neocortical volume (the neocortex is the very top layer of brain; see Fig. 17.2). A more recent analysis offered further confirmation of

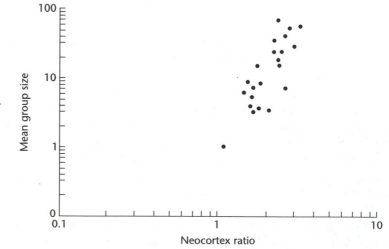

Figure 17.2 The relationship between neocortex ratio and group size in simian primates (monkeys and apes). Neocortex ratio refers to the volume of the neocortex (very top layer of brain) taken as a ratio of the rest of the brain (neocortex/non-neocortex brain). Note the very strong relationship between the two measures, in that as group size increases so does the neocortex ratio. (Adapted from Dunbar, 1996, p. 63.)

Dunbar's conclusion (Clark, Mitra, & Wang, 2001). Put simply, what these studies show is that primates living in larger social groups have more neocortex. It seems that as a primate's social world becomes increasingly complex, more cortex is required to evaluate and monitor the group's shifting social dynamics (who's going with whom, who's on top, who's miffed at whom, etc.).

The close connection between the neocortex and social group size allowed Dunbar to calculate the average social group size for humans based on our brain size, a number that turned out to be about 150. In other words, regardless of whether one lives in a small town or a huge metropolis, the circle of acquaintances and friends with whom one has relationships should be no more than about 150. Considerable evidence supports this prediction (see Dunbar, 1996, pp. 69–79, for a summary). For example, the most stable hunter–gatherer units, the clans or bands, are composed of about 150 members. The earliest farming villages of the Near East, dated at around 5,000 BCE, had about 150 residents. More recently, after an extensive study, the Church of England concluded that the ideal size for its congregations was 200 or less. The most common stand-alone military fighting units, companies, average about 170 soldiers. Finally, sociological studies examining the question of how many people a single individual believes he or she knows well enough to request a favor of have tended to settle on about 135, not far at all from Dunbar's 150. All of this provides support for Dunbar's notion that our brains have evolved to allow us to navigate within a restricted social sphere that tops out at around 150 people.

What does this have to do with the evolution of spoken language? The answer is that to form a stable social group, some mechanism must be used to establish and maintain social relationships. In our primate cousins, this mechanism is called **grooming**. Grooming is the action when one ape meticulously picks and combs through the hair and skin of another, detangling matted hair, pulling off dirt and parasites, and generally just cleaning up. Grooming is no trivial pursuit. Keeping hair and skin hygienically fit is essential to avoid infections and illness, heal cuts and wounds, and maintain overall good health. In addition, grooming serves an important social function in establishing and reinforcing relational bonds between apes. Grooming requires that one ape invest a significant amount of time and effort in the well-being of another. During the course of grooming, endogenous opiates are released and act as primary reinforcers in the bonding between the groomer and groomee (Kaverne, Marinez, & Tuite, 1989). Studies have confirmed a relationship between the amount of time a pair spends grooming together and their willingness to support each other in conflict situations (Dunbar, 1988, p. 253). As their time commitments become more stressed because of the demands of growing infants, mother baboons will continue to resist reductions in the amount of time they spend grooming, often by sacrificing badly needed rest (Dunbar & Dunbar, 1988). The importance of grooming to the creation of a socially cohesive group is reflected in the fact that among primates it can consume up to 20% of the group's time during waking hours (Iwamoto & Dunbar, 1983). When a sufficient amount of time cannot be dedicated to grooming, social stability is sacrificed and groups often fragment and disintegrate (Dunbar, 1993). However, grooming time can cut into the amount of time needed for other important activities, such as foraging and rest. Dunbar estimated that a group can allocate, at most, about 25% of its time to grooming. If a group size reaches a level at which more than this is necessary to keep the peace, then trouble is in the offing.

It was just this sort of trouble that, according to Dunbar, befell *H. erectus* between 500,000 and 250,000 years ago, as evolutionary pressures forced them into larger, more complex social groups. Based on *H. erectus's* cranial capacity, group size and grooming time estimates can be calculated that indicate that the proportion of time necessary for grooming would have well exceeded the maximum found in any known primate group (Aiello & Dunbar, 1993). In short, *H. erectus* could not have used the typical, primate manual form of grooming to construct and maintain the large social groups necessary for its own survival (Fig. 17.3). New forms of grooming had to be invented: vocal grooming, or gossiping. Vocal grooming, Dunbar argued, would have been a much more efficient means of massaging relationships, because a socially satisfying vocal exchange requires far less time and energy than manual grooming and may involve more than two individuals. In support of his theory, Dunbar pointed out that, across many different cultures, estimates of the proportion of time in an average day that people spend in social conversation ranges around the predicted 20%, based on primate grooming time (Fig. 17.4; Dunbar, 1998, pp. 96–98, for summary). In addition, Dunbar's studies and others found that 60%–70% of what people talk about is social in nature; that is, they discuss personal relationships, likes and dislikes, personal experiences, other people's behavior, and other similar topics (Dunbar, 1996, pp. 120–123)—exactly the sort of things you might expect two apes to discuss while grooming! Moreover, sex differences in conversational style also conform to evolutionary expectations. Female conversations typically focus on getting to know another person, whereas exchanges between males more often serve to establish status within a relationship (Coates, 1993; Tannen, 1996).

We like to think that spoken language evolved so that humans could exchange vital bits of information about hunting, child rearing, and the like. However, if Dunbar was correct, we talk not because of any pressing need to exchange critical

Figure 17.3 The estimated proportion of time spent grooming for various hominin species, based on predicted group size. Predicted group size was calculated based on estimated neocortex ratios based on total brain volume indicated by fossil crania. The bottom dashed line (20%) represents the maximum grooming time observed among primates (geleda baboons). Note that both the Australopiths (gray circles) and *Homo habilis* (filled circles) fall near to this proportion. However, by about .5 million years ago, *Homo erectus* (black rectangles) was well beyond this proportion at about 30%. It is hypothesized that to maintain cohesive groups, erectus would have needed to "invent" a new form of grooming, vocal grooming, to survive. (Adapted from Dunbar, 1996, p. 114.)

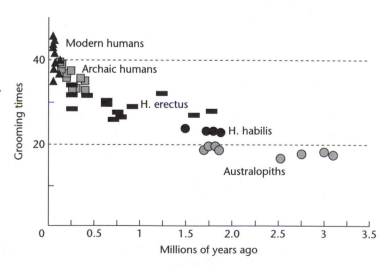

Society	Exonomy	Activity	Hrs/day	%*	Source
Dundee, Scotland	Industrial	Conversation	3.3	20.6	Emler (1994)
Kapanara, (New Guinea)	Horicultural	Social interaction	3.1	19.4	Grossman (1984)
Maasai (Tanzania)	Pastoralist	Leisure	2.8	17.5	Biran (1996)
Central African Republic	Agricultural	Non-work (leisure, dances, visits)	2.7	16.8	Berio (1984)
Nepal	Agricultural	Leisure/social	5.2	32.3	Berio (1984)
Ivory Coast, Africa	Agricultural	Social	1.2	7.2	Berio (1984)
Upper Volta, Africa	Agricultural	Free time (social, religion, errands)	3.3	23.6	McSweeney (1979)

*Assuming a 16-hr waking day (see, for example, Berio 1984)

Figure 17.4 Cross-cultural estimates of the time spent in social conversation. Note that five of the seven studies report that about 20% of the average day is spent in social conversation. (Adapted from Dunbar, 1998, p. 97.)

information but just to make nice, to reinforce social bonds, to make friends and be friends. And we do this mostly by just informal chit-chat and gossip. This function should not be sold short, however. If our hominin ancestors had not figured out how to (really evolved to) keep large, complex groups from imploding around them, then we probably would not be here. Moving from manual grooming to vocal grooming may have been a crucial factor in keeping the peace eons ago. Our vocal behavior exhibits those characteristics one might expect if its purpose is to establish and maintain social relationships in a manner similar to grooming functions in ape and monkey groups.

The Talk of Our Ancestors

If *H. erectus* or other archaic hominins did speak, what did they sound like? Would we recognize their talk as language, or would it sound more like the grunts, hoots, and howls of present-day apes? Like so many issues we have dealt with in this chapter, there is no definitive answer. However, a couple of lines of research cast a dim light on this intriguing issue.

Protolanguage and Other Catastrophes

One approach to this issue is to look at how present-day language evolves in the absence of its normal developmental context. Two well-documented examples are: (1) the development of language among 19th- and early 20th-century plantation workers in Hawaii, and (2) the spontaneous development of sign language among deaf children in Nicaragua. Let's start with the first. In the 19th century, workers from many different countries, including Japan, China, Korea, the Philippines, and Portugal, were imported to Hawaii to work on the plantations. These monolinguistic adult workers had to find some way of communicating with each other as well as with their English-speaking employers and the Hawaiian-speaking natives. In time, they developed a common stock of words from their different languages that could be strung together in very brief, single-idea, present-tense utterances. For example, one might say to another "you nani hanahana" (you want work?), which has words from three different languages: English, Japanese, and Hawaiian (Roberts, 1993, 1996; Bickerton, 1998; Bickerton & Odo, 1976). This language was referred to as a **pidgin.** The children of these workers, however, developed a much different common language. Their language involved a more complex syntax that allowed for the embedding of clauses within statements and tense markers to signify events in the past, present, and future ("you work tomorrow, inside the house, after I call"). This new **creole** language emerged spontaneously in a single generation and possessed a syntax unlike that of any of the children's native languages. Its structure, however, was similar to that of creoles throughout the world.

A similar process was observed with deaf children in Nicaragua in the late 1970s and early 1980s. Nicaragua under the Somoza regime had no institutionalized settings for the education of the deaf. To communicate with their parents and siblings, deaf children developed a form of "home sign" language that varied from one household to another. When Somoza was overthrown in 1979, the new government created community-based schools for the deaf. Within these schools, deaf children, each of whom had his or her own unique home sign language, had to learn to communicate with each other. Their situation was not all that different from the plantation workers in Hawaii, except that their languages were manual rather than spoken. These children (most of whom were 10 years old or older) developed a simple common sign language, not all that different from the vocal pidgin used by the Hawaiian plantation workers. When a younger group of deaf children later were introduced into the school, they proceeded to construct a more complex common sign language with more sophisticated syntax and a hierarchical-based structure. As with the plantation workers, a process of pidgin to creole was observed in "one generation" (so to speak) in sign (Bickerton, 1998, pp. 628–630; Kegl & Iwata, 1989).

These accounts, according to linguist Derek Bickerton (1990, 1995), provide evidence that the evolution of language occurs not in gradual increments but in wide, discrete steps, a process that he called **catastrophic evolution.** The first stage of language, which he termed **protolanguage**, is equivalent in form to pidgin language. This language is found not only among human adults under some circumstances but also among language-trained apes and human 2-year-olds. Protolanguage can be likened to the stringing of words on a bead, with one simple idea expressed (e.g., "Bill watch John" or "John go home"). The fact that many creatures, including apes, dolphins, sea lions, and birds, have been trained to create protolinguistic utterances suggests that an evolved capacity for protolanguage is widespread in the animal world. Protolanguage differs, however, from "**real**" **language**, in that it lacks any hierarchical and recursive syntax that allows for the embedding of clauses and the expression of complex ideas ("Bill watched as John was heading home"). Real language, with its sophisticated syntax, emerges suddenly and completely. The fact that no intermediate forms of language between protolanguage and real language have been observed provides support for Bickerton's catastrophic evolutionary process. Furthermore, contended Bickerton, the archeological record is consistent with a catastrophic onset of real language. For nearly a million years, the tools and culture of *H. erectus* remained stagnant. Then, about 40,000 years ago, in one precipitous onslaught, tools and culture made a radical advance. These stages correspond to a long period of protolanguage, followed by a sudden emergence of a new species, *H. sapiens*, and a new form of vocal communication, real language. *H. erectus* and other archaic species would have had a spoken language then, only it would have been a pidgin form of language, a simplistic "here and now" stringing together of short two- or three-word bursts. If Bickerton is correct, then Kanzi and human 2-year-olds provide rough echoes of what language would have been like among our now long-extinct ancestors.

Comparative Anatomy

Another approach to the question of ancient hominin speech involves anatomical comparisons of the speech apparatus. One of the important reasons that humans can talk is that our mouths and throats contain structures that permit the creation and articulation of precise speech sounds. For example, unlike apes, our larynx (which contains the vocal cords) is low in the throat at the base of the pharynx (the long tube descending from the mouth). As air is pushed up through the larynx, the vocal cords can adjust to vibrate the air in different ways and at different frequencies, not unlike a reed in a wind instrument. This air then can be further modified as it passes up the pharynx to the articulators in the mouth: the tongue, teeth, and lips. The tongue, teeth, and lips can restrict, constrict, and stop the flow of air to form various consonant sounds, such as those associated with the letters p, t, or n. The tubular distance between the low-slung larynx and the mouth allows for the precise manipulation of air necessary for the creation of the phonemes of speech. Apes cannot talk because their larynxes are high in their throats, which is an excellent arrangement for breathing and eating simultaneously but a poor one for talking (Fig. 17.5). With this knowledge in hand, researchers can ask whether our hominin ancestors had vocal tracts similar to humans (with a low-placed larynx) or apes (with a high-placed larynx).

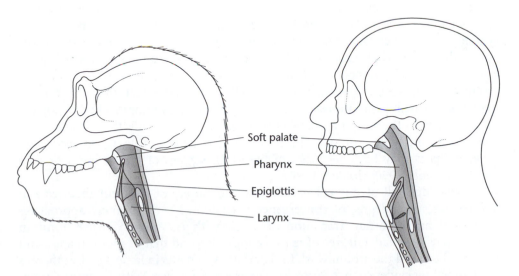

Soft palate

Pharynx

Epiglottis

Larynx

Figure 17.5 A comparison of the vocal tracts of a chimpanzee (left) and a human adult (right). Note how much lower the larynx is in the throat of the human. Also note the "arching" of the human cranial base where the pharynx descends, as opposed to the more flattened chimp cranial base. (Adapted from Relethford, 2000, p. 393.)

This approach seems reasonable enough, but it runs into a serious problem. Larynxes, pharynxes, and other vocal structures do not fossilize. Skulls do, however, and some of their properties can be used to ascertain the condition of the vocal structures. To have a high-positioned larynx, one must also have a cranial base (or bottom) that is relatively flat and horizontal. This allows the pharynx to run quite a distance horizontally along the base of the skull, providing room for the larynx. By contrast, the base of the human cranium is less flat and more arched, with very little room for a horizontally running pharynx (Fig. 17.5). Instead, the pharynx must bend at almost a right angle and descend vertically down the neck, with the larynx at its bottom. Thus, the question of what kind of vocal apparatus (human-like or ape-like) our ancestors had reduces to a question about their cranial bases.

Analysis of the cranial bases of *Australopithecus* showed them to be flat and ape-like, indicating a high-positioned larynx incapable of articulate speech (Laitman & Heimbuch, 1982; Lieberman, 1975). The basicranium of *H. erectus*, however, was more arched and human-like, although not to the same degree as modern humans (Stringer, 1992). It is interesting to note that Neanderthals appear to have had vocal tracts less human-like than *H. erectus*, suggesting that their vocal capacity was no better and maybe even worse than some older hominin species (Lieberman, 1998).

Other anatomical evidence has been brought to bear on the question of ancient hominin speech. For example, the nearly complete skeleton of Turkana Boy (*H. erectus/ergaster*) allowed a rare examination of an ancient vertebral column. This is important, because the diameter of the column provides information about the size of the spinal cord, which, in turn, tells us something about the state of the nervous system. In Turkana Boy, the spinal column was comparable in diameter to modern humans, except that it was narrower through the chest area (MacLarnon, 1993; Walker, 1996). This may indicate that *H. erectus* had less voluntary control over the breathing apparatus, thus placing limitations on the ability to produce spoken language. Another bit of evidence comes from measuring the size of the hypoglossal canal, the hole at the base of the skull through which passes the motor nerve connecting the brain and the tongue. Control of the tongue is essential to articulate speech, which is reflected in the fact that the human hypoglossal canal is 1.8 times larger than that of apes. Australopiths had hypoglossal canals about the size of apes, whereas later erectus, Neanderthals, and archaic *Homo* had canals about on par with us. At the tongue level at least, *H. erectus* and other archaics may have been as capable as *H. sapiens* of producing articulate speech (Duchin,1990; Holden, 1999).

What does all of this tell us? Despite the variety of different theories and approaches, some degree of convergence is evident. Nearly all these approaches agree that an important transition occurred with *H. erectus*. Earlier hominin species may have had a degree of motor control beyond that of modern apes, and this may have laid the groundwork for later developments in language. But there is no compelling evidence that *Australopithecus* had language. With *H. erectus*, however, a number of factors suggest that important trends toward the evolution of language were in place. Group sizes were becoming larger, with more advanced tools and culture. Vocal grooming rather than manual grooming may have been necessary to achieve social cohesion. Rituals involving symbolic dance and ceremony may have helped to solidify groups into trusting communities where honest information exchange would have been advantageous to both message sender and receiver. Anatomical changes may have allowed for greater speech capacity and the production of a protolanguage with simple, short, present-tense utterances. "Real" language, with complex syntax and hierarchical structure, may have been the result of a slow, gradual evolutionary process, as many have argued (Corballis, 1991; Deacon, 1997; Pinker, 1994), or it may have crashed down upon our ancestors in a sudden, catastrophic evolutionary event, as Bickerton and others have envisioned (Bickerton, 1995; Noble & Davidson, 1996). There seems little doubt, however, that by the time of the Upper Paleolithic revolution, *H. sapiens sapiens* had this gift firmly in hand (or mind) and used it to create a unique culture and singular position within the natural world.

SUMMARY

Language possesses many characteristics, such as arbitrariness, discreteness, syntax, and symbolic reference, which make it an extraordinarily flexible form of communication. Many elements of human language can be seen in a limited form in other animals. Ape language studies, especially the Kanzi project, have shown how these elements can be expanded into a system of communication that is vaguely human in nature. However, a number of factors have conspired to make the evolution of language in nonhuman species an (as of yet) impossible proposition. Foremost is the fact that language requires honest vocal signaling from signaler to receiver, and honest vocal signals can hold no fitness advantage to the signaler. In humans, this obstacle was overcome in the form of trusting communities, where honest vocal signals could hold fitness advantages for both signaler and receivers.

Theories abound concerning the way trusting communities emerged in human evolution. Many theories see rituals surrounding reproduction and male provisioning as keys to this evolution, but finding convincing evidence of this is challenging. Some theories envision language evolution as a gradual process, but at least one theory has proposed that language emerged catastrophically, in a sudden onslaught. According to this view, protolanguages (similar to pidgin languages) would have suddenly given way to full-blown language, with no intermediate steps. Anatomical comparisons of ape, hominin, and human suggest that speech probably was not present in early hominin species but may have been present in later species, such as *H. erectus*.

KEY WORDS

arbitrariness	intervention	real language
autocuing	Kanzi	referential
conscious control	mimesis	ritual
cranial base	morphemes	syntax
creole	particulate principle	trusting communities
discreteness	phonemes	Vickie
generativity	pidgin	Washoe
grooming	protolanguage	

REVIEW QUESTIONS

1. Describe some of the studies in animal syntax and symbolic reference. What capabilities do these studies demonstrate in animals that are similar to and different from humans?

2. Define arbitrariness, discreteness, generativity, and intervention. How do these characteristics provide an almost limitless potential for the communicative power of language?

3. Summarize the abilities that Kanzi has demonstrated regarding syntax, symbolic reference, and language comprehension. How do they compare with human language abilities?

4. What is mimesis, and what role might it have played in the evolution of human language?

5. What is protolanguage, and how does it differ from real language?

6. Describe some of the different evolutionary scenarios that have been proposed for the evolution of trusting communities necessary for language. What evidence is there to support these ideas?

7. How can anatomical comparisons help to uncover the language capacities of our hominin ancestors?

SUGGESTED READINGS

Deacon, T. (1997). *The symbolic species.* New York: W.W. Norton.

Donald, M. (2001). *A mind so rare.* New York: W. W. Norton.

Dunbar, R. (1996). *Grooming, gossip, and the evolution of language.* Cambridge, MA: Harvard University Press.

Huford, J.R., Studdert-Kennedy, M., & Knight, C. (1998). *Approaches to the evolution of language.* Cambridge: Cambridge University Press.

Noble, W., & Davidson, I. (1996). *Human evolution, language and mind.* New York: Cambridge University Press.

WEB SITES

www.gsu.edu/~wwwlrc/biographies/kanzi.html excellent site for learning more about the Kanzi project

http://arts.uwaterloo.ca/~acheyne/index.html a site with many links for resources on the evolution of language.

www.pitt.edu/~mattf/EvolLangList.html home page of the Evolution of Language List, many valuable links to other sites and resources on the evolution of language.

18

Right, Wrong, and a Sense of Self

Behaving Like Animals

"It is dangerous to show man too clearly how much he resembles the beast, without at the same time showing him his greatness. It is also dangerous to allow him too clear a vision of his greatness without his baseness. It is even more dangerous to leave him in ignorance of both."

THIS MAY SEEM LIKE SOMETHING DARWIN would have said, but it was written (precisely) 2 centuries before *Origin of Species* by French mathematician and philosopher Blaise Pascal (1659; fragment 347). Hundreds of years before Darwin, thoughtful people were already contemplating humanity's close connection to the natural world and the way this connection altered our self-perception. If we think ourselves too special, too distinct from our animal cousins, then we risk becoming arrogant and reckless with the natural world around us. On the other hand, if we think ourselves mere animals, then do we not risk behaving as such? It seems curious that for most of our history we have regarded the latter possibility as more troubling than the former. The thoughtless "inhuman" cruelty we associate with animals seems somehow more disturbing than any calculated, mindful cruelty. This is strange when you consider that our greatest atrocities, including torture, mass murder, and genocide, typically require a degree of consideration and planning unknown to other species.

Why, then, the great aversion to behaving like an animal? Why not encourage more "animal-like" behavior if it means curbing some of the more extreme forms of human violence? The answer most likely rests with our perception of animals as amoral creatures—creatures incapable of comprehending moral codes. Even if we do not always follow such codes or if we apply them inconsistently, it is better to be capable of moral reasoning then to be forever ignorant of right and wrong. Our moral reasoning did not simply fall into our laps from the heavens above. It too evolved slowly over the countless millennia. Can we be so sure, then, that there are no traces of a moral sense in our animal cousins? In this chapter, we will address the evolutionary origins of that most cherished of human capacities: moral thought, a sense of right and wrong and its intimate connection with a sense of self.

Animal Morality?

The boy lay motionless as Binty approached. Slowly, cautiously, she lifted him and cradled him in her arms. He had fallen quite a distance, and the impact had rendered him unconscious, helpless. Without a word, she carried him over to the caretaker's door and gently set him down. Except for the fact that Binty was a female gorilla, the foregoing incident would not have been worthy of national news coverage. However, Binty *was* a gorilla, and the boy had accidentally fallen into her enclosure on a 1996 visit to Chicago's Brookfield Zoo. A video camera captured the event, making Binty a national heroine. Was Binty acting altruistically? Did she empathize with the boy's helpless state and simply try to "do the right thing?" Maybe. But what do we conclude, then, about the actions of sharks when they chew off the arms and legs of innocent surfers? Or when chimpanzees rip the limbs from screaming monkeys and gnaw away placidly, oblivious to their victims' suffering? Does the apparent lack of empathy in these animals indicate that they are sadistic and evil? These are difficult questions to address philosophically and even more difficult to tackle scientifically. Despite this, some researchers have tried. Their results, although certainly not conclusive, are intriguing.

In the 1950s and 1960s, a classic set of experiments was performed to see if the lowly rat was capable of altruism. A rat was trained to press a lever to obtain food. After having learned this association, the rules were changed, so that sometimes a press on the lever produced food and other times it delivered a shock to a genetically unrelated rat visible in an adjacent cage (Church, 1959). Under these circumstances, rats stopped pressing the bar (thus forfeiting food) to avoid shocking another rat. Was this an example of self-sacrificial behavior for the benefit of another?

In another experiment, rats were trained to press a bar that lowered a Styrofoam block that was suspended in midair. Because lowering the block was of no direct benefit to the rat, the training required shocking the rat if it failed to press the bar that lowered the block. When the shock contingency was removed, rats quickly stopped pressing the bar. However, when another rat was suspended in midair, understandably distressed about that predicament, the other rat resumed bar pressing to lower it to safety. Because the shock contingency had been removed, the rat doing the bar pressing received no direct benefit for its action, other than relieving the distress of another rat. But perhaps the bar-pressing rat did receive a direct benefit in the cessation of the squealing and screaming of its hanging mate. Experiments have shown that rats will bar press in order to remove unpleasant auditory stimuli from their environments. They also tend to find white noise more annoying than rat squeals (Lavery & Foley, 1963). These experiments are suggestive and open up the possibility of rat altruism, but they cannot eliminate the possibility that rats do nice things for selfish reasons (Hauser, 2000, pp. 219–224, for an excellent summary and discussion of these studies).

Primate studies have been even more suggestive when it comes to demonstrations of "real" altruism. In a very early study conducted in the 1960s, rhesus monkeys were taught to pull chains to receive a food reward. After this, however, the consequence of pulling a chain was altered, so that pulling one chain produced a food reward and another delivered a shock to a monkey visible in an adjacent cage. All monkeys responded by differentially avoiding the chain that delivered the shock, but two monkeys went even further. They abstained from pulling any chains for several days, thus willingly sacrificing food to be certain not to harm another monkey (Miller, 1967). It was also observed that monkeys who knew each other were more likely to behave altruistically toward one another.

More recently, Frans de Waal (de Waal, 1997; de Waal & Berger, 2000) showed that capuchin monkeys willingly share with one another, especially if they can see each other and work together to achieve a goal. In one study, two monkeys were placed in side-by-side cages separated by a mesh partition. When one monkey was provided with food, instead of monopolizing it by remaining on the side of the cage opposite the partition, the monkey spontaneously went over to the partition to drop food pieces and allow the other monkey to gather them up. Using a similar set-up, de Waal also had monkeys engage in either a solo or cooperative food acquisition task. While in their side-by-side cages, monkeys were presented with two bowls on a tray just outside the cages, so that only one bowl was accessible to each cage. Each monkey was provided with a pull bar that allowed him or her to pull the tray forward toward the cage, thus putting the bowl within reach (Fig. 18.1). In the solo task, only one bowl was filled with food. The monkey whose cage was across from the filled bowl could then pull the bar and get the bowl. On the cooperative task, only one bowl was filled, but the tray was weighted so that both monkeys had to pull on their bars together to move the tray forward. The results showed that the monkeys were significantly more likely to share the food on the cooperative trials than on the solo trials (Fig. 18.2). When forced to work together so that only one could benefit, the one getting the benefit was more generous than when the reward was achieved alone. However, cooperation broke down when the mesh barrier was replaced with an opaque one. For cooperation and the subsequent sharing of rewards, the monkeys must be able to monitor each other's contribution to the cause (Mendres & de Waal, 2000).

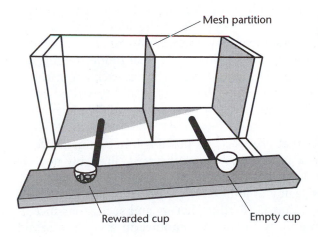

Figure 18.1 Apparatus used in the de Waal studies on primate cooperation. A monkey is placed in each of the side-by-side cages, separated by a mesh partition. A tray sits outside of the cages with cups placed so that one cup is available to each cage. One cup contains a food reward; the other does not. A handle runs from the tray to each of the cages, allowing the monkey to pull the tray forward to get access to a cup. A sample trial would work as follows: Imagine two monkeys, each in a cage. The cup on the left is baited with apple slices, the cup on the right is empty. On a *solo* trial the tray would be weighted so that the monkey in the left cage could pull the handle, move the tray forward, and get to the baited cup. On a *cooperation* trial, the tray would be weighted so that the monkey in the left cage would need the help of the monkey in the right cage to move the tray forward. With both monkeys pulling on their respective handles, the tray could be moved forward so that the left monkey could get to the baited cup. Will that monkey share the spoils of their joint effort? (Adapted from de Waal & Berger, 2000, p. 653.)

Mesh partition

Rewarded cup   Empty cup

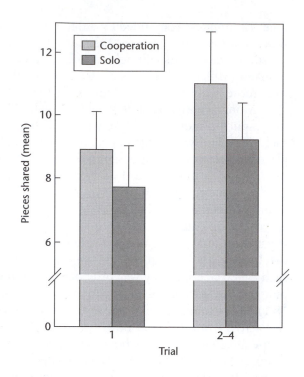

Figure 18.2 Average number of apple pieces shared on both cooperation (light bar) and solo (dark bar) trials. Sharing was found to be significantly greater on cooperation trials than on solo trials. (Adapted from de Waal & Berger, 2000.)

Observations of primates in more natural settings also have provided evidence of an incipient moral sense. In his book *Good Natured: The Origins of Right and Wrong in Humans and Other Animals*, de Waal (1996) provided examples of what he regarded as ape and monkey empathy, friendship, tolerance, and peacemaking. He recounted the story of Mozu, a Japanese macaque, who was born without hands and feet. Despite her malformities, she has managed to survive more than 18 years and produce five healthy offspring. Although she seems to get little in the way of special consideration from her troop mates, she does appear to enjoy a certain tolerance that even humans sometimes withhold from others who are different. In the animal world of "survival of the fittest," de Waal found the survival and success of Mozu an attractive puzzlement. Similar stories exist about chimpanzees, among whom orphaned infants may be adopted and raised by other adults or, at times, apes may actively intervene to defuse potentially violent disputes between conspecifics.

Does this evidence indicate that primates and possibly other animals live by certain conscious moral precepts, such as "do unto others..."? Probably not. De Waal (de Waal & Berger, 2000) suggested that primates possess "**attitudinal reciprocity.**" By cooperating and engaging in joint efforts, primates engender a positive attitude toward one another, thus facilitating sharing and social tolerance. A cooperative partner also is more likely to support another in a conflict or aid another in a hunt and share the spoils. Thus, for social species such as primates, getting others to like you by sharing and cooperating with them can have individual fitness pay-offs in terms of increased status, resources, and social support. Deacon (1997) concurred with the general gist of this thinking, adding that many animals have the capacity for some degree of empathy. Many species can detect the emotional state of another, based on extrinsic cues, and are often inclined to mimic that state, such as when one purring cat encounters another, rubs against it, and causes the second to begin purring as well. Moreover, many species can bring their emotional states into congruence with one another based on a shared external stimulus. For example, an alarm call from one monkey can cause another to scan the sky and become aroused as well. Where animals falter is in being able to mentally represent the world from the perspective of another. Animals, according to Deacon, lack the symbolic mental function that permits one to model the world from another's point of view and state of mind. For Deacon, this is the very essence of human morality: the ability to understand the mind of another.

It is on this point that the most profound difference between humans and other animals arises. The human ability to empathize seems to be of a deeper quality than that of any other animal. We *can* imagine what it is like to see the world from another's perspective. Somewhere over the course of hominin evolution, the ability to resonate with the thoughts and feelings of other members of our species reached unparalleled heights. It is this capacity that is central to our moral sense and our desire to construct moral codes. We want people to "do unto others..." because we can envision what it is like *to be* the other. Most researchers also agree that the ability to understand the mind of another is closely linked with one's own sense of self (Gallup, 1982, 1998; Gopnick, 1993; Hobson, 1993; Humphrey, 1983). To have insight into another's mind, one must first have an awareness of one's own mind and a sense of individual existence. Understanding the evolution of morality requires an understanding of the evolution of a sense of self. Thus, before returning directly to the issue of morality, we must first explore the issues of self-awareness and other-awareness.

Primate Self-Awareness

"Self-awareness is, then, one of the most fundamental, possibly *the* most fundamental, characteristic of the human species....Self-awareness has, however, brought in its train somber companions—fear, anxiety, and death-awareness.... A being who knows that he will die arose from ancestors who did not know" (Dobzhansky, 1967, pp. 68–69). To be self-aware is to know what it is like to be alive and thus to dread life's loss. The irony implicit in Dobzhansky's statement is that our awareness of death evolved from creatures who had no awareness that they were even alive! But how numb to their own lives are other animals, especially the apes who are our closest relatives?

This might seem like a difficult question to answer, but, in the late 1960s, Gordon Gallup devised the **mirror test**, an ingenious test of chimpanzee self-awareness. Gallup observed the reactions of common chimpanzees and two species of monkeys when they were allowed to see their mirror reflections (Gallup, 1970). The animals were individually given access to a mirror for 8 hours per day for up to 14 days. Initially, the chimps and the monkeys treated their reflections as if they were other animals. After about 3 days of exposure, the chimps' behavior changed dramatically. Instead of continuing to exhibit socially directed behaviors, the chimps engaged in an increasing number of self-directed behaviors, such as grooming and inspecting body parts they normally could not see. The chimps seemed to recognize that the chimp in the mirror was a reflection of themselves (not another chimp) and began to use the reflection as a means of gaining visual access to body parts normally only available through touch (much like a person using a mirror to inspect a bald spot or the fit of a pair of jeans). In contrast, the monkeys showed no marked changes in behavior over the study period.

Next, Gallup anesthetized the animals and placed a bright red mark on one eyebrow and one ear of each animal. The mark left no olfactory, tactile, or direct visual cues to its presence. When placed before the mirror, the chimpanzees spent a considerable amount of time inspecting the marks, seeming to recognize that the mark was a rather strange part of *their* bodies. The amount of time they spent touching and examining the mark far exceeded that of a control condition in which chimps were marked but not exposed to the mirror. Once again, the monkeys showed no special interest in the mark, and, in a follow-up study, Gallup, McClure, Hill, and Bundy (1971) showed that chimps raised in social isolation also showed no special interest in the marks.

The significance of Gallup's work was that it suggested a qualitative divergence in the self-awareness of great apes and monkeys. Apes had a concept of themselves: an internalized identity that permitted recognition of an external representation of themselves (the mirror image). They understood themselves as creatures with a distinct physical existence, one that permitted them to be both observers (as when looking in the mirror) and the observed (as when recognizing the mirror-reflected image as themselves). This was a level of self-awareness (sometimes called "**objective self-awareness**"; Sedikides & Skowronski, 1997) that was beyond the capacity of monkeys. Further studies sought to confirm the presence of this important distinction. Evidence for mirror recognition in other great apes, such as orangutans (Lethmate & Dücker, 1973; Miles, 1994; Suarez & Gallup, 1981) and bonobos (Hyatt & Hopkins, 1994), was found, along with a failure of recognition in most monkey species (Anderson, 1983; Lethmate & Dünker, 1973; Mitchell & Anderson, 1993; Suarez & Gallup, 1986). However, a few anomalies arose. One great ape, the gorilla, did not pass the mirror test (Suarez & Gallup, 1981; Ledbetter & Basen, 1982), and a few studies reported mirror self-recognition in some monkeys (Boccia, 1994; Hauser, Kralik, Botto-Mahan, Garrett, & Oser, 1995; Thompson & Boatright-Horowitz, 1994). Some researchers have argued that the failure of monkeys to pass the mirror test does not represent a phylogenetic divergence in self-representational abilities between monkeys and great apes but, instead, results from behavioral differences between the species. Face-to-face gazes between monkeys are often used as threat cues and are therefore avoided. Novak (1996) overcame this tendency by training rhesus monkeys to look at each other and then subsequently presented them with the mirror. These subjects did show evidence of self-recognition.

The failure of most gorillas in the mirror test has been a perplexing issue. Although most studies have shown no evidence of self-recognition in gorillas, a study by Patterson and Cohen (1994) is an exception. Their subject was the human-raised gorilla Koko, who has also been taught to use sign language for communication. The experimenters surreptitiously placed a colored mark above Koko's eyebrows and waited to see her reaction before the mirror. She noticed it immediately, inspected it closely and studied her reflection intently in the mirror. Why did Koko pass when most gorillas failed? As a human-encultured subject, Koko may not be representative of the typical gorilla. In the wild, gorillas are behaviorally similar to many monkeys, in that looking directly at another is usually avoided. Their gentle, tactile exploratory activities may not dispose them to treat the mirror in a manner conducive to discovering its reflective properties (Byrne, 1995). Koko's upbringing may have altered this usual pattern.

According to this line of thinking, gorillas do possess a self-representation like that of other great apes, but certain behavioral tendencies must be overcome for evidence of this to emerge. Povinelli (1994) appeared to agree with this general assessment but saw deeper evolutionary and genetic factors at work. He contended that, during the course of their evolutionary history, gorillas may have undergone a reversal in some of their developmental and cognitive traits, including the ability for self-recognition. The capacity for self-recognition may be present genetically, but the instructions that would allow for the expression of such an ability have been shut down. Alterations in development (such as those that might be associated with Koko's anomalous rearing) could serve to reinstate the expression of these dormant abilities.

Donald (1991) concurred that behavioral difference between gorillas and chimps may be an important factor in the mirror test but asserted that these differences may lead to real differences in self-representational abilities. Gorillas and monkeys use their hands relatively more for locomotion, whereas chimpanzees' hands are freer for manipulative and exploratory acts. Using the hands in this manner brings together the tactile and proprioceptive senses under the guidance of vision. When exploring with the hands, vision is directed at one's own body and bodily activities as opposed to being directed at the external environment (as in locomotion). This could lead to a more sophisticated sense of self, one that is revealed in the mirror test. Chimps and humans also differ in the degree to which they use the hands as manipulative and exploratory tools, and, once again, this difference may be an important factor in self-representational differences between these species.

We are left, however, with the unresolved issue of what the ape and monkey differences in the mirror test results represent. Most researchers see the ape and monkey difference in self-recognition as a real one and interpret these results as indicating a divergence in self-awareness between the monkey and great ape evolutionary lines (Byrne, 1995; Gallup, 1994; Povinelli, 1998). The type of self-awareness necessary to recognize one's image in a mirror arose in the common ancestor of the great apes and humans after the monkey branch had already diverged. Tomasello and Call (1997), however, are more cautious, noting that monkey and ape differences in many areas have been exaggerated and more work needs to be done on the behavioral differences between the ways monkeys and apes approach the mirror situation before firm conclusions can be drawn.

Although a number of researchers have raised questions and criticisms of the mirror test and its interpretation (see, for example, Neisser, 1993; Oakley, 1985; Rochat, 1995; Tomasello & Call, 1997), most researchers appear comfortable with it as an indicator of self-awareness. Given that this is justified, then, mirror self-recognition also tells us something about a primate's level of *other* understanding.

If a sense of self evolved before the chimpanzee and hominin lines separated, then an understanding of other minds should also be present in great apes. It may be that humans are not alone when it comes to being able to contemplate the thoughts and feelings of others. Great apes may have a "theory of mind."

Theory of Mind

A **theory of mind** refers to the ability to attribute mental states to others and to use those attributions as a means of explaining and predicting behaviors (Premack & Woodruff, 1978). This ability does not appear in humans until about 3.5 or 4 years of age. With little effort or difficulty, humans draw conclusions about the thoughts, motives, intentions, and emotions of other humans, based on external behavioral and situational cues. It is this ability to make inferences about the mental lives of others that is the source of our vast capacity for both good and evil. When we see another enduring hardship or suffering a terrible loss, we can project ourselves into those circumstances, examine our own potential emotions and thoughts, and thereby gain an empathetic understanding of another's plight. Human compassion is powerful, because it can be based not just on behavioral evidence of need but on a real sense of the inner anguish of those we seek to help. By the same token, however, understanding the inner lives of others confers on us the power to inflict and increase the pain of others in ways that less cognitively endowed creatures could never imagine. A theory of mind is a potent tool, and, although its use can sometimes be reckless, it seems to be a natural and ubiquitous component of human social judgment. But to what extent is it a uniquely human attribute? Gallup's experimental work suggested that apes might indeed be capable of a theory of mind, and naturalistic observations lend even more credence to that notion.

Machiavellian Apes

If one were convinced that apes possessed a theory of mind and could understand the goals, intentions, motivations, and attitudes of others, then what behaviors would one look for to support such a conviction? As a highly social species, chimpanzees provide ample opportunity for the close examination of complex social interactions over extended periods of time. At about the same time that Gallup began speculating about the chimpanzee theory of mind, de Waal published *Chimpanzee Politics: Power and Sex Among Apes* (1982). The book described years of observation of the chimpanzee social world and seemed to contain exactly the sort of behavioral tendencies one might expect of an animal that can contemplate what others must be thinking. de Waal described numerous instances of chimpanzee deception, counterdeception, alliance formation, reciprocity, and double-crossing. For example, a male chimp might cover external signs of sexual arousal or fear to avoid tipping off another chimp to his intentions. de Waal (1986) also recounted the way an angry male chimp would feign an appeasement gesture (holding out its hand) only to spring a surprise attack on a competitor. Goodall (1986) reported that a young chimpanzee managed to get others to leave a feeding station by arising and walking off in a deliberate "I am the leader" fashion. The others followed, which allowed the youngster to secretly double back and get the food. Byrne (1995) reported that a young baboon, Paul, managed to obtain food from adults by using his high-ranking mother as a tool. After observing an adult female secure a difficult-to-obtain food item, Paul moved close to the adult and let out a scream, which immediately brought the youngster's mother to the rescue. Not wishing to tangle with Paul's mother, the adult female baboon ran off, leaving the food for Paul.

In all of these instances, it seems that the animals must have had some understanding of what was going on in the minds of others to successfully execute the described behavior. For instance, it seems very easy to assume that little Paul thought to himself, "Hmmm. How can I get that food from Hairy Wilma over there? I've got it! If I scream, Mom will think that Wilma is hurting me and then chase her off. I'll get the food!" Because wild primates lack language, these thoughts obviously could not be internalized as such, but an understanding of their own motives and the internal motives of others would be underlying these behaviors.

One of the most extensive studies of deception among primates was carried out by Byrne and Whiten (1990), who compiled 253 accounts of what could have been regarded as tactical deception by nonhuman primates. The researchers analyzed these accounts by asking a series of questions, such as: (1) Are there alternative explanations for the behavior other than tactical deception? (2) Is there evidence of another animal being led to believe something that was untrue? (3) Are the communication patterns used by the animals sufficiently understood so as to draw valid conclusions? Of the original 253 accounts, only 117 instances qualified as convincing examples of primate deception. Of these, however, only 18 (15%) passed the authors' criteria for "intentional deception," involving an indication of some understanding of the mind of another (among apes only, this proportion rose to 30%).

Laboratory Tests of the Theory of Mind

Field observations are suggestive, but controlled studies are necessary for definitive answers. A number of studies have been carried out that exploit the close connection between visual attention and state of mind.

We humans are visually dominated creatures. Most of the animal world places its trust in the olfactory system (even your dog is not convinced it's you until he gives you a good sniff), but humans trust the eyes more than other senses. Our colloquialisms (e.g., "seeing is believing") and our science bear this out. When the senses are placed into conflict, such as when a person feels something that is square but sees a rectangle, vision typically wins the day (Welch & Warren, 1980). It is not surprising, then, that humans pay close attention to the eyes when assessing what others know about the world. If I walk into a classroom full of students and notice a number of students staring at the ceiling, I'm likely to snatch a look upward to see what's going on. It's so automatic, it's hard to resist! This is so because, from a very early age, humans learn that seeing corresponds to attention. What is being looked at is usually what a person is thinking about. A child witnessing his or her mother looking at a favorite vase shattered on the kitchen floor has a pretty good idea of mom's mental state. Thus, the first step in constructing a theory of mind may be recognizing the connection between *where* another allocates visual attention and *what* they are likely to be thinking about.

Chimpanzees also show a heightened sensitivity to the eyes of another. Chimpanzees will follow the gaze of another chimp or human and attempt to lock onto whatever the other is attending to. In addition, de Waal (1996) reported that reconciliations between rival chimps often require a mutual gaze into the eyes of the other or the appeasing gestures are not trusted. Does this mean that, like humans, chimpanzees understand that vision is connected to thought? Daniel Povinelli (Povinelli & Eddy, 1996) addressed this question by taking advantage of the chimpanzee's natural begging gesture (holding out the hand). In the lab, he and his colleagues taught young chimpanzees to beg for a food treat from the experimenter. On test trials, the chimps were allowed to beg to either an experimenter with a blindfold around the eyes or another with a blindfold around the mouth. Surprisingly, the chimpanzees begged randomly to either one, showing no sensitivity to the fact that only the experimenter who could see them could mentally interpret the significance of their begging gesture.

In other conditions, the chimpanzees were confronted with one experimenter who could see them and another with either a bucket on the head or hands over the eyes. Again, the chimps begged randomly, completely disregarding the visual status of the experimenter. The chimps apparently did not understand the role that visual attention plays in the mental state of another. Additional experiments demonstrated that chimpanzees also failed to discriminate between an experimenter whose back was turned and another whose back was turned but who was looking over the shoulder at the chimps. Over time, the chimpanzees' performance improved, but their behavior strongly suggested that they were following (sometimes sophisticated) perceptual rules, such as: "beg to the one whose face is visible" or "beg to the one whose face is visible, unless both faces are equally visible, then beg to the one whose eyes are visible" (Povinelli & Prince, 1998). Further evidence of this was found in another study in which chimpanzees were presented with an experimenter who was either looking directly at one of two covers (under which there was food) or was staring at a spot above one of the covers. The experimenters reasoned that if a subject understood that eye fixation indicated knowledge about an object, then the subjects would choose the cover when it was being looked at and would choose randomly when nothing was being directly looked at. This was exactly what 3-year-old children did when they were tested in these conditions. Chimpanzees, however, performed similarly in both conditions, choosing the cover to which the head of the experimenter was oriented whether it was being looked at or not. In other words, it was the external context that cued their acts, not inferences about another's mental state (Povinelli, Bierschwale, & Cech, 1999).

Other studies have looked at whether apes can distinguish between the intentional and accidental acts of another. Human developmental studies have indicated that by age 3 children are able to consider the intentions of an individual when judging the consequences of an act and can distinguish between accidental and intended outcomes (Nelson, 1980; Nelson-LeGall, 1985; Yuill, 1984). Studies with chimpanzees, however, present a more ambiguous picture of their ability to separate the intentional from the accidental. Povinelli, Perilloux, Reaux, and Bierschwale (1998) trained young chimpanzees to point to experimenters to receive food rewards. Then the apes were presented with different experimenters who either accidentally spilled juice or intentionally dumped juice that was intended for the chimp. The experimenters hypothesized that if the chimps made a distinction between accidental and intentional acts, they would show a preference for the "accidental" experimenter, because the "intentional" experimenter could not be relied upon to relinquish the reward. Later, however, when chimps were allowed to point to either of the two experimenters to receive a reward, they showed no preference. Similar results were found when a food reward intended for the chimp was either intentionally consumed by the experimenter or was unexpectedly snatched from one experimenter and consumed by another. Premack (1986) reported a similar inability to discriminate intentional from accidental behaviors for the human-encultured ape, Sarah.

At least one study, however, has yielded conflicting findings. Call and Tomasello (1998) trained orangutans and chimpanzees to obtain food by retrieving it from a box marked by the experimenter. Experimenters then either intentionally placed markers or accidentally dropped markers onto boxes. Both orangs and chimps showed a clear preference for boxes marked intentionally rather than accidentally. This suggests that these apes could distinguish intentional versus accidental actions on the part of another. A potentially important distinction between this study and those of Povinelli cited earlier is that in this study apes were required to distinguish intentional versus accidental behaviors directed at objects (how was the box marked?), whereas Povinelli required apes to interpret intentional and accidental behaviors as indicators of internal dispositions (was the person intentionally mean?). There may be different levels of intentional analysis, only some of which are accessible to nonhuman primates.

Middle Ground on Theory of Mind?

The current state of ape "theory of mind" research has spawned skeptics (such as Povinelli) and believers (such as Gallup). However, recent work (Hare, Call, Agnetta, & Tomasello, 2000; Hare, Call, & Tomasello, 2001) has opened up the possibility of a middle ground between these extremes. These researchers question the ecological validity of many of the testing procedures used to support the idea that chimpanzees have no "theory of mind." Their studies have exploited a paradigm of subordinate–dominant competition, which they contend is a more realistic model of the chimpanzee social world. In their procedure, food was hidden in such a way that a dominant chimp was either aware or unaware of its location. Monitoring the whole process was a subordinate chimp. When given the opportunity to retrieve the food, subordinates showed a clear preference for the food at locations unknown to the dominant (Fig. 18.3). The subordinates seemed sensitive to what the dominants did or did not know about food locations, which suggests that under some circumstances chimps are aware of another's state of mind (or knowledge).

Based on these findings, Hare et al. (2001) were critical of theorists who take an either/or approach to ape theory of mind (they either have it or they don't). Instead, these authors contend that apes may understand that another's level of knowledge or awareness can differ from their own. Apes have difficulty, however, when it comes to using this understanding as a basis for constructing the way the world looks from another's perspective. So chimp A may realize that chimp B is unaware of X, but chimp A probably does not realize how lacking knowledge of X

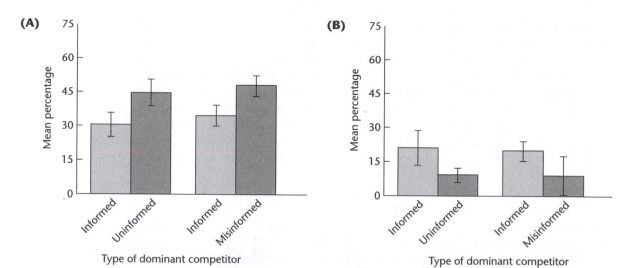

Figure 18.3 **(A)** Mean percentage of pieces of food obtained by a subordinate chimp when the dominant chimp was either aware (informed) or unaware (uninformed or misinformed) about the location of the food. Note that subordinate chimps always obtain significantly more food when dominants were either uninformed or misinformed. **(B)** The percentage of trials on which the subordinate failed to approach a location where food was hidden when the dominant was either aware or unaware of the food's location. Note that the subordinates were more avoidant of the food when the dominants were aware of its location. This difference between informed and uninformed was significant, but the difference between informed and misinformed fell short of significance. (Adapted from Hare et al., 2001, p. 143.)

affects chimp B's entire interpretation of the current situation. Chimp A cannot put herself in B's place and imagine what the world must be like if one does not know X. Thus, the conclusion by Hare et al. (2000) converges with Deacon's (1997) assessment that animals lack the symbolic function necessary to see the world from another's perspective. We come back then to a familiar theme: humans may not be alone in possessing a capacity for empathy and self/other understanding, but our ability to use that capacity to construct an alternative perspective exceeds that of other species.

The Ancestral Sense of Self and Other

The importance of "theory of mind" and "sense of self" research in apes is that it may provide insight into the capacities of the common ancestor of the ape and hominin. Characteristics shared by species of common descent are likely to have been present in the common ancestor of those species. Thus, if chimpanzees and other great apes show evidence of a self/other sense similar to that of humans, then our common ancestor probably possessed that ability as well. Baron-Cohen (1999) evaluated two hypotheses regarding the evolution of the human sense of self and other. Believers in an ape theory of mind are likely to adopt the **6-million-year hypothesis**, which contends that a human-like self/other sense was present in the common ancestor and is shared by humans and great apes (Byrne & Whiten, 1991; Mithen, 1996; Whiten, 1999). Baron-Cohen (1999), however, doubted this hypothesis and, instead, found a **40,000-year hypothesis** more convincing. This, he contended, is more in line with the archeological evidence, especially the impressive cultural artifacts that appear only with the Upper Paleolithic. If we reject an "either/or" approach and follow the middle ground prescribed by Hare, Call, and Tomasello (2001), then it might be the case that a certain self/other sense was present in our common ancestor. It may not, however, have been the same as that of modern humans (or great apes, for that matter). What might it have been like?

Dan Povinelli contended that Gallup's mirror test tapped a more primitive **kinesthetic sense of self**, not an elaborate human-like sense of self. Povinelli and James Cant spent several months in the Sumatran rain forest, carefully observing the impressive acrobatics of orangutans. These 100–200-pound tree dwellers have a manner of movement that would score high marks from even the most jaded or corrupt gymnastics judge. With meticulous grace, they methodically swing, twist, and maneuver themselves from branch to branch, gracefully suspended by any of their four limbs. Because their great weight bends and stresses the branches on which they swing, orangutans must constantly monitor their body position and locomotive progress, quickly adjusting to any unexpected weaknesses in the canopy.

From their observations, Povinelli and Cant (1995) concluded that the Miocene ancestor of the great apes and humans faced a serious problem. As their body size increased, the challenges of locomotion in an arboreal environment became increasingly difficult and life threatening. How can a large-bodied animal maneuver in a three-dimensional space in which size, weight, momentum, distance, orientation, and other factors must all be balanced to effectively get from one place to another? To negotiate this environment without literally breaking one's neck would require a high-level kinesthetic self-representation. According to Povinelli and Cant's **clambering hypothesis**, the ancient ancestor of the great apes and humans must have possessed a keen understanding of its own body and body movements. This kinesthetic sense of self is what allowed it to plan and execute sophisticated movements among the tree branches high above the rain forest floor. The echoes of this ancient self-representation are still present in the great apes today, including humans. It was this sense of self that Gallup revealed with the mirror test and that very young children display when they demonstrate mirror recognition but fail other more demanding tests of self-knowledge (e.g., Povinelli, Landau, and Perilloux, 1996). An important feature of the kinesthetic sense of self, as envisioned by Povinelli and Cant, is that it is primarily a physical, movement-oriented self-representation with few (if any) concomitant psychological implications. This understanding of self is not necessarily projected onto another. If Povinelli and Cant (1995) were correct, then the evolution of the human sense of self began by simply understanding the physical body and how it moved, an understanding that would be largely shared with other great apes. This seems reasonable, given that humans and apes have very similar somatosensory and motor cortex body representations (although the cortical areas dedicated to the hands and face are larger in humans; Bear, Connors, & Paradiso, 1996).

Evolving the Human Sense of Self

If the kinesthetic sense of self is something humans share with apes, then it is likely that this trait was present in our common ancestor. However, over the 5 million years that chimpanzees and hominins have been on separate evolutionary tracks, this sense may well have evolved differently in the two species. At the end of the first year of life, the cognitive development of human infants diverges notably from that of chimpanzees (Hallock & Worobey, 1984; Mathieu & Bergeron, 1981). One important aspect of this divergence is that human children become intensely curious about object–object relations, whereas apes focus on body–object relations. Poti and Spinozzi (1994) related this difference to the role of locomotion and the actions of the hands in ontogeny. Young chimpanzees are mobile sooner than human children and are able to locomote independently to objects at an earlier stage of cognitive development. Because of their relative immobility, human children are restricted to hand–object manipulations that extend into later stages of cognitive development. Thus, by the end of the first year of life, for the chimp the relationship of body to object becomes prominent, whereas the relationship of hand to object is paramount for the child. This difference may well have an important impact on the development of one's sense of self. The visually guided movements of the hand are more refined and subtle and are a more indirect way of exploring the external world than the more gross movements of the trunk and limbs. With the hand, one becomes both an acute observer of one's own actions on the environment *and* the agent of those actions (Wilson, 1998). The borders of the self are more fully explored and the detachment of objects from the self are more distinctly experienced. The bipedalism of *Australopithecus* would have allowed it increased opportunities for the types of visually guided hand movements likely to heighten the degree of physical self-awareness. The increased motor control inherent in the mimetic acts attributed to *Homo erectus* (such as toolmaking) make it reasonable to suppose that physical self-awareness may have advanced further in this species. However, the only (literally) hard evidence that we have concerning the time at which this physical sense of self took on deeper psychological qualities comes in the form of artifacts marking the advent of the Upper Paleolithic.

We have already reviewed the art, artifacts, and other symbolic remnants of the Cro-Magnons of Europe dating back 20,000–30,000 years. Their relevance in this context is in what they tell us about our ancestors' level of self-awareness. The pottery, body adornments, carvings, and drawings of these ancient humans are believed to have played an important social function. As human communities became more complex, the roles of individuals within those communities became more difficult to define and organize. Art helped solved the problem of who held what responsibilities within the tribe (Stringer & McKie, 1996). An externalized symbol, such as a certain necklace, cut of clothing, or style of bead, could signify rank, marital status, clan membership, or even who the best hunter was. In other words, the symbol marked the self—not just the *physical* self but a deeply personal, *psychological* self as well. In fact, according to anthropologist Randall White, the explosion of artwork and symbols that occurred at the transition of the Upper Paleolithic period represented the new-found human capacity to construct multiple selves through the use of external symbols and ornaments. Chimpanzees may have an individual sense of self, but they do not possess a sense of self that can be manipulated; that is, constructed and reconstructed with the aid of external supports. "We aren't born with our complete social identity," said White. "It's a constructed phenomenon. I view the use of beads and pendants as one of the ways early Upper Paleolithic people were constructing their social identities" (Shreeve, 1995, p. 321).

As Dobzhansky indicated, with self-awareness comes death-awareness. The Upper Paleolithic also brought with it evidence of a heightened understanding of the significance of death, most notably attested to by the Sungir burial site and its elaborately adorned corpses. But were the Cro-Magnons the first to recognize the significance of death and to hope for an afterlife beyond the grave?

A number of researchers have speculated in the scientific literature that a profound sense of death and spirituality may pre-date Cro-Magnons. Neanderthal burial sites dating back to the Middle Paleolithic period show evidence of deliberate and possibly symbolic organization. For example, it is difficult to attribute the shape and depth of such sites as La Chapelle-aux-Saints, Le Ferrassie, and Le Moustier in France to natural processes. It seems the bodies were intentionally and carefully interred. Moreover, concentrations of flower pollen found at the Shanidar site in Iraq or the arrangement of animal horns at the Teshik Tash site in Uzbekistan have been interpreted as having ritualistic or religious significance. Many researchers have pointed out that, although these sites may offer evidence of deliberate burial, that does not necessarily imply religious or symbolic significance (Gargett, 1989). Neanderthals may have had strong social bonds that compelled them to treat their dead respectfully, but ritualistic or religious elements were not necessarily tied to these practices. Chase and Dibble (1987) argued that most of the supposedly symbolic grave artifacts can be explained more easily as objects accidentally added to the site by the burial activity or by later natural processes, such as weather events or animal activity. Mellars (1996) seemed to concur with this thinking, noting that the case for a symbolic dimension to Neanderthal burial sites remains "at best unproven." Any uncertainty vanishes, however, when confronted with burial sites of the Upper Paleolithic. Thus, it is only by about 40,000 years ago that we can be reasonably assured that a fully "human" sense of self and other had emerged, with all the moral ramifications that entails.

The Evolution of Morality

A sense of self and other are necessary elements of any real moral sense, but human morality possesses other attributes that must have emerged over the course of our evolution. Dennis Krebs (1998) argued that human morality evolved along three tracks: (1) deference to authority, (2) reciprocity leading to altruism, and (3) devotion. Let's look at each of these and the aspects of morality that they entail.

Deference to Authority: Moral Laws

Deference to authority refers to the human tendency to accept moral laws and proscriptions. Human morality is often characterized by an authoritative set of teachings or divinely inspired laws that stipulate which behaviors are understood as moral or immoral by a certain culture. Hammurabi's code may be the oldest documented example. Others include the Ten Commandments in the Judeo-Christian tradition, the Eightfold Path of Buddhism, and the Five Confucian texts of Chinese culture. Krebs saw the origins of this moral deference in the hierarchical social systems common among primates. Because social hierarchy is a shared trait of nearly all great apes and humans, it seems reasonable that hominins arose from an ancestor who also had this trait. Before authoritative moral rules were articulated, our behaviors were regulated by the authority of a dominant alpha. A selective advantage would accrue to those who managed to satisfy individual fitness interests while minimizing conflicts with the alpha. Humans come from a

---

KEY CONTRIBUTIONS

Moral Codes and Moral Emotions

BOX 18.1 One of the key assumptions of evolutionary psychology is that it is our *emotional* makeup that has been most directly affected by natural selection. Our desires, motivations, gut feelings, and various other emotional "pushes" and "pulls," which so often inexplicably compel us down one path or another, represent adaptations that allowed our ancestors to survive and reproduce. From this perspective, then, the origins of human morality must be emotional in nature. Long before our ancestors could rationally articulate their beliefs about right and wrong, they operated based on what *felt* right or wrong. The deep evolutionary origins of morality are moral emotions. Only much later did humans attempt to take these vague dispositions and express them as moral laws. Even today, scientists, philosophers, and theologians continue to struggle with the translation of moral feelings into moral principles. Why is it that some actions feel right but violate a moral law, or that some moral laws feel so unjust or immoral when put into practice? Why is there so often a disconnection between what we *think* is right versus what *feel* we should do?

A recent experiment showed that the schism between moral codes and moral emotions extends all the way down to the brain level. Green, Sommerville, Nystrom, Darley, & Cohen (2001) used functional magnetic resonance imaging (fMRI) to monitor brain activity as subjects contemplated various moral dilemmas. fMRI allows researchers to measure blood flow and oxygen levels to different parts of the brain while subjects engage in cognitive tasks. Increased blood flow to a certain area of the brain generally indicates that that area is more active.

Green and colleagues presented subjects with two different types of moral dilemmas: *moral–personal* and *moral–impersonal.* An example of a moral–personal dilemma would be the following: Suppose a train is running out of control and is set to strike and kill five people along the track. You can stop the train by pushing an unsuspecting large man off a footbridge above the track. The man would fall onto the track, and his body would successfully stop the train before it strikes the five people. Should you take this action to save the five people?

A moral–impersonal dilemma would be pretty much the same, but, instead of pushing a man onto the track to stop the train, you could throw a switch that diverts the train to an alternative track on which there is only one person and not five. Thus, the critical difference between the moral–personal and moral–impersonal dilemmas lies in the means used to accomplish some end. In moral–personal dilemmas, one must directly (personally) cause harm to another, whereas in the moral–impersonal ones, the harm is caused indirectly. When presented with moral–personal dilemmas, most people respond "no." In other words, they contend that it is wrong to directly harm another (push someone onto the tracks, for example), even if they are trying to a save a larger number of others. However, when presented with moral–impersonal dilemmas of exactly the same kind, most people respond "yes." In other words, it is okay to flip a switch that results in the death of another person if you are saving a larger number of others in the process. This is intriguing, because in both cases the end result is the same: one person is sacrificed to save five. Moral laws would seem to dictate that both cases should be treated the same; either both are morally acceptable or both are unacceptable. It may be that in assessing these dilemmas people are not trying to apply a moral principle as much as they are simply following their moral emotions.

Figure 18.A shows the increase in brain activity as measured by fMRI for different brain structures while subjects pondered either moral–personal (dark bars) or moral–impersonal (light bars) dilemmas (note that subjects also were presented nonmoral scenarios, and

long line of creatures who evolved to "work within" a given system to achieve personal (really genetic) gain. With the emergence of symbolic thought and language, hominins were capable of codifying the rules of their group's system and, in some cases, attaching divine authority to them (see Box 18.1 for more on moral codes and moral emotions).

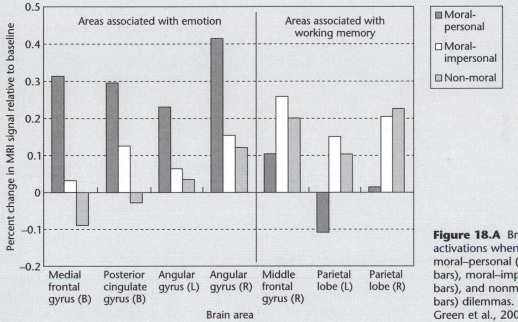

Figure 18.A Brain area activations when pondering moral–personal (dark gray bars), moral–impersonal (white bars), and nonmoral (light gray bars) dilemmas. (Adapted from Green et al., 2001, p. 2106.)

these are shown on the graph). Note that those parts of the brain associated with emotions (medial frontal gyrus, posterior cingulate gyrus, and the left and right angular gyri) show significant increases in activation for the moral–personal compared with the moral–impersonal dilemmas. Although they produce the same ends, the brain does not treat moral–personal and moral–impersonal situations the same. We seem emotionally repelled by the fact that we must personally harm another to save others.

We did not evolve as moral philosophers but as practical actors. These findings may help to shed light on why knowing moral laws (and even agreeing with them on a rational level) may not necessarily lead to

moral behavior. We may transgress a moral law because the law feels wrong and the action feels right. Does this mean that our moral feelings are always truly moral? Certainly not, because our feelings evolved not to compel us to be good but to be adaptive. The important lesson seems to be that if we honestly believe that certain moral laws are truly good, then to follow them we must find ways of getting our emotions in line with our rational assessment of right and wrong. The truly moral person may have to find ways of becoming passionate about what he or she has rationally determined to be right. Recall that the Good Samaritan was "moved to pity," whereas others knew the rightness of pity but failed to act.

Source: **Green, J.D., Sommerville, R.B., Nystrom, L.E., Darley, J.M., & Cohen, J.D. (2001).** An fMRI investigation of emotional engagement in moral judgement. *Science, 293,* 2105–2108.

Reciprocity: A Sense of Justice

Reciprocity, like hierarchy, is also a widespread trait of the primate social world. Flack and de Waal (2000) reviewed a vast array of literature on primate food sharing and other forms of reciprocal exchange. They cited evidence suggesting that apes and some monkeys keep tabs on who has been a generous sharer and who has been stingy and that behavior is adjusted accordingly, sharing more with the generous and withholding or taking retribution on the stingy. Although their conclusions have stirred controversy (see, for example, Bernstein, 2000; Kagan, 2000), the evidence does raise the possibility that a budding sense of **justice** may have been present in our common ancestor. One would expect that reciprocal sharing and generosity would be practiced initially only with kin. Thus, one's kindness would continue to benefit one's genes. However, as hominin societies became more complex and reciprocal exchanges became more involved, the hominin sense of fairness also would have evolved so that individuals could continue to reap the benefits of group stability. Enlarged groups would have contained extended family, "in-laws," friends, and others with no direct genetic links. Individuals within groups that successfully broadened reciprocity beyond immediate kin would have enjoyed fitness advantages over individuals in smaller, less inclusive groups in the competition for scarce resources. These conditions helped promote the evolution of a more altruistic beyond-kin-but-within-the-group sense of fairness. Consistent with this evolutionary explanation is the fact that even today, we humans often find it difficult to apply our principles of justice and fairness to out-group members (e.g., those of other races, religions, or tribes). Natural selection can take you only so far.

Devotion: A Sense of Concern

A final track for the evolution of morality involves sexual selection for devotion. As hominin females became increasingly burdened by their offspring, pair bonding and male investment would have become more critical to individual fitness. Female hominins would have found a selective advantage in choosing males who formed strong emotional bonds with them and their offspring and, as a result, willingly shared resources with them. An advantage would be had for males who selected females who willingly restricted their sexual activities to their mates. Both sexes would have exerted pressure on the other for aspects of **devotion**, an emotional bonding that caused certain behaviors (such as cheating on one's commitments) to produce feelings of guilt. Parker's (1998) model of evolution of emotions (discussed in chapter 7) fits with this reasoning.

From Moral Authority to Justice and Devotion

Given what we know about the background of hominin evolution, it is also possible to sketch out the most likely sequence of the emergence of these three moral tracks. Boehm (2000) noted that both social hierarchy and coalition formation are common traits of chimpanzees, bonobos, and humans, making them likely characteristics of the ape/hominin common ancestor. He further noted the widespread presence of egalitarianism among hunter–gatherer societies. These observations led him to formulate an evolutionary scenario of a rigid primate social hierarchy slowly giving way to hunter–gatherer egalitarianism. Initially, hominins existed in strict, alpha-dominated, hierarchical groups. From the standpoint of moral evolution, then, deference to authority would have been our oldest form of social regulation. From this beginning, senses of justice and devotion would have followed.

Over the course of our evolution, subordinates formed increasingly effective coalitions designed to curb the excesses of alpha domination (what Boehm, 2000, called **alpha bullying**), thereby offering fitness advantages to individual coalition members (Krebs, 2000). Competition from other groups and other ecological factors would have bestowed advantages on individuals who were part of ever larger, more effectively cooperative coalitions (Alexander, 1987). A challenge to the construction of increasingly larger, cooperative coalitions would have been the presence of individual deviants—those who tried to reap benefits from the coalition without making appropriate sacrifices. Bingham (1999; also see chapter 9) argued that coalitional enforcement in the form of group stoning or other weapon-aided, punishment-at-a-distance may very well have served the function of suppressing cheaters. It was in this context that the evolution of a sense of fairness may have held a selective advantage. Those able to reliably distinguish debts owed and paid would have been most likely to avoid the detrimental fitness effects of being cheated by another or punished by the group. Eventually, with the advent of language, the implicit moral guidelines of the group could be expressed more explicitly and gossip could be used to more effectively identify cheaters. Furthermore, physical sanctioning of cheaters could be replaced by verbal castigation and ridicule, often very effectively used by hunter–gatherer cultures (see, for example, Turnbull, 1961).

At the same time that selection pressures would have made larger, more cooperative groups beneficial to individual fitness, sexual selection would have been operating to hone the hominin sense of commitment, sexual propriety, and affection for offspring and mates. The hominin sense of fairness and justice, originally fostered in the reciprocity of coalitions, would have intermingled with issues of sexual fidelity, paternity certainty, and the maintenance of group stability through standards of sexual conduct. Boehm (2000) argued that modern human morality tends to be inordinately preoccupied with these issues (potentially because of their importance in our evolutionary history), and also that hunter–gatherer societies have proved quite effective in regulating sexual offenses.

Is It Science?

Although interesting and plausible, it must be admitted that our evolutionary conjectures about the origins of morality currently lack any form of rigorous testing. Boehm's (2000) model, for example, which posits a subordinate coup of alpha domination may sound quite reasonable. At present, however, it is not clear what testable hypotheses might be derived that could support or falsify the idea (see Bernstein, 2000). We therefore must understand the evolution of human morality to be an emerging area in which theories and ideas are being put forth but in which the real task of scientific evaluation remains to be done. Science, however, starts with ideas, and the ideas proposed on this issue are at least promising. It may fall to the next generation of thinkers, perhaps someone reading this book, to take the next step.

"I and My Brother..."

An old Arab saying captures our evolutionary moral inheritance: "I and my brother against my cousin. I and my cousin against the stranger." We are by nature designed to be selective, rather than universal, in the way we employ our moral implements. Remember that evolution is no moralist. Traits evolve because they incur a fitness advantage on the organism, not because they are good. Thus, evolution has designed us to be as moral as we need to be to gain a fitness advantage for ourselves, and that is it. This is one of the reasons why human moral concern is often so difficult to apply equitably beyond the boundaries of kin, clan, or tribe. Whether it was the Romans and Barbarians, Christians and Infidels, Jews and Canaanites, Hindus and Muslims, or Hutus and Tutsis, the ease with which we have casually shed the moral regard usually held for in-group members when dealing with out-group members is frightening. However, it is also quite understandable. In our ancestral past, being moral toward a fellow group member yielded reciprocal rewards, status, and other considerations that could enhance fitness. Out-group members would have been of little use, except as competitors by whose elimination we could prove our mate worthiness and elevate our status. We didn't need to be moral to them, so we weren't and, all too often, aren't.

Centuries ago, philosophers such as Hobbes and Rousseau debated whether man's nature was inherently evil or good. Now we know it is neither. We are not born innately good or evil but with an evolved propensity to figure out how good we need to be to obtain maximal rewards or, as Robert Wright (1994) put it, how much cheating we can get away with. The acclaimed developmentalist Jean Piaget (1932) was struck by how common lying was among children. "The tendency to tell lies," he wrote, "is...natural...spontaneous and universal" (p. 139). Subsequent research confirmed his suspicion (Krout, 1931; Vasek, 1986). Children may be born liars, but the degree to which they persist in lying as they get older depends a great deal on whether or not their parents reprimand them for lying, how much lying their parents do, and generally how much parental supervision they get. This is all consistent with the notion that children naturally "test" to see how much lying is acceptable in their environments—an early start on figuring out how moral one needs to be.

Understanding the foundations from which our morality emerged helps us to appreciate the challenge of being a truly moral species (or individual). Although we have a natural tendency toward reciprocity, we are not naturally fair in reciprocal arrangements. By evolutionary design, we are creatures who want to get a bit more than we give. We naturally want to check our morality before it costs us more than we get back, and we have little if any natural proclivity toward embracing out-group members in the same envelope of concern and respect with which we surround our own group. With this in mind, it becomes easy to see why so many of us eagerly applaud religious sentiments such as universal love, the golden rule, and turning the other cheek, but so few actually practice them. Real morality does not come naturally. Truly "doing unto others..." is a challenge, and loving one's enemies is downright unfit. Nature can take you only so far. Blessed is the species that can reach for morality, for they have a chance of being more than just moral enough.

SUMMARY

Experimental tests of animal empathy suggest that many animals are able to detect and respond to the distress of another animal. However, it is unclear if their response is based on a real empathic understanding of another's plight or a desire to simply terminate another's unpleasant distress signals. To determine if an animal truly "empathizes" with another, one must establish that the animal is capable of possessing a "theory of mind" or, put another way, is able to understand the mental states of another.

Theory of mind tests in primates have produced a complicated picture. Most apes are capable of passing the mirror test, indicating that they do have a certain level of self-awareness, which suggests that they also possess a certain degree of other-awareness. Field observations of deception among primates add additional evidence to the idea of a primate theory of mind. However, laboratory studies indicate that chimpanzees often behave based on visual cues and not on an understanding of another's mental state. Some studies, however, suggest that chimps are aware of some aspects of another's mental state but are unable to use that information to understand how the world looks from another's perspective. It may be that the ability to comprehend alternative perspectives is a mental attribute that evolved along the hominin line after its split from the chimpanzee line.

It has been suggested that the evolution of human moral thinking has evolved along three tracks: (1) deference to moral authority, (2) reciprocity and justice, and (3) devotion and commitment. Each of these emerged out of different aspects of the hominin social evolutionary context. Deference to authoritative moral codes may have its roots in our primate hierarchical social heritage. A sense of justice may have come from the reciprocity and relative egalitarianism of coalitions that arose to regulate alpha bullying. Notions of commitment, fidelity, and sexual propriety may have come from male–female pair bonds. All of this may have engendered in us a limited form of morality, based in moral emotions, that served hominin fitness interests.

KEY TERMS

40,000-year hypothesis	deference to authority	mirror test
alpha bullying	devotion	objective self-awareness
attitudinal reciprocity	justice	6-million-year hypothesis
clambering hypothesis	kinesthetic sense of self	theory of mind

REVIEW QUESTIONS

1. Describe the mirror test and what it suggests about primate self-awareness.

2. What is a theory of mind? Describe the evidence for and against theory of mind in nonhuman primates.

3. What is a kinesthetic self-awareness? How might it have evolved, and how is it different from a self-awareness that allows for empathy?

4. What is meant by alpha bullying? What form of morality may be associated with it, and what form of morality may have evolved in opposition to it?

5. Why might it be argued that our evolved morality is limited in form? What are its limitations? Is it true morality?

SUGGESTED READINGS

de Waal, F. (1996). *Good natured.* Cambridge, MA: Harvard University Press.

Katz, L. (2000). *Evolutionary origins of morality.* New York: Imprint Academic.

Macphail, E.M. (1998). *The evolution of consciousness.* Oxford: Oxford University Press.

Ridley, M. (1996). *The origins of virtue.* New York: Viking.

WEB SITES

www.bun.kyoto-u.ac.jp/~suchii/D.onM.html good site from the University of Kyoto on Darwin's writings on the evolution of morality.

www.imprint-academic.demon.co.uk/books/Katz.html article by Leonard Katz on the evolution of morality.

www.theatlantic.com/issues/98apr/biomoral.htm article from the Atlantic Monthly by E.O. Wilson on the biological basis of morality, deals also with many philosophical and theological issues.

Epilogue: A Moral to the Story?

For but an eyeblink of time, let the ceaseless journey hesitate in meditative silence. *Homo sapiens sapiens* have arrived and are privileged to look back longingly at the landscape traversed. In a reflective gaze unique to this species, we can ponder the meaning of a seemingly meaningless odyssey. But for us, odyssey must have meaning, for such is the essence of this species. We are the species that constructs meaning. And, oddly enough, there is meaning in this odyssey—strange, wonderful, paradoxical meaning.

If we ask, what it is that made us human, an answer emerges. It is clear that all the obvious traits—our upright stance, our big brains, our spoken language, our naked skin, our dexterous hands, and even our bloated sex organs—are not the basis of our humanity. What made us human was that we somehow managed to use those traits to create deeply penetrating relationships with other humans. These relationships, in turn, furthered the evolution of those traits. In isolation, *Homo sapiens sapiens* is nothing more than a naked ape. In solitude, there is no extraordinary intellect, no science, no art, no language, no music, nothing that any of us would identify as the unique and laudable qualities of humanity. All of the distinctive traits so admired in our species, all the best of what we are, resulted from evolution within human communities. We evolved in the context of an unprecedented interdependence with one another. We needed each other, and it was that need that made all the difference on this journey. *What made us human was other humans!*

This might give us cause to wonder. In our headlong rush to secure every manner of *individual* freedoms, rights, conveniences, and comforts, what effect might these have on the very thing that made us human: the overwhelming need for one another?

Glossary

abstract physical causes Physical causes, such as mass and force, that operate beyond the superficial perceived qualities of objects.

acceptance Integration with warmth and affection into a social network; Fredrickson sees this as a critical element in understanding the adaptive significance of happiness.

Acheulean tools Category of hominin stone tools that arose about 1.4 million years ago; usually associated with *Homo erectus* and characterized by the bifacial hand axe.

active teaching Term describing a teaching situation in which information is intentionally transmitted from teacher to learner and in which the teacher is sensitive to and adjusts activities to accommodate the learner's level of knowledge.

adaptive restraints The tendency to consider only a restricted set of possible solutions or alternatives when confronted with a stimulus or event that could be interpreted in a multitude of ways.

agreeableness Term describing a personality trait characterized by the presence of a cooperative attitude.

allopatric speciation The creation of a new species through a process in which a subpopulation is isolated from a main group and therefore sets off on its own evolutionary track.

alpha bullying The tendency of alpha males to use threat, intimidation, and violence to dominate a group; Boehm asserted that the evolution of a sense of justice would have been necessary to curb alpha bullying.

altricial Helpless; born in a state of nervous system immaturity and needing constant care for survival.

anagenesis A pattern of evolutionary change marked by the transformation of a single species into a new species over time.

arbitrariness A characteristic of language in which the elemental parts of the language (for example, phonemic sounds) have no inherent meaning but are endowed with meaning by the way they are combined with other elements.

archaic *Homo sapiens* Term describing a species of hominin that arose about .5 million years ago, with physical characteristics that made it distinct from both *Homo erectus* and modern humans.

archival data   Data collected from past research.

assortative mating   The tendency for mate choices to be nonrandom; often associated with variables that increase genetic relatedness.

asymmetry of affective experience effect   Term describing the fact that negative emotions brought on by unfortunate events are experienced more strongly than positive emotions brought on by fortunate events.

attachment   Emotional bonding of one organism to another; most commonly found between mother and offspring.

attitudinal reciprocity   Term used by de Waal to explain why monkeys (and presumably apes) share with one another and return favors. By doing so, they engender a cooperative tendency in others that can have fitness payoffs for the giver.

attraction   Positive affective or psychological "pull" toward a person or object.

Aurignacian tools   Term describing the more complex tools associated with the Upper Paleolithic period.

Australopithecines (more recently called Australopiths)   Genus of hominin that arose in Africa more than 4 million years ago, whose important characteristics included bipedal locomotion, an ape-sized brain, and large face and teeth.

Australopiths   *see Australopithecine.*

autocuing   Term used by Donald to describe the ability to voluntarily access one's own mind.

availability of investing males   Important factor in determining the reproductive strategies of females; as females perceive more males to be interested and available for long-term investing in offspring, females tend to opt for long-term mating strategies.

base rate neglect   A reasoning deficit with which an individual fails to take into account the prevalence of some variable in the population.

behavioral ecological approach   An approach to understanding the social and behavioral tendencies of extinct hominins by combining the range of social behaviors available to them (often by phylogenetic comparisons) with the likely alterations arising from changing environments.

blindness   The notion that natural selection cannot "foresee" future circumstances and can only adapt organisms based on their present traits and current environmental conditions.

catastrophism   The notion that earth's major geological features were produced as result of cataclysmic events, such as the Biblical great flood.

cerebrotype   Term describing brain organization; focuses on the relative sizes of 11 different brain structures

chance and law   Refers in evolutionary theory to the idea that evolution is a combination of chance events (for example, random genetic mutations or contingent historical and environmental circumstances) and lawful processes (for example, natural selection).

cheat detection   Ability to determine if someone is failing to carry through on a social agreement; believed by some evolutionary psychologists to be an example of a domain-specific mental adaptation in humans.

chemotaxis   Ability of single-celled organisms, such as amoebas, to move away from noxious chemical environments and toward more beneficial ones.

cladogenesis   Pattern of evolutionary change marked by a single species splitting or branching off into two or more species over time.

clambering hypothesis   Hypothesis espoused by Povinelli and Cant asserting that apes, increasing in size over the course of evolution, would have needed to develop a kinesthetic sense of self to be able to plan and execute locomotor movements in the dangerous high canopy of their habitats.

coalitional enforcement   Term used by Bingham to describe collective enforcement of social norms. It is hypothesized that this sort of group pressure would have been necessary to inhibit cheating and allow cooperative groups to evolve.

commitment problem   Situation in which an individual experiences difficulty in determining whether another individual is entering a cooperative relationship for the long-term good of both parties or for his or her short-term benefit.

common ancestor   Ancestral species to which two or more concurrent species can trace their evolutionary origins

competition   In evolutionary theory, the notion that organisms must struggle against one another for limited resources to secure what they need to survive and reproduce.

conceptual understanding of number   An understanding of the way in which the quantity signified by a number relates to the entire system of values of which that number is part.

conscious control   Ability to voluntarily monitor and direct one's own behaviors; it is asserted that certain aspects of language must be under conscious control.

consumption as parental investment   Term describing the theory that, in industrialized societies, parents may compete against each other not by having more offspring but by lavishly provisioning only a few or single offspring.

contingency   In evolutionary theory, the notion that the course of evolution can be significantly affected by unpredictable historical and environmental events.

copulatory vigilance   Male reproductive strategy in which the male monitors the female to make sure she does not copulate with another male; believed to have arisen as ovulation became more concealed in females.

core theory   Fundamental explanatory principle underlying a theory.

cranial base   Base or bottom profile of the skull; in humans, the cranial base is arched or flexed, a configuration associated with the lowering of the larynx.

creole   Hybrid language created by the combination of two or more languages.

cross-cultural comparisons   Analyses of subjects from different cultures.

cross-species comparisons   Comparisons done on different species

cuckolded   Term describing a male who has been duped into expending resources on an offspring that does not carry his genetic material.

cuckoldry   Mating strategy in which the female obtains resources from a long-term partner but genetic material from a short-term partner.

cultural determinism   Theory that human nature results from or is determined by cultural factors, with biology playing little or no role

cultural dimorphism   Term used by Miller to describe the disproportional contribution of males in the economic, social, and cultural spheres of society; these are manifested as display behaviors designed to enhance a male's status and, ultimately, reproductive success.

daughter guarding   Tendency of fathers to closely monitor daughters to control their sexual activity.

deception   Process of misleading; in evolution, deceptive tendencies could prove advantageous if an organism could induce others to perform nonreciprocated acts of altruism.

deference to authority   Asserted by some evolutionists to be the first step in the evolution of a sense of morality; because of the hierarchical nature of primate groups, human ancestors would have accepted the "moral" teachings of an alpha male as authoritative.

deference to higher status   Tendency to allow those of higher status to gain more from reciprocal relationships.

developmental module   Specialized mental adaptation appearing early in life, such as the ability to recognize faces or to ascribe intentionality to another.

devotion   Emotional attachment to another; a sense of devotion is thought by some to have been a precursor to moral thinking.

discreteness   Fact that elemental parts of language retain their integrity when combined with other parts and do not mix or blend in the creation of meaning.

discriminative hedonic amplifiers   Term used by Johnston to describe the adaptive function played by emotions in filtering and amplifying fitness-relevant stimuli.

disengaging from unattainable goals   Term describing a potential adaptive function of depression in which the depressive feelings compel the individual to preserve energy and resources by discontinuing the pursuit of a goal that cannot be achieved.

division of labor hypothesis   Hypothesis that maintains that males and females engaged in different activities over the course of human evolution and thus were subjected to different selection pressures.

docility   Adaptive tendency of organisms, especially humans, to unquestioningly accept cultural teachings.

domain specificity   Important concept of the evolutionary approach that claims that the human mind is composed of specialized modules designed by natural selection for specific adaptive purposes (for example, a face recognition module).

dominance   Power or influence exerted by an individual; believed by many to be an important personality characteristic.

emulation   Re-creation of the general goal-directed behaviors of another.

encephalization   Term describing the enlargement of the brain relative to the body over the course of evolution.

encephalization quotient (EQ)   Cross-species brain size comparison measure that scales the actual size of the brain against the expected brain size predicted by body size.

environment of evolutionary adaptedness (EEA)   Sum total of the selection pressures responsible for a specific adaptive structure. In evolutionary psychology, the EEA is also often used to describe a time span in evolutionary history (.5 million years ago or so) when human ancestors were engaged in a hunter–gathering lifestyle and when most of our important physical and psychological adaptations evolved.

episodic minds   Term used by Donald to describe minds in which access is restricted by current environmental cues so that they operate almost exclusively in the "here and now." Donald asserts that ape minds are of this type.

ethology   Branch of biology that studies the behavior of animals under natural conditions

evolution   Descent with modification; the change in organisms over time.

evolutionary byproduct   Structure or trait that results from evolutionary processes but does not directly solve an adaptive problem and, thus, is not considered an adaptation.

evolved social reasoning   Term describing the notion that humans have evolved to apply our reasoning power to social situations rather than to abstract problems of logic.

executive functions   Functions of the brain, often localized in the frontal lobe, that involve such activities as planning, reasoning, causal attribution, and organization and coordination of movement.

experimental test   Test in which variables are manipulated and controlled so that causal inferences can be made.

face recognition   Ability to identify faces; often thought to be an innate capacity of newborns.

female choice   Term describing the fact that females are often highly selective when choosing mating partners. Their choices can then affect which male traits become prevalent in future generations.

first fictions   Term used by Baron-Cohen to describe the first evidence of abstract, symbolic artifacts found in Upper Paleolithic remains.

fitness   Term in evolutionary theory to describing the probability of survival and reproduction of an organism.

five-jawed cradle   Type of grip in which an object is surrounded by four fingers on one side and the thumb on the other.

fixed action patterns   Stereotypic, species-specific behaviors triggered by specific environmental stimuli.

foramen magnum   Opening in the cranium at which the spine enters.

40,000 year hypothesis   The hypothesis that humans did not develop a "sense of self" until about 40,000 years ago, at the time of the Upper Paleolithic revolution.

friendship   Relationship of mutual reciprocity and affective concern.

future (un)certainty   Important factor in determining female reproductive strategies. As the future become uncertain, females tend to adopt short-term mating strategies.

game theory   Approach to understanding and studying the evolution of cooperation that involves mathematical modeling of the cost and benefits of different strategies of social interaction

generative praxis   Ability to decompose motor movements into subunits and recombine them to form new movements

genetic concern   Affective bond between two organisms rooted in their genetic relatedness.

genetic determinism   Notion that an organism's physical and/or behavioral traits are determined by its genetic endowment

grandparental investment   Contribution in effort, energy, and resources expended by grandparents in the care and upbringing of their children's offspring.

gravity error   Mistake made by children and animals based on their misapplication of the effects of gravity on falling objects.

green beard   Term used by Dawkins to describe a phenotypic trait that might signal to another the presence of common genes.

handicap principle   Term used by Zahavi to describe certain male traits that presumably signal good genes. These traits place the male metabolically or physically at risk, thus demonstrating that the male has the capacity to endure hardship and continue to function.

harem   Arrangement in which many females share a single male mate

hedonic treadmill effect   Term describing the way in which positive feelings associated with external events diminish as one adapts to current circumstances.

Homo erectus   Species of hominin that arose about 1.8 million years ago; characterized by a significant increase in brain size as well as more advanced social organization.

Homo habilis   Species of early hominin that arose about 2 million years ago; one of the first early toolmakers.

Homo rudolfensis   Species of early hominin that arose about 2 million years ago with more primitive facial characteristics than *H. habilis* but a larger brain.

Homo sapiens sapiens   Species of hominin that arose about 200,000 years ago; another term for modern humans.

Homo   Genus of hominin that arose about 2 million years ago in Africa; characterized by relatively large brain size and increasing dependence on social organization for survival.

honest signals   Term used to describe the adaptive function of emotions that provide trustworthy signals about an organism's internal state.

hunter–gatherers   Term describing those humans and human ancestors who lived in mobile groups surviving on hunted meat and locally gathered edibles.

hypothesis   A theory-derived prediction that, whenever possible, is put to an experimental test to evaluate the power of the theory.

Igf2   Male-imprinted gene that drives high metabolic resource investment in the fetus and placenta.

impossible entities   Term describing some abstract artifacts of the Upper Paleolithic.

imprinted genes   Genes that express their associated traits only when they are either maternally or paternally inherited.

indicators of domesticity   Signals used by a female to assess a male's commitment to provide resources to her and her offspring

interactionist approach   Idea that human psychology is best understood as an interaction between genetic endowment and environmental circumstances.

intervention   Characteristic of language describing the way in which language interposes itself between the internal state of the organism and its external expression.

intra- and intersexual selection   Two forms of sexual selection. Intrasexual selection refers to male competition for access to females. Intersexual selection refers to female choice of specific males as mates.

just so stories   A plausible but, as of yet, untested idea about the way in which a specific trait may have evolved.

justice   Fairness, equity. Some evolutionists have asserted that group egalitarianism might have emerged as a means of curbing the power of an alpha male (*see alpha bullying*).

Kanzi   The language-trained bonobo of Sue Savage-Rumbaugh; probably the most linguistically competent ape alive.

kinesthetic sense of self   Awareness of one's own body and bodily movements.

kinship   Term describing the genetic and familial relatedness of individuals, including offspring, siblings, cousins, etc.

K-selected species   Generally larger, more slowly maturing species in which parents produce fewer offspring but invest more heavily in their upbringing.

!Kung   The !Kung San of southern Africa, one of the most extensively studied extant hunter–gatherer groups.

Levallois technique   Stone toolmaking technique whereby a prepared core is used in the creation of a tool.

looming stimulus   Stimulus that causes retinal image size to steadily increase, indicating that an object is approaching the observer.

lunate sulcus   Brain fissure between the occipital and parietal lobes; has shifted rearward over the course of hominin evolution, thus allowing expansion of the parietal lobe.

M6p   Female-imprinted gene that counteracts the effects of paternally inherited *Igf2*.

Madonna/whore dichotomy   Term describing a categorical mode of male thinking used by males to judge females in association with two types of reproductive opportunities: long-term committed and short-term uncommitted.

male competition   Struggle of males against one another for access to females, who, because of the relatively scarcity of eggs, are a highly valued reproductive resource.

male parental investment Term describing the effort and resources expended by males in the care and upbringing of their offspring.

mate copying Mating strategy in which one individual attempts to steal another's mate.

maternity certainty The fact that females have no confusion over which offspring carry their genetic material.

meat-for-sex deal Term describing the evolved cooperative social arrangement between males and females for maintaining an extended pair bond capable of successfully raising offspring

mimesis Ability to consciously control and refine movement and thus endow it with representational properties.

mirror test Test used by Gallup and others to measure the sense of self of animals. When presented with a mirror does the animal treat the image as another animal or as a reflection of the self?

monogamy Social arrangement in which each sex has one exclusive partner. Technically speaking, monogamy is defined by the fact that reproductive variance for both sexes is equal.

morphemes Smallest units of meaning in a language.

Müller's ratchet Term used to describe the fact that damaging mutations can build up quickly in asexually reproducing species

multimale polygyny Social arrangement in which many males share multiple female partners (such as in chimpanzee societies).

multiregional model Model of human evolution asserting that modern humans arose gradually in many different parts of the world, emerging from the regionally present stock of archaic hominins.

mutation Copy error in the replication of DNA.

mutualism Cooperative arrangement in which the parties involved reap an immediate mutual reward that could not be attained alone.

natural selection The major mechanism of evolutionary change whereby the inherited traits of some organisms allow them to survive and reproduce in greater abundance than others, thus ensuring that those advantageous traits will be passed on to the next generation at the expense of other less advantageous traits.

naturalistic fallacy Mistaken notion that it is philosophically acceptable to derive moral statements ("oughts") from naturalistic conditions ("is").

Neanderthals Species of hominin that arose about 250,000 years ago and was adapted to the conditions of Ice Age Europe.

neocortex ratio Proportion comparing volume of neocortex with the rest of the brain.

neomammalian brain Term used by McLean to describe the very top layer of brain, in which the most sophisticated forms of thinking take place.

neophilia Love of novelty; Miller asserts that neophilia might have signaled the presence of intelligence in a potential mate.

objective self-awareness   Level of self-awareness at which one realizes that one can be both the observer as well as the observed, both the subject and object of mental processes.

oblique power grip   Grip in which all the fingers are brought across the palm in one direction and the thumb in the other, so that an object such as a club or hammer can be held securely.

old mammalian brain   Term used by McLean to describe the subcortical structures, such as the limbic system, in which emotional behavior originates.

Oldowan tools   Category of stone tools that arose about 2.6 million years ago; most often associated with late Australopiths and early *Homo.*

pad-to-side grip   Grip in which the the thumb is pressed against the side of the index finger; used for holding and manipulating small objects.

pair bond enhancers   Those aspects of male and female bodies (for example, breasts or penis) that serve to enhance sexual pleasure and therefore help to maintain a long-term sexually exclusive relationship between two partners.

parental investment   Effort and resources dedicated to one offspring at the expense of other current or future offspring.

parent–infant conflict   Term used by Trivers to describe the often conflicting fitness interests of parents and their offspring.

particulate principle   Idea that language can create new meanings by virtue of the fact that its meaningful elements retain their integrity when combined with other meaningful elements. Thus meanings are added or combined and not blended when new words or phrases are formed. Language can then explore new combinations and new meanings rather than being restricted to the meaning space bounded by the current morphological units.

paternity certainty   Degree to which a male can be assured that an offspring he is raising does, in fact, carry his genes.

paternity uncertainty   Fact that males can never be certain whether mate's offspring actually carries his genes.

patriarchy   Male-dominated society.

perceived mate value   An individual's assessment of his or her own standing as a potential mate.

perception   Ability to interpret or give meaning to an external signal without having direct contact with that signal.

percussion technique   Toolmaking technique in which a core is struck at an acute angle by a hammerstone to remove a sharp-edged flake.

phonemes   Basic units of sound in a language.

phylogenetic approach   Approach used to study hominin social or behavior traits; traits of the common ancestor are identified by using traits common to extant species who all share a single ancestor.

pidgin   Primitive form of language lacking recursive syntax; formed by the combination of two or more languages.

Pithecanthropus erectus   Celebrated missing link sought by Dubois.

planning depth   Term used by Binford to describe the ability to engage in future planning.

polygyny   Single male with multiple wives.

praxis   Ability to organize a sequence of purposeful motor movements that are not bound by the spatial constraints of the environment.

preadaptation   Idea that a structure adapted by natural selection for one purpose may be used later for another purpose.

precocial   Born in a state of relative nervous system maturity and able to quickly begin to take care of oneself.

pregnancy sickness   Nausea experienced by pregnant women and associated with certain foods or smells; often called "morning sickness."

prepared learner   Term describing one whose genetic predispositions make it easier to acquire some skills and knowledge.

prepared learning   Term describing the fact that the acquisition of some stimulus–response patterns, often ones with high adaptive value, is aided by genetic predisposition.

preparedness   Predisposition to quickly and efficiently acquire certain adaptive skills and knowledge.

prepotency   Predisposition to respond strongly to certain stimulus patterns that have important survival and reproductive value.

prisoner's dilemma   Term describing a scenario in which players must choose to cooperate or not cooperate with a partner and in which the benefits of these choices depend, in part, on their partners' choices.

prosopagnosia   Inability to recognize faces; usually caused by damage to the temporal lobe.

protolanguage   Language, such as pidgin, lacking hierarchical and recursive syntax and therefore limited in use to expressing ideas of the "here and now." Asserted by Bickerton to be the form of language that preceded "real" language in human evolution.

pseudopathology   Response (especially an emotional response) that served an adaptive function in an organism's past evolutionary history but may be maladaptive under current circumstances.

rational soul   Philosophical term used to explain the presence of human reasoning power.

real language   Human language as we know it today, complete with sophisticated syntax (*see also protolanguage*).

reciprocal altruism   Any behavior that reduces one's own fitness while benefiting the fitness of another; performed with expectations that at some point in the future the recipient will do likewise.

reciprocity   Bestowing a beneficial act on another in repayment for an earlier act by the current recipient; return of a favor or benefit.

Red Queen   Term describing the fact that a population must continue to evolve in order to "keep up" with competitors.

referential   Characteristic of language by which words and phrases direct attention or point the mind toward other environmental objects or ideas.

reproductive strategies   Evolved tendencies in reproductive behavior exhibited by different organisms.

reproductive value   Number of future offspring a person of a given age is likely to produce.

reproductive variance   Degree to which offspring production varies from one organism to another.

reptilian brain   Term used by McLean to describe the evolutionarily oldest brain structures (for example, the brainstem), in which basic survival and reproductive behaviors originate

resource extraction   Strategy whereby a female attempts to obtain resources from a male, often by using short-term mating. Hrdy asserts that concealed ovulation may have aided the use of this strategy.

resource holding potential   Internal assessment of one's own capacity to obtain and secure resources necessary for survival and believed by some to be a precursor to self-esteem.

ritual   Stylized or symbolic activities that carry meaning or represent something meaningful to a group of people. Deacon, Donald, and others have asserted that ritual behavior may have been a step in the evolution of language.

r-selected species   Generally smaller, more quickly maturing species in which parents have many offspring but invest very little in their care and upbringing.

runaway selection   Self-reinforcing cycle in which a preference for a specific trait in one sex (usually male) can cause that trait to evolve inordinately and rapidly.

satiation   State of being physically or psychologically satisfied.

security   Freedom from threats to person or resources.

seeds of confusion   Term used by Hrdy to describe a female mating strategy whereby the female mates with many males to confuse the identity of offspring paternity.

self-deception   Dishonesty with oneself; applied to evolution, self-deception may be an advantageous strategy, because those who do not consciously realize that they are being deceptive will emit few if any signals revealing their exploitative intentions.

self-serving bias   Interpretation of events in a way that best preserves an individual's status or interests.

sensations   Processing of outside stimuli by nervous system receptors.

serial monogamy   Having a succession of mates singly over time.

sexual dimorphism in maturation rates   Fact that females typically show secondary sexual characteristics before being fertile, whereas males typically become fertile before showing secondary sexual characteristics.

sexual selection   Along with natural selection, another mechanism that can drive evolutionary change. Sexual selection refers to the fact that traits can be selected because they provide an advantage in securing mates, rather than directly benefiting survival and reproduction.

Sherlock Holmes reasoning   Ability to deduce unseen causes from available evidence.

single origin model (also called "out of Africa" model)   Model of human evolution that asserts that modern humans arose rather abruptly in Africa and then spanned out across the globe, replacing the resident hominin populations (also sometimes called the "replacement model").

6-million-year hypothesis   Idea that a sense of self was present in the common ancestor of humans and chimpanzees before their evolutionary branching.

smoke detector principle   Term describing the potential adaptive value of anxiety, whereby feelings of anxiety may signal a potential threat to one's welfare.

social competition hypothesis   Hypothesis regarding the evolutionary origins of depression, whereby depressive feelings serve the adaptive function of pulling one away from potentially damaging social competition.

social ostracism   Collective shunning of an individual, often for failing to conform to group norms.

social referencing   Use of others' reactions (especially caregivers and adults) as a means of determining the proper emotional reaction to an event.

sociobiology   Field of study defined by Wilson; seeks to use Darwinian principles to understand the social and cooperative behavior of animals, including humans.

Solutrean blades   Blades created in the Upper Paleolithic with a purpose that appears to be more aesthetic than practical.

stance phase   Part of the walking cycle that occurs between the heel strike on the ground and the push-off of the big toe; the foot is flat or nearly flat to the ground, and the knee is locked.

status   Relative standing of the individual in a social group; when applied to evolutionary theory, social status is a critical goal for males in gaining maximal access to females and for females to ensure resources for their offspring.

subitization   Ability to understand number based on pattern recognition.

survey/questionnaire approach   Method of research involving the use of surveys and questionnaires as means of testing hypotheses

swing phase   Part of the walk cycle that occurs after the push-off of the big toe and before the heel strike of the foot to the ground; the leg is airborne and the knee bent.

syntax   Rules of language that allow for the creation of "lawful" expressions.

taxonomic constraint   Tendency of children to associate related words by category rather than function.

testes size   Size of male testes; often signals the degree of sperm competition that currently exists or did exist in the evolutionary past of a species.

theory of mind   Tendency to ascribe mental states to other organisms; understanding that others have thoughts, motivations, and intentions that drive their behaviors; ability to attribute mental states to others and use those states as a means of explaining and predicting behavior.

three-jawed chuck grip   Grip in which the first three figures surround the object on one side with the thumb on the other; for holding and manipulating small objects.

trap tube task (*see tube task*)   Version of the tube task in which a trap is used to complicate the extraction of food.

Trivers–Willard effect   Tendency of parents to invest more heavily in offspring of greater potential reproductive value.

trusting communities   Communities in which honest expressions can be traded off for status, thus providing a fitness advantage for both signalers and receivers; asserted by many evolutionists to be a necessary prerequisite to the evolution of language.

tube task   Reasoning task used extensively by Visalberghi to study primate thinking. In the task, subject must figure out how to remove a morsel of food from a transparent tube.

ultimate and proximate explanations   Proximate explanation uses relatively immediate factors as causal mechanisms; ultimate explanation invokes overarching evolutionary principles as causal mechanisms. For example, boys seek social status to gain friends and get dates, a proximate explanation. Boys seeks status because the friends and dates that status affords would have provided fitness advantages in our evolutionary past, an ultimate explanation.

unconscious mind   Term describing mental operations that occur below one's conscious awareness.

uniformitarianism   Notion that Earth's major geological features resulted from slow action of natural processes at work over long spans of time.

unimale polygyny   Social arrangement in which a single male has multiple female mates.

universals   Principles that generalize across cultures and environments.

Upper Paleolithic revolution   Rather sudden emergence of sophisticated tools and symbolic artifacts around 40,000 years ago in Europe; often cited as the first evidence of modern human behavior.

upsuck hypothesis   Hypothesis asserting that the purpose of female orgasm is to facilitate fertilization by pulling sperm farther up the reproductive tract.

valgus angle   Inward angle of the femur as it runs from the hip socket to the knee.

Vicki   One of the first language-trained apes; the effort was largely a failure, because she was able to produce only a few spoken words.

violence inhibition mechanism   Mental mechanism proposed by Blair in which an individual is sensitive to submissive signals in others and responds with moral emotions and withdrawal behaviors; believed to be dysfunctional in psychopaths.

warmth   Positive emotional feelings that are inherently self-rewarding and arise from familial closeness.

Washoe   One of the first sign language-trained apes. After the failure of Vicki (*see Vicki*), researchers concentrated on teaching manual rather than spoken language to apes. Washoe was able to master a vocabulary of more than 100 signs.

whole object assumption   Tendency of children to associate a word label with an entire object rather than a property of that object.

References

Abbot, E. (2000). *A History of celibacy*. New York: Scribner.

Aiello, L.C. (1992). Allometry and the analysis of size and shape in human evolution. *Journal of Human Evolution, 22*, 127–147.

Aiello, L.C. (1994). Variable but singular. *Nature, 368*, 399–400.

Aiello, L.C., & Dean, M.C. (1990). *An introduction to human evolutionary anatomy*. London: Academic Press.

Aiello, L.C., & Dunbar, R.I.M. (1993). Neocortex size, group size and the evolution of language. *Current Anthropology, 34*, 184–193.

Aigner, J.S. (1978). Important archaeological remains from North China. In F. Ikawa-Smith (Ed.), *Early paleolithic in South and East Asia* (pp. 163–232). The Hague: Mouton.

Ainsworth, M.D. (1963). The development of infant-mother attachment among the Ganda. In D.M. Foss (Ed.), *Determinants of infant behavior*, (Vol. 2, pp. 67–104). New York: John Wiley & Sons.

Ainsworth, M.D.S. (1967). *Infancy in Uganda: Infant care and the growth of love*. Baltimore: Johns Hopkins University Press.

Ainsworth, M.D.S., Blehar, M., Waters, E., & Wall, S. (1978). *Patterns of attachment: A psychological study of the strange situation*. Hillsdale, NJ: Erlbaum.

Aitchison, J. (1998). On discontinuing the continuity-discontinuity debate. In J.R. Hurford, M. Studdert–Kennedy, & C. Knight (Eds.), *Approaches to the evolution of language: Social and cognitive bases* (pp. 17–29). Cambridge, MA: Cambridge University Press.

Alexander, R.D. (1975). The search for a general theory of behavior. *Behavioral Science, 20*, 77–100.

Alexander, R.D. (1979). *Darwinism and human affairs*. London: Pittman Publishing Ltd.

Alexander, R.D. (1987). *The biology of moral systems*. New York: Aldine de Gruyter.

Alexander, R.D., Hoogland, J.L., Howard, R.D., Noonan, K.M., & Sherman, P.W. (1979). Sexual dimorphisms and breeding systems in pinnipeds, ungulates, primates, and humans. In N. Chagnon & W. Irons (Eds.), *Evolutionary biology and human social behavior: An anthropological perspective* (pp. 402–435). North Scituate, MA: Duxbury Press.

Allman, J.M.(1999). *Evolving brains*. New York: Scientific American Library.

Allman, J., Rosin, A., Kumar, R., & Hasenstaub, A. (1998). Parenting and survival in anthropoid primates: Caretakers live longer. *Proceedings of the National Academy of Sciences, 95*, 6866–6869.

Alp, R. (1997). "Stepping-sticks" and "seat-sticks": New types of tools used by wild chimpanzees (*Pan troglodytes*) in Sierra Leone. *American Journal of Primatology, 41*, 45–52.

Altmann, J., Hausfater, G., & Altmann, S.A. (1988). Determinants of reproductive success in savanna baboons, *Papio cynocephalus*. In T.H. Clutton-Brock (Ed.), *Reproductive success* (pp. 403–418). Chicago: University of Chicago Press.

Ambrose, S. (2001). Paleolithic technology and human evolution. *Science, 291,* 1748–1752.

Anderson, A.K., & Phelps, E.K. (2001). Lesions of the human amygdala impair enhanced perception of emotionally salient events. *Nature, 411*, 305–309.

Anderson, J.R. (1983). Responses to mirror image stimulation and assessment of self-recognition in mirror- and peer-reared stumptail macaques. *Quarterly Journal of Experimental Psychology, 35B*, 201–212.

Andersson, M. (1982). Female choice selects for extreme tail length in widow bird. *Nature, 299*, 818–820.

Andrews, P.J. (1984). An alternative interpretation of the characters used to define *Homo erectus. Courier Forschungsinstitut Senckenberg, 69,*167–175.

Annett, M. (1985). *Left, right, hand and brain: The right shift theory*. London: Erlbaum.

Annett, M., & Annett, J. (1991). Handedness for eating in gorillas. *Cortex, 27*, 269–275.

Archer, J. (1988). *The behavioral biology of aggression*. Cambridge, MA: Cambridge University Press.

Ardener, E. (1956). *Coastal Bantu of the Cameroons*. London: International African Institute.

Ardener, E. (1975). Belief and the problem of women. In S. Ardener (Ed.), *Perceiving Women* (pp. 1–17). London: Dent.

Ardrey, R. (1976). *The hunting hypothesis*. New York: Atheneum.

Aristotle. (ca. 350 BC; 1934). Nicomachaen ethics. In H. Rackham (Trans.), *Aristotle in 23 Volumes.* Cambridge, MA: Harvard University Press.

Armelagos, G.J., & Dewey, J.R. (1970). Evolutionary response to human infectious diseases. *Bioscience, 157,* 638–644.

Athanasiou, R., Shaver, P., & Tavis, C. (1970, July). Sex. *Psychology Today,* 37–52.

Avise, J.C. (1998). *The genetic gods: Evolution and belief in human affairs.* Cambridge, MA: Harvard University Press.

Axelrod, R. (1984). *The evolution of cooperation.* New York: Basic Books.

Ayala, F.J. (1995). The difference of being human: Ethical behavior as an evolutionary byproduct. In H. Rolston (Ed.), *Biology, ethics, and the origins of life* (pp. 117–135). Boston: Jones & Bartlett.

Baillargeon, R. (1987). Object permanence in 3½- and 4½-month-old infants. *Developmental Psychology, 23,* 655–664.

Baillargeon, R. (1995). Physical reasoning in infancy. In M. Gazzaniga (Ed.), *The cognitive neurosciences* (pp. 181–204). Cambridge, MA: MIT Press.

Baker, R. (1996). *Sperm wars: The science of sex.* New York: Basic Books.

Baker, R.R., & Bellis, M.A. (1989). Number of sperm in human ejaculates varies in accordance with sperm competition theory. *Animal Behaviour, 37,* 867–869.

Baker, R.R., & Bellis, M.A. (1993a). Human sperm competition: Ejaculate adjustment by males and the function of masturbation. *Animal Behaviour, 46,* 861–885.

Baker, R.R., & Bellis, M.A. (1993b). Human sperm competition: Ejaculate manipulation by females and a function for the female orgasm. *Animal Behaviour, 46,* 886–909.

Baker, R.R., & Bellis, M.A. (1995). *Human sperm competition.* London: Chapman & Hall.

Baldwin, D.A. (2000). Interpersonal understanding fuels knowledge acquisition. *Current Directions in Psychological Science, 9,* 40–45.

Baldwin, D.A., & Tomasello, M. (1998). Word learning: A window on early pragmatic understanding. In E. Clark (Ed.), *The proceedings of the 29th Annual Child Language Research Forum* (pp. 3–23). Chicago: CSL Publications.

Baldwin, D.A., Baird, J.A., Saylor, M.M., & Clark, M.A. (2001). Infants parse dynamic action. *Child Development, 72,* 708–717.

Baldwin, D.A., Markman, E.M., Bill, B., Desjardins, R.N., & Irwin, J.M. (1996). Infant's reliance on social criterion for establishing word-object relations. *Child Development, 67,* 3135–3153.

Balogh, R.D., & Porter, R.H. (1986). Olfactory preferences resulting from mere exposure in human neonates. *Infant Behavior and Development, 9,* 395–401.

Bandura, A. (1969). Social learning theory of identificatory processes. In D.A. Goslin (Ed.), *Handbook of social the-ory and research* (pp. 231–262). Chicago: Rand-McNally.

Banich, M.T. (1997). *Neuropsychology.* New York: Houghton-Mifflin.

Bard, K.A., Fragaszy, D., and Visalberghi, E. (1995). Acquisition and comprehension of tool-using behavior by young chimpanzees (*Pan troglodytes*): Effects of age and modeling. *International Journal of Comparative Psychology, 8,* 1–22.

Barkow, J. (1989). *Darwin, sex, and status: Biological approaches to mind and culture.* Toronto: University of Toronto Press.

Barkow, J., Cosmides, L., & Tooby, J. (1992). *The adapted mind: Evolutionary psychology and the generation of culture.* New York: Oxford University Press.

Baron-Cohen, S. (1987). Autism and symbolic play. *British Journal of Developmental Psychology, 5,* 139–148.

Baron-Cohen, S. (1995). *Mindblindness.* Cambridge, MA: MIT Press.

Baron-Cohen, S. (1997a). How to build a baby that can read minds: Cognitive mechanisms in mind reading. In S. Baron-Cohen (Ed.), *The maladapted mind* (pp. 207–239). East Sussex, UK: Psychology Press.

Baron-Cohen, S. (1997b). *The maladapted mind: Classic readings in evolutionary psychopathology.* East Sussex, UK: Psychology Press.

Baron-Cohen, S. (1999). The evolution of a theory of mind. In M.C. Corballis & S.E.G. Lea (Eds.), *The descent of mind: Psychological perspectives of hominid evolution* (pp. 261–277). Oxford, UK: Oxford University Press.

Baron-Cohen, S., Baldwin, D.A., & Crowson, M. (1997). Do children with autism use the speaker's direction of gaze strategy to crack the code of language? *Child Development, 68,* 48–57.

Baron-Cohen, S., Leslie, A.M., & Frith, U. (1985). Does the autistic child have a 'theory of mind'? *Cognition, 21,* 37–46.

Baron-Cohen, S., Leslie, A.M., & Frith, U. (1986). Mechanical, behavioral, and intentional understanding of picture stories in autistic children. *British Journal of Developmental Psychology, 4,* 113–125.

Baron-Cohen, S., Ring, H., Moriarty, J., Schmidt, P., Costa, D., & Ell, P. (1994). Recognition of mental state terms: A clinical study of children with autism, and functional neuroimaging study of normal adults. *British Journal of Psychiatry, 165,* 640–649.

Barrera, M.E., & Maurer, D. (1981). Recognition of mother's photographed face by the three-month-old infant. *Child Development, 52,* 714–716.

Barret–Ducrocq, F. (1989). *Love in the time of Victoria.* New York: Penguin Books.

Barrett, K.C. (1995). A functionalist approach to shame and guilt. In J.P. Tangney & K.W. Fischer (Eds.), *Self-conscious emotions: The psychology of shame, guilt, embarrassment, and pride* (pp. 25–63). New York: The Guilford Press.

Barrow, J. (1991). *Theories of everything*. Oxford, UK: Oxford University Press

Bar-Yosef, O., Vandermeersch, B., Arensburg, B., Belfer-Cohen, A., Goldberg, P., Laville, H., et al. (1992). The excavations in Kebara Cave, Mt. Carmel. *Current Anthropology, 33,* 497–550.

Bateman, A.J. (1948). Intra-sexual selection in *Drosophila*. *Heredity, 2,* 349–368.

Baumeister, R.F., & Leary, M.R. (1995). The need to belong: Desire for interpersonal attachments as a fundamental human motivation. *Psychological Bulletin, 117,* 497–529.

Beal, V. (1971). Nutritional studies during pregnancy. I: Changes in intakes of calories, carbohydrates, fat, protein, and calcium. *Journal of the American Dietetic Association, 58,* 312–320.

Bear, M., Connors, B., & Paradiso, M. (1996). *Neuroscience: Exploring the brain*. Baltimore: Williams & Wilkins.

Bechara, A., Damasio, A.R., Damasio, H., & Anderson, S. (1994). Insensitivity to future consequences following damage to human prefrontal cortex. *Cognition, 50,* 7–12.

Bechara, A., Tranel, D., Damasio, H., & Damasio, A.R. (1993). Failure to respond autonomically in anticipation of future outcomes following damage to human prefrontal cortex. *Society for Neuroscience, 19,* 791.

Begley, D.J., Firth, J.A., & Hoult, J.R.S. (1980). *Human reproduction and developmental biology*. Bristol, England: J.W. Arrowsmith.

Begun, D.R., & Walker, A. (1993). The endocast. In A. Walker & R.E.F. Leakey (Eds.), *The Nariokotome Homo erectus skeleton* (pp. 326–358). Cambridge MA: Harvard University Press.

Bekoff, M., & Byers, J. (1998). *Animal play*. Cambridge, UK: Cambridge University Press.

Berard, J.D., Nurnberg, P., Epplen, J.T., & Schmidtke, J. (1993). Male rank, reproductive behavior, and reproductive success in free-ranging rhesus macaques. *Primates, 34,* 481–489.

Bercovitch, F.B. (1988). Coalitions, cooperation and reproductive tactics among adult male baboons. *Animal Behaviour, 36,* 1198–1209.

Bercovitch, F.B. (1995). Female cooperation, consortship maintenance, and male mating success in savanna baboons. *Animal Behavior, 50(1),* 137–149.

Bereczkei, T., & Csanaky, A. (1996). Mate choice, marital success, and reproduction in a modern society. *Ethology and Sociobiology, 17,* 17–35.

Bernds, W.P., & Barash, D.P. (1979). Early termination of parental investment in mammals, including humans. In N.A. Chagnon & W. Irons (Eds.), *Evolutionary biology and human social behavior: An anthropological perspective* (pp. 487–506). North Scituate, MA: Duxbury.

Berndt, C.H. (1970). Digging sticks and spears, or the two-sex model. In Gale, F. (Ed.), *Woman's role in aboriginal society. Australian Aboriginal Studies 36*. Canberra, Australia: Australian Institute of Aboriginal Studies.

Bernstein, I.S. (2000a). Logic and human morality: An attractive if untestable scenario. *Journal of Consciousness Studies, 7(1–2),* 105–107.

Bernstein, I.S. (2000b). The law of parsimony prevails; Missing premises allow any conclusion. *Journal of Consciousness Studies, 7(1–2),* 31–38.

Berry, J.W. (1966). Temme and Eskimo perceptual skills. *International Journal of Psychology, 1,* 207–229.

Berscheid, E. (1985). Interpersonal attraction. In G. Lindzey & E. Aronson (Eds.), *Handbook of social psychology* (pp. 413–484). New York: Academic Press.

Berscheid, E., & Walster, E.H. (1978). *Interpersonal attraction*. Reading MA: Addison-Wesley.

Betzig, L.L. (1982). Despotism and differential reproduction: A cross-cultural correlation of conflict asymmetry, hierarchy, and degree of polygyny. *Ethology and Sociobiology, 3,* 209–221.

Betzig, L.L. (1986). *Despotism and differential reproduction: A Darwinian view of history*. New York: Aldine de Gruyter.

Betzig, L.L. (1992). Roman polygyny. *Ethology and Sociobiology, 13,* 309–349.

Betzig, L.L. (1993). Where are the bastard's daddies? *Behavioral and Brain Sciences, 16,* 285–295.

Betzig, L., Borgerhoff Mulder, M., & Turke, P. (Eds.). (1988). *Human reproductive behaviour: A Darwinian perspective,* New York: Cambridge University Press.

Betzig, L.L., & Turke, P. (1986). Parental investment by sex on Ifaluk. *Ethology and Sociobiology, 7,* 29–37.

Bever, T. (1992). The logical and extrinsic sources sources of modularity. In M. Gunner & M. Maratsos (Eds.), *Modularity and constraints in language and cognition* (pp. 179–212). Hillsdale, NJ: Erlbaum.

Bickerton, D. (1990). *Language and species*. Chicago: University of Chicago Press.

Bickerton, D. (1995). *Language and human behavior*. Seattle: University of Washington Press.

Bickerton, D. (1998a). Catastrophic evolution: The case for a single step from protolanguage to full human language. In J.R. Hurford, M. Studdert-Kennedy, & C. Knight (Eds.), *Approaches to the evolution of language: Social and cognitive bases* (pp. 341–358). Cambridge, MA: Cambridge University Press.

Bickerton, D. (1998b). The creation and re-creation of language. In C. Crawford & D.L. Krebs (Eds.), *Handbook of evolutionary psychology* (pp. 613–634). Mahwah, NJ: Lawrence Erlbaum Associates.

Bickerton, D., & Odo, C. (1976). *General phonology and pidgin syntax*. Final report on National Science Foundation Grant No. GS-39748, Vol. 1. University of Hawaii, mimeo.

Binford, L.R. (1985). Human ancestors: Changing views of their behavior. *Journal of Anthropological Archaeology, 4,* 292–327.

Binford, L.R. (1989). Isolating the transitions to cultural adaptations: An organizational approach. In E. Trinkhaus (Ed.), *The emergence of modern humans:*

Biocultural adaptations in the later Pleistocene. Cambridge, UK: Cambridge Unversity Press.

Binford, L.R. (1992, Feb.). Hard evidence. *Discover,* 44–51.

Bingham, P.M. (1999). Human uniqueness: A general theory. *The Quarterly Review of Biology, 74,* 133–169.

Birdsall, N. (1980). Population growth and poverty in the developing world. *Population Bulletin, 35,* 3–46.

Birkhead, T.R., Moore, H.D.M., & Bedford, J.M. (1997). Sex, science and sensationalism. *Trends in Ecology and Evolution, 12,* 121–122.

Birx, J. (1991). *Interpreting evolution: Charles Darwin and Teilhard de Chardin.* Buffalo, NY: Prometheus Books.

Bischoff, J.L., Soler, N., Marot, J., & Julia, R. (1989). Abrupt Mousterian/Aurignacian boundary at c. 40 ka bp: Accelerator 14C dates from L'Arbreda Cave (Catalunya, Spain). *Journal of Archaeological Science, 16,* 563–576.

Blacking, J. (1985). Movement, dance, music and the Venda girls' initiation cycle. In P. Spencer (Ed.), *Society and the dance. The social anthropology of process and performance* (pp. 64–91). Cambridge, UK: Cambridge University Press.

Blair, R.J.R. (1995). A cognitive developmental approach to morality: Investigating the psychopath. *Cognition, 57,* 1–29.

Blair, R.J.R., Jones, L., Clark, F., & Smith, M. (1997). The psychopathic individual: A lack of resposiveness to distress cues. *Psychophysiology, 34,* 192–198.

Bloom, P. (1999). The evolution of certain novel human capacities. In M.C. Corballis & S.E.G. Lea (Eds.), *The descent of mind: Psychological perspectives of hominid evolution* (pp. 295–310). Oxford, UK: Oxford University Press.

Boccia, M. L. (1994). Mirror behavior in macaques. In S.T. Parker, R.W. Mitchell, & M.L. Boccia (Eds.), *Self-awareness in animals and humans: Developmental persepectives* (pp. 350–360). Cambridge, UK: Cambridge University Press.

Boddy, J. (1982). Womb as oasis: The symbolic context of pharaonic circumcision in rural northern Sudan. *American Ethnologist, 9(4),* 682–698.

Boehm, C. (2000). Conflict and the evolution of social control. *Journal of Consciousness Studies, 7(1–2),* 79–101.

Boesch, C. (1991). Teaching among wild chimpanzees. *Animal Behaviour, 41,* 530–532.

Boesch, C. (1994). Cooperative hunting in wild chimpanzees. *Animal Behaviour, 48,* 653–667.

Boesch, C., & Boesch, H. (1984). Mental map in wild chimpanzees: An analysis of hammer transports for nut cracking. *Primates, 25,* 160–170.

Boesch, C., & Boesch, H. (1989). Hunting behavior of wild chimpanzees in the Tai National Park. *American Journal of Physical Anthropology, 78,* 547–573.

Borgerhoff Mulder, M. (1987). Reproductive success of three Kipsigis cohorts. In T.H. Clutton-Brock (Ed.), *Reproductive success: Studies of selection and adaptation in constrasting breeding systems* (pp. 419–435). Chicago: University of Chicago Press.

Borgerhoff Mulder, M. (1988). Kipsigis bridewealth payments. In L.L. Betzig, M. Borgerhoff Mulder, & P.W. Turke (Eds.), *Human reproductive behavior: A Darwinian perspective* (pp. 65–82). Cambridge, UK: Cambridge University Press.

Boswell, J. (1990). *The kindness of strangers: The abandonment of children in Western Europe from Late Antiquity to the Renaissance.* New York: Vintage Press.

Bower, B. (2001). Faces of perception. *Science News, 160,* 1–7.

Bowlby, J. (1969). *Attachment and loss: Vol. 1. Attachment.* New York: Basic Books.

Bowlby, J. (1988). *A Secure base: Parent–child attachment and healthy human development.* New York: Basic Books.

Bowlby, J. (1990). *Charles Darwin: A new life.* New York: W.W. Norton.

Bownds, M.D. (1999). *The biology of mind.* Bethesda, MD: Fitzgerald Science Press.

Boysen, S.T. (1996). "More is less": The distribution of rule-governed resource distribution in chimpanzees. In A.E. Russon, K.A. Bard, & S.T. Parker (Eds.), *Reaching into thought: The minds of the great apes* (pp. 177–189). Cambridge, UK: Cambridge University Press.

Boysen, S.T. and Berntson, G.G. (1995). Responses to quantity: Perceptual versus cognitive mechanisms in chimpanzees (*Pan troglodytes*). *Journal of Comparative Psychology, 21,* 82–86.

Bräuer, G. (1984). A craniological approach to the origin of anatomically modern *Homo sapiens* in Africa and implications for the appearance of modern Europeans. In F.H. Smith & F. Spencer (Eds.), *The origins of modern humans: A world survey of the fossil evidence.* New York: Alan R. Liss.

Bräuer, G., & Mbua, E. (1992). *Homo erectus* features used in cladistics and their variability in Asian and African hominids. *Journal of Human Evolution, 22,* 79–108.

Bräuer, G., & Schultz, M. (1996). The morphological affinities of the Plio-Pleistocene mandible from Dmanisi, Georgia. *Journal of Human Evolution, 30,* 445–481.

Bresard, B., & Bresson, F. (1987). Reaching or manipulation: Left or right? *Behavioral and Brain Sciences, 10,* 265–266.

Brewer, D.D., Potterat, J.J., Garrett, S.B., Muth, S.Q., Roberts, J.M., Kasprzyk, D., et al. (2000). Prostitution and the sex discrepancy in reported number of sexual partners. *Procedings of the National Academy of Sciences, USA, 97,* 12385–12388.

Brewer, M.B., & Lui, L.N. (1989). The primacy of age and sex in the structure of person categories. *Social Cognition, 3,* 262–274.

Brogman, P. (1990). *The fighting never stopped: A comprehensive guide to world conflict since 1945.* New York: Vintage Press.

Bronson, G.W. (1972). Infants' reactions to unfamiliar persons and novel objects. *Monographs of the Society for Research in Child Development, 32,* (3, Serial # 148).

Brooke, J.H. (1991). *Science and religion: Some historical perspectives.* Cambridge, UK: Cambridge University Press.

Brooks, M. (2000, Oct. 28). What's love got to do with it? *New Scientist, 168,* 38–41.

Brown, F.H., Harris, J., Leakey, R., & Walker, A. (1985). Early *Homo erectus* skeleton from west Lake Turkana, Kenya. *Nature, 316,* 788–792.

Brown, J., Kahn, E., & Hartman, T. (1997). Profet, profits, and proof: Do nausea and vomiting of early pregnancy protect women from "harmful" vegetables? *American Journal of Obstetrics and Gynecology, 176,* 179–181.

Brunet, M., Beauvilain, A., Coppens, Y.K., Heintz, E., Moutaye, A.H.E., & Pilbeam, D. (1996). *Australopithecus bahrelghazali,* a new species of early hominid from Koro Toro region, Chad. *Comptes Rendus de l'Academie des Sciences, Paris,* series 2a, *322,* 907–913.

Buehlman, K.T., Gottman, J.M., & Katz, L.F. (1992). How a couple view their past predicts their future: Predicting divorce from an oral history interview. *Journal of Family Psychology, 5,* 295–318.

Bueler, L.E. (1973). *Wild dogs of the world.* New York: Stein & Day.

Bunn, H.T. (1986). Patterns of skeletal representation and hominid subsistence activities at Olduvai Gorge, Tanzania, and Koobi Fora, Kenya. *Journal of Human Evolution, 15,* 673–690.

Bunn, H.T., & Kroll, E.M. (1986). Systematic butchery by Plio/Pleistocene hominids at Olduvai Gorge, Tanzania. *Current Anthropology, 5,* 431–452.

Burgess, E.W., & Wallin, P. (1943). Homogamy in social characteristics. *American Journal of Sociology, 49,* 109–124.

Burke, A., Heuer, F., & Reisberg, D. (1992). Remembering emotional events. *Memory and Cognition, 20,* 277–290.

Burley, N. (1988). Wild zebra finches have band color preferences. *Animal Behavior, 36,* 1235–1237.

Burnet, F.M. (1959). *The clonal selection theory of acquired immunity.* London: Cambridge University Press.

Burnett, J. (Lord Monboddo) (1773). *The origin and progress of language.* (Vols. I–IV). Edinburgh: A. Kincaid.

Burton, L.M. (1990). Teenage childbearing as an alternative life-course strategy in multigeneration black families. *Human Nature, 1,* 123–143.

Bushnell, I.W.R., Sai, F., & Mullin, J.T. (1989). Neonatal recognition of the mother's face. *British Journal of Developmental Psychology, 7,* 3–15.

Buss, D.M. (1989). Sex differences in human mate preferences: Evolutionary hypotheses test in 37 cultures. *Behavioral and Brain Sciences, 12,* 1–49.

Buss, D.M. (1992a). Manipulation in close relationships: Five personality factors in interactional context. *Journal of Personality, 60,* 477–499.

Buss, D.M. (1992b). Mate preference mechanisms: Consequences for partner choice and intrasexual competition. In J. Barkow, L. Cosmides, & J. Tooby (Eds.), *The adapted mind: Evolutionary psychology and the generation of culture* (pp. 249–266). New York: Oxford University Press.

Buss, D.M. (1994). *The evolution of desire.* New York: Basic Books.

Buss, D.M. (1996). Social adaptation and five major factors in personality. In J.S. Wiggins (Ed.), *The five factor theory of personality* (pp. 180–207). New York: Guilford Press.

Buss, D.M. (1998). The psychology of human mate selection: Exploring the complexity of the strategic repertoire. In C. Crawford & D.L. Krebs. *Handbook of evolutionary psychology* (pp. 405–429). Mahwah, NJ: Lawrence Erlbaum.

Buss, D.M. (2000). The evolution of happiness. *American Psychologist, 55 (1),* 15–23.

Buss, D.M., & Dedden, L.A. (1990). Derogation of competitors. *Journal of Social and Personal Relationships, 7,* 395–422.

Buss, D.M., Larsen, R.J., Westen, D., & Semmelroth, J. (1992). Sex differences in jealousy: Evolution, physiology, and psychology. *Psychological Science, 3,* 251–255.

Buss, D.M., & Schmitt, D.P. (1993). Sexual strategies theory: An evolutionary perspective on human mating. *Psychological Review, 100,* 204–232.

Byrne, R.W. (1993). The complex leaf-gathering skills of mountain gorillas (*Gorilla g. beringei*): Variability and standardization. *American Journal of Primatology, 31,* 241–261.

Byrne, R.W. (1995). *The thinking ape: Evolutionary origins of intelligence.* Oxford, UK: Oxford University Press.

Byrne, R.W. (1996). The misunderstood ape: The cognitive skills of the gorilla. In A.E. Russon, K.A. Bard, & S. T. Parker (Eds.), *Reaching into thought: The minds of the great apes* (pp. 111–130). Cambridge, UK: Cambridge University Press.

Byrne, R.W. (1999). Human cognitive evolution. In M.C. Corballis & S.E.G. Lea (Eds.), *The descent of mind: Psychological perspective on hominid evolution* (pp. 71–87). Oxford, UK: Oxford University Press.

Byrne, R.W., & Byrne, J.M. (1991). Hand preferences in the skilled gathering tasks of mountain gorillas (*Gorilla g. berengei*). *Cortex, 27,* 512–546.

Byrne, R.W., & Whiten, A. (1988). *Machiavellian intelligence: Social expertise and the evolution of intellect in monkeys, apes, and humans.* Oxford, UK: Clarendon Press.

Byrne, R.W., & Whiten, A.(1990). Tactical deception in primates: The 1990 database. *Primate Report, 27,* 1–101.

Byrne, R.W., & Whiten, A. (1991). Computation and mindreading in primate tactical deception. In A. Whiten (Ed.), *Natural theories of mind* (pp. 127–141). Oxford, UK: Blackwell.

Cabrera Valdés, V., & Bischoff, J.L. (1989). Accelerator 14C dates for early Upper Paleolithic (Basal Aurignacian) at El Castillo Cave (Spain). *Journal of Archaeological Science, 16,* 577–584.

Cain, W.S. (1982). Odor identification by males and females: Predictions versus performance. *Chemical Senses, 7*, 129–142.

Call, J., & Tomasello, M. (1994a). The production and comprehension of referential pointing by orangutans (*Pongo pygmaeus*). *Journal of Comparative Psychology, 108*, 307–317.

Call, J., & Tomasello, M. (1994b). The social learning of tool use by orangutans (*Pongo pymaeus*). *Journal of Human Evolution, 9*, 297–313.

Call, J., & Tomasello, M. (1998). Distinguishing intentional from accidental actions in orangutans (*Pongo pygmaeus*), chimpanzees (*Pan troglodytes*), and human children (*Homo sapiens*). *Journal of Comparative Psychology, 28*, 362–367.

Calne, D.B. (1999). *Within reason: Rationality and human behavior.* New York: Pantheon Books.

Calvin, W.H. (1983a). A stone's throw and its launch window: timing precision and its implications for language and hominid brains. *Journal of Theoretical Biology, 104*, 121–135.

Calvin, W.H. (1983b). *The throwing madonna.* New York: McGraw-Hill.

Calvin, W.H. (1990). *The ascent of mind: Ice Age climates and the evolution of intelligence.* New York: Bantam.

Calvin, W.H. (1993). The unitary hypothesis: A common neural circuitry for novel manipulations, language, plan-ahead, and throwing? In K.R. Gibson & T. Ingold (Eds.), *Tools, language, and cognition in human evolution* (pp. 230–250). Cambridge, UK: Cambridge University Press.

Campbell, J.C. (1992). If I can't have you, no one can: Issues of power and control in homicide of female partners. In J. Radford & D.E.H. Russell (Eds.), *Femicide* (pp. 99–113). New York: Twayne.

Cann, R.L., Stoneking, M., & Wilson, A.C. (1987). Mitochondrial DNA and human evolution. *Nature, 325*, 31–36.

Cantalupo, C., & Hopkins, W.D. (2001). Asymmetric Broca's area in great apes. *Nature, 414*, 505

Carey, J. (1992). *The intellectuals and the masses.* London: Faber and Faber.

Carlsmith, L. (1964). Effect of early father absence on scholastic aptitude. *Harvard Educational Review, 34*, 3–21.

Case, A.C., Lin, I.-F., & McLanahan, S. (1999). Household resource allocation in stepfamilies: Darwin reflects on the plight of Cinderella. *American Economic Review, 89*, 234–238.

Case, A.C., Lin, I-F., & McLanahan, S. (2000a). Educational attainment in blended families. *National Bureau of Economic Research Working Paper # 7874.* Washington, DC: National Bureau of Economic Research.

Case, A.C., Lin, I.-F., & McLanahan, S. (2000b). How hungry is the selfish gene. *Economic Journal, 110*, 781–804.

Case, A.C., Lin, I.-F., & McLanahan, S. (2001). Educational attainment of siblings in stepfamilies. *Evolution and Human Behavior, 22*, 269–289.

Case, A.C., & Paxson, C. (2001). Mothers and others: Who invests in children's health? *Journal of Health Economics, 20*, 301–328.

Cashdan, E. (1993). Attracting mates: Effects of paternal investment on mate attraction. *Ethology and Sociobiology, 14*, 1–24.

Casscells, W., Schoenberger, A., & Grayboys, T. (1978). Interpretation by physicians of clinical laboratory results. *New England Journal of Medicine, 299*, 999–1000.

Catchpole, C.K. (1980). Sexual selection and the evolution of complex song among European warblers of the genus *Acrocephalus. Behavior, 74*, 149–166.

Catchpole, C.K. (1987). Bird song, sexual selection and female choice. *Trends in Evolution and Ecology, 2*, 94–97.

Cavalli-Sforza, L.L., Menozzi, P., & Piazza, A. (1994). *The history and geography of human genes.* Princeton, NJ: Princeton University Press.

Cernoch, J.M., & Porter, R.H. (1985). Recognition of maternal axillary odors by infants. *Child Development, 56*, 1593–1598.

Chagnon, N. (1988). Life histories, blood revenge, and warfare in a tribal population. *Science, 239*, 985–992.

Chagnon, N. (1997). *Yanomamo: the fierce people.* 5th ed. Fort Worth, TX: Harcourt Brace.

Chalmeau, R., & Gallo, A. (1996). Cooperation in primates: Critical analysis of behavioural criteria. *Behavioural Processes 35*, 101–111.

Chalmeau, R. (1994). Do chimpanzees cooperate in a learning task? *Primates, 35(3)*, 385–392.

Chance, M.R.A. (1962). Social behavior and primate evolution. In M.F.A. Montagu (Ed.), *Culture and the evolution of man* (pp. 84–130). Oxford, UK: Oxford University Press.

Charman, T., & Baron-Cohen, S. (1992). Understanding beliefs and drawings: a further test of the metarepresentation theory in autism. *Journal of Child Psychology and Psychiatry, 33*, 1105–112.

Charmie, J., & Nsuly, S. (1981). Sex differences in remarriage and spouse selection. *Demography, 18*, 332–348.

Chase, P.G., & Dibble, H.L. (1987). Middle Paleolithic symbolism: A review of current evidence and interpretations. *Journal of Anthropological Archeology, 6*, 263–296.

Chen, P.W., & Holyoak, K.J. (1985). Pragmatic reasoning schemas. *Cognitive Psychology, 17*, 391–416.

Chen, P.W., Holyoak, K.J., Nisbett, R.E., & Oliver, L.M. (1986). Pragmatic versus syntactic approaches to training deductive reasoning. *Cognitive Psychology, 18*, 293–328.

Cheney, D.L., & Seyfarth, R.M. (1990). *How monkeys see the world.* Chicago: University of Chicago Press.

Chevalier-Skolnikoff, S. (1973). Facial expression of emotions in nonhuman primates. In P. Ekman (Ed.), *Darwin and facial expression* (pp. 11–90). New York: Academic Press.

Chimbos, P.D. (1978). *Marital violence: A study of interspousal homicide.* San Francisco: R&E Research Associates.

Chisholm, J.S. (1993). Death, hope, and sex: Life-history theory and the development of reproductive strategies. *Current Anthropology, 34*, 1–46.

Christiansen, K.O. (1977). A review of studies of criminality among twins. In S.A. Mednick & K.O. Christiansen (Eds.), *Biosocial bases of criminal behavior.* New York: Gardner Press.

Christianson, S-A. (1992). Emotional stress and eyewitness memory: A critical review. *Psychological Bulletin, 112*, 284–309.

Church, R.M. (1959). Emotional reactions of rats to the pain of others. *Journal of Comparative and Physiological Psychology, 52*, 132–134.

Clark, A. (1997). *Being there: Putting brain, body and world together again.* Cambridge, MA: MIT Press.

Clark, A. (2001). *Mindware: An introduction to the philosophy of cognitive science.* New York: Oxford University Press.

Clark, D.A., Mitra, P.P., & Wang, S. S-H. (2001). Scalable architecture in mammalian brains. *Nature, 411*, 189–193.

Clark, R.J., & Tobias, P.V. (1995). Sterkfontein member 2 foot bones of the oldest South African hominind. *Science, 269*, 521–524.

Clarke, A.C. (1952). An examination of the operation of residential propinquity as a factor in mate selection. *American Sociological Review, 27*, 17–22.

Clarke, A.L., & Low, B.S. (1992). Ecological correlates of human dispersal in 19th century Sweden. *Animal Behaviour, 44*, 677–693.

Claus, R., Hoppen, H.O., & Karg, H. (1981). The secret of truffles: A steroidal pheromone? *Experientia, 37*, 1178–1179.

Clements, H. (1983). *Alfred Russel Wallace: Biologist and social reformer.* London: Huchinson.

Clements, W.A., & Perner, J. (1994). Implicit understanding of belief. *Cognitive Development, 9*, 377–95.

Cleveland, J., & Snowdon, C.T. (1981). The complex vocal repertoire of the adult cotton-top tamarin. (*Saguinus oedipus oedipus*). *Zeitschrift fur Tierpsychologie, 58*, 231–70.

Cloninger, C.R., & Gottesman, I.I. (1987). Genetic and environmental factors in anti-social behavior disorders. In S.A. Mednick, Terrie E. Moffitt, & S.A. Stack (Eds.), *The causes of crime: New biological approaches.* Cambridge, MA: Cambridge University Press.

Clutton-Brock, T.H., Albon, S.D., & Guinness, F.E. (1984). Maternal dominance, breeding success, and birth sex ratios in red deer. *Nature, 308*, 358–360.

Clutton-Brock, T.H., & McComb, K. (1993). Experimental tests of copying and mate choice in fallow deer (*Dama dama*). *Behavioral Ecology, 4*, 191–193.

Clutton-Brock, T.H., & Vincent, A.J.C. (1991). Sexual selection and the potential reproductive rates of males and females. *Nature, 351*, 58–60.

Coates, J. (1993). *Men, women, and language.* New York: Longman.

Cohen, L.E., & Machalek, R. (1988). A general theory of expropriative crime: An evolutionary ecological approach. *American Journal of Sociobiology, 94(3)*, 465–501.

Cohen, M.N. (1989). *Health and the rise of civilization.* New Haven, CT: Yale University Press.

Constable, J.L., Ashley, M.V., Goodall, J., & Pusey, A.E. (2001). Noninvasive paternity assignment in Gombe chimpazees. *Molecular Ecology, 10*, 1279–1300.

Cook, E.W., Hodes, R.L., & Lang, P.J. (1986). Preparedness and phobia: Effects of stimulus content on human visceral conditioning. *Journal of Abnormal Psychology, 95*, 195–207.

Cook, M., & Mineka, S. (1989). Observational conditioning of fear to fear-relevant versus fear-irrelevant stimuli in rhesus monkeys. *Journal of Abnormal Psychology, 98*, 448–459.

Coolidge, F.L., & Wynn, T. (2001). Executive functions of the frontal lobes and the evolutionary acendancy of *Homo sapiens. Cambridge Archaeological Journal, 11*, in press.

Corballis, M.C. (1989). Laterality and human evolution. *Psychological Review, 96*, 492–505.

Corballis, M.C. (1991). *The lopsided ape.* Oxford, UK: Oxford University Press.

Corballis, M.C. (1999). Phylogeny from apes to humans. In M.C. Corballis & S.E.G. Lea (Eds.), *The descent of mind* (pp. 40–70). Oxford, UK: Oxford University Press.

Core, F. (1994, Feb–March). Women and the restructuring of employment. *OECD Observer.*

Coruccini, R.S. (1992). Bootstrap approaches to estimating confidence intervals for molecular dissimilarities and resultant trees. *Journal of Human Evolution, 23*, 481–493.

Cosmides, L. (1989). The logic of social exchange: Has natural selection shaped how humans reason? Studies with the Wason selection task. *Cognition, 31*, 187–276.

Cosmides, L. (1994, August). *Emergence of evolutionary psychology.* Distinguished early career address at the meeting of the American Psychology Association, Los Angeles, CA.

Cosmides, L., & Tooby, J. (1989). Evolutionary psychology and the generation of culture: Part II. A computational theory of social exchange. *Ethology and Sociobiology, 10*, 51–97.

Cosmides, L., & Tooby, J. (1992). Cognitive adaptations for social exchange. In J. Barkow, L. Cosmides, & J. Tooby (Eds.), *The adapted mind* (pp. 163–228). New York: Oxford.

Cosmides, L., & Tooby, J. (1996). Are humans good intuitive statisticians after all? Rethinking some conclusions from the literature on judgement under uncertainty. *Cognition, 58*, 1–73.

Cosmides, L., & Tooby, J. (2000). Evolutionary psychology and the emotions. In M. Lewis & J.M. Haviland-Jones (Eds.), *The handbook of emotions.* New York: The Guilford Press.

Cowlishaw, G., & Mace, R. (1996). Cross-cultural patterns of marriage and inheritance: A phylogenetic approach. *Ethology and Sociobiology, 17*, 87–97.

Crawford, C. (1998). Environments and adaptations: Then and now. In C. Crawford & D.L. Krebs (Eds.), *The handbook of evolutionary psychology* (pp. 275–302). Mahwah, NJ: L. Erlbaum.

Crawford, C.B., Salter, B., & Jang, K.L. (1989). Human grief: Is its intensity related to the reproductive value of the deceased? *Ethology and Sociobiology, 10*, 297–307.

Crawford, M.P. (1937). The cooperative solving of problems by young chimpanzees. *Comparative Psychology Monographs, 14*, 1–88.

Crawford, M.P. (1941). The cooperative solving by chimpanzees of problems requiring serial responses to color cues. *Journal of Social Psychology, 13*, 259–280.

Cronin, H. (1991). *The ant and the peacock.* Cambridge, UK: Cambridge University Press.

Cronk, L. (1991). Wealth, status, and reproductive success among the Mukogodo of Kenya. *American Anthropology, 93*, 345–360.

Crow, J.F. (1999). The odds of losing at genetic roulette. *Nature 397*, 293–294.

Crudgington, H., & Shiva-Jothy, M. (2000). Genital damage, kicking, and early death. *Nature, 407*, 855–56.

Cummins, D.D. (1999). Early emergence of cheater detection in human development. Paper presented at the annual meeting of the Human Behavior and Evolution Society, Salt Lake City, UT.

Cunningham, M., Dugatkin, L.A., & Lundy, D. (2001). Who's hot and who's not: Mate copying in humans. Manuscript submitted for publication.

Cunnigham, M., Roberts, A.R., Barbee, A.P., Druen, P.B., & Wu, C. (1995). Their ideas of beauty are, on the whole, the same as ours: Consistency and variability in cross-cultural perception of female attractiveness. *Journal of Personality and Social Psychology, 68*, 261–279.

Cutler, W.B., Preti, G., Krieger, A., Huggins, G.R., Garcia, C.R., & Lawley, H.J. (1986). Human axillary secretions influence women's menstrual cycles: The role of donor extract from men. *Hormones and Behavior, 20*, 463–473.

Daly, M., & Wilson, M. (1982). Homicide and kinship. *American Anthropologist, 84*, 372–378.

Daly, M., & Wilson, M. (1983). *Sex, evolution and behavior* (2nd ed.). Boston: Willard Grant.

Daly, M., & Wilson, M.I. (1985). Child abuse and other risks of not living with both parents. *Ethology and Sociobiology, 6*, 197–210.

Daly, M., & Wilson, M.I. (1988a). *Homicide.* New York: Aldine deGruyter.

Daly, M., & Wilson, M.I. (1988b). Evolutionary social psychology and family homicide. *Science, 242*, 519–524.

Daly, M., & Wilson, M. (1990). Killing the competition: Female/female and male/male homicide. *Human Nature, 1*, 81–107.

Daly, M., & Wilson, M. I. (1994). Some differential attributes of lethal assaults on small children by stepfathers versus genetic fathers. *Ethology and Sociobiology, 15*, 207–217.

Daly, M., & Wilson, M.I. (1998). Psychology of family violence. In C. Crawford & D.L. Krebs (Eds.), *Handbook of evolutionary psychology* (pp. 431–456). Mahwah, NJ: Erlbaum.

Daly, M., Wilson, M.I., & Weghorst, S.J. (1982). Male sexual jealousy. *Ethology and Sociobiology, 3*, 11–27.

Damasio, A.R. (1994). *Decartes' error: Emotion, reason, and the human brain.* New York: Avon Books.

Damasio, A.R., Tranel, D., & Damasio, H. (1991). Somatic markers and the guidance of behavior: Theory and preliminary testing. In H.S. Levin, H.M. Eisenberg, & A.L. Benton (Eds.), *Frontal lobe function and dysfunction* (pp. 217–229). New York: Oxford University Press.

Darlington, C.D. (1969). *The evolution of man and society.* New York: Simon and Schuster.

Darwin, C. (1859). *On the origin of species by natural selection.* London: John Murray.

Darwin, C. (1871). *The descent of man.* London: John Murray.

Darwin, C. (1872/1965). *The expression of emotions in man and animals.* Chicago: University of Chicago Press.

David, N.C. (1973). On Upper Palaeolithic society, ecology, and technological change: The Noaillian case. In A.C. Renfrew (Ed.), *The explanation of cultural change* (pp. 277–303). London: Duckworth.

Davidson, I., & Noble, W. (1992). Why the first colonization of the Australian region is the earliest evidence of modern human behavior. *Archaeology in Oceania, 27*, 135–142.

Davidson, R.J. (1993). The neuropsychology of emotion and affective style. In M. Lewis & J.M. Haviland (Eds.), *Handbook of emotions* (pp. 143–154). New York: Guilford.

Dawkins, R. (1976). *The selfish gene.* Oxford, UK: Oxford University Press.

Dawkins, R. (1986). *The blind watchmaker.* New York: W. W. Norton.

Day, M.H. (1972). The Omo human skeletal remains. In F.H. Bordes (Ed.), *The origin of* Homo sapiens. Paris: UNESCO.

Day, M.H., & Stringer, C.B. (1982). A reconsideration of the Omo-Kibish remains and the *erectus–sapiens* transition. In M.A. de Lumley (Ed.), *L'Homo erectus et la place de l'homme de Tautavel parmi les hominidés fossiles.* Nice: Centre National de la Recherche Scientifique.

Denig, E.T. (1961). *Five indian tribes of the upper Missouri: Sioux, Arickaras, Assiniboines, Cree, Crows.* Norman, OK: University of Oklahoma Press.

Deacon, T. (1988). Human brain evolution: II. Embryology and brain allometry. In H. Jerison & I. Jerison (Eds.), *Intelligence and evolutionary biology* (pp. 383–415). New York: Springer-Verlag.

Deacon, T. (1995). Why a brain capable of language evolved only once: Prefrontal cortex and symbol learning. In B. Velikovsky (Ed.), *Social and biological origins of language.* Mahwah, NJ: L. Erlbaum.

Deacon, T.W. (1997). *The symbolic species: The co-evolution of language and the brain*. New York: W.W. Norton.

DeCasper, A.J., & Fifer, W.P. (1980). Of human bonding: Newborns prefer their mothers' voices. *Science, 208,* 1174–1176.

DeCasper, A.J., & Spence, M.J. (1986). Prenatal maternal speech influences newborns' perception of speech sounds. *Infant Behavior and Development, 9,* 133–150.

Deichmann, U. (1966). *Biologists under Hitler*. Cambridge, MA: Harvard University Press.

Delbruck, M. (1986). *Mind from matter? An essay on evolutionary epistemology*. Palo Alto, CA: Blackwell Scientific.

Dennell, R. (1997). The world's oldest spears. *Nature, 385,* 767–768.

Dennett, D. (1996). *Kinds of minds*. New York: Basic Books.

Dennis, W. (1940). Does culture appreciably affect patterns of infant behavior? *Journal of Social Psychology, 12,* 305–317.

Dessalles, J.L. (1998). Altruism, status, and the origin of relevance. In J.R. Hurford, M. Studdert-Kennedy, & C. Knight (Eds.), *Approaches to the evolution of language: Social and cognitive bases* (pp. 130–147). Cambridge, MA: Cambridge University Press.

Diamond, J. (1997). *Why is sex fun? The evolution of human sexuality*. London: Weidenfeld and Nicolson.

de Waal, F. (1982). *Chimpanzee politics: Power and sex among apes*. London: Jonathan Cape.

de Waal, F.B.M. (1986). Deception in the natural communication of chimpanzees. In R.W. Mitchell & N.S. Thompson (Eds.), *Deception: Perspectives on human and nonhuman deceit* (pp. 221–244). Albany, NY: SUNY Press.

de Waal, F.B.M. (1987). Tension regulation and nonreproductive functions of sex in captive bonobos (*Pan paniscus*). *National Geographic Research, 3,* 318–335.

de Waal, F.B.M. (1989). Food sharing and reciprocal obligations among chimpanzees. *Human Evolution, 18,* 433–459.

de Waal, F.B.M. (1995, March). Bonobo sex and society. *Scientific American,* 82–88.

de Waal, F.B.M. (1996). *Good natured: The origins of right and wrong in humans and other animals*. Cambridge, MA: Harvard University Press.

de Waal, F.B.M. (1997). Food transfers through mesh in brown capuchins. *Journal of Comparative Psychology, 111,* 370–378.

de Waal, F.B.M., & Berger, M.L. (2000). Payment for labour in monkeys. *Nature, 404,* 563.

de Waal, F., & Lanting, F. (1997). *Bonobo: The forgotten ape*. Berkley, CA: University of California Press.

de Waal, F.B.M., & Luttrell, L.M. (1988). Mechanisms of social reciprocity in three primate species: Symmetrical relationship characteristics or cognition? *Ethology and Sociobiology, 9,* 101–118.

Dickemann, M. (1979). Female infanticide, reproductive strategies, and social stratification: A preliminary model. In N.A. Chagnon & W. Irons (Eds.), *Evolutionary biology and human social behavior: An anthropological perspective* (pp. 321–368). North Scituate, MA: Duxbury Press.

Dickemann, M. (1981). Paternal confidence and dowry competition: Biocultural analysis of purdah. In R.D. Alexander & D.W. Tinkle (Eds.), *Natural selection and social behavior: Recent research and new theory* (pp. 417–438). New York: Chiron Press.

Diekmann, A., Jungbauer-Gans, M., Krassig, H., & Lorenz, S. (1996). Social status and aggression: A field study analyzed by survival analysis. *Journal of Social Psychology, 136,* 761–768.

Diener, E., Suh, E.M., Lucas, R.E., & Smith, H.L. (1999). Subjective well-being: Three decades of progress. *Psychological Bulletin, 125,* 276–302.

Dittus, W.P.J. (1998). Birth sex ratios in toque macaques and other mammals: Integrating the effects of maternal condition and competition. *Behavioral Ecology and Sociobiology, 44,* 149–160.

Dobzhansky, T.G. (1967). *The biology of ultimate concern*. New York: New American Library.

Dobzhansky, T. (1973). Nothing in biology makes sense except in the light of evolution. *American Biology Teacher, 35,* 125–129.

Donald, M. (1991). *Origins of the human mind: three stages in the evolution of culture and cognition*. Cambridge, MA: Harvard University Press.

Donald, M. (1993). Human cognitive evolution: What we were, what we are becoming. *Social Research, 60,* 143–170.

Donald, M. (1998). Mimesis and the executive suite: missing links in language evolution. In J. Hurford, M. Studdert-Kennedy, & C. Knight (Eds.), *Approaches to the evolution of language: Social and cognitive bases* (pp. 44–67). Cambridge, UK: Cambridge University Press.

Donald, M. (1999). The preconditions for the evolution of protolanguages. In M.C. Corballis & S.E.G. Lea (Eds.), *The descent of mind* (139–154). Oxford, UK: Oxford University Press.

Doob, A.N., & Gross, A.E. (1968). Status of frustrator as an inhibitor of horn-honking responses. *Journal of Social Psychology, 76,* 213–218.

Doty, R.L., Shaman, P., Applebaum, S.L., Giberson, R. Siksorski, L., & Rosenberg, L. (1984). Smell identification ability: Changes with age. *Science, 226,* 1441–1443.

Draper, P., & Harpending, H. (1982). Father absence and reproductive strategy: An evolutionary perspective. *Journal of Anthropological Research, 38,* 255–273.

Duchaine, B., Cosmides, L., & Tooby, J. (2001). Evolutionary psychology and the brain. *Current Opinion in Neurobiology, 11,* 225–230.

Duchin, L.E. (1990). The evolution of articulate speech: Comparative anatomy of the oral cavity in *Pan* and *Homo. Journal of Human Evolution, 19,* 687–697.

Duffy, J.D., & Campbell, J.J. (1994). The regional prefrontal syndromes: A theoretical and clinical overview. *Journal of Neuropsychiatry and Clinical Neurosciences, 6,* 379–387.

Dugatkin, L. (1992). Sexual selection and imitation: Females copy mate choice of others. *American Naturalist, 139*, 1384–1389.

Dugatkin, L.A. (2001) The imitation factor: Evolution beyond the gene. New York: The Free Press.

Duke, P.M., Carlsmith, J.M., Jennings, D., Martin, J.A., Dornbusch, S.M., Gross, R.T., et al. (1982). Educational correlates of early and late sexual maturation in adolescence. *Journal of Pediatrics, 100*, 633–637.

Dunbar, R. (1988). *Primate social systems.* London: Croom Helm.

Dunbar, R.I.M. (1992). Neocortex size as a constraint on group size in primates. *Journal of Human Evolution, 20*, 469–493.

Dunbar, R.I.M. (1993). Time: A hidden constraint on the behavioral ecology of baboons. *Behavioral Ecology and Sociobiology, 31*, 35–49.

Dunbar, R. (1996). *Grooming, gossip, and the evolution of language.* Cambridge, MA: Harvard University Press.

Dunbar, R. (1998). Theory of mind and the evolution of language. J.R. Hurford, M. Studdert-Kennedy, & C. Knight (Eds.), *Approaches to the evolution of language: Social and cognitive bases* (pp. 92–110). Cambridge, MA: Cambridge University Press.

Dunbar, R.I.M., & Dunbar, P. (1988). Maternal time budgets of gelada baboons. *Animal Behaviour, 36*, 970–980.

Dunker, K. (1945). On problem solving. *Psychological Monographs, 58*, (5, Entire No. 270).

Dunn, F.L. (1968). Epidemiological factors: Health and disease among hunter–gatherers. In R.B. Lee & I. DeVore (Eds.), *Man the hunter* (pp. 221–228). Chicago: Aldine de Gruyter.

Dyson, F. (2000). *Progress in religion.* Acceptance speech for the Templeton Prize, presented May 16 at the National Cathedral, Washington, D.C.

Eagly, A.H., & Wood, W. (1999). The origins of sex differences in human behavior. *American Psychologist, 54*, 408–423.

Eals, M., & Silverman, I. (1994). The hunter–gatherer theory of spatial sex differences: Proximate factors mediating the female advantage in recall of object arrays. *Ethology and Sociobiology, 15*, 95–105.

Easterbrook, J.A. (1959). The effect of emotion on cue utilization and the organization of behavior. *Psychological Review, 66*, 183–201.

Eaves, L., Silberg, J., Hewitt, J.K., Meyer, J., Rutter, M., Simonoff, E., et al. (1993). Genes, personality, and psychopathology: A latent class analysis of liability to symptoms of attention-deficit hyperactivity disorder in twins. In R. Plomin & G.E. McClearn (Eds.), *Nature, nurture, and psychology* (pp. 285–303). Washington, D.C.: APA Books.

Eberhard, W.G. (1985). *Sexual selection and animal genitalia.* Cambridge, MA: Harvard University Press.

Eddy, D.M. (1982). Probabilistic reasoning in clinical medicine: Problems and opportunities. In D. Kahneman, P. Slovik, & A. Tversky (Eds.), *Judgment under uncertainty: Heuristics and biases* (pp. 249–267). Cambridge, UK: Cambridge University Press.

Egeland, J.A., & Hostetter, A.M. (1983). Amish study: I. Affective disorders among the Amish, 1976–1980. *American Journal of Psychiatry 140*, 56–61.

Eibl-Eibesfeldt, I. (1972). Similarities and differences between cultures in expressive movements. In R.A. Hinde (Ed.), *Nonverbal communication* (pp. 297–311). Cambridge, UK: Cambridge University Press.

Eisley, L. (1958). *Darwin's century.* New York: Doubleday.

Ekman, P. (1972). Universals and cultural differences in facial expressions of emotion. In J. Cole (Ed.), *Nebraska symposium on motivation, 19* (pp. 207–284). Lincoln, NE: University of Nebraska Press.

Ekman, P. (1973). Cross-cultural studies of facial expression. In P. Ekman (Ed.), *Darwin and facial expressions* (pp. 169–222). New York: Academic Press.

Ekman, P. (1992). *Telling lies.* New York: W.W. Norton.

Ekman, P., & Davidson, R.J. (1993). Voluntary smiling changes regional brain activity. *Psychological Science, 4*, 342–345.

Ellis, B.J., & Garber, J. (2000). Psychosocial antecedents of pubertal maturation in girls: Parental psychopathology, stepfather presence, and family and martial stress. *Child Development, 71*, 485–501.

Ellis, B.J., McFayden-Ketchum, S., Dodge, K.A., Pettit, G.S., & Bates, J.E. (1999). Quality of early family relationships and individual differences in the timing of pubertal maturation in girls: A longitudinal test of an evolutionary model. *Journal of Personality and Social Psychology, 77*, 387– 401.

Ellis, L. (1988). Criminal behavior and r/K selection: An extension of gene-based evolutionary theory. *Personality and Individual Differences, 9*, 697–708.

Epley, N., & Dunning, D. (2001). Feeling "holier than thou": Are self-serving assessments produced by errors in self- or social prediction? *Journal of Personality and Social Psychology, 79*, 861–875.

Erdal, D., & Whiten, A. (1994). On human egalitarianism: An evolutionary product of Machiavellian status escalation? *Current Anthropology, 35*, 175–183.

Erdal, D., & Whiten, A. (1996). Egalitarianism and Machiavellian intelligence in human evolution. In P. Mellars & K. Gibson (Eds.), *Modelling the early human mind* (pp. 139–150). Cambridge, UK: McDonald Institute Monographs.

Erikson, C.J., & Zenone, P.G. (1976). Courtship differences in male ring doves: Avoidance of cuckoldry? *Science, 192*, 1353–1354.

Eyre-Walker, A., & Keightley, P.D. (1999). High genomic deleterious mutation rates in hominids. *Nature, 397*, 344–347.

Eysenck, H.J., & Gudjonsson, G.H. (1989). *The causes and cures of criminality.* London: Plenum Press.

Fadiman, J.A. (1982). *An oral history of tribal warfare: the Meru of Mt. Kenya.* Athens, OH: Ohio University Press.

Fady, J.C. (1972). Absence de cooperation de type instrumental en melieu naturel chez *Papio papio*. *Behaviour, 43,* 157–164.

Falk, D. (1980). A re-analysis of the South African australopithecine natural endocast. *American Journal of Physical Anthropology, 53,* 525–539.

Falk, D. (1983). Cerebral cortices of East African early hominids. *Science, 222,* 1072–1074.

Falk, D. (1985). Apples, oranges and the lunate sulcus. *American Journal of Physical Anthropology, 67,* 313–315.

Falk, D. (1986). Evolution of cranial blood drainage in hominids. *American Journal of Physical Anthropology, 70,* 311–324.

Falk, D. (1987). Brain lateralization in primates and its evolution in hominids. *Yearbook of Physical Anthropology, 30,* 107–125.

Falk, D. (1990). Brain evolution in *Homo*—The radiator theory. *Behavioral and Brain Sciences, 13,* 333–343.

Falk, D. (1991). 3.5 million years of hominid brain evolution. *Seminars in the Neurosciences, 3,* 409–416.

Farah, M.J., Rabinowitz, C., Quinn, G.E., & Liu, G.T. (2000). Early commitment of neural substrates for face recognition. *Cognitive Neuropsychology, 17,* 177–123.

Feibel, C.S., Agnew, N., Latimer, B., Demas, M., Marshall, F., & Waane, S.A.C. (1995). The Laetoli hominid footprints: A preliminary report on conservation and scientific restudy. *Evolutionary Anthropology, 4,* 149–154.

Feibel, C.S., Brown, F.H., & McDougall, I. (1989). Stratigraphic context of fossil hominids from the Omo Group deposits. *American Journal of Physical Anthropology, 78,* 595–622.

Feingold, A. (1990). Gender differences in effects of physical attractiveness on romantic attraction: A comparison across five research paradigms. *Journal of Personality and Social Psychology, 59,* 981–993.

Feingold, A. (1992). Gender differences in mate selection peferences: A test of the parental investment model. *Psychological Bulletin, 112,* 125–139.

Feinman, S., & Lewis, M. (1983). Social referencing at 10 months: A second-order effect on infants' responses to strangers. *Child Development, 54,* 878–887.

Fifer, F.C. (1987). The adoption of bipedalism by the hominids: A new hypothesis. *Human Evolution, 2,* 135–147.

Fisher, H. (1992). *Anatomy of love: The Natural history of monogamy, adultery, and divorce.* New York: Simon & Schuster.

Fisher, R.A. (1930). *The genetical theory of natural selection.* Oxford, UK: Clarendon Press.

Flack, J.C., & de Waal, F.B.M. (2000). 'Any animal whatever' Darwinian building blocks of morality in monkeys and apes. *Journal of Consciousness Studies, 7*(1–2), 1–29.

Flaxman, S.M., & Sherman, P.W. (2000). Morning sickness: A mechanism for protecting mother and embryo. *Quarterly Review of Biology, 75,* 113–148.

Fleagle, J.G., Kay, R.R., & Simons, E.L. (1980). Sexual dimorphism in early anthropoids. *Nature, 287,* 328–330.

Flinn, M.V. (1986). Correlates of reproductive success in a Caribbean village. *Human Ecology, 14,* 225–243.

Flinn, M.V. (1988a). Parent–offspring interactions in a Caribbean village: Daughter guarding. In L. Betzig, M. Borgerhoff Mulder, & P. Turke (Eds.), *Human reproductive behavior* (pp. 189–200). Cambridge, UK: Cambridge University Press.

Flinn, M.V. (1988b). Step- and genetic parent/offspring relationships in a Caribbean village. *Ethology and Sociobiology, 9,* 335–369.

Floyd, C. (2000). Virtuous species: The biological origins of human morality—An interview with Frans de Waal. *Science and Spirit, 11*(1), 14–16.

Fodor, J. (2000). Why we are so good at catching cheaters. *Cognition, 75,* 29–32.

Foley, R. (1987). Hominid species and stone tool assemblages. *Antiquity, 61,* 380–392.

Foley, R.A. (1989). The evolution of hominid social behaviour. In V. Standen & R.A. Foley (Eds.), *Comparative socioecology* (pp. 473–494). Oxford, UK: Blackwell Scientific Publications.

Foley, R.A. (1990). The causes of brain enlargement in human evolution. *Behavioral and Brain Sciences, 13,* 354–356.

Foley, R.A. (1991). How many hominid species should there be? *Journal of Human Evolution, 20,* 413–427.

Foley, R. (1992). Ecology and energetics of encephalization in hominid evolution. In A. Whiten & E.M. Widdowson (Eds.), *Foraging strategies and the natural diet of monkeys, apes, and humans* (pp. 63–72). Oxford, UK: Oxford University Press.

Foley, R.A. (1995). *Humans before humanity.* Oxford, UK: Blackwell Publishers.

Foley, R.A., & Lee, P.C. (1989). Finite social space, evolutionary pathways and reconstructing hominid behavior. *Science, 243,* 901–906.

Foley, R.A., & Lee, P.C. (1995). Finite social space and the evolution of human social behavior. In S. Shennan & J. Steele (Eds.), *Archaeology of human ancestry* (pp. 47–66). London: Routledge.

Forbes, L.S. (1997). The evolutionary biology of spontaneous abortion in humans. *Trends in Ecology and Evolution, 12,* 446–450.

Fossey, D. (1983). *Gorillas in the mist.* Boston: Houghton Mifflin.

Fox, E., Lester, V., Russo, R., Bowles, R.J., Pichler, A., & Dutton, K. (2000). Facial expressions of emotion: Are angry faces detected more efficiently? *Cognition and Emotion, 14,* 61–92.

Fox, R., & McDaniel, C. (1982). The perception of biological motion by human infants. *Science, 218,* 486–487.

Frank, R.H. (1988). *Passions within reason: The strategic role of the emotions.* New York: W.W. Norton.

Frank, R.H., Gilovich, T., & Regan, D.T. (1993). The evolution of one-shot cooperation. *Ethology and Sociobiology, 14,* 247–256.

Frank, M.G., & Ekman, P. (1997). The ability to detect deceit generalizes across different types of high-stakes lies. *Journal of Personality and Social Psychology, 72,* 1429–1439.

Franzoi, R.L., & Herzog, M.E. (1987). Judging physcial attractiveness: What body aspects do we use? *Personality and Social Psychology Bulletin, 13,*19–33.

Frayer, D.W. (1986). Cranial variation at Mladec and the relationship between Mousterian and Upper Paleolithic hominids. *Anthropos, 23,* 243–256.

Fredrickson, B.L. (1998). What good are positive emotions? *Review of General Psychology, 2,* 300–319.

Fredrickson, B.L. (2000, March 7). Cultivating positive emotions to optimize health and well-being. *Prevention and Treatment, 3.* Article 001a. Retrieved March 15, 2002, from www.journals.apa.org/prevention/volume3/pre0030001a.html.

Freeman, D. (1983). *Margaret Mead and Samoa: The making and unmaking of an anthropological myth.* Cambridge, MA: Harvard University Press.

Furuichi, T. (1992). The prolonged estrus of females and factors influencing mating in a wild group of bonobos (*Pan Paniscus)* in Wamba, Zaire. In N. Itoiga, Y. Sugiyama, G.P. Sackett, & K.R. Thompson (Eds.), *Topics in primatology, 2: Behavior, ecology and conservation* (179–190). Tokyo: University of Tokyo Press.

Gabunia, L., Vekua, A., Lordkipanidze, D., Swisher, C.C., Ferring, R., Justus, A., et al. (2000). Earliest Pleistocene hominid cranial remains from Dmanisi, Republic of Georgia. *Science, 288,* 1019–1025.

Gagneux, P., Boesch, C., & Woodruff, D.S. (1999). Female reproductive strategies, paternity and community structure in wild West African Chimpanzees. *Animal Behavior, 57,* 9–12.

Galea, L.A.M., & Kimura, D. (1993). Sex differences in route learning. *Personality and Individual Differences, 14,* 53–65.

Galdikas, B. Social and reproductive behavior of wild adolescent female orangutans. In R.D. Nadler, B.M.F. Galdikas, L.K. Sheeran, & N. Rosen (Eds.), *The neglected ape* (pp. 163–182). New York: Plenum Press.

Gallistel, C.R. (2000). The replacement of general purpose learning models with adaptively specialized learning modules. In M.S. Gazzaniga (Ed.), *The new cognitive neurosciences* (pp. 1179–1191). Cambridge, MA: MIT Press.

Gallup, G., Jr. (1970). Chimpanzees: self–recognition. *Science, 167,* 86–87.

Gallup, G., Jr. (1982). Self-awareness and the emergence of mind in primates. *American Journal of Primatology, 2,* 237–248.

Gallup, G., Jr. (1994). Self-recognition: Research strategies and experimental design. In S.T. Parker, R.W. Mitchell, & M.L. Boccia (Eds.), *Self-awareness in animals and humans: Developmental perspectives* (pp. 35–50). Cambridge, UK: Cambridge University Press.

Gallup, G., Jr. (1998, November). Can animals empathize? Yes. *Scientific American.* Special Issue on Intelligence. Retrieved March 15, 2002, from www.sciam.com/specialissues/1198intelligence/1198gallup.html.

Gallup, G., Jr., McClure, M.K., Hill, S.D., & Bundy, R.A. (1971). Capacity for self-recognition in differentially reared chimpanzees. *Psychological Record, 21,* 69–74.

Gamble, C. (1986). *The Palaeolithic settlement of Europe.* Cambridge, UK: Cambridge University Press.

Gamble, C. (1993). *Timewalkers: The pre-history of global colonization.* London: Penguin.

Gangestad, S.W., & Buss, D.M. (1993). Pathogen prevalence and human mate preferences. *Ethology and Sociobiology, 14,* 89–96.

Gangestad, S.W., & Thornhill, R. (1997). Human sexual selection and developmental stability. In J.A. Simpson & D.T. Kenrick (Eds.), *Evolutionary social psychology* (pp. 169–175). Mahwah, NJ: Erlbaum.

Gangestad, S.W., Thornhill, R., & Yeo, R.A. (1994). Facial attractiveness, developmental stability, and fluctuating asymmetry. *Ethology and Sociobiology, 15,* 73–85.

Gardner, R.A., Gardner, B.T., & Van Cantfort, T.E. (1989). *Teaching sign language to chimpanzees.* Albany: State University of New York Press.

Gargett, R. H. (1989). Grave shortcomings: The evidence for Neanderthal burial. *Current Anthropology, 30,* 157–190.

Gaulin, S.J.C. (1980). Sexual dimorphism in the human post-reproductive life-span: Possible causes. *Journal of Human Evolution, 9,* 227–232.

Gaulin, S.J.C., & Fitzgerald, R.W. (1986). Sex differences in spatial ability: An evolutionary hypothesis and test. *The American Naturalist, 127,* 74–88.

Gaulin, S.J.C., McBurney, D., & Brakeman-Wartell, S. (1997). Matrilateral biases in the investment of aunts and uncles: A consequence and measure of paternity uncertainty. *Human Nature, 8,* 139–151.

Gaulin, S.J.C., & Robbins, C.J. (1991). Trivers-Willard effect in contemporary North American Society. *American Journal of Physical Anthropology, 85,* 61–68.

Gauthier, I., & Nelson, C.A. (2001). The development of face expertise. *Current Opinion in Neurobiology, 11,* 219–224.

Gauthier, I., Tarr, M.J., Anderson, A.W., Skudlarski, P., & Gore, J.C. (1999). Activation of the middle fusiform 'face area' increases with expertise in recognizing novel objects. *Nature Neuroscience, 2,* 568–580.

Gazzaniga, M.S., & Smylie, C.S. (1990). Hemispheric mechansims controlling voluntary and spontaneous facial expressions. *Journal of Cognitive Neuroscience, 2,* 239–245.

Gazzaniga, M.S., Ivry, R.B., & Mangun G.R. (1998). *Cognitive neuroscience: The biology of the mind.* New York: W. W. Norton.

Geary, D.C. (1998). *Male, female: The evolution of human sex differences.* Washington, D.C.: American Psychological Association.

Gelder, M.G., & Marks, J.M. (1970). Transsexualism and faradic stimulation: In R. Green (Ed.), *Transsexualism and sex reassignment.* Baltimore: Johns Hopkins University Press.

Gell-Mann, M (1994). *The quark and the jaguar.* New York: W.H. Freeman and Co.

Georgia State University Language Research Center Web site. Retrieved March 14, 2002, from www.gsu.edu/~wwwlrc/biographies/kanzi.html.

Gergely, G., Nadasdy, Z., Csibra, G., & Biro, S. (1995). Taking the intentional stance at 12 months of age. *Cognition, 56,* 165–193.

Geronimus, A.T. (1987). On teenage childbearing and neonatal mortality in the United States. *Population and Development Review, 13,* 245–279.

Geronimus, A.T. (1991). Teenage childbearing and social and reproductive disadvantage: The evolution of complex questions and the demise of simple answers. *Family Relations, 40,* 463–471.

Ghesquiere, J., Martin, R.D., & Newcombe, F. (1985). *Human sexual dimorphism.* Washington, DC: Taylor & Francis.

Ghiglieri, M.P. (1989). Hominid sociobiology and hominid social evolution. In P. G. Heltne & L.A. Marquardt (Eds.), *Understanding chimpanzees* (pp. 370–379). Cambridge, MA: Harvard University Press.

Gibbons, A. (1996). Did Neanderthals lose an evolutionary "arms" race? *Science, 272,* 1586–1587.

Gibson, R.M., Bradbury, J.W., & Vehrencamp, S.L. (1991). Mate choice in lekking sage grouse: The roles of vocal display, female site fidelity and copying. *Behavioral Ecology, 2,* 165–180.

Gigerenzer, G., & Hoffrage, U. (1995). How to improve Bayesian reasoning without instruction. *Psychological Review, 102,* 684–704.

Gigerenzer, G., & Hug, U. (1992). Domain specific reasoning: Social contracts, cheating, and perspective change. *Cognition, 43,* 127–171.

Giglieri, M.P. (1987). Sociobiology of the great apes and the hominid ancestor. *Journal of Human Evolution, 16,* 319–357.

Gilligan, C. (1982, 1993). *In a different voice: Psychological theory and women's development.* Cambridge, MA: Harvard University Press.

Gilligan, C. (1997). In a different voice. In J.L. Nelson (Ed.), *Human nature: Lynchburg College symposium readings* (pp. 132–139). Lanham, MD: University Press of America.

Gilovich, T., Vallone, R., & Tversky, A. (1985). The hot hand in basketball: On the misperception of random sequences. *Cognitive Psychology, 17,* 295–314.

Gindhart, P.S. (1973). Growth standards for the tibia and radius in children aged one month through eighteen years. *American Journal of Physical Anthropology, 39,* 41–48.

Gleitman, H. (1991). *Psychology* (3rd ed.). New York: W.W. Norton.

Goldberg, L.R. (1990). An alternative 'description of personality': the Big Five structure. *Journal of Personality and Social Psychology, 59,* 1216–1229.

Goldstein, E.B. (1999). *Sensation and perception.* Pacific Grove, CA: Brooks/Cole.

Goleman, D. (1998). *Working with emotional intelligence.* NewYork: Bantam Books.

Goodall, J. (1968). Expressive movements and communication in free-ranging chimpanzees: A preliminary report. In P.C. Jay (Ed.), *Primates: Studies in adaptation and variability* (pp. 313–374). New York: Holt, Rinehart & Winston.

Goodall, J. (1986). *The chimpanzees of Gombe: Patterns of behavior.* Cambridge, MA: Harvard University Press.

Goodall, J. (1990). *Through a window.* Boston: Houghton Mifflin Company.

Goode, E. (2000, March 14). Human nature: Born or made. Evolutionary theorists provoke an uproar. *New York Times: Science Times.*

Goodenough, F.L., & Brian, C.R. (1929). Certain factors underlying the acquisition of motor skill by pre-school children. *Journal of Experimental Psychology, 12,* 127–155.

Goodman, M. (19xx) A personal account of the origins of a new paradigm. *Molecular Phylogenetics and Evolution, 5,* 269–285.

Goodman, M., Bailey, W.J., Hayasaka, K., Stanhope, M.J., Slightom, J., & Czelusniak, J. (1994). Molecular evidence on primate phylogeny from DNA sequences. *American Journal of Physical Anthropology, 94,* 3–24.

Gopnik, A. (1993). How we know our minds: The illusion of first-person knowledge of intentionality. *Behavioral and Brain Sciences, 16,* 1–14.

Gould, J.L. (1990). Honeybee cognition. *Cognition, 37,* 83–103.

Gould, J.L., & Gould, C.G. (1997). *Sexual selection: Mate choice and courtship in nature.* New York: W.H. Freeman and Co.

Gould, J.L., & Gould, C.G. (1998). *The honeybee.* New York: Freeman.

Gould, S.J. (1986). Evolution and the triumph of homology, or why history matters. *American Scientist, 74,* 60–69.

Gould, S.J. (1991). Exaptation: A crucial tool for evolutionary psychology. *Journal of Social Issues, 47,* 43–58.

Gould, S.J. (1998). *Rocks of ages: Science and religion in the fullness of life.* New York: Ballantine Books.

Gouras, P. (1991). Color vision. In E.R. Kandel, J. H. Schwartz, & T.M. Jessell (Eds.), *Principles of neuroscience* (3rd ed.) (pp. 467–480). New York: Elsevier.

Gowlett, J.A.J. (1984). Mental abilities of early man. In R. Foley (Ed.), *Hominid evolution and community ecology* (pp. 167–192). London: Academic Press.

Gowlett, J.A.J. (1992). Tools—the Palaeolithic record. In S. Jones, R. Martin, & D. Pilbeam (Eds.), *The Cambridge encyclopedia of human evolution* (pp. 350–360). Cambridge, UK: Cambridge University Press.

Graber, J.A., Brooks-Gunn, J., & Warren, M.P. (1995). The antecedents of menarcheal age: Heredity, family environment and stressful life events. *Child Development, 66,* 346–359.

Grammer, K. (1992). Variations on a theme: Age dependent mate selection in humans. *Behavioral and Brain Sciences, 15,* 100–102.

Grammer, K., Dittami, J., & Fischmann, B. (1993). Changes in female sexual advertisement according to menstrual cycle. Paper presented at the annual meeting of the Human Behavior and Evolution Society, Syracuse, NY.

Granrud, C.E., & Yonas, A. (1984). Infants' perception of pictorially specified interposition. *Journal of Experimental Child Psychology, 37,* 500–511.

Granrud, C.E., Yonas, A., & Opland, E.A. (1985). Infants' sensitivity to the depth cue of shading. *Perception & Psychophysics, 37,* 415–419.

Green, J.D., Sommerville, R.B., Nystrom, L.E., Darley, J.M., & Cohen, J.D. (2001). An fMRI investigation of emotional engagement in moral judgement. *Science, 293,* 2105–2108.

Greenfield, P.M., & Savage-Rumbaugh, E.S. (1991). Imitation, grammatical development and the invention of protogrammar by an ape. In N.A. Krasnegor, D.M. Rumbaugh, R.L. Schiefelbusch, & M. Studdert-Kennedy (Eds.), *Biological and behavioral determinants of language development* (pp. 235–258). Hillside, NJ: Lawrence Erlbaum Associates.

Gregory, R.L. (1970). *The intelligent eye.* New York: McGraw–Hill.

Groen, G., Wunderlich, A.P., Spitzer, M., Tomczak, R., & Riepe, M.W. (2000). Brain activation during human navigation: Gender-different neural networks as substrate of performance. *Nature Neuroscience, 3,* 404–408.

Groves, C.P. (1989). *A theory of human and primate evolution.* Oxford, UK: Clarendon Press.

Guiard, Y. (1987). Asymmetric division of labor in human skilled bimanual action: The kinematic chain as a model. *Journal of Motor Behavior, 19,* 486–517.

Gut, E. (1989). *Productive and unproductive depression: Success or failure of a vital process.* New York: Basic Books.

Gutierres, S.E., Kenrick, D.T., & Partch, J.J. (1999). Beauty, dominance and the dating game: Contrast effects in self-assessment reflect gender differences in mate selection. *Personality and Social Psychology Bulletin, 25,* 1126–1134.

Hackworth, D.H. (1989). *About face: The odyssey of an American warrior.* New York: Simon & Schuster.

Hager, L.D. (1997). *Women in human evolution.* London: Routledge.

Haggerty, M.E. (1913). Plumbing the minds of apes. *McClures Magazine, 41,* 151–154.

Haig, D. (1993). Genetic conflicts in human pregnancy. *The Quarterly Review of Biology, 68,* 495–532.

Hailman, J.P., & Ficken, M.S. (1987). Combinatorial animal communication with computable syntax: Chick-a-dee calling qualifies as "language" by structural linguistics. *Animal Beahvior, 34,* 1899–1901.

Hailman, J.P., Ficken, M.S., & Ficken, R.W. (1985). The "chick-a-dee" calls of *Parus atricapillus*: A recombinant system of animal communication compared with written English. *Semiotica, 56,* 191–224.

Hailman, J.P., Ficken, M.S., & Ficken, R.W. (1987). Constraints on the structure of combinatorial "chick-a-dee" calls. *Ethology, 75,* 62–80.

Hallock, M.B., & Worobey, J. (1984). Cognitive development in chimpanzee infants (*Pan troglodytes*). *Journal of Human Evolution, 13,* 441–447.

Halpern, D.F. (1989). *Thought and knowledge: An introduction to critical thinking.* Hillsdale, NJ: Erlbaum.

Halpern, D.F. (1992). *Sex differences in cognitive abilities.* Hillsdale, NJ: Erlbaum.

Hamilton, W.D. (1964). The genetical evolution of social behavior. I and II. *Journal of Theoretical Biology, 7,* 1–52.

Hammer, M.F., Spurdle, A.B., Karafet, T., Bonner, M.R., Wood, E.T., Novoletto, A., et al., (1997). The geographic distribution of human Y chromosome variation. *Genetics, 145,* 787–805.

Hammond, G.R. (1990). Manual performance asymmetries. In G.R. Hammond (Ed.), *Cerebral control of speech and limb movements* (pp. 59–77). Amsterdam: North-Holland.

Hansen, C.H., & Hansen, R.D. (1988). Finding faces in the crowd: An anger superiority effect. *Journal of Personality and Social Psychology, 54,* 917–924.

Harcourt, A.H., & de Waal, F.B.M. (1992). *Coalitions and alliances in humans and other animals.* Oxford, UK: Oxford University Press.

Harcourt, A.H., Harvey, P.H., Larson, S.G., & Short, R.V. (1981). Testis weight, body weight, and breeding system in primates. *Nature, 293,* 55–57.

Hare, B., Call, J., Agnetta, B., & Tomasello, M. (2000). Chimpanzees know what conspecifics do and do not see. *Animal Behaviour, 59,* 771–785.

Hare, B., Call, J., & Tomasello, M. (2001). Do chimpanzees know what conspecifics know? *Animal Behaviour, 61,* 139–151.

Harris, J.W.K. (1983). Cultural beginnings. *African Archaeological Review, 1,* 3–31.

Hart, B.L. (1990). Behavioral adaptations to pathogens and parasites: Five strategies. *Neuroscience and Biobehavioral Review, 14,* 273–294.

Hartung, J. (1982). Polygyny and the inheritance of wealth. *Current Anthropology, 23,* 1–12.

Hartwig-Scherer, S., & Martin, R.D. (1991). Was "Lucy" more human than her "child?" *Journal of Human Evolution, 21,* 439–449.

Hasegawa, M., Kishino, H., & Yano, T. (1989). Estimation of branching dates among primates by molecular clocks of nuclear DNA which slowed down in Hominoidea. *Journal of Human Evolution, 18,* 461–476.

Hasher, L., & Zacks, R. (1984). Automatic processing of fundamental information: The case of frequency of occurence. *American Psychologist, 39,* 1372–1388.

Hastie, R., & Park, B. (1986). The relationship between memory and judgment depends on whether the judgment task is memory based or on-line. *Psychological Review, 93,* 258–268.

Haugeland, J. (1985). *Artificial intelligence: The very idea.* Cambridge, MA: MIT Press.

Haught, J. (2000). *God after Darwin.* Boulder CO: Westview Press.

Hauser, M.D. (2000). *Wild minds: What animals really think*. New York: Henry Holt and Company.

Hauser, M.D. (1996). *The evolution of communication*. Cambridge, MA: MIT Press.

Hauser, M.D., Kralik, J., Botto-Mahan, C., Garrett, M., & Oser, J. (1995). Self-recognition in primates: Phylogeny and the salience of species-typical features. *Proceedings of the National Academy Sciences USA, 92*, 10811–10814.

Hauser, M.D., Teixidor, P., Field, L., & Flaherty R. (1993). Food-elicited calls in chimpanzees: Effects of food quantity and divisibility. *Animal Behavior, 45*, 817–819.

Hausler, M.H., & Schmid, P. (1995). Comparisons of the pelves of Sts 14 and AL 288–1. *Journal of Human Evolution, 29*, 363–383.

Hawkes, K. (1993). Why hunter–gatherers work: An ancient version of the problem of public goods. *Current Anthropology, 34*, 341–361.

Hawkes, K., O'Connell, J.F., & Blurton-Jones, N.G. (1997). Hazda women's time allocation, offspring provisioning, and the evolution of long postmenopausal life spans. *Current Anthropology, 38*, 551–577.

Hawkes, K., O'Connell, J.F., Blurton-Jones, N.G., Alvarez, H., & Charnov, E.L. (1998). Grandmothering, menopause, and the evolution of human life histories. *Proceedings of the National Academy of Sciences USA, 95*, 1336–1339.

Hayashi, R.H. (1979). Physiological adjustments in pregnancy. In R.W. Huff & C.J. Pauerstein (Eds.), *Human reproduction: Physiology and pathophysiology* (pp. 310–331). New York: Wiley.

Hayes, K.J., & Hayes, C. (1951). The intellectual development of a home-raised chimpanzee. *Proceedings of the American Philosophical Society, 95*, 105–109.

Henshaw, S.K., Forrest, J.D., & Blaine, E.B. (1984). Abortion services in the United States. *Family Planning Perspectives, 16*, 119–127.

Hertz, R.S., & Cahill, E.D. (1997). Differential use of sensory information in sexual behavior as a function of gender. *Human Nature, 8*, 275–286.

Hewlett, B.S. (1988). Sexual selection and paternal investment among Aka Pymies. In L. Betzig, M. Borgerhoff Mulder, & P. Turke (Eds.), *Human reproductive behaviour: A Darwinian perspective*. New York: Cambridge University Press.

Hickok, G. Bellugi, U., & Klima, E.S. (1996).The neurobiology of sign language and its implications for the neural basis of language. *Nature, 381*, 699–702.

Hill, A., Ward, S., Deino, A., Curtis, G., & Drake, R. (1992). Earliest *Homo. Nature, 355*, 719–722.

Hill, C.T., Rubin, L., & Peplau, L.A. (1976). Breakups before marriage: The end of 103 affairs. *Journal of Social Issues, 32*, 147–168.

Hill, E.M., & Low, B. (1990). Contemporary abortion patterns: A life history approach. *Ethology and Sociobiology, 13*, 35–48.

Hill, E., Nocks, E., & Gardner, L. (1987). Physical attractiveness: Manipulation by physique and status displays. *Ethology and Sociobiology, 8*, 143–154.

Hill, E., & Wenzl, P.A. (1981). Variation in ornamentation and behavior in a discotheque for females observed at different menstrual phases. Paper presented at the annual meeting of the Animal Behavior Society, Knoxville TN.

Hill, J.P., Holmbeck, G.N., Marlow, L., Green, T.M., & Lynch, M.E. (1985). Menarcheal status and parent-child relations in families of seventh-grade girls. *Journal of Youth and Adolescence, 14*, 301–316.

Hill, K., & Hurtado, M. (1996). *Demographic/life history of Ache foragers*. Hawthorne, NY: Aldine de Gruyter.

Hill, K., & Kaplan, H. (1994). On why male foragers hunt and share food. *Current Anthropology, 34*, 701–706.

Hill, K., & Kaplan, H. (1988). Trade-offs in male and female reproductive strategies among the Ache. In L. Betzig, M. Borgerhoff Mulder, & P. Turke (Eds.), *Human reproductive behavior: A Darwinian perspective* (pp. 277–306). New York: Cambridge University Press.

Hirshleifer, J. (1987). On the emotions as guarantors of threats and promises. In J. Dupre (Ed.), *The latest on the best: Essays on evolution and optimality* (pp. 307–326). Cambridge, MA: Bradford Books.

Hobson, R.P. (1993). *Autism and the development of mind*. Hillsdale NJ: Lawrance Erlbaum.

Hoch, S.J., & Tschirgi, J.E. (1983). Cue redundancy and extra-logical inferences in a deductive reasoning task. *Memory and Cognition, 11,* 200–209.

Hockett, C.F. (1963). The problem of universals in language. In J.H. Grenberg (Ed.), *Universals of language*. Cambridge, MA: MIT Press.

Hoffman, D.D. (1998). *Visual intelligence: How we create what we see*. New York: W.W. Norton.

Hoffman, M.L. (1977). Sex differences in empathy and related behaviors. *Psychological Bulletin, 84*, 712–722.

Hogan, R. (1983). A socioanalytic theory of personality. In M.M. Page (Ed.), *Personality: Current theory and research* (pp. 55–89). Lincoln, NB: University of Nebraska Press.

Holden, C. (1999). Neanderthals left speechless? *Science, 283*, 1111.

Holland, B., & Rice, W.R. (1999). Experimental removal of sexual selection reverses intersexual antagonistic coevolution and removes reproductive load. *Proceedings of the National Academy of Science USA, 96*, 5083–5088.

Holloway, R.L. (1979). Brain size, allometry, and reorganization: Toward a synthesis. In M. Hahn, C. Jensen, & B. Dudek (Eds.), *Development and evolution of brain size*. New York: Academic Press.

Holloway, R.L. (1981a). Revisiting the South African Taung australopithecine endocast: The position of the lunate sulcus as determined by the stereoplotting technique. *American Journal of Physcial Anthropology, 56*, 43–58.

Holloway, R.L. (1981b). Culture, symbols, and human brain evolution. *Dialectical Anthropology, 5*, 287–303.

Holloway, R.L. (1984). The Taung endocast and the lunate sulcus: A rejection of the hypothesis of its anterior position. *American Journal of Physical Anthropology, 64*, 285–287.

Holloway, R.L. (1996). Evolution of the hominid brain. In A. Lock & C.R. Peters (Eds.), *The handbook of symbolic evolution* (pp. 74–125). Oxford, UK: Oxford University Press.

Hood, B. (1995). Gravity rules for 2–4-year-olds? *Cognitive Development, 10*, 577–598.

Hood, B., Hauser, M.D., Anderson, L., & Santos, L. (1999). Gravity biases in a non-human primate? *Developmental Science, 2*, 35–41.

Hopkins, W.D. (1996). Chimpanzee handedness revisited: 55 years since Finch (1941). *Psychonomic Bulletin and Review, 3*, 449–57.

Hopkins, W.D., & Leavens, D.A. (1998). Hand use and gestural communication in chimpanzees (*Pan troglodytes*). *Journal of Comparative Psychology, 112*, 95–99.

Hopkins, W.D., & Rabinowitz, D.M. (1997). Manual specialisation and tool use in captive chimpanzees (*Pan troglodytes*): The effect of unimanual and bimanual strategies on hand preference. *Laterality, 2*, 267–277.

Hopkins, W.D., & Savage-Rumbaugh, E.S. (1991). Vocal communication as a function of differential rearing experiences in *Pan paniscus*. *International Journal of Primatology, 12*, 559–583.

Houde, A.E. (1997). *Sex, color and mate choice in guppies.* Princeton, NJ: Princeton University Press.

Howell, N. (1979). *Demography of the dobe !Kung.* New York: Academic Press.

Hrdy, S.B. (1977). *The langurs of Abu.* Cambridge, MA: Harvard University Press.

Hrdy, S.B. (1979). Infanticide among animals: A review, classification, and examination of the implications for the reproductive strategies of females. *Ethology and Sociobiology, 1*, 13–40.

Hrdy, S.B. (1981). *The woman that never evolved.* Cambride, MA: Havard University Press.

Humphrey, N.K. (1983). *Consciousness regained.* Oxford, UK: Oxford University Press.

Humphrey, N.K (1992). *A history of the mind.* New York: Simon & Schuster.

Humphrey, N. (1998, October). *Necessity as the mother of invention: How cognitive deficit may have advanced the human mind.* Paper presented at the Human Cognitive Specializations conference, University of Louisiana, New Iberia, LA.

Hunt, M. (1974). *Sexual Behavior in the 70's.* Chicago: Playboy Press.

Huxley, R.R. (2000). Nausea and vomiting in early pregnancy: Its role in placental development. *Obstetrics & Gynecology, 95*, 779–782.

Hyatt, C.W., & Hopkins, W.D. (1994). Self-awareness in bonobos and chimpanzees: A comparative perspective. In S.T. Parker, R.W. Mitchell, & M.L. Boccia (Eds.), *Self-awareness in animals and humans: Developmental perspectives* (pp. 248–253). Cambridge, UK: Cambridge University Press

Inglehart, R. (1990). *Culture shift in advanced industrial society.* Princeton, NJ: Princeton University Press.

Ingman, M., Kaessmann, H., Paabo, S., & Gyllensten, U. (2000). Mitochondrial genome variation and the origin of modern humans. *Nature, 408*, 708–713.

Insel, T.R. (2000). Toward a neurobiology of attachment. *Review of General Psychology, 4*, 176–185.

Irons, W. (1979). Natural selection, adaptation, and human social behavior. In N. A. Chagnon and W. Irons (Eds.), *Evolutionary biology and human social behavior: An anthropological perspective* (pp. 4–39). North Scituate, MA: Duxbury.

Isaac, B. (1987). Throwing and human evolution. *African Archeological Review, 5*, 3–17.

Isaac, G.L. (1986). Foundation stones: Early artifacts as indicators of activities and abilities. In G.N. Bailey and P. Callow (Eds.), *Stone Age prehistory.* Cambridge, UK: Cambridge University Press.

Isbell, L.A., & Young, T.P. (1996). The evolution of bipedalism in hominids and reduced group size in chimpanzees. *Journal of Human Evolution, 30*, 389–397.

Iwamoto, T., & Dunbar, R.I.M (1983). Thermoregulation, habitat quality and the behavioural ecology of gelada baboons. *Journal of Animal Ecology, 52*, 357–366.

Iwaniuk, A.N., Nelson, J.E., & Pellis, S.M. (2001). Do big-brained animals play more? Comparative analyses of play and relative brain size in mammals. *Journal of Comparative Psychology, 115*, 29–41.

Izard, C.E. (1977). *Human emotions.* New York: Plenum Press.

Izquierdo, I., & McGaugh, J. (1985). Effect of a novel experience prior to training or testing on retention of an inhibitory avoidance response in mice: Involvement of an opioid system. *Behavioral and Neural Biology, 44*, 228–238.

Jablonski, N.G., & Chaplin, G. (1993). Origin of habitual terrestrial bipedalism in the ancestor of Hominidae. *Journal of Human Evolution, 24*, 259–280.

Jacob, F. (1982). *The possible and the actual.* Seattle: University of Washington Press.

Jahoda, G. (1980). Sex and ethnic differences on a spatial-perceptual task: Some hypotheses tested. *British Journal of Psychology, 71*, 425–431.

Janicki, M., & Krebs, D.L. (1998). Evolutionary approaches to culture. In C. Crawford & D.L. Krebs (Eds.), *The handbook of evolutionary psychology* (pp. 163–208). Mahwah, NJ: L. Erlbaum.

Janov, A. (2000). *The biology of love.* Amherst, NY: Prometheus Books.

Jansson, L., & Lars-Govan, O. (1982). Behavioral treatments for agoraphobia: An evaluative review. *Clinical Psychology Review, 2*, 353–375.

Jardine, R., & Martin, N-G. (1983). Spatial ability and throwing accuracy. *Behavior Genetics, 13*, 331–340.

Jellema, L.M., Latimer, B., & Walker, A. (1993). The skull. In A. Walker & R. Leakey (Eds.), *The Nariokotome* Homo erectus *skeleton* (pp. 294–325). Cambridge MA: Harvard University Press.

Jensen, A.R. (1978). How much can we boost IQ and scholastic achievement? *Harvard Educational Review, 11,* 1–223.

Jerison, H. J. (1973). *The evolution of the brain and intelligence.* New York: Academic Press.

Jerne, N.K. (1985). The generative grammar of the immune system. *Science, 229,* 1057–1059.

Jessor, S.L., & Jessor, R. (1974). Materal ideology and adolescent problem behavior. *Developmental Psychology, 10,* 246–254.

Johanson, D.C., & Edey, M.E. (1981). *Lucy: The beginings of humankind.* New York: Simon & Schuster.

Johanson, D.C., & White, T.D. (1979). A systematic assessment of early African hominids. *Science, 203,* 321–330.

John Paul II (1997). The Pope's message on evolution. *Quarterly Review of Biology, 72,* 377–383.

Johnson, S.P., & Aslin, R.N. (1995). Perception of object unity in 2-month-old infants. *Developmental Psychology, 31,* 739–745.

Johnston, V.S. (1999). *Why we feel: The science of human emotion.* Cambridge, MA: Perseus Books.

Johnston, V.S., & Franklin, M. (1993). Is beauty in the eye of the beholder? *Ethology and Sociobiology, 14(3),* 183–199.

Jolly, A. (1985). *The evolution of primate behavior.* New York: MacMillan.

Jolly, A. (1998). Pair-bonding, female aggression, and the evolution of lemur societies. *Folia Primatologica, 69*(Suppl.), 1–13.

Jolly, A. (1999). *Lucy's legacy: Sex and intelligence in human evolution.* Cambridge, MA: Harvard University Press.

Jones, B., & Mishkin, M. (1972). Limbic lesions and the problems of stimulus-reinforcement associations. *Experimental Neurology, 36,* 362–377,

Jones, M.C. (1957). The later careers of boys who were early- or late-maturing. *Child Development, 28,* 113–128.

Jones, M.C. (1965). Psychological correlates of somatic development. *Child Development, 36,* 899–911.

Jones, M.C., & Bayley, N. (1950). Physcial maturing among boys as related to behavior. *Journal of Educational Psychology, 41,* 129–148.

Jorde, L.B., Bamshad, M., & Rogers, A.R. (1998). Using mitochondrial and nuclear DNA markers to reconstruct human evolution. *BioEssays, 20,* 126–136.

Judd, D.B., & Kelly, K.L. (1965). The ISCC-NBS method of designating colors and a dictionary of color names (2nd ed.). *US National Bureau of Standards Circular 553.* Washington, DC: US Government Printing Office.

Jungers, W.L. (1988). Relative joint size and hominid locomotor adaptations with implications for the evolution of hominid bipedalism. *Journal of Human Evolution, 17,* 247.

Jurgens, U., Kirzinger, A., & von Cramon, D. (1982). The effects of deep-reaching lesions in the coritcal face area on phonation. A combined case report and experimental monkey study. *Cortex, 18,* 125–139.

Kagan, J. (2000). Human morality is distinctive. *Journal of Consciousness Studies, 7(1–2),* 46–48.

Kahneman, D., & Tversky, A. (1984). Choices, values, and frames. *American Psychologist, 39,* 341–350.

Kanwisher, N. (2000). Domain specificity in face perception. *Nature Neuroscience, 3,* 759.

Kanwisher, N., McDermott, J., & Chun, M.M. (1997). The fusiform face area: A module in human extrastriate cortex specialized for face perception. *Journal of Neuroscience, 17,* 4302–4311.

Karnow, S. (1983). *Vietnam: A history.* New York: Penguin Books.

Kater, M.H. (1989). *Doctors under Hitler.* Chapel Hill: University of North Carolina Press.

Katkin, E.S., Wiens, S., & Ohman, A. (2001). Nonconscious fear conditioning, visceral perception, and the development of gut feelings. *Psychological Science, 12,* 366–370.

Kauffman, S. (1995). *At home in the universe.* New York: Oxford University Press

Ke, Y., Su, B., Song, X., Lu, D., Chen, L., Li, H., et al. (2001). African origin of modern humans in East Asia: A tale of 12,000 Y Chromosomes. *Science, 292,* 1151–1153.

Keeley, J.H. (1977). The functions of Paleolithic flint tools. *Scientific American, 237,* 108–127.

Keeley, L.H. (1996). *War before civilization.* New York: Oxford University Press.

Keeley, L.H., & Toth, N. (1981). Microwear polishes on early stone tools from Koobi Fora, Kenya. *Nature, 293,* 464–465.

Kegl, J., & Iwata, G.A.(1989). *Lenguaje de signos Nicaraguense: A pidgin sheds light on the "Creole" ASL.* Proceedings of the 4th annual meeting of the Pacific Linguistics Society, Eugene, OR.

Keightley, P.D., & Eyre-Walker, A. (2000). Deleterious mutations and the evolution of sex. *Science, 290,* 331–333.

Kemp, S. (1990). *Medieval psychology.* Westport, CT: Greenwood Press.

Kemp, S. (1996). *Cognitive psychology in the Middle Ages.* Westport, CT: Greenwood Press.

Kempenaers, B., Everding, S., Bishop, C., Boag, P., & Robertson, R.J. (2001). Extra-pair paternity and the reproductive role of male floaters in the tree swallow (*Tachycineta bicolor*). *Behavioral Ecology and Sociology, 49,* 251–259.

Kenrick, D.T., Dantchik, A., & MacFarlane, S. (1983). Personality, environment and criminal behavior: An evolutionary perspective. In W.S. Laufer & J.M. Day (Eds.), *Personality theory, moral development and criminal behavior* (pp. 217–242). Lexington, KY: Lexington Books.

Kenrick, D.T., Gutierres, S.E, & Goldberg, L. (1989). Influence of erotica on ratings of strangers and mates. *Journal of Experimental Social Psychology, 25,* 159–167.

Kenrick, D.T., & Keefe, R.C. (1992). Age preferences in mates reflect sex differences in reproductive strategies. *Behavioral and Brain Sciences, 15,* 75–133.

Kenrick, D.T., Keefe, R.C., Gabrielidis, C., & Cornelius, J.S. (1996). Adolescents' age preferences for dating partners: Support for an evolutionary model of life history patterns. *Child Development, 67,* 1499–1511.

Kenrick, D.T., Neuberg, S.L., Zierk, K.L., & Krones, J.M. (1994). Evolution and social cognition: Contrast effects as a function of sex, dominance and physical attractiveness. *Personality and Social Psychology Bulletin, 20,* 210–217.

Kenrick, D.T., Sadalla, E.K., Groth, G., & Trost, M.R. (1990). Evolution, traits, and the stages of human courtship: Qualifying the parental investment model. *Journal of Personality, 58,* 97–115.

Kenrick, D.T., Sadalla, E.K., & Keefe, R.C. (1998). Evolutionary cognitive psychology: The missing heart of modern cognitive science. In C. Crawford & D.L. Krebs (Eds.), *Handbook of evolutionary psychology* (pp. 485–514). Mahwah, NJ: Erlbaum.

Kessin, R.H., & Van Lookeren Campagne, M.M. (1992). The development of a social amoeba. *American Scientist, 80,* 556–565.

Kessler, R.C., McGonagle, K.A., Zhao, S., Nelson, C.B., Hughes, M., Eshelman, S., et al. (1994). Lifetime and 12-month prevalence of DSM-III-R psychiatric disorders in the United States: Results from the national comorbidity survey. *Archives of General Psychiatry, 51,* 8–19.

Keverne, E.B. (1996), Genomic imprinting and the differential roles of parental genomes in brain development. *Developmental Brain Research, 92,* 91.

Keverne, E.B., Martinez, N.D., & Tuite, B. (1989). Beta-endorphin concentrations in cerebrospinal fluid of monkeys are influenced by grooming relationships. *Psychoneuroendocrinology, 14,* 155–161.

Kinsey, A.C., Pomeroy, W.B., & Martin, C.E. (1948). *Sexual behavior in the human male.* Philadelphia: Saunders.

Kinsey, A.C., Pomeroy, W.B., & Martin, C.E. (1953). *Sexual behavior in the human female.* Philadelphia: Saunders.

Kitcher, P. (1993). The evolution of human altruism. *Journal of Philosophy, 90,* 497–516.

Klein, R. (2000). Archeology and the evolution of human behavior. *Evolutionary Anthropology, 9,* 17–36.

Klein, R.G. (1999). *The human career: Human biological and cultural origins.* Chicago: University of Chicago Press.

Klinger, E. (1998). The search for meaning in evolutionary perspective and its clinical implications. In P.T.P. Wong & P.S. Fry (Eds.), *The human quest for meaning: A handbook of psychological research and clinical applications* (pp. 27–50). Mahwah, NJ: Lawrence Erlbaum Associates.

Knauft, B.M. (1991). Violence and sociality in human evolution. *Current Anthropology, 32,* 391–428.

Knecht, H. (1993). Early Upper Paleolithic approaches to bone and antler projectile technolgy. In G. Peterkin, H. Bricker, & P. Mellars (Eds.), *Hunting and animal exploitation in the later Palaeolithic and Mesolithic of Eurasia* (pp. 33–48). Washington, D.C.: The American Anthropological Association.

Knight, C. (1991). *Blood relations: Menstruation and the origins of culture.* New Haven, CT: Yale University Press.

Knight, C. (1998). Ritual speech coevolution: A solution to the problem of deception. In J.R. Hurford, M. Studdert-Kennedy, & C. Knight (Eds.), *Approaches to the evolution of Language: Social and cognitive bases* (pp. 68–91). Cambridge, MA: Cambridge University Press.

Knight, C.D., Power, C., & Watts, I. (1995). The human symbolic revolution: A Darwinian account. *Cambridge Archeological Journal, 5(1),* 75–114.

Koenig, R. (2001). Creationism takes root where Europe, Asia meet. *Science, 292,* 1286–1287.

Kohlberg, L. (1969). Stage and sequence: The cognitive developmental approach to socialization. In D.A. Goslin (Ed.), *Handbook of socialization theory of research* (pp. 347–480). Chicago: Rand McNally.

Kohlberg, L., & Candee, D. (1984). The relationship of moral judgment to moral action. In W.M. Kurtines & L. Gewirtz (Eds.), *Morality, moral behavior, and moral development* (pp. 52–73). New York: John Wiley & Sons.

Kortlandt, A. (1972). *New perspectives on ape and human evolution.* Amsterdam: Stichting voor Psychobiologie.

Kotovsky, L., & Baillargeon, R. (1998). Calibration-based reasoning about collision events in 11-month-old infants. *Cognition, 67,* 311–51.

Kozlowski, J.K. (1990). A multi-aspectual approach to the origins of the Upper Palaeolithic in Europe. In P. Mellars (Ed.), *The emergence of modern humans: An archaeological perspective* (pp. 419–437). Edinburgh: Edinburgh University Press.

Krebs, D.L. (1998). The evolution of moral behaviors. In C. Crawford and D.L. Krebs (Eds.), *Handbook of evolutionary psychology: Ideas, issues and applications* (pp. 337–368). Mahwah, NJ: Lawrence Erlbaum Associates.

Krebs, D. (2000). As moral as we need to be. *Journal of Consciousness Studies, 7(1–2),* 139–143.

Krebs, J.R., & Dawkins, R. (1984). Animal signals: Mind-reading and manipulation. In J.R. Krebs, N.B. Davies (Eds.), *Behavioral ecology: An evolutionary approach* (2nd ed.) (pp. 380–402). Oxford, UK: Blackwell Scientific Publications.

Krings, M., Stone, A., Schmitz, R.W., Krainitzki, H., Soneking, M., & Paabo, S. (1997). Neanderthal DNA sequences and the origin of modern humans. *Cell, 90,* 19–30.

Krout, M.H. (1931). The psychology of children's lies. *Journal of Abnormal and Social Psychology, 26,* 1–27.

Kummer, H. (1995). *Inquest of the sacred baboon: A scientist's journey.* Princeton, NJ: Princeton University Press.

Kummer, H.W., Gotz, W., & Angst, W. (1974). Triadic differentiation: An inhibitory process protecting pair bonds in baboons. *Behavior, 49,* 62–87.

Kunzig, R. (1999, August). Learning to love Neanderthals. *Discover,* 69–75.

Lacreuse, A., Parr, L.A., Smith, H.M., & Hopkins, W.D. (1999). Hand preference for a haptic task in chimpanzees (*Pan troglodytes*). *International Journal of Primatology, 20,* 867–881.

LaFreniere, P.J. (2000). *Emotional development: A biosocial perspective.* Belmont, CA: Wadsworth.

Laitman, J.T., & Heimbuch, R.C. (1982). The basicranium of Plio-Pleistocene hominids as an indicator of their upper respiratory sytems. *American Journal of Physical Anthropology, 59,* 323–344.

Lancaster, J.B. (1973). On the evolution of tool-using behavior. In C.L. Brace & J. Metress (Eds.), *Man in evolutionary perspective* (pp. 79–90). New York: Wiley.

Landolt, J.A., Lalumiere, M.L., & Quinsey, V.L. (1995). Sex differences in intra-sex variations in human mating tactics: An evolutionary approach. *Ethology and Sociobiology, 15,* 3–24.

Lane, H. (1984). *When the mind hears.* New York: Random House.

Langlois, J.H., & Roggman, L.A. (1990). Attractive faces are only average. *Psychological Science, 1,* 115–121.

Laumann, E.O., Michael, R.T., Gagnon, J.H., & Michaels, S. (1994). *The social organization of sexuality: Sexual practices in the United States.* Chicago: University of Chicago Press.

Lavery, J.J., & Foley, P.J. (1963). Altruism or arousal in the rat? *Science, 140,* 172–173.

Law, D.J., Pellegrino, J.W., Mitchell, S.R., Fischer, S.C., McDonald, T.P., & Hunt, E.B. (1993). Perceptual and cognitive factors governing performance in comparative arrival-time judgments. *Journal of Experimental Psychology: Human Perception and Performance, 19,* 1183–1199.

Lawick-Goodall, J. van (1968). The behavior of free-living chimpanzees in the Gombe Stream Reserve. *Animal Behavior Monographs, 1,* 161–311.

Leakey, L. (1976). A summary and discussion of the archeological evidence from Bed I and Bed II, Olduvai Gorge, Tanzania. In G.L. Isaac and E.R. McGowan (Eds.), *Human origins: Louis Leakey and the East African evidence* (pp. 431–459). Menlo Park, CA: Benjamin.

Leakey, M., & Hay, R. L. (1979). Pliocene footprints in the Laetolil Beds at Laetoli, northern Tanzania. *Nature, 278,* 317–323.

Leakey R.E., & Lewin R. (1992): *Origins reconsidered: In search of what makes us human.* New York: Doubleday.

Leakey, R.E.F., & Walker, A. (1976). *Australopithecus, Homo erectus,* and the single species hypothesis. *Nature* 261, 572–574.

Leakey, R.E.F., & Walker, A. (1985). Further hominids from the Plio-Pleistocene of Koobi Fora, Kenya. *American Journal of Physical Anthropology* 67, 135–163.

LeBoeuf, B., & Reiter, J., (1988). Lifetime reproductive success in Northern elephant seals. In T.H. Clutton-Brock (Ed.), *Reproductive success: Studies of individual variation in contrasting breeding systems* (pp. 344–383). Chicago: University of Chicago Press.

Lecours, A.R., & Joanette, Y. (1980). Linguistic and other aspects of paroxysmal aphasia. *Brain and Language, 10,* 1–23.

Ledbetter, D.H., & Basen, J.A. (1982). Failure to demonstrate self-recognition in gorillas. *American Journal of Primatology, 2,* 307–310.

LeDoux, J. (1996). *The emotional brain: The mysterious underpinnings of emotional life.* New York: Simon & Schuster.

Lee, P.C. (1994). Social structure and evolution. In P. Slater & T. Halliday (Eds.), *Behavior and evolution* (pp. 266–303). Cambridge, UK: Cambridge University Press.

Lee, R.B. (1979). *The !Kung San: Men, Women and Work in a Foraging Society.* Cambridge, UK: Cambridge University Press.

Lee, R.B., & DeVore, I. (1968). *Man the hunter.* Chicago: University of Chicago Press.

Leekam, S., & Perner, J. (1991). Does the autistic child have a metarepresentational deficit? *Cognition, 40,* 203–218.

Leger, D.W., Owings, D.H., & Gelfand, D.L. (1980). Single-note vocalizations of California ground squirrels: Graded signals and situation-specificity of predator and socially evoked calls. *Zeitschift fur Tierpsychologie, 52,* 227–246.

Leibowitz, A., Eisen, M., & Chow, W.K. (1985). An economic model of teenage pregnancy decision-making. *Demography, 23,* 67–77.

Lerner, G. (1986). *The creation of patriarchy.* New York: Oxford University Press.

Lerner, I.M., & Libby, W.J. (1976). *Heredity, evolution, and society.* San Francisco: W.H. Freeman.

Lerner, M.J., Somers, D.G., Reid, D., Chiriboga, D., & Tierney, M. (1991). Adult children as caregivers: Egocentric biases in judgments of sibling contributions. *Gerontologist, 31,* 746–755.

Leslie, A.M. (1982). The perception of causality in infants. *Perception, 11,* 173–186.

Leslie, A.M., & Keeble, S. (1987). Do six-month-old infants perceive causality? *Cognition, 25,* 265–288.

Leslie, A.M., & Thaiss, L. (1992). Domain specificity in conceptual development: Neuropsychological evidence from autism. *Cognition, 43,* 225–251.

Less, A. (1983). Introduction. In J. Von Lang & C. Cibyll (Eds.), *Eichmann interrogated* (pp. v–xxii). New York: Farrar, Strauss, Giroux.

Lethmate, J., & Ducker, G. (1973). Untersuchungen zum selbsterkennen im spiegel bei orangutans und einigen anderen affenarten. *Zeitschrift fur Tierpsychology, 33,* 248–269.

Lewin, R. (1987). *Bones of contention.* New York: Simon and Schuster.

Lewin, R. (1998). *Principles of human evolution.* London: Blackwell Science.

Lewis, H.B. (1971). *Shame and guilt in neurosis.* New York: International Universities Press.

Lewis, K.P. (2000). A comparative study of primate play behaviour: Implications for the study of cognition. *Folia Primatologica, 71,* 417–421.

Lhermitte, F. (1983). "Utilization behaviour" and its relation to lesions of the frontal lobes. *Brain, 106,* 237–255.

Lhermitte, F., Pillon, B., & Serdaru, M. (1986). Human anatomy and the frontal lobes. Part I: Imitation and utilization behavior: A neuropsychological study of 75 patients. *Annals of Neurology, 19,* 326–334.

Lieberman, D.E. (1993). The rise and fall of seasonal mobility among hunter–gatherers: The case of the Southern Levant. *Current Anthropology, 34,* 599–631.

Lieberman, D.E., & Shea, J.J. (1994). Behavioral differences between archaic and modern humans in the Levantine Mousterian. *American Anthropologist, 96,* 300–332.

Lieberman, P. (1975). *On the origins of language: An introduction to the evolution of speech.* New York: Macmillan.

Lieberman, P. (1984). *The biology and the evolution of language.* Cambridge, MA: Harvard University Press.

Lieberman, P. (1991). *Uniquely human: The evolution of speech, thought, and selfless behavior.* Cambridge, MA: Harvard University Press.

Lieberman, P. (1998). *Eve spoke: Human language and human evolution.* New York: W.W. Norton and Company.

Lightcap, J.L., Kurland J.A., & Burgess, R.L. (1982). Child abuse: A test of some predictions from evolutionary biology. *Ethology and Sociobiology, 3,* 61–67.

Limongelli, L., Boysen, S.T., & Visalberghi, E. (1995). Comprehension of cause-effect relations in a tool-using task by chimpanzees (*Pan troglodytes*). *Journal of Comparative Psychology, 109,* 18–26.

Lindberg, D. (1992). *The beginnings of Western science.* Chicago: University of Chicago Press.

Lindly, J.M., & Clark, G.A. (1990). Symbolism and modern human origins. *Current Anthropology, 31,* 233–261.

Linn, M.C., & Peterson, A.C. (1986). Emergence and characterization of sex differences in spatial abilities: A meta-analysis. *Child Development, 56,* 1479–1498.

Littlefield, C.H., & Rushton, J.P. (1986). When a child dies: The sociobiology of bereavement. *Journal of Personality and Social Psychology, 51,* 797–802.

Lively, C.M. (1987). Red Queen hypothesis supported by parasitism in sexual and clonal fish. *Nature, 344,* 864–866.

Livson, N., & Peskin, H. (1980). Perspectives on adolescence from longitudinal research. In J. Adelson (Ed.), *Handbook of adolescent psychology.* New York: Wiley.

Locke, A. (1999). On the recent origin of symbolically mediated language and its implications for psychological science. In M.C. Corballis & S.E.G. Lea (Eds.), *The descent of mind* (pp. 324–355). Oxford, UK: Oxford University Press.

Lomborg, B. (1993). The structure of solutions in the iterated prisoner's dilemma. Paper presented at Gruter Institute Conference on the Uses of Biology in the Study of Law, Squaw Valley, CA.

Lovejoy, O.C. (1981). The origin of man. *Science, 221,* 341–350.

Lovejoy, O.C. (1988). The evolution of human walking. *Scientific American, 259,* 118–125.

Low, B. (1991). Reproductive life in 19th-century Sweden: An evolutionary perspective on demographic phenomena. *Ethology and Sociobiology, 12,* 411–448.

Low, B.S. (1979). Sexual selection and human ornamentation. In N. Chagnon & W. Irons (Eds.), *Evolutionary Biology and Human Social Behavior* (pp. 462–486). North Sciuate, MA: Duxbury Press.

Low, B.S. (1998). The evolution of human life histories. In C. Crawford & D.L. Krebs (Eds.), *Handbook of evolutionary psychology* (pp. 131–161). Mahwah, NJ: L. Erlbaum.

Low, B.S. (2000). *Why sex matters: A Darwinian look at human behavior.* Princeton, NJ: Princeton University Press.

Low, B., Alexander, R.M., & Noonan, K.M. (1987). Human hips, breasts, and buttocks: Is fat deceptive? *Ethology and Sociobiology, 8,* 249–257.

Luebbert, M.C. (1999). The survival value of forgiveness. In D.H. Rosen & M.C. Luebbert (Eds.), *The evolution of the psyche* (pp. 169–187). Westport, CT.: Praeger Pub.

Luria, A.R. (1976). *Cognitive development: Its cultural and social foundations.* Cambridge, MA: Harvard University Press.

Lykken, D. (1999). *Happiness.* New York: Golden Books.

Lykken, D.T., & Tellegen, A. (1993). Is human mating adventitious or the result of lawful choice? A twin study of mate selection. *Journal of Personality and Social Psychology, 65,* 56–68.

Lynn, R. (1992). Sex differences on the differential aptitude test in British and American adolescents. *Educational Psychology, 12,* 101–106.

MacDonald, K. (1990). Mechanisms of sexual egalitarianism in Western Europe. *Ethology and Sociobiology, 11,* 195–238.

MacDonald, K. (1992). Warmth as a developmental construct: An evolutionary analysis. *Child Development, 63,* 753–773.

MacFarlane, A. (1977). *The psychology of childbirth.* Cambridge, MA: Harvard University Press.

MacKay, D.G. (1987). *The organization of perception and action: A theory for language and other cognitive skills.* New York: Springer.

Mackey, W.C. (1984). The placenta: The celibate sibling. *Journal of Human Evolution, 13,* 449–455.

MacLarnon, A. (1993). The vertebrate canal. In A. Walker & R. Leakey (Eds.), *The Nariokotome* Homo erectus *skeleton* (pp. 359–390). Cambridge MA: Harvard University Press.

MacLean, P.D. (1990). *The triune brain in evolution: Role of paleocerebral functions.* New York: Plenum Press.

MacLean, P.D. (1993). Cerebral evolution of emotion. In M. Lewis & J.M. Haviland (Eds.), *Handbook of emotion* (pp. 67–86). New York: Guilford.

MacNeilage, P.F., Studdert-Kennedy, M.G., & Lindblom, B. (1987). Primate handedness reconsidered. *Behavioral and Brain Sciences, 10,* 247–303.

Mahoney, S.A. (1980). Cost of locomotion and heat balance during rest and running from 0 to 55 degrees C. in a patas monkey. *Journal of Applied Physiology: Respiratory, Environmental, and Excercise Physiology, 49,* 789–800.

Malcolm, J.R., & Marten, K. (1982). Natural selection and the communal rearing of pups in African wild dogs (*Lycaon pictus*). *Behavioral Ecology and Sociobiology, 10,* 1–13.

Malinowski, B. (1929). *The sexual life of savages in north western Melanesia: An ethnographic account of courtship, marriage and family life among the natives of the Trobriand Islands, British New Guinea.* New York: Harcourt Brace.

Mann, J. (1992). Nurturance or negligence: Maternal psychology and behavioral preference among preterm twins. In J. Barkow, L. Cosmides, & J. Tooby (Eds.), *The adapted mind: Evolutionary psychology and the generation of culture* (pp. 367–390). New York: Oxford University Press.

Mann, V.A., Sasanuma, S., Sakuma, N., & Masaki, S. (1990). Sex differences in cognitive ablities: A cross-cultural perspective. *Neuropsychologia, 28,* 1063–1077.

Marchant, L.F., & McGrew, W.C. (1996) Laterality of limb function in wild chimpanzees of Gombe National Park: comprehensive study of spontaneous activities. *Journal of Human Evolution, 30,* 427–443

Margulis, L. (1981). *Symbiosis in cell evolution.* San Francisco: W.H. Freeman and Co.

Margulis, L., & Sagan, D. (1986). *Origins of sex: Three billion years of genetic recombination.* New Haven, CT: Yale University Press.

Margulis, L., & Sagan, D. (1991). *Mystery dance: On the evolution of human sexuality.* New York: Summit Books.

Markman, E.M. (1989). *Categorization and naming in children: Problems of induction.* Cambridge, MA: MIT Press.

Markman, E.M. (1990). Constraints children place on word meanings. *Cognitive Science, 14,* 57–77.

Markman, E.M., & Hutchinson, J.E. (1984). Children's sensitivity to constraints on word meaning: Taxonomic vs. thematic relations. *Cognitive Psychology, 16,* 1–27.

Marks, I.M. (1969). *Fears and phobias.* New York: Academic Press.

Marks, I.M. (1987). *Fears, phobias, and rituals.* New York: Oxford University Press.

Marks, I.M., Boulougouris, J., & Marset, P. (1971). Flooding versus desensitization in the treatment of phobic patients. A cross-over study. *British Journal of Psychiatry, 119,* 353–375.

Marks, I.M., & Neese, R.M. (1994). Fear and fitness: An evolutionary analysis of anxiety disorders. *Ethology and Sociobiology, 15,* 247–261.

Marks, J. (1994). Blood will tell (won't it?). *American Journal of Physical Anthropology, 94,* 59–79.

Marler, P., & Peters, S. (1989). Species differences in auditory responsiveness in early vocal learning. In R.J. Dooling & S.H. Hulse (Eds.), *The comparative psychology of audition: Perceiving complex sounds* (pp. 243–273). Hillsdale, NJ: Erlbaum.

Marler, P., & Pickert, R. (1984). Species-universal microstructure in the learned song of the swamp sparrow (*Melospiza georgiana*). *Animal Behavior, 32,* 673–689.

Marshall, J.T., Jr., & Marshall, E.R. (1976). Gibbons and their territorial songs. *Science, 193,* 235–237.

Martin, R.D. (1986). Primates: A definition. In B. Wood, L. Martin, & P. Andrews (Eds.), *Major topics in primate and human evolution.* London: Academic Press.

Martin, R.D. (1989). *Primate origins and evolution: A phylogenetic reconstruction.* London: Chapman and Hall.

Martin, R.D., Willner, L.A., & Dettling, A. (1994). The evolution of sexual size dimorphism in primates. In R.V. Short & E. Balaban (Eds.), *The differences between the sexes* (pp. 159–200). Cambridge, UK: Cambridge University Press.

Marzke, M.W. (1986). Tool use and the evolution of hominid hands and bipedality. In J.G. Else & P.C. Lee (Eds.), *Proceedings of the Tenth Congress of the International Primatology Society, 1,* 203–209. Cambridge, UK: Cambridge University Press.

Marzke, M.W. (1994). Evolution. In K.M.B. Bennett & U. Castiello (Eds.), *Insights into the reach to grasp movement* (Chapter 2). Amsterdam: Elsevier Science.

Marzke, M.W. (1996). Evolution of the hand and bipedality. In A. Lock & C.R. Peters (Eds.), *Handbook of human symbolic evolution* (pp. 126–154). Oxford, UK: Clarendon Press.

Marzke, M.W. (1997). Precision grips, hand morphology, and tools. *American Journal of Physical Anthropology, 102,* 91–110.

Mascie-Taylor, C.G.N., & Vandenberg, S. (1988). Assortative mating for IQ and personality due to propinquity and personal preference. *Behavior Genetics, 18,* 339–345.

Mason, J., & Wrangham, R. (1991). Intergroup aggression in chimpanzees and humans. *Current Anthropology, 32,* 369–390.

Mason, W.A., & Hollis, J.H. (1962). Communication between young rhesus monkeys. *Animal Behaviour, 10,* 211–221.

Mathieu, M., & Bergeron, G. (1981). Piagetian assessment on cognitive development in chimpanzee (*Pan troglodytes*). In A. B. Chiarelli & R. S. Corruccini (Eds.), *Primate behavior and sociobiology* (pp. 142–147). Berlin: Springer-Verlag.

Matsuda, H., & Harada, Y. (1990). Evolutionary stable stalk to spore ratio in cellular slime molds and the law of equalization of net incomes. *Journal of Theoretical Biology 147,* 329–344.

Matsuzawa, T. (1985). Use of numbers by a chimpanzee. *Nature, 315,* 57–59.

Matsuzawa, T. (1994). Field experiments on use of stone tools in the wild. In R.W. Wrangham, W.C. McGrew, F.B.M. de Waal, & P.G. Heltne (Eds.), *Chimpanzee cultures* (pp. 351–370). Cambridge, MA: Harvard University Press.

Matsuzawa, T. (1999). Cultural and social contexts of tool use in chimpanzees. In M.D. Hauser & M. Konishi (Eds.), *The design of animal communication.* Cambridge, MA: MIT Press.

Maynard–Smith, J. (1982). *Evolution and the theory of games.* Cambridge, UK: Cambridge University Press.

Maynard Smith, J. (1984, November). Science and myth. *Natural History, 93,* 11–24.

Mazur, A., & Booth, A. (1998). Testosterone and dominance in men. *Behavioral and Brain Sciences, 21,* 353–371.

McBurney, D.H., Gaulin, S.J.C., Devineni, T., & Adams, C. (1997). Superior spatial memory of women: Stronger evidence for the gathering hypothesis. *Evolution and Human Behavior, 18,* 165–174.

McComb, K., Packer, C., & Pusey, A. (1994). Roaring and numerical assessment in contests between groups of female lions, *Panthera leo. Animal Behaviour, 47,* 379–387.

McCrae, R.R., & John, O.P. (1992). An introduction to the five-factor model and its applications. *Journal of Personality, 60,* 175–216.

McGee, M.G. (1979). Human spatial abilities: Psychometric studies and environmental, genetic, hormonal, and neurological influences. *Psychological Bulletin, 80,* 889–918.

McGrew, W.C. (1992). *Chimpanzee material culture.* Cambridge, UK: Cambridge University Press.

McGuire, M.T., Troisi, A., & Raleigh, M.M. (1997). Depression in evolutionary context. In S. Baron-Cohen (Ed.), *The maladaptive mind.* (pp. 255–282). East Sussex, UK: Psychology Press.

McHenry, H.M. (1986). The first bipeds: A comparison of the *A. afarensis* and *A. africanus* postcranium and implications for the evoution of bipedalism. *Journal of Human Evolution, 15,* 177–191.

McHenry, H. (1991). Sexual dimorphism in *Australopithecus afarensis. Journal of Human Evolution, 20,* 21–32.

McHenry, H.M. (1992). How big were early hominids? *Evolutionary Anthropology, 1,* 15–20.

McHenry, H.M. & Berger, L.R. (1996). Apelike body proportions in *Australopithecus africanus* and their implications for the origin of *Homo. American Journal of Physical Anthropology, 22*(Suppl.), 163–164.

McHenry, H., & Berger, L.R. (1998). Body proportions in *Australopithecus afarensis* and *A. africanus* and the origin of the genus *Homo. Journal of Human Evolution, 35,* 1–22.

McKinney, H.L. (1972). *Wallace and natural selection.* New Haven, CT: Yale University Press.

McLeod, A. (2001). Changing patterns of teenage pregnancy: population-based study of small areas. *British Medical Journal, 323,* 199–203.

McPherron, S. (2000). Handaxes as a measure of the mental capabilities of early hominids. *Journal of Achaeological Science, 27,* 655–633.

Mealey, L. (1995). The sociobiology of sociopathy: An integrated model. *Behavioral and Brain Sciences, 18,* 523–541.

Mealey, L., & Mackey, W. (1990). Variation in offspring sex ratio in women of differing social status. *Ethology and Sociobiology, 11,* 83–95.

Medin, D.L., & Ross, B.H. (1997). *Cognitive psychology.* New York: Harcourt Brace.

Mellars, P.A. (1985). The ecological basis of social complexity in the Upper Paleolithic of southwestern France. In T.D. Price & J. A. Brown (Eds.), *Prehistoric hunter-gatherers: The emergence of cultural complexity* (pp. 271–297). Orlando, FL: Academic Press.

Mellars, P.A. (1989a). Major issues in the emergence of modern humans. *Current Anthropology, 30,* 349–385.

Mellars, P.A. (1989b). Technological changes across the Middle-Upper Palaeolithic transition: Technological, social, and cognitive perspectives. In P. Mellars & C. Stringer (Eds.), *The human revolution: Behavioral and biological perspectives on the origins of modern humans* (pp. 338–365). Princeton, NJ: Princeton University Press.

Mellars, P.A. (1996). *The Neanderthal legacy.* Princeton, NJ: Princeton University Press.

Melton, L. (2000, October). Womb wars. *Scientific American.* Retrieved March 14, 2002, from www.sciam.com/2000/1000issue/1000scicit6.html.

Meltzoff, A. (1995). Understanding the intentions of others: Re-enactment of intended acts by 18-month-old children. *Developmental Psychology, 24,* 838–850.

Meltzoff, A.N., & Moore, M.K. (1977). Imitations of facial and gestures by human neonates. *Nature, 198,* 75–78.

Meltzoff, A.N., & Moore, M.K. (1995). Infants' understanding of people and things: From body imitation to folk psychology. In J.L. Bermudez, A. Marcel, & N. Eilen (Eds.), *The body and the self* (pp. 43–70). Cambridge, UK: Cambridge University Press.

Mendres, K.A., & de Waal, F.B.M. (2000). Capuchins do cooperate: The advantage of an intuitive task. *Animal Behaviour, 60,* 523–529.

Miles, H.L.W. (1990). The cognitive foundations for reference in a signing orangutan. In S.T. Parker & K.R. Gibson (Eds.), *"Language" and intelligence in monkeys and apes* (pp. 511–539). Cambridge, UK: Cambridge University Press.

Miles, H.L.W. (1994). ME CHANTEK: The development of self–awareness in a signing orangutan. In S.T. Parker, R.W. Mitchell, & M.L. Boccia (Eds.), *Self-awareness in animals and humans: Developmental perspectives* (pp. 254–272). Cambridge, UK: Cambridge University Press.

Milgram, S. (1970). The experience of living in cities. *Science, 167,* 1461–1468.

Milinski, M., & Wedekind, C. (2001). Evidence for MHC-correlated perfume preferences in humans. *Behavioral Ecology, 12,* 140–149.

Miller, D.T., & Ross, M. (1975). Self-serving biases in the attribution of causality: Fact or fiction? *Psychological Bulletin 82,* 213–225.

Miller, G.F. (1995, June). Darwinian demographics of cultural production. Paper presented at the 7th Annual Meeting of the Human Behavior and Evolution Society. Santa Barbara, CA: University of California at Santa Barbara.

Miller, G.F. (1998). How mate choice shaped human nature: A review of sexual selection and human evolution. In C. Crawford & D.L. Krebs (Eds.), *Handbook of evolutionary psychology* (pp. 87–129). Mahwah, NJ: L. Erlbaum.

Miller, G.F. (1999). Sexual selection for cultural displays. In R. Dunbar, C. Knight, & C. Power (Eds.), *The evolution of culture* (pp. 71–91). Edinburgh: Edinburgh U. Press.

Miller, G.F. (2000). *The mating mind: How sexual choice shaped the evolution of human nature.* New York: Doubleday.

Miller, R.E. (1967). Experimental approaches to the physiological and behavioral concomitants of affective communication in rhesus monkeys. In S.A. Altmann (Ed.), *Social communication among primates.* Chicago: University of Chicago Press.

Mineka, S. Davidson, M., Cook, M., & Keir, R. (1984). Observational conditioning of snake fear in rhesus monkeys. *Journal of Abnormal Psychology, 93,* 355–372.

Mischel, W. (1976). *Introduction to personality* (2nd ed.). New York: Holt Rinehart & Winston.

Mitani, J.C. (1994). Ethological studies of chimpanzee vocal behavior. In R.W. Wrangham, W.C. McGrew, F.B.M. de Waal, and P.G. Heltne (Eds.), *Chimpanzee cultures.* Cambridge, MA, and London: Harvard University Press.

Mitani, J.C., & Brandt, K.L. (1994). Social factors influence the acoustic variability in the long-distance calls of male chipmanzees. *Ethology, 96,* 233–252.

Mitchell, R.W., & Anderson, J.R. (1993). Discrimination learning of scratching, but failure to obtain imitation and self-recognition in a long-tailed macaque. *Primates, 34,* 301–309.

Mithen, S. (1994). Technology and society during the Middle Pleistocene. *Cambridge Archaeological Journal, 4,* 3–32.

Mithen, S. (1996). *The prehistory of the mind.* London: Thames and Hudson.

Miyake, K., Chen, S., & Campos, J. (1985). Infant temperment, mother's mode of interaction, and attachment in Japan. In I. Bretherton & E. Waters (Eds.), Growing points in attachment theory and research. *Monographs of the Society for Research in Child Development, 50,* (1/2, Serial # 209), 276–279.

Moehlman, P. (1979). Jackel helpers and pup survival. *Nature, 277,* 382–383.

Moffitt, T.E., Caspi, A., Belsky, J., & Silva, P.A. (1992). Childhood experience and the onset of menarche: A test of a sociobiological hypothesis. *Child Development, 63,* 47–58.

Moller, A.P. (1992). Female swallow preferences for symmetrical male sexual ornaments. *Nature, 357,* 238–240.

Moller, A.P., & Pomiankowski, A. (1993). Fluctuating asymmetry and sexual selection. *Genetica, 89,* 267–279.

Moller, A.P., & Thornhill, R. (1998). Bilateral symmetry and sexual selection: A meta-analysis. *The American Naturalist, 151,* 174–192.

Morgan, E. (1985). *The descent of woman.* London: Souvenir Press.

Morris, D. (1967). *The naked ape.* New York: McGraw-Hill.

Murphy, N., & Ellis, G.F.R. (1996). *On the moral nature of the universe: Theology, cosmology, and ethics.* Minneapolis, MN: Fortress Press.

Myers, A.A., & Giller, P.S. (1988). *Analytical biogeography.* London: Chapman and Hall.

Myers, D. (2000). The funds, friends, and faith of happy people. *American Psychologist, 55,* 56–67.

Myers, D.G., & Diener, E. (1995). Who is happy? *Psychological Science, 6,* 10–19.

Nagell, K., Olguin, R.S., & Tomasello, M. (1993). Processes of social learning in the tool use of chimpanzees (*Pan troglodytes*). *Journal of Comparative Psychology, 107,* 174–186.

Neisser, U. (1993). The self-perceived. In U. Neisser (ed.), *The perceived self* (pp. 3–21). Cambridge, UK: Cambridge University Press.

Nelson, C. (2001). The development and neural basis of face recognition. *Infant and Child Development, 10,* 3–18.

Nelson, C.A. (1993). The recognition of facial expressions in infancy: Behavioral and electrophysiological correlates. In B. de Boysson–Bardies, S. de Schonen, P. Jusczyk, P. MacNeilage, & J. Morton (Eds.), *Developmental neurocognition: Face and speech processing in the first year of life* (pp. 187–193). Hingham, MA: Kluwer Academic Press.

Nelson, S.A. (1980). Factors influencing young children's use of motives and outcomes as moral criteria. *Child Development, 51,* 823–829.

Nelson-LeGall, S.A. (1985). Motive-outcome matching and outcome foreseeability: Effects on attribution of intentionality and moral judgments. *Developmental Psychology, 21,* 332–337.

Nesse, R.M. (1987). An evolutionary perspective on panic disorder and agoraphobia. *Ethology and Sociobiology, 8,* 735–835.

Nesse, R.M. (1990). Evolutionary explanations of emotions. *Human Nature, 1,* 261–289.

Nesse, R.M. (2000). Is depression an adaptation? *Archives of General Psychiatry 57,* 14–20.

Nesse, R.M., & Williams, G.C. (1994). *Why we get sick.* New York: Times Books.

Niewoehner, W.A. (2001). Behavioural inferences from the Skhul/Qafzeh early modern human hand remains. *Proceedings of the National Academy of Sciences, 98,* 2979 –2984.

Nishida, T., Hasegawa, T., Hayaki, H., Takahata, Y., & Uehara, S. (1992). Meat-sharing as a coalition strategy by an alpha male chimpanzee? In T. Nishida, W.C. McGrew, P. Marler, M. Pickford, & F.B.M. de Waal (Eds.), *Topics in primatology. Human origins* (pp. 159–174). Tokyo: University of Tokyo Press.

Noad, M.J., Cato, D.H., Bryden, M.M., Jenner, M.N., & Jenner, K.C.S. (2000). Cultural revolution in whale songs. *Nature, 408,* 537.

Noble, W., & Davidson, I. (1996). *Human evolution, language and mind: A psychological and archaeological inquiry.* Cambridge, UK: Cambridge University Press.

Noe, R. (1992). Alliance formation among male baboons: Shopping for the profitable partners. In A.H. Harcourt & F.B.M. de Waal (Eds.), *Coalitions and alliances in humans and other animals.* Oxford, UK: Oxford University Press.

Novak, M. (1996). Self-recognition in rhesus macaques. Paper presented at a meeting of the International Primatological Society, Madison, WI.

Nowak, M.A., & Sigmund, K. (1998). Evolution of indirect reciprocity by image scoring. *Nature, 393,* 573–577.

Nowak, M.A., May R.M., & Sigmund, K. (1995). The arithmetics of mutual help. *Scientific American, 272,* 50–55.

Nucci, L. (1981). Conceptions of personal issues: a domain distinct from moral or societal concepts. *Child Development, 52,* 114–121.

Numbers, R.L. (1998). *Darwinism comes to America.* Cambridge, MA: Harvard University Press.

O'Connell, J.F., Hawkes, K., & Blurton Jones, N.G. (1999). Grandmothering and the evolution of *Homo erectus. Journal of Human Evolution, 35,* 461–485.

Oakley, D.A. (1985). Cognition and imagery in animals. In D. Oakley (Ed.), *Brain and mind.* London: Methuen.

Ohman, A., & Dimberg, U. (1984). An evolutionary perspective on human social behavior. In W.M. Waid (Ed.), *Sociopsychology.* New York: Springer.

Ohman, A., Dimberg, U., & Ost, L.G. (1985). Biological constraints on the fear response. In S. Reiss & R. Bootsin (Eds.), *Theoretical issues in behavior therapy* (pp. 123–175). New York: Academic Press.

Ohman, A., Eriksson, A., & Olofsson, L. (1973). One trial learning and superior resistance to extinction of autonomic responses conditioned to potentially phobic stimuli. *Journal of Comparative and Physiological Psychology, 88,* 619–627.

Ohman, A., Flykt, A., & Esteves, F. (2001). Emotion drives attention: Detecting the snake in the grass. *Journal of Experimental Psychology, 130,* 466–478.

Oldroyd, B.P., Smolenski, A.J., Cornuet, J.-M., & Corzier, R.H. (1994). Anarchy in the beehive. *Nature, 371,* 749.

Ong, W. (1982). *Orality and literacy: The technologizing of the word.* New York: Methuen.

Oross, S., Francis, E., Mauk, D., & Fox, R. (1987). The Ames window illusion: Perception of illusory motion by human infants. Special issue: The ontogenesis of perception. *Journal of Experimental Psychology: Human Perception and Performance, 13,* 609–613.

Owens, D.D., & Owens, M.J. (1984). Helping behavior in brown hyenas. *Nature, 308,* 843–845.

Owings, D.H., Hennessy, D.F., Leger, D.W., & Gladney, A.B. (1986). Different functions of alarm calling for different time scales: a preliminary report on ground squirrels. *Behavior, 99,* 101–116.

Packer, C. (1977). Reciprocal altruism in olive baboons (*Papio anubis*). *Nature, 265,* 441–443.

Packer, C., Herbst, L., Pusey, A.E., Bygott, J. D., Hanby, J.P., Cairns, S. J., et al. (1988). Reproductive success of lions. In T.H. Clutton-Brock (Ed.), *Reproductive success* (pp. 363–383). Chicago: University of Chicago Press.

Packer, C., Lewis, S., & Pusey, A.E. (1992). A comparative analysis of non-offspring nursing. *Animal Behavior, 43,* 265–281.

Packer, C., Tatar, M., & Collins, A. (1998). Reproductive cessation in female mammals. *Nature, 392,* 807–811.

Parker, G.A. (1974). Assessment strategy and the evolution of fighting behaviour. *Journal of Theoretical Biology, 47,* 223–243.

Parker, M. (1995). Rethinking female circumcision. *Africa, 64(4),* 506–523.

Parker, S.T. (1998). A social selection model for the evolution and adaptive significance of self-conscious emotions. In M. Ferrari & R. Sternberg (Eds.), *Self-awareness: Its nature and development.* New York: The Guilford Press.

Parnell, R.J., & Buchanan-Smith, H.M. (2001). Animal behaviour: An unusual social display by gorillas. *Nature, 412,* 294.

Pascal, B. (1659) *Pensées.* Translated by W.F. Trotter. Retrieved on March 14, 2002, from www.orst.edu/instruct/phl302/texts/pascal/pensees-contents.html.

Pascalis, O., & de Schonen, S. (1994). Recognition memory in 3- to 4-day-old human neonates. *NeuroReport, 5,* 1721–1724.

Pascalis, O., de Schonen, S., Morton, J., Deruelle, C., & Fabre-Grenet, M. (1995). Mother's face recognition by neonates: a replication and extension. *Infant Behavior and Development, 18,* 79–85.

Passingham, R.E. (1982). *The human primate.* San Francisco: W. H. Freeman.

Patterson, F., & Linden, E. (1981). *The education of Koko.* New York: Owl Books.

Patterson, F.G.P., & Cohen, R.H. (1994). Self-recognition and self-awareness in lowland gorillas. In S.T. Parker, R.W. Mitchell, & M.L. Boccia (Eds.), *Self-awareness in animals and humans: Developmental perspectives* (pp. 273–290). Cambridge, UK: Cambridge University Press.

Payne, D. (1991). Characterology, media and rhetoric. In B.E. Gronbeck, T.J. Farrell, & P. Soukup (Eds.), *Media, consciousness and culture: Explorations of Walter Ong's thought* (pp. 223–252). Newbury Park, CA: Sage.

Payne, K.B., & Payne, R.S. (1985). Large-scale changes over 19 years in songs of humpback whales in Bermuda. *Zeitschrift fur Tierpsychologie, 68,* 89–114.

Payne, K.B., Tyack, P., & Payne, R.S. (1984). Progessive changes in the songs of humpback whales (*Megaptera novaeangliae*): A detailed analysis of two seasons in Hawaii. In R. Payne (Ed.), *Communication and behavior of whales* (pp. 9–57). Boulder, CO: Westview.

Pecins-Thompson, M., Brown, N., & Bethea, C. (1998). Regulation of serotonin re-uptake transporter mRNA expression by ovarian steriods in rhesus monkeys. *Molecular Brain Research, 53,* 120–129.

Pennington, B.F., & Ozonoff, S. (1996). Executive functions and developmental psychopathology. *Journal of Child Psychology and Psychiatry, 37,* 51–87.

Penton-Voak, I.S., & Perrett, D.I. (2000). Female preference for male faces changes cyclically: Further evidence. *Evolution and Human Behavior, 21,* 39–48.

Penton-Voak, I. S., Perrett, D., Castles, D., Burt, M., Koyabashi, T., & Murray, L.K. (1999). Female preferences for male faces change cyclically. *Nature, 399,* 741–742.

Pepperberg, I.M. (1994). Numerical competence in an African gray parrot (*Psittacus erithacus*). *Journal of Comparative Psychology, 108,* 36–44.

Persson, I. (1990). The third dimension-equal status between Swedish women and men. In I. Persson (Ed.). *Generating equality in the welfare state: The Swedish experience* (pp. 223–244). Oslo, Norway: Norwegian University Press.

Perusse, D. (1993). Cultural and reproductive success in industrial societies: Testing the relationship and proximate and ultimate levels. *Behavioral and Brain Sciences, 16,* 267–322.

Perusse, D. (1994). Mate choice in modern societies: Testing evolutionary hypotheses with behavioral data. *Human Nature, 5,* 255–278.

Petit, O., Desportes, C., & Thierry, B. (1992). Differential probability of "coproduction" in two species of macaque (*Macaca Tonkeana, M. mulatta*). *Ethology, 90,* 107–120.

Phears and phobias. (1984, August/September). *Public Opinion,* p. 32.

Piaget, J. (1932). *The moral judgment of the child.* New York: The Free Press.

Pilbeam, D.R. (1986). Hominoid evolution and hominoid origins. *American Anthropologist* 88, 295–312.

Pilbeam, D. (1996). Genetic and morphological records of the Hominidea and hominid origins: A synthesis. *Molecular Phylogenetics and Evolution, 5,* 155–168.

Pinker, S. (1994). *The language instinct.* New York: Morrow.

Pinker, S. (1997). *How the mind works.* New York: W.W. Norton.

Plomin, R., & DeFries, J.C. (1985). *Origins of individual differences in infancy: The Colorado Adoption Project.* Orlando, FL: Academic Press.

Plooij, F.X. (1978). Tool-use during chimpanzee's bushpig hunt. *Carnivore, 1,* 103–6.

Plotkin, H. (1994). *Darwin machines and the nature of knowledge.* Cambridge, MA: Harvard University Press.

Plotkin, H. (1997). *Evolution in Mind.* Cambridge, MA: Harvard Unversity.

Plutchik, R. (1980). A general psychoevolutionary theory of emotion. In R. Plutchik & H. Kellerman (Eds.), *Emotion: Theory, research, and experience* (*1*, pp. 3–32). New York: Academic Press.

Podos, J., Peters, S., Rudnicky, T., Marler, P., & Nowicki, S. (1992). The organization of song repertoires in song sparrows: Themes and variations. *Ethology, 90,* 89–106.

Polk, K. (1994). *When men kill: Scenarios of masculine violence.* Cambridge, MA: Cambridge University Press.

Porteous, S.D. (1965). *Porteous maze test: Fifty years of application.* Palo Alto, CA: Pacific Books

Porter, R.H., Cernoch, J.M., & McLaughlin, F.J. (1983). Maternal recognition of neonates through olfactory cues. *Physiology & Behavior, 30,* 151–154.

Porter, R.H., & Moore, J.D. (1981). Human kin recognition by olfactory cues. *Physiology and Behavior, 27,* 493–495.

Posner, R.A. (1992). *Sex and reason.* Cambridge, MA: Harvard University Press.

Poti, P., & Spinozzi, G. (1994). Early sensorimotor development in chimpanzees (*Pan troglodytes*). *Journal of Comparative Psychology, 108,* 93–103.

Poundstone, W. (1992). *Prisoner's dilemma: John von Neumann, game theory and the puzzle of the bomb.* Oxford, UK: Oxford University.

Povinelli, D.J. (1994). How to create self-recognizing gorillas (but don't try it on macaques). In S.T. Parker, R.W. Mitchell, & M.L. Boccia (Eds.), *Self-awareness in animals and humans: Developmental perspectives* (pp. 291–294). Cambridge, UK: Cambridge University Press.

Povinelli, D. J. (1998, November). Can animals empathize? Maybe not. *Scientific American,* special issue on intelligence. Retrieved on March 14, 2002, from www.sciam.com/specialissues/1198intelligence/1198povinelli.html.

Povinelli, D.J. (2000). *Folk physics for apes: the chimpanzee's theory of how the world works.* Oxford, UK: Oxford University Press.

Povinelli, D.J., Bierschwale, D.T., & Cech, C.G. (1999). Comprehension of seeing as a referential act in young children, but not juvenile chimpanzees. *British Journal of Developmental Psychology, 17,* 37–60.

Povinelli, D.J., & Cant, J.G.H. (1995). Arboreal clambering and the evolution of self-conception. *Quarterly Review of Biology, 70,* 393–421.

Povinelli, D.J., & Eddy, T.J. (1996). What young chimpanzees know about seeing. *Monographs of the Society for Research in Child Development, 61* (2, serial No. 247).

Povinelli, D.J., Landau, K.R., & Perilloux, H.K. (1996). Self-recognition in young children using delayed vesus live feedback: Evidence of a developmental asynchrony. *Child Development, 67,* 1540–1554.

Povinelli, D.J., Nelson, K.E., & Boysen, S.T. (1992). Comprehension of role reversal in chimpanzees: evidence of empathy? *Animal Behavior, 43,* 633–640.

Povinelli, D.J., Parks, K.A., & Novak, M.A. (1992). Role reversal by rhesus monkeys, but no evidence of empathy. *Animal Behavior, 44,* 269–281.

Povinelli, D.J., Perilloux, H.K., Reaux, J.E., & Beirschwale, D.T. (1998). Young and juvenile chimpazees' (*Pan troglodytes*) reactions to intentional versus accidental and inadvertent actions. *Behavioral Processes, 42,* 205–218.

Povinelli, D.J., & Prince, C.G. (1998). When self met other. In M. Ferrari & R. J. Sternberg (Eds.), *Self-awareness: Its nature and development.* New York: The Guilford Press.

Povinelli, D.J., Reaux, J.E., Bierschwale, D.T., Allain, A.D., & Simon, B.B. (1997). Exploitation of pointing as a referential gesture in young children, but not adolescent chimpanzees. *Cognitive Development, 12,* 423–461.

Power, C. (1998). Old wives' tales: The gossip hypothesis and the reliability of cheap signals. In J.R. Hurford, M.

Studdert–Kennedy, and C. Knight (Eds.), *Approaches to the evolution of language: Social and cognitive bases* (pp. 111–129). Cambridge, MA: Cambridge University Press.

Power, C., & Watts, I. (1996). Female strategies and collective behaviour. The archeology of earliest *Homo sapiens sapiens*. In J. Steele and S. Shennan (Eds.), *The archeology of human ancestry. Power, sex and tradition*. London: Routledge, 306–330.

Powers, E.A. (1971). Thirty years of research on ideal mate characteristics: What do we know? *International Journal of Sociology of the Family, 1*, 207–215.

Pratto, R., & John, O.P. (1991). Automatic vigilance: The attention-grabbing power of negative social information. *Journal of Personality and Social Psychology, 61*, 380–391.

Premack, D. (1976). *Intelligence in ape and man*. Hillsdale, NJ: Erlbaum.

Premack, D. (1986). *Gavagai!* Cambridge, MA: MIT Press.

Premack, D., & Premack, A.J. (1983). *The mind of an ape*. New York: W.W. Norton.

Premack, D., & Premack, A.J. (1994). Levels of causal understanding in chimpanzees and children. *Cognition, 50*, 347–362.

Premack, D., & Premack, A.J. (1995). Origins of human social competence. In M. Gazzaniga (Ed.), *The cognitive neurosciences* (pp. 205–218). Cambridge, MA: MIT Press.

Premack, D., & Premack, A.J. (1997). Infants attribute value ± to the goal-directed actions of self-propelled objects. *Journal of Cognitive Neuroscience, 9*, 848–856.

Premack, D., & Woodruff, G. (1978). Does the chimpanzee have a theory of mind? *Behavioral and Brain Sciences, 4*, 515–526.

Preti, G., Cutler, W.B., Garcia, C.R., Huggins, G.R., & Lawley, H.J. (1986). Human axillary secretions influence women's menstrual cycles: The role of donor extract of females. *Hormones and Behavior, 20*, 474–482.

Price, J., Sloman, L., Gardner, R., Jr, Gilbert, P., & Rohde, P. (1994). The social competition hypothesis of depression. *British Journal of Psychiatry, 164*, 309–315.

Profet, M. (1992). Pregnancy sickness as adaptation: A deterrent to maternal ingestion of teratogens. In J. Barkow, L. Cosmides, & J. Tooby (Eds.), *The adapted mind: Evolutionary psychology and the generation of culture* (pp. 327–365). New York: Oxford University Press.

Quinn, P.C., Eimas, P.D., & Tarr, M.J. (2001). Perceptual categorization of cat and dog silhouettes by 3- and 4-month-old infants. *Journal of Experimental Child Psychology, 79*, 78–94.

Raemaekers, J.J., Raemaekers, P.M., & Haimoff, E.H. (1984). Loud calls of the gibbons (*Hylobates lar*): Repertoire, organization and context. *Behavior, 91*, 146–189.

Raine, A. (1993). *The psychopathology of crime: Criminal behavior as a clinical disorder*. San Diego, CA: Academic Press.

Raine, A., & Dunkin, J. (1990). The genetic and psychophysiological basis of antisocial behavior: Implications for counseling and therapy. *Journal of Counseling and Development, 68*, 637–644.

Raine, A., & Venables, P.H. (1984). Tonic heart rate level, social class and antisocial behavior in adolescents. *Biological Psychology, 18*, 123–132.

Rak, Y. (1990). On the differences between two pelvises of Mousterian context from the Qafzeh and Kebara caves, Israel. *American Journal of Physical Anthropology, 81*, 323–332.

Rak, Y., & Arensburg, B. (1987). Kebara 2 Neanderthal pelvis: First look at a complete inlet. *American Journal of Physical Anthropology, 73*, 227–231.

Ramachandran, V.S., & Blakeslee, S. (1998). *Phantoms in the mind*. New York: William Morrow.

Ratnieks, F.L. (1988). Reproductive harmony via mutual policing by workers in Eusocial Hymenoptera. *American Naturalist, 132*, 217–236.

Reader, J. (1981). *Missing links*. London: Collins.

Real, L. (1991). Animal choice behavior and the evolution of cognitive architecture. *Science, 253*, 980–986.

Regan, P.C. (1996). Rhythms of desire: The association between menstrual cycle phases and female sexual desire. *Canadian Journal of Human Sexuality, 5*, 145–156.

Reisberg, D. (2001). *Cognition: Exploring the science of the mind*. New York: W.W. Norton.

Reissland, N. (1988). Neonatal imitation in the first hour of life: Observations in rural Nepal. *Developmental Psychology, 24*, 464–469.

Relethford, J.H. (1998). Genetics of human origins and diversity. *Annual Review of Anthropology 27*, 1–23.

Reynolds, J.D., & Harvey, P.H. (1994). Sexual selection and the evolution of sex differences. In R.V. Short & E. Balaban (Eds.), *The differences between the sexes* (pp. 53–70). Cambridge, UK: Cambridge University Press.

Rhudy, J.L., & Meagher, M.W. (2000). Fear and anxiety: Divergent effects on human pain thresholds. *Pain, 84*, 65–75.

Rice, W. (1996). Sexually antagonistic male adaptation triggered by experimental arrest of female evolution. *Nature, 381*, 232–234.

Richards, M.P., Pettitt, P.B., Trinkhaus, E., Smith, F.H., Paunovic, M., & Karavanic, I. (2000). Neanderthal diet at Vindija and Neanderthal predation: The evidence from stable isotopes. *Proceedings of the National Academy of Sciences USA, 97*, 7663–7666.

Richmond, B.G., Begun, D.R., & Strait, D.S. (2001). The origin of human bipedalism: The knuckle-walking hypothesis revisited. *Yearbook of Physical Anthropology, 44*, 70–105.

Richmond, B.G., & Jungers, W.L. (1995). Size variation and sexual dimorphism in *Australopithecus afarensis* and living hominioids. *Journal of Human Evolution, 29*, 229–245.

Richmond, B.G., & Strait, D.S. (2000). Evidence that humans evolved from a knuckle-walking ancestor. *Nature, 404*, 382–385.

Ridley, M. (1996). *The origins of virtue*. New York: Viking Press.

Ristau, C.A., & Robbins, D. (1982). Language in the great apes: A critical review. In J.S. Rosenblatt, R.A. Hinde, C. Beer, & M.C. Busnel (Eds.), *Advances in the study of behavior* (Vol.12, pp.142–255.). New York: Academic Press.

Roberts, B.W., & Robins, R.W. (2000). Broad dispositions, broad aspirations: The intersection of personality traits and major life goals. *Personality and Social Psychology Bulletin, 26,* 1284–1296.

Roberts, C.J., & Lowe, C.R. (1975). Where have all the conceptions gone? *Lancet, 1,* 498–499.

Roberts, J. (1993). *The transformation of Hawaiian plantation pidgin and the emergence of Hawaii Creole English.* Paper presented at the conference of the Society for Pidgin and Creole Linguistics, Amsterdam, The Netherlands.

Roberts, J. (1996). Pidgin Hawaiian: A sociohistorical study. *Journal of Pidgin and Creole Languages, 10,* 1–63.

Robins, L.N., Tipp, J., & Przybeck, T. (1991). Antisocial personality. In L.N. Robins & D.A. Reiger (Eds.), *Psychiatric disorders in America* (pp. 258–290). New York: Free Press.

Robinson, J.G. (1979). An analysis of the organization of vocal communication in the titi monkey (*Callicebus moloch*). *Zeitschrift fur Tierpsychologie, 49,* 381–405.

Robinson, J.G. (1984). Syntactic structures in the vocalizations of wedge-capped capuchin monkeys (*Cebus nigrivittatus*). *Behavior, 90,* 46–79.

Rochat, P. (1995). Early objectification of the self. In P. Rochat (Ed.), *The self in infancy* (pp. 53–71). Amsterdam: North Holland Press.

Rock, I. (1983). *The logic of perception.* Cambridge, MA: MIT Press.

Rodman, P.S. (1984). Foraging and social systems of orangutans and chimpanzees. In P.S. Rodman & J.G.H. Cant (Eds.), *Adapations for foraging in nonhuman primates* (pp. 134–160). New York: Columbia University Press.

Rodman, P.S., & McHenry, H.M. (1980). Bioenergetics of hominid bipedalism. *American Journal of Physical Anthropology, 52,* 103–106.

Rogers, J. (1993). The phylogenetic relationships among *Homo, Pan* and *Gorilla. Journal of Human Evolution, 25,* 201–215.

Roland, P.E. (1993). *Brain activation.* New York: Wiley-Liss.

Rolston, H. (1999). *Genes, genesis, and God.* Cambridge, UK: Cambridge University Press.

Rosenberg, K., & Trevathan, W. (1995). Bipedalism and human birth: The obstetrical dilemma revisited. *Evolutionary Anthropology, 4,* 161–168.

Roskaft, E., Wara, A., & Viken, A. (1992). Repoductive success in relation to resource-access and parental age in a small Norwegian farming parish during the period 1700–1900. *Ethology and Sociobiology, 13,* 443–461.

Ross, M., & Sicoly, F. (1979). Egocentric biases in availability and attribution. *Journal of Personality and Social Psychology, 37,* 322–336.

Ruff, C.B. (1994). Morphological adaptation to climate in modern and fossil hominids. *Yearbook of Physical Anthropology, 37,* 65–107.

Russell, B. (1945). *The history of Western philosophy.* New York: Simon and Schuster.

Ruvolo, M. (1994). Molecular evolutionary processes and conflicting gene trees. *American Journal of Physical Anthropology, 94,* 89–113.

Ruvolo, M.D. (1996). A new approach to studying modern human origins. *Molecular Phylogenetics and Evolution, 5,* 202–219.

Ruvolo, M.D., Pan, S., Zehr, S., Goldberg, T., Disotell, T.R., & von Dornum, M. (1994). Gene trees and hominoid phylogeny. *Proceedings of the National Academy of Science USA, 91,* 8900–8904.

Sahlins, M. (1972). *Stone Age economics.* Chicago: Aldine–Atherton.

Sanday, P.R. (1981). *Female power and male dominance: On the origins of sexual inequality.* New York: Cambridge University Press.

Sapolsky, R. (1992). *Stress, the aging brain, and the mechanisms of neuron death.* Cambridge, MA: MIT Press.

Sapolsky, R.M. (1994). *Why zebras don't get ulcers: A guide to stress, stress-related diseases, and coping.* New York: W.H. Freeman.

Sarich, V.M., & Wilson, A.C. (1967). Immunological time scale for hominid evolution. *Science, 158,* 1200–1203.

Satterfeld, J.H. (1987). Childhood diagnostic and neurophysiological predictors of teenage arrest rates: An eight-year prospective study. In S.A. Mednick, T.E. Moffitt, & S.A. Stack (Eds.), *The causes of crime: New biological approaches.* Cambridge, MA: Cambridge University Press.

Savage-Rumbaugh, E.S. (1984). *Pan paniscus* and *Pan troglodytes*: Contrasts in preverbal communicative competence. In R.L. Susman (Ed.), *The pygmy chimpanzee: Evolutionary biology and behavior* (pp. 395–413). New York: Plenum Press.

Savage-Rumbaugh, E.S., & Lewin, R. (1994). *Kanzi, the ape at the brink of the human mind.* New York: John Wiley and Sons.

Savage-Rumbaugh, E.S., McDonald, K., Sevcik, R., Hopkins, W., & Rupert, E. (1986). Spontaneous symbol acquisition and communicative use by pygmy chimpanzee (*Pan paniscus*). *Journal of Experimental Psychology: General, 115,* 211–235.

Savage-Rumbaugh, E.S., Murphy, J., Sevcik, R.A., Brakke, K.E., Williams, S.L., & Rumbaugh, D.M. (1993). Language comprehension in ape and child. *Monographs of the Society for Research in Child Development, 58(3–4),* no.233.

Savage-Rumbaugh, E.S., Rumbaugh, D.M., & Boysen, S. (1978). Linguistically mediated tool use and exchange by chimpanzees (*Pan troglodytes*). *Behavioral and Brain Sciences, 4,* 539–554.

Savic, I., Berglund, H., Gulyas, B., & Roland, P. (2001). Smelling of odorous sex hormone-like compound causes sex-differentiated hypothalamic activation in humans. *Neuron, 31*, 661–668.

Schaller, G. (1972). *The Serengeti lion: A study of predator-prey relations.* Chicago: University of Chicago Press.

Scheel, D., & Packer, C. (1991). Group hunting behavior of lions: A search for cooperation. *Animal Behavior, 41*, 711–722.

Schick, K.D., & Toth, N. (1993). *Making silent stones speak: Human evolution and the dawn of technology.* New York: Simon & Schuster.

Schiff, W. (1965). Perception of impending collision. *Psychological Monographs, 79*, 1–26.

Schmid, P. (1983). A reconstruction of skeleton A.L. 288-1 (Hadar) and its consequences. *Folia Primatologica, 40*, 283–306.

Schrenk, F., Bromage, T.G., Betzler, C.G., Ring, U., & Juwayeyi, Y.M. (1993). Oldest *Homo* and Pliocene bio-geography of the Malawi Rift. *Nature, 365*, 833–836.

Scully, G.W. (1997). Murder by the state. *New York Times*, section 4, December 14, p.7.

Secular, R., & Blake, R., (1994). *Perception.* New York: McGraw–Hill.

Sedikides, C., & Skowronski, J.J. (1997). The symbolic self in evolutionary context. *Personality and Social Psychology Review. 1*, 80–102.

Segerstrale, U. (2000). *Defenders of truth.* Oxford, UK: Oxford University Press.

Seielstad, M.T., Minch, E., & Cavalli–Sforza, L. (1998). Genetic evidence for a higher female migration rate in humans. *Nature Genetics, 20*, 278–280.

Seligman, M. (1970). On the generality of the laws of learning. *Psychological Review, 77*, 407–418.

Semaw, S., Renne, P., Harris, J.W.K., Feibel, C.S., Bernor, R.L., Fesseha, N., et al. (1997). 2.5-million-year-old stone tools from Gona, Ethiopia. *Nature, 385*, 333–336.

Semenov, S.A. (1964). *Prehistoric technology.* London: Cory, McAdams, & MacKay.

Senut, B., & Tardieu, C. (1985). Functional aspects of Plio-Pleistocene hominid limb bones: Implications for tax-onomy and phylogeny. In E. Delson (Ed.), *Ancestors: The hard evidence.* New York: Alan R. Liss.

Seyfarth, R.M., Cheney, D.L., & Marler, P. (1980). Monkey responses to three different alarm calls: Evidence of predator classification and semantic communication. *Science, 210*, 801–803.

Shaffer, D.R. (1993). *Developmental psychology.* Pacific Grove, CA: Brooks/Cole.

Shaller, S. (1991). *A man without words.* New York: Summit Press.

Sharman, G.B. (1976). Evolution of viviparity in mam-mals. In C.R. Austin & R.V. Short (Eds.), *Reproduction in mammals: Book 6. The evolution of reproduction* (pp. 32–70). Cambridge, UK: Cambridge University Press.

Sherry, D.F., & Schacter, D.L. (1987). The evolution of multiple memory systems. *Psychological Review, 94*, 439–454.

Short, R.V., & Balaban, E. (1994). *The differences between the sexes.* Cambridge, UK: Cambridge University Press.

Shostak, M. (1981) *Nisa: The life and words of a !Kung woman.* Cambridge, MA: Harvard University Press.

Shreeve, J. (1995). *The Neanderthal enigma.* New York: William Morrow.

Sibley, C.G., & Alquist, J.E. (1987). The phylogeny of hominid primates as indicated by DNA-DNA hybridization. *Journal of Molecular Evolution, 20*, 1–15.

Siegfried, B., Netto, C., & Izquierdo, I. (1987). Exposure to novely induces naltrexone-reversible analgesia in rats. *Behavioral Neuroscience, 101*, 436–438.

Sigg, H., & Falett, J. (1985). Experiments on the respect of possession and property in hamadryas baboons. *Animal Behavior, 33*, 978–84.

Silberglied, R.E., Shepard, J.G., & Dickinson, J.L. (1984). Eunuchs: The role of apyrene sperm in Lepidotera. *American Naturalist, 123*, 255–265.

Silverman, I., & Eals, M. (1992). Sex differences in spatial abilities: Evolutionary theory and data. In J. H. Barkow, L. Cosmides, & J. Tooby (Eds.), *The adapted mind: Evolutionary psychology and the generation of culture* (pp. 533–549). New York: Oxford University Press.

Silverman, I., & Phillips, K. (1998). The evolutionary psy-chology of spatial sex differences. In C. Crawford & D.L. Krebs (Eds.), *Handbook of evolutionary psychology* (pp. 595–612). Mahwah, N.J.: Erlbaum.

Simion, F., Cassia, V.M., Turati, C., & Valenza, E. (2001). The origins of face perception: Specific versus non-specific mechanisms. *Infant and Child Development, 10*, 59–65.

Simion, F., Valenza, E., & Umilta, C. (1998). Mechanisms underlying face preference at birth. In F. Simion & G. Butterworth (Eds.), *The development of sensory, motor and cognitive capacities in early infancy: From perception to cognition.* Hove, UK: Psychology Press.

Simon, H.A. (1983). *Reason in human affairs.* Stanford CA: Stanford University Press.

Simon, H.A. (1990). A mechanism for social selection and successful altruism. *Science, 250*, 1665–1668.

Simonton, D.K. (1988). Age and outstanding achievement: What do we know after a century of research? *Psychological Bulletin, 104*, 251–267.

Sinclair, A.R.E., Leakey, M.D., & Norton-Griffiths, M. (1986). Migration and hominid bipedalism. *Nature, 324*, 307–308.

Singh, D. (1993). Adaptive significance of female physical attractiveness: Role of waist-to-hip ratio. *Journal of Personality and Social Psychology, 85*, 293–307.

Singh, D., & Bronstad, P.M. (2001). Female body odour is a potential cue to ovulation. *Proceedings of the Royal Society: Biological Sciences, 268*, 797–801.

Singh, D., & Young, R.K. (1995). Body weight, waist-to-hip ratio, breasts, and hips: Role in judgments of female attractiveness and desirability for relationships. *Ethology and Sociobiology, 16*, 483–507.

Slater, A., & Quinn, P.C. (2001). Face recognition in the newborn infant. *Infant and Child Development, 10*, 21–24.

Slater, A., von der Schulenburg, C., Brown, E., Badenoch, M., Butterworth, G., Parsons, S., et al. (1998). Newborn infants prefer attractive faces. *Infant Behavior and Development, 21,* 345–354.

Slaughter, V., & Gopnick, A. (1997). Conceptual coherence in the child's theory of mind: Training children to understand belief. *Child Development, 67,* 2967–2988.

Slavin, M.O. (1985). The origins of psychic conflict and the adaptive functions of repression: An evolutionary biological view. *Psychoanalysis and Contemporary Thought, 8,* 407–440.

Small, M. (1988). Female primate behavior and conception: Are there really sperm to spare? *Current Anthropology, 29,* 81–100.

Small, M. (1993). *Female choices: Sexual behavior of female primates.* Ithaca, NY: Cornell University Press.

Small, M. (1998). *Our babies, ourselves: How biology and culture shape the way we parent.* New York: Anchor Books.

Smart, Y.C., Roberts, T.K., Clancy, R.L., & Cripps, A.W. (1981). Early pregnancy factor: Its role in mammalian reproduction—research review. *Fertility and Sterility, 35,* 397.

Smetana, J., Kelly, M., & Twentyman, C.T. (1984). Abused, neglected and nonmaltreated children's conception of moral and social-conventional transgressions. *Child Development, 55,* 277–287.

Smith, E.E., & Medin, D.L. (1981). *Categories and concepts.* Cambridge, MA: Harvard University Press.

Smith, M.S. (1998). Research in developmental sociobiology: Parenting and family behavior. In K.B. MacDonald (Ed.), *Sociobiological perspectives in human development* (pp. 271–292). New York: Springer-Verlag.

Smith, M.S., Kish, B.J., & Crawford, C.B. (1987). Inheritance of wealth as human kin investment. *Ethology and Sociobiology, 8,* 171–182.

Smuts, B.B. (1985). *Sex and friendship in baboons.* New York: Aldine.

Smuts, B.B. (1987). Sexual competition and mate choice. In B.B. Smuts, D.L. Cheney, R.M. Seyfarth, R.W. Wrangham, & T.T. Struhsaker (Eds.), *Primate societies* (pp. 385–399). Chicago: University of Chicago Press.

Smuts, B.B., Cheney, D.L., Seyfarth, R.M., Wrangham, R.W., & Struhsaker, T.T. (1985). *Primate societies.* Chicago: University of Chicago Press.

Smuts, B.B., & Gubernick, D.J. (1992). Male-infant relationships in nonhuman primates: Parental investment or mating effort? In B.S. Hewlett (Ed.), *Father-child relations: Cultural and biosocial contexts.* Chicago: Aldine de Gruyter.

Smuts, B.B., & Smuts, R.W. (1992). Male aggression and sexual coercion of female nonhuman primates and other mammals: Evidence and theoretical implication. *Advances in the study of behavior, 22,* 1–61. London: Academic Press.

Soffer, O. (1994). Ancestral lifeways in Eurasia—the Middle and Upper Paleolithic records. In M. Nitecki & D. Nitecki (Eds.), *Origins of anatomically modern humans* (pp. 101–119). New York: Plenum Press.

Song, M., Smetana, J.G., & Kim, S.Y. (1987). Korean children's conception of moral and conventional transgressions. *Developmental Psychology, 23,* 577–582.

Sorabji, R. (1993). *Animal minds and human morals.* Ithaca, NY: Cornell University Press.

Sorensen, M.V., & Leonard, W.R. (2001). Neanderthal energetics and foraging efficiency. *Journal of Human Evolution, 40,* 483–495.

Sperry, R.W. (1952). Neurology and the mind-brain problem. *American Scientist, 40,* 291–312.

Spitz, R. (1965). *The first year of life.* New York: International Universities Press.

Sponheimer, M., & Lee-Thorp, J.A. (1999). Isotopic evidence for the diet of an early hominid, *Australopithecus africanus. Science, 283,* 368–370.

Spoor, F., Wood, B.A., & Zonneveld, F. (1996). Evidence for a link between human semicircular canal size and bipedal behavior. *Journal of Human Evolution, 30,* 183–187.

Spuhler, J.N. (1968). Assortative mating with respect to physical characteristics. *Social Biology, 15,* 128–140.

Sroufe, L.A. (1977). Wariness of strangers and the study of infant development. *Child Development, 48,* 731–746.

Starks, P.T., & Blackie, C. A. (2000). The relationship between serial monogamy and rape in the United States (1960–1995). *Proceedings of the Royal Society of London.*

Stearns, S.C. (1987). The evolution of sex and the difference it makes. In S.C. Stearns (Ed.), *The evolution of sex and its consequences* (pp. 15–31). Basel, Switzerland: Birkhauser.

Steblay, N.J. (1992). A meta-analytic review of the weapon focus effect. *Law and Human Behavior, 16,* 413–424.

Steel, J., & Shennen, S., Eds. (1995). *The archeology of human ancestry.* London: Routledge.

Steklis, H.D., & Marchant, L.F. (1987). Primate handedness: Reaching and grasping for straws? *Behavioral and Brain Sciences, 10,* 284–286.

Steudel, K. (1996). Limb morphology, bipedal gait, and the energetics of hominid locomotion. *American Journal of Physical Anthropology, 99,* 345–355.

Stevens, S.S. (1961). The psychophysics of sensory function. In W.A. Rosenblith (Ed.), *Sensory communication* (pp. 1–33). Cambridge, MA: MIT Press.

Stevenson, J. (1992). Evidence for a genetic etiology in hyperactivity in children. *Behavior Genetics, 22,* 337–44.

Stoneking, M. (1993). DNA and recent human evolution. *Evolutionary Anthropology, 2,* 60–73.

Straus, L.G. (1994). Upper Paleolithic origins and radiocarbon calibration: More new evidence from Spain. *Evolutionary Anthropology 2,* 195–198.

Straus, L.G. (1997). The Iberian situation between 40,000 and 30,000 B.P., in light of European models of migration and convergence. In G.A. Clark & C.M. Willermet (Eds.), *Conceptual issues in modern human origins research* (pp. 235–252). New York: Aldine de Gruyter.

Stringer, C.B. (1990, December). The emergence of modern humans. *Scientific American,* 98–104.

Stringer, C.B. (1992). Evolution of early humans. In S. Jones, R. Martin, & D. Pilbeam (Eds.), *The Cambridge encyclopedia of human evolution* (pp. 241–251). Cambridge, UK: Cambridge University Press.

Stringer, C., & McKie, R. (1996). *African exodus: The origins of modern humanity.* New York: Henry Holt.

Studdert-Kennedy, M. (1998). The particulate origins of language generativity: From syllable to gesture. In J.R. Hurford, M. Studdert-Kennedy, & C. Knight (Eds.), *Approaches to the evolution of language: Social and cognitive bases* (pp. 202–221). Cambridge, MA: Cambridge University Press.

Suarez, S.D., & Gallup, G., Jr. (1981). Self-recognition in chimpanzees and orangutans, but not gorillas. *Journal of Human Evolution, 10,* 175–188.

Suarez, S.D., & Gallup, G., Jr. (1986). Social responding to mirrors in rhesus macaques (*Macaca mulatta*): Effects of changing mirror location. *American Journal of Primatology, 11,* 239–244.

Surbey, M.K. (1990). Family composition, stress, and human menarche. In T.E. Ziegler & F.B. Bercovitch (Eds.), *The Socioendocrinology of primate reproduction* (pp. 11–32). New York: Wiley.

Surbey, M.K. (1998). Developmental psychology and modern Darwinism. In C. Crawford & D.L. Krebs (Eds.), *Handbook of evolutionary psychology* (pp. 369–404). Mahwah, N.J.: Erlbaum.

Susanne, C., & Lepage, Y. (1988). Assortative mating for anthropometric characteristics. In C.G.N. Mascie-Taylor & A.J. Boyce (Eds.), *Human mating patterns: Society for the Study of Human Biology Symposium Series #28* (pp. 61–82). Cambridge, MA: Cambridge University Press.

Susman, E.J., Nottelman, E.D., Inhoff-Germain, G.E., Dorn, L.D., Cutler, G.B., Loriaux, D.L., et al. (1985). The relationship of development and social-emotional behavior in young adolescents. *Journal of Youth and Adolescence, 14,* 245–264.

Susman, R.L. (1994). Fossile evidence for early hominid tool use. *Science, 265,* 1570–1573.

Susman, R.L. (1988). Hand of *Paranthropus robustus* from Member 1, Swartkrans. *Science, 240,* 781–784.

Susman, R.L., Stern, J.T., & Jungers, W.L. (1984). Arboreality and bipedality in the Hadar hominids. *Folia Primatologica, 43,* 113–156.

Sutton, H.E., & Wanger, R.P. (1985). *Genetics: A human concern.* New York: MacMillan.

Swedish Institute (Feb. 2000). Fact Sheet on Sweden, "Equality between Women and Men." Accessed on March 14, 2002, at www.si.se/docs/infosweden/engelska/fs82.pdf

Swisher, C.C.I., Curits, G.H., Jacob, T., Getty, A.G., Suprijo, A., & Widiasmoro. (1994). Age of the earliest known hominids in Java, Indonesia. *Science, 263,* 1118–1121.

Swisher, C. C., Rink, W. J., Antón, S. C., Schwarcz, H. P., Curtis, G. H., Suprijo, A., et al. (1996). Latest *Homo erectus* of Java: Potential contemporaneity with *Homo sapiens* in Southeast Asia. *Science, 274,* 1870–1874.

Symons, D. (1979). *The evolution of human sexuality.* Oxford, UK: Oxford University Press.

Szalay, F.S., & Costello, R.K. (1991) . Evolution of permanent estrus displays in hominids. *Journal of Human Evolution, 20,* 439–464.

Taborin, Y. (1993). Shells of the French Aurignacian and Perigordian. In H. Knecht, A. Pike-Tay, & R. White (Eds.), *Before Lascaux: The complex record of the early Upper Paleolithic* (pp. 211–229). Boca Raton, FL: CRC Press.

Tager-Flusberg, H. (1992). Autistic children's talk about psychological states: Deficits in the early acquisition of a theory of mind. *Child Development, 63,* 161–172.

Takahata, Y., Ihobe, H., & Idani, G. (1996). Comparing copulations of chimpanzees and bonobos: Do females exhibit proceptivity or receptivity? In W.C. McGrew, L.F. Marchant, & T. Nishida (Eds.), *Great ape societies* (pp. 146–155). Cambridge, UK: Cambridge University Press.

Tangney, J.P., & Fischer, K.W. (1995). *Self-conscious emotions: The psychology of shame, guilt, embarrassment, and pride.* New York: The Guilford Press.

Tangney, J.P. (1990). Assessing individual differences in proneness to shame and guilt: Development of the self-conscious affect and attribution inventory. *Journal of Personality and Social Psychology, 59,* 102–111.

Tannen, D. (1996). *Talking nine to five.* London: Virago.

Tanner, J.M. (1990). *Fetus to man: Physical growth from conception to maturity.* Cambridge, MA: Harvard University Press.

Tattersall, I. (1993) *The human odyssey: Four million years of human evolution.* New York: Prentice Hall.

Tattersall, I. (1995). *The fossil trail.* New York: Oxford University Press.

Tattersall, I. (1998). *Becoming Human: Evolution and Human Uniqueness.* Oxford: Oxford University Press.

Taylor, C.R., Heglund, N.C., & Maloiy, G.M.O. (1982). Energetics and mechanics of terrestrial locomotion. I. Metabolic energy consumption as a function of speed and body size in birds and mammals. *Journal of Experimental Biology, 97,* 1–21.

Taylor, C.R., & Rountree, V.J. (1973). Running on two or four legs: Which consumes less energy? *Science, 179,* 186–187.

Tchernov, E. (1992). Biochronology, paleoecology, and dispersal events of hominids in the southern Levant. In T. Akazawa, K. Aoki, & T. Kimura (Eds.), *The evolution and dispersal of modern humans in Asia.* Tokyo: Hokusen-Sha.

Templeton, A.R. (1992). Human origins and analysis of mitochondrial DNA sequences. *Science, 255,* 737.

Templeton, A.R. (1993). The "Eve" hypothesis: A genetic critique and reanalysis. *American Anthropologist, 95,* 51–72.

Terrace, H.S., Petitto, L.A., Sanders, R.J., and Bever, T.G. (1979). Can an ape create a sentence? *Science, 206,* 891–902.

"The war between the sexes" (1994). *The Economist,* March 5, pp. 80–81.

Thelen, E. (1995). Motor development: A new synthesis. *American Psychologist, 50,* 79–95.

Thelen, E., & Fisher, D.M. (1983). The organization of spontaneous leg movements in newborn infants. *Journal of Motor Behavior, 15,* 353–377.

Thelen, E., & Smith, L.B. (1994). *A dynamic systems approach to the development of cognition and action.* Cambridge, MA: MIT Press.

Thieme, H. (1997). Lower Paleolithic hunting spears from Germany. *Nature, 385,* 807–810.

Thiessen, D. (1999). Social influences on human assortative mating. In M.C. Corballis & S.E.G. Lea (Eds.), *The descent of mind* (pp. 311–323). Oxford, UK: Oxford University Press.

Thiessen, D., & Gregg, B. (1980). Human assortative mating and genetic equilibrium: An evolutionary perspective. *Ethology and Sociobiology, 1,* 111–140.

Thiessen, D., Young, R.K., & Delgado, M. (1997). Social pressures for assortative mating. *Personality and Individual Differences, 22,* 157–164.

Thomas, J.R., & French, K.E. (1985). Gender differences across age in motor performance: A meta-analysis. *Psychological Bulletin, 98,* 260–282.

Thompson, A.P. (1983). Extramarital sex: A review of the research literature. *Journal of Sex Research, 19,* 1–22.

Thompson, R.L., & Boatright-Horowitz, S.L. (1994). The question of mirror-mediated self-recognition in apes and monkeys: Some new results and reservations. In S.T. Parker, R.W. Mitchell, & M.L. Boccia (Eds.), *Self-awareness in animals and humans: Developmental perspectives* (pp. 330–349). Cambridge, UK: Cambridge University Press.

Thornhill, R. (1976). Sexual selection and paternal investment in insects. *American Naturalist, 110,* 153–163.

Thornhill, R., & Gangestad, S.W. (1993). Human facial beauty: Averageness, symmetry and parasite resistance. *Human Nature, 4,* 237–269.

Thornhill, R., & Gangestad, S.W. (1999). The scent of symmetry: A human sex pheromone that signals fitness? *Evolution and Human Behavior, 20,* 175–201.

Tinbergen, N. (1951). *The study of instinct.* Oxford, UK: Clarendon Press.

Tinbergen, N., & Kuenen, D.J. (1939). Uber die auslosenden und richtungsgebenden Reizsituationen der Sperrbewegung von jungen Drosseln (*Turdus m. merula L.* und *T.e.ericetorum* Turdon) *Zeitschrift fur Teirpsychologie,3,* 37–60. [Roughly translated, "About the releasing and directional-giving attraction situations of the blocking movement of young thrushes,"]

Tobias, P.V. (1991). *Olduvai gorge.* Vol. 4. *The skulls, endocasts and teeth of* Homo habilis. Cambridge, UK: Cambridge University Press.

Tobias, P.V. (1987). The brain of *Homo habilis*: A new level of organization in cerebral evolution. *Journal of Human Evolution, 16,* 741–761.

Tomasello, M. (1994). Can an ape understand a sentence? A review of language comprehension in ape and child by E.S. Savage-Rumbaugh et al. *Language and Communication, 14,* 377–390.

Tomasello, M. (2000). Perceiving intentions and learning words in the second year of life. In M. Bowerman & S. Levinson (Eds.), *Language acquisition and conceptual development* (pp. 132–158). Cambridge, UK: Cambridge University Press.

Tomasello, M., & Barton, M. (1994). Learning words in nonostensive contexts. *Developmental Psychology, 30,* 639–650.

Tomasello, M., & Call, J. (1997). *Primate cognition.* New York: Oxford University Press.

Tomasello, M., Savage-Rumbaugh, S. & Kruger, A.C. (1993). Imitative learning of actions on objects by children, chimpanzees, and encultured chimpanzees. *Child Development, 64,* 1688–1705.

Tomasello, M., Strosberg, R., & Akhtar, N. (1996). Eighteen-month-old children learn words in non-ostensive contexts. *Journal of Child Language, 22,* 1–20.

Tooby, J., & Cosmides, L. (1992). The psychological foundations of culture. In J.H. Barkow, L. Cosmides, & J. Tooby (Eds.), *The adapted mind: Evolutionary psychology and the generation of culture* (pp. 19–136). New York: Oxford University Press.

Tooby, J., & Devore, I. (1987). The reconstruction of hominid behavioral evolution through strategic modeling. In W.G. Kinzey (Ed.), *The evolution of human behavior: Primate models* (pp. 183–237). Albany, NY: SUNY Press.

Tooke, W., & Camire, L. (1991). Patterns of deception in intersexual and intrasexual mating strategies. *Ethology and Sociobiology, 12,* 345–364.

Toth, N. (1985). Archeological evidence for preferential right-handedness in the Lower and Middle Pleistocene, and its possible implications. *Journal of Human Evolution, 14,* 607–614.

Toth, N., & Schick, K. (1993). Early stone industries and inferences regarding language and cognition. In K.R. Gibson & T. Ingold (Eds.), *Tools, language, and cognition in human evolution* (pp. 346–62). Cambridge, UK: Cambridge University Press.

Toth, N., Schick, K., Savage-Rumbaugh, E.S., Sevcik, R.A., & Rumbaugh, D. (1993). *Pan* the tool-maker; investigations into the stone tool-making capabilities of a bonobo (*Pan paniscus*). *Journal of Archeological Science, 20,* 81–91.

Tranel, D., Damasio, A., & Damasio, H. (1988). Intact recognition of facial expressions, gender, and age in patients with impaired recognition of face identity. *Neurology, 38,* 690–696.

Treisman, A.M., & Gelade, G. (1980). A feature integration theory of attention. *Cognitive Psychology, 12,* 97–136.

Treisman, M. (1995). The multiregional and single origin hypotheses of the evolution of modern man: A reconciliation. *Journal of Theoretical Biology, 173,* 23–29.

Trevathan, W. (1987). *Human birth: An evolutionary perspective.* New York: Aldine de Gruyter.

Trinkaus, E. (1986). Neanderthals and the origins of modern humans. *Annual Review of Anthropology, 15,* 193–218.

Trinkaus, E. (1992). Morphological contrasts between the Near Eastern Qafezeh–Skhul and late archaic human samples: Grounds for a behavioral difference? In T. Akazawa, K Aoki, & T. Kimura (Eds.), *The evolution and dispersal of modern humans in Asia* (pp. 278–294). Tokyo: Hakusen–Sha.

Trivers, R.L. (1971). The evolution of reciprocal altruism. *Quarterly Review of Biology, 46,* 35–57.

Trivers, R.L.(1972). Parental investment and sexual selection. In B. Campbell (Ed.), *Sexual selection and the descent of man: 1871–1971.* (pp. 136–179). Chicago: Aldine de Gruyter.

Trivers, R.L. (1974). Parent-offspring conflict. *American Zooloogist, 14,* 247–262.

Trivers, R.L.(1985). *Social evolution.* Merlo Park, CA: Benjamin/Cummings.

Trivers, R.L., & Willard, D.E. (1973). Natural selection of parental ability to vary the sex ratio of offspring. *Science, 179,* 90–92.

Troyer, J. (2000). Human and other natures. *Journal of Consciousness Studies, 7,* 62–66.

Turke, P.W., & Betzig, L.L. (1985). Those who can do: Wealth, status, and reproductive success on Ifaluk. *Ethology and Sociobiology, 6,* 79–87.

Turnbull, C.M. (1961). *The forest people: A study of the pygmies of the Congo.* New York: Simon and Schuster.

Tuttle, R.H. (1981). Evolution of hominid bipedalism and prehensile capabilities. *Philosophical Transactions of the Royal Society of London.* ser. B, *292,* 89–94.

Tuttle, R.H. (1990). The pitted pattern of Laetoli feet. *Natural History, 1990,* 60–65.

Tuttle, R.H., Webb, D., Weidl, E., & Baksh, M. (1990). Further progress on the Laetoli trails. *Journal of Archeological Science, 17,* 347–362.

Tylor, E.B. (1889). On a method of investigating the development of institutions: Applied to laws of marrige and descent. *Journal of the Royal Anthropological Institute, 18,* 245–269.

Ujhelyi, M. (1998). Long-call structure in apes as a possible precursor to spoken language. In J.R. Hurford, M. Studdert–Kennedy, & C. Knight (Eds.), *Approaches to the evolution of Language: Social and cognitive bases* (pp. 177–189). Cambridge, MA: Cambridge University Press.

Ulbaek, I. (1998). The origin of language and cognition. In J.R. Hurford, M. Studdert–Kennedy, & C. Knight (Eds.), *Approaches to the evolution of language: Social and cognitive bases* (pp. 30–43). Cambridge, MA: Cambridge University Press.

Valiente-Noailles, C. (1993). *The Kua. Life and soul of the central Kalahari bushman.* Rotterdam, The Netherlands: Balkema.

Van Hooff, J.A.R.A.M. (1972). A comparative approach to the phylogeny of laughter and smiling. In R.A. Hinde (Ed.), *Nonverbal communication* (pp. 209–241). Cambridge, UK: Cambridge University Press.

Van Hooff, J.A.R.A.M., and Van Schaik, C.P. (1992). Cooperation in competition: the ecology of primate bonds. In A. Harcourt and F.B.M. de Waal (Eds.), *Coalitions and alliances in humans and other animals.* Oxford, UK: Oxford University Press.

Van Schaik, C.P., & Hrdy, S.B. (1991). Intensity of local resource competition shapes the relationship between maternal rank and sex ratios at birth in cercopithecine primates. *American Naturalist, 138,* 1555–1562.

Vasek, M.E. (1986). Lying as a skill: The development of deception in children. In R.W. Mitchell & N.S. Thompson (Eds.), *Deception: Persepectives on human and nonhuman deceit.* Albany, NY: SUNY Press.

Velle, W. (1987). Sex differences in sensory functions. *Perspectives in Biology and Medicine, 30,* 490–522.

Vines, G. (1997). Imprinted genes suggest your cortex may derive from your mother, *New Scientist* 3 May. Retrieved March 14, 2002, from http://dhushara.tripod.com/book/socio/imprint.htm

Visalberghi, E., Fragaszy, D.M., & Savage-Rumbaugh, S. (1995). Performance in a tool-using task by common chimpanzees (*Pan troglodytes*), bonobos (*Pan paniscus*), an orangutan (*Pongo pygmaeus*) and capuchin monkeys (*Cebus apella*). *Journal of Comparative Psychology, 109,* 52–60.

Visalberghi, E., & Limongelli, L. (1994). Lack of comprehension of cause-effect relations in tool-using capuchin monkeys (*Cebus apella*). *Journal of Comparative Psychology, 108,* 15–22.

Visalberghi, E., Quarantotti, B.P., & Tranchida, F. (2000). Solving a cooperative task without taking into account the partner's behavior: The case with capuchin monkeys (*Cebus apella*). *Journal of Comparative Psychology, 114,* 297–301.

Visalberghi, E., & Trinca, L. (1989). Tool use in capuchin monkeys: Distinguishing between performing and understanding. *Primates, 30,* 511–521.

Vogel, J. (1990). Inequality in Sweden: Trends and current situation. In I. Persson (Ed.), *Generating equality in the welfare state: The Swedish experience* (pp. 37–74). Oslo, Norway: Norwegian University Press.

Voland, E. (1988). Differential infant and child mortality in evolutionary perspective: Data from late 17th to 19th century Ostfriesland. In L. Betzig, M. Borgerhoff Mulder, & P. Turke (Eds.), *Human reproductive behavior* (pp. 253–276)). Cambridge, UK: Cambridge University Press.

Voland, E., & Engel, C. (1990). Female choice in humans: A conditional mate selection strategy of the Kummerhorn women (Germany 1720–1874). *Ethology and Sociobiology, 84,* 144–154.

Von Humbolt, W. (1836/1972). *Linguistic variability and intellectual development.* Translated by G.C. Buck and F.A. Raven. Philadelphia: University of Pennsylvania Press.

Vrana, P.B., Guan, X.-J., Ingram, R.S., & Tilghman, S.M. (1998). Genomic imprinting is disrupted in interspecific *Peromyscus* hybrids. *Nature Genetics, 20,* 362–365.

Walker, A. (1996). *The wisdom of the bones: In search of human origins.* New York: Knopf.

Walker, A. C., & Leakey, R.E.F. (1978). The hominids of East Turkana. *Scientific American, 239 (2),* 54–66.

Walker, A., & Leakey, R. (1993). The postcranial bones. In A. Walker & R. Leakey (Eds.), *The Nariokotome* Homo erectus *skeleton* (pp.95–160). Berlin: Springer.

Walker, L.J. (1984). Sex differences in the development of moral reasoning: A critical review. *Child Development, 55,* 677–691.

Wallace, A.R. (1903). *Man's place in the universe.* New York: McClure/Phillips.

Walsh, A. (1993). Love styles, masculinity/femininity, physical attractiveness and sexual behavior: A test of evolutionary theory. *Ethology and Sociobiology, 14,* 25–38.

Walton, G.E., Bower, N.J.A., & Bower, T.G.R. (1992). Recognition of familiar faces by newborns. *Infant Behavior and Development, 15,* 265–269.

Ward, S.L, Newcombe, N., & Overton, W.F. (1986) Turn left at the church, or three miles north: A study of direction giving and sex differences. *Environment and Behavior, 18,* 192–213.

Washburn, S.L., & Moore, R. (1980). *Ape into human: A study of human evolution.* Boston: Little, Brown.

Wason, P.C. (1996). Reasoning. In B.M. Foss (Ed.), *New horizons in psychology* (Vol. 1; pp. 135–151). Harmondsworth, UK: Penguin.

Wason, P.C. & Evans, J. St. B.T. (1975). Dual processes in reasoning. *Cognition 3,* 141–154.

Wason, P.C. & Johnson-Laird, P.N. (1972). *Psychology of reasoning: Structure and content.* London: Batsford.

Wasser, S.K., & Barash, D.P. (1983). Reproductive suppression among female mammals: Implications for biomedicine and sexual selection theory. *The Quarterly Review of Biology, 58,* 513–538.

Watson, N.V., & Kimura, D. (1989). Right-handed superiority for throwing but not for intercepting. *Neuropsychologia, 27,*1399–1414.

Watson, R.I., & Evans, D. (1991). *The great psychologists.* New York: Harper Collins.

Watts, D.P. (1989). Infanticide in mountain gorillas: New cases and reconsideration of the evidence. *Ethology, 81,* 1–18.

Watts, D.P. (1990). Ecology of gorillas and its relation to female transfer in mountain gorillas. *International Journal of Primatology, 11,* 21–46.

Waxman, S.R., & Hall, D.G. (1993). The development of a linkage between count nouns and object categories: Evidence from 15 to 21 month old infants. *Child Development, 64,* 1224–1241.

Wedekind, C., & Furi, S. (1997). Body odor preferences in men and women: Do they aim for specific MHC combinations or simply heterozygosity? *Proceedings of the Royal Society of London, B 264,* 1471–1479.

Wedekind, C., Seebeck, T., Bettens, F., & Paepke, A.J. (1995). MHC-dependent mate preferences in humans. *Proceedings of the Royal Society of London, B 260,* 245–249.

Weigel, M., & Weigel, R. (1989). Nausea and vomiting of early pregnancy and pregnancy outcome. An epidemiological study. *British Journal of Obstetrics and Gynecology, 96,* 1304–1311.

Weindling, P. (1989). *Health, race, and German politics between National Unification and Nazism, 1870–1945.* Cambridge, UK: Cambridge University Press.

Weisfeld, G.E., & Billings, R. (1988). Observations on adolescence. In K.B. MacDonald (Ed.), *Sociobiological perspectives on human development* (pp. 207–233). New York: Spring-Verlag.

Weiss, D.L., & Slosnerick, M. (1981). Attitudes toward sexual and nonsexual extramarital involvments among a sample of college students. *Journal of Marriage and Family, 43,* 349–358.

Weitoft, G.R., Haglund, B., & Rosén, M. (2000). Mortality among lone mothers in Sweden. *Lancet, 355,* 1215–1219.

Welch, A.M., Semlitsch, R.D., & Gerhardt, C.H. (1998). Call duration as an indicator of genetic quality in male grey tree frogs. *Science, 280,* 1928–30.

Welch, R.B., & Warren, D. H. (1980). Immediate perceptual response to intersensory discrepancy. *Psychological Bulletin, 88,* 638–667.

West-Eberhard, M.J. (1991). Sexual selection and social behavior. In M.H. Robinson & L. Tiger (Eds.), *Man and beast revisited.* Washington, D.C.: Smithsonian Institution Press.

Westergaard, G.C., Liv, C., Haynie, M.K., Suomi, S.J. (2000). A comparative study of aimed throwing by monkeys and humans. *Neuropsychologia, 38,* 1511–1517.

Wheeler, P.E. (1994). The thermoregulatory advantage of heat storage and shade-seeking behavior to hominids foraging in equitorial savannah environments. *Journal of Human Evolution, 26,* 339–350.

White, M.J.D. (1978). *Modes of speciation.* San Francisco: W.H. Freeman.

White, R. (1993a). Technological and social dimensions of 'Aurignacian-age' body ornaments across Europe. In H. Knecht, A. Pike-Tay, & R. White (Eds.), *Before Lascaux: The complex record of the Early Upper Paleolithic* (pp. 277–300). Boca Raton, FL: CRC Press.

White, R. (1993b). The dawn of adornment. *Natural History, 1193,* 60–67.

White, T.D. (1994). *Australopithecus ramidus,* a new species of early hominid from Aramis, Ethiopia. *Nature, 371,* 306–312.

Whiten, A. (1991). The emergence of mind reading. In A. Whiten (Ed.), *Natural theories of mind.* Oxford, UK: Basil Blackwell.

Whiten, A. (1999). The evolution of deep social mind in humans. In M.C. Corballis & S.E.G. Lea (Eds.), *The Descent of Mind* (pp. 173–193). Oxford, UK: Oxford University Press

Widom, C.S. (1976). Interpersonal and personal construct systems in psychopaths. *Journal of Consulting and Clinical Psychology, 44,* 614–623.

Wigner, E. (1960). The unreasonable effectiveness of mathematics in the natural sciences. *Communications in Pure and Applied Mathematics, 13,* 1–14

Wilkins, W.K., & Wakefield, J. (1995). Brain evolution and neurolinguistic preconditions. *Behavioral and Brain Sciences. 18*, 161–226.

Wilkinson, G.S. (1984). Reciprocal food sharing in the vampire bat. *Nature, 308,* 181–184.

Willatts, P. (1984). The stage-IV infant's solutions of problems requiring the use of supports. *Infant Behavior and Development, 7,* 125–134.

Williams, B. (1993). *Shame and necessity.* Berkeley, CA: University of California Press.

Williams, G.C. (1966). *Adaptation and natural selection: A critique of some current evolutionary thought.* Princeton, NJ: Princeton University Press.

Williams, G.C. (1975). *Sex and evolution.* Princeton, NJ: Princeton University Press.

Williams, G.C. (1992). *Natural selection: Domains, levels, and challenges.* Oxford, UK: Oxford University Press.

Willingham, D.B. (2001). *Cognition: The thinking animal.* Upper Saddle River, NJ: Prentice Hall.

Wilson, A.C., & Cann, R.L. (1992, April). The recent African genesis of humans. *Scientific American,* 68–73.

Wilson, E.O. (1975). *Sociobiology: The new synthesis.* Cambridge, MA: Harvard University Press.

Wilson, E.O. (1992). *The diversity of life.* Cambridge, MA: Harvard University Press.

Wilson, E.O. (1994). *Naturalist.* Washington, D.C.: Island Press.

Wilson, F.R. (1998). *The hand: How its use shapes the brain, language, and human culture.* New York: Pantheon Books.

Wilson, J.Q., & Herrnstein, R.J. (1985). *Crime and human nature.* New York: Simon and Schuster Pub.

Wilson, M.I., & Daly, M. (1992). The man who mistook his wife for a chattel. In J.H. Barkow, L. Cosmides, & J. Tooby (Eds.), *The adapted mind* (pp. 289–322). New York: Oxford University Press.

Wilson, M.I., & Daly, M. (1993). An evolutionary psychological perspective on male sexual proprietariness and violence against wives. *Violence & Victims, 8,* 271–294.

Wilson, M.I., Daly, M., & Weghorst, S.J. (1980). Household composition and the risk of child abuse and neglect. *Journal of Biosocial Science, 12,* 333–340.

Wilson, M.I., Daly, M. & Wright, C. (1993). Uxoricide in Canada: Demographic risk patterns. *Canadian Journal of Criminology, 35,* 331–361.

Wilson, P.J. (1980). *Man: The promising primate.* New Haven, CT: Yale University Press.

Wimmer, H., & Perner, J. (1983). Beliefs about beliefs: Representational and constraining function of wrong beliefs in young children's understanding of deception. *Cognition, 13,* 103–128.

Winter, W., & Oxnard, C.E. (2001). Evolutionary radiations and convergences in the structural organization of mammalian brains. *Nature, 409,* 710–714.

Wolf, A.P. (1995). *Sexual attraction and childhood association: A Chinese brief for Edward Westermarck.* Stanford, CA: Stanford University Press.

Wolpoff, M.H. (1980). *Paleoanthropology.* New York: Knopf.

Wolpoff, M. H, (1996). *Human evolution.* New York: McGraw-Hill.

Wolpoff, M.H., Hawks, J., Frayer, D.W., & Hunley, K. (2001). Modern human ancestry at the peripheries: A test of the replacement theory. *Science, 291,* 293–297.

Wolpoff, M.H., Thorne, A.G., Smith, F.H., Frayer, D.W., & Pope, G.G. (1994). Multiregional evolution: a worldwide source for modern human populations. In M.H. Nitecki & D.V. Nitecki (Eds.), *Origins of anatomically modern humans* (pp. 175–199). New York: Plenum Press.

Wolpoff, M.H., Zhi, W.X., & Thorne, A.G., (1984). Modern *Homo sapiens* origins: A general theory of hominid evolution involving the fossil evidence from East Asia. In F. Smith & F. Spencer (Eds.), *The origin of modern humans: A world survey of fossil evidence* (pp. 411–483). New York: Alan Liss.

Wood, B. (1992). Origin and evolution of the genus *Homo. Nature, 355,* 783–790.

Wood, B. (1997). The oldest whodunit in the world. *Nature 385,* 292–293.

Wood, B., & Richmond, B.G. (2000). Human evolution: Taxonomy and paleobiology. *Journal of Anatomy, 196,* 19–60.

Woodburn, J. (1982). Egalitarian societies. *Man, 17,* 431–451.

Woolfendon, G.E., & FitzPatrick, J.W. (1984). *The Florida scrub jay: Demography of a cooperative breeding bird.* Princeton: Princeton University Press.

Wrangham, R.W. (1980). An ecological model of female-bonded groups. *Behaviour, 75,* 262–300.

Wrangham, R.W. (1987). The significance of African apes for reconstructing human evolution. In W.G. Kinzey (Ed.), *The evolution of human behavior: Primate models* (pp. 51–71). Stony Brook, NY: SUNY Press.

Wrangham, R.W., & Peterson, D. (1996). *Demonic males.* Boston: Houghton Mifflin.

Wright, R. (1994). *The moral animal.* New York: Vintage Books.

Wright, R. (2000). *Non-zero: The logic of human destiny.* New York: Vintage Books.

Wright, R.V.S. (1972). Imitative learning of a flaked-tool technology: The case of an orangutan. *Mankind, 8,* 296–306.

Wu, R., & Lin, S. (1983). Peking Man. *Scientific American, 248,* 86–95.

Wynn, T. (1979). The intelligence of later Acheulean hominids. *Man, 14,* 379–391.

Wynn, T. (1985). Piaget, stone tools and the evolution of human intelligence. *World Archaeology, 17,* 32–43.

Wynn, T. (1993a). Layers of thinking in tool behavior. In K.R. Gibson & T. Ingold (Eds.), *Tools, language and cognition in human evolution* (pp. 389–405). Cambridge, UK: Cambridge University Press.

Wynn, T. (1993b). Two developments in the mind of early *Homo. Journal of Anthropology and Archeology, 12,* 299–322.

Wynn, T. (1996). The evolution of tools and symbolic behaviour. In A.J. Lock & C.R. Peters (Eds.), *Handbook of human symbolic evolution* (pp. 263–287). Oxford, UK: Clarendon Press.

Wynn, T., & McGrew, W.C. (1989). An ape's eye view of the Oldowan. *Man, 24,* 383–398.

Wynn, T., & Tierson, F. (1990). Regional comparison of the shapes of later Acheulean handaxes. *American Anthropologist, 92,* 73–84.

Wynne-Edwards, V.C. (1962). *Animal dispersion in relation to social behavior.* Edinburgh: Oliver & Boyd.

Wysocki, C.J., Pierce, J.D., & Gilbert, A.N. (1991). Geographic, cross-cultural and individual variation in human olfaction. In T.V. Getchell, R.L. Doty, L.M. Bartoshuk, & J.B. Snow, Jr. (Eds.), *Smell and taste in health and disease* (pp. 287–313). New York: Raven Press.

Yaguello, M. (1991). *Lunatic lovers of language: Imaginary languages and their inventors.* Translated by Catherine Stater, London: Athlone. Originally: *Les fous du language: des langues imaginaires et de leurs inventeurs.* Paris: Editions du Seuil (1984).

Yonas, A., Cleaves, W., & Pettersen, L. (1978). Development of sensitivity to pictorial depth. *Science, 200,* 77–79.

Yuill, N. (1984). Young children's coordination of motive and outcome in judgements of satisfaction and morality. *British Journal of Developmental Psychology, 2,* 73–81.

Zahavi, A. (1975). Mate selection—a selection of handicap. *Journal of Theoretical Biology, 53,* 205–214

Zihlman, A. (1997). The Paleolithic glass ceiling: Women in human evolution. In L.D. Hager (Ed.), *Women in human evolution* (pp. 91–113). London: Routledge.

Name Index

Subject Index